Microsoft System Center 2016 Service Manager Cookbook

Second Edition

Discover over 100 practical recipes to help you master the art of IT service management for your organization

Anders Asp (MVP)
Andreas Baumgarten (MVP)
Steve Beaumont (MVP)
Steve Buchanan (MVP)
Dieter Gasser

BIRMINGHAM - MUMBAI

Microsoft System Center 2016 Service Manager Cookbook

Second Edition

First published: October 2012

Second edition: February 2017

Production reference: 1200217

Published by Packt Publishing Ltd.
Livery Place
35 Livery Street
Birmingham
B3 2PB, UK.

ISBN 978-1-78646-489-7

www.packtpub.com

Credits

Authors

Anders Asp (MVP)
Andreas Baumgarten (MVP)
Steve Beaumont (MVP)
Steve Buchanan (MVP)
Dieter Gasser

Copy Editor

Safis Editing

Reviewers

Rafael Delgado
Samuel Erskine

Project Coordinator

Judie Jose

Acquisition Editor

Vinay Argekar

Proofreader

Safis Editing

Content Development Editor

Amedh Pohad

Indexer

Aishwarya Gangawane

Technical Editor

Mohit Hassija

Production Coordinator

Aparna Bhagat

Foreword

System Center Service Manager 2016 (SCSM 2016) is the latest revision of the Service Manager product line and Microsoft's full IT Service Management (ITSM) solution.

SCSM 2016 is the seamless connector and interface between the System Center products as well as being the gateway to modern service management in the cloud.

Service Manager helps IT organizations streamline Incident Management, Problem Management, Change Management, Release Management, Request Fulfillment, Self-Service, and reporting.

This release of System Center Service Manager (2016) proves that the product is alive and well. SCSM 2016 will officially be supported by Microsoft through to 2027. The product continues to be implemented worldwide with various configuration scenarios, ranging from traditional ITSM to business-scenario-driven automation and interfacing with multi-vendor cloud platforms.

SCSM 2016's many enhancements include better overall performance, stability of the data warehouse, faster workflows/groups and queues, faster console, improved connectors (AD/SCCM), and the all new HTML5 self-service portal. These enhancements and improvements show the commitment from the Microsoft Service Manager product team to the customer and the product's future.

This new edition of the Service Manager cookbook builds on the simplification of ITSM shared through the internationally bestselling *Microsoft System Center 2012 Service Manager Cookbook*. The authors (many of them Microsoft MVPs and technology consultants) set out to arm you with everything you need to become a Service Manager Rockstar and provide a rock solid ITSM solution to your organization.

This book is full of valuable insight and experiences from real-world Service Manager implementations. The book is written in the Packt style, which provides the reader with independent task-oriented steps to achieve specific SCSM objectives. The authors recommend that you read the first two chapters as a background for subsequent chapters, if you are new to SCSM and process-oriented software products. The book, however, may be read in your order of interest, but where relevant, the authors refer to dependent recipes in other chapters.

Samuel Erskine

Microsoft MCT and MVP

About the Authors

Anders Asp (MVP) is a Principal Consultant at Lumagate AB with focus on ITSM and automation in the hybrid cloud. He is very active in the community and can regularly be seen speaking at different events, teaching courses, blogging on his blog at www.scsm.se, or answering questions on different forums. For his work in the community, he was awarded the Microsoft MVP award in the Cloud and Datacenter area for the first time in 2012 and has since then been renewed as MVP every year.

Anders has been working with Service Manager since 2009, when the product was still in early beta, and has provided endless feedback to Microsoft and seen the product evolve to what it is today. Besides Service Manager, he is also very fond of the whole Microsoft Operations Management Suite and helps customers embrace the management capabilities it offers.

> *I wish to thank all my family and friends for always being supportive and encouraging! A special thanks to my two daughters for always putting a smile on my face and giving me the energy boost needed when things are though. Thanks Anna for being helpful when my planning isn't on top. I would also like to thank all the co-authors for making this book possible.Last but not least, thanks to the Service Manager team and the whole Service Manager community.*

Andreas Baumgarten (MVP) is a Microsoft MVP and works as an IT Architect with the German IT service provider H&D International Group. He has been working as an IT professional for more than 20 years. Microsoft technologies have always accompanied him, and he can also look back on more than 14 years' experience as a Microsoft Certified Trainer.

Since 2008, he has been responsible for the field of Microsoft System Center technology consulting and ever since has taken part in Microsoft System Center Service Manager (2010, 2012, 2012 R2 and 2016); additionally, he has participated in the Microsoft System Center Technology Adoption Program with H&D since many years.

With his deep inside-technology know-how and his broad experience across the Microsoft System Center product family and IT management, he now designs and develops private and hybrid cloud solutions for customers all over Germany and Europe.

In October 2016 he was awarded the Microsoft Most Valuable Professional (MVP) title for System Center Cloud and Datacenter Management for the fifth year in a row.

> *A special thanks goes to my very good friend Samuel Erskine for his help and review of my chapters. Thanks a lot buddy! I would like to thank my colleague Patrick Hersing from H&D International Group for his helping hand and support with some content of this book. The book was only possible due to the efforts of a great team. I would like to acknowledge and thank my co-authors Steve Buchanan, Anders Asp, Steve Beaumont and Dieter Gasser. It was a pleasure and great fun to work with you again!*

Steve Beaumont (MVP) has worked for more years than he cares to admit within IT, starting with desktop support. He is now the Product Development Director of PowerONPlatforms and a Microsoft MVP within the Cloud and Datacenter Management area, where he helps organizations realize the benefits of the hybrid cloud. He is also a co-author of the Microsoft System Center 2012 Service Manager, Orchestrator, and Operations Manager cookbooks. Steve can also be found speaking at various events and blogging either at `http://systemcenter.ninja` or `http://www.poweronplatforms.com/news-and-blogs/`, where he covers all things System Center and Azure related to design, deployment, and optimization.

His passion for everything about System Center, Azure, and IT systems management reflects through all areas of his work, presentation, and day-to-day life in the form of new and innovative solutions brought to the market by PowerONPlatforms.

> *A special thanks goes to my very good friend Samuel Erskine for his help and review of my chapters. Thanks a lot buddy!*

Steve Buchanan (MVP), MCSE, ITIL, is a regional solutions director with Concurrency, a five-time Microsoft Cloud and Data Center MVP, and author of several technical books focused on the System Center platform. Steve has been an IT Professional for 17+ years in various positions, ranging from infrastructure architect to IT manager. Steve is focused on digitally transforming IT departments through service management, systems management, and cloud technologies.

Steve has authored the following books:

- *System Center 2012 Service Manager Unleashed, Sams Publishing*
- *Microsoft System Center Data Protection Manager 2012 SP1, Packt*
- *Microsoft Data Protection Manager 2010, Packt*

Steve holds the following certifications: A +, Linux +, MCSA, MCITP: Server Administrator, MCSE: Private Cloud, and ITIL 2011 Foundation.

Steve stays active in the System Center community and enjoys blogging about his adventures in the world of IT at www.buchatech.com.

First and foremost, I give thanks to God for making all things possible. Thanks to my family, especially my wife and sons, for giving the time to work on opportunities like this. I would like to thank Sam Erskine for bringing me into this book. I also want to thank all of the other authors on the project, Andreas Baumgarten, Dieter Gasser, Anders Asp, and Steve Beaumont, for allowing me to be a part of this team. You guys are some of the best in this space! Also thanks to the Microsoft Service Manager product group team Rahul Gupta, Harsh Verma, and others, along with the SCSM community.

Dieter Gasser is an IT consultant and the management partner of itnetX AG, headquartered in Switzerland. He has a strong focus on the delivery and customization of Service Manager.

Dieter has been working in IT for more than 13 years, and has focused on Microsoft technologies. He started his career as an application and database developer, and later became the IT manager of an international manufacturing company.

In 2010, he entered the systems management and automation market. With both his technical and managerial backgrounds, he has focused on Service Manager. Together with his colleagues, he delivers data center management, automation, and cloud solutions based on Microsoft System Center to customers all across Switzerland.

I would like to thank Sam Erskine for making the first edition of this book possible, and to all my friends and my co-authors Andreas Baumgarten, Steve Buchanan, Anders Asp and Steve Beaumont for the great fun in working with you.

About the Reviewers

Rafael Delgado is an IT Professional with over 12 years' experience and is a Cloud Management Engineer at PowerON. He is currently working across the delivery and development teams, implementing and designing innovative cloud and System Center suite solutions. He spent the majority of his IT career working in local government in a wide range of areas from service desk, desktop support to third-line infrastructure management.

Rafael is passionate about giving back to the IT community, you can find his blog at `http://sysctr.info`, focusing on all things System Center, PowerShell, Azure Automation, Power BI and more. He is also the creator of the Service Manager and Configuration Manager Power BI dashboards which can be found on the TechNet gallery `https://gallery.technet.microsoft.com/Power-BI-SCCM-Dashboard-d1b7e688` / `https://gallery.technet.microsoft.com/PowerON-Power-BI-SCSM-e1c02a22`. His Twitter handle is `@Raf_Delgado`.

Samuel Erskine is a Microsoft MCT and MVP, and works as a service management and cloud consultant. He is an author, systems specialist, and trainer specializing in System Center and MS Cloud technologies. He is the content designer and lead author of three Microsoft System Center Cookbooks and co-author of two System Center Unleashed books.

www.PacktPub.com

For support files and downloads related to your book, please visit www.PacktPub.com.

Did you know that Packt offers eBook versions of every book published, with PDF and ePub files available? You can upgrade to the eBook version at www.PacktPub.com and as a print book customer, you are entitled to a discount on the eBook copy. Get in touch with us at service@packtpub.com for more details.

At www.PacktPub.com, you can also read a collection of free technical articles, sign up for a range of free newsletters and receive exclusive discounts and offers on Packt books and eBooks.

https://www.packtpub.com/mapt

Get the most in-demand software skills with Mapt. Mapt gives you full access to all Packt books and video courses, as well as industry-leading tools to help you plan your personal development and advance your career.

Why subscribe?

- Fully searchable across every book published by Packt
- Copy and paste, print, and bookmark content
- On demand and accessible via a web browser

Customer Feedback

Thanks for purchasing this Packt book. At Packt, quality is at the heart of our editorial process. To help us improve, please leave us an honest review on this book's Amazon page at `https://www.amazon.com/dp/1786464896`.

If you'd like to join our team of regular reviewers, you can e-mail us at `customerreviews@packtpub.com`. We award our regular reviewers with free eBooks and videos in exchange for their valuable feedback. Help us be relentless in improving our products!

Table of Contents

Preface

The Microsoft System Center 2016 Service Manager Cookbook - Second Edition is a collection of recipes from Service Manager experts brought to you from the field. This book sets out to guide the reader through all aspects of deploying, configuring, and maintaining a Service Manager environment. In this book you will find information that is needed to help you leverage the new features and functionality of the Service Manager 2016 version.

This book has value for beginners and experienced Service Manager administrators. A beginner can read chapter by chapter moving from no Service Manager to a fully functional environment or an experienced Service Manager administrator can go straight to chapters containing recipes that pertain to their need.

What this book covers

Chapter 1, *ITSM and ITIL Frameworks and Processes*, aims to provide a background into the creation of processes aligned with ITIL and MOF (Microsoft Operations Framework) principles and explains some of the key areas and how they relate to Service Manager 2016.

Chapter 2, *Personalizing SCSM 2016 Administration*, covers the initial process-dependent critical settings and tasks a Service Manager administrator would need to configure after successfully installing the product.

Chapter 3, *Configuring Service Level Agreements (SLAs)*, delves into the Service-Level Agreement areas of Service Manager 2012 and provides you with recipes that simplify the implementation of this complex topic.

Chapter 4, *Building the Configuration Management Database (CMDB)*, shows Service Manager Administrators are how to build the SCSM Configuration Management Database (CMDB). The recipes in this chapter include various options, from a manual approach right through to automating the importing of information from external systems.

Chapter 5, *Deploying Service Request Fulfillment*, provides recipes to configure the Service Catalog with different Service and Request Offerings in SCSM 2016.

Chapter 6, *Deploying and Configuring the HTML 5 Self-Service Portal*, teaches you the ins and outs of planning the new HTML5 portal, deploying the portal, overall configuration, and finally how to customize it to have the look and feel you want. After reading this chapter, you will be armed and ready to spin up the new HTML5 portal as a part of your Service Manager deployment.

Chapter 7, *Working with Incident and Problem Management*, contains recipes related to the Incident and Problem processes. This chapter contains things such as creating tasks, templates, how to configure the Exchange connector, and how to extend the incident class.

Chapter 8, *Designing and Configuring Change Management and Release Management*, covers the details of Change Management and Release Management in SCSM 2016.

Chapter 9, *Implementing Security Roles*, explains the details of Security Roles and how they can be used to control access to different objects in SCSM 2016.

Chapter 10, *Working with the Data Warehouse and Reporting*, walks you through the various options of using the Service Manager Data Warehouse to gain insight into the data stored in the Service Manager database.

Chapter 11, *Extending SCSM with Advanced Personalization*, is the chapter where you will be able to see how to perform more advanced customizations of Service Manager. This chapter contains recipes around installing and using the Authoring Tool in different ways, but it also includes recipes around how to manually edit the XML of management packs.

Chapter 12, *Automating Service Manager 2016*, teaches you how to work smart and efficient by automating things in Service Manager. This chapter covers different ways of automating Service Manager with the use of custom workflows, PowerShell, and Orchestrator.

Chapter 13, *What's New in SCSM 2016 and Upgrading from SCSM 2012 R2*, explains the new features of SCSM 2016 and walks you through the process of planning and performing an upgrade from SCSM 2012 R2.

Appendix A, *Community Extensions and Third-party Commercial SCSM Solutions*, contains useful community extensions and third-party solutions for SCSM 2016.

Appendix B, *Useful Websites and Community Resources*, lists some helpful websites and communities for System Center Service Manager.

What you need for this book

In order to complete all the recipes in this book, you will need a minimum of three servers configured with System Center Service Manager 2016 RTM, in the following configurations:

Server 1: System Center Service Manager 2016 management server hosting the CMDB and workflow role

Server 2: System Center Service Manager 2016 management server hosting the data warehouse role

Server 3: System Center Service Manager 2016 management server hosting the HTML5 self-service portal

The required software and deployment guides of System Center Service Manager 2016 can be found at the following official Microsoft website:

```
https://technet.microsoft.com/en-us/system-center-docs/sm/deploy/deploy-depl
oying-system-center-2016-service-manager
```

We recommend using the online Microsoft resource due to the frequency of updates to the products' supported requirements.

Who this book is for

The target audience of this book is SCSM administrators and process owners responsible for implementing ITSM processes in the scope of the product. The recipes in this book range from beginner-level to expert-level SCSM administration expertise. The ultimate goal is to provide you with knowledge to enhance your existing skills and, more importantly, to share real-world experience from seasoned technology implementers.

Sections

In this book, you will find several headings that appear frequently (Getting ready, How to do it, How it works, There's more, and See also).

To give clear instructions on how to complete a recipe, we use these sections as follows:

Getting ready

This section tells you what to expect in the recipe, and describes how to set up any software or any preliminary settings required for the recipe.

How to do it…

This section contains the steps required to follow the recipe.

How it works…

This section usually consists of a detailed explanation of what happened in the previous section.

There's more…

This section consists of additional information about the recipe in order to make the reader more knowledgeable about the recipe.

See also

This section provides helpful links to other useful information for the recipe.

Conventions

In this book, you will find a number of text styles that distinguish between different kinds of information. Here are some examples of these styles and an explanation of their meaning.

Code words in text, database table names, folder names, filenames, file extensions, pathnames, dummy URLs, user input, and Twitter handles are shown as follows: "The old work items in the working database (the database name is ServiceManager by default) slows down the console and provides a negative experience for the service management team."

A block of code is set as follows:

```
$date = $date.ToString("dd.MM.yyyy") # 24.09.2016
```

Any command-line input or output is written as follows:

```
Set-ExecutionPolicy RemoteSigned
```

New terms and **important words** are shown in bold. Words that you see on the screen, for example, in menus or dialog boxes, appear in the text like this: "Select **Work Items | Review** and adjust retention times (in days) to reflect how long the items should be kept in the SCSM database."

Warnings or important notes appear in a box like this.

Tips and tricks appear like this.

Reader feedback

Feedback from our readers is always welcome. Let us know what you think about this book-what you liked or disliked. Reader feedback is important for us as it helps us develop titles that you will really get the most out of.

To send us general feedback, simply e-mail feedback@packtpub.com, and mention the book's title in the subject of your message.

If there is a topic that you have expertise in and you are interested in either writing or contributing to a book, see our author guide at www.packtpub.com/authors.

Customer support

Now that you are the proud owner of a Packt book, we have a number of things to help you to get the most from your purchase.

Downloading the example code

You can download the example code files for this book from your account at http://www.packtpub.com. If you purchased this book elsewhere, you can visit http://www.packtpub.com/support and register to have the files e-mailed directly to you.

You can download the code files by following these steps:

1. Log in or register to our website using your e-mail address and password.
2. Hover the mouse pointer on the **SUPPORT** tab at the top.
3. Click on **Code Downloads & Errata**.
4. Enter the name of the book in the **Search** box.
5. Select the book for which you're looking to download the code files.
6. Choose from the drop-down menu where you purchased this book from.
7. Click on **Code Download**.

You can also download the code files by clicking on the **Code Files** button on the book's webpage at the Packt Publishing website. This page can be accessed by entering the book's name in the **Search** box. Please note that you need to be logged in to your Packt account.

Once the file is downloaded, please make sure that you unzip or extract the folder using the latest version of:

- WinRAR / 7-Zip for Windows
- Zipeg / iZip / UnRarX for Mac
- 7-Zip / PeaZip for Linux

The code bundle for the book is also hosted on GitHub at `https://github.com/PacktPubl ishing/Microsoft-System-Center-2016-Service-Manager-Cookbook-Second-Edition`. We also have other code bundles from our rich catalog of books and videos available at `htt ps://github.com/PacktPublishing/`. Check them out!

Downloading the color images of this book

We also provide you with a PDF file that has color images of the screenshots/diagrams used in this book. The color images will help you better understand the changes in the output. You can download this file from `https://www.packtpub.com/sites/default/files/down loads/MicrosoftSystemCenter2016ServiceManagerCookbookSecondEdition_ColorImag es.pdf`.

Errata

Although we have taken every care to ensure the accuracy of our content, mistakes do happen. If you find a mistake in one of our books-maybe a mistake in the text or the code-we would be grateful if you could report this to us. By doing so, you can save other readers from frustration and help us improve subsequent versions of this book. If you find any errata, please report them by visiting `http://www.packtpub.com/submit-errata`, selecting your book, clicking on the **Errata Submission Form** link, and entering the details of your errata. Once your errata are verified, your submission will be accepted and the errata will be uploaded to our website or added to any list of existing errata under the Errata section of that title.

To view the previously submitted errata, go to `https://www.packtpub.com/books/conten t/support`and enter the name of the book in the search field. The required information will appear under the **Errata** section.

Piracy

Piracy of copyrighted material on the Internet is an ongoing problem across all media. At Packt, we take the protection of our copyright and licenses very seriously. If you come across any illegal copies of our works in any form on the Internet, please provide us with the location address or website name immediately so that we can pursue a remedy.

Please contact us at `copyright@packtpub.com` with a link to the suspected pirated material.

We appreciate your help in protecting our authors and our ability to bring you valuable content.

Questions

If you have a problem with any aspect of this book, you can contact us at `questions@packtpub.com`, and we will do our best to address the problem.

1
ITSM and ITIL Frameworks and Processes

This chapter aims to provide a background into the creation of processes aligned with ITIL and **Microsoft Operations Framework** (**MOF**) principles and explains some of the key areas and how they relate to Service Manager; specifically, we will cover the following areas:

- Understanding ITSM frameworks
- ITIL© processes
- Creating an Asset Management process
- Creating a Configuration Management System (CMS) process
- Creating a Service Request Fulfilment process
- Creating an Incident and Problem Management process
- Creating a Change and Release Management process
- Creating an IT Service Desk
- The Service Level Management process
- Dependencies and relationships between ITSM processes

Introduction

System Center 2016 Service Manager (**SCSM**) is built on the principles of the **Information Technology Infrastructure Library** (**ITIL©**) and the operational principles of the Microsoft Operations Framework (MOF). This chapter discusses the operational execution of these principles in real-world implementations.

There are various books and online resources available to you on ITIL© and MOF. The authors recommend you review and research the principles of ITIL© and MOF in the areas in the scope of your SCSM implementation.

The goal of creating processes, regardless of the framework, is to move your organization or teams from using individual flexible approaches to using an agreed uniform policy-driven best practice approach to meet your objectives. This approach is usually described as process maturity.

ITIL© is commonly described as an industry-recognized process framework. MOF is the Microsoft standard for the execution of the processes typically using (but not limited to) Microsoft products.

Understanding ITSM frameworks

This recipe provides a summary analysis of the **IT Service Management** (**ITSM**) frameworks in general and what they mean to each organization.

Getting ready

A general understanding of the objectives of standards and frameworks is required for this recipe.

How to do it...

Plan to invest in one or more of the following:

- Buy this book

- Research the subject of frameworks using your preferred method of learning

- Attend an accredited training course in the subject

- Adopt and adapt frameworks to your specific organization needs, strategies, and capabilities

How it works...

IT Service Management is a broad term used to describe a process-focused approach to IT management. The goal for most organizations is to implement a service-focused approach to delivering IT dependent services to the end customer.

The industry standard approach for achieving the ITSM objective is to use best-in-class standards as a guide. Examples of common industry frameworks include, but are not limited to, the following:

- Information Technology Infrastructure Library (ITIL©)
- Microsoft Operations Framework (MOF)
- Core Practices

Frameworks are guides and can be compared to the rules of a game (for example, soccer). In a game, the rules provide a consistent approach but do not limit the individual or team strategy. Another critical factor is individual creativity, which, when championed, often leads to a strategic advantage.

ITSM frameworks work best for organizations when the adoption is personalized to the organizations specific strategies and internal capabilities.

ITIL© processes

This recipe provides a summary discussion of the current ITIL© V3 processes.

Getting ready

The authors recommend that you read the *Understanding ITSM frameworks* recipe.

How to do it...

Plan to do one or more of the following:

- Attend one or more ITIL© training courses in the recommended order
- Invest in the ITIL© official book(s) and complementary books
- Use the vast free resources on the Internet

- Implement and improve your organizational ITSM processes using the ITIL© knowledge as a guide
- Review and update your processes in line with organization strategies and capabilities

How it works...

ITIL© processes take a repeatable cyclic approach to ITSM organization underpinned by continual service improvements. The ITIL© goals are aimed at ensuring the following for the organization:

- Plans for services
- Catalogues and tracks IT services
- Introduces new services with minimal risks
- Manages and operates active services consistently
- Performs maintenance and updates to existing services with minimum risk and maximum value to the business
- Continually monitors and improves the services delivered to the business

The official phases of ITIL© are as follows:

- Service Strategy
- Service Design
- Service Transition
- Service Operation
- Continual Service Improvement

SCSM is a technology capability enabler of a subset of the ITIL© processes. It is important to follow the principle of **People**, **Processes**, and **Products**. SCSM is a product that complements your organizations agreed processes and needs people to implement, manage, and continually improve the overall IT service strategy.

ITIL© implementation is not mandatory for SCSM deployment, but an understanding of ITIL© is recommended.

See also

Appendix B, *Useful Websites and Community Resources* provides a list of useful websites for ITIL© and is highly recommended by the authors.

Creating an Asset Management process

This recipe will provide steps for creating a sample Asset Management process.

Getting ready

For this recipe, the authors recommend you read up on the difference between asset inventory and asset management as an organizational process.

How to do it...

Asset Management is a life cycle process, which tracks an IT asset with its associated financial data from when the asset is requested to when the asset is retired, as shown in the following figure:

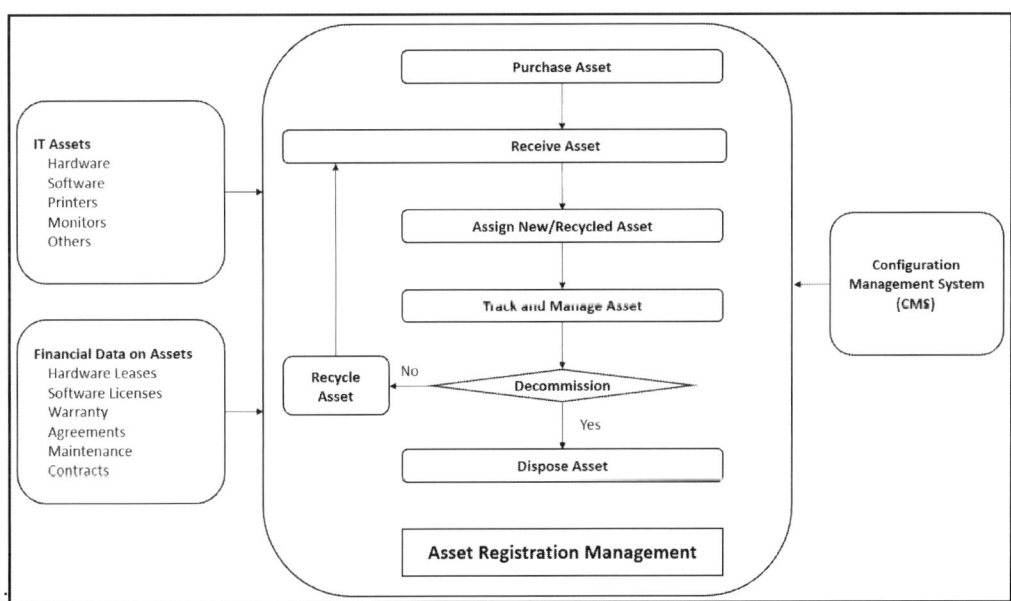

An example of the steps for creating an Asset Management process is as follows:

1. Agree and document the organization's asset management policy.
2. Document the operational process to support the asset management policy.
3. Create and assign people roles to manage the process. At a minimum, you should plan to include the following:

    -   Hardware Asset Managers
    -   Hardware Asset Inventory agents
    -   Software Asset Managers
    -   Software Asset Inventory agents

4. Identify and agree on an asset register management system. An asset register in its basic form is a manual process. In advanced scenarios, you may be able to automate this process with a tool such as a bar-code scanner. It should capture the following:

    -   Capture the IT asset type
    -   Capture financial information
    -   Align the IT asset to its financial data
    -   Capture the input to a Configuration Management system (CMS)
    -   Continually aligned to the CMS

5. Implement Asset Management in SCSM using one of the following methods:

    -   Manually extend the **Configuration Items** (**CI**) class to include financial data for assets
    -   Purchase an asset management solution for SCSM (for example, Provance IT Asset Management Pack for SCSM or Cireson Asset Management)

6. Continually review the policy and operational process. The goal of this step is to improve the process and ensure compliance.

How it works...

Asset Management begins and ends with people and ultimately can cost or add value to a business. A non-IT related analogy is the lessons from retail stock takes, which typically happen annually. The stock take is the best opportunity for a retail shop to get the most accurate figure for its profit or loss on stock. Two forms of lost revenues are as follows:

* Damaged goods
* Missing goods

IT asset management is the stock take required for all your technological assets, and its resultant analysis for intelligent decision making to provide factual compliance measurements. The IT equivalent of the stock take process is referred to as audits for software and hardware. SCSM with partner extensions or in-house authoring provides 80 % of the Asset Management for the organization. People and process critically account for the high value of 20 percent.

There's more...

There are various tools (products) labeled as Asset Management tools. The true Asset Management tools should have the capability of tracking assets from order to decommissioning, and in some cases, recommissioning.

Asset Management is an end-to-end process, and the tools are enablers of successful implementation. Successful Asset Management organization programs recognize the full life cycle management of assets.

See also

See the *Using the SCSM Authoring Tool* and *Extending Service Manager classes* recipes in Chapter 11, *Extending SCSM with Advanced Personalization*, for advanced recipes on management pack authoring.

Creating a Configuration Management System (CMS) process

This recipe provides steps for creating a Configuration Management System process.

Getting ready

This recipe is focused on a Configuration Management System (CMS) process using SCSM. The CMS process differs from a **Configuration Management Database (CMDB)**. A CMS combines one or more CMDBs. SCSM implements a CMS within its CMDB by merging data from multiple CMDBs including the following:

- **Active directory (AD)**
- **System Center Configuration Manager (ConfigMgr)**
- **System Center Operations Manager (OpsMgr)**

This recipe is focused on how you create a CMS process with SCSM using AD, ConfigMgr, and OpsMgr.

How to do it...

An example of the steps for creating a CMS process is as follows:

1. Plan to agree and document the organization configuration management policy.
2. Document the operational process to support the configuration management policy.
3. Create and assign people roles to manage the process.
4. Install and configure the CMDB systems in scope (in this example, AD, ConfigMgr, and OpsMgr).
5. Add the AD capable assets to the AD CMDB.
6. Discover the AD joined assets with ConfigMgr and deploy the ConfigMgr agent.
7. Discover the AD joined assets with OpsMgr and deploy the OpsMgr agent.
8. Configure the AD connector for SCSM and synchronize the data from AD with SCSM.
9. Configure the ConfigMgr connector and synchronize the data from ConfigMgr with SCSM.

10. Configure the OpsMgr connector and synchronize the data from OpsMgr with SCSM.
11. The CMS example structure is shown in the following figure:

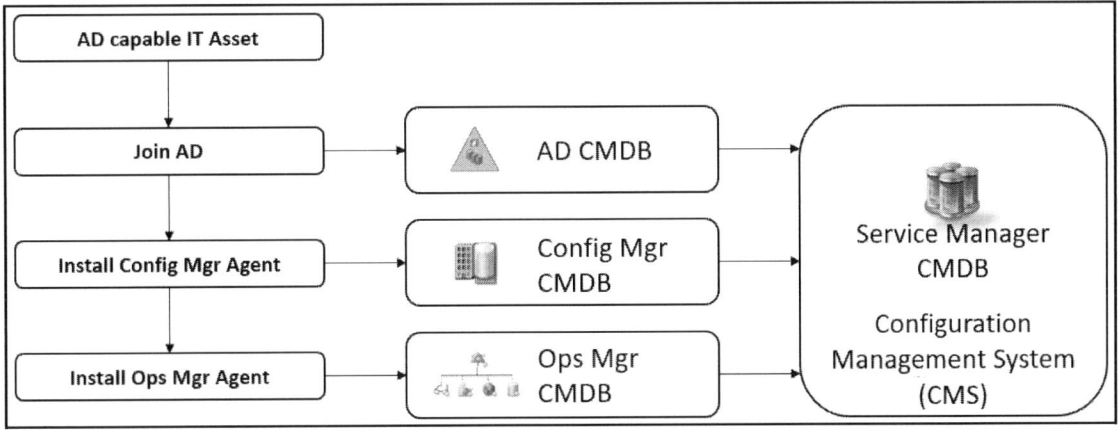

How it works...

SCSM addresses the technology requirements of a CMS process by providing a simplified and consistent framework for connecting multiple CMDBs. In the example, the three CMDBs provide information, which SCSM merges to provide a single view of the asset. Using a database server as our asset, here's an example:

- AD provides the computer details and information registered in the AD CMDB
- ConfigMgr provides information on the hardware and software of the asset (for example, 64-bit operating system with Microsoft SQL Server 2014)
- OpsMgr provides information on what databases are installed on the computer

SCSM presents a consolidated view of this information to the analyst and is dynamically refreshed by the owner of the data.

SCSM builds the ITIL© process on its CMDB, which is a dynamic CMS. The CMS approach ensures that the data accuracy and management is performed at the source (AD, ConfigMgr, OpsMgr, or another supported connector). This approach removes the risk of data inconsistency typical of other systems where the IT Service Management (ITSM) tool does not automatically synchronize with CMDBs in scope.

See also

- The *Importing Active Directory configuration items* recipe in Chapter 4, *Building the Configuration Management Database (CMDB)*
- The *Importing Configuration Manager configuration items* recipe in Chapter 4, *Building the Configuration Management Database (CMDB)*
- The *Importing Operations Manager configuration items* recipe in Chapter 4, *Building the Configuration Management Database (CMDB)*

Creating a Service Request Fulfilment process

This recipe provides guidance on creating an organization Service Request Fulfillment process.

Getting ready

Service Request Fulfillment is typically a process put in place to support a proactive approach to providing services to customers.

How to do it...

An example of the steps for creating a Service Request Fulfillment process is as follows:

1. Agree and document the organization Service Request Fulfillment policy.
2. Document the operational process to support the Service Request Fulfillment policy.
3. Create and assign people roles to manage the process.
4. Create a service catalog of the organization services available to the end customers.
5. Sort the services by categories. Here are two examples of category types:

   - Approval required services
   - Non-approval required services (standard services)

6. Agree and establish the organization-supported channels for requesting services. Examples of channels include the following:

- Phone calls into the service desk
- E-mail
- Self-service Web Portal

7. Publish the list of services and provide guidance on how to order services, including approval processes and costs.
8. Provide training and guidance to the support teams responsible for Service Request Fulfillment.
9. Plan to review the process and improve the service based on customer feedback and technological advances. An example of a Service Request Fulfillment process structure is shown in the following figure:

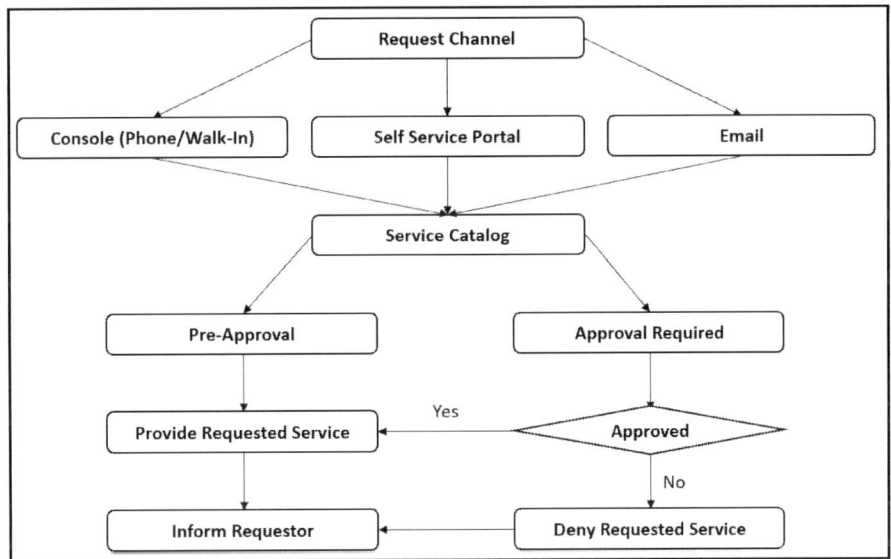

How it works...

A Service Request Fulfillment process aims to address the proactive goals of ITSM. Some of the common objectives when establishing this process are as follows:

- Provide predictable services at a known cost.
- Engage customers by using predictable published channels of service delivery.
- Improve the change management processes. A repeatable change request with a low risk known outcome may qualify for a published Service Request with a simpler approval process.
- Provide visibility and proactive management of services in the service catalog.

Service Requests are typically requests for services that do not require change management, but may or may not require approval. As an example, we can have a process for requesting access to a special printer or a request for premium software.

Creating an Incident and Problem Management process

This recipe discusses creating an Incident and Problem Management process.

Getting ready

In Incident Management, we focus on restoring a service to its known mode of operation before an unplanned interruption. Problem Management requires you to focus on understanding the actual cause of the interruption with the goal of providing a permanent resolution.

The ITIL© framework books and online resources discuss best practices for Incident and Problem Management processes. You must plan to review and understand Incident and Problem Management principles as a prerequisite to creating the processes.

How to do it...

An example of the steps for creating an Incident and Problem Management process is as follows.

Incident Management

Here are the example steps specific to an Incident Management process:

1. Agree and document the organization Incident Management policy.
2. Document the operational process to support the Incident Management policy. This should include but not be limited to the following:

   - Support hours
   - Classification categories
   - Escalation procedures

3. Create and assign people roles to manage the process, for example, Service Desk analysts:

   - Desktop support
   - Infrastructure analyst
   - Service Desk managers

4. We typically have two channels for Incident Management:

- Service Desk team-created incidents (using the SCSM console Sample process steps from incident creation to priority allocation) are shown in the following figure:

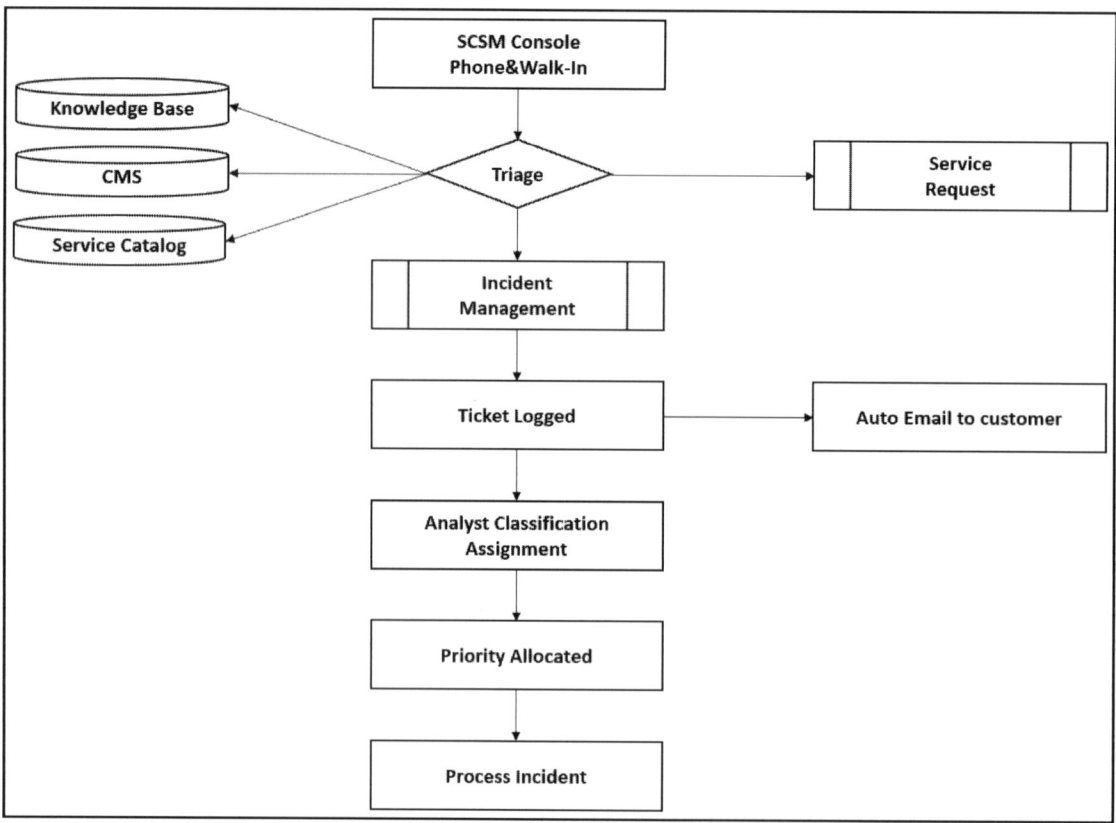

- Automated or end user self-service created incidents (end user web portal, e-mail, or automatic system event driven). Sample process steps from incident creation to priority allocation are shown in the following figure:

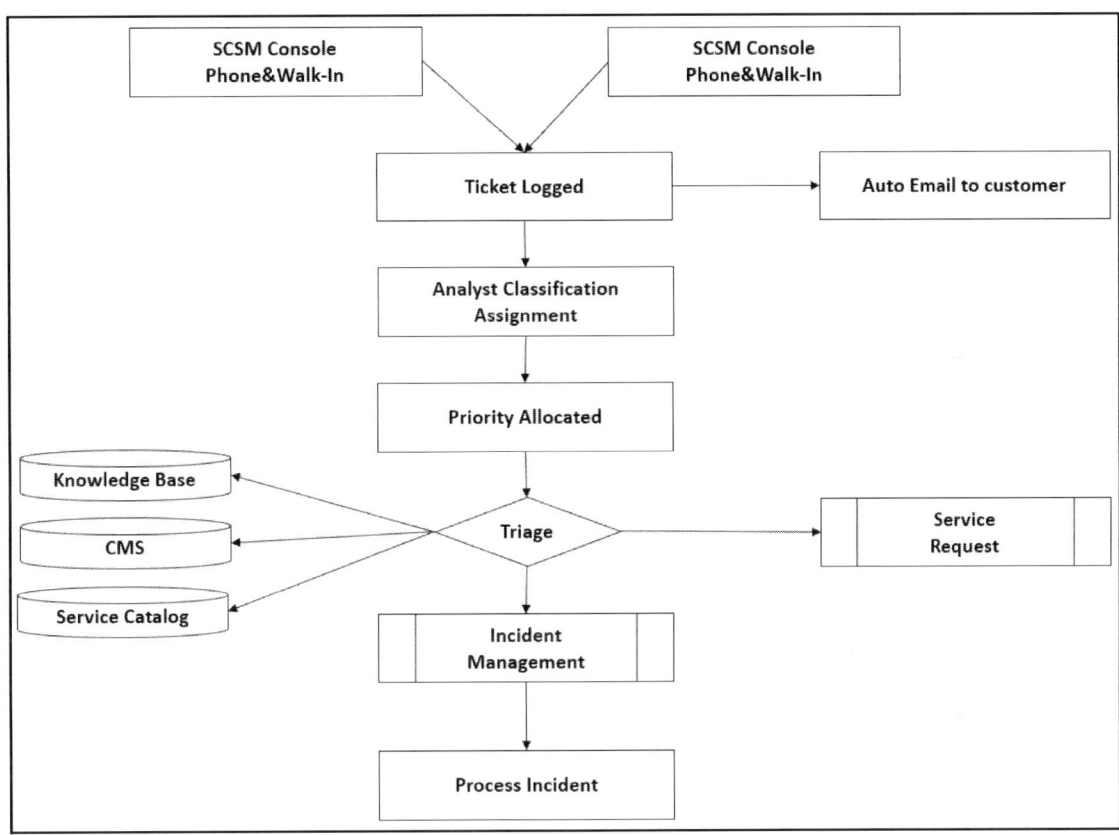

5. The difference between the two typical channels is how the incident is initially categorized (triage). The next step, Process Incident, involves the creation of a process flow to match how the Incident Management team manage the incident based on your policies and procedures. An example is shown in the following figure:

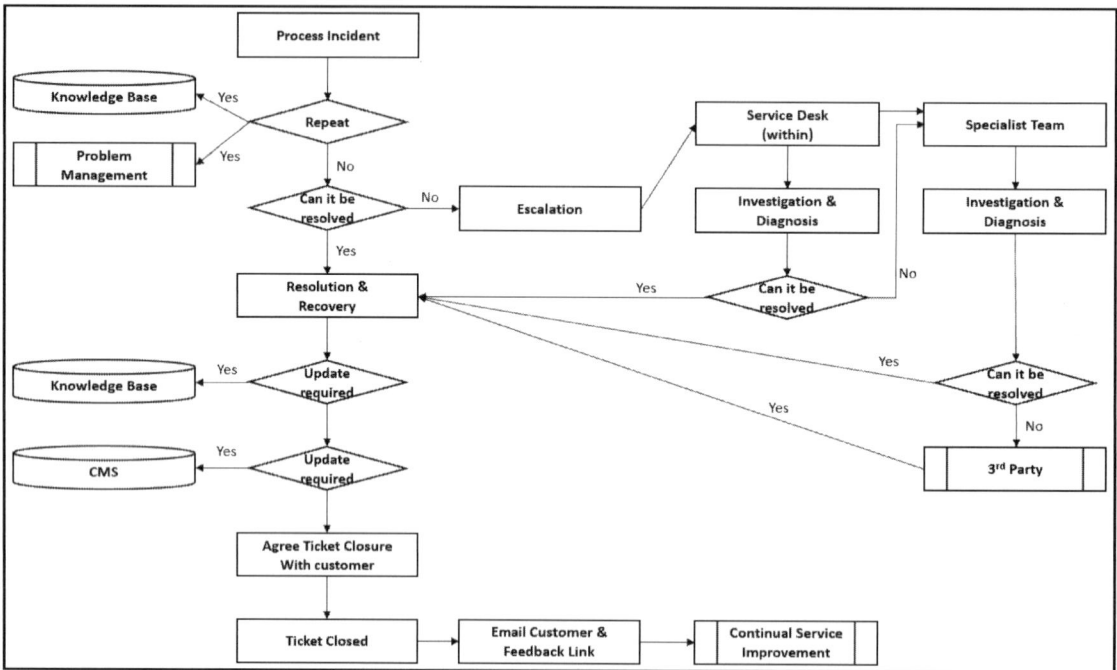

- Monitor and report on the performance of the Incident Management process. The aim is to improve the process, and also identify incidents that require Problem Management.

Problem Management

Here are the example steps specific to a Problem Management process:

1. Agree and document the organization Problem Management policy.
2. Document the operational process to support the Problem Management policy.
3. Create and assign people roles to manage the process, for example:

   - Problem analysts

- Problem managers

4. Review the Incident Management process with the aim of identifying instances of the following type:

 - Repeated issues over a defined period (for example, monthly, quarterly, or annually)
 - Incidents with known workarounds (typically implies there is an opportunity for root cause investigation)

5. Perform detailed investigation on incidents escalated to Problem Management using internal experts or third-party external support.
6. Create a change request for problems with known permanent fixes.

How it works...

Incident Management is about getting services that people rely on back to an agreed operational state as soon as possible. An example of Incident Management is a customer who is unable to access their documents:

1. On investigation, we find that the issue is with the laptop assigned to the customer.
2. We issue the customer with a loan laptop and confirm access to their document.

The previous steps will resolve the incident, but we still have a problem. What is wrong with the customer's laptop?

The answer to the question is Problem Management. We use Problem Management to identify the true (root) cause of the issue. We can continue with our scenario from Incident Management:

1. The desktop engineering team identifies the issue as a network hardware device failure in the laptop.
2. The team also identifies that this issue has been happening to a number of laptops over the last quarter.
3. The team also identifies through asset management that we purchased a set of laptops from a vendor and all the issues relate to this set.
4. We escalate to the vendor and get a driver fix.
5. A change request is raised to proactively apply the fix to all laptops from the set.

The fix applied to all laptops in scope resolves the issue on the original laptop. We can close the problem, and also change the original status of the incident to closed. A final best practice will be to create a knowledge article about this known issue and its corresponding fix.

The previous examples illustrate how Incident Management and Problem Management work in practice.

Creating a Change and Release Management process

This recipe discusses creating a Change and Release Management process for an organization.

Getting ready

In Change Management, we focus on enhancing existing services, service components, or introducing new services and components without an unplanned interruption to existing services. Release Management focuses on when the changes are implemented and manages planned interruption to services.

The ITIL© framework online resources delve much deeper into the best practices for the Change and Release Management processes. You must plan to review and understand Change and Release Management principles as a prerequisite to creating the processes.

How to do it...

An example of the steps for creating a Change and Release Management process is as follows:

1. Agree and document the organization Change and Release Management policy with the aim of identifying the following:

   - Change types and categories
   - Change type priorities
   - Policy owner

2. Create and continually update a service map for all services and applications in scope of Change and Release Management. Examples include but are not limited to the following types of service: infrastructure services, messaging services, and collaboration services. A best practice industry approach is the RACI model:

- **Responsible (R)**: Who is responsible for the service or service component?
- **Accountable (A)**: Who is accountable for the service? This is typically the assigned business unit application owner.
- **Consulted (C)**: Who is consulted about the service operations? Typically, this is a support team acting as the subject matter experts.
- **Informed (I)**: Who is informed about service availability?

3. Document the operational process to support the Change and Release Management policy. The operational procedures should include the following:
   - Technical approvers and management approvers
   - Plan for proxy approvers to cover expected or non-expected absence of main approvers
   - Maintenance schedules (approved change implementation windows)
   - Release process structure:
     - By change stage
     - By change type
     - By maintenance window

4. Create and assign people roles to manage the process, for example:

- Change managers
- Release managers
- Change implementers (this would be a logical role as implementers will vary based on the change type and related service)

5. Review the Change and Release Management process with the aim of identifying instances of the following type:

- Candidates for Service Request fulfillment (changes that have been successfully validated as low risk and low impact based on an agreed number of successful implementation results).
- Changes requiring re-classification, for example, a minor change that results in a major outage due to an identified dependency service.
- Release window adjustment due to a business process schedule change, for example, a financial audit application used during peak accounting periods may require a special release window.

6. The Change and Release Management process, once established, typically has the following operational states:
  - Initiate
  - Approve:
    - Technical (validation from a technical perspective)
    - Management (validation from a cost and business risk perspective)
  - Implement and release:
    - Implementation steps and owners (who does it and how)
    - Release schedule alignment (when it gets done)
  - Post implementation review, for example:
    - Successful in the time allocated
    - Successful but overrun time allocated
    - Failed
    - Resubmission

The following figure provides an example of the process from the change initiation stage:

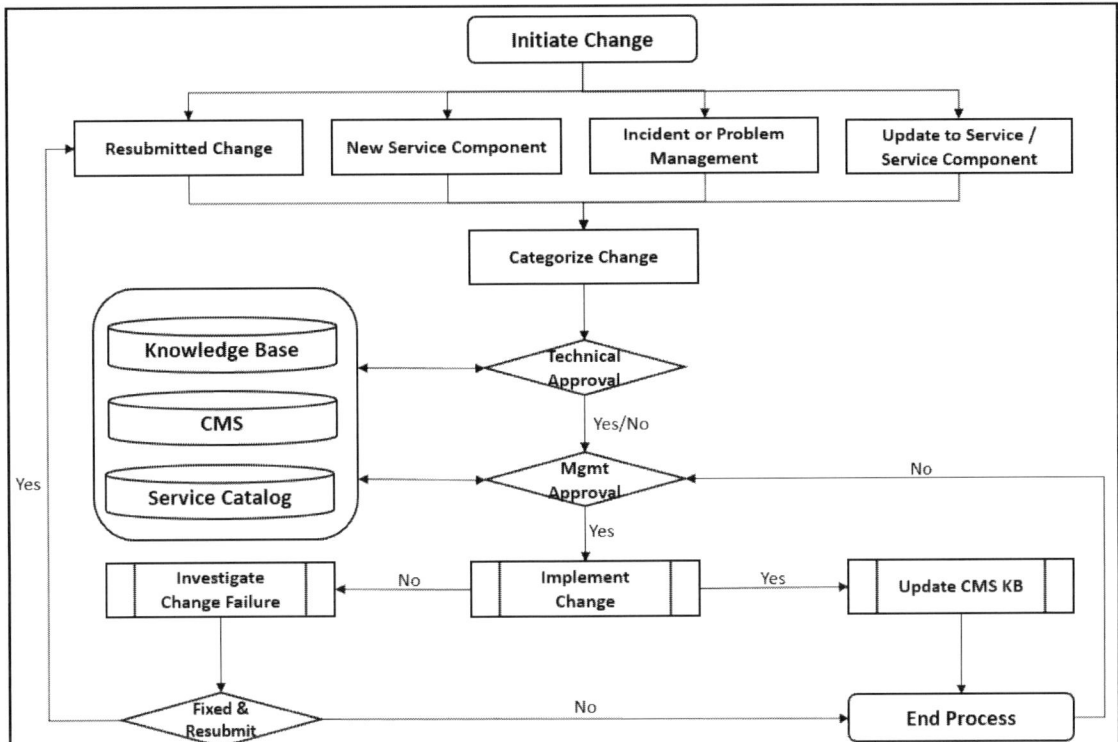

How it works...

In Change Management, we use Release Management principles to coordinate multiple changes in cases where these changes may impact on each other. We focus on the following areas when creating and implementing Change Management:

- Organization culture:
    - Successful Change Management creation requires complete buy-in from the whole organization
    - Exceptions and breaches of Change Management are opportunities to educate and refine the process as appropriate
    - Change Management is a journey, not a destination (expect changing conditions and adapt as appropriate)

- Categorization and classification:
    - What type of change, and how does it impact existing services?
    - How important is the change?
- Approvals:
    - Who has the authority to approve?
    - Who has the best knowledge on the impact and risk to the existing services?
    - Cost justification
- Post implementation analysis:
    - Unplanned impact of changes
    - Configuration management updates and service catalogue maintenance
    - Lessons learned (Knowledge Management)

There's more...

Release Management can be as follows:

- **Simple**: Manage the forward change schedule
    - Multiple changes that affect the same service component requires coordination
    - Multiple changes grouped and released during the same maintenance window
- **Complex**:
    - Extension of application life cycle management.
    - New software developed in house.
    - Patch Management is a candidate for Release Management.
    - Release Management is a discipline with broad and wide coverage. A best practice for creating the process is this: you should plan to assign a Release Management expert. The process should also have a supported agreed organizational policy.

Creating an IT Service Desk

This section provides an example of what is typically required to create an IT Service Desk.

Getting ready

Service Desks are organization-specific but share a common goal. The goal of most Service Desks is to be the central point of contact for customers in the following areas:

- Request for services
- Unplanned outages or interruptions to services
- Feedback channels for improvement to existing services
- Coordination and tracking of active requests and incidents

A prerequisite for creating a Service Desk process is to define what role it would play in the overall ITSM strategy.

Service Desks principles are defined in the ITIL© Service Operations books. Plan to review the industry best practices before creating an organization-specific version.

How to do it...

There are three main types of Service Desk:

- **Local Service Desk**: A Service desk in each customer's geographic location, independently managing support services
- **Central Service Desk**: One service desk that supports all geographic locations and offers a consolidated picture of issues and requests across the organization
- **Virtual Service Desk**: Use technology to manage either of the first two types from any location

The successful Service Desk process is based on communication and coordination. Here are some categories of tools you must plan to implement to support the process:

- Integrated Service Management and Operations Management systems (for example, the Microsoft System Center Management product)
- Advanced telephony systems (for example, auto-routing, hunt groups, **Computer Telephony Integration (CTI)**, **Voice Over Internet Protocol (VOIP)**)
- **Interactive Voice Response (IVR)** systems
- Electronic communication (voice, video, mobile, intranet, Internet, and e-mail systems)
- Knowledge, search, and diagnostic tools
- Automated operations and Network Management tools

Here are the common functions the Service Desk should aim to perform:

- Receive calls and act as the first-line customer liaison
- Record and track incidents and complaints
- Keep customers informed about request status and progress
- Make an initial assessment of requests, attempt to resolve them, or escalate as appropriate
- Manage the request and issues life cycle, including closure and verification
- Communicate planned changes and disruption to services
- Coordinate hierarchical and functional escalations
- Highlight customer and service desk personnel training opportunities
- Monitor and track **Service Level Agreements (SLAs)** and **Operational Level Agreements (OLAs)**
- Report on customer trends and service desk performance

How it works...

The service desk process, once established, should deliver the following:

- Act to lower the total cost of IT ownership
- Support the integration and management of the service portfolio and catalogue
- Make efficient use of resources and technology
- Optimize investments and the management of business support services

A service desk should aim to provide a unified and simplified experience to the customers it serves.

The Service Level Management process

Service Level Management (SLM) is the foundation and underpinning element of ITSM. This recipe looks at the common input components of SLM and the deliverables of the process. SLM typically can be applied internally, externally, or both. The external application of SLM can be complex as it typically requires legal contracts with external providers outside an organization. In this recipe, our focus will be on the internal execution of SLM.

Getting ready

SLM is a vital organization function. The goal of SLM is to ensure that the customers' expectations are met in line with formal published agreements. We must be able to consistently capture the inputs, and accurately report on the adherence or non-compliance to the agreed SLM objectives. We must have organization buy-in and a full understanding of SLM through official ITIL© material, or appropriate training in the SLM discipline.

How to do it...

SLM is the key to all processes and functions in ITIL©. The common area in SLM is Service Level Agreements (SLAs. We will use Incident Management and Service Request Fulfillment to implement this:

1. Agree and publish Service Level Agreements for Incident Management response times and resolution times. The following table provides an example of the SLM inputs for five categories (priority) of incidents based on urgency and impact. The second table provides an example of the SLM inputs for the Service Request Fulfillment:

Incident Priority	Target first response	Target resolution time
1	30 minutes	4 hours
2	2 hours	8 hours
3	8 hours	24 hours
4	16 hours	80 hours
5	24 hours	120 hours
Service Request priority	Target first response	Target implementation
1	8 hours	16 hours
2	16 hours	24 hours
3	24 hours	72 hours

2. Install and configure an appropriate ITSM tool with SLM implementation capabilities (for example, SCSM).
3. Configure the tool with the details of the organization SLM requirements.

4. Capture the SLM metrics. Examples of some incident metrics are as follows:
    *   Number of SLA breaches
    *   Average time to resolve incidents
    *   Number of incidents per week/month/quarter

5. Monitor the operational adherence to the SLM metric.

6. Report and adjust the appropriate execution of the processes to ensure adherence is in line with the agreed SLM objectives.

How it works...

Service Level Management is what we use to ensure that IT capabilities are aligned with customer expectations of the services provided by IT. The successful implementation of SLM involves creating agreements between the supplier of services (IT and supporting third parties), and the consumer of the services (business customers). A driver for successful SLM is when an organization commits to compliance with industry-recognized standards. The following standards are typical drivers:

*   ISO 9001
*   ISO 27001
*   ITIL© certification

The overall goal is to ensure services are delivered at the right cost to the expectations of the service consumers. SLM is at its most effective when we create credible agreements, report proactively on performance of the service, and accurately capture the service consumer's feedback (for example, using customer satisfaction surveys).

Dependencies and relationships between ITSM processes

Technically, all ITSM processes in this chapter can be implemented independently in SCSM. Based on best practice, an order of implementing the process is recommended.

Getting ready

A general understanding of the objectives of ITSM frameworks is required for this recipe. Also, a basic understanding of all ITSM processes described in this chapter is required.

How to do it…

The following figure provides a diagram of information flow, trigger options, and relationships between the ITSM processes in SCSM:

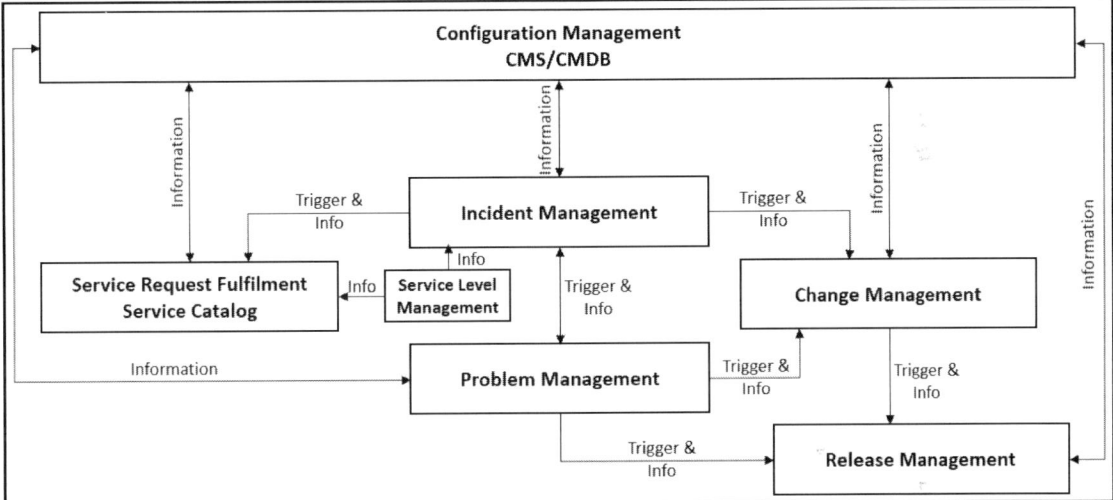

The order of implementing the different ITSM processes in SCSM depends on the requirement of each individual organization, which might differ. In general, some combinations and orders of ITSM processes are a best practice to the successful implementation of SCSM.

Option 1:

1. Configuration Management
2. Incident Management
3. Problem Management

Option 2:

1. Configuration Management
2. Service Request Fulfillment (Service Catalog)

Option 3:

1. Configuration Management
2. Incident Management
3. Combination of the following:
4. Problem Management
5. Change Management
6. Release Management

Option 4:

1. Configuration Management
2. Incident Management
3. Combination of the following:
4. Problem Management
5. Change Management
6. Service Request Fulfillment
7. Release Management

The Incident Management and Service Request Fulfillment are typically supported by the Service Level Management (SLM). SLM provides information on the Service Level Agreements (SLAs) for the respective processes.

How it works...

The Configuration Management process with the Configuration Management System (CMS also commonly known as the Configuration Management Database (CMDB, provides technical information and details for all IT components (Configuration Items, CIs) for all other ITSM processes in SCSM. In addition, all ITSM processes update the CMS/CMDB with relevant information as each process is executed during its life cycle.

Incident Management is responsible for the fast remediation of disrupted IT services. Information from the Incident Records (Incident Ticket) can be used in the Problem Management process as related Problem Records. This is helpful in order to create workarounds, create Known Errors, discover the root cause of an incident, and optimize the IT services.

The Incident Management and the Problem Management processes can trigger required changes of an IT services. These changes are logged in Change Records in Change Management. A Change Record will contain different types of related activities (Review Activities, Manual Activities).

If the change is approved and all related activities in the Change Management process are completed, Release Management is responsible for rolling out the change to the affected IT service components. This will be logged as a Release Record with all the related activities of the roll-out.

An incident can also trigger a Service Request to provide a new service. For instance, an incident with the issue *Can't open a file because of missing application on a client computer* can be resolved by a Service Request to install the required application on the client computer.

The Service Level Management with defined Service Level Agreements supports the Incident Management and Service Request Fulfillment processes to monitor and report on the agreed SLM objectives.

2
Personalizing SCSM 2016 Administration

In this chapter, we will provide recipes for the initial configuration tasks an SCSM administrator should perform following a successful installation of the environment. We will cover the following areas and topics:

- Configuring how long to keep your SCSM data
- Configuring the Incident Management global settings
- Configuring the Problem Management global settings
- Configuring the Service Requests, Activity, Release, Knowledge, and Change Management global settings
- Configuring the behavior of child incidents when resolving, reactivating, and closing the parent incident
- Configuring the priority and urgency for your SLA targets
- Creating Management Packs to save your SCSM personalization
- Creating a configuration item group
- Creating a basic queue
- Creating SCSM console tasks
- Configuring global e-mail notification infrastructure settings
- Creating formatted e-mail notification templates

Introduction

The Microsoft System Center Service Manager (SCSM) console is where you will configure and manage typical settings and activities associated with the IT Infrastructure Library (ITILÂ®) and Microsoft Management Framework (MOF) processes implemented by the product. This chapter will provide steps for the global settings and some basic activities you may want to perform, before delving into the configuration and management of the supported product processes.

The settings addressed by this chapter have a significant impact on the behavior of Work Items and Configuration Items. In some cases, there is no retrospective application of the settings to existing items. The authors recommend you review and apply the settings in this chapter as a first step in the full configuration of your environment, after installation of the product.

Configuring how long to keep your SCSM data

This recipe provides the steps required to configure how long SCSM retains the data presented in the console. We will also provide steps on how long to retain data for historical use.

Getting ready

You need to ensure you have successfully installed the SCSM product, are a user in the SCSM Administrators role, and have the SCSM console open.

How to do it…

The following steps will guide you through the process of configuring the retention period in SCSM:

1. Navigate to **Service Manager Console** | **Administration** | **Settings** | **Data Retention Settings** and click on **Properties** under **Tasks**, as shown in the following screenshot:

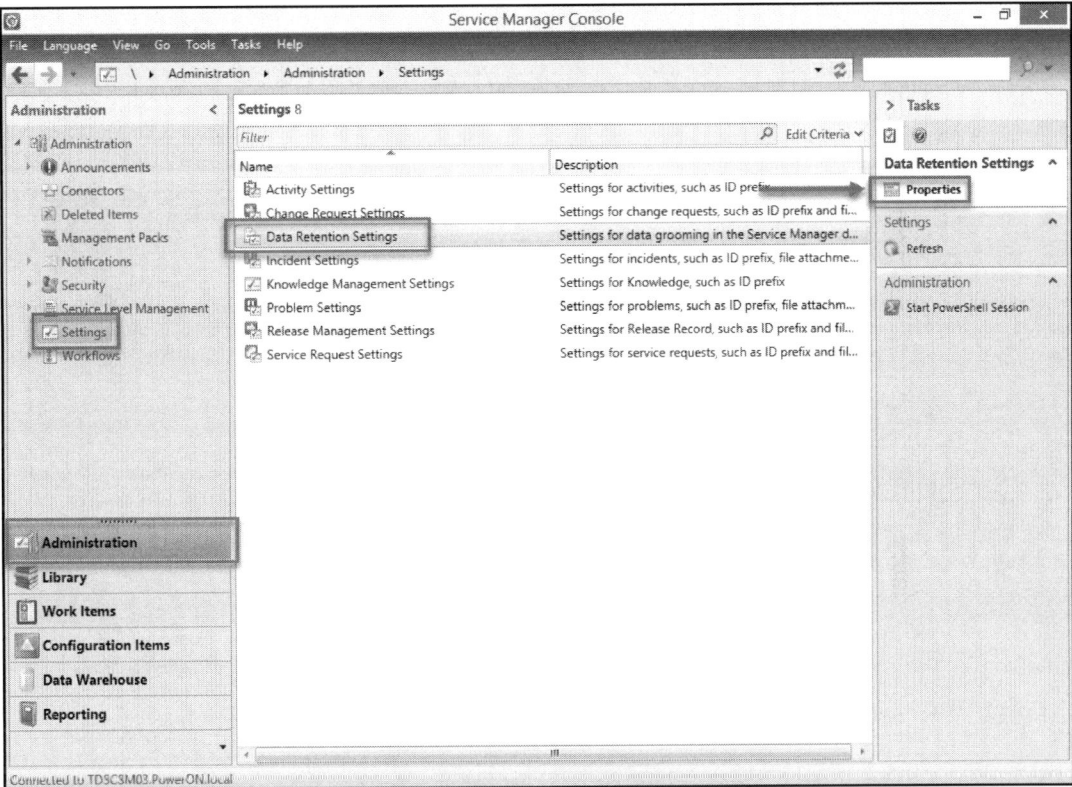

2. Select **Work Items | Review** and adjust retention times (in days) to reflect how long the items should be kept in the SCSM database:

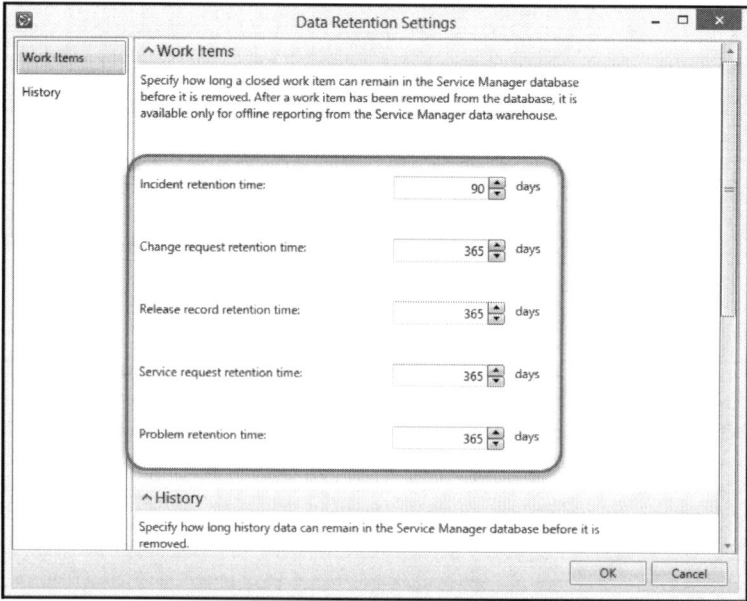

3. Select **History | Review** and adjust the history retention times (in days) to reflect how long the history of items should be kept in the SCSM database:

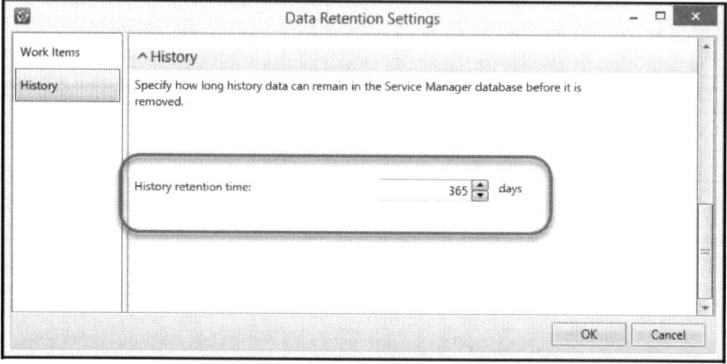

4. Click on **OK** to confirm the data retention settings.

How it works...

SCSM, by default, has grooming settings in place to keep the performance of the product at its most desired state. There are two types of data in SCSM:

- **Configuration Items**: These are typically the console objects you see in the Configuration Items node and are of the class type `configuration item`. The Configuration Items are typically introduced and maintained by the connectors (for example, the Active Directory connector imports the users, computers, and printer Configuration Items).
- **Work Items**: These are typically the objects you see in the Work Items node of the console and are of the class type `work item`. These objects are associated with their respective process class (for example, the incident management Work Items class for all incidents).

The retention settings are related to the Work Items class. The Work Items class, for example, incidents, cannot be deleted from the console. An automated deletion process using the data retention settings you specify is responsible for removing the Work Items data from the SCSM database. The automated process for deleting items is known as grooming. It is important to note that the criterion uses the following formula to groom (delete) the respective Work Items data:

Delete the work item type (for example, incident) with a status = Closed and has not been modified in x days (where x is the number of days you set for the respective work items type).

You must plan to have a data warehouse configuration with the following desired objectives of typical best practice organizations:

- **Improve the performance and efficiency of the console**: The old work items in the working database (the database name is `ServiceManager` by default) slows down the console and provides a negative experience for the service management team.
- **Historical retention and reporting**: You need to install and configure a data warehouse in order to have reporting capabilities. The data warehouse is optimized for reporting and is the recommended option for retaining the old Work or Configuration Items information.

A data warehouse combined with optimal data retention settings will provide your environment with the desired objectives.

There's more...

This recipe focused on the Work Item grooming and provided instructions to that effect. Configuration Items are also groomed but are controlled by the connectors, and the delete actions are manually performed by an SCSM administrator with the relevant role in the console.

Additionally, grooming has an internal schedule. The schedule control requires you to export and edit the internal management packs. The default schedule is midnight every day and it is run on the server that is assigned the workflow role. (This is typically the first management server unless you manually move the role.)

Configuration Items data grooming using the console

The Configuration Items displayed in the console can be manually deleted. The console user needs to be either an Advanced Operator, or an Administrator role user to perform a delete action. For example, you can delete a user in the console by selecting the **Delete** task in the console, as shown in the following screenshot:

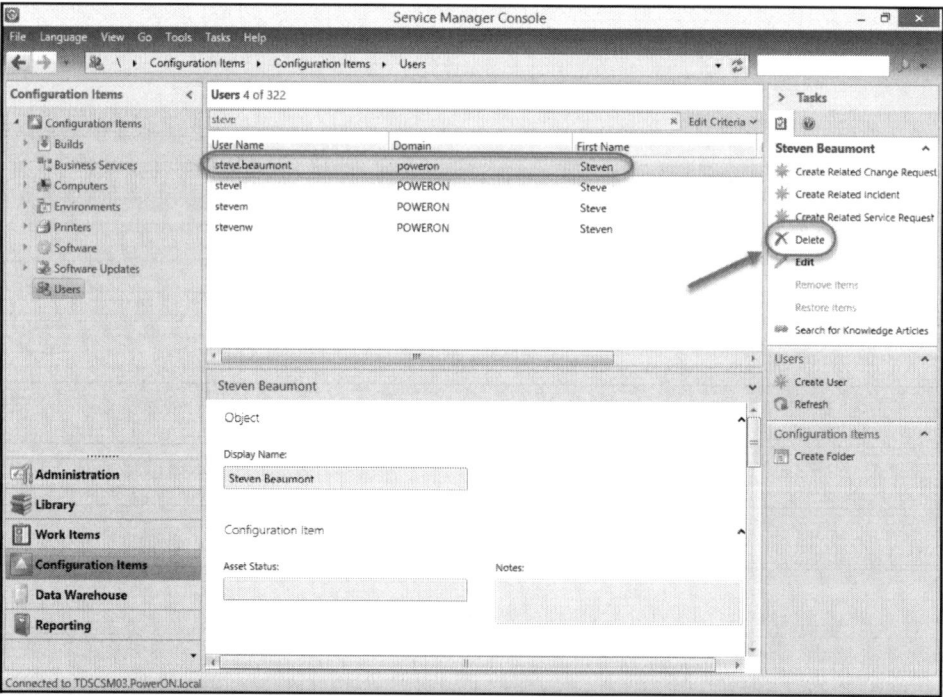

The delete action marks the Configuration Items in scope for automated grooming and does not perform an immediate removal from the database. The Configuration Items will not show in the Configuration Items space and will be marked with a status of *pending delete* in the database. The deleted item will be placed in the **Deleted items** node and can be restored by an Administrator, if the action is performed before the internal grooming process runs. Note that if the Configuration Items is from an active connector then it would be re-imported into the database and displayed the next time the connector is synchronized. You must delete the object from the source (for example, Active Directory) if it is a Configuration Items from a connector.

The history setting determines how long Configuration Items are kept in the **Deleted items** node outside the normal connector behavior.

See also

Modifying grooming settings is performed in the respective management pack responsible for the grooming process. This type of modification is typically performed in the authoring tool or an XML editor.

- See the *Using the SCSM Authoring Tool* and *Creating new classes* recipes in `Chapter 11`, *Extending SCSM with Advanced Personalization,* for advanced recipes on management pack authoring
- `Appendix B`, *Useful Websites and Community Resources,* provides a list of useful websites with comprehensive advanced instructions on authoring and configuring SCSM

Configuring the Incident Management global settings

This recipe will provide the steps required to configure the general settings, which apply to all incident class Work Items. We will also provide steps on how to assign a default support group for new incidents.

Getting ready

You need to ensure you have successfully installed the SCSM product, are a user in the SCSM Administrators role, and have the SCSM console open. Plan a naming standard for the process prefix and agree a size limitation for attachments.

Follow the list creation instructions in `Chapter 7`, *Working with Incident and Problem Management*, to create a new list item for the *Incident Tier Queue* list called *Service Desk 1 Line*.

How to do it...

The following steps will guide you through the process of configuring the global settings for incident management:

1. Navigate to **Service Manager Console | Administration | Settings | Incident Settings** and click on **Properties** under **Tasks**, as shown in the following screenshot:

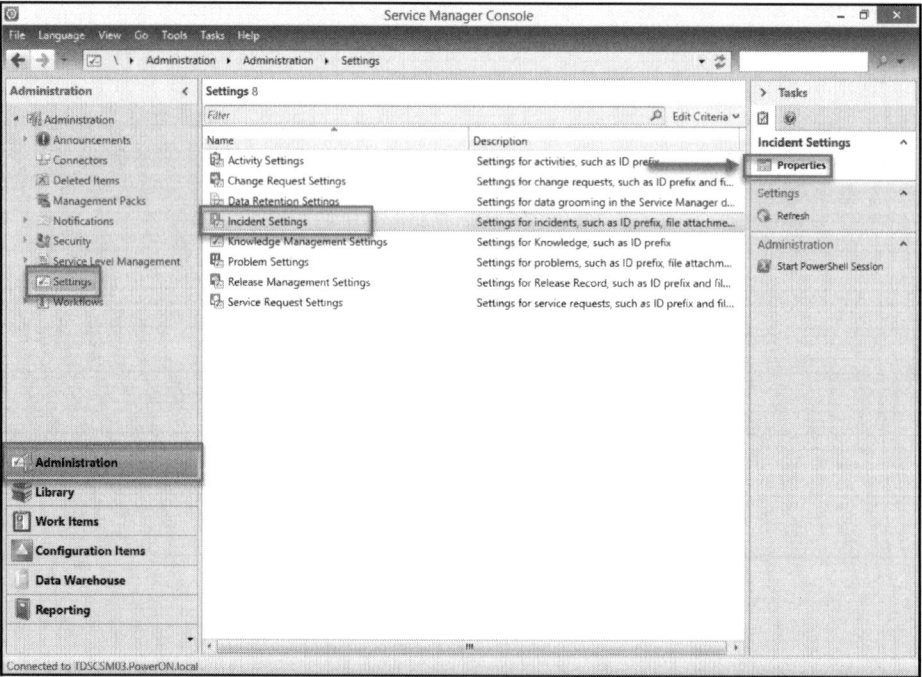

2. Click on **General** and configure the following settings to your organization's standard:

- **Prefix: IR**
- **Maximum number of attached files: 10** (default setting)
- **Maximum size (KB): 2048** (default setting)
- **Default support group: Service Desk** (a custom Incident Tier queue list item)

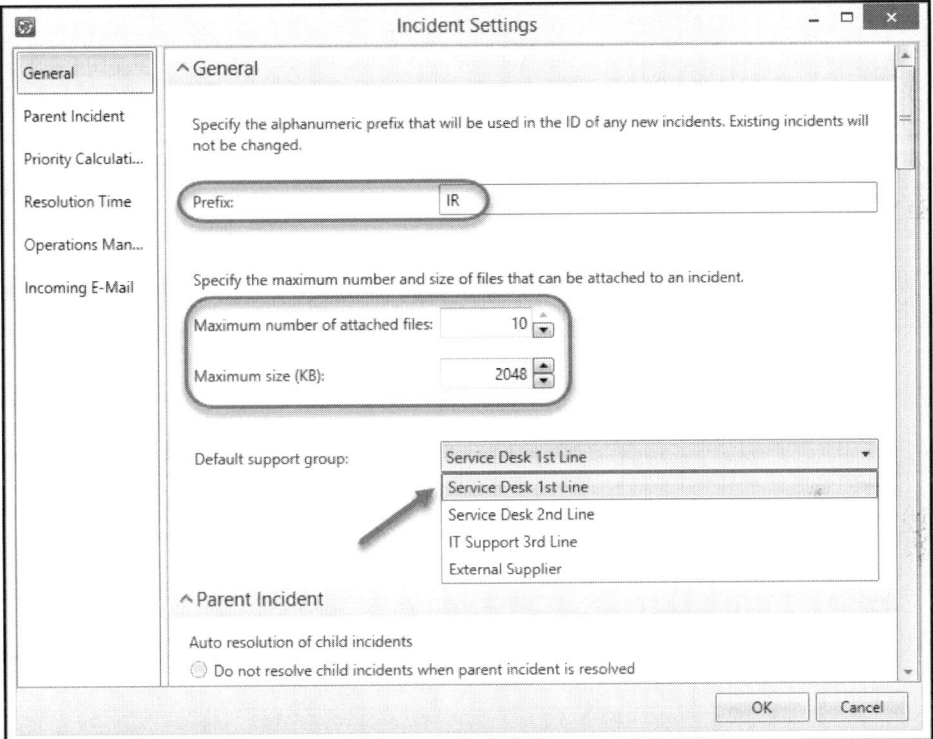

3. Review the settings and click on **OK**.

How it works...

The global settings we have configured will apply to all incidents you create. Prefix is the first part of the incident reference number. It is automatically generated and is always higher than the last incident number in the database. The attachment settings apply to how many files you, or a user using the self-service portal, can attach to the incident. The attachment size is used to specify the maximum size of a file that can be attached. The final setting, **Default support group**, is the logical group to whom the incident is assigned.

Configuring the Problem Management global settings

This recipe will provide the steps required to configure the general settings, which apply to all problem class Work Items.

Getting ready

You need to ensure you have successfully installed the SCSM product, are a user in the SCSM Administrators role, and have the SCSM console open. Plan a naming standard for the process prefix and agree a size limitation for attachments. You also need to consider values to define the priorities of a problem using an impact/urgency matrix.

In this chapter, see the *Configuring the priority and urgency for your SLA targets* recipe for more information on how to configure the priority matrix.

How to do it…

The following steps will guide you through the process of configuring the global settings for problem management:

1. Navigate to **Service Manager Console** ❘ **Administration** ❘ **Settings** ❘ **Problem Settings** and click on **Properties** under **Tasks**, as shown in the following screenshot:

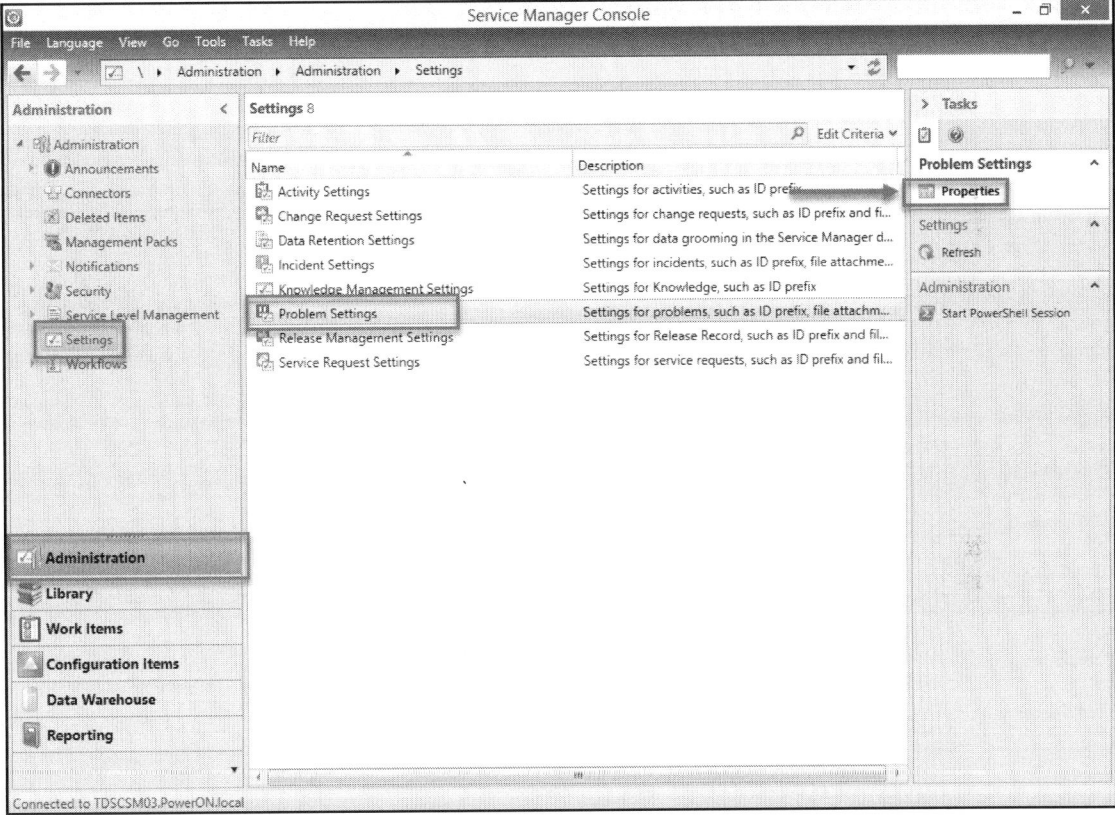

2. Click on General and configure the following settings to your organization's standard:

- **Prefix: PR**
- **Maximum number of attached files: 10** (default setting)
- **Maximum size (KB): 2048** (default setting)

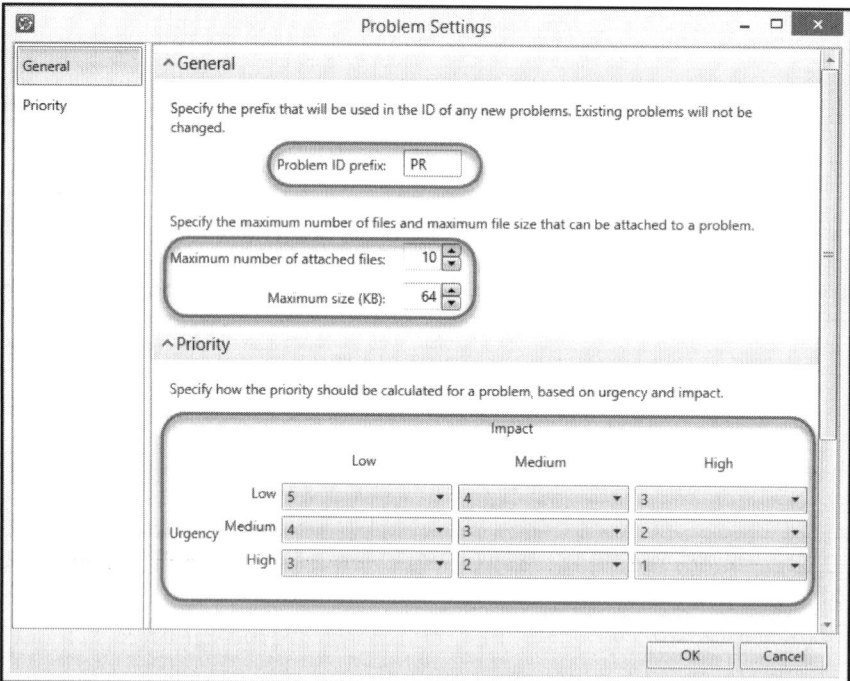

3. Use the **Priority** section to drop down and select values that correspond to your priority of a problem based on the impact and urgency.
4. Review the settings and click on **OK**.

How it works...

The global settings we have configured will apply to all problems you create. The prefix is the first part of the problem reference number. It is automatically generated and is always higher than the last problem number in the database. The attachment settings apply to how many files you can attach to the problem. The attachment size is used to specify the maximum size of a file that can be attached.

The priority settings allow you to define a matrix that when logging a problem in the console allows a priority rating to be assigned based on the combinations of impact and urgency chosen. This priority can then be used in the configuration of queues and SLAs, for example.

Configuring the Service Requests, Activity, Release, Knowledge, and Change Management global settings

This recipe will provide the steps required to configure the general settings, which apply to all Service Requests, all Activity class types, Release, Knowledge, and Change Management class Work Items.

Getting ready

You must ensure you have successfully installed the SCSM product, are a user in the SCSM Administrators role, and have the SCSM console open. Plan a naming standard for the process prefix and agree a size limitation for attachments.

How to do it...

The following steps will guide you through the process of configuring other global settings:

1. Navigate to **Service Manager Console** | **Administration** | **Settings** | **Knowledge Management Settings** and click on **Properties** under **Tasks**, as shown in the following screenshot:

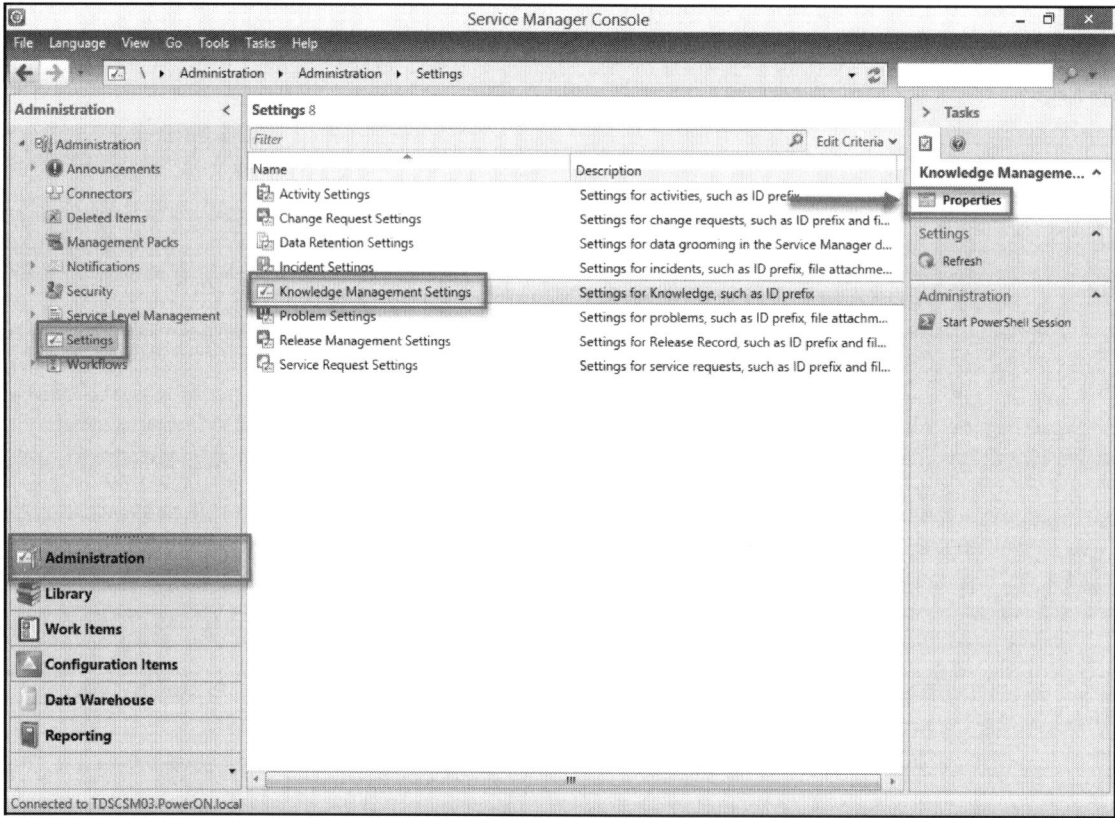

2. Type your organization's agreed prefix under **Knowledge article prefix:** (for example, replace the default **KA** with **KB**). Click on **OK** to commit your change:

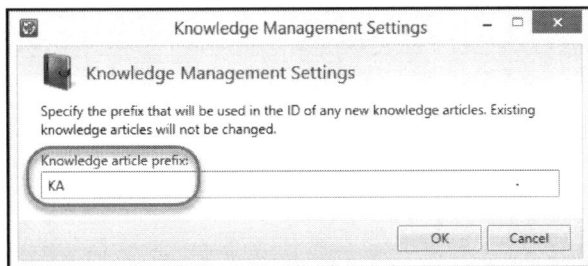

3. Repeat Step 1 and this time select **Service Request Settings**. Type in the agreed prefix and the organization's agreed standard for service request attachments. Click on **OK** to commit your change:

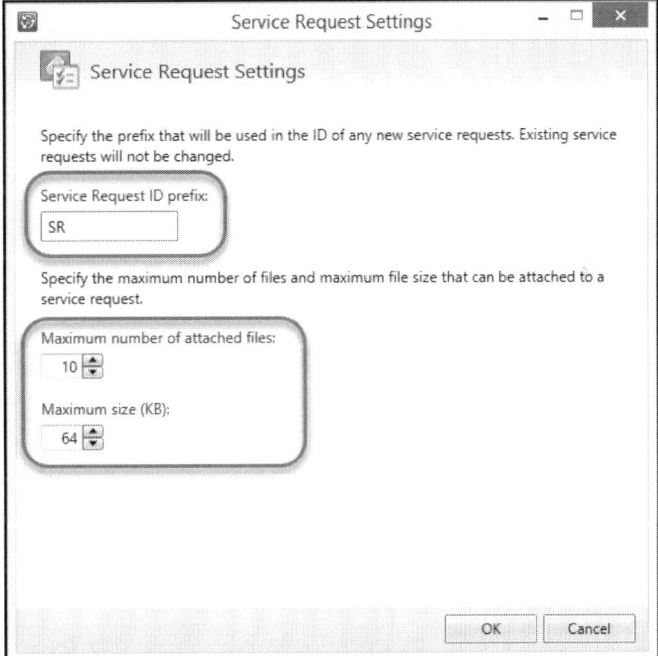

4. Repeat Step 1 and this time select **Activity Settings**. Type in the agreed relevant **Activity prefix**. Click on OK to commit your change:

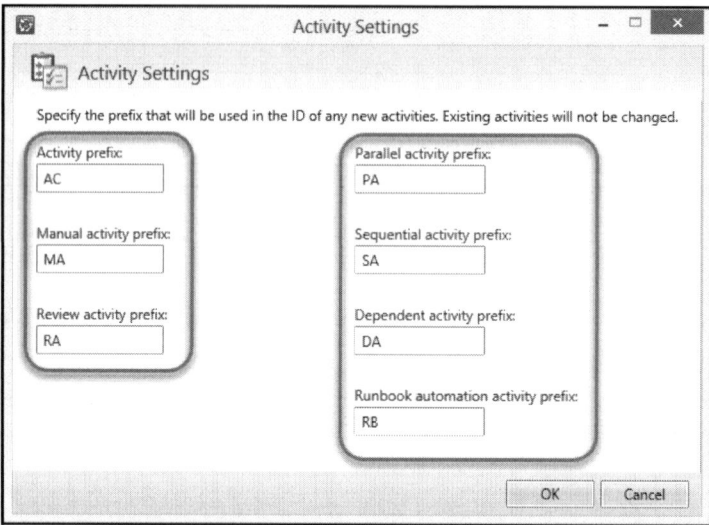

5. Repeat Step 1 and this time select **Release Management Settings**. Type in the agreed prefix and the organization's agreed standard for Release Management attachments. Click on **OK** to commit your change:

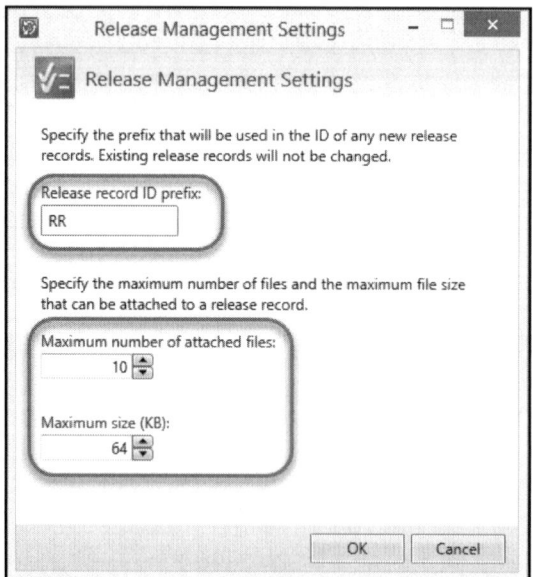

6. Repeat Step 1 and this time select **Change Management Settings**. Type in the agreed prefix and the organization's agreed standard for Change Management attachments. Click on **OK** to commit your change:

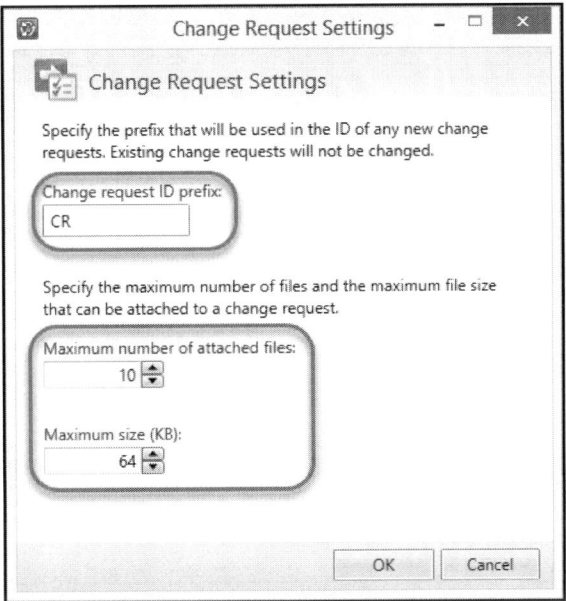

How it works…

This recipe has two components that you must decide on before applying them to the settings:

- Prefix settings
- File attachment settings, including the size per file

Working with prefix settings

SCSM by default has the prefix configured. You have the option to change the default settings to one relevant to your organization. The authors recommend you document changes to these settings and perform any changes before you go into production use. The prefix will also have an impact in reports and query-based settings.

File attachment settings

The default file settings in SCSM may not meet your organization's requirements. You have the option to increase the size and the number of files you can attach to Service Requests, Change, and Release Management records. You can view the file attachments by selecting the Related Items tab of the relevant supported process.

Configuring the behavior of child incidents when resolving, reactivating, and closing the parent incident

SCSM supports parent child relationships for the incident class. This recipe provides the steps required for the automatic configuration of child incidents, when there is a change to the parent incident.

Getting ready

You must ensure you have successfully installed the SCSM product, are a user in the SCSM Administrators role, and have the SCSM console open.

How to do it...

There are three options you can configure for the parent incident settings, as follows:

- Auto resolution of child incidents
- Auto reactivation of child incidents
- Status of child incidents when linked to a parent

These three options are discussed in the next section:

1. Navigate to **Service Manager Console** | **Administration** | **Settings** | **Incident Settings** and click on **Properties** under **Tasks**.
2. Select the **Parent Incident** tab on the left and set the following:

   - **Auto resolution of child incidents**
   - **Auto reactivation of child incidents**

- **Status of active child incidents when linked to a parent:**

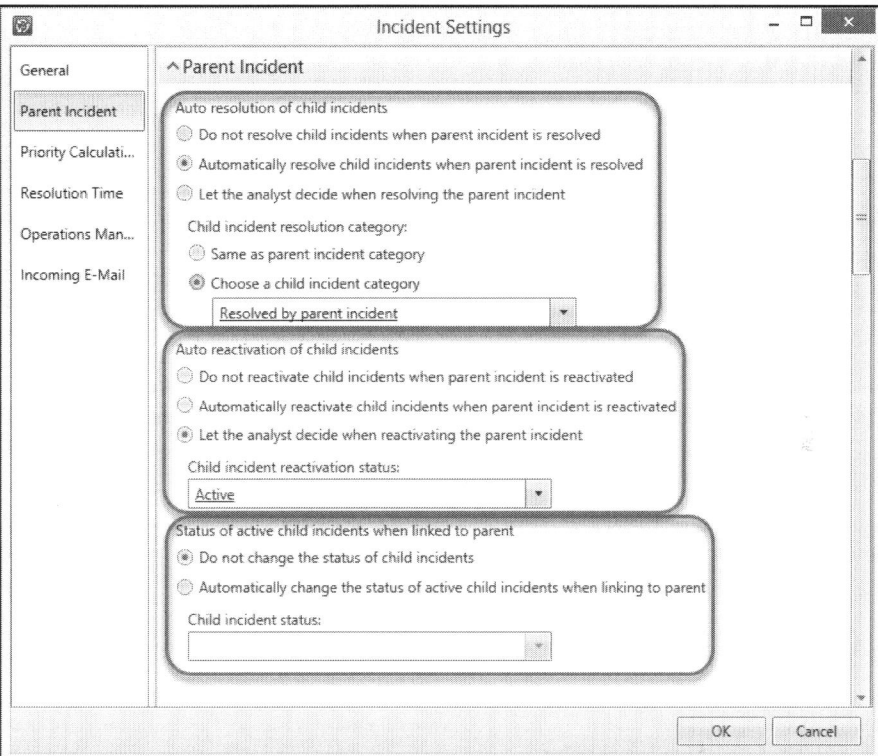

3. Click on **OK** to confirm the **Parent Incident** settings.

How it works...

The parent incident settings provide you with a means to standardize by using three options. The explanation of how these three options work is as follows.

Auto resolution of child incidents

This option should be set to reflect the agreed Incident Management process. The options you select have an impact on the SLA you set for incidents and the resulting reports. In the example settings, we set the option to **Automatically resolve child incidents when parent incident is resolved** and set the **Child incident resolution category** value to **Resolved by parent incident**.

The result of the example setting is a reduction of manual activity and the ability to report accurately on linked incidents. Selecting any of the other two options will require a manual action to the child incidents and may be prone to human error.

Auto reactivation of child incidents

This action is the opposite of the auto resolution setting. Child incidents linked with the parent can either be automatically reactivated, manually activated, or controlled by the SCSM analyst. In the example, we show a setting where the action is to allow the analysts decide.

The approach gives the analysts control over the number of child incidents to reactivate. The configuration every organization selects should be aligned with the policies and procedures agreed for Incident Management.

Status of child incidents when linked with a parent

The final option provides us with an ability to change the child status when we link it to a parent incident. SCSM automatically displays the parent incident as a link in the child incident form. Parent incident forms have an additional tab for child incidents. In the example, this is set to **Do not change the status of child incidents**. Due to the automatic behavior, you should plan to use a status change only if your internal processes require you to do so, or you have a need to report on the status.

Configuring the priority and urgency for your SLA targets

In this recipe, we will provide the steps to configure the priority and urgency settings in SCSM. The example we will use for the configuration is an organization with Priority 1 to 5 SLAs.

Getting ready

The input required for this task is a table with the values for calculating the matrix.

The following table is an example of a five priority matrix:

		Impact		
		Low	Medium	High
Urgency	Low	5	4	3
	Medium	4	3	2
	High	3	2	1

How to do it…You must ensure you have successfully installed the SCSM product, are a user in the SCSM Administrators role, and have the SCSM console open.

The following steps will guide you through the process of configuring the priority and urgency for your SLA targets:

1. Navigate to **Service Manager Console** | **Administration** | **Settings** | **Incident Settings** and click on **Properties** under **Tasks**.
2. Select the **Priority Calculation** tab on the left and fill the settings in using the **Priority Calculation** matrix table:

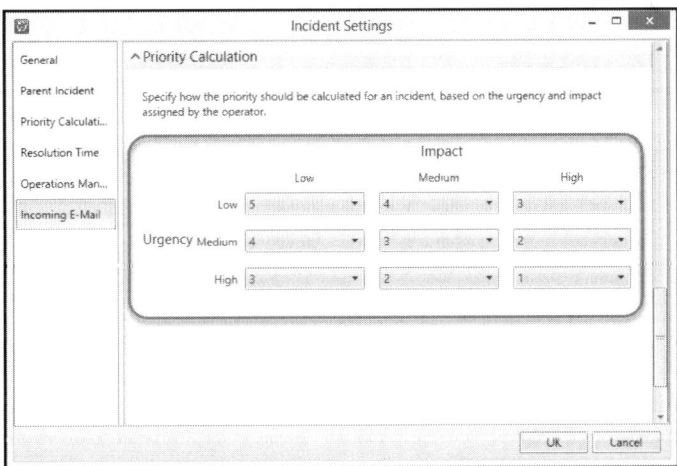

3. Click on **OK** to confirm the priority calculation settings.

How it works...

The priority that is assigned to an incident is determined using the priority calculation table. There are two mandatory selections when you create an incident, as follows:

- **Impact**: What is the effect of on incident on the business service? The values available in a default installation are low, medium, or high. The selected value will depend on the organization process. The value can be modified to change the priority.
- **Urgency**: How soon do we need to bring the service back on line? The values available in a default installation are low, medium, and high.

Using the example table, we can determine that an incident with a **low** impact and **medium** urgency will be set to priority **4**:

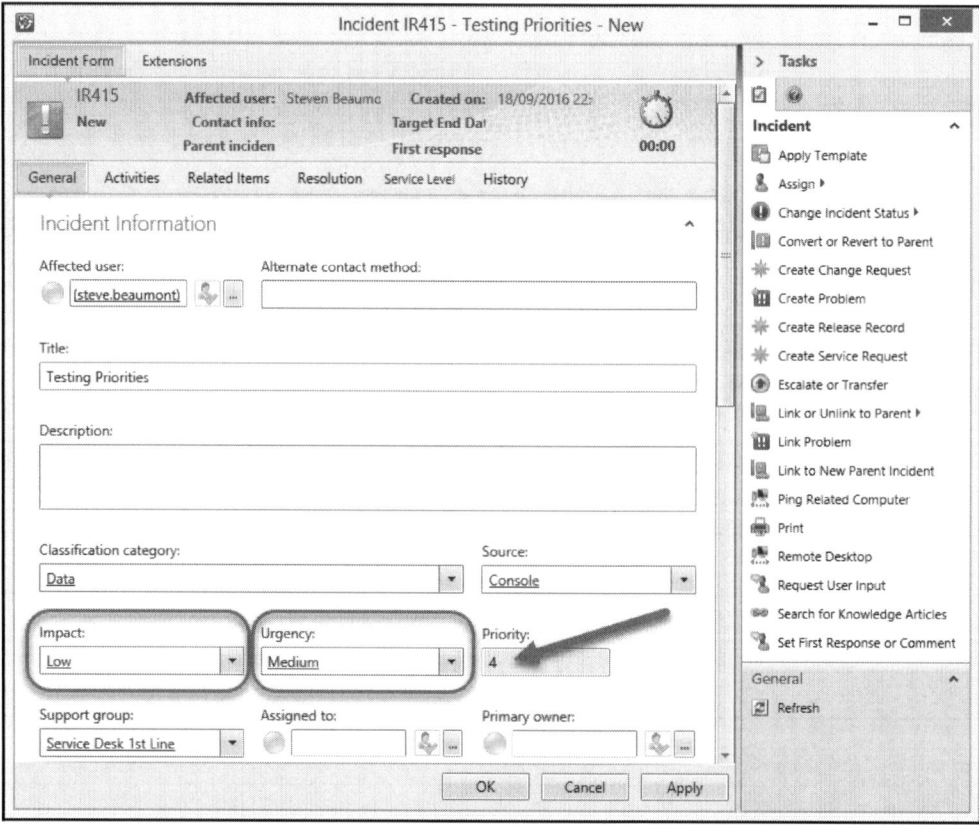

See also

- See the *Creating Incident Management SLAs* recipe in `Chapter 3`, *Configuring Service Level Agreements (SLAs)*, which covers the SLA configuration using the priority settings as a dependence configuration

Creating Management Packs to save your SCSM personalization

This recipe details the steps for creating a Management Pack in which to save your customizations. Management Packs are an XML storage format that hold customizations such as new folders, views, and queues, right through to new class types.

Getting ready

You need to ensure you have successfully installed the SCSM product, are a user in the SCSM Administrator role, and have the SCSM console open.

You should also think about adopting a naming convention for your management packs and utilization of a prefix to the naming convention to easily identify management packs custom to your organization.

How to do it...

The following steps will guide you through the process of creating a management pack for personalizations:

1. Navigate to **Service Manager Console** | **Administration** | **Management Packs** and click on **Create Management Pack** under **Tasks:**

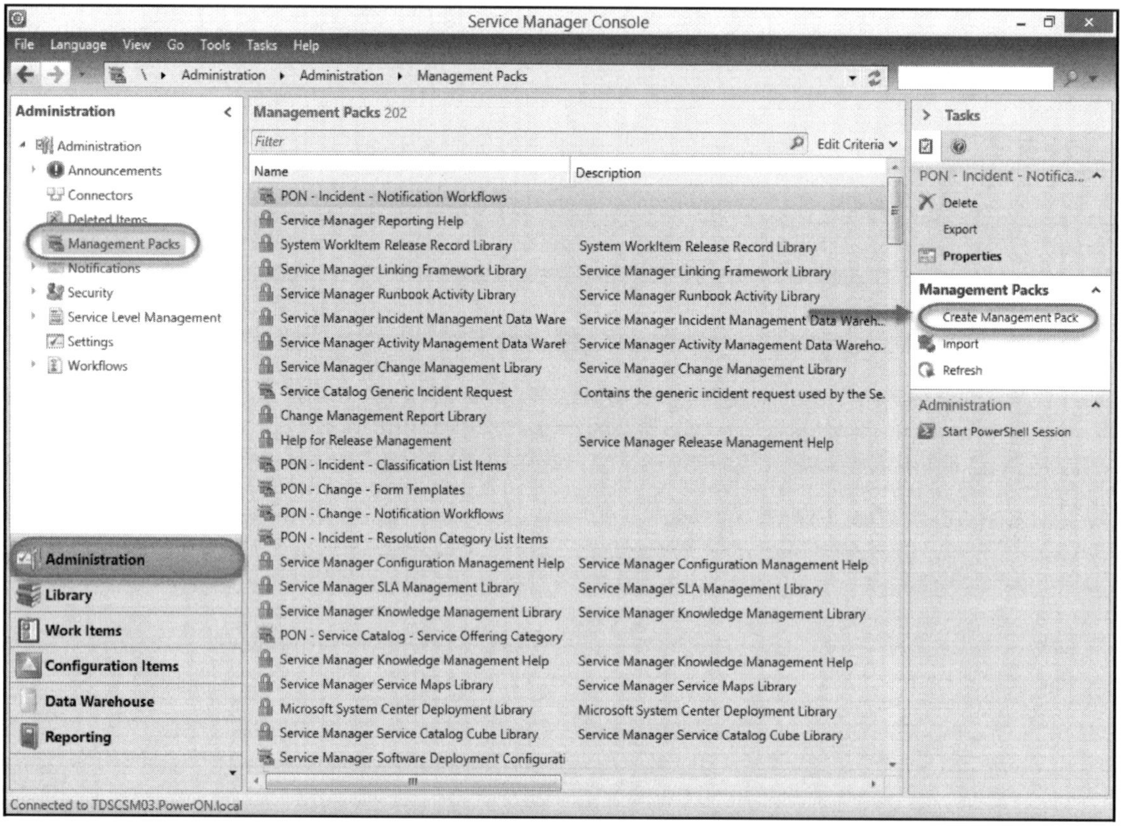

2. Provide a **Name** – PON - Incident - Lists.

   The name used above as an example for the management pack uses a naming convention of:
   <Organization Short Name> - <Class> - <Type of content>
   Adopting this type of naming convention makes it very easy to quickly identify management packs custom to your organization and their expected contents.

3. Provide a **Description** – Custom Management Pack that contains all lists related to Incidents.

4. Click **OK**:

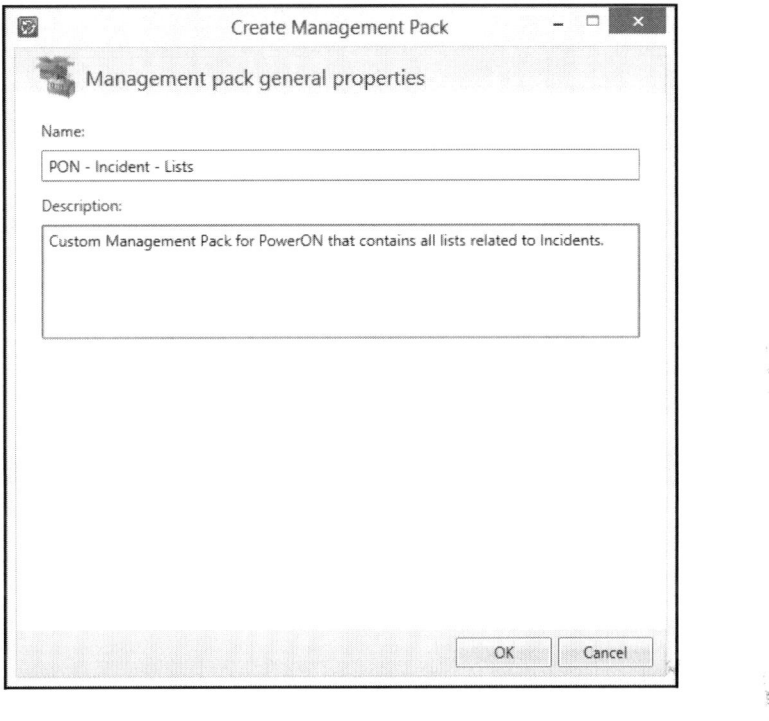

How it works...

SCSM stores its configuration in management packs. There are three types of management pack:

- **Unsealed**: This type of management pack is what you create when you create a management pack in the console using the steps outlined in this recipe, or when you create a management pack in the Authoring tool. Unsealed management packs have an .XML file extension. This type of management pack allows you to save your configuration or delete existing configurations that are stored in them using the SCSM console.

- **Sealed**: This is a management pack that is, in effect, a read-only configuration store. The settings stored in this type of management pack cannot be edited in the SCSM console. You have to store changes to the configuration associated with this management pack in an unsealed management pack or edit the original unsealed version of the management pack.
- **Bundle**: This type of management pack is a special type of a sealed management pack and has an .MBP file extension. A bundle typically contains more than one management pack and associated resources like icons.

The only option when you create a management pack in the console is the display name and the description. Management Packs created via the console are stored directly within the SCSM database, but are able to be exported for manual editing later. The filename of a management pack that was initially created in the console is by default <GUID>.XML when exported. Do not change this filename unless you are specifically updating the internal GUID within the management pack as well. Changing the filename can be error prone.

See also

- The *Creating priority queues* recipe in Chapter 3, *Configuring Service Level Agreements (SLAs)*, for other scenarios related to the use of queues

Creating a configuration item group

You can use groups within Service Manager to logically group and manage configuration items (CIs). Groups can contain either CIs of the same class or mixed classes and can be either a static group (by manually adding certain CIs) or a dynamic group (by specifying the rules).

How to do it...

The following steps will guide you through the process of creating a CI group:

1. In the **Service Manager** console, navigate to the **Library** workspace, expand **Library**, and click on **Groups**.
2. In the task pane, on the right-hand side, click on **Create Group**.
3. Review the information on the **Create Group Wizard** screen then click on **Next**.

4. On the **General** screen, provide a name for the group and a description. For this recipe, name the group **VIP** Users and provide a description of **All VIP IT Service Users**.

5. Under **Management pack**, drop the list down and select your custom management pack to store this group in, and then click on **Next**.

6. If you wish to manually specify any specific objects, on the **Included Members** screen, click on **Add**. For this recipe, simply click on **Next** on the screen to skip.

7. On the **Dynamic Members** screen click the **...** button next to the box under the text **Specify the class and add criteria to build your query**.

8. On the **Select a class** screen that opens, filter the list by typing in the box and select the **User** class. Click on **OK**.

9. Use the filter box under **Available properties** to find **Department**, select it, and click on **Add**. Then alter the **Criteria** to **contains** and type **Management**:

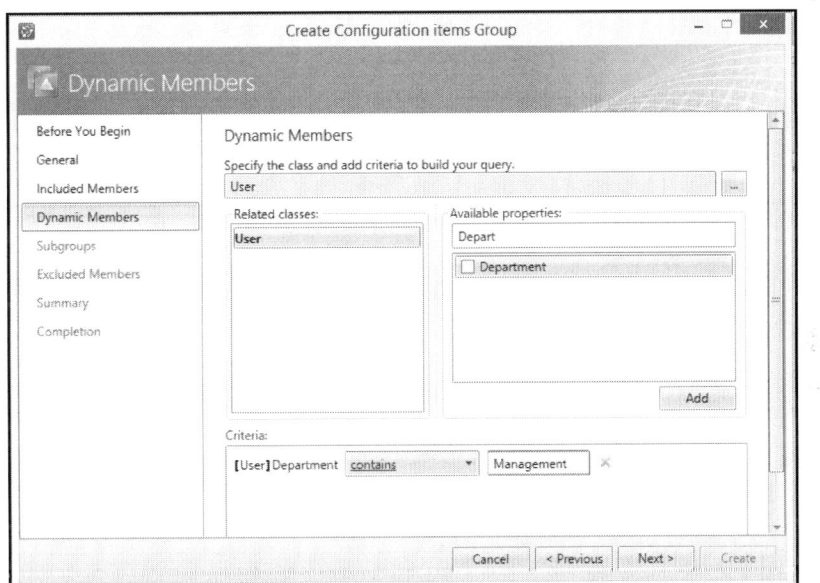

 This will create a group containing all users that have management as part of their department description that is either pulled from Active Directory or manually specified.

10. Click on **Next**.

11. On the **Subgroups** page, you can specify other groups that already exist to combine them into one group. For example, if you had two separate groups, one for the senior managers and one for the line managers, you could create an all managers group and use this to simply add both the groups without having to use the dynamic members section. For this recipe, just click on **Next** to skip the screen.

12. On the **Excluded Members** screen, you can choose objects to specifically exclude from the list that might get picked up by any dynamic rules or other groups that you don't want in this list. For this recipe, just click on **Next** to skip the screen.

13. Review the information on the **Summary** screen then click on **Create**.

14. Once the **Completion** screen shows that the group has been created successfully, click on **Close**.

How it works...

A **group** is a logical grouping of configuration items stored within the CMDB. Once you have created a group, you can use it within security roles to restrict access, as criteria for notification subscriptions, or even as criteria for reports.

There's more...

This recipe showed how to create a group containing users, but you can create groups for other CIs too.

Creating other groups containing other CI types

You can use this recipe and change the object type to select anything stored within the CMDB to build groups containing other Cis, such as a group to hold all the virtual servers, by varying Steps 8 and 9. Also, you can manually assign items by adding them in Step 6 and skipping Steps 7, 8, and 9 instead.

Creating a basic queue

This recipe details the steps for creating a SCSM queue. Queues in SCSM are specific to each process. You cannot combine classes, so in this example we will create a queue for a support group called *Service Desk*.

Getting ready

You need to ensure you have successfully installed the SCSM product, are a user in the SCSM Administrator role, and have the SCSM console open.

Follow the list creation instructions in `Chapter 7`, *Working with Incident and Problem Management*, to create a new list item for the *Incident Tier Queue* list called *Service Desk*.

How to do it...

The following steps will guide you through the process of creating a basic queue:

1. Open the SCSM Console. Navigate to **Library** | **Queues** and click on **Create Queue**:

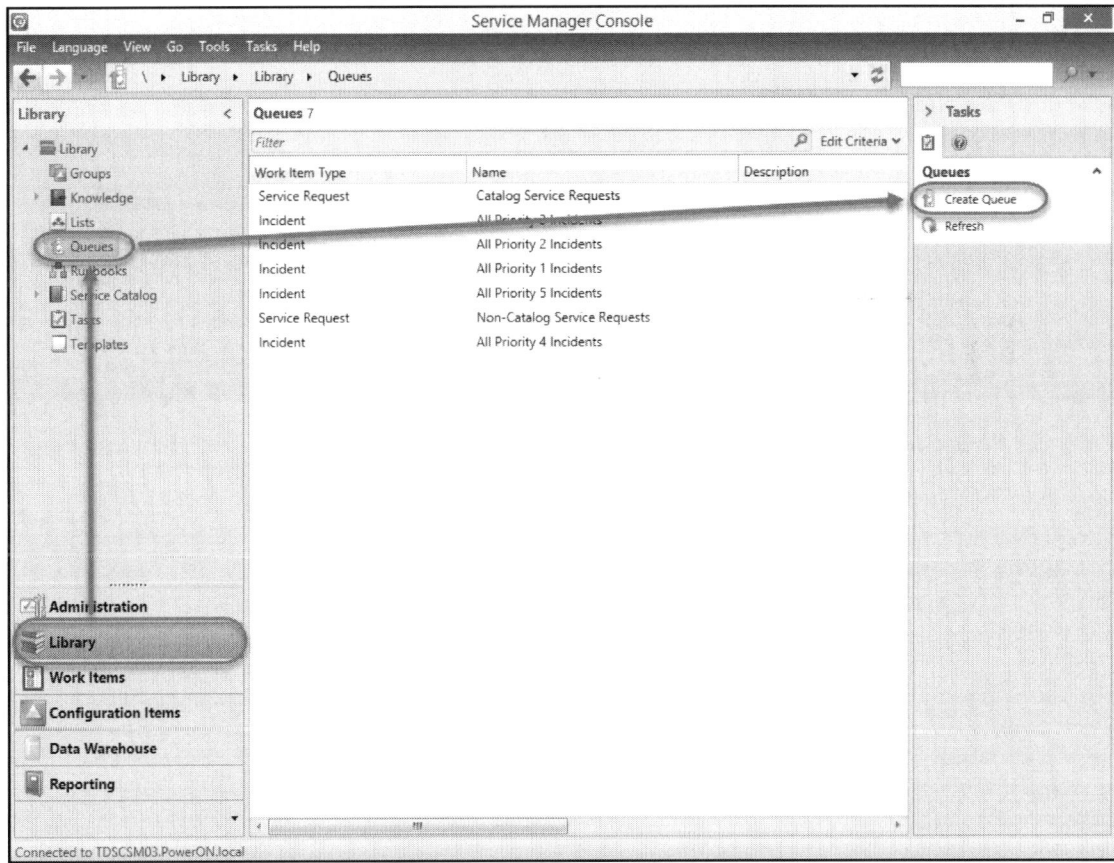

2. Click on **Next**. Provide a queue name and description. For this recipe, use the queue name `Incident - Service Desk 1st Line` and a description of `All Incidents with a support group of Service Desk 1st Line`.

3. Under **Work item type**, click on **...** and select **Incident** as the work item type.

4. Under **Management pack**, select a custom management pack (for example, **PON – Incident – Queues**). Click on **Next**:

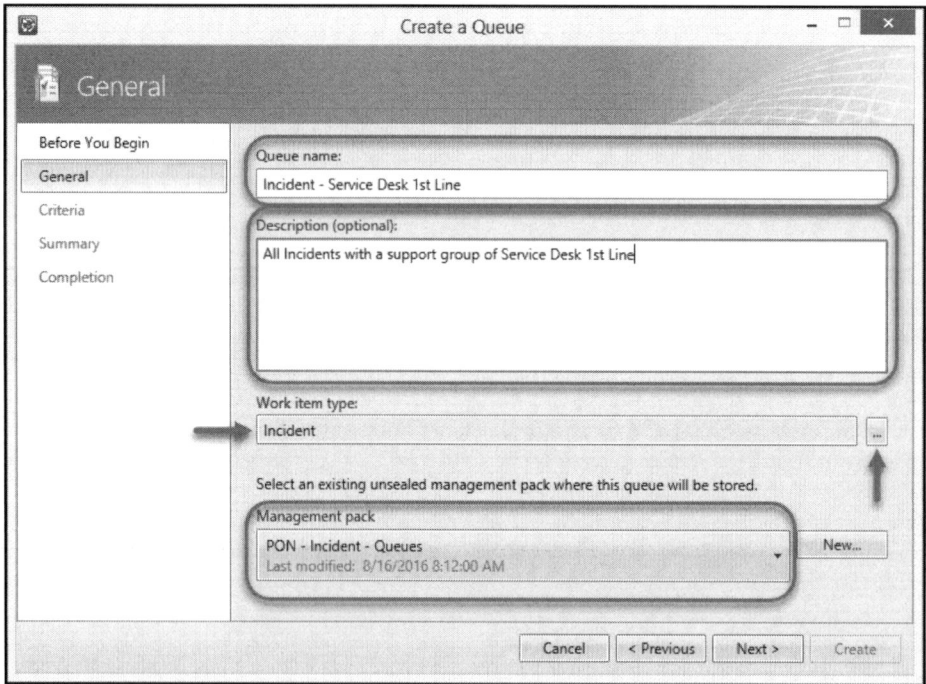

5. For the criteria, select **Support** Group under **Available properties** on the right and click on **Add**:

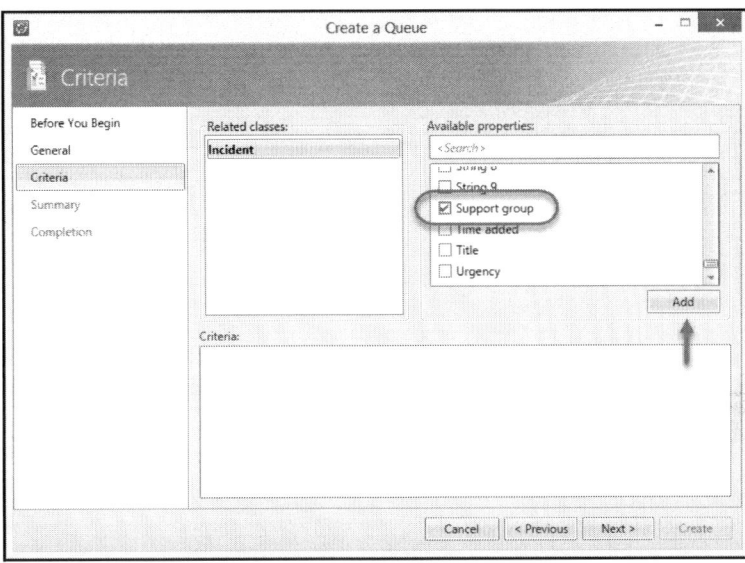

6. Set **Criteria** to **equals Service Desk 1st Line**. Click on **Next**. Review **Summary** and click on **Create** to complete the queue creation:

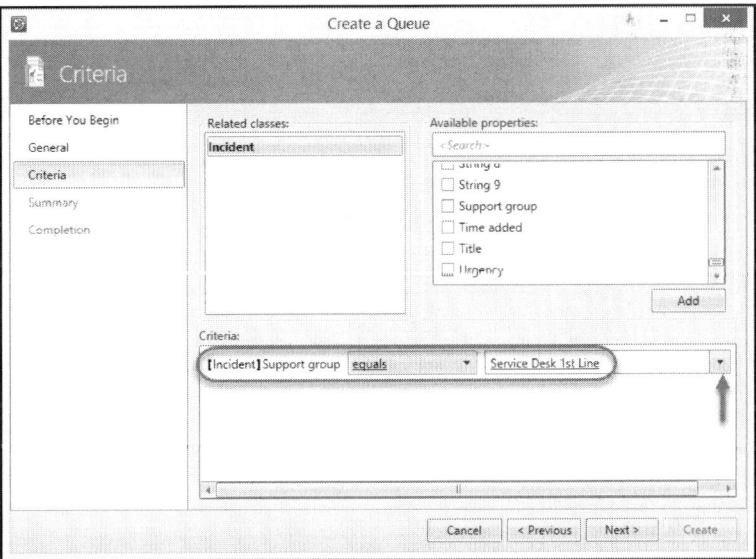

How it works...

In SCSM, what you see in the console are called views. How much of what you see depends on your role and what your queue is allowed to see.

Think about a "queue to a view". When you create a queue for a specific class (for example, incidents), you are able to filter and restrict what the users who match the queue criteria can see in the console, and what actions they can perform.

In the example steps, we can create a new Incident role where only the Service Desk queue is selected. This would have the effect of only showing users associated with that role incidents where the support group is set to Service Desk 1st Line.

See also

- The *Creating priority queues* recipe in `Chapter 3`, *Configuring Service Level Agreements (SLAs)*, for other scenarios related to the use of queues

Creating SCSM console tasks

This recipe details the steps for creating a SCSM custom console task. Console tasks in SCSM provide you with a method to add quickly accessible common tasks to the SCSM console that can leverage properties of the class that they are scoped to.

Getting ready

You need to ensure you have successfully installed the SCSM product, are a user in the SCSM Administrator role, and have the SCSM console open.

You will also require the SCSM console installed on your device.

How to do it...

The following steps will guide you through the process of creating a console task:

1. Open the SCSM Console. Navigate to **Library** | **Tasks** and click on **Create Task:**

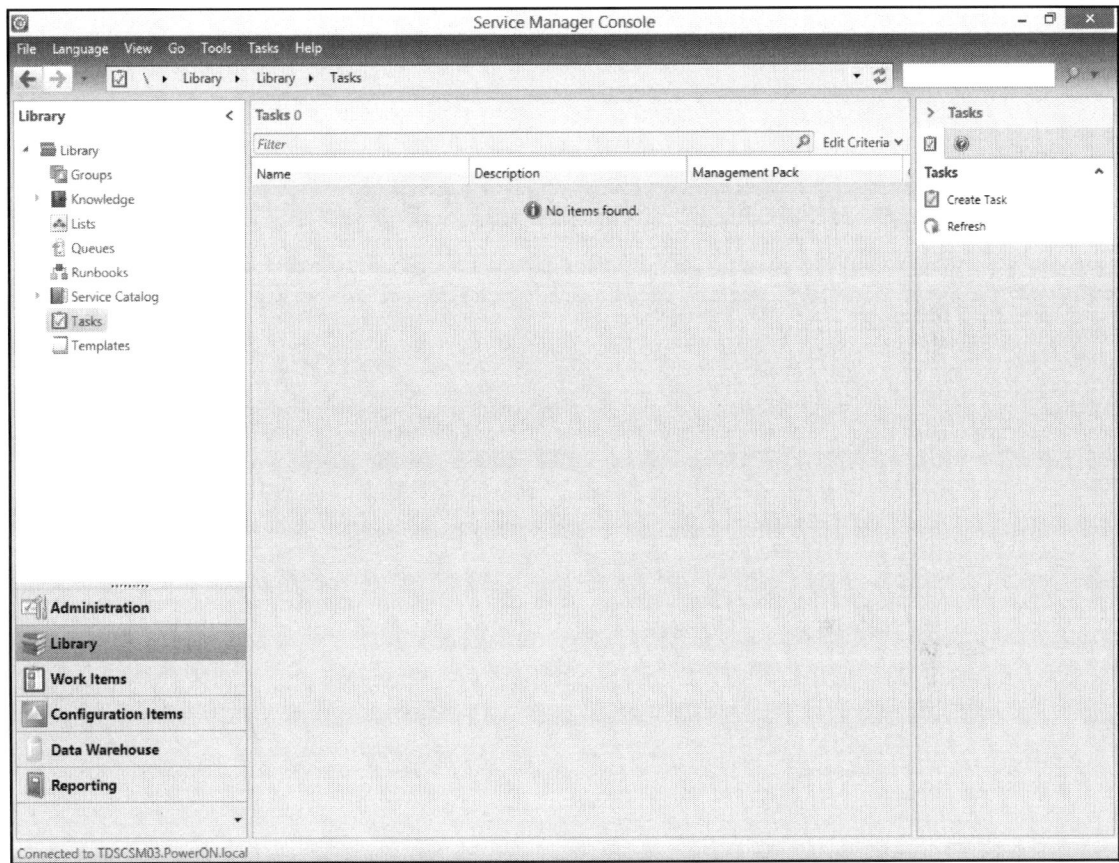

2. Click on **Next**. Provide a task name and description. For this recipe, use the task name `Launch ConfigMgr Remote Control` and a description of `Launches the System Center Configuration Manager Remote Control tool.`

3. Under **Target class**, click on **...** and select **Incident** as the target class type.

4. Under **Management pack**, select a custom management pack (for example, **PON – Incident – Tasks**). Click on **Next**:

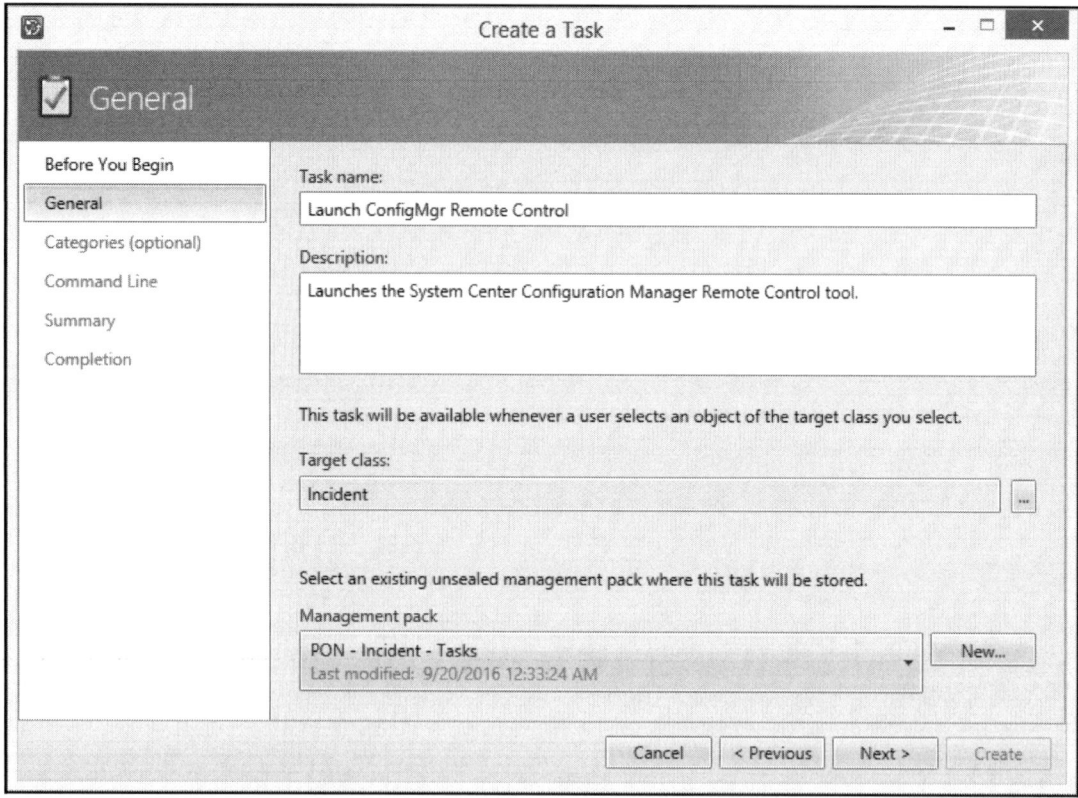

5. Leave the **Categories (optional)** selections unticked.

6. Enter the **full path to command** as: `C:\Program Files (x86)\Microsoft Configuration Manager\AdminConsole\bin\i386\CmRcViewer.exe`

7. Click **Insert Property**.

8. Choose the related class of **About Configuration Item**, search for and select **Principal Name** under the **Windows Computer** available properties, and click **Add:**

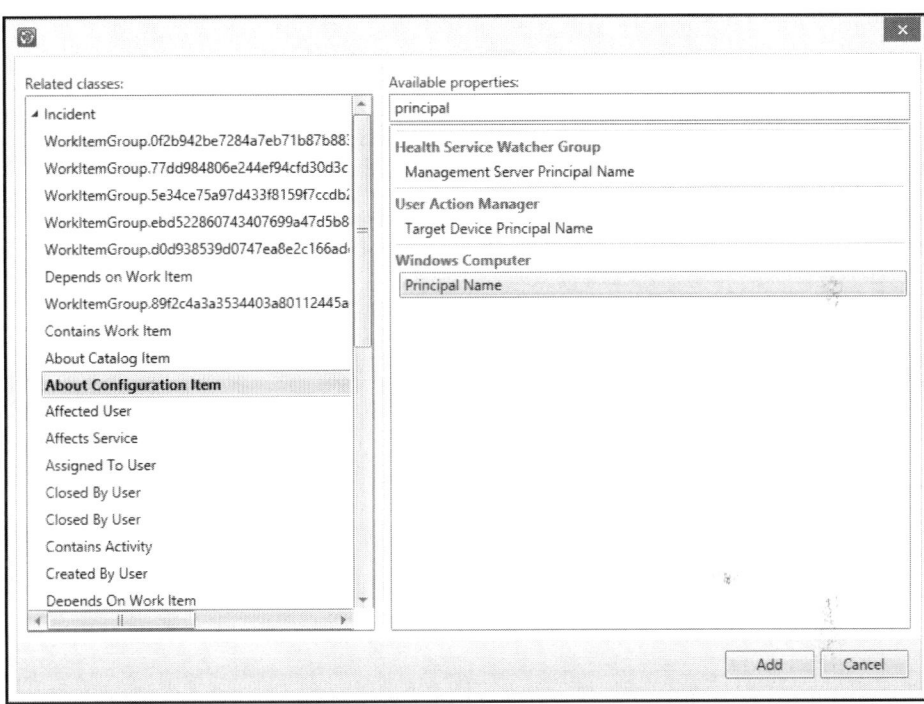

9. Untick the options for **Log in action log when this task is run** and **Show output when this task is run**:

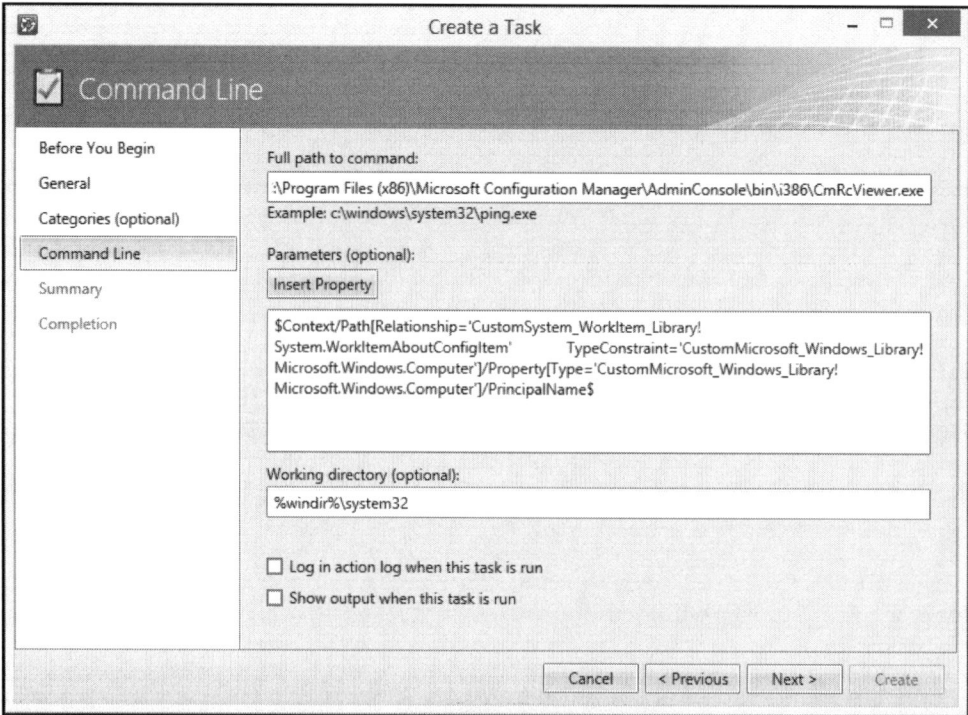

10. Click **Create** on the summary screen, then click **Close**.

How it works...

In SCSM you have a task pane on the right of all the windows in the console. Creating a custom task for the ConfigMgr remote control tool and selecting the target class of Incident scopes this task to only be visible when working with Incidents:

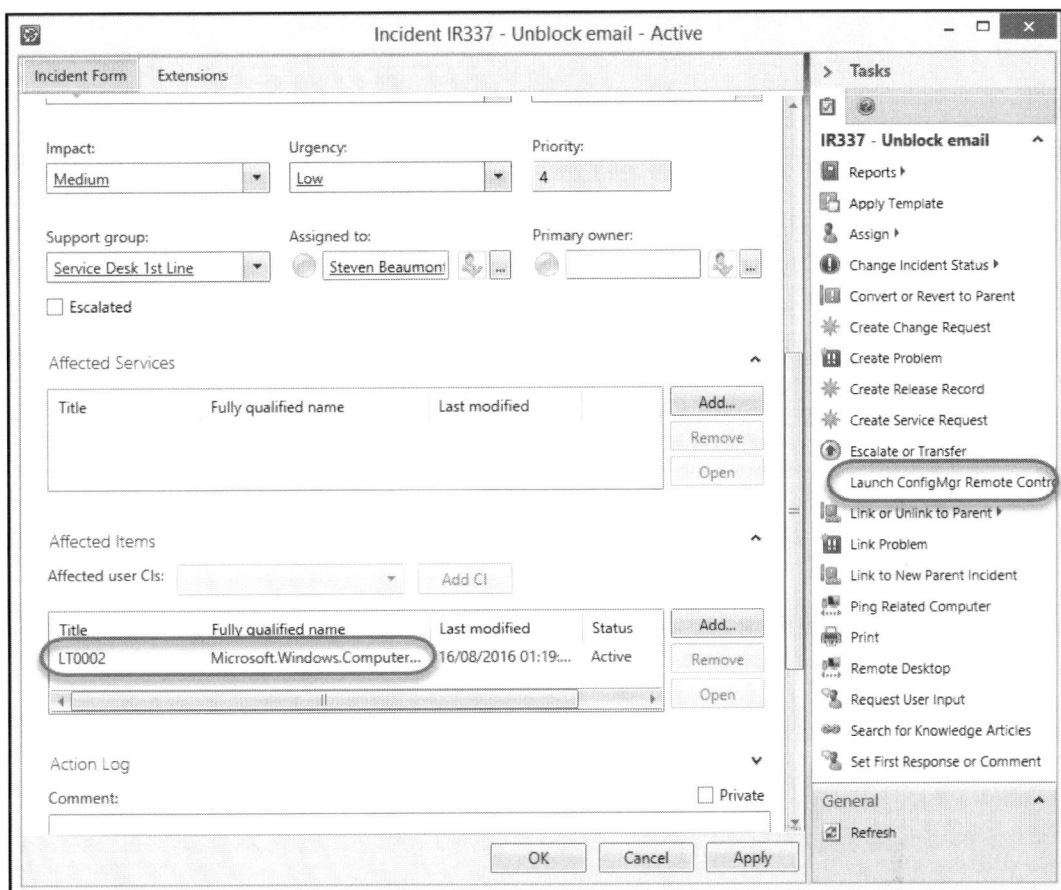

Using the Insert Property button to choose the computer name supplies the name of the computer CI related to the incident as a parameter to the remote control tool, causing it to immediately try to connect when launched.

Configuring global e-mail notification infrastructure settings

SCSM has numerous notification capabilities. The e-mail notification capabilities require you to configure global infrastructure settings. This recipe provides the steps to complete the infrastructure settings the e-mail functionality depends on.

Getting ready

Ensure you have a SCSM-supported SMTP server and have configured your infrastructure to allow the SCSM Management server to send e-mails. Record the following details:

- Fully Qualified Domain Name (FQDN) of the SMTP server
- The return e-mail address for notifications
- The configured allowed port for SMTP communication

You must also ensure that you are in the SCSM Administrator role and have the SCSM console open.

How to do it...

The following steps will guide you through the process of configuring the settings for e-mail notifications:

1. Navigate to **Service Manager Console** | **Administration** | **Notification** | **Channels** | **Email Notification Channel** and click on **Properties** under **Tasks**, as shown in the following screenshot:

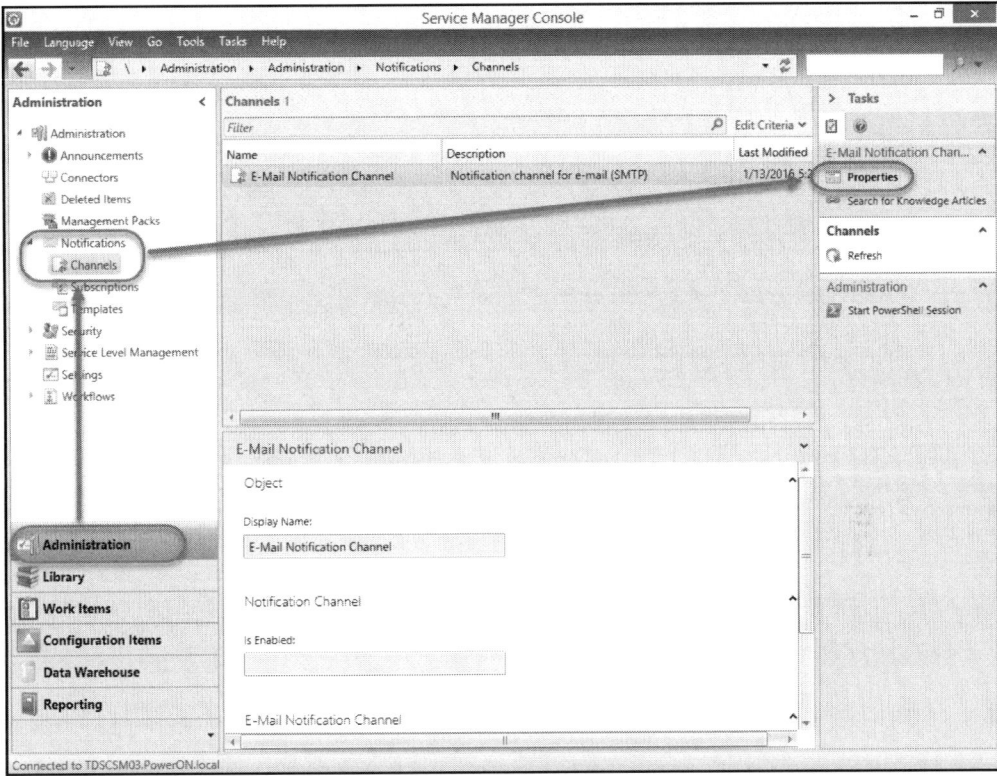

2. Tick **Enable e-mail notification**. Click on **Add...**

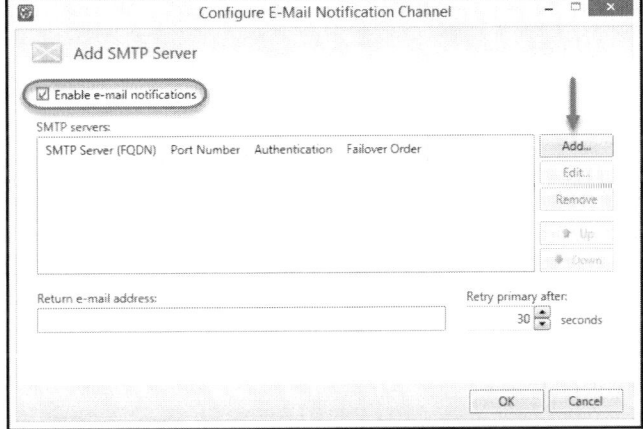

3. Type in the FQDN of the SMTP server, accept or change the default port, accept or change the default authentication, and then click on **OK**.

4. Type in the **Return e-mail address**. Review the settings and click on **OK** to confirm:

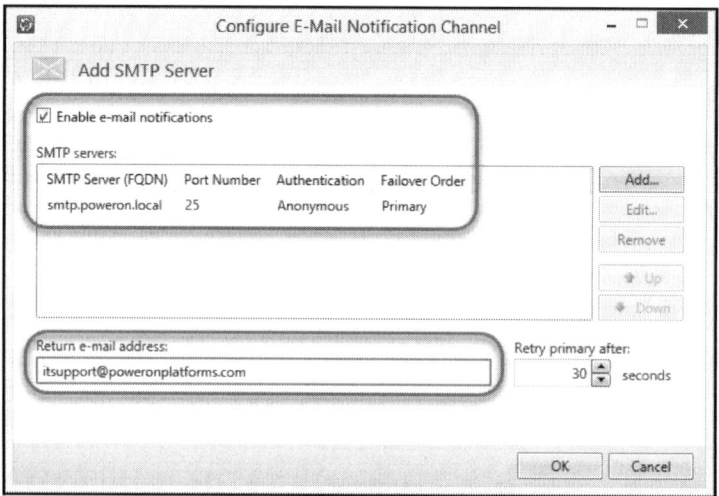

How it works...

The SMTP server configuration enables the e-mail notification function. When you configure the e-mail notification either through a workflow setting or subscription, the SMTP server(s) is/are used to route the e-mail to the targeted recipient.

Creating formatted e-mail notification templates

This recipe discusses the steps required to create a rich text formatted e-mail template.

Getting ready

This procedure requires you to have a copy on Microsoft Word 2007 or above installed. You must be in the SCSM Administrator role and have the SCSM console open.

We will use an incident notification as an example. We will create a template for sending the affected user the following incident details:

- The ID of the Incident
- Affected users name
- Title
- Description
- Status
- Priority

How to do it…

The following steps will guide you through the process of how to create an e-mail notification template:

1. Create a new Word document and design the format of your notification e-mail with the details of the properties to be sent, using new lines to separate each property:

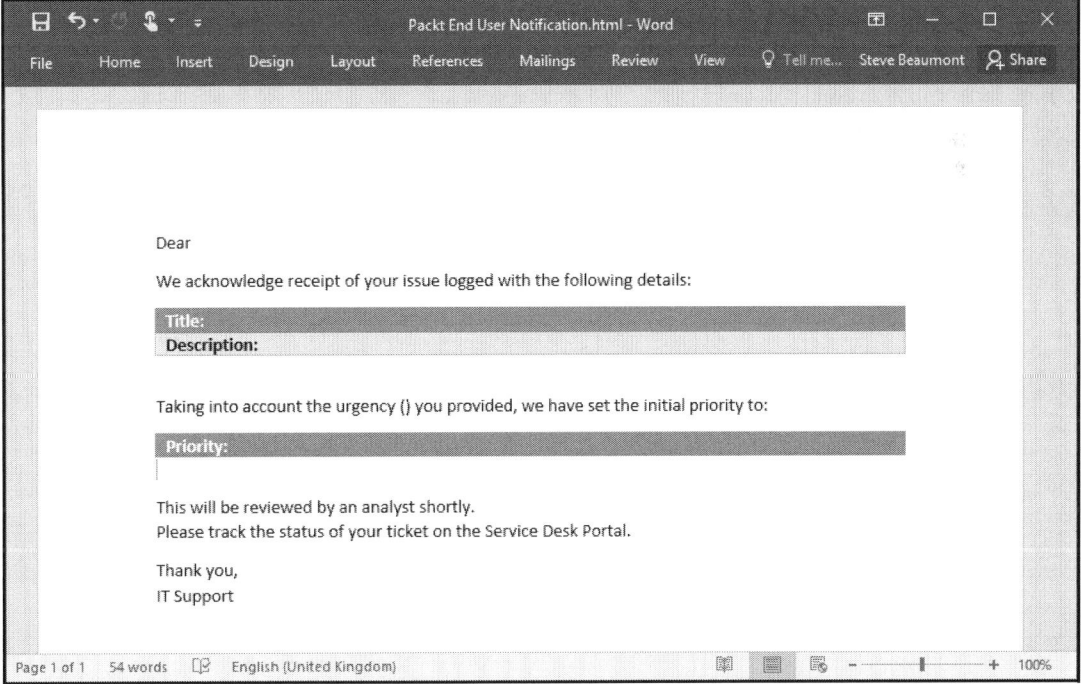

2. Save the file as a **Web Page, Filtered (*.htm, *.html)** file:

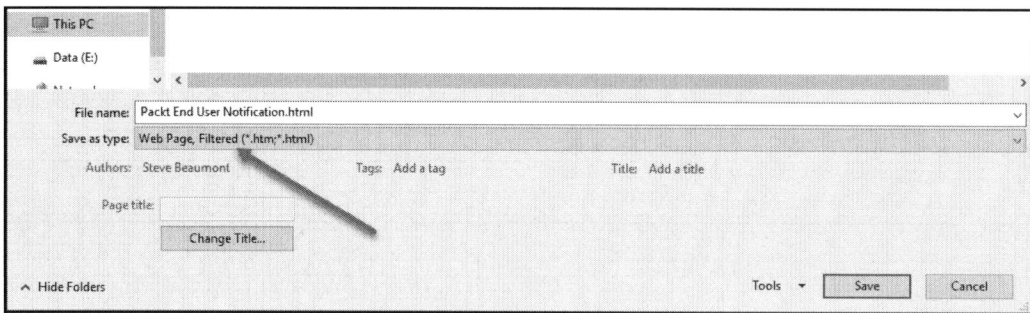

3. Navigate to the file location. Open the file with Notepad and copy the text.
4. Navigate to **SCSM Console | Administration | Notifications | Templates** and select **Create E-Mail Template** from the **Tasks** workspace:

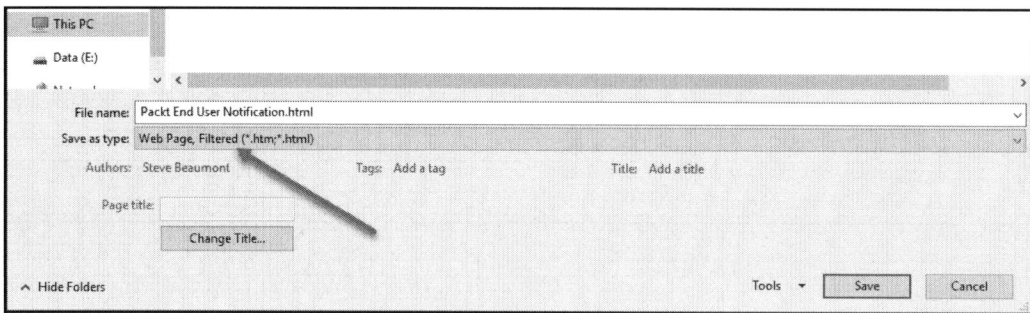

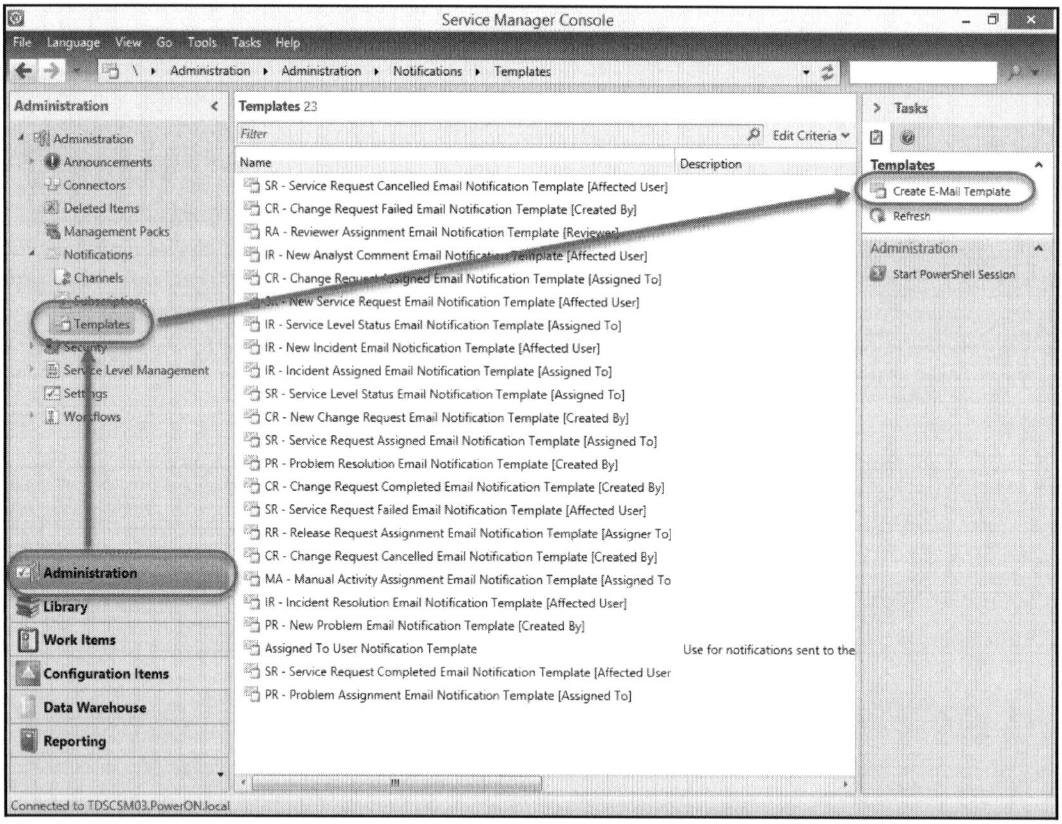

5. Configure the following for the general settings:

- **Notification template name**: `Packt End User Notification`
- **Description**: `HTML formatted message for new Incidents`
- **Target class**: Click on **Browse...** and select **Incident**
- Management pack: Select a custom management pack (for example, **PON – Incident – Notification Templates**)
- Click on **Next**:

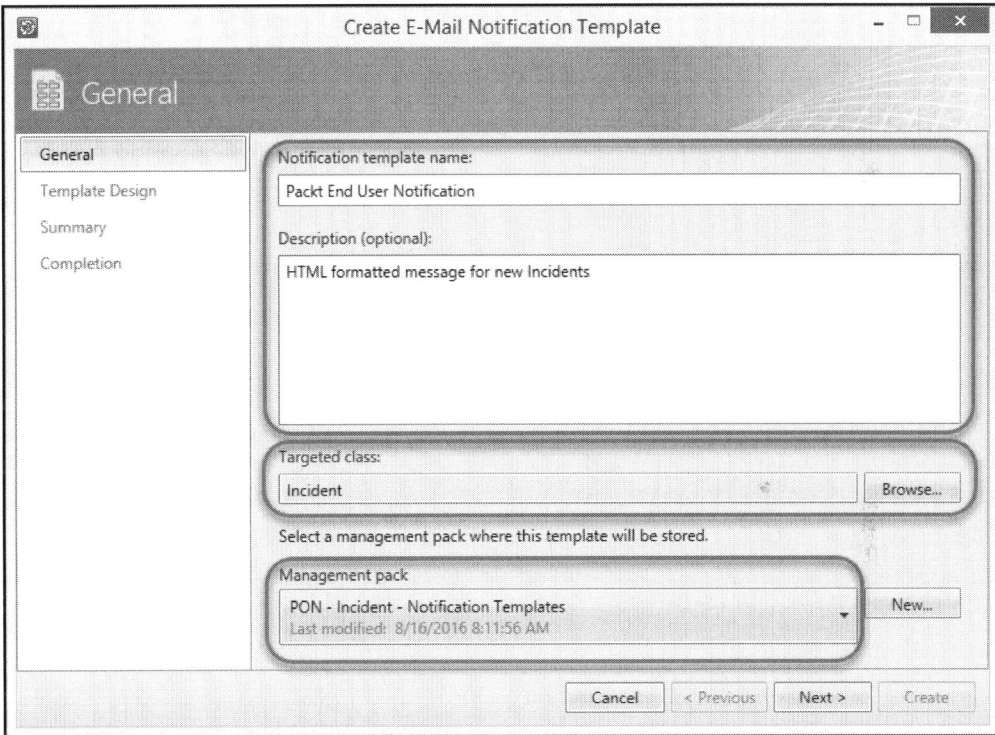

6. Tick the **Send as HTML** checkbox and type a descriptive message in the **Message subject** field.

7. Paste the details from Step 3 into the **Message body** field:

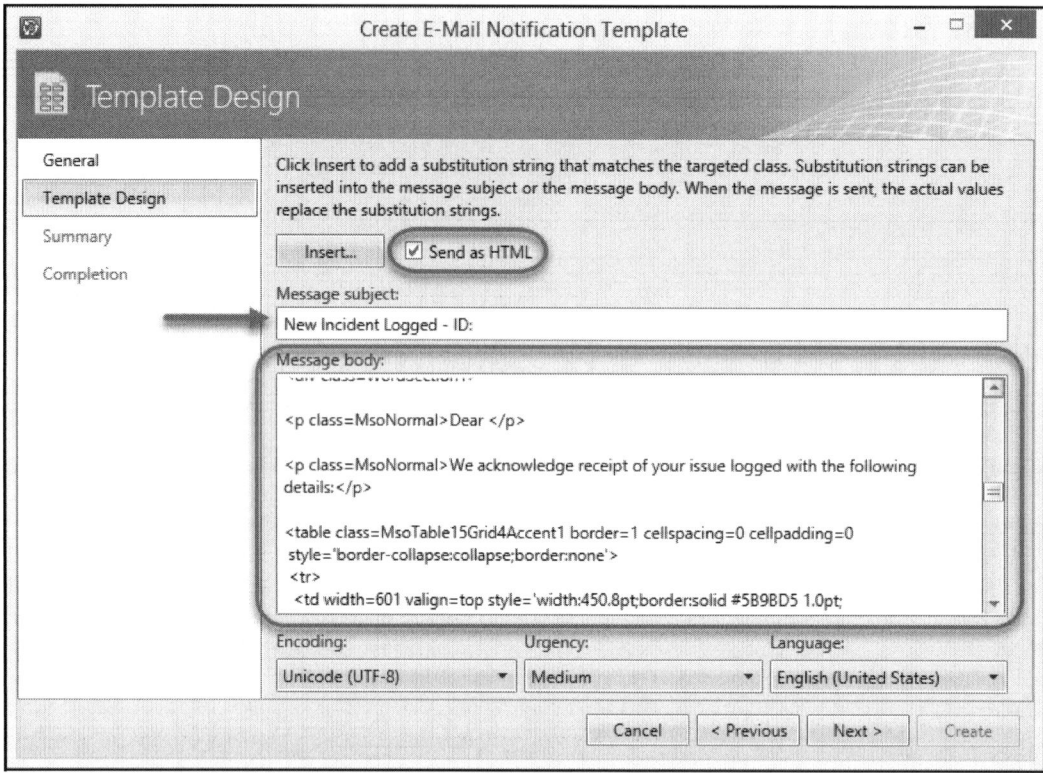

8. Find the various places where you want to insert the properties from the *Getting ready* section of this recipe. Click on **Insert...** to select the property and click on **Add**:

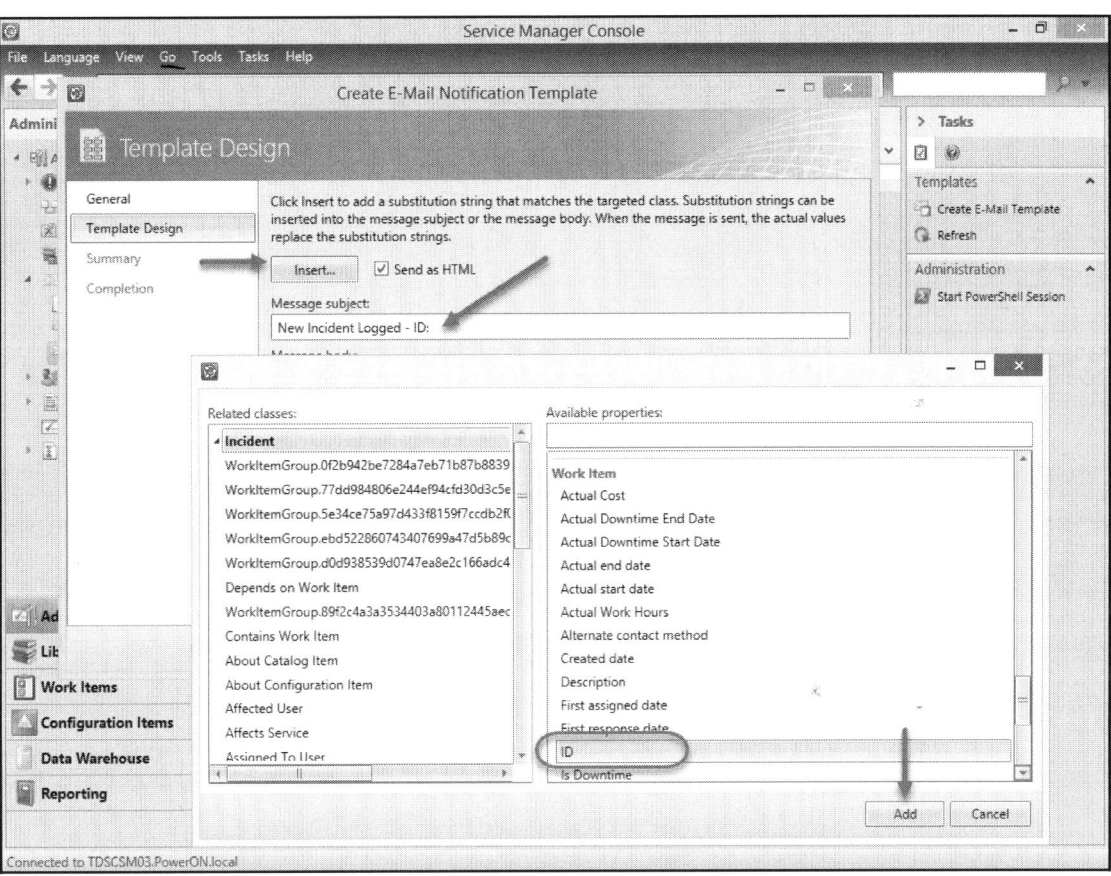

9. Repeat the previous step for all properties in the scope:

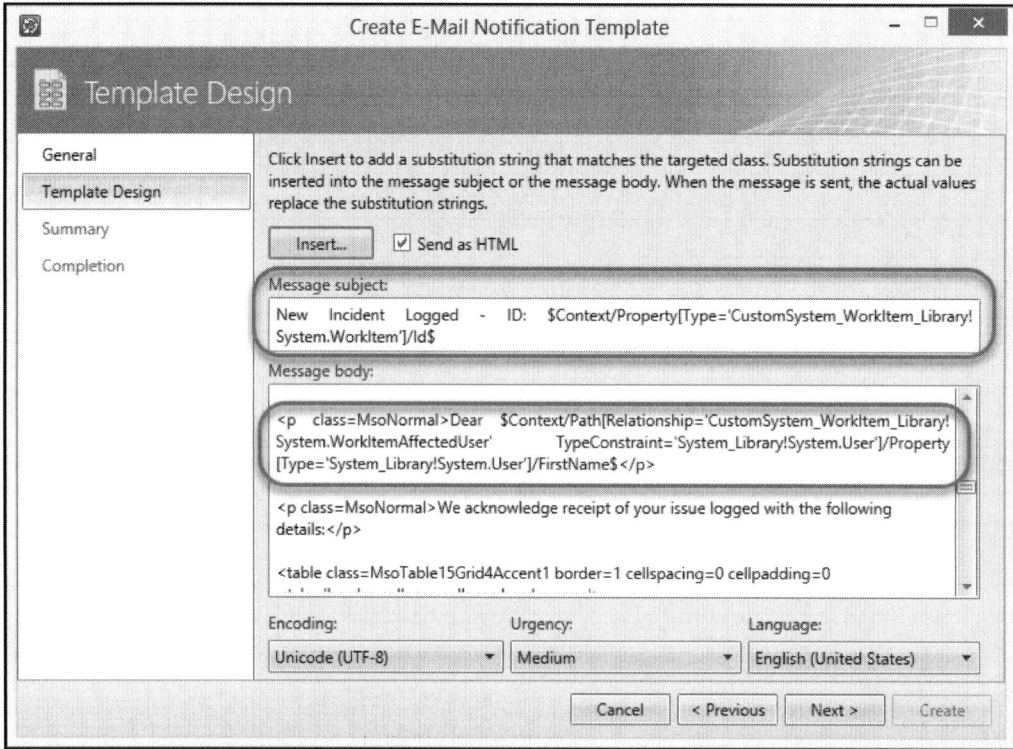

10. Click on **Next**. Verify the details and click on **Create**.

11. The template is created for use and can be selected for incident class notifications, for example, sending an e-mail to the affected user:

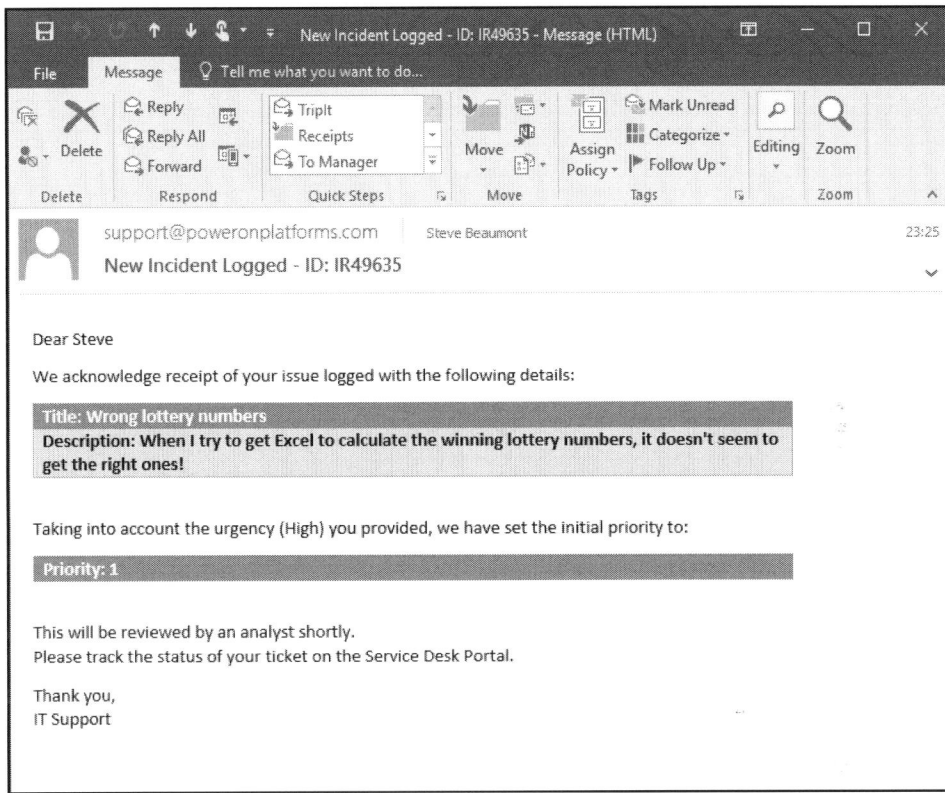

How it works...

By default, the e-mail notification templates you create in the SCSM console do not get formatted as HTML. This applies even if you select the **Send as HTML** option.

You have two choices if you want the message to be in true HTML format:

- Manually type the HTML tags to format the message
- Use an HTML-capable editor to save the format as described in the recipe steps

See also

- The *Setting up SLA notifications for warning and breaches* recipe in Chapter 3, *Configuring Service Level Agreements (SLAs)*, discusses SLA notification and provides examples of using the notification templates you create

3
Configuring Service Level Agreements (SLAs)

In this chapter, we will provide recipes to tailor SCSM to your environment. Specifically, we will cover the area of setting up the SLA functions of Service Manager with the following tasks:

- Creating priority queues
- Configuring business hours and non-working days
- Creating SLA metrics
- Creating SLOs
- Creating Incident Management SLAs
- Creating Service Request SLAs
- Viewing SLA warnings and breaches
- Setting up SLA notifications for warnings and breaches
- Creating repeated notifications before SLA breaches with escalation

Introduction

SLAs in ITILÂ® and IT Service Management terms allow two parties to set out an agreement on how a specific service will be delivered by one to the other.

In this chapter, we will provide recipes to configure Service Manager 2016's SLA engine. We will define how it will handle the tracking of Incidents and Service Requests against defined SLAs, how to view the progress of work items against these SLAs, and how to configure SCSM 2016 to alert users when work items are nearing, or have breached, these SLAs.

As with most areas of configuration within Service Manager 2016, the organization must define its processes before implementing the Service Manager feature. For example, this chapter assumes that SLAs are already in place and agreed with your customers and metrics relating to areas such as resolution time or response times, mapped to priorities are defined.

Creating priority queues

This recipe will define a number of queues related to your defined priority for work items such as Incidents and Service Requests. These queues will then be mapped to Service Level Objectives (SLOs).

Getting ready

For this recipe, it is required that you have already followed the *Configuring priority and urgency for your SLA targets* recipe in `Chapter 2`, *Personalizing SCSM 2016 Administration*, for configuring your priority matrix according to the impact and urgency definitions of your organization, and that you have custom management packs in place to store your queue customizations.

How to do it...

The following steps will guide you through the process of creating priority queues:

1. Navigate to the **Queues** folder in the **Library** section of the **Service Manager 2016** console.
2. Choose **Create Queue** from the taskbar on the right-hand side of the console.
3. Review the information on the **Before You Begin** screen of the **Create Queue Wizard** and click on **Next**.
4. Enter a queue name that describes the queue. In this example, we will name it `Incident SLA Queue - Priority 1` to describe a queue holding Incidents with a priority of 1. Then click on the **...** selection button next to the **Work item type** textbox:

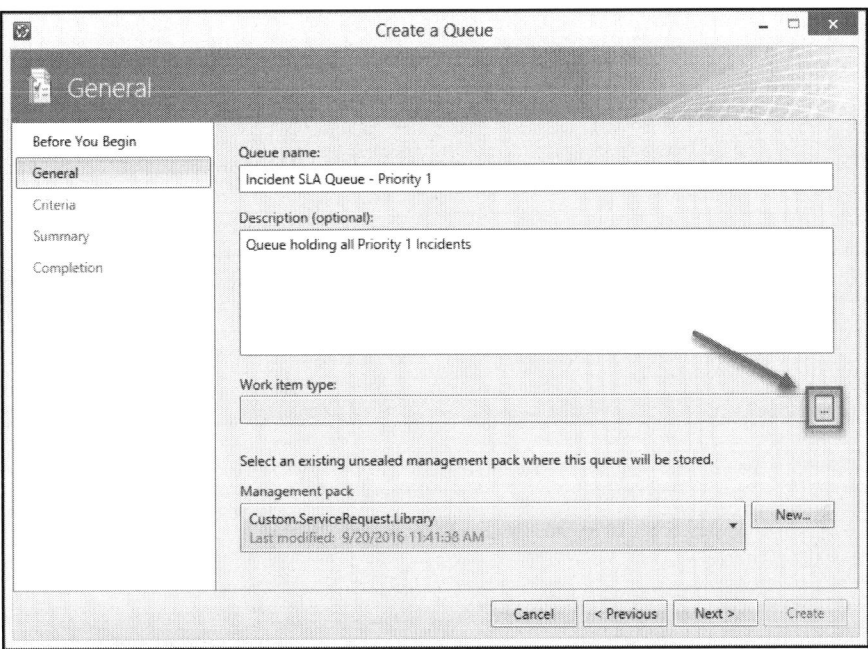

5. Use the filter box to scope the choices down to Incident Work Items, choose **Incident**, and then click **OK**:

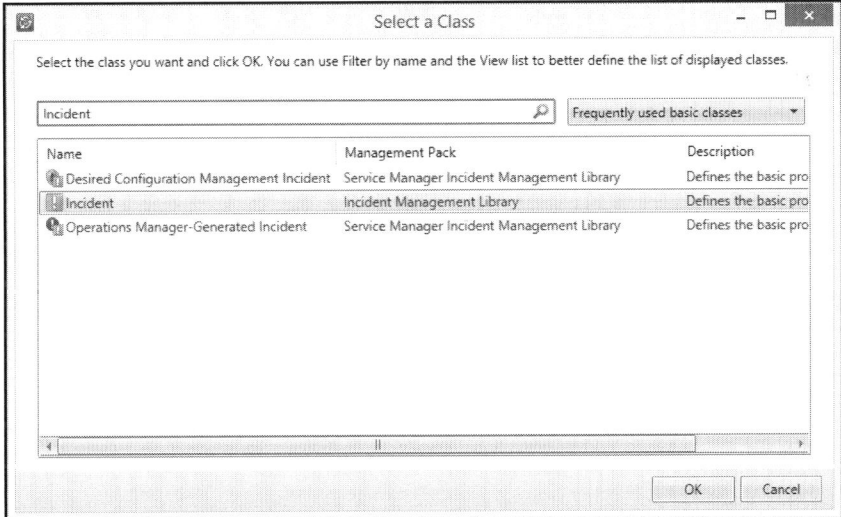

6. Choose your custom Incident Management Pack from the selection list and click on **Next**.

Refer to `Chapter 2`, *Personalizing SCSM 2016 Administration*, for more information on custom management packs.

7. Use the **Search** box under **Available properties** to drop the list down to **Priority**. Tick the box next to **Priority** and then click on **Add**:

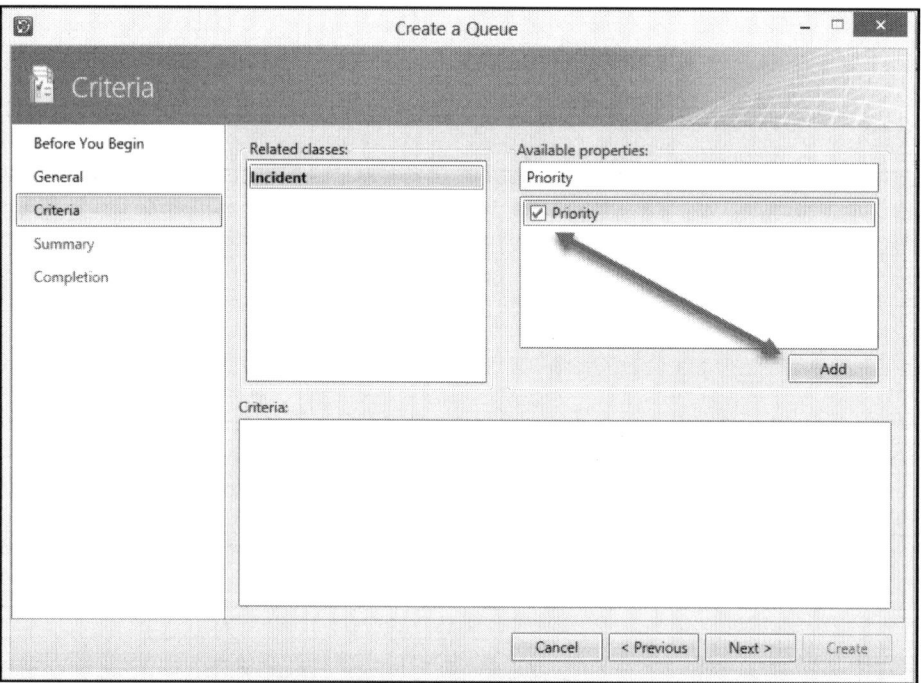

8. Change the criteria for **[Trouble Ticket] Priority**, using the drop-down list, to **equals** and supply the Priority value; in this example, we will give a value of 1. Click on **Next**:

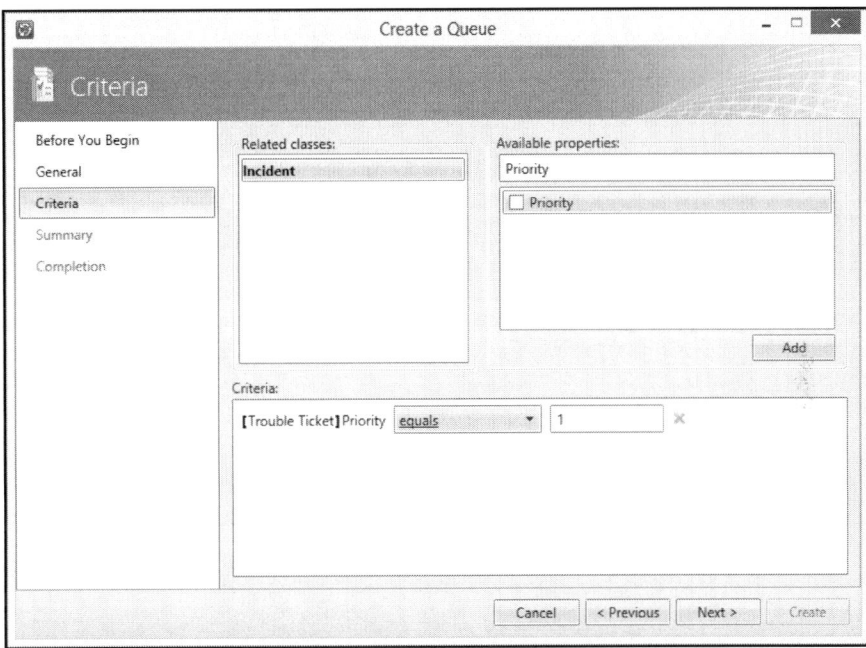

9. Review the **Summary** screen of the wizard and then click on **Create**.
10. You have now successfully created a queue. Click on **Close** to complete the wizard.
11. Repeat this process for each priority you want to link an SLO to.

How it works...

Creating a queue allows Service Manager to group similar work items that meet specified criteria, such as all Incidents with a priority of 1. Service Manager can use these queues to scope actions. Using this grouping of work items, we have a target to apply a Service Level Objective (SLO) to.

There's more…

This recipe requires you to repeat the steps for each priority you would like to apply an SLO to.

Repeat each step, but change key information such as the name, priority value, and description to reflect the priority you are creating the queue for. For example, for an Incident Priority 3 queue, make the changes as reflected in the following screenshots:

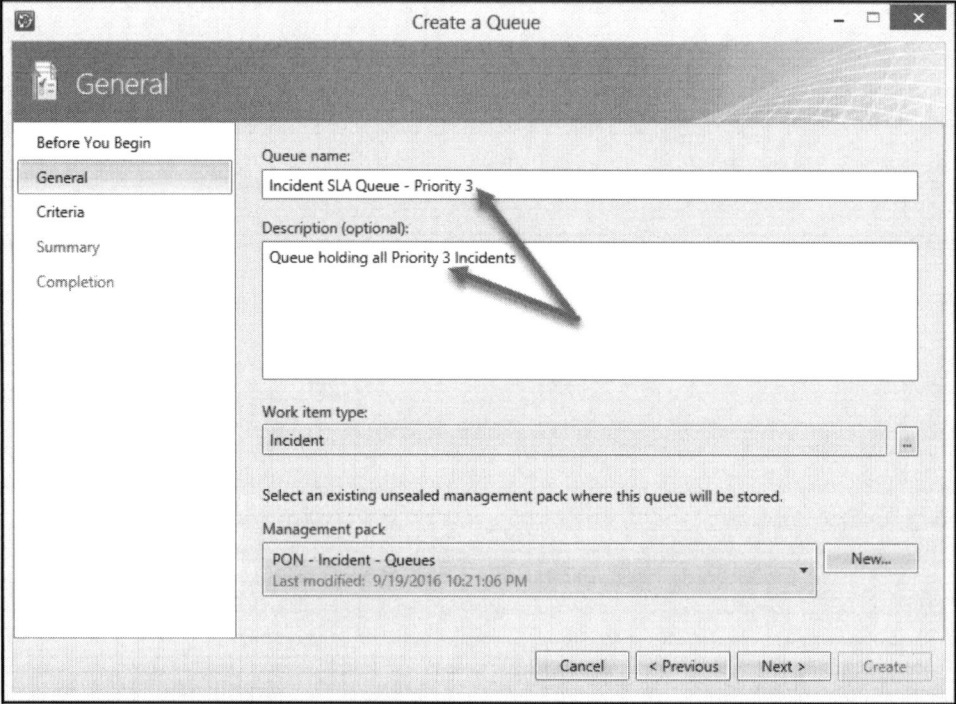

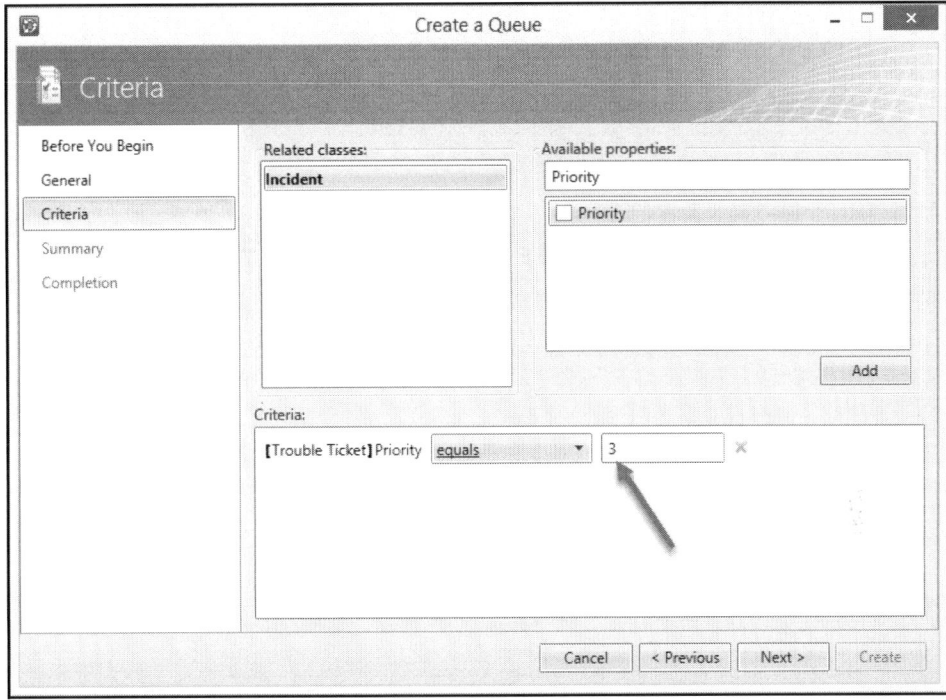

Service Request queues

Queues can be created to define any type of grouping of supported process work items in scope for SLA management.

For example, you may wish to repeat this recipe for the **Service Request** process class.

Repeat the recipe but select **Service Request** as the work item type in the wizard, and then choose the defining criteria for the queue related to the **Service Request** class:

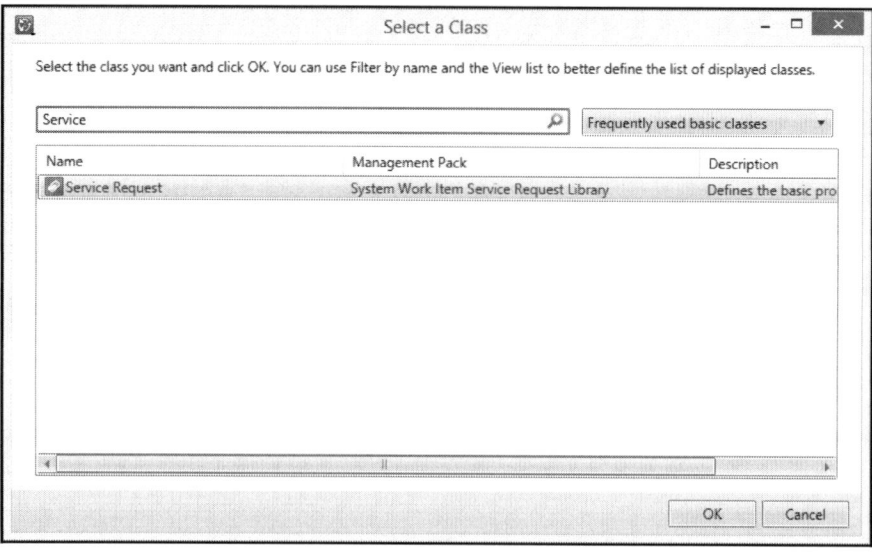

You can also use this recipe, but instead of defining the criteria for the queue based on priority, you could choose the category of the incident, say, **Hardware**:

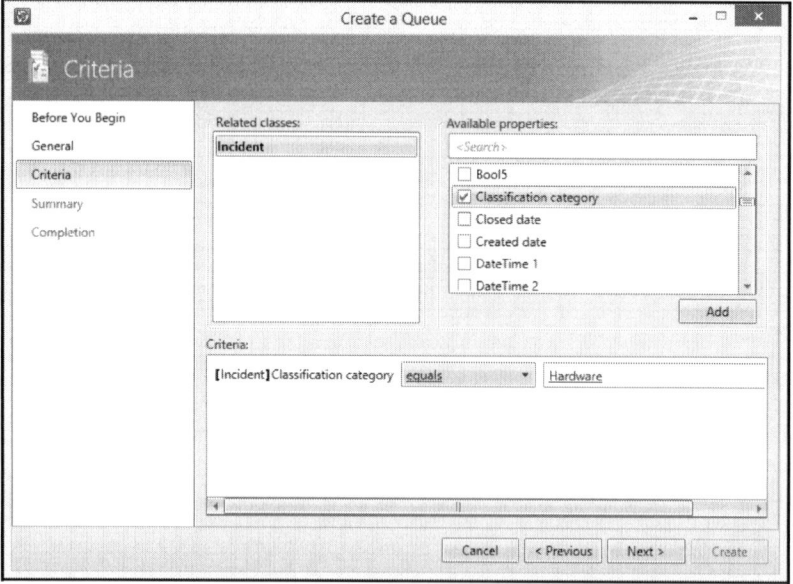

Further queue types

If the incident class was extended to capture whether the affected user was a VIP, you would be able to define a VIP queue and give those work items matching that criteria a different resolution time SLA.

See also

- The *Configuring priority and urgency for your SLA targets* recipe in `Chapter 2`, *Personalizing SCSM 2016 Administration*
- The *Creating management packs to save your SCSM personalization* recipe in `Chapter 2`, *Personalizing SCSM 2016 Administration*

Configuring business hours and non-working days

This recipe will define the hours that your business offers services, which allows calculation of resolution and response times against SLAs.

Getting ready

For this recipe, it is required that you have already assessed the business hours that your IT services will offer to your organization, and that you have custom management packs in place to store your queue customizations.

How to do it...

The following steps will guide you through the process of configuring business hours and non-working days within Service Manager:

1. Under **Administration**, expand **Service Level Management** and then click on **Calendar**.

2. Under **Tasks** on the right-hand side of the screen, click on **Create Calendar**.

3. Give the calendar a meaningful name; in this example, we have used `Core Business Hours`:

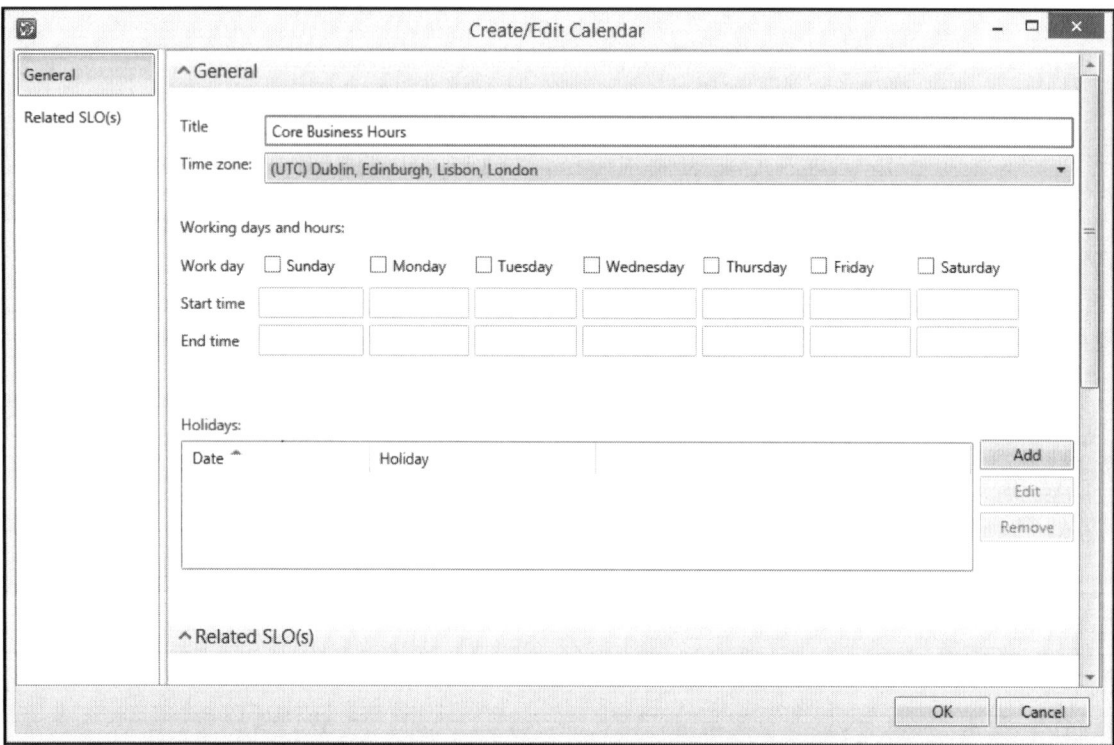

4. Choose the relevant time zone.

5. Place a check mark against all the days for which you offer services.

6. Under each working day, enter a start time and an end time in the `00:00:00` format, for example, `8` am should be entered as `08:00:00`:

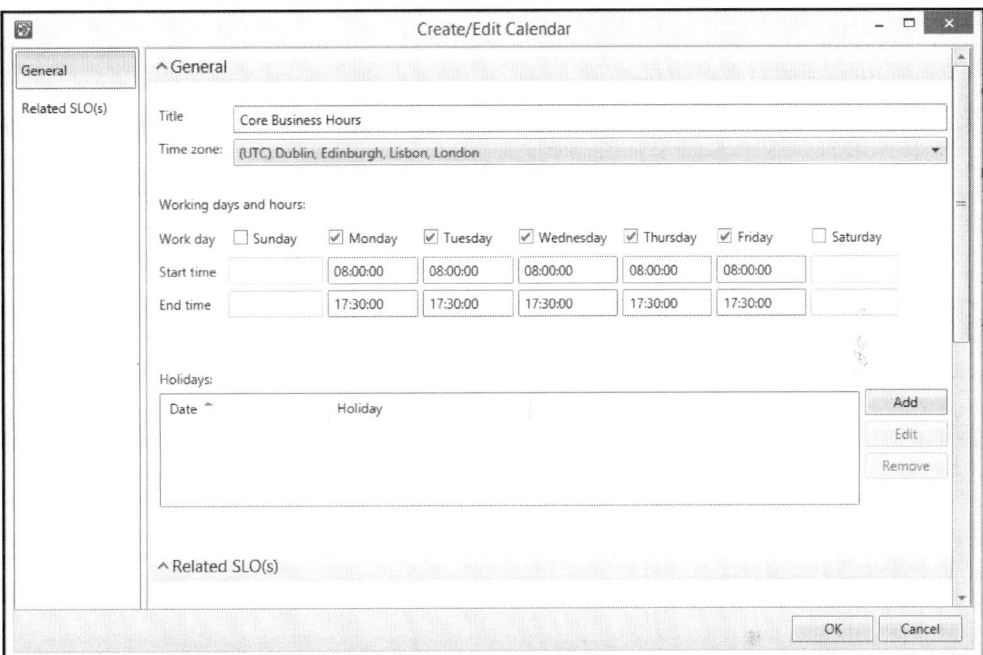

7. You can also specify the non-working days using the **Holidays** section; under the **Holidays** pane, click on **Add**.

8. In the **Add Holiday** window that opens enter a name for the Holiday, for example, `New Year's Day`.

9. Either manually enter the date in the format relevant for your regional settings (for example, for the United Kingdom regional settings, use DD/MM/YYYY) or use the visual calendar by clicking on the button to the right of the date entry textbox:

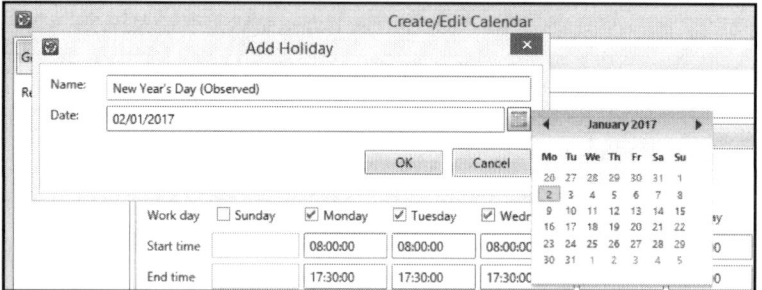

10. Click on **OK** for each holiday. Once all holidays have been added, click on **OK** to close the **Create/Edit Calendar** window.

How it works...

When you specify the business hours and non-working days, Service Manager will take these into consideration when calculating SLA metrics, such as resolution time and first response time for all work items that are affected by the calendar.

There's more...

A calendar on its own has no impact on service levels. The calendar is one part of the SLO configuration. The rest of this chapter provides additional recipes to complete the configuration.

Adding holidays in bulk

Adding holidays manually can be a very time consuming process. Our co-author Anders Asp has automated the process using PowerShell to import a list of holidays.

 You can download the script and read about the process on the TechNet Gallery at `http://gallery.technet.microsoft.com/Generate-SCSMHolidaysCSVps1 -a32722ce`.

Creating SLA metrics

Using SLA metrics in Service Manager, we can define what is measured within an SLA. For this recipe, we will show how to create a metric to measure the resolution time of an Incident.

How to do it...

The following steps will guide you through the process of creating SLA metrics in Service Manager:

1. Under **Administration**, expand **Service Level Management** and then click on **Metric**.
2. Under **Tasks** on the right-hand side of the screen, click on **Create Metric**.
3. Supply a title for the metric. In this example, we will use `Resolution Time` and a description.
4. Click on the **Browse...** button next to the class field and use the filter box in the **Select a Class** window that opens to select **Incident**. Click on **OK**.
5. Use the drop-down list for **Start Date** and choose **Created date**.

6. Use the drop-down list for **End** Date and choose **Resolved date**:

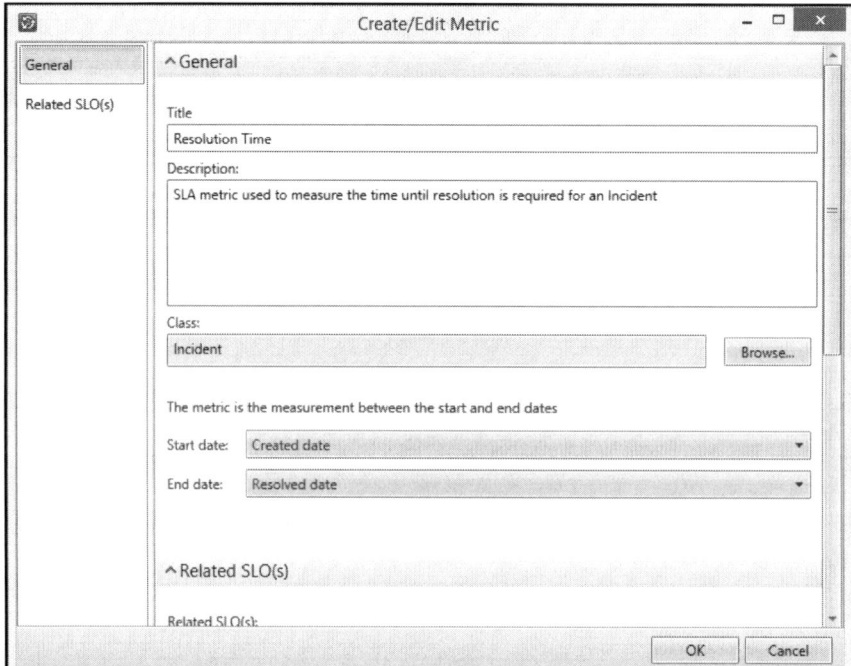

7. Click on **OK**.

How it works...

Creating a metric defines what you want Service Manager to track, within your SLA definition. So, when an item falls outside the parameters, you can start a notification and escalation process.

Creating SLOs

This recipe will show you how to create a SLO, which is used within Service Manager to create the relationships between the queues, service levels, calendars, and metrics. The SLO will define the timings to trigger warnings or breaches of service levels.

Getting ready

To create an SLO, you will need to have already created the following:

- Queues that correspond to each service level
- Metrics to measure differences in the start and end times of an incident
- A calendar to define business working hours

You will also need custom management packs in place to store your SLO customizations.

How to do it...

The following steps will guide you through the process of creating SLOs within Service Manager:

1. Under **Administration**, expand **Service Level Management** and then click on **Service Level Objectives**.
2. Under **Tasks** on the right-hand side of the screen, click on **Create Service Level Objective**.
3. Review the **Before You Begin** information and then click on **Next**.
4. Provide a title and description relevant to the Service Level Objective you are creating.

   For this recipe, we will create an SLO for a Priority 1 Incident, and so we will set this SLO's Title to `Incident Resolution Time SLO – Priority 1` with a meaningful description.

5. Click on the **Browse...** button next to the **Class** textbox and use the filter box in the **Select a Class** window that opens to select **Incident**. Click on **OK**.

6. Use the drop-down list under the **Management pack** heading to select your custom management pack for storing SLA related customizations to.

7. If you are planning to use this SLO immediately then leave the **Enabled** checkbox ticked. Only untick this if you plan to create/stage SLOs before setting up SLA functions:

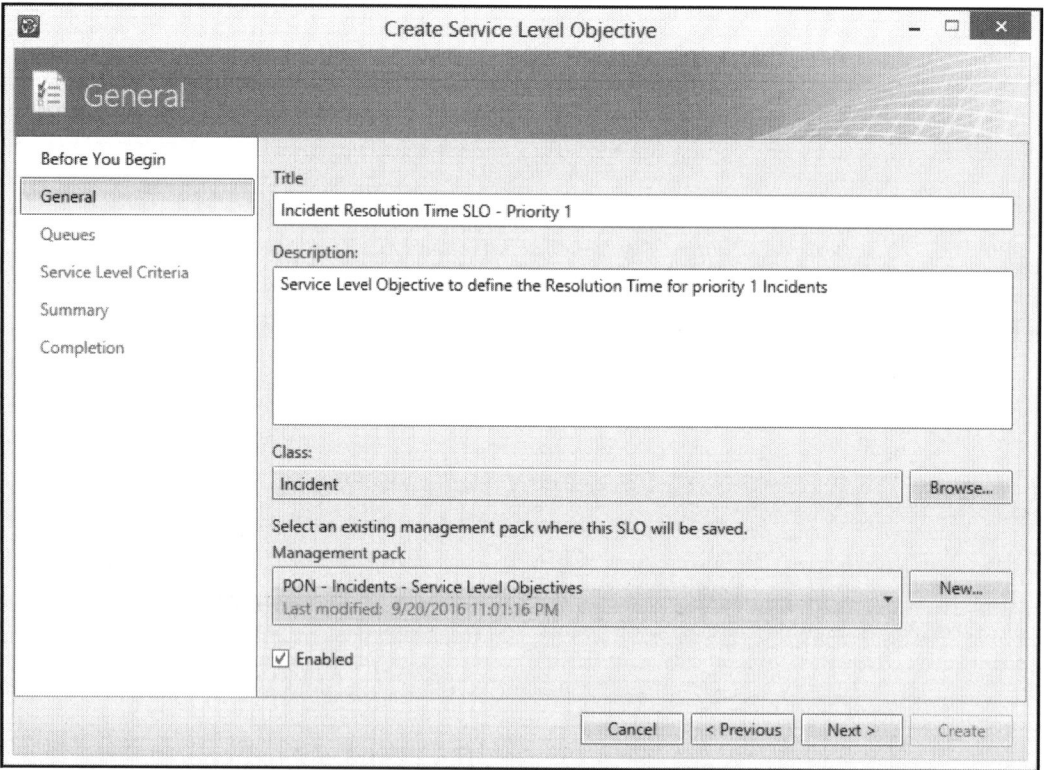

8. Click on **Next**.

9. Choose the queue you created previously in the *Creating priority queues* recipe of this chapter, which relates to the priority of incidents for this SLO.

   In this recipe, use the queue named **Incident SLA Queue – Priority 1**:

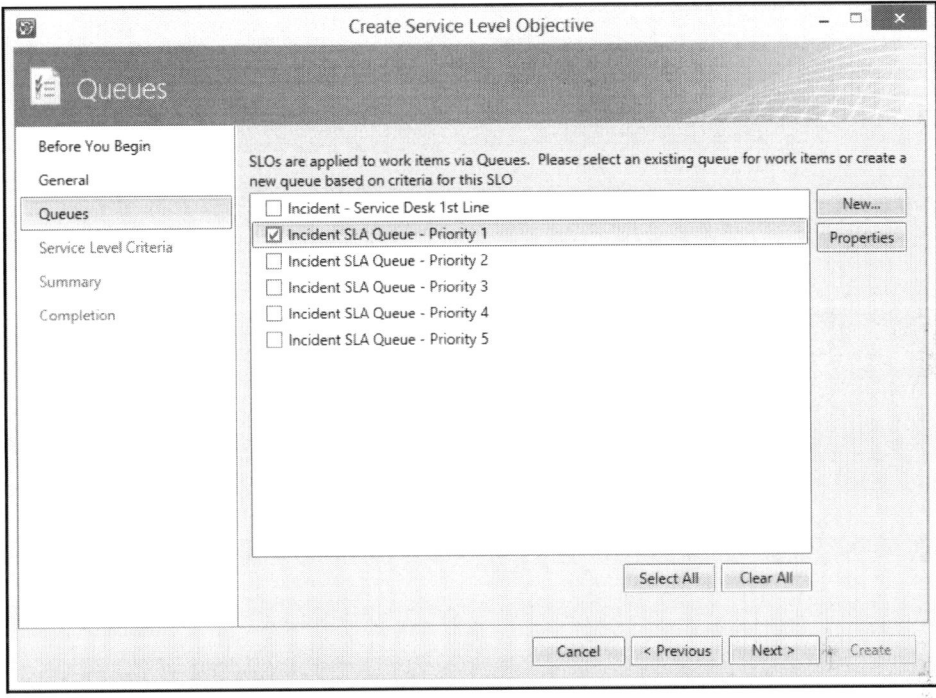

10. Click on **Next**.
11. On the **Service Level Criteria** screen, choose the **Calendar** that you want to associate this SLO with.

    For this recipe, choose the **Business Hours** calendar that was created during the *Configuring business hours and non-working days* recipe in this chapter.

12. Under **Metric**, use the drop-down list to select the time metric you wish to measure against.

    Following along with the examples, select the **Resolution Time** metric.

13. Define the target time period before a breach would occur for this metric by entering a value under target.

   For our Priority 1 Resolution, enter **4 Hours** to define the time period before an incident would change to a breach SLA status.

14. Define the target time period before a warning would occur for this metric by entering a value under **Warning threshold**.

   For our Priority 1 Resolution, enter **2 Hours** to define the time period before an incident would change to a warning SLA status:

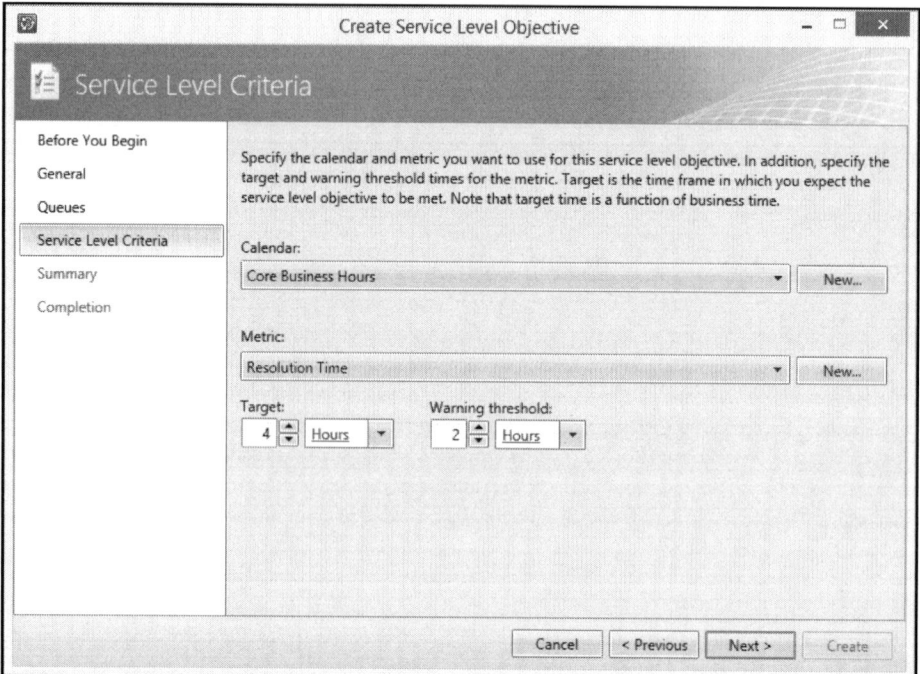

15. Click on **Next**.
16. Review the Information on the **Summary** page, and when ready, click on **Create**.
17. Once the SLO has been created and a successful message is displayed, click on **Close**.

How it works...

When you configure a SLO, you're pulling together three components, queues, calendars, and metrics. These three components are defined and illustrated as follows:

- **Queues**: Work items this SLO will be applied to
- **Calendar**: Days and hours that services are offered on
- **Metric**: Items that are measured

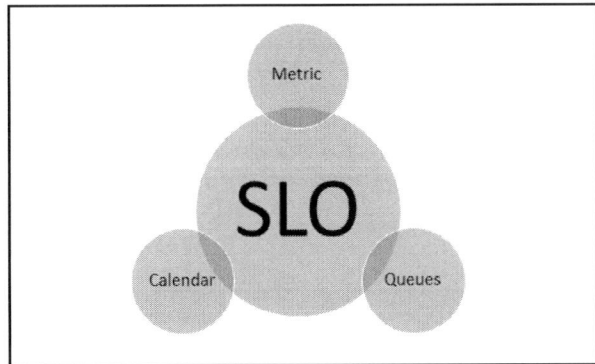

See also

- The *Creating SLA metrics* recipe
- The *Creating priority queues* recipe
- The *Configuring business hours and non-working days* recipe
- The *Creating management packs to save your SCSM personalization* recipe in Chapter 2, *Personalizing SCSM 2016 Administration*

Creating Incident Management SLAs

Service Manager has different classes of work items for which SLAs can be configured. This recipe will show how to set up SLA management of the Incident class for two common SLA categories, First Response Time and Resolution Time.

Getting ready

You should be familiar with the following recipes:

- *Creating SLA metrics*
- *Creating priority queues*
- *Configuring business hours and non-working days*
- *Creating Service Level Objectives*
- *Creating management packs to save your SCSM personalization* in `Chapter 2`, *Personalizing SCSM 2016 Administration*

How to do it…

The following steps will guide you through the process of creating the incident management SLAs.

Resolution Time SLA

Perform the following steps in this order:

1. **Creating Priority Queues**: Repeat the *Creating priority queues* recipe until you have a queue for each priority. Usually, this will be five queues for Priority 1 – 5 Incident types. Each time you create a new queue, ensure that the name, description, and value for priority change to reflect the priority.

2. **Configuring business hours and non-working days**: Only one calendar is required based on the hours/days that you provide Incident Management services to your customers.

3. **Creating SLA metrics**: Use the example in the recipe for Resolution Time based on Created Date and Resolved Date.

4. **Creating Service Level Objectives**: Create a SLO for each priority; usually, this will be five SLOs for Priority 1 – 5 Incident types. Each time you create a new SLO, ensure that the name and description change to reflect the priority it is based upon and ensure that the correct priority queue is also selected.

For each SLO, you will need to supply a target and warning threshold value. The following table shows common values that can be used, but it should reflect your organization's specifically defined requirements and/or agreements with your customers:

Priority	Target	Warning threshold
Priority 1	4 hours	2 hours
Priority 2	8 hours	4 hours
Priority 3	24 hours	12 hours
Priority 4	80 hours	40 hours
Priority 5	160 hours	80 hours

First Response Time SLA

Perform the following recipes in this order:

1. **Creating Priority Queues**: Keep repeating the *Creating priority queues* recipe until you have a queue for each priority; usually, this will be five queues for Priority 1 – 5 Incident types. Each time you create a new queue, ensure that the name and description change to reflect the priority. You may have already created the queues for the Resolution Time SLA configuration. You can reuse the same queues; do not set up new queues based on the same priorities just with new names for response time SLAs.

2. **Configuring business hours and non-working days**: Only one calendar is required, based on the hours/days that you provide Incident Management services to your customers. Again, the same calendar used for the Resolution Time SLA configuration can be reused.

3. **Creating SLA metrics**: Follow the recipe, but instead of using Created Date and Resolved Date, this time use the following:

   - Start date: Created date
   - End date: First Response date

4. **Creating Service Level Objectives**: Create a SLO for each priority; usually, this will be five SLOs for Priority 1 – 5 Incident types. Each time you create a new SLO ensure that the name and description change to reflect the priority it is based upon and ensure that the correct priority queue is also selected. Select the First Response Time metric you created in the previous step.

For each SLO, you will need to supply a target and warning threshold value. The following table shows common values that can be used, but should reflect your organizations specifically defined requirements and/or agreements with your customers:

Priority	Target	Warning threshold
Priority 1	30 minutes	15 minutes
Priority 2	2 hours	1 hours
Priority 3	8 hours	4 hours
Priority 4	16 hours	8 hours
Priority 5	24 hours	12 hours

How it works...

By defining the different parts that make up your organizations requirements and tying them together with a SLO, Service Manager now enables you to model your SLA requirements and keep track of how the service is performing. The ability to measure when incidents are nearing or have breached their SLA allows for escalations to be put in place, preferably before a breach, and for notifications to be sent to those people that need to be informed.

Creating Service Request SLAs

Service Manager has different classes of work items for which SLAs can be configured. This recipe will show how to set up SLA management for the Service Request class scoped to Implementation Time.

Getting ready

Be familiar with the following recipes:

- *Creating SLA metrics*
- *Creating priority queues*
- *Configuring business hours and non-working days*
- *Creating Service Level Objectives*
- *Creating management Packs to save your SCSM personalization* in `Chapter 2,` *Personalizing SCSM 2016 Administration*

How to do it...

We will refer to the previous recipes. The main change is to ensure the work item class, where referenced, is changed to target the **Service Request** class, as shown in the following screenshot:

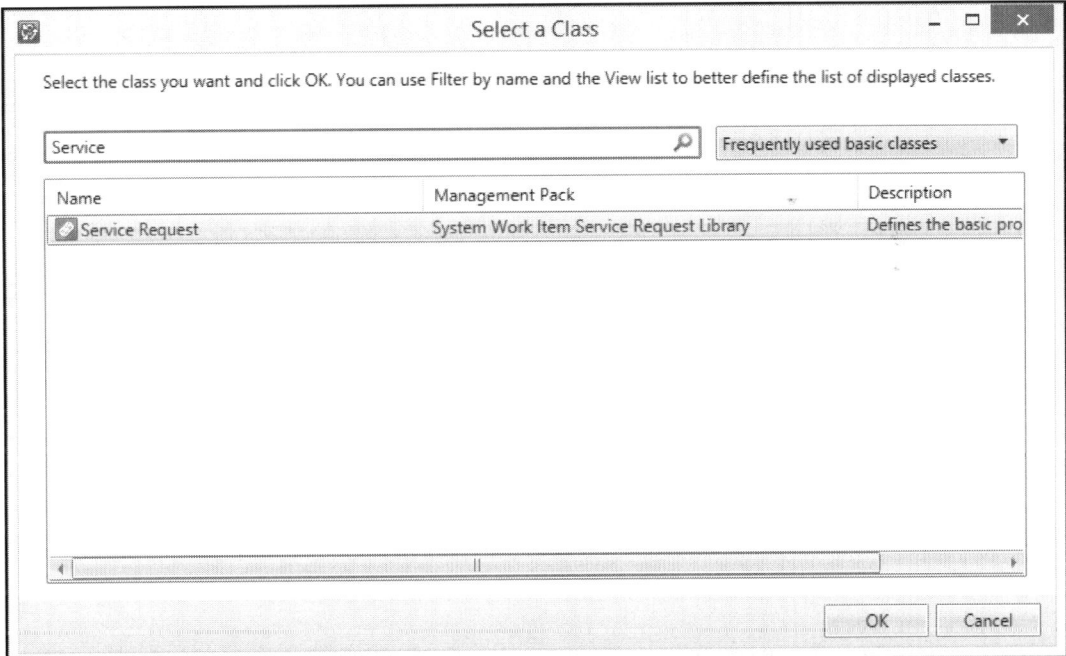

Implementation Time SLA

Perform the following recipes in this order:

1. **Creating Priority Queues**: Follow the *Creating Priority Queues* recipe, but each time you create a new queue, ensure that the name and description are changed to reflect the priority and that they are for Service Requests.

 Ensure that during the creation, the class is changed to Service Request. This will give you a different choice of priority for Service Requests. With incidents, you specified a numeric value. With Service Requests, use the drop-down selection list to choose the priority of **Low**, **Medium**, **High**, or **Immediate**:

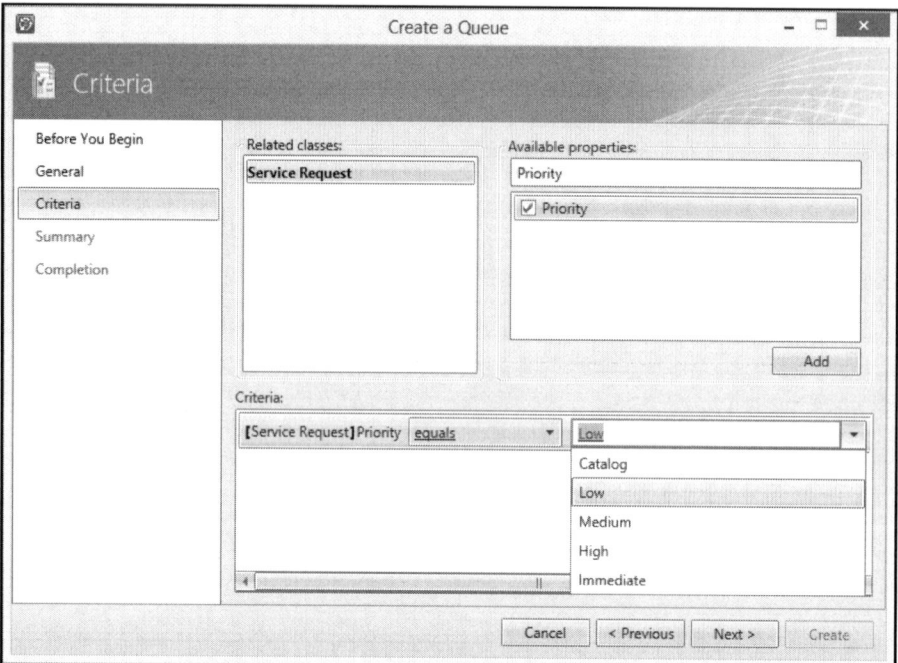

2. **Configuring business hours and non-working days**: Only one calendar is required based on the hours/days that you provide Service Request services to your customers. This could be the same calendar used for Incident Management, depending on your individual organization.

3. **Creating SLA metrics**: Use the example in the recipe, but change the class to **Service Request** and **End date** to **Completed Date**, as shown in the following screenshot:

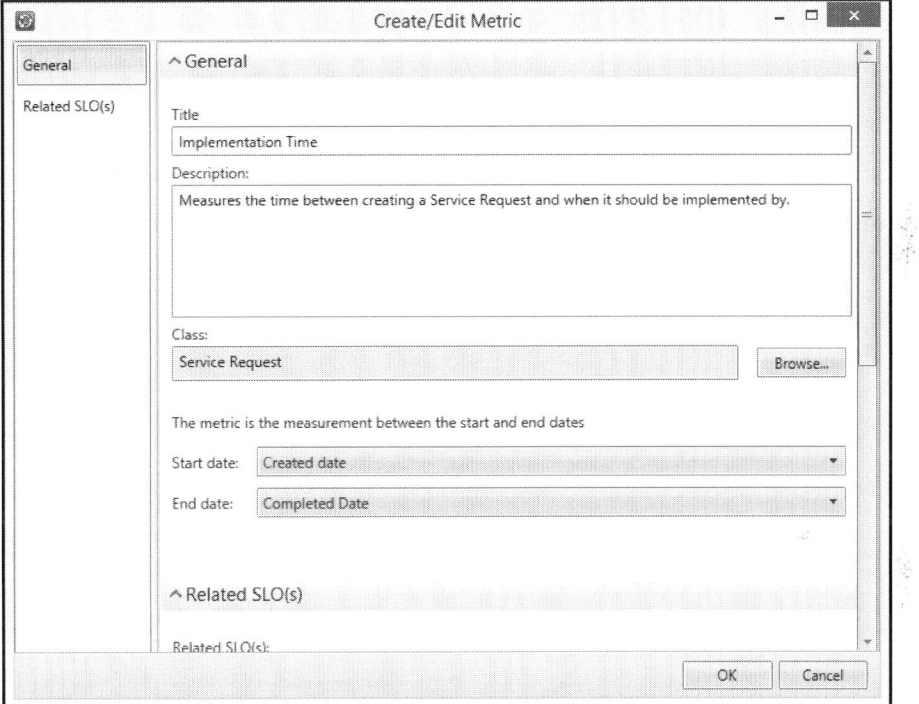

4. **Creating Service Level Objectives**: Create a SLO for each priority; usually this will be 4 SLOs for Priority **Low**, **Medium**, **High**, or **Immediate** Service Request types. Each time you create a new SLO, ensure that the name and description change to reflect the respective Service Request SLO and its Priority. Ensure that the correct priority queue for Service Requests is also selected.

For each SLO, you will need to supply a target and warning threshold value. The following table shows common values that can be used, but should reflect your organization's specifically defined requirements and/or agreements with your customers:

Priority	Target	Warning threshold
Immediate	9 hours	6 hours
High	45 hours	33 hours
Medium	90 hours	67 hours
Low	180 hours	180 hours

How it works...

By defining the different parts that make up your organization's requirements and tying them together with a SLO, Service Manager now enables you to model your SLA requirements and keep track of how the service is performing. This recipe provides steps to implement Service Request specific SLAs using the unique properties of the service request process.

Viewing SLA warnings and breaches

After setting up SLAs within Service Manager, it would be rather useful to actually see how work items are performing against the SLAs you've defined. There are a few places where we can see some of this information.

Getting ready

In order to view SLA information in the SCSM console, you need to have completed the previous recipes in this chapter.

How to do it...

The following steps will guide you through the process of viewing SLA warnings and breaches within Service Manager:

1. Navigate to the **Work Items** node of the console, expand the **Incident Management** folder, and then click on **Incidents with Service Level Breached**.
2. This should display a list of all incidents that have breached their SLA in the center of the console.
3. Highlight an incident and either double-click it or choose **Edit** from the tasks pane on the right-hand side.
4. When the breached incident form opens, it should be immediately obvious that there has been a breach of SLA on this incident from the yellow bar that is now present and the red exclamation mark next to the **Service Level** tab, as shown in the following screenshot:

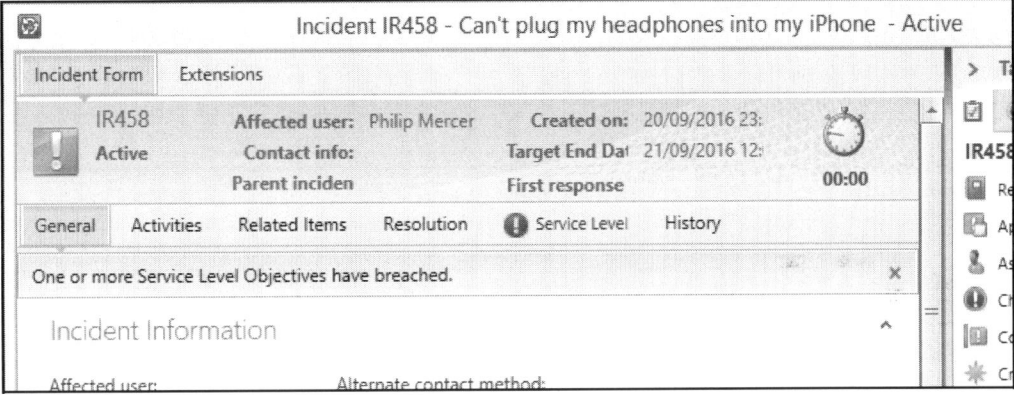

5. Clicking on the **Service Level** tab allows you to see more information related to the SLA, as shown in the following screenshot:

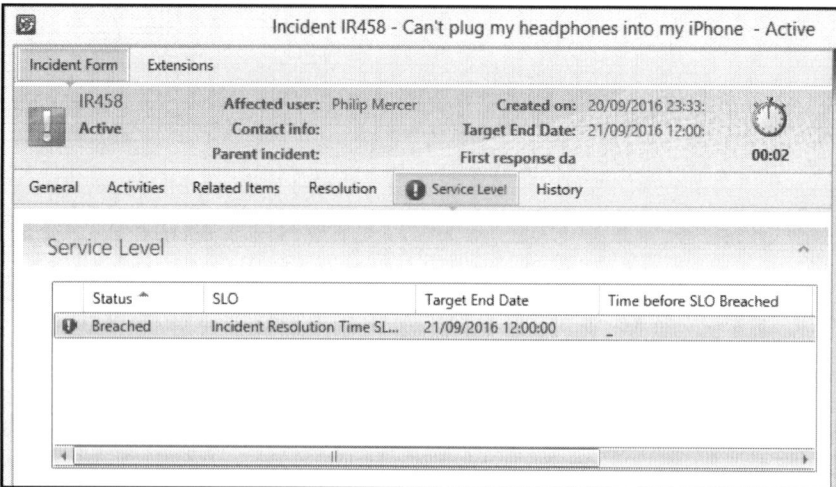

6. Depending on how the incident has been routed and the SLAs defined within you organization, it is possible to see multiple Service Levels displayed:

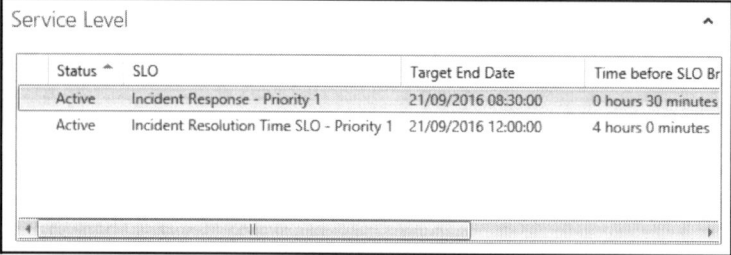

How it works...

Once a queue has been defined that targets incidents and has an SLO mapped to that queue, service levels are assigned to the members of that queue. The Service Level information is made available within the forms for the work items in scope of the configuration.

By default, Service Manager has two views to help with Service Level monitoring/management: **Incidents with Service Level Breached** and **Incidents with Service Level Warning**.

There's more…

Service Manager provides you with the ability to display SLA information in a color-coded format.

RAG status in console

You can create custom views to get what is known as a Red, Amber, Green (RAG) status in the main console without having to open each incident:

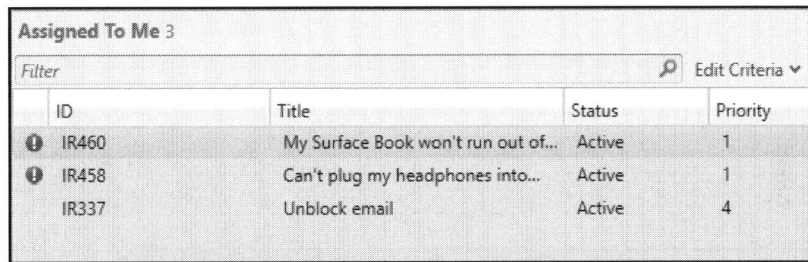

Setting up SLA notifications for warnings and breaches

This recipe will show you how to configure Service Manager to send an e-mail notification when a work item moves into either an SLA warning or breach state.

Getting ready

Ensure Service Levels are fully configured by following the previous recipes in this chapter.

It is also assumed that you have set up an SMTP channel for e-mail.

How to do it...

The following steps will guide you through the process of creating notifications within Service Manager for when an SLA goes into warning or breach:

1. Navigate to the **Administration** node of the **Service Manager** console, expand the **Notifications** folder, and click on **Templates**.
2. Click on **Create E-Mail Template** in the tasks pane on the right-hand side of the console.
3. Provide a title for the template and a description.
4. Click on the **Browse** button next to the targeted class box.
5. In the **Select a Class** window, use the drop-down box next to the search filter to change it from **Frequently used basic classes** to **All basic classes** and then filter the list to find **Service Level Instance Time Information**:

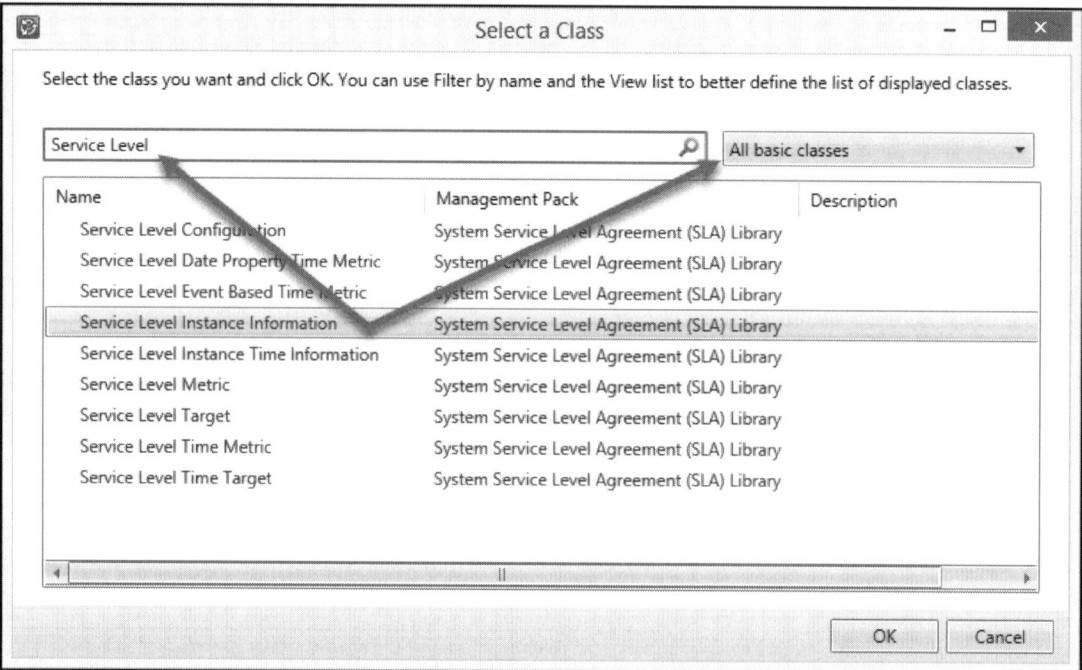

6. Choose the relevant custom management pack to store this customization in and click on **Next**:

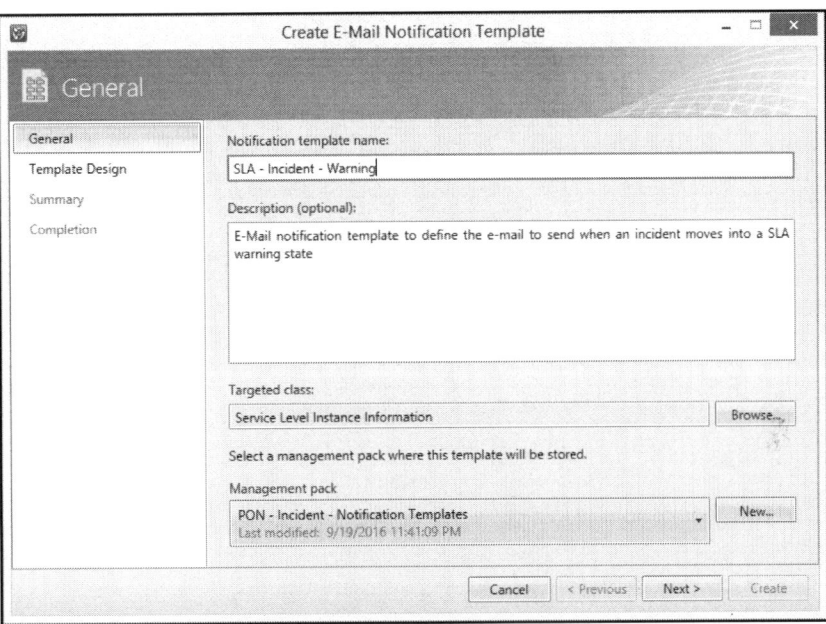

7. You can now design the template for the e-mail, including what information you would like to include.

You can type custom text, or you can use the **Insert...** button to insert tokens, or a combination of both:

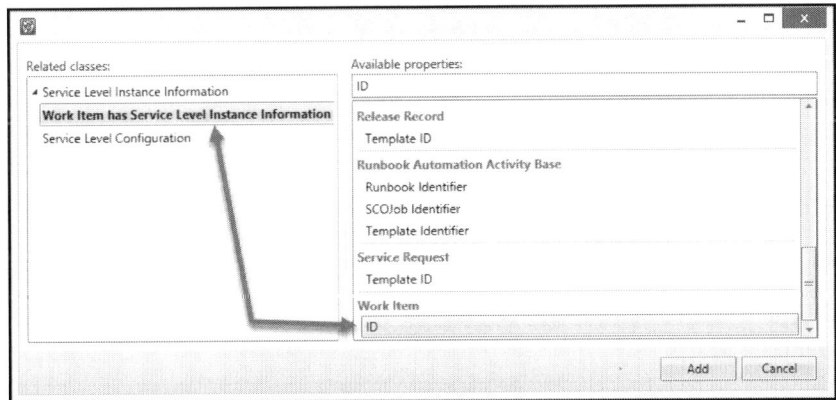

These tokens will dynamically resolve to information stored within Service Manager. For example, using the **Select Property** screen that opens and choosing **ID** under the **Work Item has Service Level Instance Information** work item will provide this token string back to the e-mail template design screen:

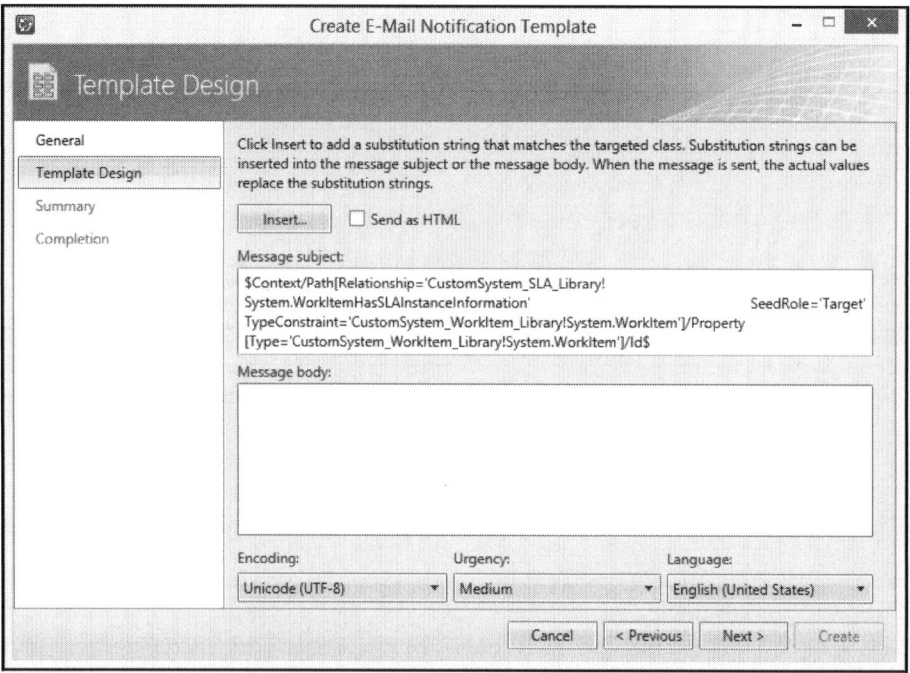

This long text will actually resolve the ID of the affected work item with the SLA breach, so if it was an incident, the ID might be IR324, for example.

If you intend to use the Exchange Connector with Service Manager then it is advisable to wrap any incident IDs with square brackets, for example, [IR324].

To do this, just add the opening bracket "[" before the token and the closing bracket "]" after the token.

For example, using the token shown in the screenshot, this would now look like the following:

```
[$Context/Path[Relationship='CustomSystem_SLA_Library!
System.WorkItemHasSLAInstanceInformation'SeedRole=
'Target'TypeConstraint='CustomSystem_SLA_Library!
System.WorkItem']/Property[Type=CustomSystem_SLA_
Library!System.WorkItem]/Id$]
```

8. Add more meaningful text around any tokens used; for example, in the message subject before the Work Item ID, add something meaningful such as SLA Warning - Incident::

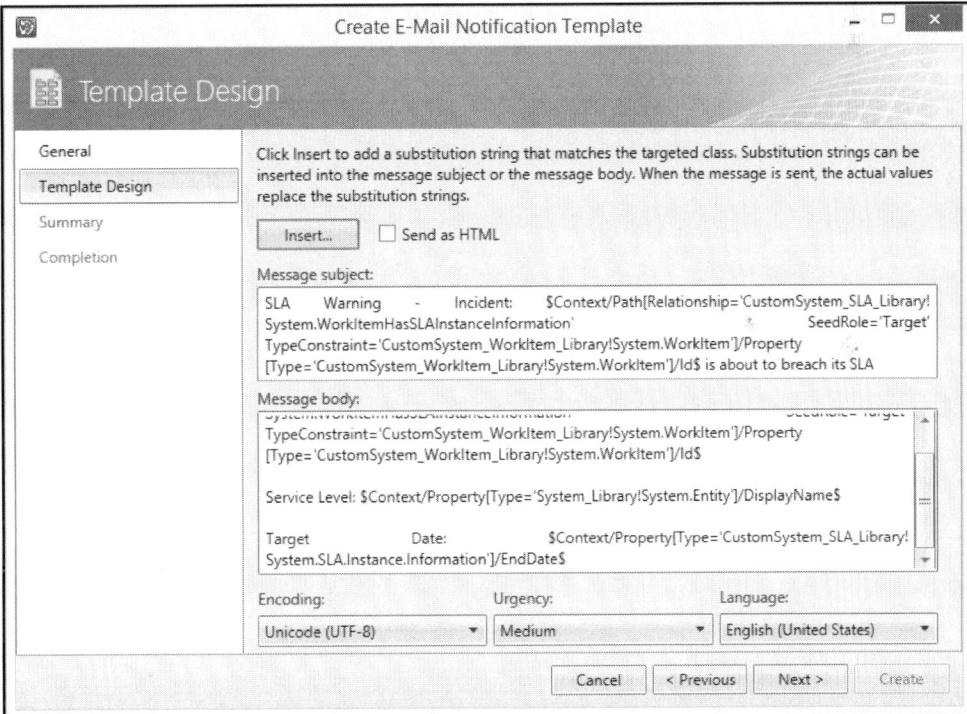

9. Click on **Next** when editing of the content is complete.
10. Review the **Summary** screen and click on **Create**.
11. Once it is completed, click on **Close**.

12. Navigate to the **Administration** node of the **Service Manager** console, expand the **Notifications** folder, and click on **Subscriptions**.

13. Click on **Create Subscription** in the tasks pane on the right-hand side of the console.

14. Click on **Next** on the **Before You Begin** screen.

15. Provide a title and a description for the subscription.

16. Use the drop-down list for **When to notify** and choose **When an object of the selected class is updated**.

17. Change the **Targeted** class to **Service Level Instance Time Information** using the **Browse**… button.

18. Select your custom management pack to store this subscription in and click on **Next**:

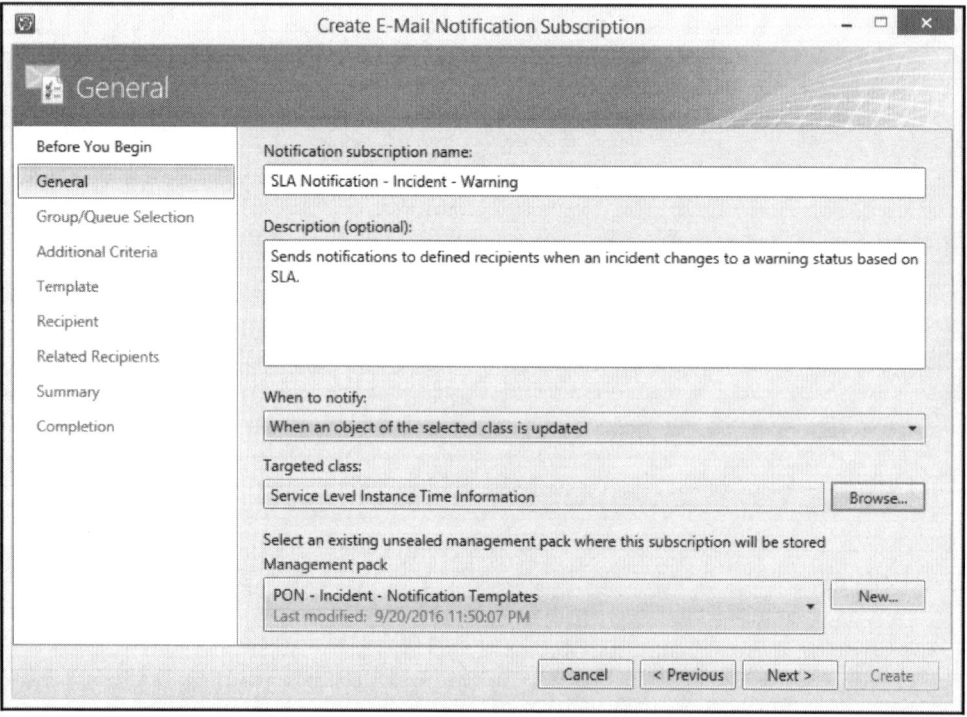

19. You can select specific groups/queues if it applies in your case, but we will skip it here and go to the additional criteria by clicking on **Next**.

    There are two tabs on the **Additional Criteria** screen, **Changed From** and **Changed To**.

20. In the **Changed From** tab, filter the properties down to find **Status** and add it as a criterion.

21. Change the validation from **equals** to **does not equal** and set the value as **Warning**:

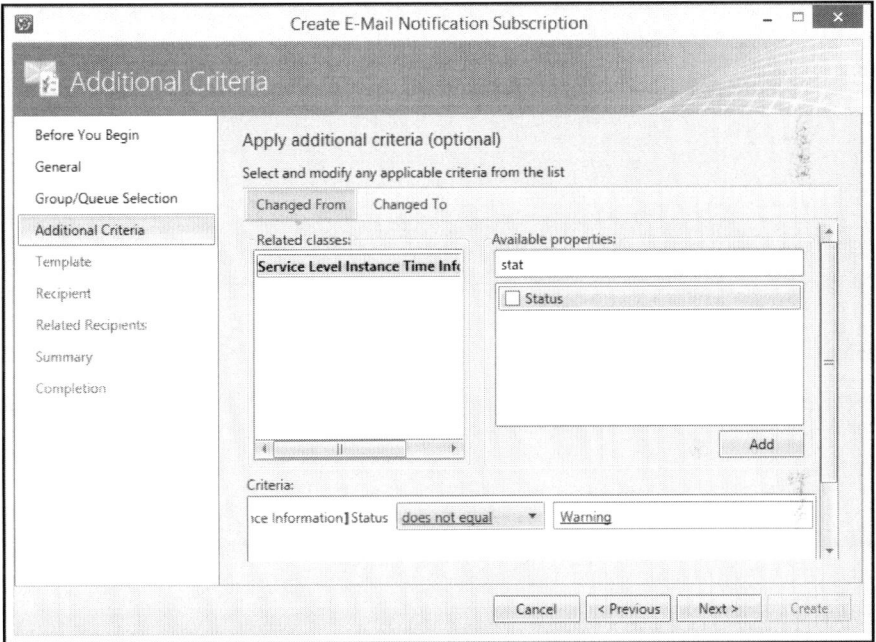

22. On the **Changed To** tab, filter the properties down to find **Status** and add it as a criterion.

23. Set the value for the criteria to **Warning**:

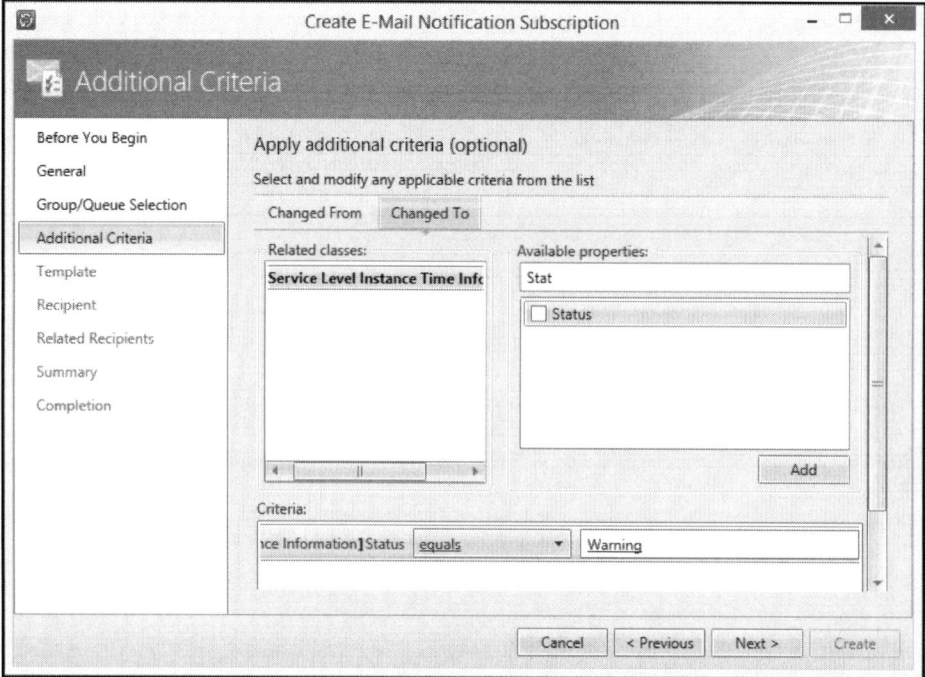

24. Click on **Next**.

25. Click on the **Select Button**, choose the e-mail notification template you created earlier in this recipe, and then click on **OK**. Click on **Next**.

26. You can either specify certain recipients to receive this notification by selecting their domain accounts from the CMDB, or click on **Next** to set up dynamic recipients.

27. Related Recipients is a feature that allows you to use relational information within the CMDB. For example, you can send the same notifications to secondary recipients.

28. Click on **Add**. On the **Select Related** Recipient screen, click on **[Work Item] Work Item has Service Level Instance Information** and then use the filter to narrow the choices down to **Assigned To User**. Select this and click on **Add**:

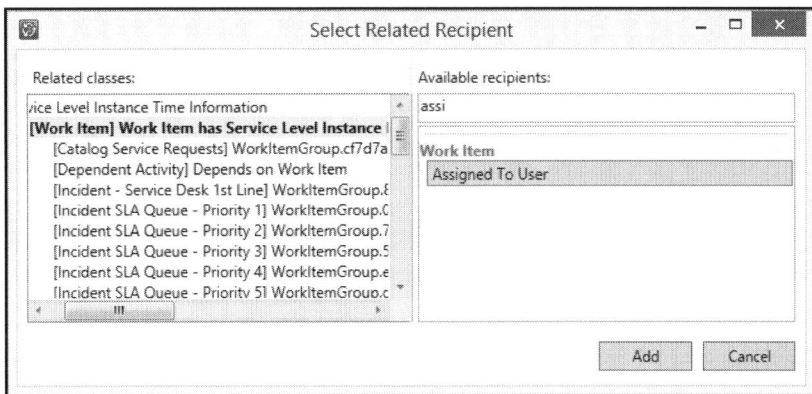

29. This adds a more dynamic nature to the e-mail subscriptions and provides flexibility. For example, we might want warning e-mails going to the assigned user for the incident, but for breaches, we might want e-mails sent to the primary owner and the person responsible for customer satisfaction, whom we would add as a direct recipient:

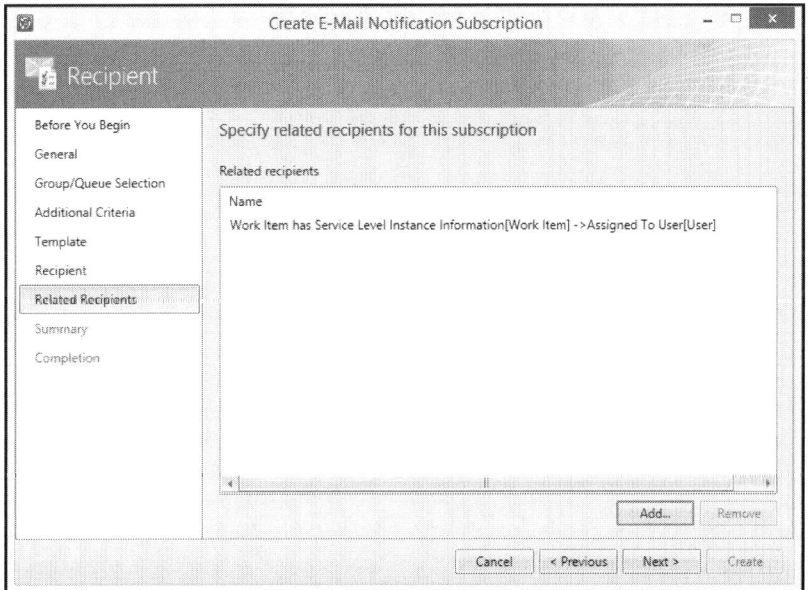

30. Click on **Next**.
31. Review the **Summary** screen and click on **Create**.
32. Once it's created, click on **Close**.

How it works...

We created a template that defined the information and layout of the message we want to send, and then we created a subscription that defines what event (change of SLA status to warning) causes the e-mail to be sent and to whom.

There's more...

This recipe can be followed for breaches of SLA rather than just warning, except for a couple of key changes.

Notification for breaches

When setting the additional criteria, we need the **Changed From** criteria setting as **equals Warning** and the **Changed To** criteria setting as **equals Breached**.

You must create a specific e-mail notification template just for breaches. Be sure to choose this template when creating the subscription.

Also, ensure names and descriptions are reflective of the intent of the notification.

Creating repeated notifications before SLA breaches with escalation

This recipe will show you how to set up a notification for incidents that are in a warning SLA status and send repeated notifications before a breach occurs, including sending a notification to an escalation point.

Getting ready

It would be advisable to perform the *Setting up SLA notifications for warning and breaches* recipe in this chapter first, as some of the principles are the same.

It is also assumed that you have set up an SMTP channel for e-mail.

How to do it...

The following steps will guide you through the process of creating notifications that repeat before an SLA breach occurs, along with escalation:

1. Navigate to the **Administration** node of the **Service Manager** console, expand the **Notifications** folder and click on **Templates**.
2. Click on **Create E-Mail Template** in the tasks pane on the right-hand side of the console.
3. Provide a title and a description for the template.
4. Click on the **Browse...** button next to the targeted class box.
5. In the **Select a Class** window, filter the list to find the **Incident** class, select it and click on **OK**:

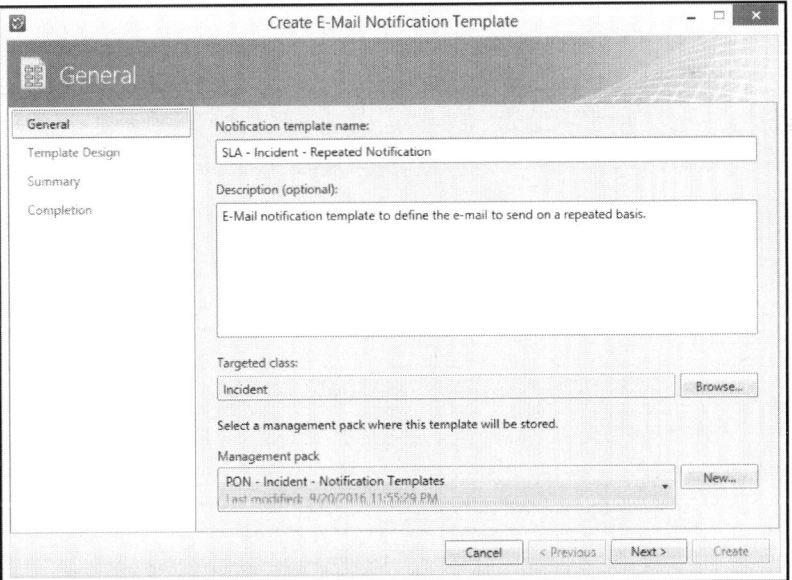

6. Choose the relevant custom management pack to store this customization in and click on **Next**.

7. You can now design the template for the e-mail, including what information you would like to include:

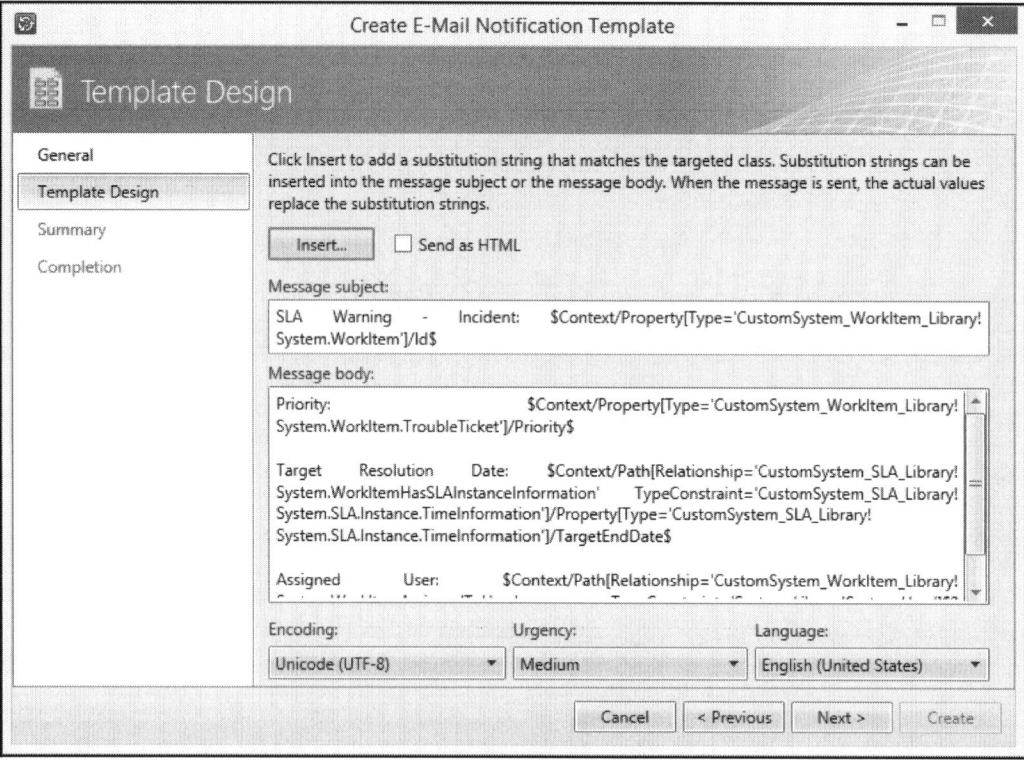

8. Click on **Next** when the content is complete.

9. Review the **Summary** screen and click on **Create**.

10. Once it is completed, click on **Close**.

11. Navigate to the **Administration** node of the **Service Manager** console, expand the **Notifications** folder, and click on **Subscriptions**.

12. Click on **Create Subscription** in the tasks pane on the right-hand side of the console.

13. Click on **Next** on the **Before You Begin** screen.

14. Provide a title and a description for the subscription.

> For repeated notifications for incidents, you will need to configure one subscription for each priority queue, so adjust the subscription name appropriately.

15. Use the drop-down list for **When to notify:** and choose **Periodically notify when objects meet a criteria**.
16. Change the **Targeted class** value to **Incident** using the **Browse...** button.
17. Select your custom management pack to store this subscription in and click on **Next**:

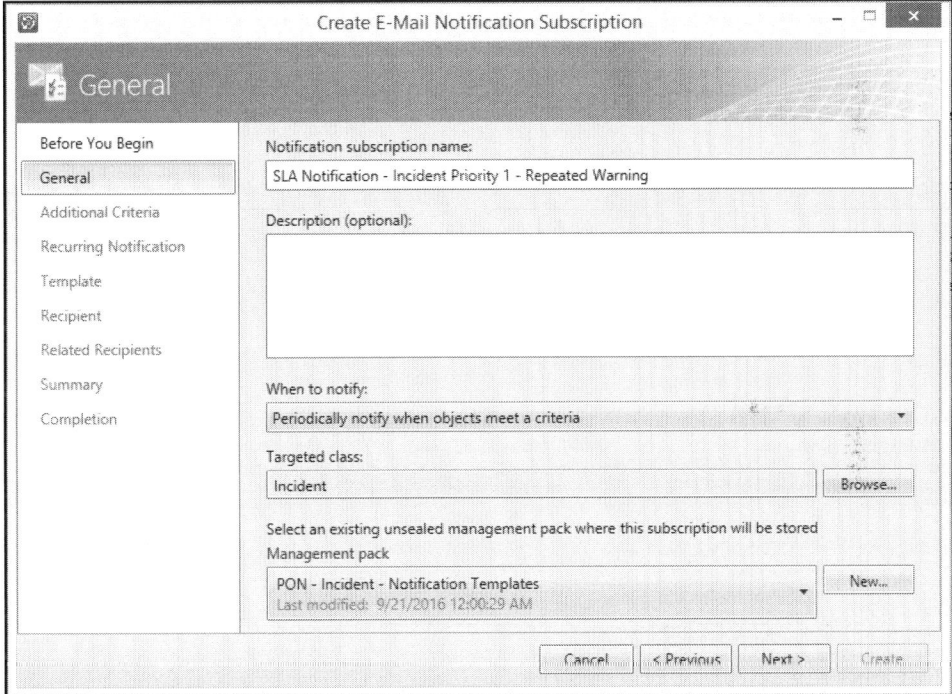

18. In the **Additional Criteria** tab, filter the properties down to find **Priority** and add it as a criterion.
19. Change the validation to **equals** and set the value as 1.

20. Expand Incident in the **Related classes** window and scroll down to select **Work Item has Service Level Instance Information**.

21. Filter the available properties to find **Status** and add that as a criterion:

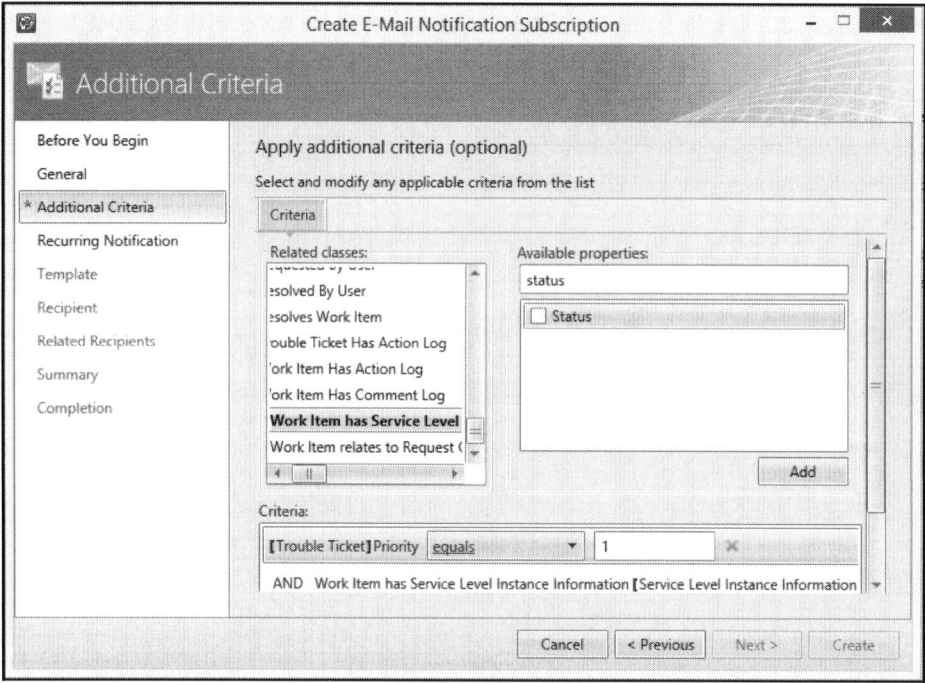

22. Change the value for **Work Item has Service Level Instance Information** to **equals Warning**:

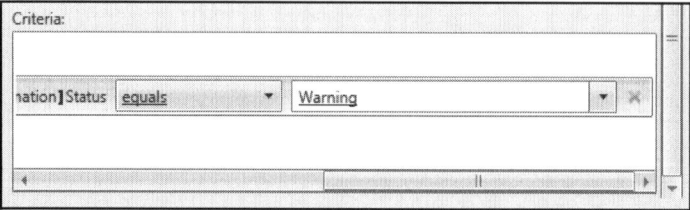

23. Click on **Next**.

24. Depending on your **Priority time** definitions, set the frequency of the recurrence of the notification.

> In previous recipes in this chapter, we defined our Priority 1 SLA to be a warning state after 15 minutes and breach after 30 minutes.

> This means you have a 15 minute time period after the incident changes to warning and before it breaches SLA, so it would be best to send a notification every three minutes, a total of four times. There isn't any point in sending a fifth notification, as that would be on or after 15 minutes, at which point a breach notification should be sent, and not another warning e-mail:

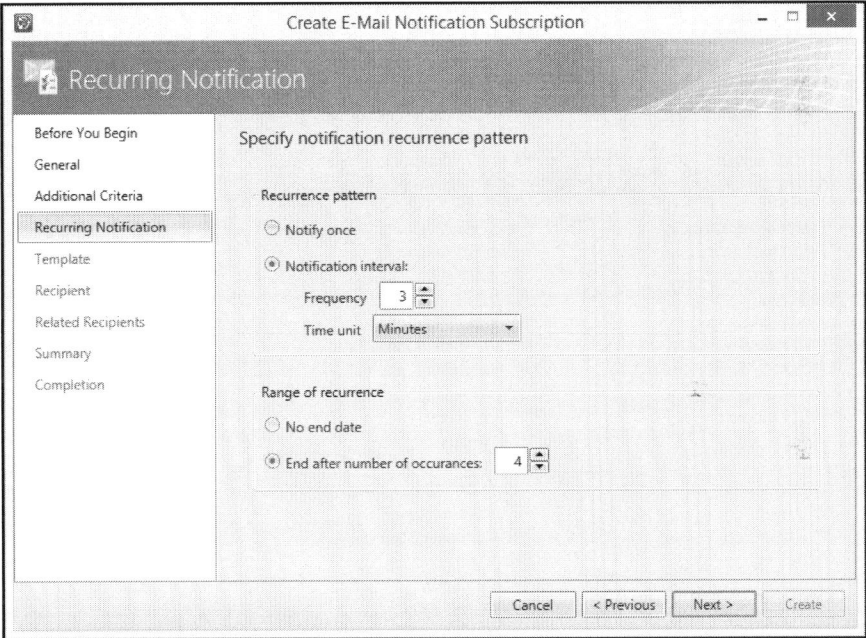

25. Click on **Next**.
26. Click on the **Select** button, choose the e-mail notification template you created earlier in this recipe, and click on **OK**. Then, click on **Next**.
27. You can either specify particular recipients to receive this notification by selecting their domain accounts from the CMDB, or click **Next** to set up dynamic recipients.

28. Related Recipients is a feature that allows you to use relational information within the CMDB. For example, you can send the same notifications to secondary recipients.

29. Click on **Add** and on the **Select Related Recipient** screen filter the available choices to **Assigned To User**. Select this and click on **Add**.

> At this point, we can also add in some escalation notifications by also adding for example the Primary Owner of the incident who may be a Line Manager, Service Desk Manager, or Team Leader, for example:

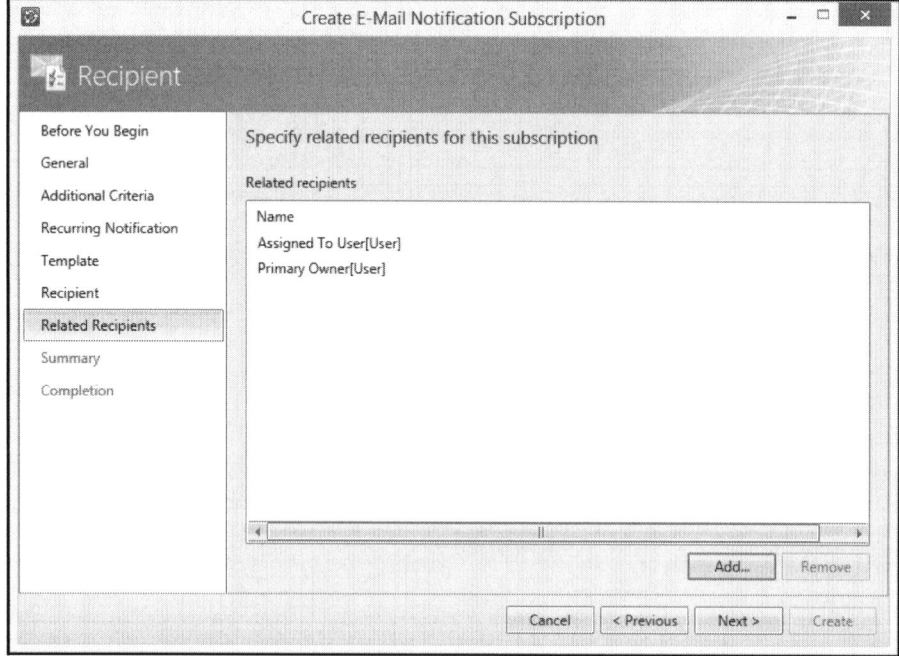

30. Click on **Next**.

31. Review the **Summary** screen, and when you are happy, click on **Create**.

32. Once created, click on **Close**.

How it works...

We created a template that defined the information and layout of the message we want to send, and then we created a subscription that defines what, at what interval, and how many times the e-mail will be sent, and to whom.

There's more...

The recipe provides steps for one priority. You may want to provide notifications for additional priorities.

Notification timings depending on priority

You will need to create a notification subscription following this recipe for each priority of work item that you would like to send out repeated notifications.

Each time you follow the recipe for a new priority, change the priority criteria to reflect the priority you are creating it for.

Also, change the notification interval and recurrence values to reflect the values for that specific priority.

Notification for breaches

This recipe can be followed for breaches of SLA rather than just warning, except for a couple of key changes.

When setting the additional criteria, the status criteria for **Work Item has Service Level Information** needs to be set to **equals Breached**.

You must create a specific e-mail notification template just for breaches. Be sure to choose this template when creating the subscription.

Also, ensure names and descriptions are reflective of the intent of the notification.

4
Building the Configuration Management Database (CMDB)

In this chapter, we will have recipes for configuring the Service Manager with information about your environment. We will specifically cover the area of setting up the Configuration Management Database (CMDB) within Service Manager, with the following tasks:

- Adding configuration items manually
- Importing Active Directory configuration items
- Importing Configuration Manager configuration items
- Importing Operations Manager configuration items
- Importing Virtual Machine Manager configuration items
- Importing Orchestrator runbooks
- Using a CSV file to import items into the CMDB
- Creating a Business Service
- Personalizing and organizing configuration item views

Introduction

In this chapter, Service Manager administrators are shown how to build the CMDB, with various options ranging from a manual approach, right through to automating the importing of information from external systems.

A **Configuration Management Database (CMDB)** is a store of information related to all the components of information systems used in an organization's IT environment. It contains the details of the **Configuration Items (CI)** within the IT infrastructure. CI can be types of components such as software, hardware, users, and clouds, and they are typically stored in the CMDB with their important attributes and relationships between other CIs.

Service Manager has the ability to create CIs through the following methods:

- Manual creation
- Importing from CSV
- Connection to Active Directory
- Connection to Configuration Manager
- Connection to Operations Manager
- Connection to Virtual Machine Manager
- Connection to Orchestrator

Adding configuration items manually

This recipe will show you how to use the Service Manager console to manually create a computer configuration item without using the connector framework or by importing any information.

How to do it...

The following steps will guide you through the process of adding CIs manually to the Service Manager CMDB:

1. In the Service Manager console navigate to **Configuration Items | Computers | All Windows Computers**.
2. Click on **Create Computer** in the task pane on the right-hand side of the console.
3. A new form screen will open.
4. Fill out the form with relevant data, ensuring any field marked with a red asterisk is filled in as they are mandatory fields.
5. Click on **OK**.

How it works...

Filling in the form submits the data to the database, creating the CI and a unique GUID identifier within the database.

There's more...

This method can be repeated for any configuration item within Service Manager. For a basic installation, this includes CIs such as the following:

- Computers/servers
- Printers
- Software
- Users
- Business services
- Builds
- Environments

Importing Active Directory configuration items

This recipe will show you how to set up the Active Directory connector, which will allow you to import users, groups, and printers from your Active Directory forest as CIs within Service Manager.

Getting ready

Before you set up the connector you will need an account within your Active Directory forest that has Read permissions to the organizational units containing the items you would like to import.

How to do it...

The following steps will guide you through the process of importing data from Active Directory into the Service Manager CMDB:

1. In the **Service Manager** console, navigate to **Administration | Connectors**.
2. In the task pane on the right-hand side click on **Create Connector** and select **Active Directory Connector**.
3. Review the information on the **Before You Begin** screen and click on **Next**.
4. Enter a name and description for the connector. In this example, I've called it `poweron.local Active Directory Connector`.

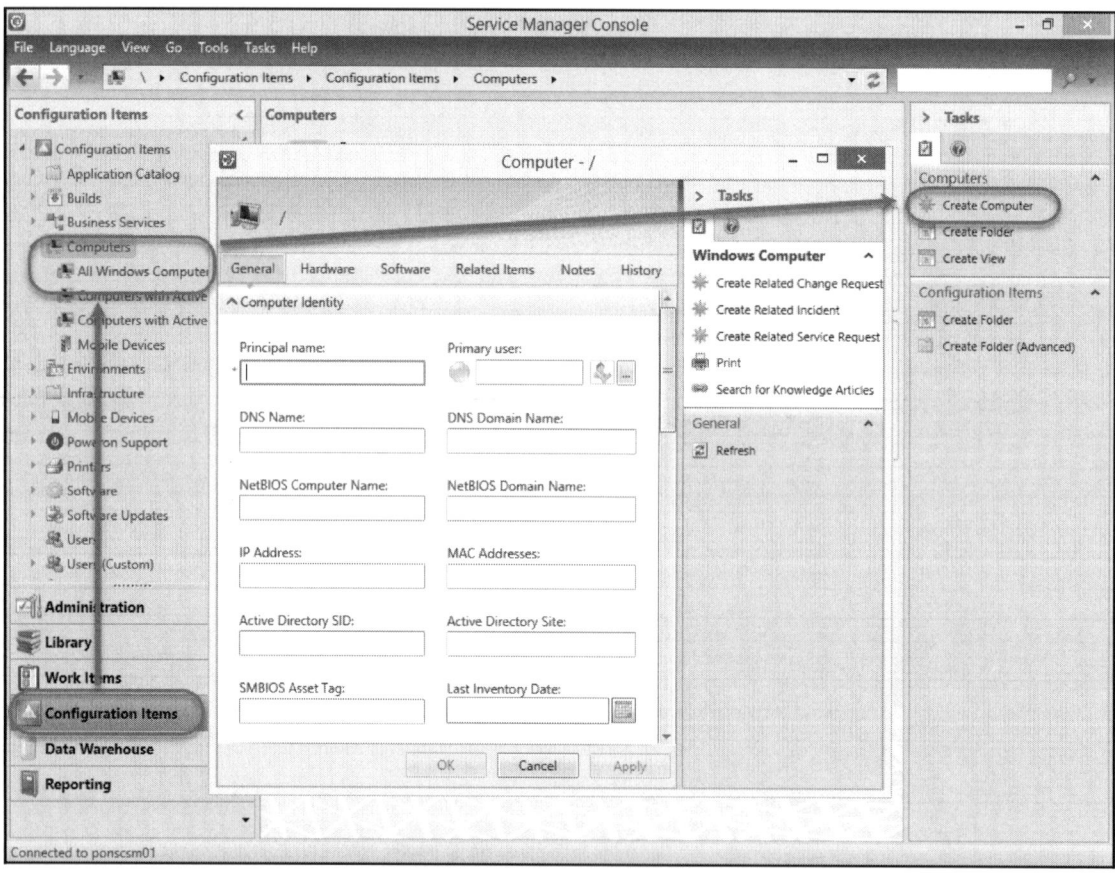

5. Ensure that the **Enable this connector** box is checked and then click on **Next**.
6. Choose to either synchronize the entire domain or a specific OU.

   In this example, I've chosen to synchronize an OU named `Cookbook`.

   A specific OU may be a more appropriate choice where the Active Directory structure may contain lots of non-relevant information and you require a more targeted import of data. Otherwise just choose to connect to the root of the domain.

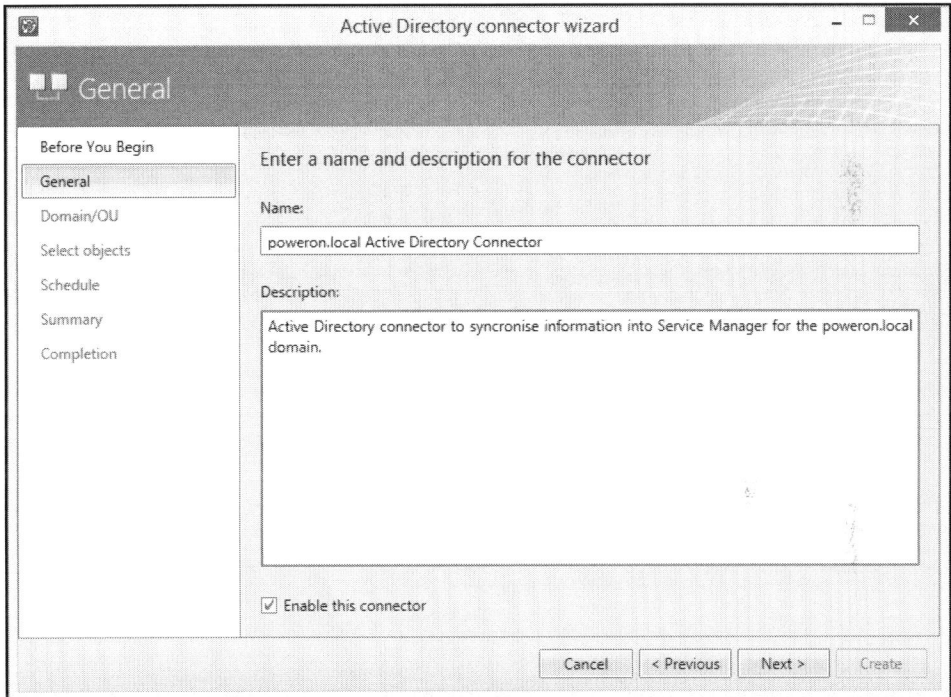

7. Next to the **Run As Account** drop-down options, click on **New** and enter the details of the account you set up before starting this recipe, which has Read rights to Active Directory. Click on **Next**. When prompted, supply the password for the account used for the connector.

8. The **Select objects** screen allows you to drill down and choose either specific objects to synchronize with this connector or provide an LDAP query to select the objects based on a custom criterion. As shown in this example, just select **All computers, printers, users and user groups**.

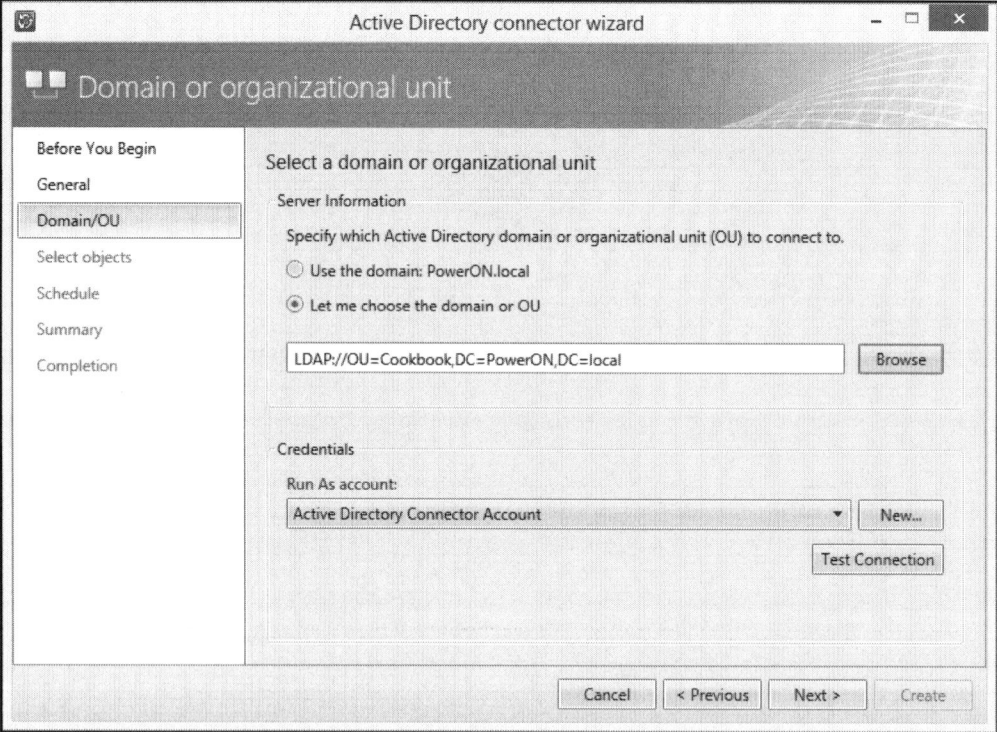

9. Ensure that the **Do not write null values for properties that are not set in Active Directory** option at the bottom of the screen is selected and click on **Next**.
10. Choose a schedule for when the connector will run then click on **Next**.
11. Review the summary and then click on **Create**.
12. When the completion screen shows that the connector was successfully created, click on **Close**.

How it works...

By default, the Active Directory connector polls Active Directory every 24 hours for new objects at the time chosen in the schedule during creation via the wizard. This can of course be altered during creation and a specific day to run chosen.

If new objects are present, they are inserted into Service Manager as new configuration items; otherwise the connector becomes dormant until the next 24-hour interval (or day specified by the schedule).

You can change this schedule via editing the connector from the console.

There's more...

The Active Directory connector can be accessed via the `Connectors` folder under the **Administration** Workspace of the Service Manager console. Select the connector and click on **Properties** from the tasks pane on the right-hand side of the console.

Mapping Active Directory domain attributes to Service Manager properties

The following link is to the Service Manager TechNet library documentation and it shows the Active Directory attribute and the corresponding Service Manager property that it maps to:

```
https://technet.microsoft.com/en-gb/system-center-docs/sm/manage/admin-appen
dix-b-mapping-active-directory-domain-services-attributes-to-properties-in-s
ystem-center-2016-service-manager.
```

Changing the Active Directory connector schedule via PowerShell

Unfortunately, changing the schedule of a connector isn't an easy PowerShell cmdlet and it requires the use of the SDK via PowerShell.

Anton Gritsenko has a good blog post here that explains how to achieve this:

```
http://blog.scsmsolutions.com/2012/03/update-ad-and-sccm-connector-scheduler-
with-powershell/.
```

Importing Configuration Manager configuration items

This recipe will show you how to set up the Configuration Manager connector, which will allow you to import information such as hardware and software information from your Configuration Manager system as CIs within Service Manager.

Getting ready

Before you set up the connector you will need an account within your Active Directory forest for the connector that has the following permissions:

- The following Configuration Manager SQL Database roles:
- smsdbrole_extract
- db_datareader
- Service Manager – Advanced Operator role

How to do it…

The following steps will guide you through the process of importing data from System Center Configuration Manager into the Service Manager CMDB:

1. In the **Service Manager** console, navigate to **Administration | Connectors**.
2. In the task pane on the right-hand side, click on **Create Connector** and select **Configuration Manager Connector**.
3. Review the **Before You Begin** screen and then click on **Next**.
4. On the **General** screen, enter a name and a description for the connector. In this example, I've called it `poweron.local Configuration Manager Connector`.

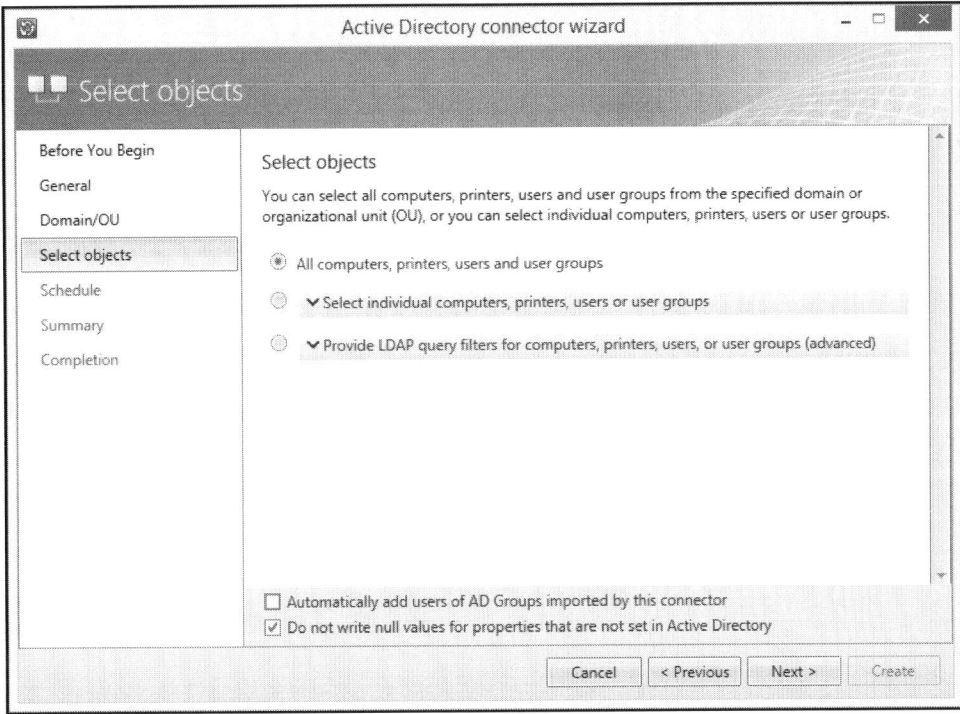

5. Ensure that **Enable** is ticked so that this connector box is enabled and then click on **Next**.

6. On the **Select Management Pack** screen, use the drop-down list under **Management Pack** to select the appropriate version of **Configuration Manager** that you wish to connect to, and then click on **Next**.

The System Center Configuration Manager 2012 connector configuration option will also support 2012 R2 and above releases, such as the Current Branch version

7. On the **Connect to System Center Configuration Manager Database** screen, supply the name of the server hosting the SQL site database (including any instance information if applicable). Then supply the name of the database. In this example, I've used PONCONFIGMGR01 as the name of the server holding the site database and COM_PON as the database name.

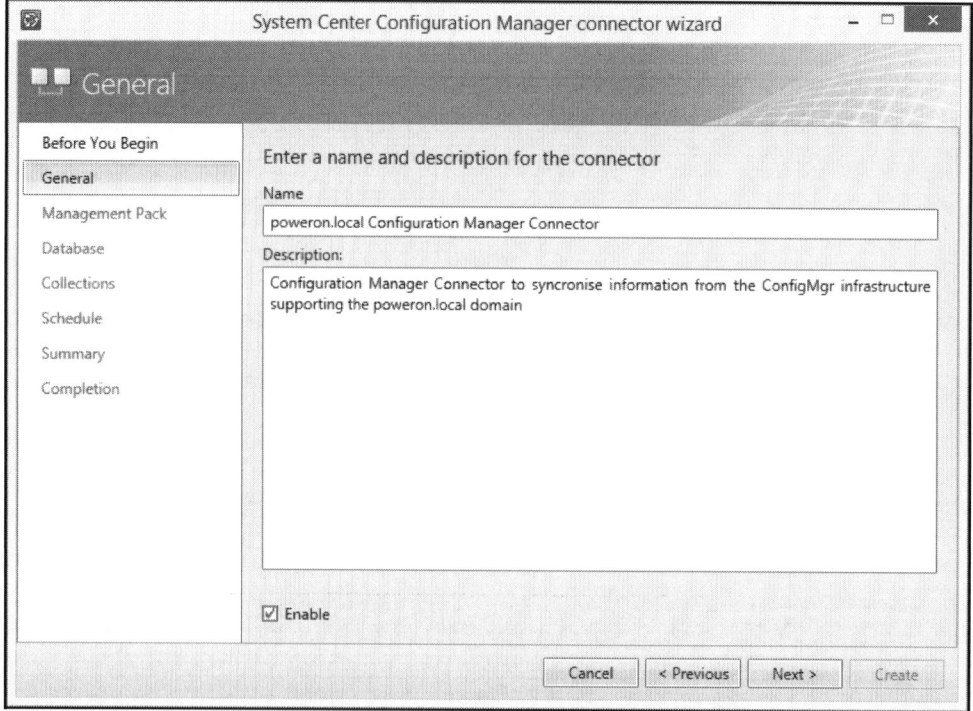

8. Next to the **Run As Account** drop-down selection, click on **New** and enter the details of the account you had set up before starting this recipe, which is a member of smsdbrole_extract and the db_datareader SQL roles for the site database.

9. Click on **Test Connection** and enter the password for the account when prompted.

10. Click on **Next**.

11. On the **Collections** screen select the collection containing the CIs you would like to synchronize, for this example, **All Desktop and Server Clients**.

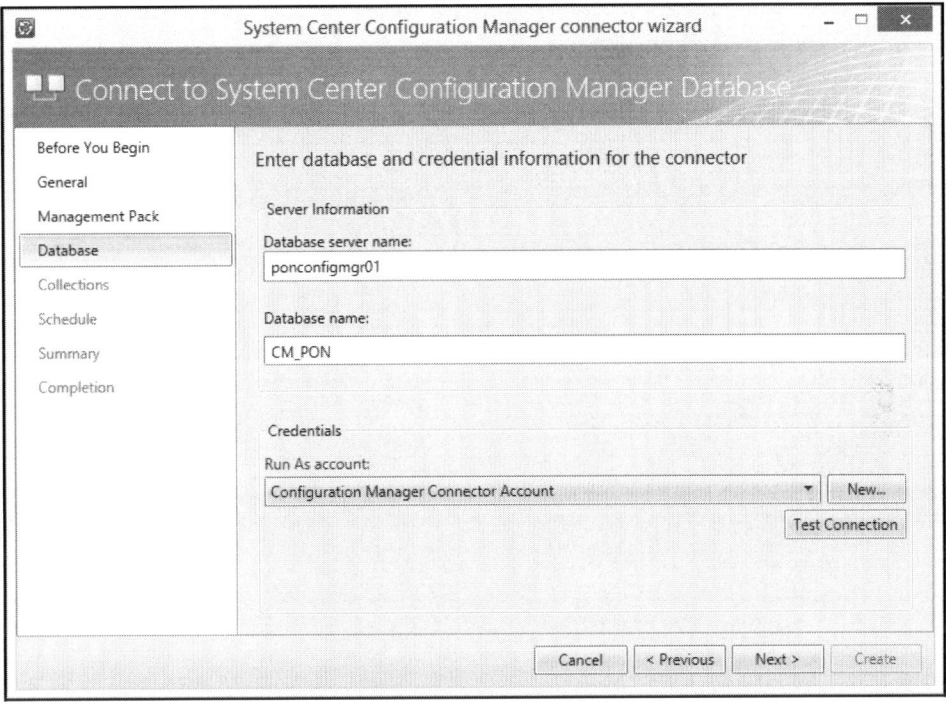

12. Ensure that the box next to **Do not write null values for properties that are not set in Configuration Manager** is checked. Click on **Next**.
13. On the **Schedule** screen, select when and how often you would like the connector to run. For this recipe, set it to every day at 06:00 and click on **Next**.
14. Review the information on the **Summary** screen and then click on **Create**.
15. Review the information on the **Confirmation** screen and then click on **Close**.

How it works...

The Service Manager connector queries the Configuration Manager database and extracts information related to computers, software, hardware, operating systems, software updates, users, and DCM baselines, and stores it within the CMDB.

Unless you are not using the Active Directory connector, it is recommended to only use a collection that is scoped to devices that have a Configuration Manager agent installed.

The purpose of the connector is to bring across hardware and software information for the CI. This information isn't present without a Configuration Manager agent on the device to collect it, therefore the extra processing involved in checking for and synchronizing non-existing data is superfluous.

There's more...

The Configuration Manager connector can be accessed via the `Connectors` folder under the **Administration** Workspace of the Service Manager console. Select the connector and click on **Properties** from the task pane on the right-hand side of the console.

Mapping Configuration Manager attributes to Service Manager properties

The following link is to the Service Manager TechNet library documentation and it shows the Configuration Manager attribute and the corresponding Service Manager property that it maps to:

```
https://technet.microsoft.com/en-gb/system-center-docs/sm/manage/admin-appen
dix-c-mapping-system-center-2016-service-manager-properties-to-configuration
-manager-database-views.
```

Importing Operations Manager configuration items

This recipe will show you how to set up the Operations Manager connector, which will allow you to import information such as (server IP addresses, SQL databases, and distributed application information from your operations manager system) as CIs within Service Manager.

Getting ready

Before you set up the connector you will need an account within your Active Directory forest for the connector that has the following permissions:

- Operations Manager – operator privileges
- Service Manager – advanced operator

For the Operations Manager connector to know what to synchronize with Service Manager, it is required that the management packs containing the classes that define the information are imported into Service Manager.

The Service Manager installation directory contains the base management packs required to get started with the Operations Manager connector.

The following steps guide you through the process of locating and importing the management packs:

1. In the **Service Manager** console, navigate to the **Administration** | **Management Packs**.
2. In the tasks pane on the right-hand side under **Management Packs**, click on **Import**.

3. On the **Select Management Packs to Import** screen, click on **Add** and navigate to the drive and directory where Service Manager is installed and choose the relevant **Operations Manager Management Packs** for the version you want to support.

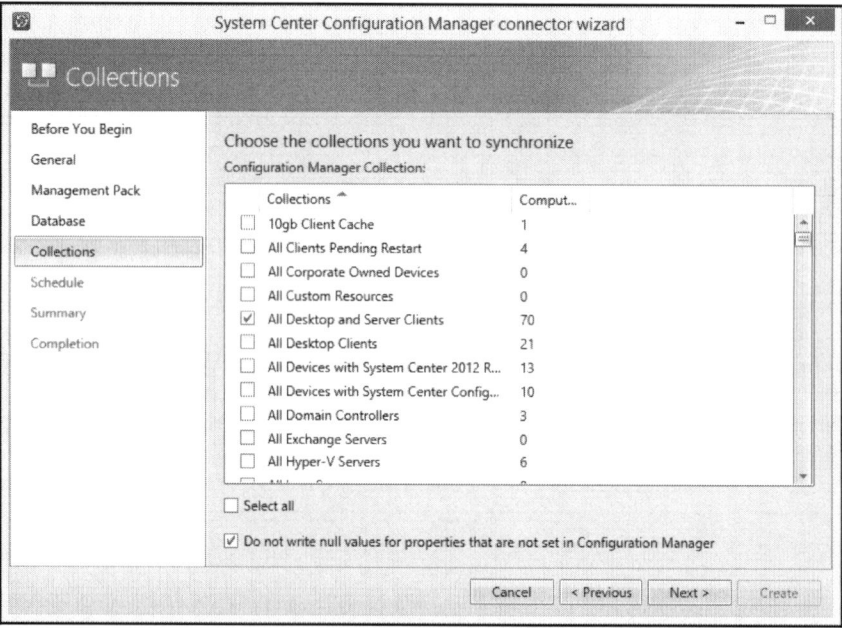

4. Click on the **Change the File Type** drop-down menu to select **MP Files (*.mp)**.
5. Select all the management packs displayed and click on **Open**.
6. On the **Import Management Packs** screen, click on **Import**.
7. When the import process is complete, click on **OK**.

How to do it...

The following steps will guide you through the process of importing data from System Center Operations Manager into the Service Manager CMDB:

1. In the **Service Manager** console, navigate to **Administration | Connectors**.
2. In the task pane on the right-hand side, click on **Create Connector** and then select **Operations Manager CI Connector**.

3. Review the **Before You Begin** screen and then click on **Next**.

4. On the **General** screen, enter a name and a description for the connector. In this example, I've called it `poweron.local Operations Manager Connector`.

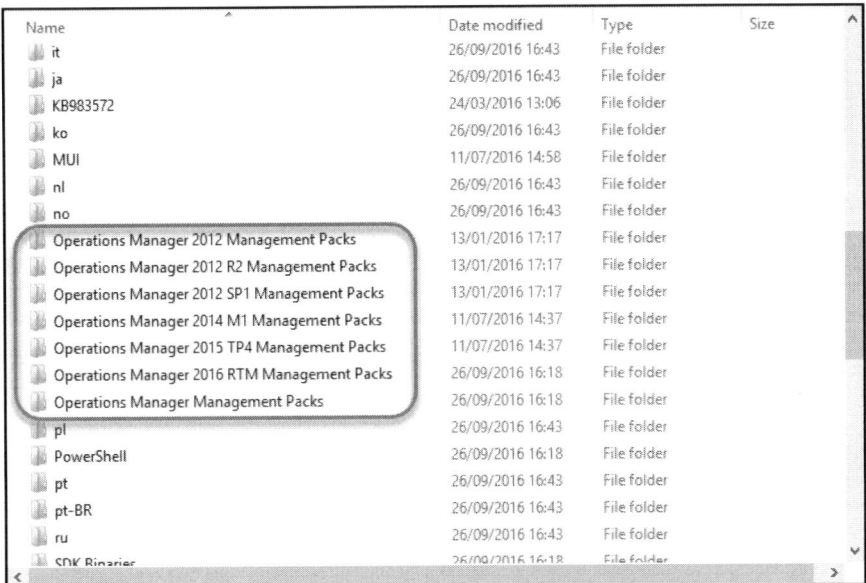

5. Ensure that the **Enable** box is checked and then click on **Next**.

6. On the **Server Details** screen in the **Server Name** box, supply the name of the server that the Operations Manager Management Server is installed on.

7. Next to the **Run As Account** drop-down menu, click on **New** and enter the details of the account you had set up before starting.

8. Click the test connection and enter the password for the account when prompted.

9. Click on **Next**.

10. On the **MP Selection** screen, check the **Select all** box and ensure that the **Do not write null values for properties that are not set in Operations Manager** box is checked. Click on **Next**.

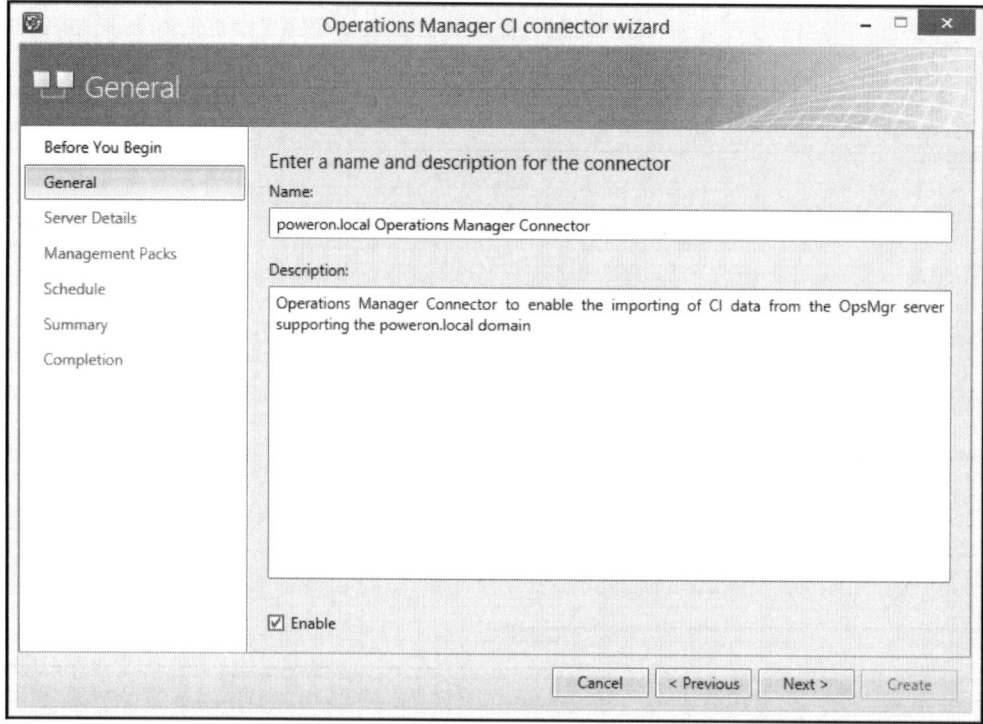

11. On the **Schedule** screen, select when and how often you would like the connector to run. For this recipe, set this to every day at 05:00 and click on **Next**.
12. Review the information on the **Summary** screen and then click on **Create**.
13. Review the information on the **Confirmation** screen and then click on **Close**.

How it works...

The Service Manager connector queries the Operations Manager Management Server and extracts information related to servers and related items and stores it within the CMDB according to the schedule specified.

There's more…

The Operations Manager connector can be accessed via the `Connectors` folder under the **Administration** Workspace of the Service Manager console. Select the connector and click on **Properties** from the task pane on the right-hand side of the console.

Adding new Operations Manager CIs

Every so often you will import new management packs into Operations Manager to extend its monitoring capabilities and/or update its management packs with newer versions. These will require importing into Service Manager to either allow these new classes of data to be brought across as CIs or to ensure that any changes to the classes within the management packs are mirrored across both systems.

First use the same method described in the *Getting ready* section of this recipe to import and browse for the updated/new management packs.

Next you must edit the Operations Manager CI connector, as follows:

1. In the Service Manager console, navigate to the **Service Manager** console to **Administration** | **Connectors**.
2. Select the **Operations Manager CI Connector**, named `PowerON.local Operations Manager Connector` in this recipe.
3. In the task pane on the right-hand side, click on **Properties**.
4. In the **Edit** screen on the left-hand side, click on **Management Packs** and then click on **Refresh**.
5. Enter the password for the account used by the Operations Manager CI Connector and click on **OK**.
6. In the **Management Packs** list, select the new management packs that you have just imported or check the **Select All** box, and click on **OK**.

Importing Virtual Machine Manager configuration items

This recipe will show you how to set up the Virtual Machine Manager connector, which will allow you to import information about your virtualization CIs and your private cloud environment.

Getting ready

Before you set up the connector you will need an account within your Active Directory forest for the connector that has the following permissions:

- Virtual Machine Manager-SCVMM Administrator Role and Local Administration Rights on the Virtual Machine Manager server
- Service Manager-Advanced Operator

You must also ensure that an Operations Manager CI connector has been created first and that the following management packs are imported:

- Relevant base Operations Manager management packs
- IIS 2003
- IIS 7
- IIS Library
- SQL Server Core Library
- Virtual Machine Manager

After these are imported, import the Virtual Machine Manager Management Pack (Microsoft.SystemCenter.VirtualMachineManager.2012.Discovery) into Service Manager and make sure that all the management packs are synchronized with the Operations Manager CI Connector.

See the *Operations Manager CI Connector* recipe for information on importing management packs, setting up the Operations Manager CI connector, and synchronizing management packs with the connector.

How to do it...

The following steps will guide you through the process of importing data from System Center Virtual Machine Manager into the Service Manager CMDB:

1. In the **Service Manager** console, navigate to **Administration | Connectors**.
2. In the task pane on the right-hand side, click on **Create Connector**. Then select **Virtual Machine Manager Connector**.
3. Review the **Before You Begin** screen and then click on **Next**.
4. On the **General** screen, enter a name for the connector and a description. In this recipe, I've called it **poweron.local Virtual Machine Manager Connector**.

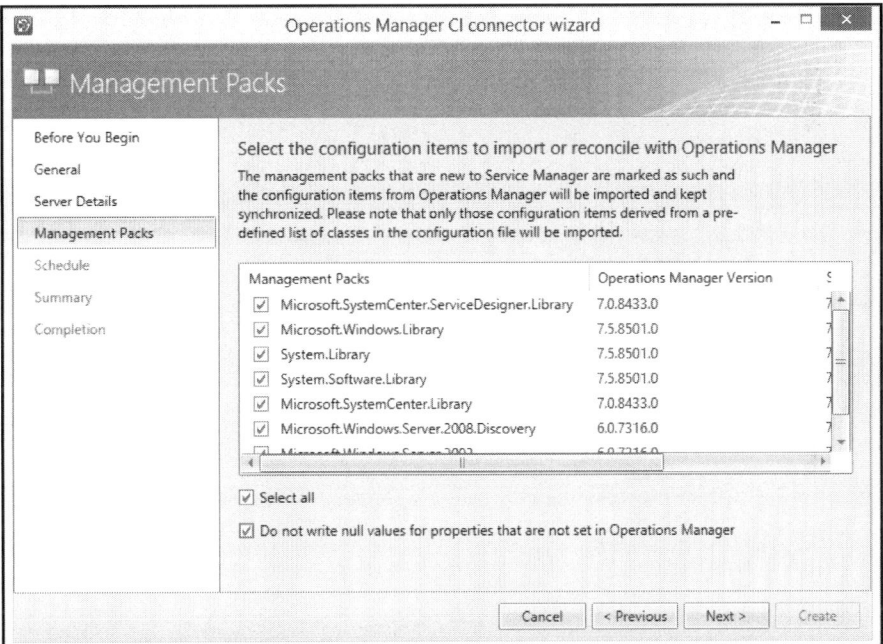

5. Ensure that the **Enable this connector** box is checked, and then click on **Next**.

6. On the **Connection** screen in the **Server Information** box, supply the name of the server that the Virtual Machine Manager is installed on. In this recipe, I've used PONSCVMM as the name of the Virtual Machine Manager Server.

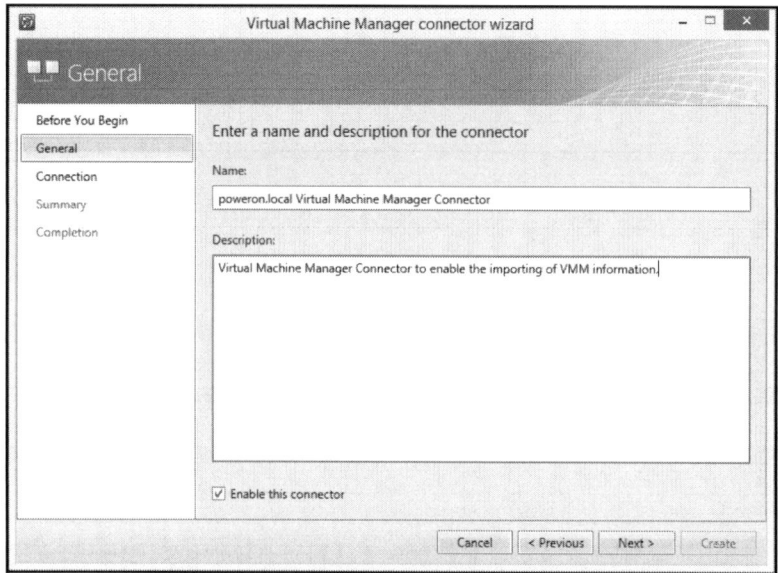

7. Next to the **Run As Account** drop-down menu click on **New** and enter the details of the account that you had set up before starting.
8. Click **Test Connection** and enter the password for the account when prompted.
9. Click on **Next**.
10. Review the information on the **Summary** screen and then click on **Create**.
11. Review the information on the **Confirmation** screen and then click on **Close**.

How it works...

Most of the CI information related to virtualization is actually brought across by the Operations Manager CI connector, which is why it is a prerequisite to have that connector set up before creating the Virtual Machine Connector. The Virtual Machine Connector syncs information relating to the Virtual Machine Manager Library to complete the CMDB information.

The items the connector syncs are as follows:

- Service templates
- VM templates
- Storage classifications
- Logical networks
- Load balancers
- Load balancer VIP templates

This extra information allows you to create items such as Service Requests that might allow a user to provision a Virtual Machine by referencing a VM Template.

There's more...

The Virtual Machine Manager connector can be accessed via the **Connectors** folder under the Administration Workspace of the Service Manager Console. Select the connector and click on **Properties** from the task pane on the right-hand side of the console.

Need to use an account that isn't a local administrator?

If you have a policy that prohibits the use of local administrator accounts, you need to manually adjust a few permissions to allow for remote PowerShell usage by the account used for the Virtual Machine Manager connector:

1. Log on to the server hosting Virtual Machine Manager as a user with administrative rights.
2. Open a PowerShell window (ensure that it's elevated with administrative rights).
3. Type the following and press *Enter:*

```
Set-PSsessionConfigurationMicrosoft.Powershell -
ShowSecurityDescriptorUI
```

4. When prompted with **are you are sure you want to perform this action**, type Y and press Enter.
5. Add the account being used for the connector and grant it **Execute (Invoke)** permission by checking the **Allow** box.
6. Click on **OK**.
7. If prompted to confirm whether **WinRM can be restarted**, type Y and press **Enter**.

Setting up a Virtual Machine Manager and Operations Manager integration

Because most of the information about your virtualization CIs comes through the Operations Manager CI Connector, it is also advisable to set up the integration feature between Virtual Machine Manager and Operations Manager via the Virtual Machine Manager console:

1. Within Operations Manager ensure that the following management packs are imported:

   - IIS 2003
   - IIS 7
   - IIS Library SQL
   - Server Core Library

2. In the **Virtual Machine Manager** console, navigate to the **Settings** workspace.
3. Click on the **System Center** settings and Operations Manager Server.
4. If no connection exists, a wizard will start.
5. Follow the wizard through and the connection will be made.

Importing Orchestrator runbooks

This recipe will show you how to set up the Orchestrator connector, which will allow you to import information about your runbooks to allow them to be used within automation activities in Service Request processes.

Getting ready

Before you set up the connector you will need an account within your Active Directory forest for the connector that has the following permissions:

- Read properties
- List contents
- Publish permissions to the root Runbook folder and all child objects

These permissions are granted via the **Runbook Designer** console.

How to do it...

The following steps will guide you through the process of importing runbook information from System Center Orchestrator into the Service Manager CMDB to allow runbooks to be used as automation activities during Service Requests:

1. In the **Service Manager** console, navigate to **Administration** | **Connectors**.
2. In the task pane on the right-hand side click on **Create Connector** and then select **Orchestrator Connector**.
3. Review the **Before You Begin** screen and then click on **Next**.
4. On the **General** screen, enter a name for the connector and a description. In this recipe, I've called it `poweron.local Orchestrator Connector`.

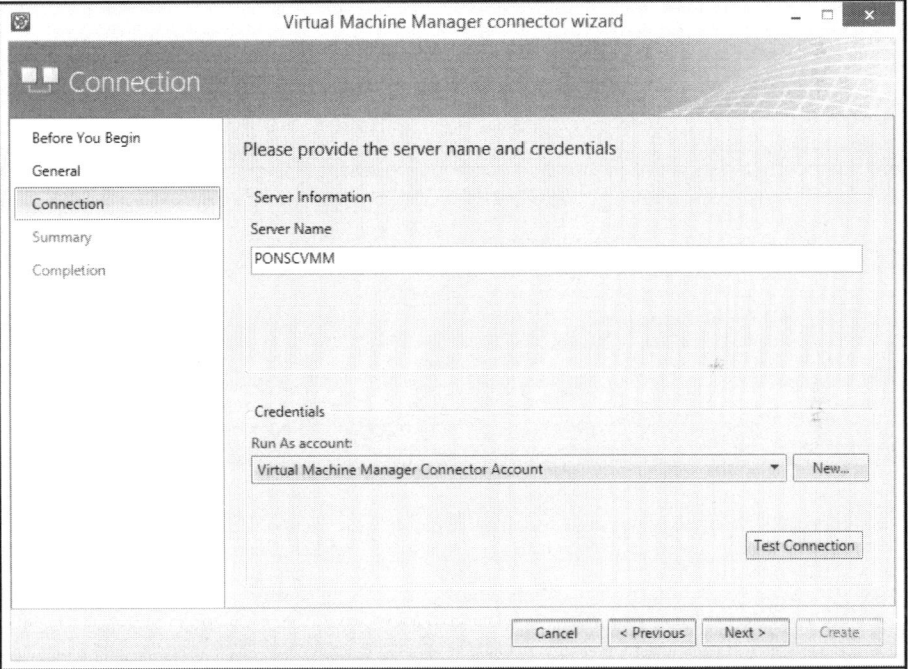

5. Ensure that the **Enable this connector** box is checked, and then click on **Next**.

6. On the **Connection** screen in the **Server Information** box, supply the URL of the Orchestrator Web Service. This is in the form of `http://<Server>:81/Orchestrator2012/Orchestrator.svc`. In this example, I've used `http://TDSCORCH01:81/Orchestrator2012/Orchestrator.svc` as the URL of the Orchestrator Web Service.

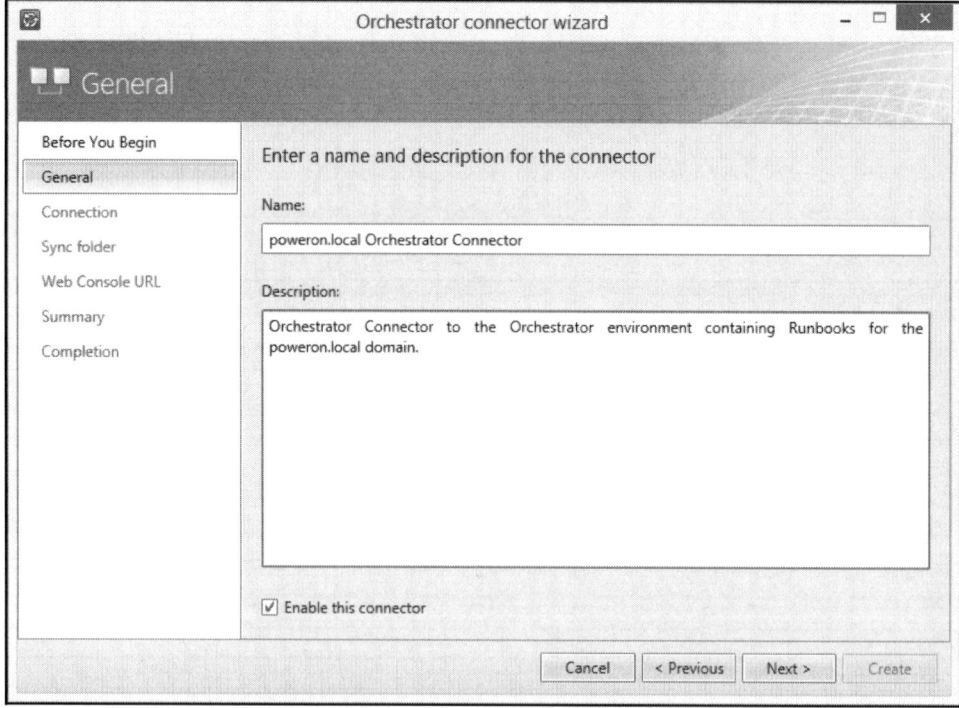

7. Next to the **Run As Account** drop-down menu, click on **New** and enter the details of the account that you set up before starting.
8. Click **Test Connection** and enter the password for the account when prompted.
9. Click on **Next**.

10. On the **Folder** screen, select the folder containing the runbooks you require to synchronize to Service Manager. For this recipe, select the root folder (shown as a \ ) to synchronize all runbooks.

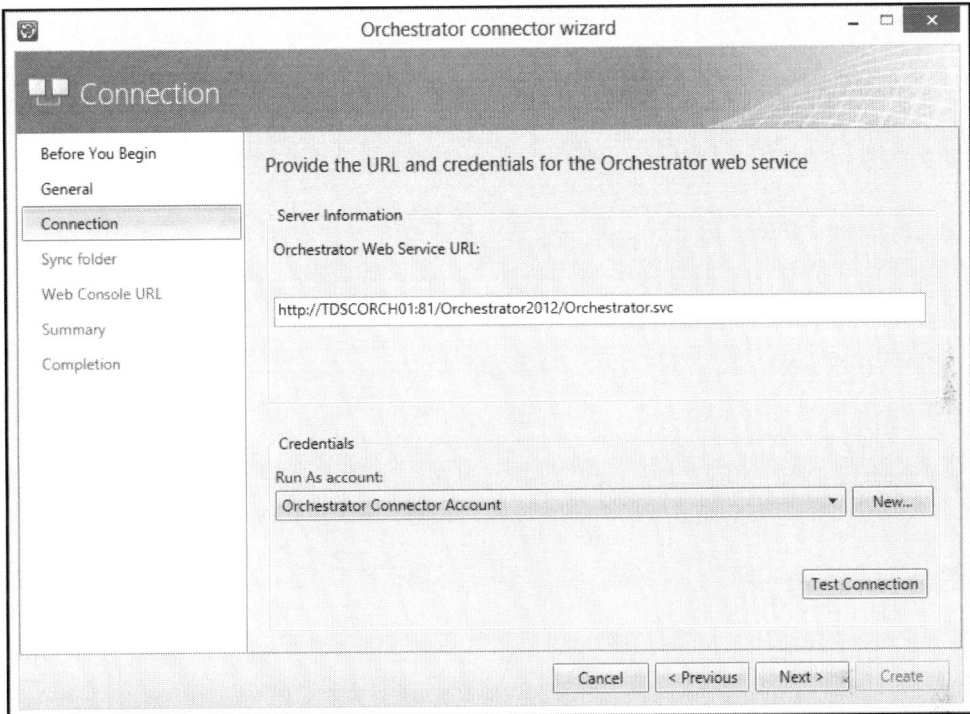

11. On the web console URL screen, type the URL for the Orchestrator web console. This is usually in the form of `http://<Server>:82`. For this recipe, I've used `http://TDSCORCH01:82`.

12. Review the information on the **Summary** screen and then click on **Create**.

13. Review the information on the **Confirmation** screen and then click on **Close**.

How it works...

The connector pulls information from the Web Service regarding what runbooks are available and the input parameters that each runbook contains. These runbooks and their parameters can then be used with automation activities. The automated activities are invoked by workflows, which use the parameters specified in the runbook CIs.

There's more...

After creating the connector, the imported information regarding the runbooks will be available for use within activities for use with Service Requests.

Where are my runbooks?

After you set up the Orchestrator connector, you will find the imported runbooks under the **Library** section of the **Service Manager** console.

Using a CSV file to import items into the CMDB

Sometimes you may want to bulk import configuration items into the CMDB. One way to do this is to import them using a **Comma-Separated Value (CSV)** file containing the CIs that relate to any class type or projection type already existing within Service Manager.

Getting ready

To import data using this method, two files are required, as follows:

- A file containing the CIs to be imported; structured in a comma-delimited method and saved with a .csv extension.
- A file that defines the class types or projection types used by all items in the CSV file. Also, this file defines the order in which the data appears as columns. The file must end with an .xml extension, and the authors recommend that you match the first part of the XML filename to the first part of the CSV filename.

How to do it...

First we need to create the data file. In this recipe, we will create a CSV file that will allow us to import some computer/server configuration items into Service Manager:

1. Open Microsoft Excel or a similar spreadsheet application.

   On the first row create the following headers:

   - Computer Name
   - Number of Physical Processors
   - Number of Logical Processors
   - IP Address

2. Then provide data, as shown in the following table:

Computer Name	Number of Physical Processors	Number of Logical Processors	IP Address
WKST01	**1**	**2**	**172.16.1.50**
WKST02	1	4	172.16.1.52
WKST03	1	2	172.16.1.57
WKST04	1	2	172.16.1.60
WKST05	1	6	172.16.1.68
Server01	2	4	172.16.1.200
Server02	2	8	172.16.1.201
Server03	4	16	172.16.1.202
Server04	4	24	172.16.1.203
Server05	1	1	172.16.1.204

3. Remove the first row with the column headings and then save the data as a CSV file called ComputerCIs.csv.

4. The resulting CSV file contents should look like the following:

```
WKST01,1,2,172.16.1.50
WKST02,1,4,172.16.1.52
WKST03,1,2,172.16.1.57
WKST04,1,2,172.16.1.60
WKST05,1,6,172.16.1.68
Server01,2,4,172.16.1.200
Server02,2,8,172.16.1.201
Server03,4,16,172.16.1.202
Server04,4,24,172.16.1.203
Server05,1,1,172.16.1.204
```

Next we need to create the XML file that defines the format and structure.

5. The information stored in the data file is aimed at creating/updating CIs of the class Windows Computer, which is defined within Service Manager as a `Microsoft.Windows.Computer` class.

6. We also have four columns of data that need mapping to the appropriate properties of the `Microsoft.Windows.Computer` class. You can either use the Authoring tool to locate the class and view the properties or you can use PowerShell.

7. Use an XML editor to create the required XML file (for example, `Notepad.exe`). The following table shows the appropriate properties for our data that we need to map the columns to:

Property	Property name
Computer Name	PrincipalName
Number of Physical Processors	PhysicalProcessors
Number of Logical Processors	LogicalProcessors
IP Address	IPAddress

8. Every XML definition file for CSV import starts with the following line:

`<CSVImportFormat>` and ends with a similar closing line:
`</CSVImportFormat>`

9. The next line defines the class type to be imported. For this recipe, that needs to be the `Microsoft.Windows.Computer` class:

```
<Class Type="Microsoft.Windows.Computer">
```

This again requires a closing tag after the properties:

```
</Class>
```

10. For each column of data within the data file, we need to specify the property of the class it requires mapping to and in the order in which they are listed within the CSV file:

```
<Property ID="PrincipalName" />
<Property ID="PhysicalProcessors" />
<Property ID="LogicalProcessors" />
<Property ID="IPAddress" />
```

11. This will give a completed XML definition file that looks like this:

```
<CSVImportFormat>
<Class Type="Microsoft.Windows.Computer">
<Property ID="PrincipalName" />
<Property ID="PhysicalProcessors" />
<Property ID="LogicalProcessors" />
<Property ID="IPAddress" />
</Class>
</CSVImportFormat>
```

12. Save this XML file as `ComputerCIs.xml`.

Finally, these two files can now be used to import data into Service Manager by following these next steps:

1. In the **Service Manager** console, navigate to the **Administration** workspace.
2. Expand **Administration** and then click on **Connectors**.
3. In the tasks pane on the right-hand side, click on **Import from CSV File**.

4. On the **Import Instances from CSV File** screen that opens, use the **Browse** buttons to locate and open the XML and CSV files that were previously created.

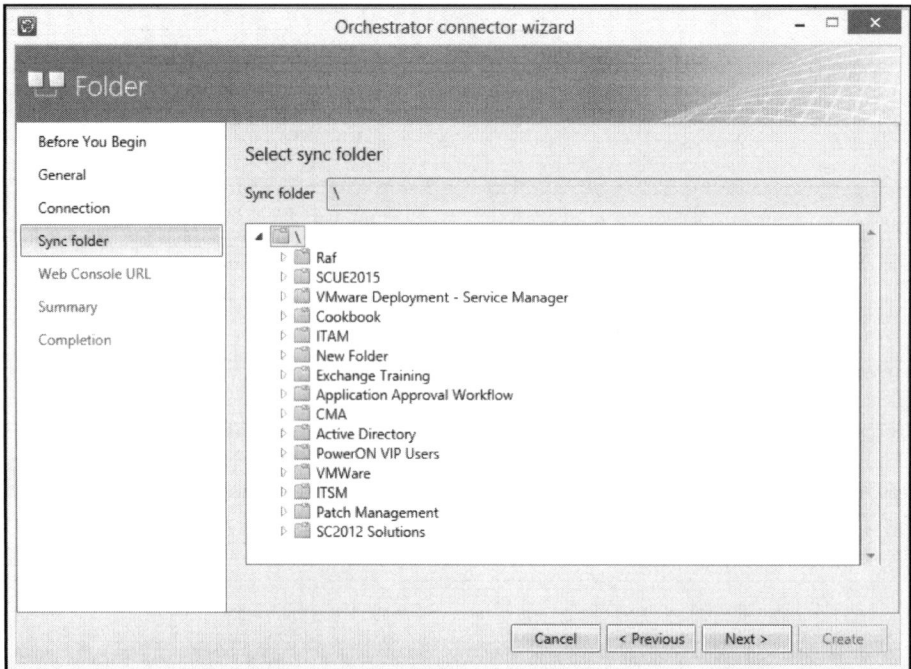

5. Click on **Import**.
6. The **Importing Instances** screen will now open and give you a progress bar for the import. If importing a large number of objects, this could take a considerable amount of time.

How it works...

By mapping the columns of data to the properties of the class you define within the XML file, it's possible to bulk import lots of data and have Service Manager match the data to the classes and properties so it can create the configuration items for you.

There's more...

The previous recipe shows the steps required to import data using a CSV file and the CSV connector, but in the following section there are some additional tips.

Using PowerShell to find the properties

Rather than having to open the Authoring tool and create a temporary management pack to view the different classes and their properties, PowerShell can be used to quickly look these up using the SCSM PowerShell Cmdlets available from CodePlex here: `http://smlets.codeplex.com/`.

For this recipe, we needed the properties for the `Windows Computer` class.

Open a PowerShell session and type the following:

```
Import-Module SMLets
$CI = Get-SCSMClass -Name Microsoft.Windows.Computer$
$CI.PropertyCollection
```

This will list all the properties directly used by the class (but not relationships).

Is CSV import just for configuration items?

No, CSV import is not just for configuration items. The CSV import method can also be used to create work items such as incidents by targeting the data at the `System.WorkItem.Incident` class by using the XML definition file and defining the properties for the data such as `Title`, `Description`, `Impact`, and `Urgency`.

This can be very useful especially for scenarios such as migrating Service Desk tools.

Complex CI importing

Sometimes you will want to import data that isn't held by just a single class, but maybe spans multiple classes and in particular class relationships.

For example, you may want to import a new computer CI, but specify the Asset Custodian for that device.

This can be achieved through the use of Type Projection and defining these in the XML definition file rather than just a single class type.

Apart from using the previous recipe and creating a new computer CI based on the information such as Computer Name, Number of Physical Processors, Number of Logical Processors, and IP Address, we also now need to specify the user details for the custodian.

The original XML definition file started with the following code:

```
<CSVImportFormat>
<Class Type="Microsoft.Windows.Computer">
```

This time the Type Projection needs to be specified first:

```
<CSVImportFormat> <Projection
Type="Microsoft.Windows.Computer.ProjectionType">
<Seed>
<Class Type="Microsoft.Windows.Computer">
```

Specify the properties as before, close the class section with the `</Class>` tag, and then ensure that the seed section is also closed with a `</Seed>` tag.

Next, the additional class information for the `Custodian` can be added by starting a new section with a `<Component Alias>` tag:

```
<Component Alias="Custodian">
<Seed>
<Class Type="System.Domain.User">
<Property ID="Domain"/>
<Property ID="UserName"/>
</Class>
</Seed>
</Component>
```

This allows the data to be added to the data file in the format of the **Domain Name** in the column after **IP Address** and then the username of the `Custodian` that should be assigned.

Finally, the `</Projection>` tag must be placed towards the bottom to close the Type Projection definition.

The final XML would look like the following:

```
<CSVImportFormat>
<Projection Type="Microsoft.Windows.Computer.ProjectionType">
<Seed>
<Class Type="Microsoft.Windows.Computer">
<Property ID="PrincipalName"/>
<Property ID="PhysicalProcessors"/>
<Property ID="LogicalProcessors"/>
<Property ID="IPAddress"/>
</Class>
</Seed>
<Component Alias="Custodian">
<Seed>
<Class Type="System.Domain.User">
```

```
<Property ID="Domain"/>
<Property ID="UserName"/>
</Class>
</Seed>
</Component>
</Projection>
</CSVImportFormat>
```

See also

- There are third-party tools that make CSV import and data mapping easier. See `Appendix A`, *Community Extensions and Third-Party Commercial SCSM Solutions* for information about Cireson's Asset Import tools and Provance's Data Management Pack.

Creating a Business Service

This recipe shows how to create a business service within Service Manager. A **business service** is a collection of information relating to an IT service such as an e-mail system, a payroll system, or other line of business service. The information about the service consists of information such as the components that make up the service (servers, databases, and websites) and properties such as availability of the service, affected users, and owner information, for example.

Getting ready

You can either manually create a business service, in which case review the *Manually creating CIs* recipe, or you can have them synchronized with information relating to distributed applications from within Operations Manager, in which case review and set up the Operations Manager CI Connector as shown in the recipe within this chapter.

This recipe will show how to create a business service based on a distributed application. Before attempting this recipe, you will need a distributed application and save it to the management pack.

You will also need all the management packs that contain items that your distributed application references, such as SQL and IIS.

How to do it...

The following steps will guide you through the process of creating a business service within Service Manager:

1. Within Operations Manager, export the management pack containing the distributed application that you want to create as a business service.

2. Within the **Service Manager** console, navigate to **Administration** | **Management Packs**.

3. On the task pane on the right-hand side of the console, click on **Import**.

4. On the **Select Management Packs to Import** screen, navigate to the management pack you exported earlier, select it, click on **Open**, and then click on **Import**.

5. If the import fails, review the error details and it most likely will reference a management pack that the one you are trying to import relies on. If so, repeat the import process, but navigate to the required management pack and import that first before the one containing your distributed application.

6. Once you have the management pack imported, navigate in the **Service Manager** console to | **Administration** | **Connectors**.

7. Select the **Operations Manager CI Connector**, and in the task pane click on **Properties**.

8. In the **Edit** screen, on the left-hand side, click on **Management Packs**, and then click on **Refresh**.

9. Enter the password for the account used by the Operations Manager CI Connector and click on **OK**.

10. In the management packs list, select the new management packs you imported and click on **OK**.

11. With the **Operations Manager CI connector** selected, click on **Synchronize Now** in the task pane.

12. Navigate in the **Service Manager** console to | **Configuration Items** | **All Business Services**.

13. Your distributed application should now be displayed under **All Business Services**.

14. Select your business service and click on **Edit** on the task pane on the right-hand side.

15. From the form screen that opens you can add additional information such as availability, operational status, owner, and affected users, as well as view the components that make up the business service as defined within Operations Manager as your distributed application.

How it works...

Service Manager uses the information in the exported management pack, from Operations Manager to create the business service CI. The business service definition in Service Manager matches the distributed application in Operations Manager due to the use of this shared management pack.

There's more...

The business services are great for storing information related to a service so they're available when creating work items, but they can also be used to automatically raise incidents.

Raising related incidents

By default, Service Manager will not connect related incidents raised from Operations Manager to Business Services. For example, an alert about a database being offline that is part of a business service will not add the business service as a related item to the incident.

This can be enabled, but it requires the alert to be generated with the same name as the business service. This requires some planning and the use of rollup monitors in the related Operations Manager instance.

Personalizing and organizing configuration item views

This recipe is designed to show you how to personalize and organize your configuration item views.

How to do it...

The following steps will guide you through how to organize CI information into personal views within Service Manager:

1. Navigate in the **Service Manager** console to the **Configuration Items** workspace, expand **Configuration Items**, and click on **Computers**.
2. Click on **Create View** on the task pane on the right-hand side.
3. Specify a name and description for the view. For this recipe, give the view a name of **All Virtual Servers**.

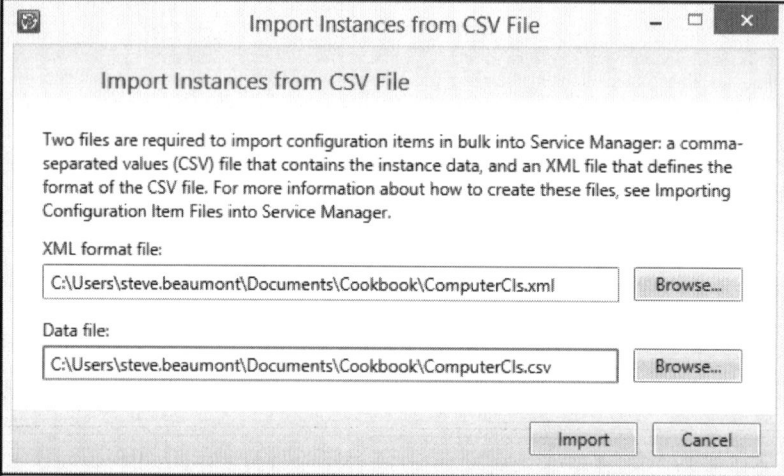

4. Click on **Criteria** on the left-hand side of the **Create View** screen.
5. Next to **Search for objects of a specific class**, click on the **Browse** button.
6. On the **Select a Class** screen, use the drop-down list to select **Combination classes** and use the filter box to find the **Computer (typical)** type projection, select it, and click on **OK**.

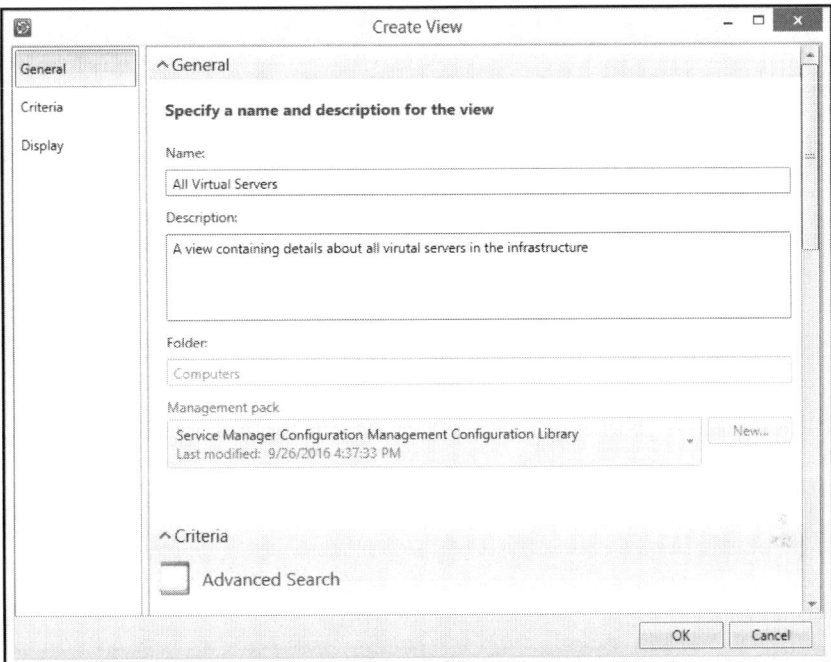

7. Under **Available properties**, select the relevant property to filter the information shown in the view. For this recipe, choose **Virtual Machine** and click on **Add**. Ensure that the criteria for **Virtual Machine** is set to: **equals** and **True**.

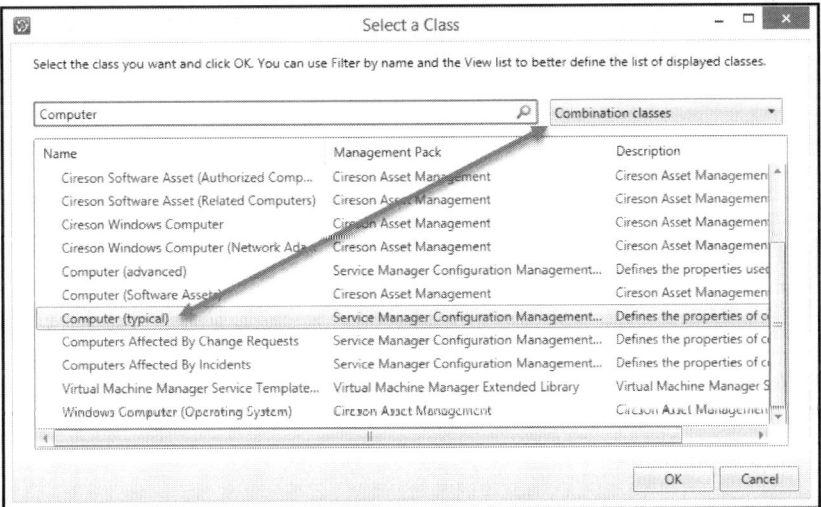

8. Click on **Display** on the left-hand side of the **Create View** screen.
9. Use this section to select the columns to display in the view. For this recipe, select only the following:

   NetBIOS Computer Name

   Then expand **Hosts Windows Operating System** and select:

   - Operating System Version Display Name
   - Physical Memory (MB)
   - Service Pack Version

10. Click on **OK**.

How it works...

This recipe walked you through the process of creating a view to display information related to the virtual servers contained within your CMDB. This recipe can be repeated to create new views based on any class or combinations of classes you select and the visible columns of data you choose to display by choosing different classes and columns in Steps 6, 7, and 9.

5
Deploying Service Request Fulfilment

In this chapter, we will provide recipes to configure Service Manager to your environment. Specifically, we will cover the Service Request Fulfillment feature of SCSM 2016 with the following tasks:

- Creating Support Groups for Service Requests
- Creating Service Request templates
- Creating Service Request activities
- Creating Service Offering categories
- Creating Service Catalog Request Offerings
- Creating Service Catalog Service Offerings
- Publishing Service Offerings and Request Offerings
- Working with Service Requests in the Self-Service Portal
- Filling in the Service Request Description with User Input from the Request Offering
- Creating Service Request notifications

Introduction

System Center 2016 Service Manager supports the ITILÂ© process, Service Request Fulfillment.

Service Request Fulfillment provides services to users created by the IT department. Typical Service Request and Service Offerings are requests for new hardware (computers, printers, and smartphones), software, user management (create, modify, or delete/disable users), requests for new virtual machines in a cloud, and many more.

The ability of SCSM 2016 to use Review Activities, Manual Activities, and Orchestrator Runbook Activities in a sequential and/or parallel order offers the opportunity to design individual process workflows for different Service Offerings.

In this chapter, we will provide the recipes to configure the basics of the Service Catalog, Service Offerings, and Request Offerings. Also, we will explain how to use the SCSM 2016 portal to create Service Requests.

Creating Support Groups for Service Requests

Using different Support Groups for Service Requests offers the opportunity for detailed and filtered reporting as well as the routing of Service Requests. The Service Request Support Groups can also be used to create different views to filter Service Requests in the SCSM 2016 console.

This recipe will show how to create the Service Request Support Groups in SCSM 2016.

Getting ready

To create Service Request Support Groups, open the SCSM 2016 console and navigate to **Library** | **Lists**. In the filter field, type **Service Request Support Group** and the list we need will be shown.

How to do it...

The following steps will show you how to create Support Groups for Service Requests:

1. Double-click on the list named **Service Request Support Group**.

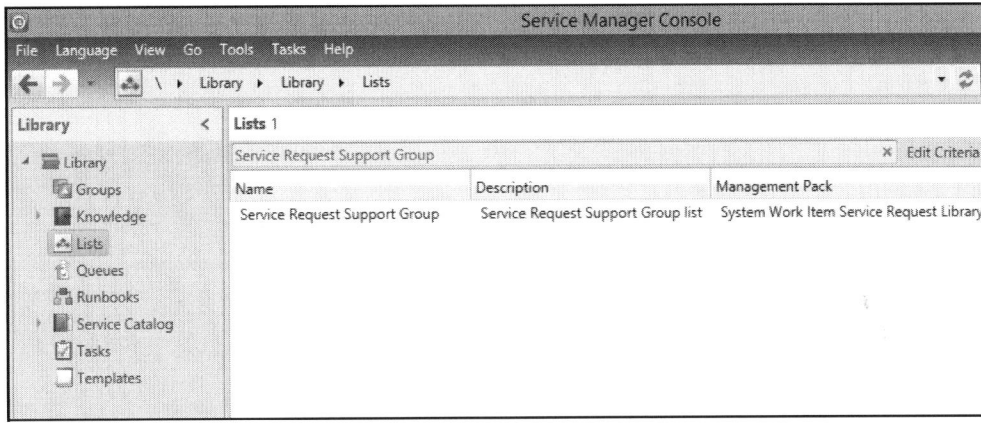

2. Click on the **Add Item** button, as shown in the following screenshot:

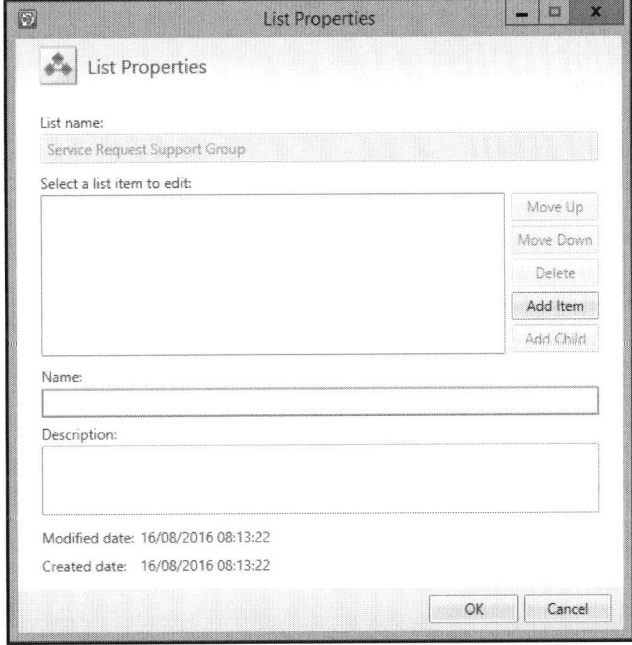

3. Choose a management pack to store the modification. Best practices and how to work with management packs are explained in the *Creating Management Packs to save your SCSM personalization* recipe in `Chapter 2`, *Personalizing SCSM 2016 Administration*:

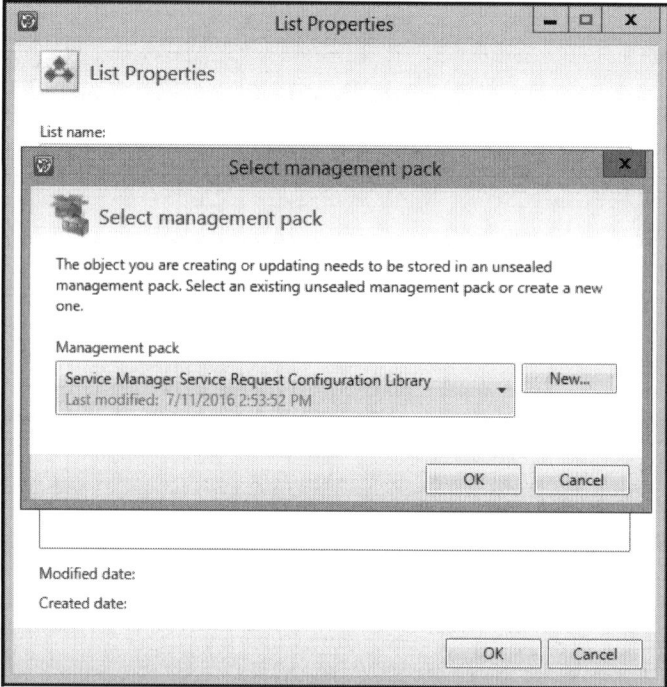

4. Select the **List Value** entry and provide a name to suit your requirements. We will choose **User Management Service Request Support Group** in this recipe:

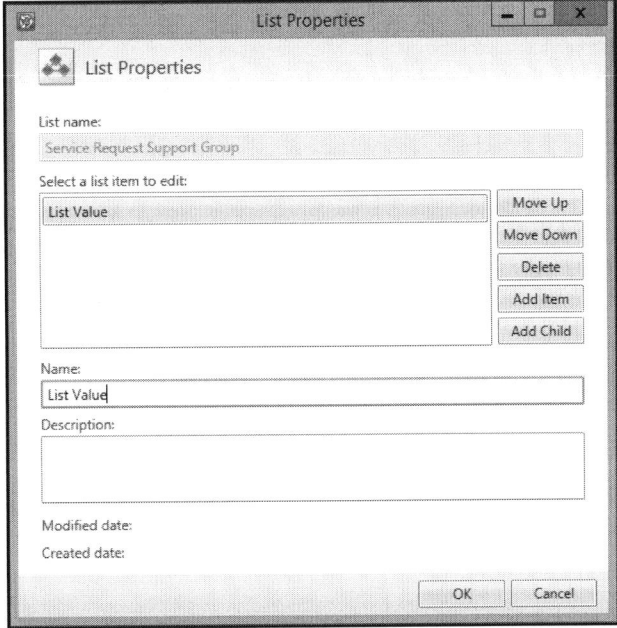

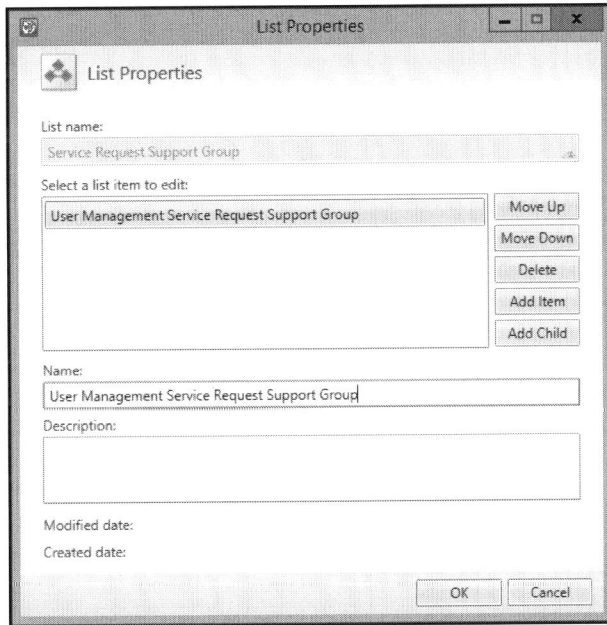

5. Add as many Service Request Support Groups as required. After you have added the required groups, click on **OK** to close the **List Properties** window.

How it works...

Service Request Support Groups can be used for filtering reports, views, and criteria for the workflows and routing of Service Requests.

There's more...

In addition to the steps provided for creating Support Groups, here is some more information about child list items, the use of Support Groups for filtering reports, and the use of this particular support group in service level management.

Creating sub (child) list items

You can also create a sub-list item. Just select the list item you want to create a child item below, and click on the **Add Child** button.

Using Support Groups for filtering in reports

The *Viewing SCSM* reports and *Analyzing data with Microsoft Excel* recipes in Chapter 10, *Working with the Data Warehouse and Reporting*, show you how to work with different criteria for filtering.

Working with management packs

The *Creating Management Packs to save your SCSM personalization* recipe in Chapter 2, *Personalizing SCSM 2016 Administration* describes how to store your customizations in management packs, as well as best practice for naming the XML files.

Service Request Groups and Service Level Agreements

Service Request Groups can be used as a criterion in **Service Level Agreements (SLAs)/Service Level Objectives (SLOs)** to filter Service Requests that belong to a SLO.

For more information on how they work please, take a look at Chapter 3, *Configuring Service Level Agreements (SLAs)*.

See also

Microsoft TechNet Library: Using the Service Catalog in System Center 2016 – Service Manager: `https://technet.microsoft.com/en-us/system-center-docs/sm/manage/adm in-using-the-service-catalog-in-system-center-2016-service-manager`.

Creating Service Request templates

Service Request templates can be used to auto-fill information in the Service Request form. These can be for example, a predefined Title, Description, Urgency, Priority, and Service Request Support Group. This recipe will describe the steps needed to create a new Service Request template.

Getting ready

To create Service Request templates open the SCSM 2016 console and navigate to **Library | Templates**.

How to do it…

The following steps explain how to create a new Service Request template:

1. Click on **Create Template**.
2. Fill in the name and description of the new template.
3. Click on the **Browse…** button beside the **Class** textbox and pick **Service Request** from the list.

4. Choose a **Management pack** to store the Service Request template. It is recommended that you use a custom management pack in our case **Custom.ServiceRequest.Library**. Click on **OK** to close the window.

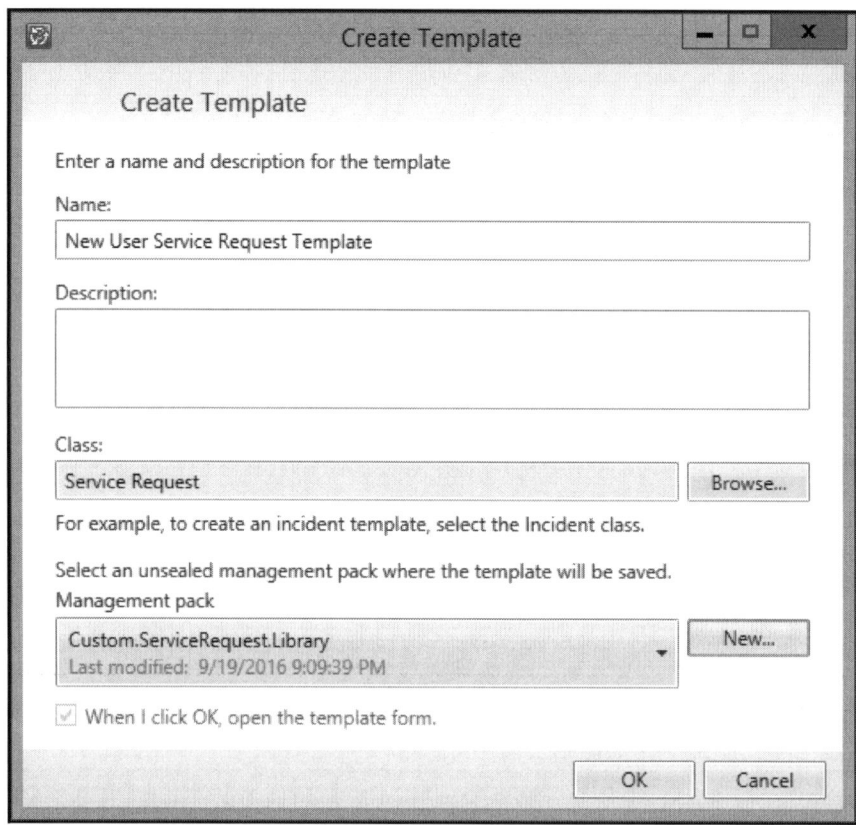

5. Fill out the fields in the **General** tab of the **Service Request Template** window. We will enter the **Title**, **Urgency**, **Priority**, **Area**, and **Support Group** we created in the previous recipe.

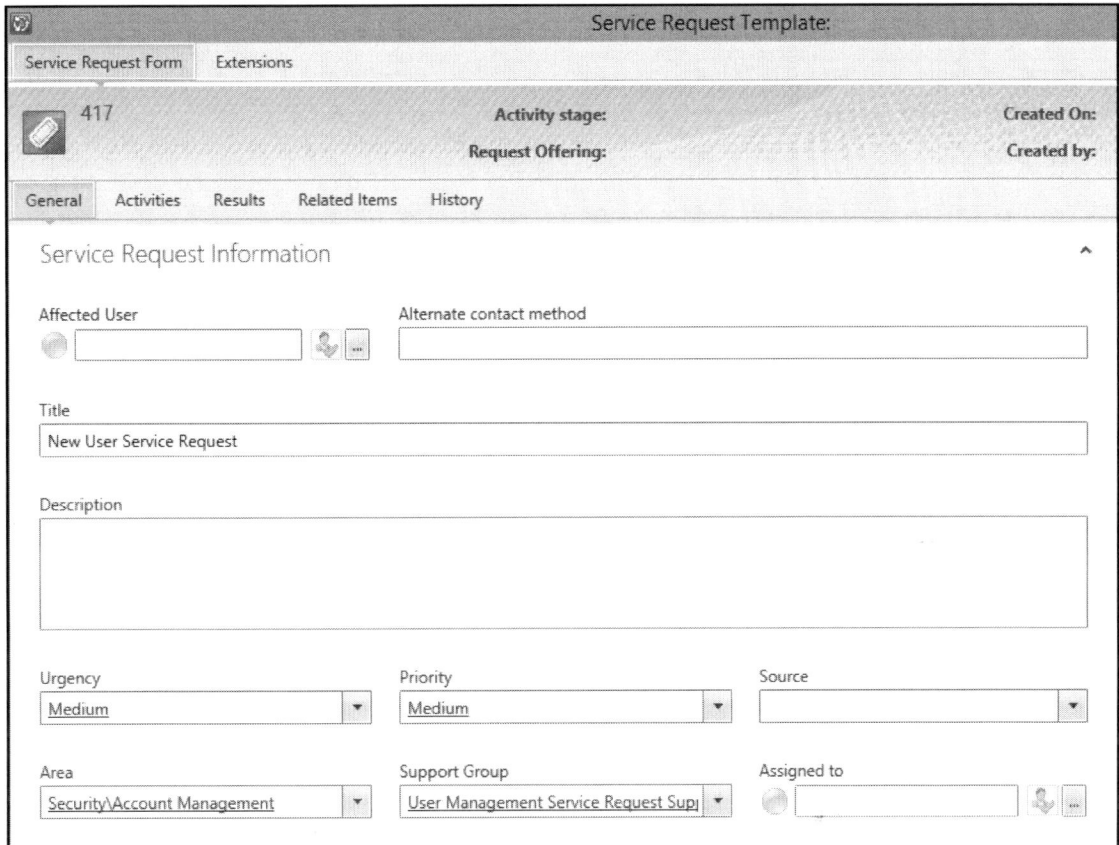

How it works...

Basically a pre-filled template in SCSM 2016 can be used to create new Work Items (for instance Incident Records, Change Requests, and Service Requests). Using templates keeps the required and optional information of Service Request forms consistent and also saves time.

There's more…

In a Service Request template you can add different types of activities. How to work with mandatory fields in a Service Request is described in the following topic.

Configuring Service Request activities in a template

In this recipe we filled out the fields of the **Service Request General** tab only. How to work with the activities on the **Activities** tab of a Service Request is described in the next recipe.

Configuring required fields of a Service Request

The fields Urgency and **Priority** are required fields in a Service Request. If you don't fill the fields in the Service Request template, you have to provide this information in each Service Request (you have to add two questions for **Urgency** and **Priority** in a Request Offering).

See also

The Microsoft TechNet Library: Using the Service Catalog in System Center 2016 – Service Manager, at

```
https://technet.microsoft.com/en-us/system-center-docs/sm/manage/admin-using-th
e-service-catalog-in-system-center-2016-service-manager
```

Creating Service Request activities

With activities, you can define the process steps that are needed to fulfill the Service Request. This recipe shows how to work with different activities such as Approval Activity and Manual Activity.

Getting ready

To create Service Request activities, open the SCSM 2016 console and navigate to **Library | Templates**. Open the Service Request template we created in the previous recipe.

How to do it…

The following are steps required to create Service Request activities:

1. In the opened **Service Request Template**, click on the **Activities** tab. Click on the **+ Activities** icon and choose **Default Review Activity** from the list. Click on **OK**:

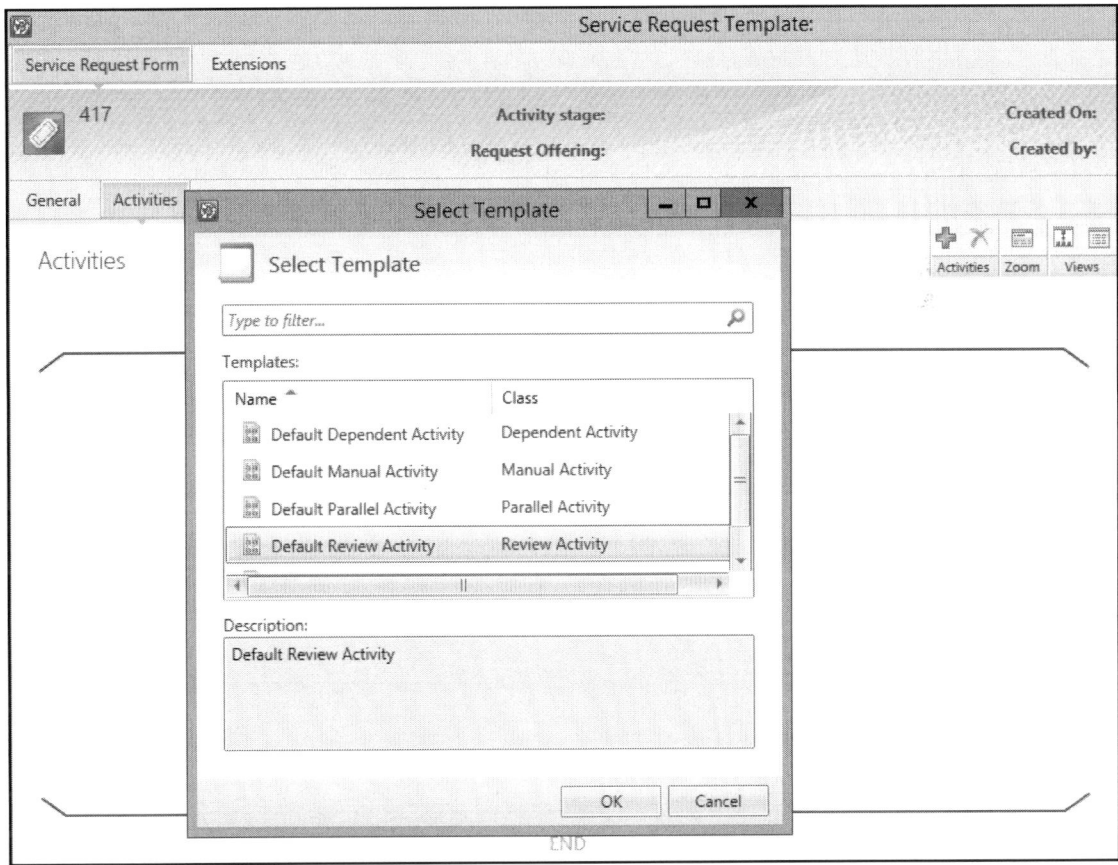

2. In the **Review** Activity form, fill in the necessary fields. We will provide a **Title** and **Description**. If approval is required from the manager of the requesting user, check the **Line Manager Should Review** checkbox. The Line Manager is the synced Manager attribute from the users' properties in the users Active Directory domain. In the **Approval Condition:** drop-down box, you can choose between **Automatic** (the approval will be done automatically), **Percentage Approval Threshold (%):** (a calculation is performed using the number of reviewers selected and the percentage, for example, in the instance where we

have three reviewers with a 50% threshold, two reviewers must approve), or **Unanimous** (all reviewers need to approve). You can add reviewers manually by clicking on **Add** and choosing the reviewer by name from the list. Click on **OK** to close the form:

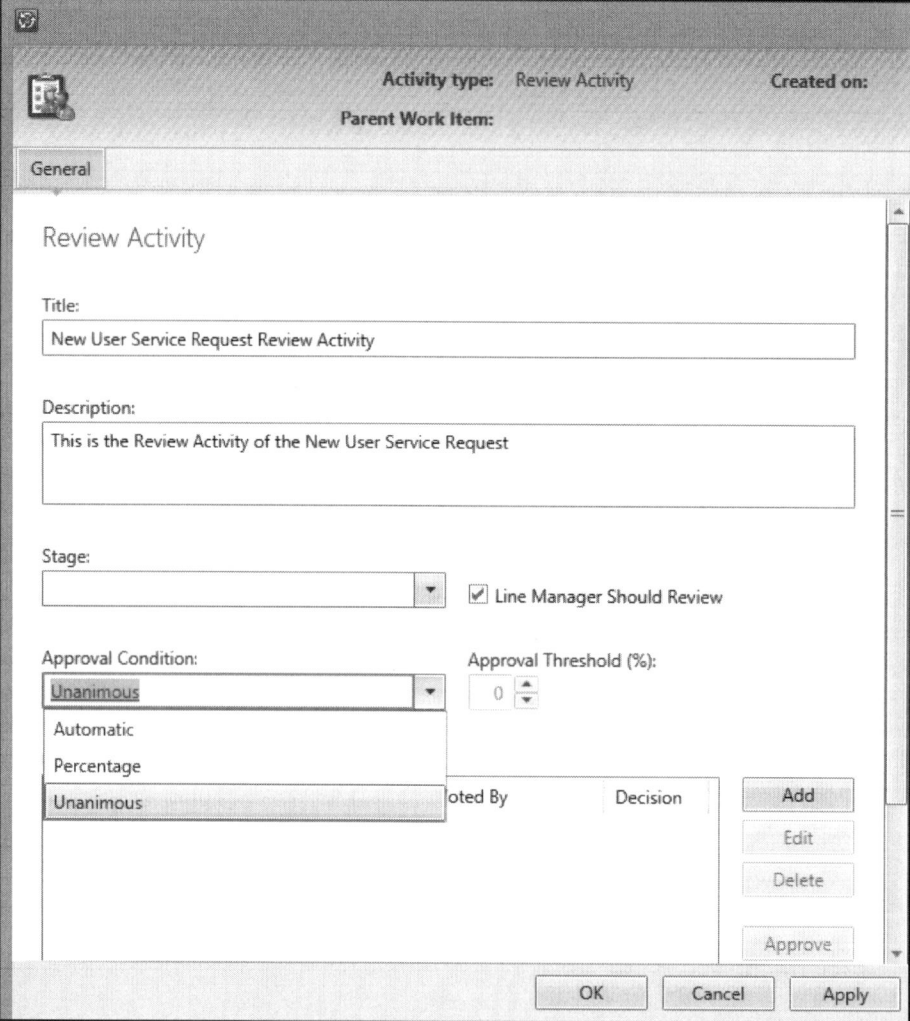

3. Click on the + **Activities** icon again. Choose **Default Manual Activity** from the list. Click on **OK** to close the window:

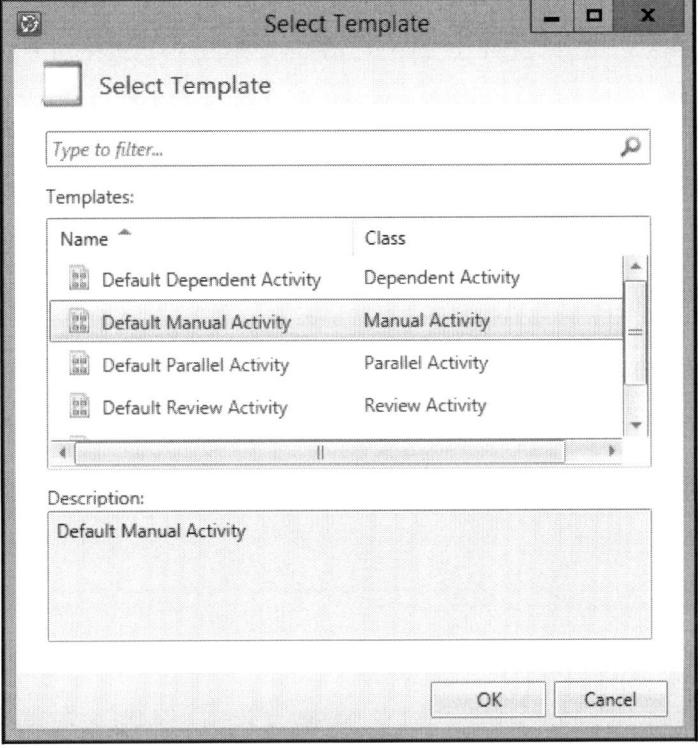

4. Fill in the necessary fields in the form. We will fill the **Title**, **Description**, **Area**, and **Priority** for this example. Click on **OK** to close the form:

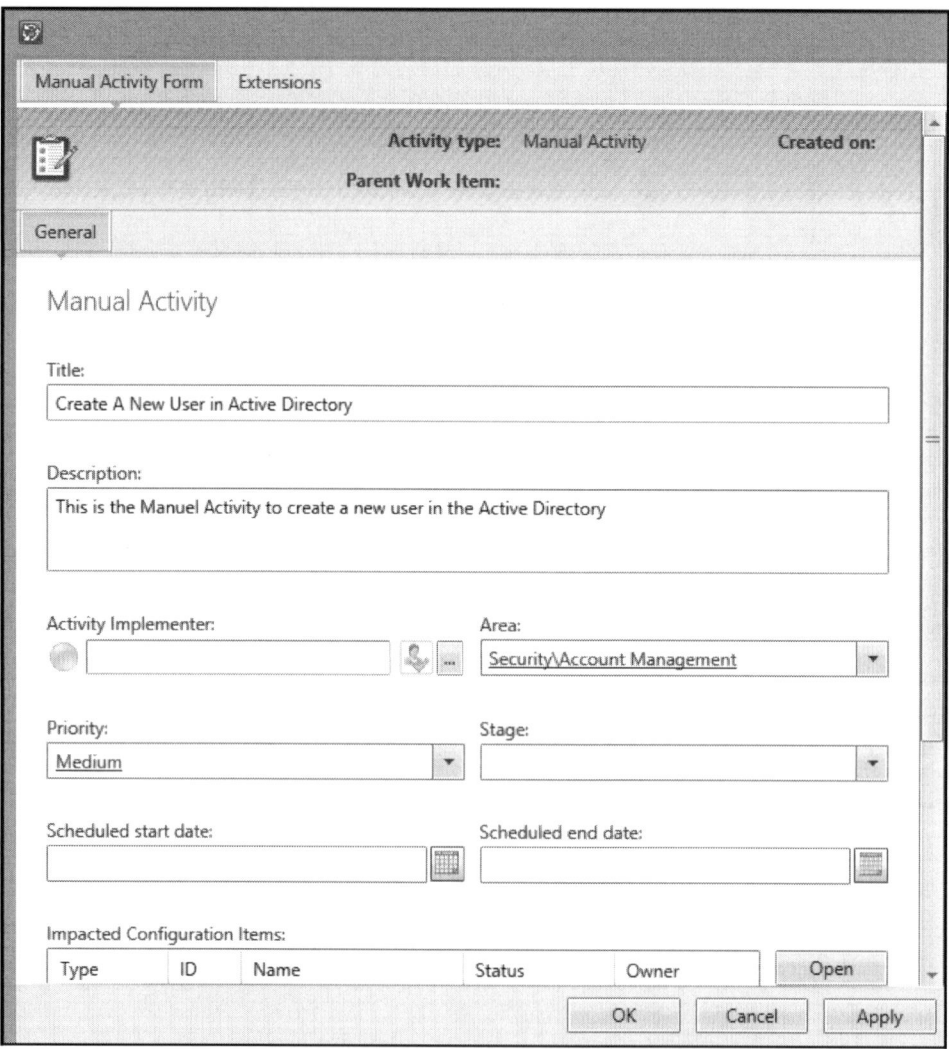

5. Add more activities related to your process requirements. Once complete, click on **OK** in the **Service Request Template** form:

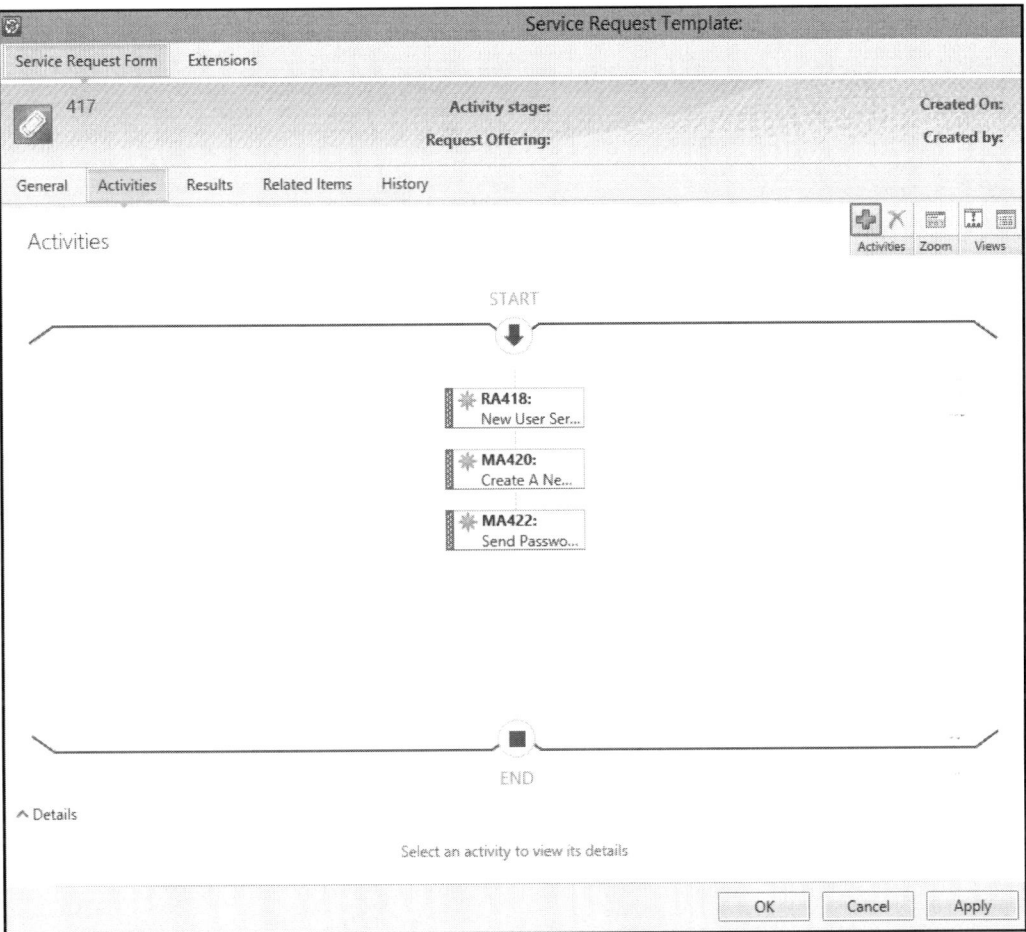

How it works...

When the Service Request template is applied to a Service Request, all pre-filled fields and all activities are inserted into the newly created Service Request.

A SCSM 2016 workflow will set the first activity to the status **In Progress**; all other activities will be set to a status of **Pending**. The Service Request will get the status **In Progress**.

There's more…

You can add different types of activities in a Service Request template.

How to configure the other activity types

For more information on other types of activities, please take a look at these Change and Release Management recipes in `Chapter 8`, *Designing and Configuring Change Management and Release Management*:

- *Creating and managing Change Management Review Activities*
- *Creating Manual Activities for Change Management*
- *Creating and managing Dependent Activities in Change Management*
- *Creating and personalizing of Change Management Parallel Activities*
- *Creating and personalizing Change Management Sequential Activities*

Adding more activities to a Service Request created with a template

You can add additional activities to Service Requests that are based on a template during the process of working with the request. Importantly, you can add more activities as long as the last activity in the Service Requested isn't completed.

See also

The Microsoft TechNet Library: Using the Service Catalog in System Center 2016 – Service Manager, at
`https://technet.microsoft.com/en-us/system-center-docs/sm/manage/admin-using-th`
`e-service-catalog-in-system-center-2016-service-manager`

Creating Service Offering categories

Service Offering categories in SCSM 2016 can be used to sort Service Offerings in the SCSM 2016 portal. The categories offer the opportunity to filter Service Requests in reports as well as views. The steps to create the Service Offering categories are shown in this recipe.

Getting ready

To create Service Offering categories, open the SCSM 2016 console and navigate to **Library | Lists**. In the filter field, type **Service Offering Category**, and the list we need will be shown.

How to do it...

1. Open the **Service Offering Category** list.
2. Click on **Add Item**.
3. Choose a management pack to store the new Service Offering category. We will choose the same management pack we used in the previous recipes, **Custom.ServiceRequest.Library**.
4. Choose a name of the new category. In this recipe, we will use **User Management**.
5. Click on **OK**:

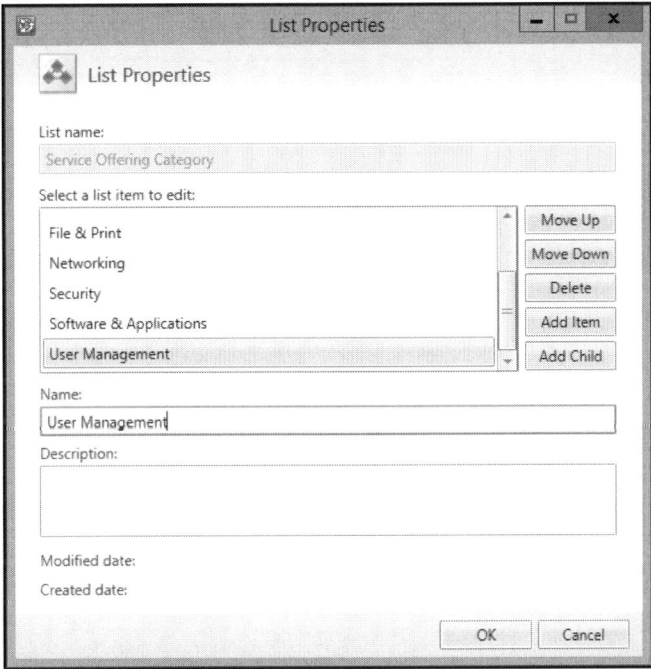

How it works...

Choosing Service Offering categories as an attribute in Service Offerings provides an opportunity to combine and sort these offerings in the SCSM 2016 portal. These categories are the first tier used to combine related types of Service Offerings/Service Requests in the SCSM 2016 portal.

There's more...

Service Request Offering categories can be used as filters in reports.

Using Service Offering categories in reports (filtering)

How filtering of reports works is described in the *Viewing SCSM reporting* recipe in Chapter 10, *Working with the Data Warehouse and Reporting*.

How to work with Excel and Analysis Services for reporting is described in the *Analyzing reports with Microsoft Excel recipe* in Chapter 10, *Working with the Data Warehouse and Reporting*.

See also

The Microsoft TechNet Library: Using the Service Catalog in System Center 2016 – Service Manager, at

https://technet.microsoft.com/en-us/system-center-docs/sm/manage/admin-using-the-service-catalog-in-system-center-2016-service-manager

Creating Service Catalog Request Offerings

Request Offerings in the SCSM 2016 Service Catalog are the different services the users can request. In the Request Offerings, the required questions to fulfill the Service Request are defined and mapped within the different forms of a Service Request.

This recipe will provide the steps required to create a Request Offering in the Service Catalog of SCSM 2016.

Getting ready

To create Request Offerings in the SCSM 2016 Service Catalog, open the SCSM 2016 console and navigate to **Library** | **Service Catalog** | **Request Offerings**.

How to do it...

To create a Service Catalog Request Offering, follow these steps:

1. Click on **Create Request Offering** in the **Tasks** pane of the SCSM 2016 console.
2. In the **Create Request Offering** wizard, read the **Before You Begin** information and click on **Next**.
3. On the **General** page, fill in a title (for example, **Request A New User In Active Directory**)
4. Optionally choose an icon. This icon will be shown in the SCSM 2016 Self-Service portal.
5. Add a short description (for example, **This Service Offerings is for requesting a new user in Active Directory**).
6. Choose a Service Request template. We will choose the Service Request template **New User Service Request Template** we created in the previous recipe.

7. Choose a management pack to store the Request Offering. In this recipe, we will use the same management pack we used previously, **Custom.ServiceRequest. Library**:

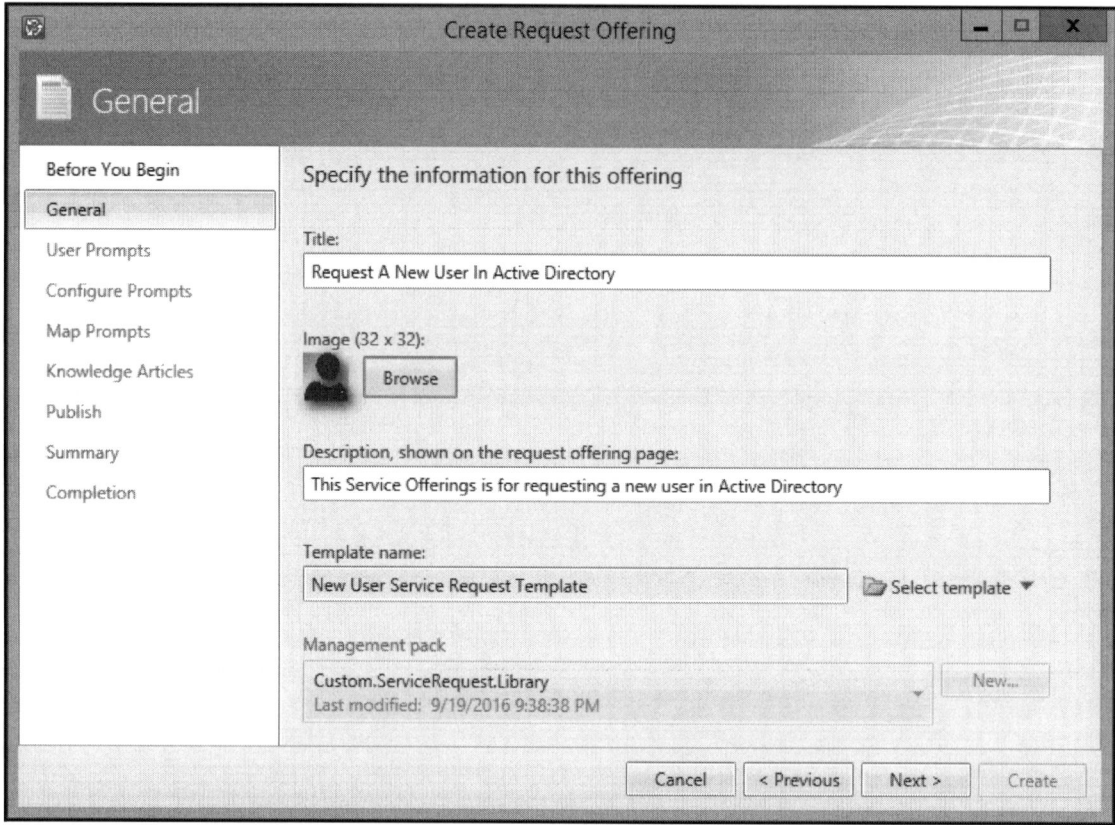

8. Click on **Next**.
9. On the **User Prompt** page, fill out **Forms Instructions**. This information will be shown in the SCSM 2016 portal to the end user.
10. Add **Prompts** or **Information Text** in the next fields. For each prompt, you can define different types. Supported prompt types are as follows:
    - Date
    - Decimal
    - File Attachment Integer
    - MP Enumeration List (content of a SCSM 2016 list you have to specify in the next step)

- Query Result (Query on the SCSM 2016 CMDB. For instance list of users, computers, and so on.)
- Simple List (A simple list available only in this Request Offering. No relation to any other list in SCSM 2016.)
- Text
- True/False

You can choose if the prompt is required, optional, or only displayed (for information).

Importantly, all prompts need to be mapped to fields in the Service Request or Activity forms in a later step. The type of the prompts must match the type of fields in the forms, **Text | String, Date/Time | Date/Time**, and so on:

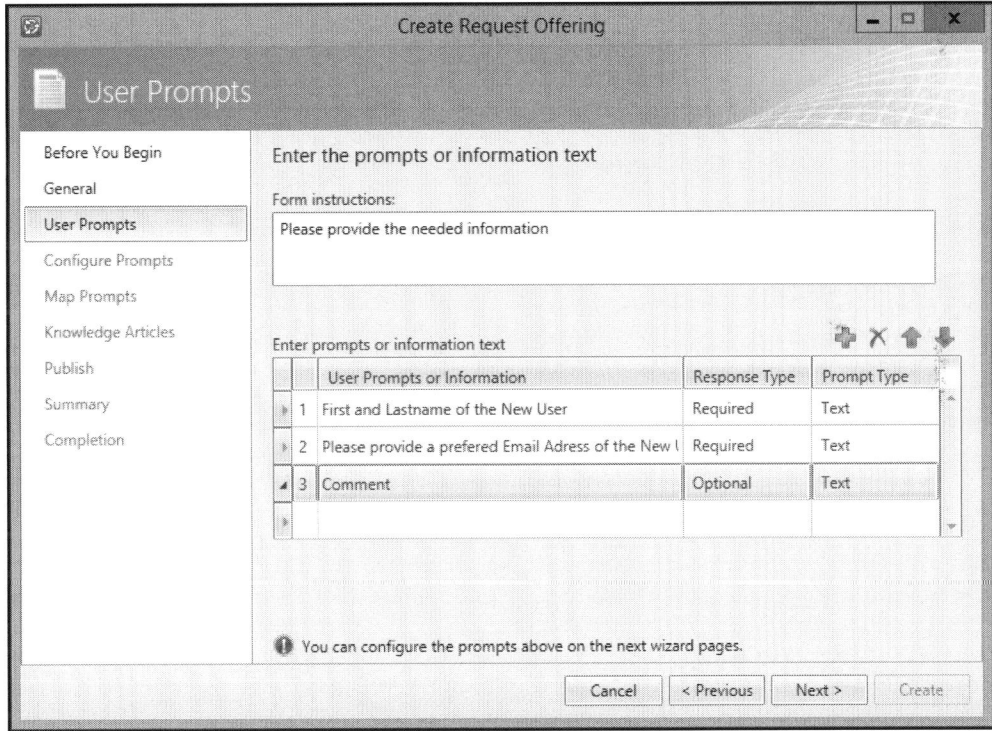

11. Click on **Next**.

12. On the next page, you can configure each prompt. For this, select the prompt and click on **Configure**. In this recipe, we will configure the text prompt of **Please provide a preferred Email Address of the New User** to be a valid e-mail format.

13. Configuring the text prompt is optional. Some of the prompt types must be configured. For instance, if you choose **Simple List** on the previous page for a prompt, you have to configure the values of the **Simple List**. Also, the **MP Enumeration List** and **Query Result** prompts need to be configured (which SCSM 2016 list you want to refer to and which SCSM 2016 class in the CDMB you want to query). Click on **OK** to close the **Configure Text Control** window:

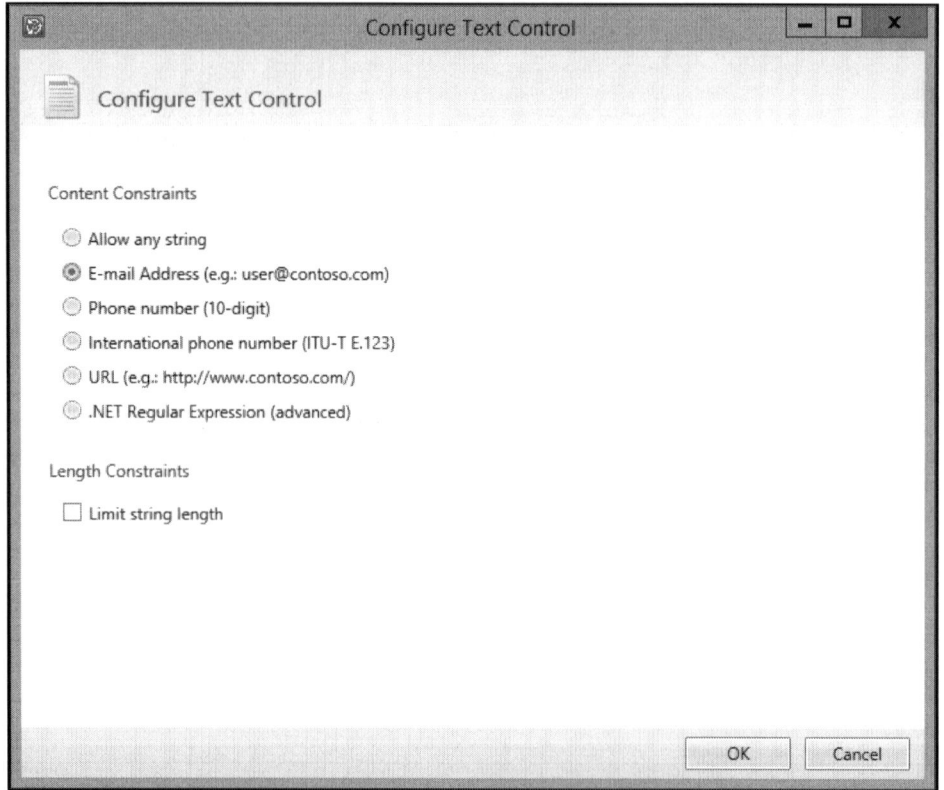

14. Click on **OK** and then on **Next** in the wizard.

15. On the **Map Prompts** page, you have to map the prompts to the **Service Request** form or the related activities of the Service Request template we chose in Step 6 of this recipe.

16. Each prompt must be mapped at least once. But you can map a prompt in different forms/fields more than once.

17. Select Service Request in the **Select an object and map its properties** pane. By default, you will only see the common properties. Activating Display all properties will show all fields of the selected object.

18. Select **Description** of the Service Request and map the prompt to the **Comment** field:

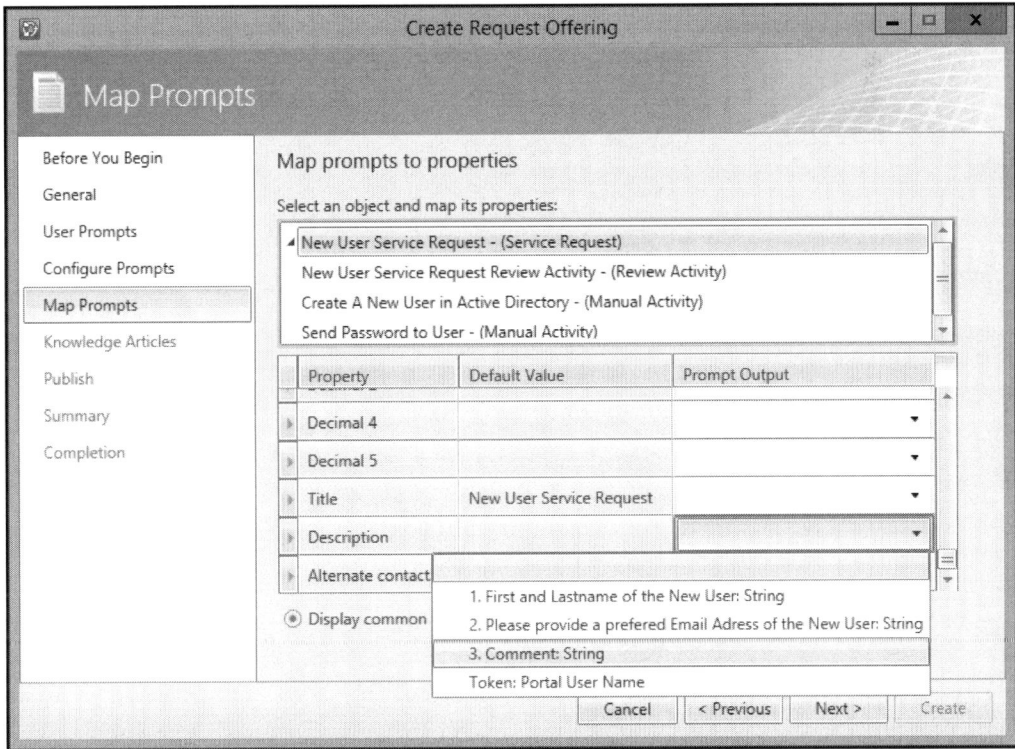

19. Select the **New User Request Service – (Service Request)** Request Approval activity and map **Description** to the prompt **First and Lastname of the New User: String**. Select the **Create A New User in Active Directory – (Manual Activity)** activity and map **Description** to the prompt **Please provide a preferred Email Address of the New User: String**.

20. In the selection form, all prompts that are mapped at least once show a tick next to them. The mapping of **Token: Portal User Name** is optional (the user who created the Service Request in the SCSM 2016 portal):

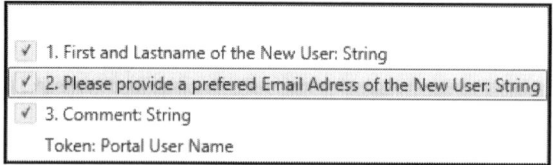

21. Click on **Next**.

22. On the **Knowledge Articles** page, relate an existing article to the Request Offering. This step is optional:

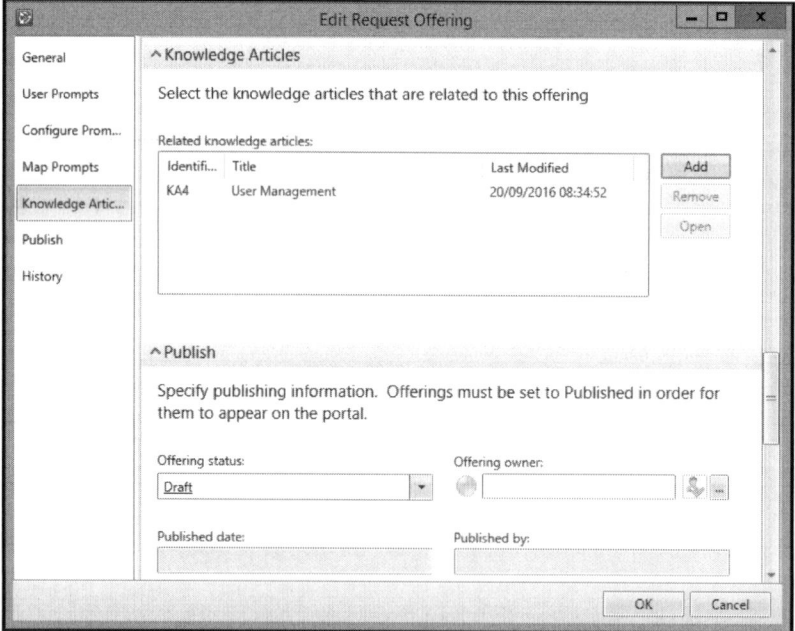

23. Click on **Next**.
24. On the **Publish** page, add an Offering owner. This owner will be responsible for this Service Offering. We will publish the Service Offering in a later recipe, named *Publishing Service Offerings and Request Offerings*.
25. Click on **Next**.
26. On the **Summary** page, verify the information and click on **Create**.

How it works...

Request Offerings, when scoped to the Service Request class, provide you with the ability to map all fields in the Service Request template form and its Activity templates to user-friendly questions. These user friendly questions are displayed in the SCSM 2016 Self-Service Portal and will also include the name, description, and an icon image of the Request Offering.

There's more...

Request Offerings can be copied. This is helpful if you need to create similar Request Offerings, for instance, in different languages.

Copying Request Offerings

You can create copies of Request Offerings, for instance, to use different languages or create almost similar Request Offerings. Follow these steps to copy an existing Request Offering:

1. Select a Request Offering you would like to copy.
2. Click on the **Create a copy** task. You can choose if you would like to create a corresponding Service Request template.
3. Open the newly created copy and make your changes.

Views for different status as of Request Offerings

In the SCSM 2016 console, there are different views of Request Offerings. This offers the opportunity to quickly navigate through the filtered list of Request Offerings.

The following views are default in SCSM 2016:

- All Service Request Offerings
- Published Request Offerings
- Draft Request Offerings
- Standalone Request Offerings

Take look at the *Publishing Service Offerings and Request Offerings* recipe.

Standalone Request Offerings

If a Request Offering isn't related to a Service Request, it is called a **Standalone Request Offering**.

This type of Request Offering is not visible in the SCSM 2016 Self-Service Portal but you can search for this Request Offering in the Portal by name.

There is a special view available for Standalone Request Offerings. You must navigate to **SCSM 2016 Console | Library | Service Catalog | Request Offerings | Standalone Request Offerings** to view this type of offering.

Adding a Request Offering to an existing Service Offering

To add a Request Offering to an existing Service Offering in the SCSM 2016 console navigate to **Library | Service Catalog | Request Offerings** (**Draft**, **Published**, or **Standalone Request Offering**).

1. Select the Request Offering and click on **Add to Service Offering** in the **Tasks** pane.
2. Select a Service Offering from the list.
3. Click on **Add**.
4. Click on **OK** to close the window.

Controlling the access to Request Offerings using Groups and User Roles in SCSM 2016

To control the access to Request Offerings to a specific group of users you can use groups and user Roles in SCSM 2016:

1. In the SCSM 2016 console, navigate to **Library** | **Groups**.
2. Click on **Create Catalog Group**.
3. Provide a name and choose a management pack.
4. Click on **Next**.
5. On the **Included Members** page, add Request Offerings from the list.
6. Click on **Next**.
7. On the **Dynamic Members** page, you can specify a criteria for dynamically selecting the offerings (for example, dynamically include **Request Offering** class where "Display Name" contains "Active Directory").
8. Click on **Next**.
9. Add existing catalog groups if needed.
10. Click on **Next**.
11. Add offerings to the excluded members (if they are added dynamically as a dynamic member).
12. Click on **Next**.
13. Verify the **Summary** screen and click on **Create**.

See also

The Microsoft TechNet Library: Using the Service Catalog in System Center 2016 – Service Manager, at https://technet.microsoft.com/en-us/system-center-docs/sm/manage/admin-using-the-service-catalog-in-system-center-2016-service-manager.

How to create and configure user roles in SCSM 2016 is described in the *Creating and managing Service Request roles*, *Creating and managing Incident Management roles*, *Creating and managing Problem Management roles*, *Creating and managing Change and Release Management roles*, and *Creating hybrid roles* recipes in Chapter 9, *Implementing Security Roles*.

Creating Service Catalog Service Offerings

Service Offerings in the SCSM 2016 Service catalog are the second tier to sort and combine Request Offerings. SCSM 2016 groups and user roles can be used to control the permission through which users are able to see and use Request Offerings in the SCSM 2016 portal.

This recipe shows the necessary configuration and steps to create Service Offerings in SCSM 2016.

Getting ready

To create Service Offerings in the SCSM 2016 Service Catalog, open the SCSM 2016 console and navigate to **Library** | **Service Catalog** | **Service Offerings**.

How to do it...

To create a Service Catalog Service Offering, follow these steps:

1. Click on **Create Service Offering** in the **Task** pane of the SCSM 2016 console.
2. Read the **Before You Begin** information and then click on **Next**.
3. In the **General** page, fill in all the information. Choose the **User Management** category we created in an earlier recipe. Choose an image:

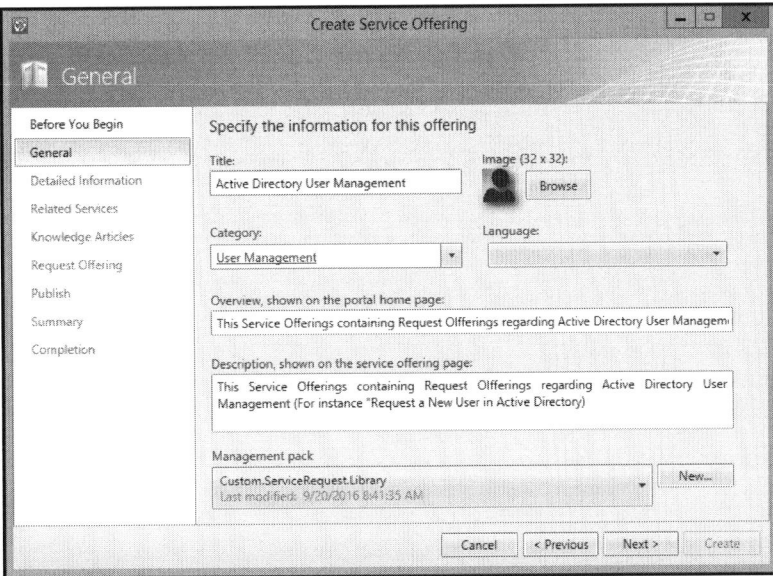

4. Click on **Next**.
5. Fill in all information in the **Detailed Information** page. This information is optional but will be helpful to the end user in the SCSM 2016 portal:

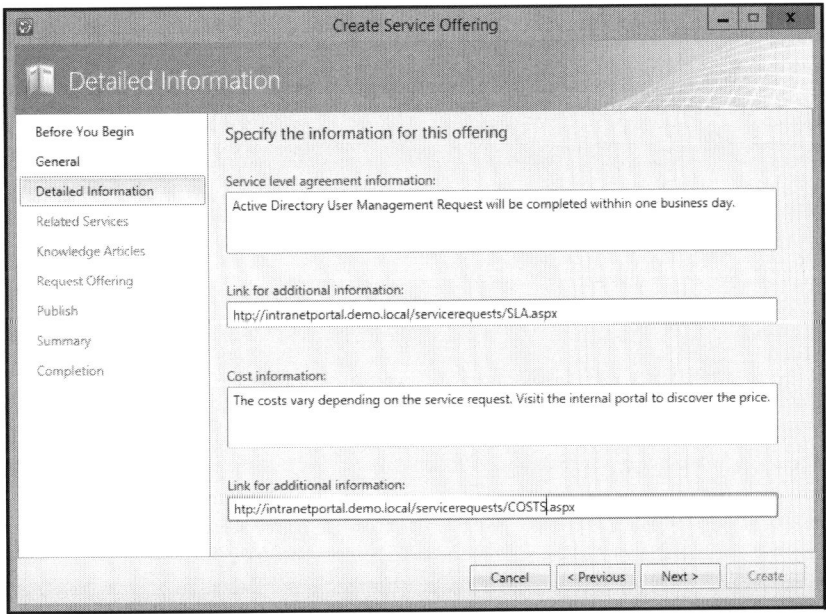

6. Click on **Next**.

7. On the **Related** Services page, you can add a Business Service of SCSM 2016. In this recipe, we will not add any related services:

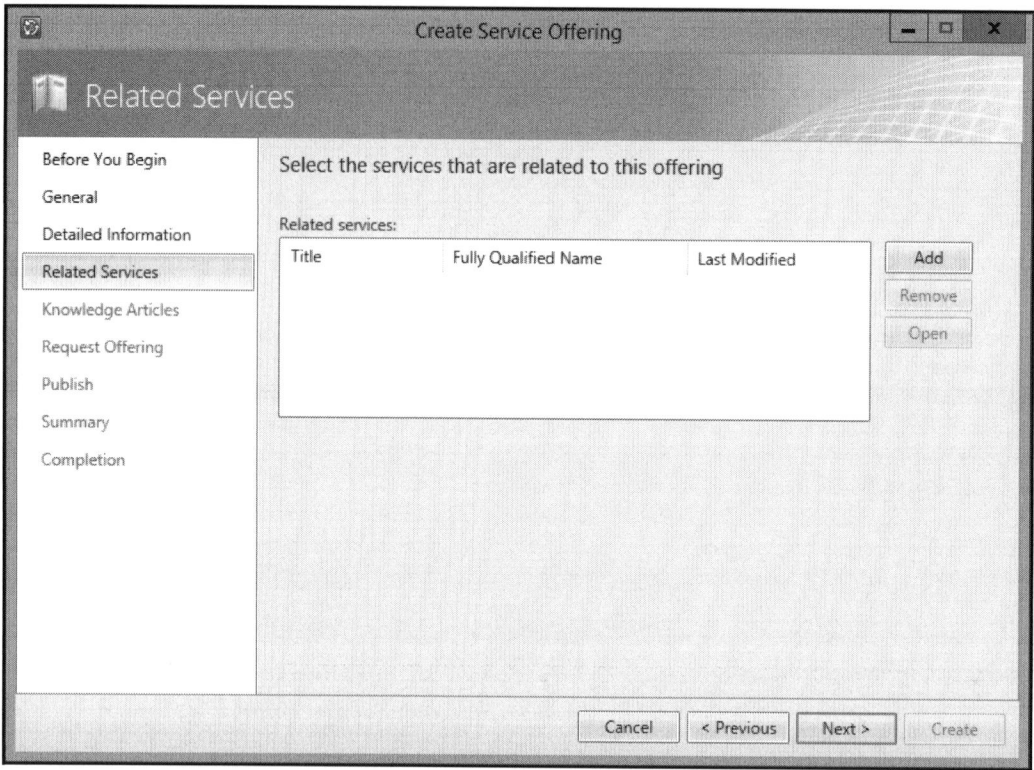

8. Click on **Next**.

9. Add a knowledge article to the Service Offering in the **Knowledge Article** page. In our recipe, we will add the **User Management** article:

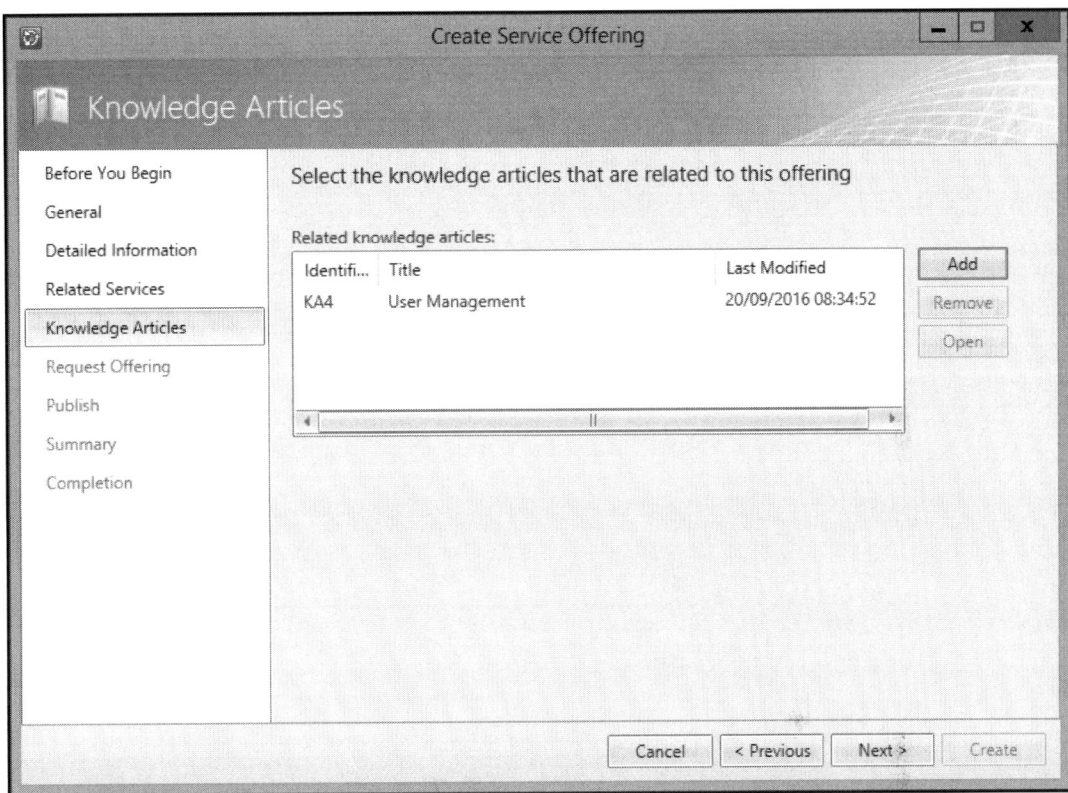

10. Click on **Next**.

11. In the **Request** Offering page add the Request Offering we created in the previous recipe. Use the filter to find the **Create New User in Active Directory** request:

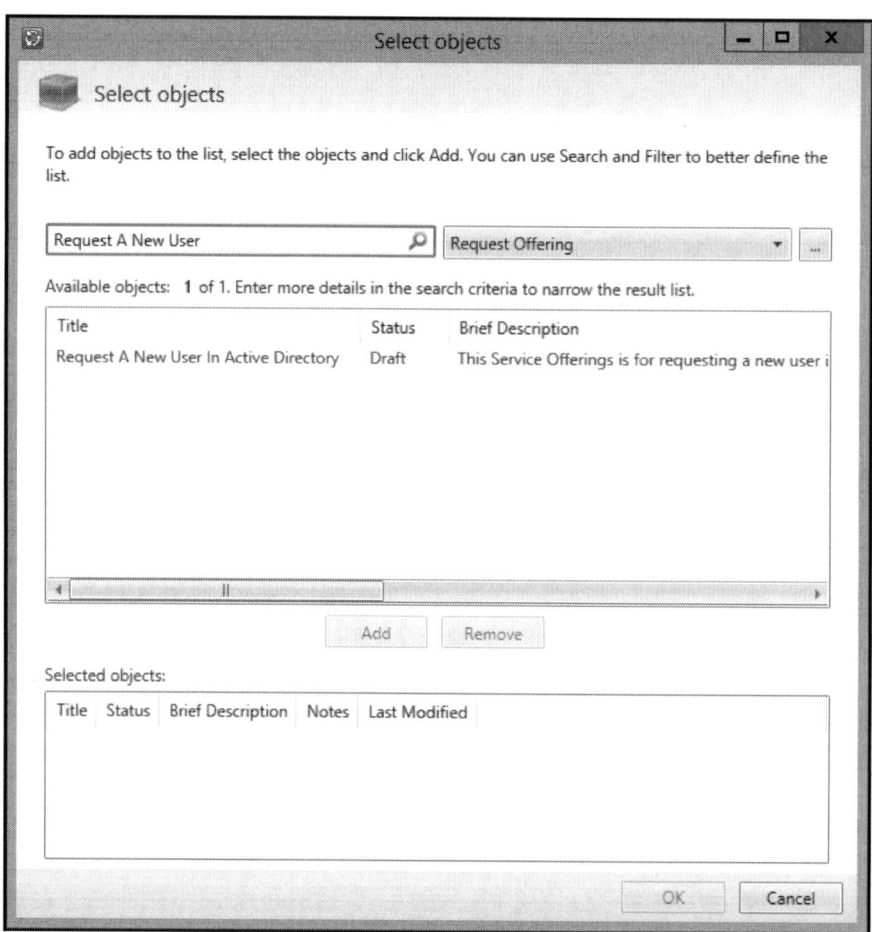

12. Select the Request Offering, click on **Add**, and then click on **OK**:

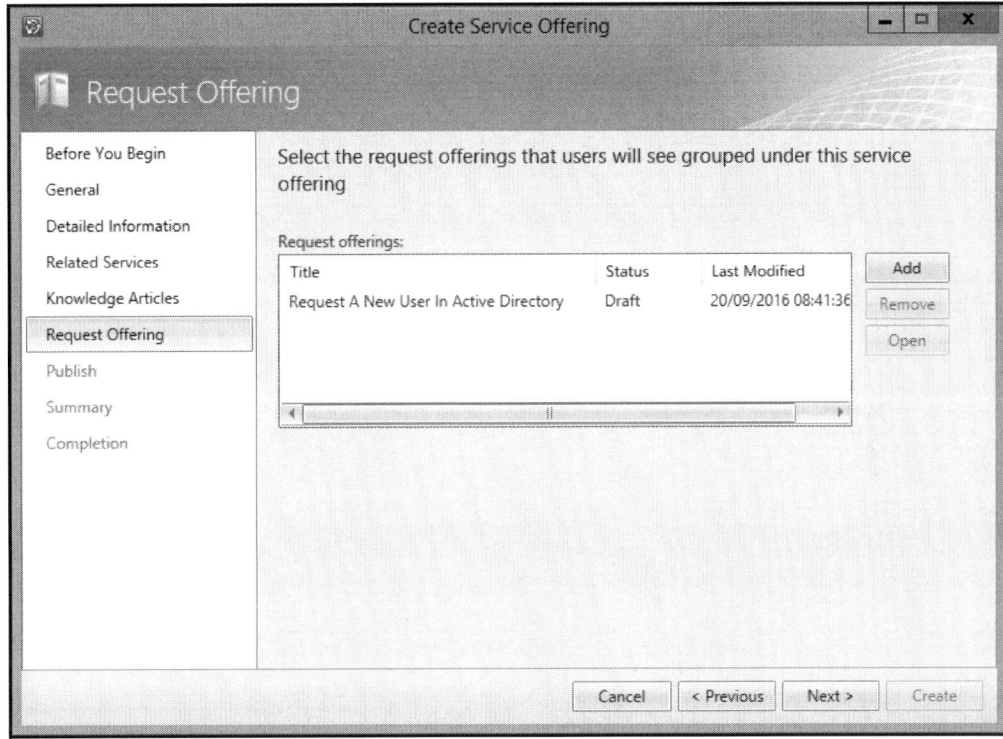

13. Click on **Next**.

14. On the **Publish** page, fill in the owner of the offering. Leave the status as **Draft**. We will work with the publishing of offerings in the next recipe:

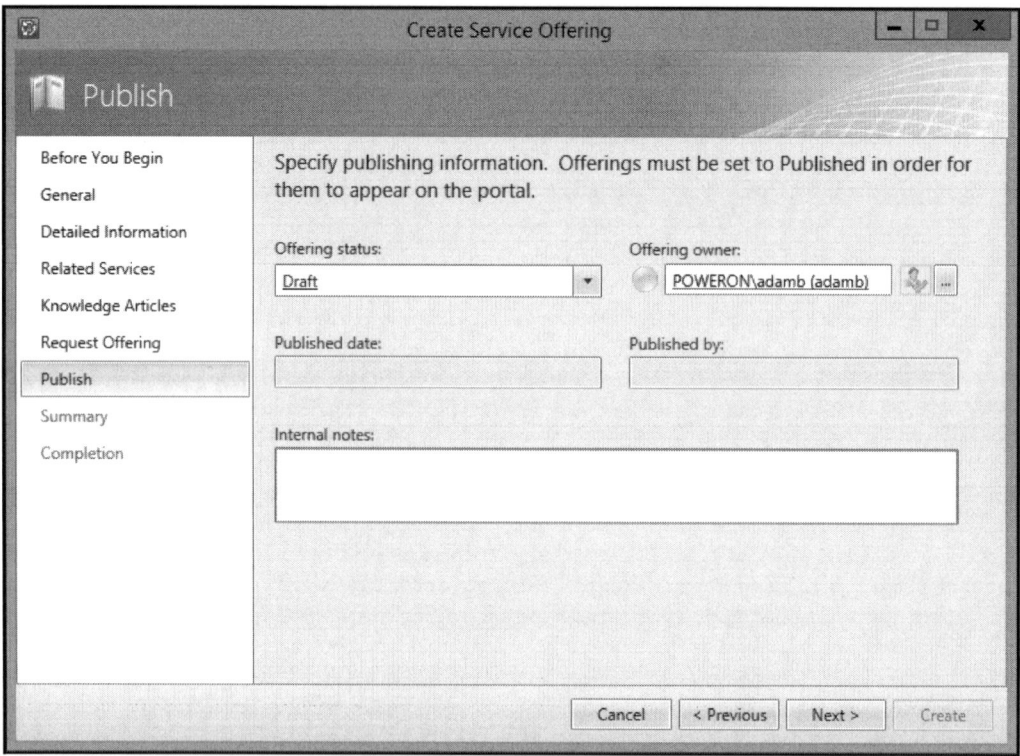

15. Click on **Next**.
16. Verify the **Summary** page and click on **Create**.

How it works...

All the information in the different pages of a Service Offering will be used to display Request Offerings grouped in categories in the SCSM 2016 portal.

There's more...

Different views can be used in the SCSM 2016 console to filter Service Offerings in different statuses.

Views for different status as of Service Offerings

In the SCSM 2016 console, there are different views for Service Offerings. This offers the opportunity to quickly navigate through the filtered list of Service Offerings.

The following views are default in SCSM 2016:

- All Service Offerings
- Draft Service Offerings
- Published Service Offerings

You could also take a look at the *Publishing Service Offerings and Request Offerings* recipe.

Controlling access to Service Offerings using groups and user roles

To control the access of Service Offerings to a specific group of users, you can use groups and user roles in SCSM 2016:

1. In the SCSM 2016 console, navigate to **Library** | **Groups**.
2. Click on **Create Catalog Group**.
3. Provide a name and choose a management pack.
4. Click on **Next**.
5. On the **Included Members** page, add offerings from the list.
6. Click on **Next**.
7. On the **Dynamic Members** page, you can specify a criteria for dynamically selecting the offerings (for example, dynamically include a Service Offering class where Display Name contains Active Directory).
8. Click on **Next**.
9. Add existing catalog groups if needed.
10. Click on **Next**.
11. Add offerings to the excluded members (if they are added dynamically as a dynamic member).
12. Click on **Next**.
13. Verify the **Summary** screen and click on **Create**.

How to create and configure user roles in SCSM 2016 is described in Chapter 9, *Implementing Security Roles*.

See also

The Microsoft TechNet Library: Using the Service Catalog in System Center 2016 – Service Manager, at `https://technet.microsoft.com/en-us/system-center-docs/sm/manage/a dmin-using-the-service-catalog-in-system-center-2016-service-manager`.

Publishing Service Offerings and Request Offerings

After creating Request and Service Offerings, as described in the previous two recipes, you need to publish both types of Offerings. As long as the Offerings are in the Draft status, they will not be visible in the SCSM 2016 portal to the end users.

A best practice for publishing Request and Service Offerings is to use Change Management with approvals for the publishing. This recipe discusses how you use Change Management with approvals to change a draft Offering into a published Offering visible in the SCSM 2016 Self-Service Portal. This will be done in two steps to publish the different Offerings. The first step is for publishing Service Offerings. The second one is for publishing Request Offerings.

Getting ready

To publish Service Offerings in the SCSM 2016 Service Catalog open SCSM 2016 console and navigate to **Library** | **Service Catalog** | **Service Offerings**.

To publish Request Offerings in the SCSM 2016 Service Catalog open SCSM 2016 console and navigate to **Library** | **Service Catalog** | **Request Offerings**.

How to do it...

To publish a Service Offering select the related Service Offering (Active Directory User Management) in the list in **SCSM 2016 Console** | **Library** | **Service Catalog** | **Service Offerings**:

1. Click on **Create Change Request to Publish** in the **Tasks** pane.
2. Choose the **Publish Offering** template from the list in the **Select Template window** and click on **OK**.

3. In the Change Request form fill in the information regarding the publishing of the Service Offering (**Title**, **Description**, **Reason**, **Created By**, **Area**, **Assigned To**, **Priority**, **Impact**, and **Risk**). For more information regarding Change Request and how they work, please take a look at `Chapter 8`, *Designing and Configuring Change Management and Release Management*:

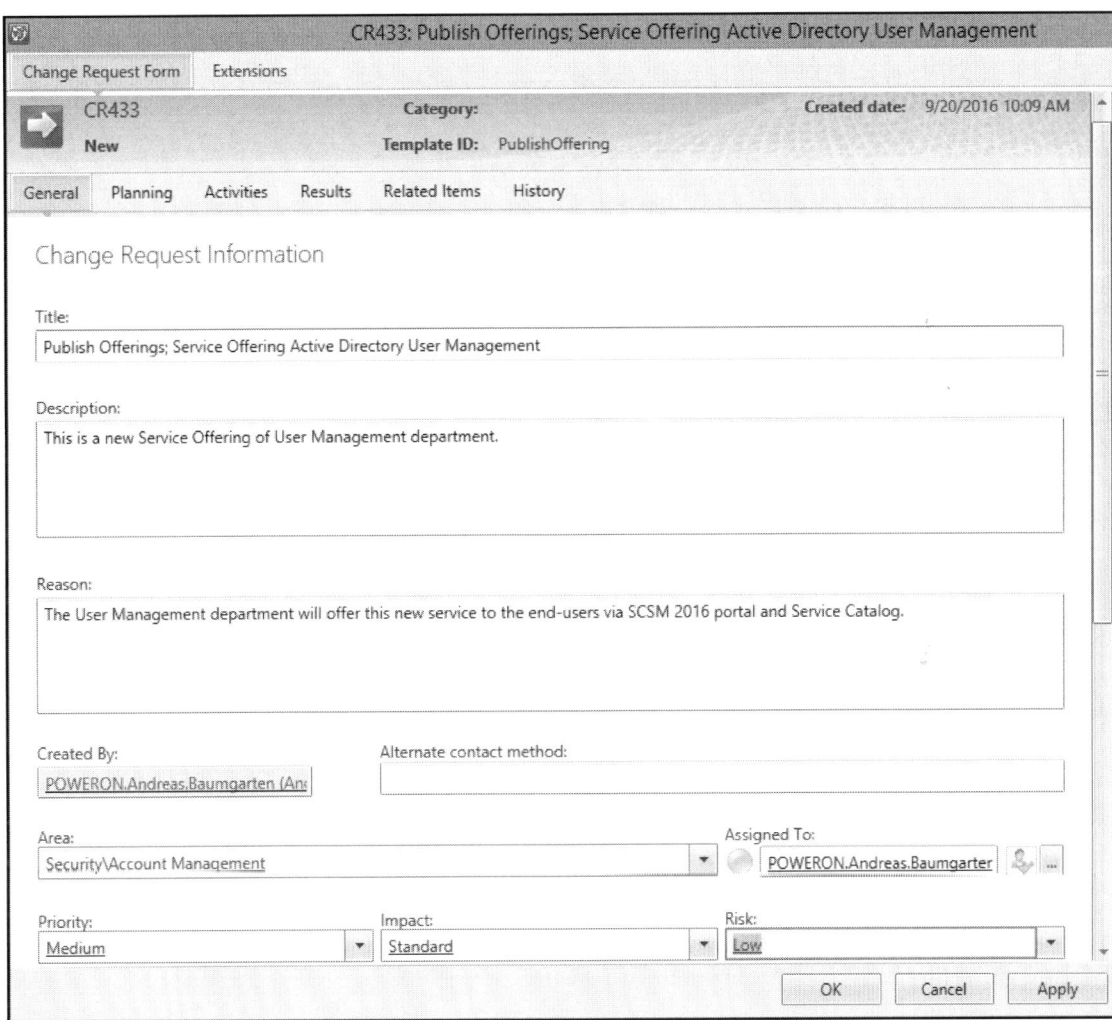

4. Click on the **Activities** tab. Verify that two activities are listed. The first Review Activity (the RA suffix) is the approval, the second (the AC suffix) is an automated activity to publish the Service Offering:

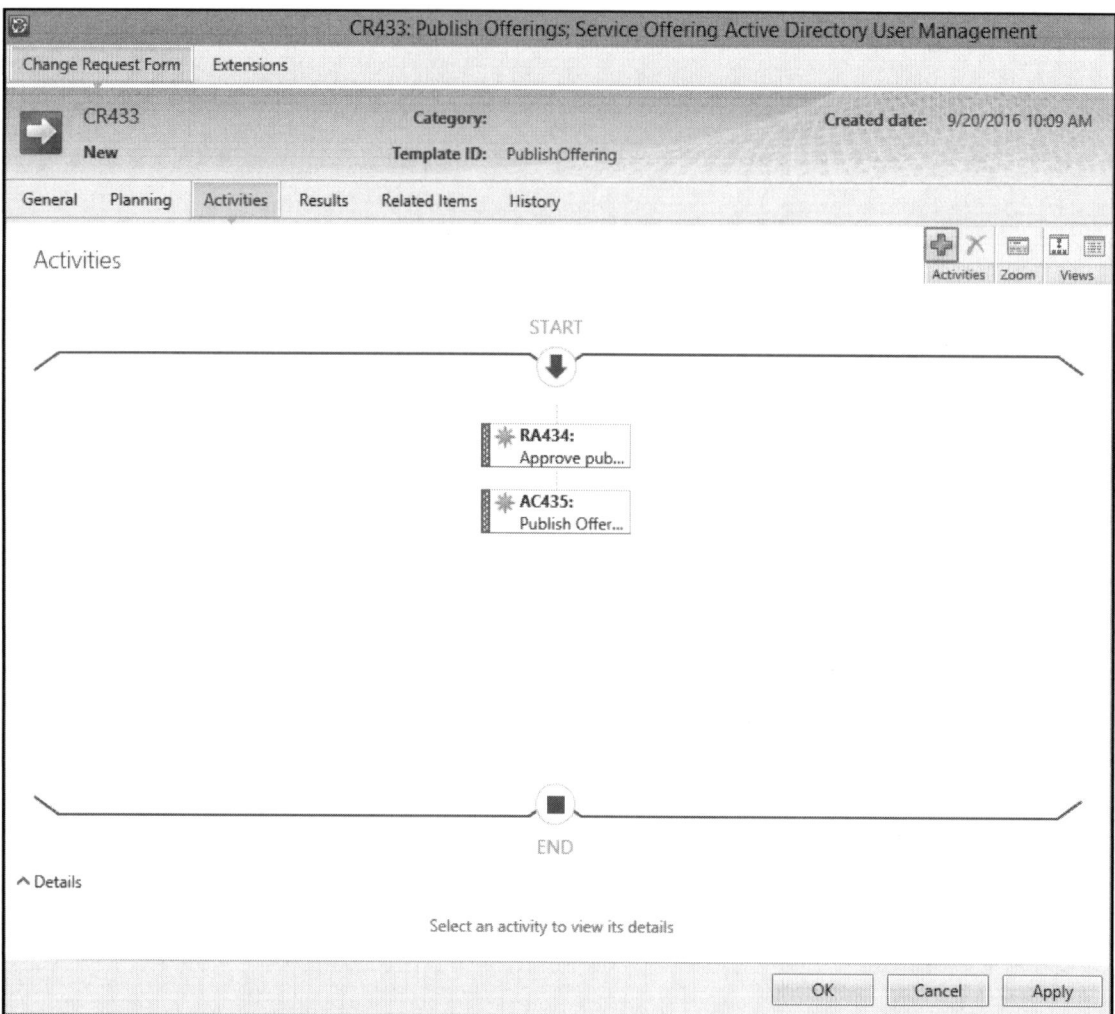

5. Add the reviewer and click on **OK in the Review Activity page:**

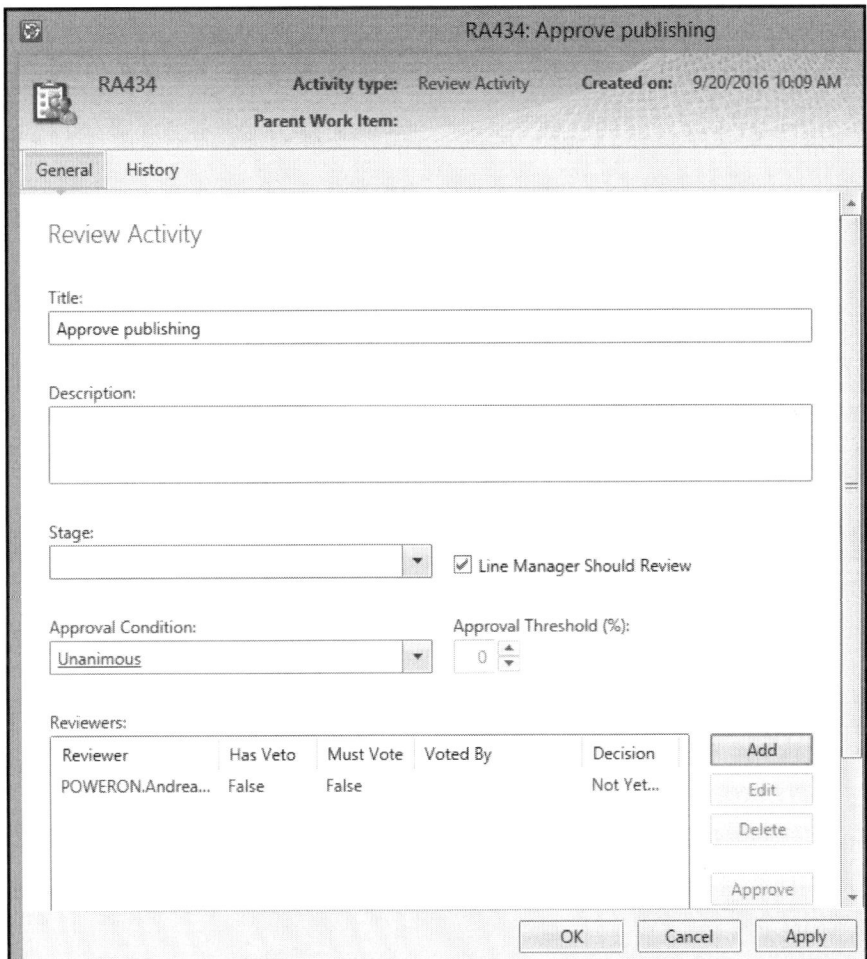

6. Close the Change Request by clicking on **OK**.

To publish a Request Offering select the related Request Offering (Request A New User in Active Directory) in the list in **SCSM 2016 Console** | **Library** | **Service Catalog** | **Request Offerings**:

1. Click on **Create Change Request to Publish** in the **Tasks** pane.
2. Choose the **Publish Offering** template from the list in the **Select Template** window and click on **OK**.
3. In the **Change Request** form, fill in the information regarding the publishing of the Request Offering (**Title**, **Description**, **Reason**, **Created By**, **Area**, **Assigned To**, **Priority**, **Impact**, and **Risk**). For more information regarding Change Request and how they work, please take a look at Chapter 8, *Designing and Configuring Change Management and Release Management*:

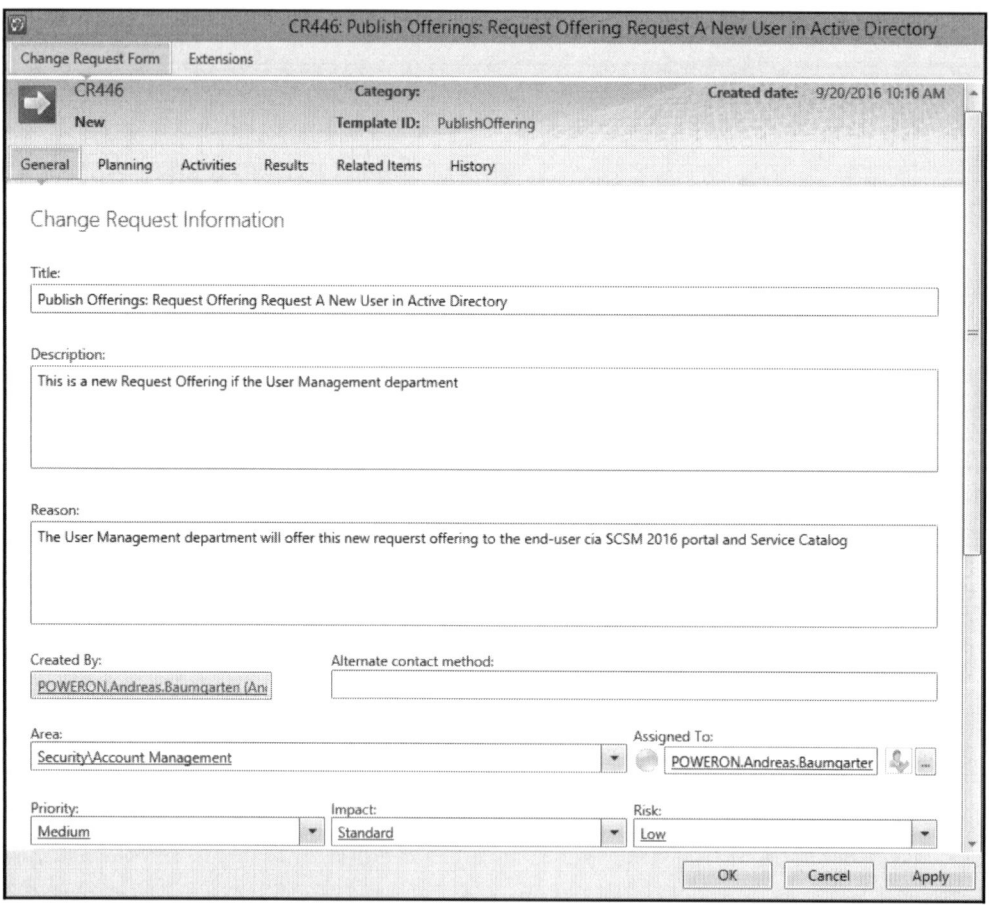

4. Click on the **Activities** tab. Verify that two activities are listed. The first Review Activity (RA suffix) is the approval, the second (AC suffix) is an automated activity to publish the Request Offering.

5. Add the reviewer and click on **OK** in the **Review Activity** page (as described in the part to publish the Service Offering).

6. Close the Change Request by clicking on **OK**.

Follow these steps to approve both Change Requests to publish the Service Offering and the Request Offering:

1. In the SCSM 2016 console, navigate to **Work Items | Activity Management | Review Activities | In-Progress Activities**.

2. Select the first Review Activity named **Approve publishing** and click on **Approve** in the **Tasks** pane.

3. Enter a comment (required) and click on **OK** to close the window.

4. Select the second Review Activity named **Approve publishing** and click on **Approve** in the **Tasks** pane.

5. Enter a comment (required) and click on **OK** to close the window:

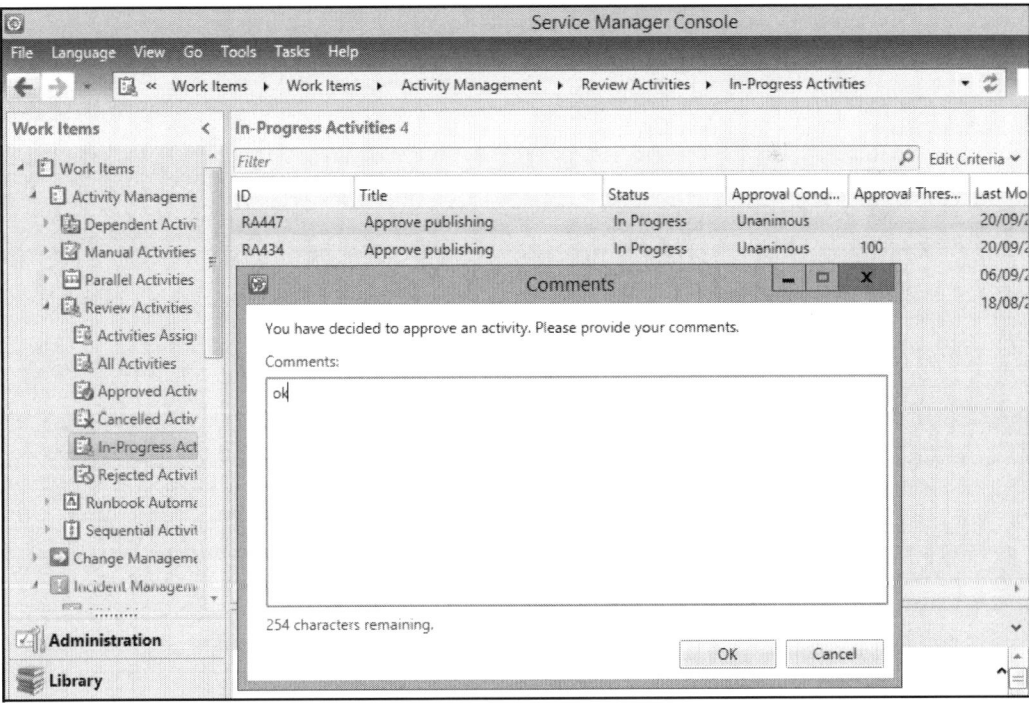

Verify the result:

1. After both Review Activities are approved, wait for a few minutes. SCSM 2016 workflows will trigger the Automated Activities to change the status for the Service Offering and Request Offering to **Published** after a few minutes.
2. In the SCSM 2016 console, navigate to **Library** | **Service Catalog** | **Service Offerings** | **Published Service Offerings**. The Service Offering we created and published during the recipes in this chapter should be listed.
3. In the SCSM 2016 console, navigate to **Library** | **Service Catalog** | **Request Offerings** | **Published Request Offerings**. The Request Offering we created and published during the recipes in this chapter should be listed.

How it works...

Change Management can be used for the publishing process of Service or Request Offerings.

After creating a related Change Request two activities are added to the Change Request record. The first activity is for reviewing and approving. The second, automated activity will be triggered by an internal SCSM 2016 workflow after the reviewer approves the first activity. The workflow will set the status of the offering to **Published**.

There is more...

Publishing and unpublishing of Service and Request Offerings can be done without involving the Change Management process.

Publishing Service and Request Offerings without the Change Management process

If no Change Management process is needed to publish the Service or Request Offering, there is a shortcut:

1. In the SCSM 2016 console, navigate to **Library** | **Service Catalog** | **Service Offerings/Request Offerings** | **Draft Service Offerings/Draft Request Offerings**.
2. Select the Service Offering or Request Offering.
3. Click on **Publish** in the **Tasks** pane.

Unpublishing a Service Offering or Request Offering

Service or Request Offerings can also be unpublished:

1. In the SCSM 2016 console, navigate to **Library** | **Service Catalog** | **Service Offerings/Request Offerings** | **Published Service Offerings/Published Request Offerings**.
2. Select the Service Offering or Request Offering.
3. Click on **Unpublish** in the **Tasks** pane.

See also

The Microsoft TechNet Library: Using the Service Catalog in System Center 2016 – Service Manager, at `https://technet.microsoft.com/en-us/system-center-docs/sm/manage/admin-using-the-service-catalog-in-system-center-2016-service-manager`.

Working with Service Requests in the Self-Service Portal

After publishing the Request Offering and Service Offering, end users can start creating Service Requests in the SCSM 2016 Self-Service Portal based on this offering.

This recipe shows how to work with the SCSM 2016 portal to submit a Service Request.

Getting ready

Open the SCSM 2016 Self-Service Portal in a browser.

By default, the URL is `https://<portalservername>:<port>`.

How to do it...

1. The following is the SCSM 2016 portal entry page:

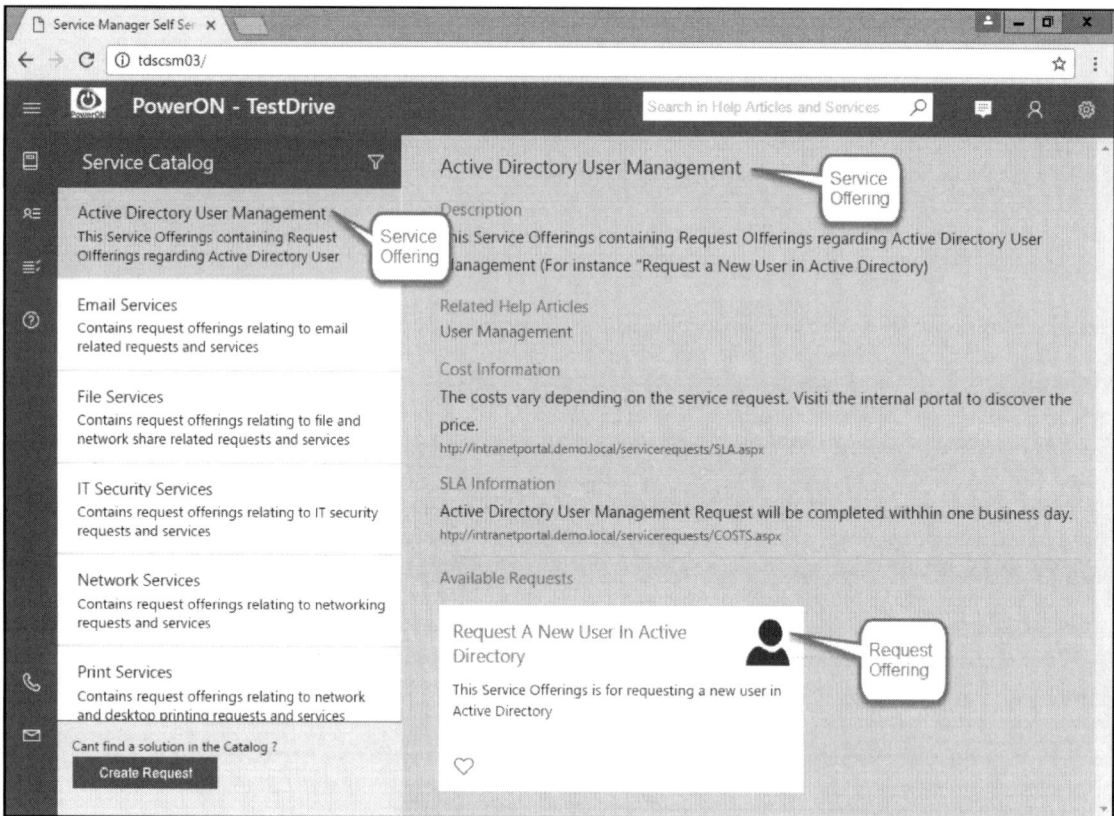

2. Click on the **Active Directory User Management Service Offering** in the **Service Catalog** section on the left side.

3. Click on **Request A New User in Active Directory**:

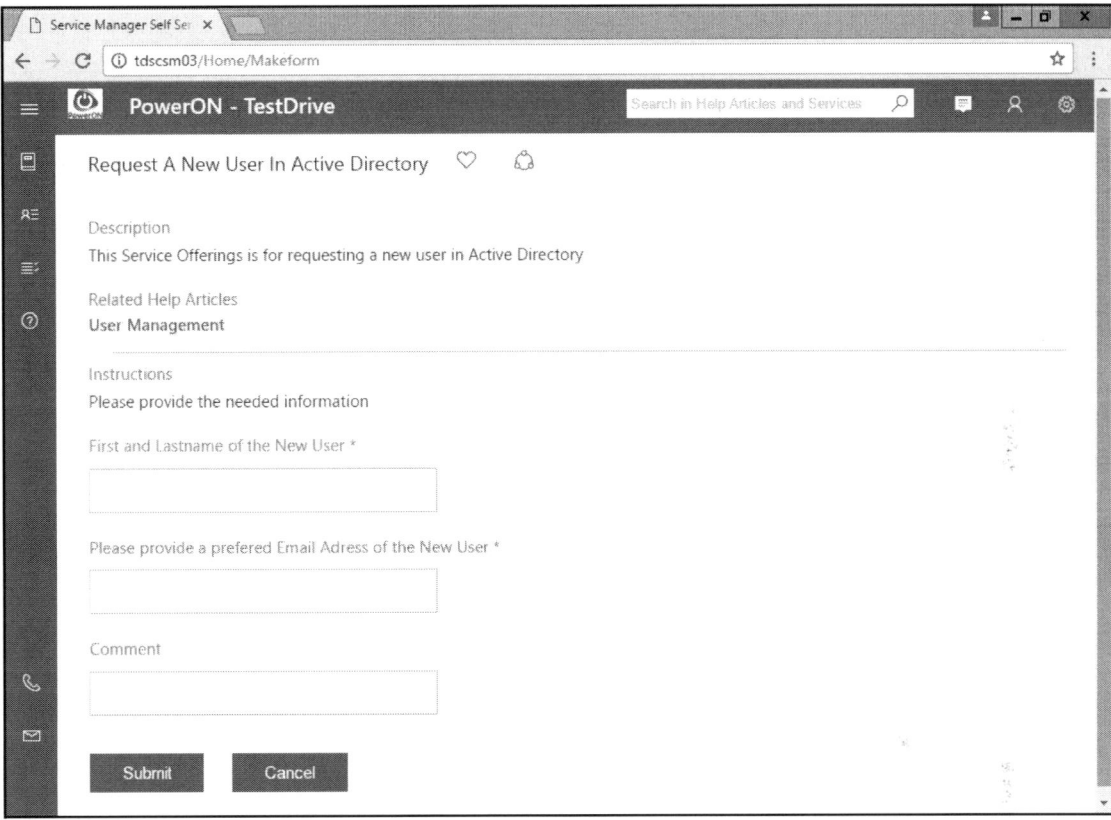

4. Provide the information in the form. Click on **Submit**.

5. After the Service Request is submitted, the end user can follow the progress of his/ her request by clicking on **My Requests** and then on the Service Request in the list:

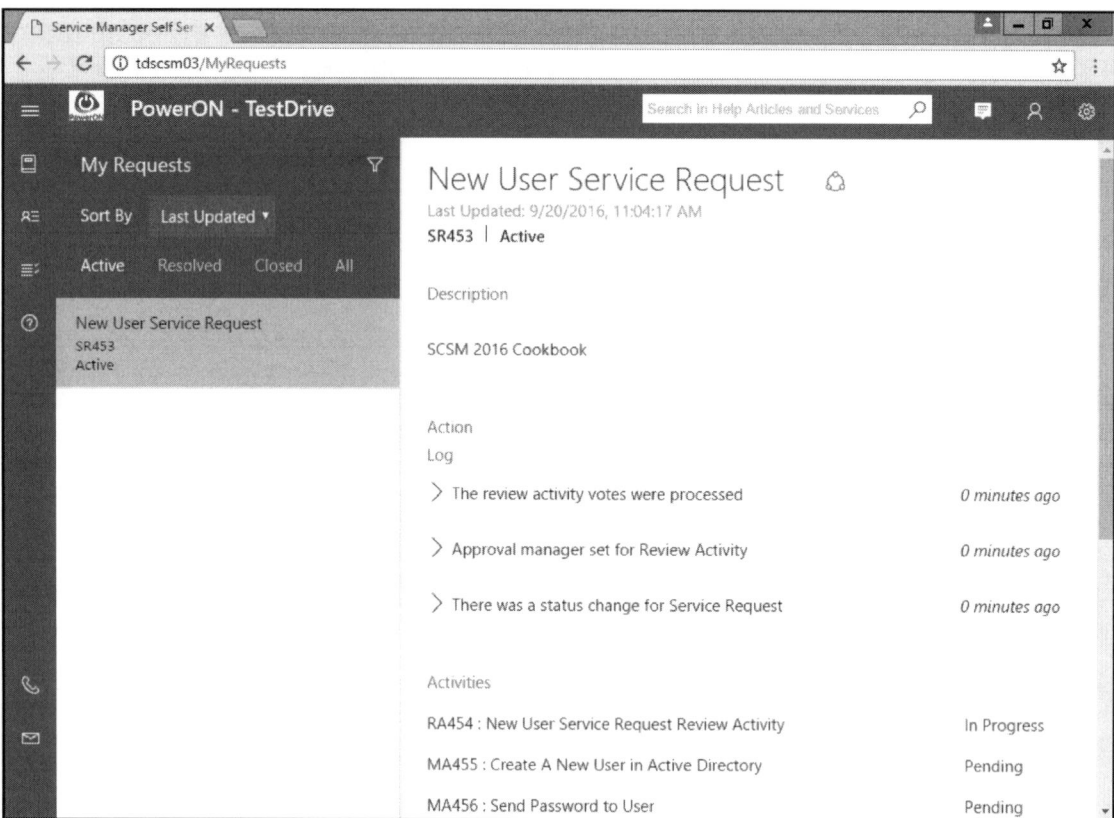

How it works...

Using the SCSM 2016 portal, it is possible for end users to raise Service Requests. Based on all the information in the Service Offering and Request Offering the user will be able to get as much information about the Service Request as possible (SLA, costs, Knowledge Articles, and the required information to fulfill the Service Request).

Also, he/she can follow the progress of his/her request in the **My Request** section of the SCSM 2016 portal.

There's more...

After submitting a Service Request, the end user can add additional input by using the SCSM 2016 Self-Service Portal.

Additional User Input after the Service Request is submitted

As long as the status of a Service Request is in progress, the end user can provide additional information to the Service Request in the SCSM 2016 portal by following these steps:

1. Open the SCSM 2016 portal in a supported SCSM 2016 web browser.
2. Click on **My Request**.
3. Click on the Service Request in the list.
4. Write the information in the **User Input** field and click on **Update**.

See also

- The Microsoft TechNet Library: Using the Service Catalog in System Center 2016 – Service Manager, at `https://technet.microsoft.com/en-us/system-center -docs/sm/manage/admin-using-the-service-catalog-in-system-center- 2016-service-manager`.

Filling in the Service Request Description with User Input from the Request Offering

In SCSM 2016 every User Input in a Service Request in the SCSM 2016 Self-Service Portal can be mapped to a property of the Service Request or a property of the related activities (for instance, related Review or Manual Activities). There is no option to do a multi-mapping of different User Inputs mapped to one property.

There is a solution available to you to solve the multi-mapping issue. To solve this requirement, a PowerShell script can be used to write the full User Input of a Service Request into the **Description** field.

Getting ready

A Service Request must be submitted in SCSM 2016 before we start. The required steps to create a Service Request are described in the *Working with Service Requests in the Self-Service Portal* recipe in this chapter. We need the ID of the created Service Request; in our example, it is SR453. If you would like to run the PowerShell script remotely (not on the SCSM 2016 management server), we need the name of the SCSM 2016 management server as well. In our example, the name of the server is TDSCSM03.

You must download and install the SCSM PowerShell cmdlets found at `http://smlets.codeplex.com/` (see the *Downloading and installing SMLets* recipe in `Chapter 12`, *Automating Service Manager 2016*).

How to do it...

On the SCSM 2016 management server start the Windows PowerShell ISE:

1. Type the following code into a new script window in **Windows PowerShell ISE**:

```
# Import SMlets module
Import-Module Smlets

#------ Variables ------

# ID of the Service Request
$id = "SR453"

# Name of the SCSM Management Server
$smDefaultComputer = "TDSCSM03"

#-----------------------

# Get Service Request Class
$srClass = Get-SCSMClass -Name System.WorkItem.ServiceRequest$

#Get Service Request Object
$srObject = Get-SCSMObject -Class $srClass -Filter "Id = $id"

# Get User Input of Service Request
$userInputContent = [XML]$srObject.UserInput

# $userInputContent = [XML]$xmlUserInput
$questions = $userInputContent.UserInputs.UserInput

 # Clear useInput variable
```

```
$userInput = ""

# If Service Request Description is not empty
if ($srObject.Description)
{
    # Build UserInput with existing description
    $userInput+= $srObject.Description + [Environment]::NewLine +
"---------------" + [Environment]::NewLine
}
# For each line in User Input of SR
foreach ($input in $questions)
{
    # If Input contains Answer Value
    if($($input.Answer) -like "<Value*")
    {
        # Set answer variable
        [xml]$answer = $input.Answer
        # for each answer varaible ...
        foreach($value in $answer.Values)
        {
                # For each item in value variable
                foreach($item in $value)
                {
                    # For each text in Item Value
                    foreach ($txt in $($item.Value))
                    {   # Build list
                        $listArray += $($txt.DisplayName)
                    }

                    # Build User Input
                    $userInput += $input.Question + " = " +
[string]::Join(" ; ",$listArray) + [Environment]::NewLine
                    $ListArray = $null
                }
        }
    }
    else
    {
            # If Input Type is a List Value
            if ($input.Type -eq "enum")
            {
            $listGuid = Get-SCSMEnumeration -Id $input.Answer
            $userInput+= $($input.Question + " = " +
$listGuid.Displayname)  + [Environment]::NewLine
            }
            # If Input Type is Date/Time value
            if ($input.Type -eq "datetime")
            {
```

```
                # Set date property
                $date = [DateTime]$input.Answer
                # Format Date/Time
                $date = $date.ToString("dd.MM.yyy")
                # Build User Input
                $userInput+= $($input.Question + " = " + $date)   +
[Environment]::NewLine
                }

        else
                {
                # Build User Input
                $userInput += $($input.Question + " = " +
$input.Answer)   + [Environment]::NewLine
                }
        }
}


# Build property has for update
$propertyHash = @{
                Description = $userInput
                }
# Update of Service Request Description field
$srObject | Set-SCSMObject -PropertyHashtable $propertyHash
```

2. Save the file as a PowerShell file with a `.ps1` extension to a filesystem location (for example, **C:\Set-SRDescriptionWithUserInput.ps1**).

3. Modify the line 7 and line 10 in the script with your SR ID and the SCSM 2016 management server name (marked in yellow):

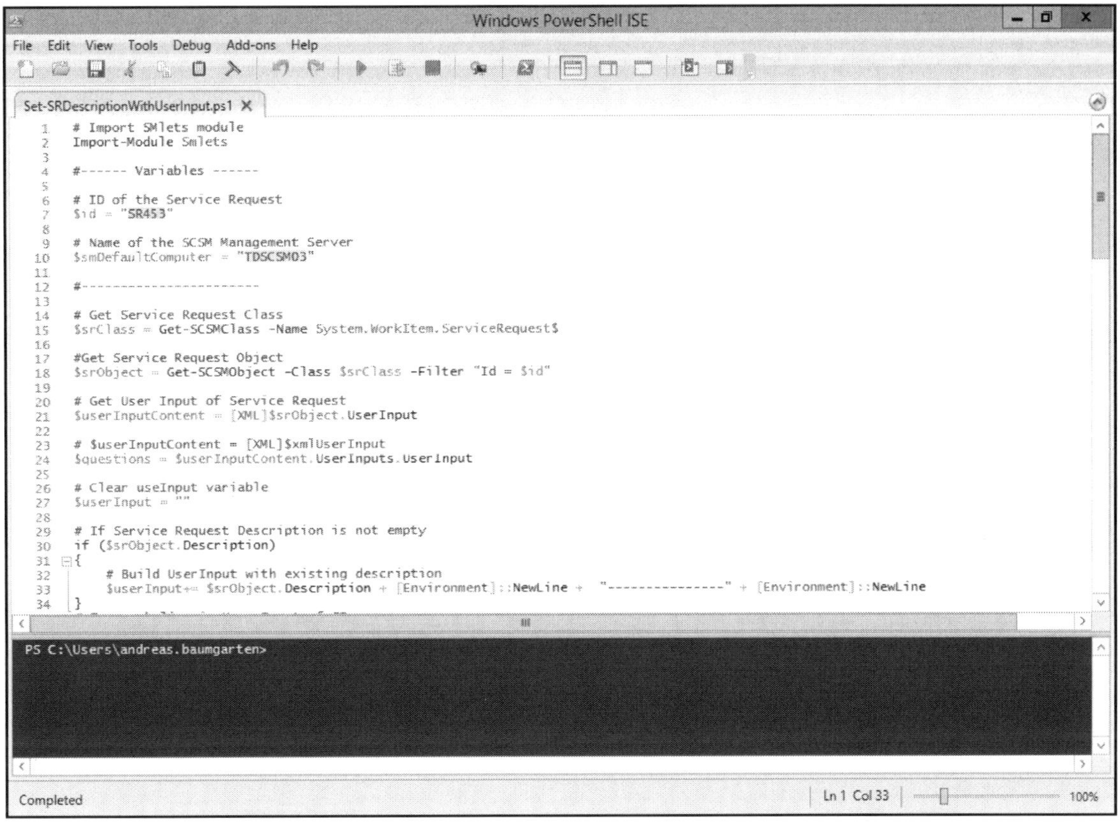

```
                              Windows PowerShell ISE                    _  □  ✕

File  Edit  View  Tools  Debug  Add-ons  Help

Set-SRDescriptionWithUserInput.ps1  ✕
    1    # Import SMlets module
    2    Import-Module Smlets
    3
    4    #------ Variables ------
    5
    6    # ID of the Service Request
    7    $id = "SR453"
    8
    9    # Name of the SCSM Management Server
   10    $smDefaultComputer = "TDSCSM03"
   11
   12    #----------------------
   13
   14    # Get Service Request Class
   15    $srClass = Get-SCSMClass -Name System.WorkItem.ServiceRequest$
   16
   17    #Get Service Request Object
   18    $srObject = Get-SCSMObject -Class $srClass -Filter "Id = $id"
   19
   20    # Get User Input of Service Request
   21    $userInputContent = [XML]$srObject.UserInput
   22
   23    # $userInputContent = [XML]$xmlUserInput
   24    $questions = $userInputContent.UserInputs.UserInput
   25
   26    # Clear useInput variable
   27    $userInput = ""
   28
   29    # If Service Request Description is not empty
   30    if ($srObject.Description)
   31  ⊟{
   32        # Build UserInput with existing description
   33        $userInput+= $srObject.Description + [Environment]::NewLine +   "---------------" + [Environment]::NewLine
   34    }

PS C:\Users\andreas.baumgarten>



Completed                                                    Ln 1  Col 33                              100%
```

4. Press *F5* or click on **Run Script in Windows PowerShell ISE.**

5. Verify in the Output window of Windows PowerShell ISE that there is no error message:

```
PS C:\Users\            > C:\Andreas\Set-SRDescriptionWithUserInput.ps1

PS C:\Users\            >
```

6. Verify the result in the **SCSM 2016 console** | **Work Items** | **Service Fulfillment** by opening the Service Request (SR453 in our example). The result should look like this:

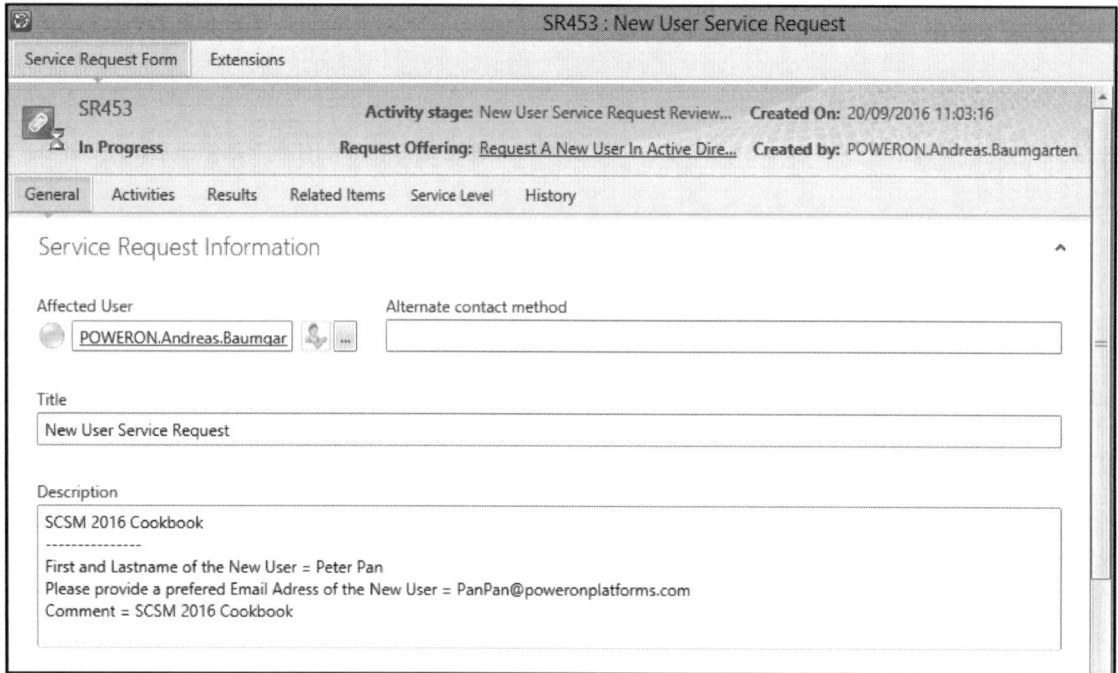

How it works...

The script starts with getting the required class (line 15) and the Service Request object filtered by ID (line 16).

The User Input of a Service Request is stored in one property (UserInput) in XML format. The XML is parsed for Question and Answer (line 20 – line 86). In this section, the script will also check if the **Description** field of the Service Request is empty or already contains text (line 29 – line 34). If there is list item or date field in the User Input, this is discovered and formatted by the PowerShell script as well (line 63 – line 78).

In lines 88 to 93, the output is prepared and the Service Request description is filled with the parsed and formatted User Input.

There's more...

Based on the specific date/time format in different countries it is maybe required to transform the date/time values in the right format.

Also the automated execution of this script might be a requirement as well.

Different date/time format for output

You can modify the date/time format in the script in line 75.

German format:

```
$date = $date.ToString("dd.MM.yyyy") # 24.09.2016
```

English UK format:

```
$date = $date.ToString("dd/MM/yyyy") # 24/09/2016
```

English US format:

```
$date = $date.ToString("MM/DD/yyyy") # 09/24/2016
```

See also...

If you need to copy the description of the Service Request in the description of all related activities (no matter which type of activities) there is a recipe in Chapter 8, *Designing and Configuring Change Management and Release Management*, called *Filling in all related Activity Descriptions with Descriptions from parent Change Requests*.

Creating Service Request notifications

In this recipe, we will configure the notification to an end user if a Service Request that he/she submitted is completed.

Getting ready

Create a notification template as described in the *Creating formatted e-mail notification templates* recipe in Chapter 2, *Personalizing SCSM 2016 Administration*, for example, Service Request Completed Notification Template.

In the SCSM 2016 console, navigate to **Administration** | **Workflow** | **Configuration**.

How to do it...

To create a Notification workflow for completed Service Requests, select **Service Request Event Workflow Configuration** and click on **Configure Workflow Rules** in the **Tasks** pane:

1. Click on **Add** in the **Configure Workflows** window.
2. Read the **Before You Begin** information and click on **Next**.
3. Provide a name and description.
4. Choose **When an object is updated** in the **Check for events** section.
5. Choose a management pack to store the information in:

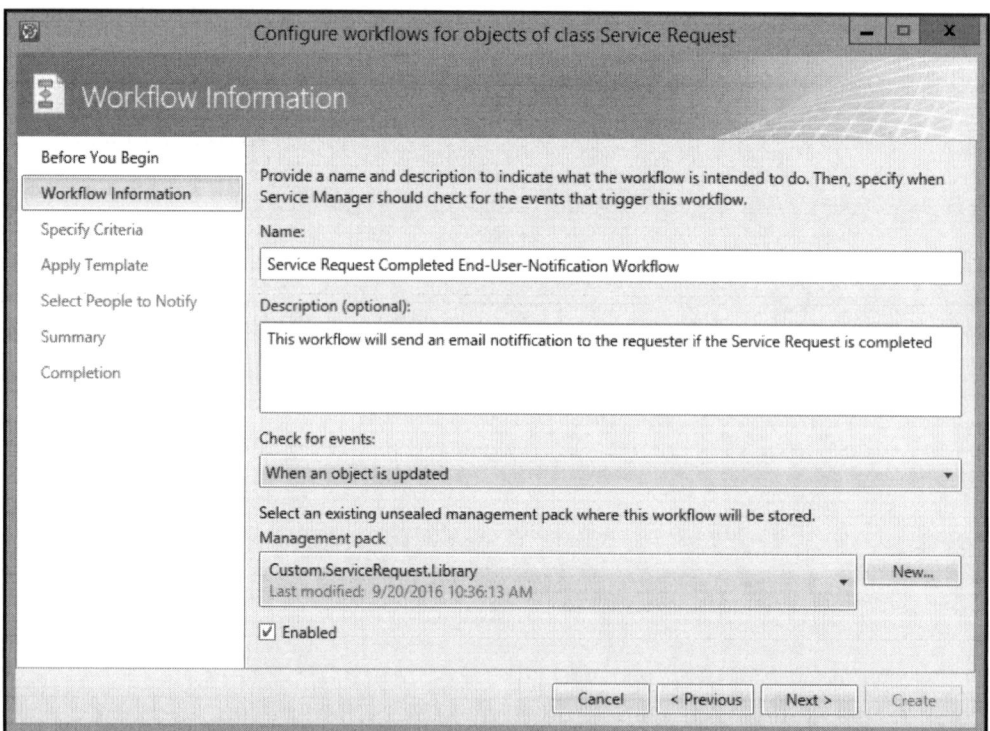

6. Click on **Next**.

7. Specify the criteria **Changed from**, **Status, does not equal**, and **Completed** in the **Specify Criteria** page:

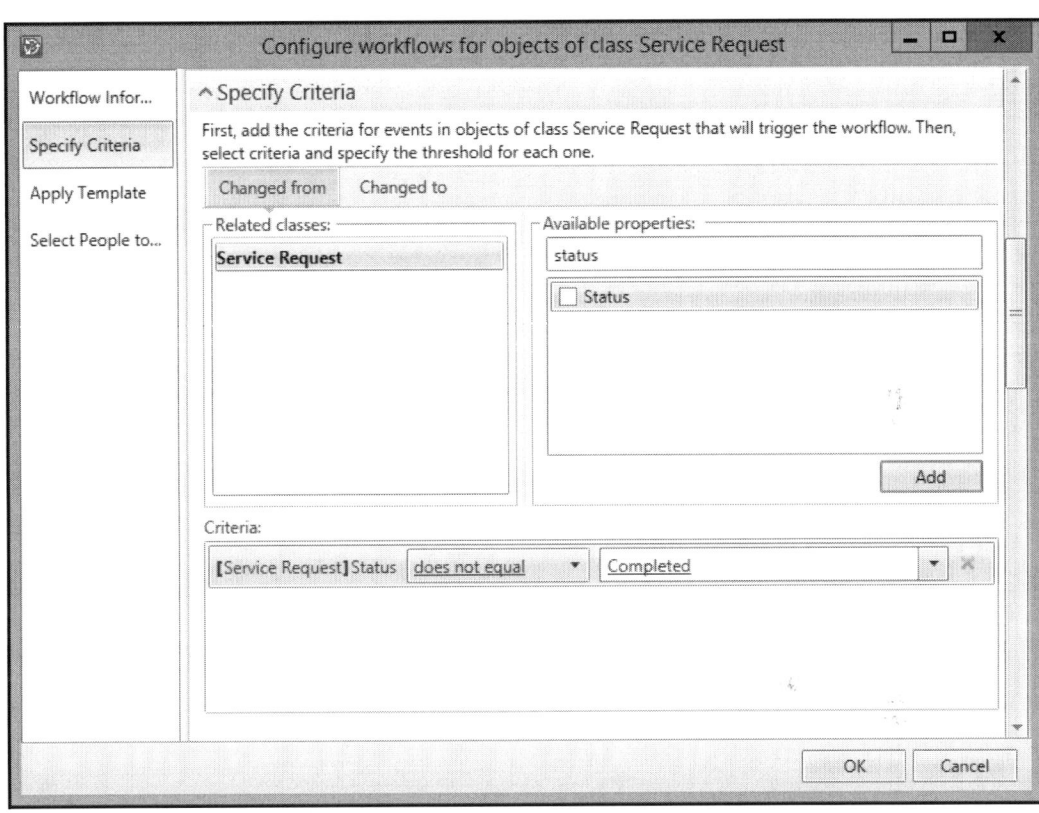

8. Specify the criteria **Changed to, Status, equals,** and **Completed** in the **Specify Criteria** page:

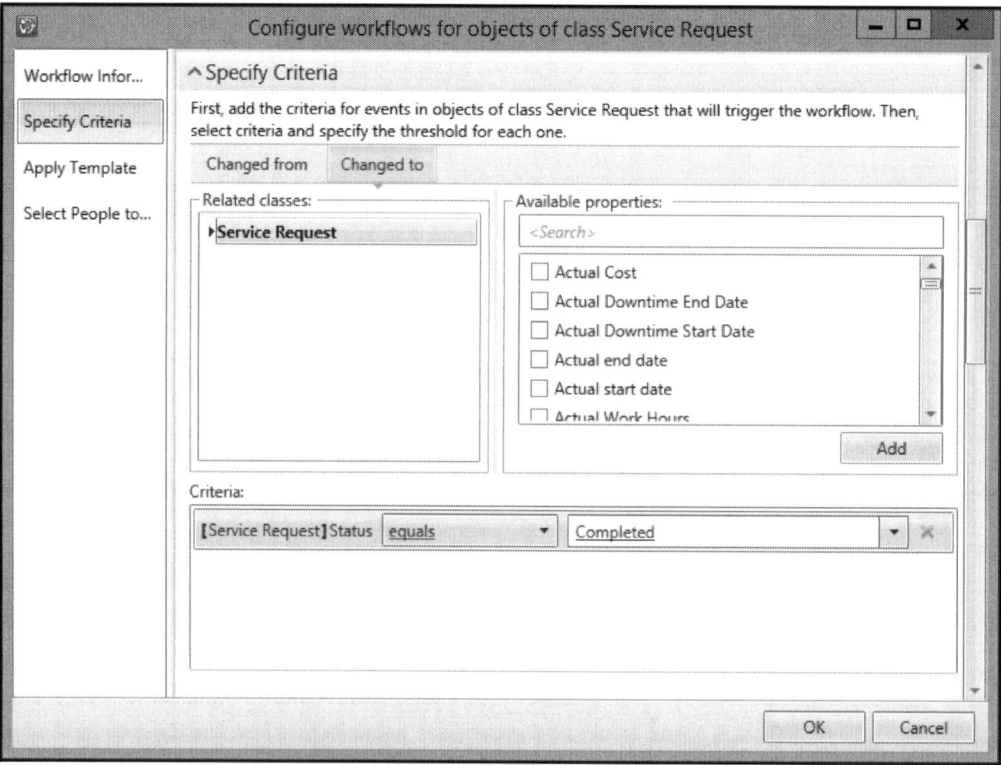

9. Click on **Next** in the **Specify Criteria** page.
10. Do not select a template in the **Apply Template** page.
11. Click on **Next** in the **Apply Template** page.
12. Check the **Enable notification** checkbox in the **Select People to Notify** page.
13. Choose **Affected User** from the **User** drop-down list.
14. Choose the message notification template you created before starting this recipe from the **Message template** drop-down list.

15. Click on **Add**:

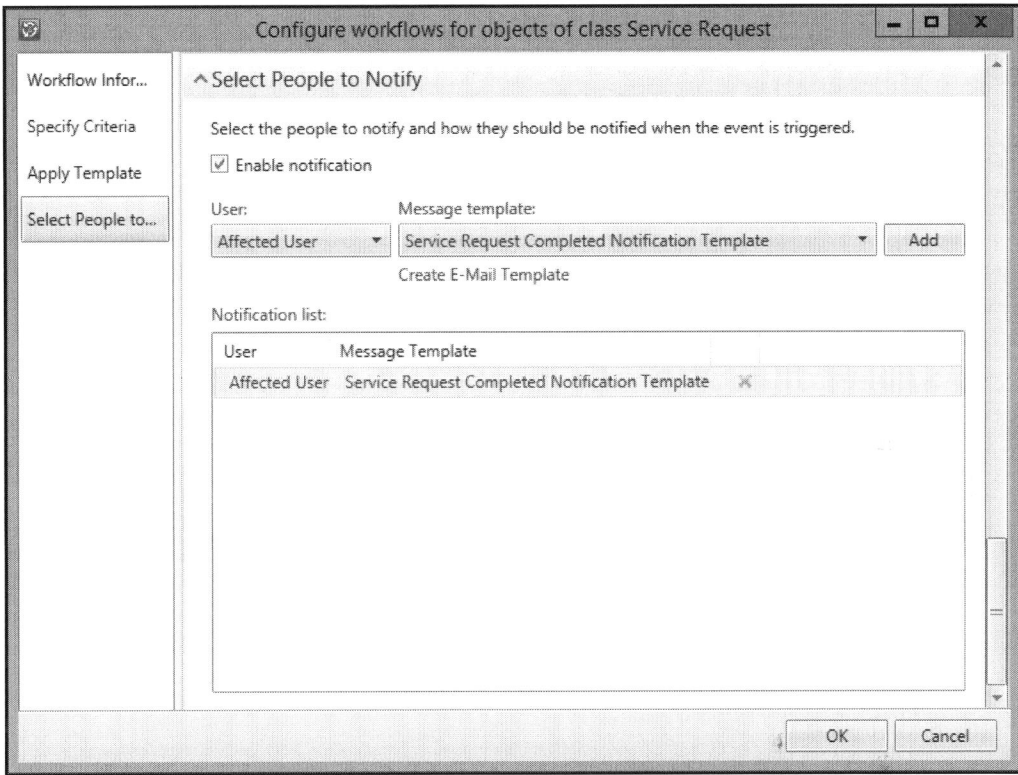

16. Click **Next** on the **Select People to Notify** page.
17. Verify the **Summary** page and then click on **Create**.
18. Click on **Close** in the **Completion** page.
19. The workflow will be visible in the list in the **Configure Workflows** window.
20. Click on **OK** to close the **Configure Workflows** window.

How it works...

The SCSM 2016 workflow engine checks in intervals to see if a condition of a defined workflow is met. If the status of a Service Request is changed from **not Completed** to **Completed,** the workflow we created in this recipe will be executed. The specified e-mail template will be used to send a message to the requester (the affected user). The requester will be informed that his Service Request is completed.

There's more...

In SCSM 2016, you can configure additional notification workflows based on the status of Service Requests.

Sending different notifications regarding a Service Request

Based on different criteria in additional workflows and different templates, the end user can also be informed if a Service Request fails (for instance, if a Service Request is "rejected" in the "Review Activity" step, for some reason).

Notification for activities in Service Requests

To send notifications on different types of activity (Review and Manual Activities), take a look at Chapter 8, *Designing and Configuring Change Management and Release Management*. There are some recipes to notify the reviewer (Review Activity) or the implementer (Manual Activity).

See also

The TechNet Library: How to View Workflow Success or Failure, at https://technet.micr osoft.com/en-us/system-center-docs/sm/manage/admin-how-to-view-workflow-succ ess-or-failure.

6
Deploying and Configuring the HTML5 Self-Service Portal

In this chapter, we will cover:

- Choosing the right deployment model
- Deploying the HTML5 Self-Service Portal
- Configuring permissions
- Configuring cache settings
- Customizing the Self-Service Portal
- Customizing the Self-Service Portal further

Introduction

In this chapter, we will look at recipes on how to design, deploy, configure, and customize the Service Manager HTML5 based Self-Service Portal.

On November 5, 2015, Microsoft released a new HMTL5 based Self-Service Portal for System Center Service Manager. This was released via Service Manager Update Rollup 8. The link for the HTML5 portal is here:

```
http://www.microsoft.com/en-in/download/details.aspx?id=49556
```

If you have Service Manager 2012 R2 with the appropriate update rollups you will need to install the portal from that link. If you have Service Manager 2016 it is included.

Microsoft moved to a faster cadence of releasing updates to the entire System Center suite a few years ago. Not only do they release fixes in the update rollups, but also new features and functionality, hence the release of this new portal via an update rollup.

Anyone that has been working with Service Manager for a while knows that the portal has left much to be desired. The old Service Manager portal was a group of Silver Light plugins that lived in SharePoint 2010. Therefore, it was exciting news to hear about the release of the new portal.

The new HTML5 Self-Service Portal has the following advantages over the previous portal:

- A modern user interface and a new service catalog with easy-to-use navigation that is based on HTML5
- It works in any browser and works well on mobile devices
- Announcements have been brought back to the portal
- The knowledge articles are now rendered in HTML, meaning they support rich text and images and don't force the user to leave the browser
- Caching technology that improves the portal performance reducing calls sent back to the database
- Ability to do rich customizations
- Ability to access direct URLs for Self-Service Portal pages
- The new portal supports the following web browsers:
    - Microsoft Edge
    - Microsoft Internet Explorer 10 and 11
    - Mozilla Firefox 42 and later
    - Google Chrome 46 and later

NOTE: The Self-Service Portal needs a screen resolution above 1024 X 768.

Choosing the right deployment model

The Service Manager HTML5 Self-Service Portal has three deployment topologies that are possible. It is important to understand the differences of these deployment to determine the one that aligns best to your environment.

Getting ready

Make sure that Service Manager is up and running and that you have sufficient privileges to the management server running the SDK. In order to complete this and the rest of the recipes in this chapter, you need to be a member of the Administrator user role within Service Manager.

How to do it…

The Service Manager Self-Service Portal can be deployed in a topology that meets your needs. The three deployment topologies are as follows:

1. Single server.

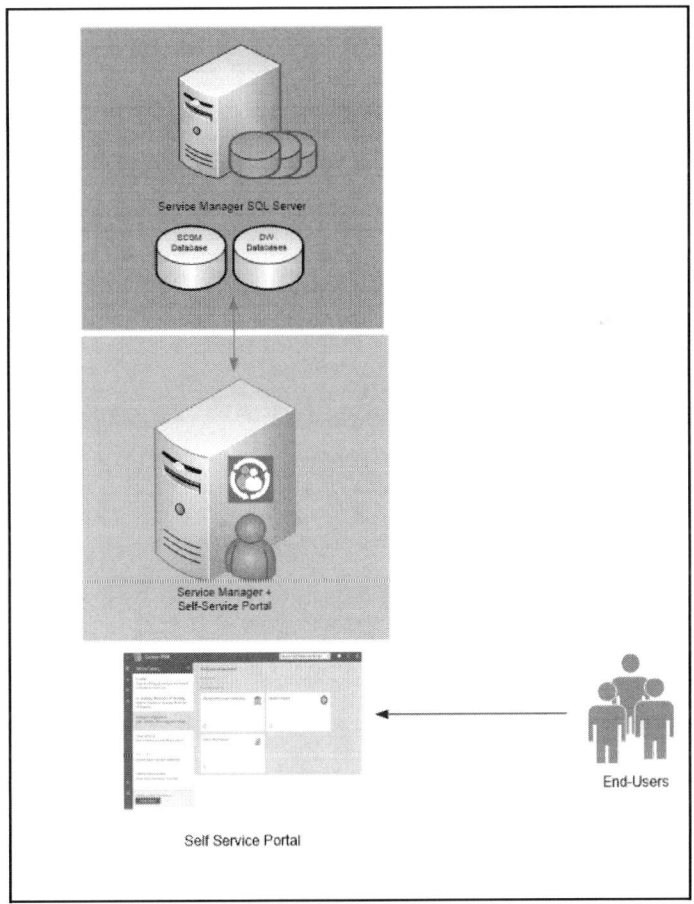

- The single server topology should be used when you want to have an all-in-one deployment of the Service Manager HTML5 Portal. The topology consists of deploying this single server as a management server in the management group and the portal. The major benefit of doing this is that the portal authenticates locally with the Service Manager SDK service and then talks directly to the Service Manager database. This simplifies the process and is by far the easiest.

2. Standalone Self Service Portal deployment.

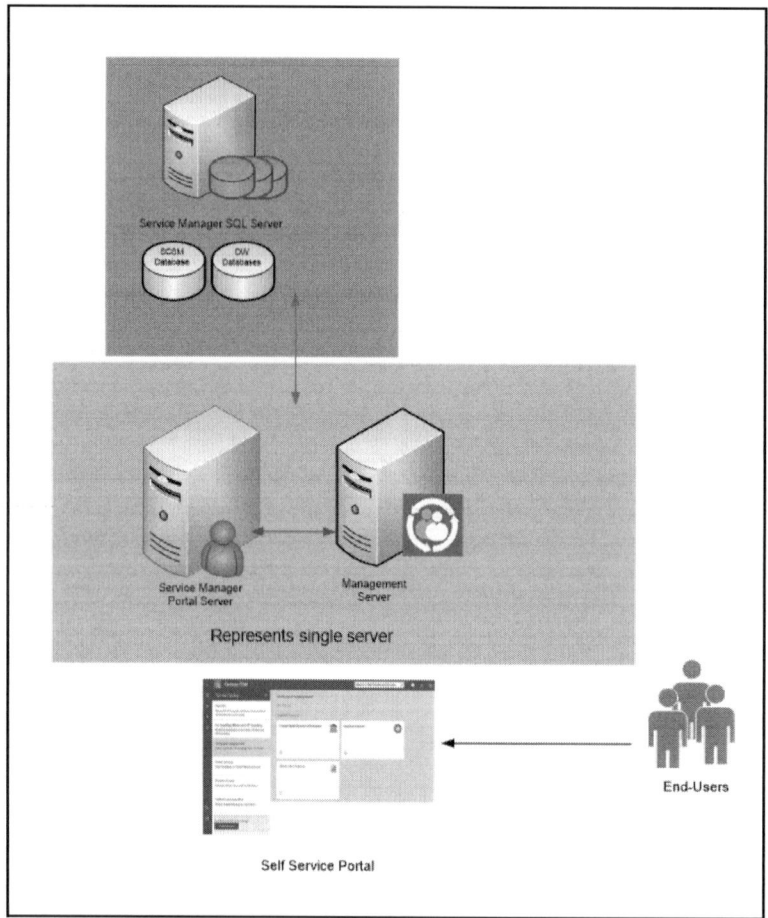

- The standalone server installs the HTML5 portal on its own server keeping the management server separate. You can use existing management servers. In this topology Kerberos will be used for authentication to the management server.

3. Load balanced web farm.

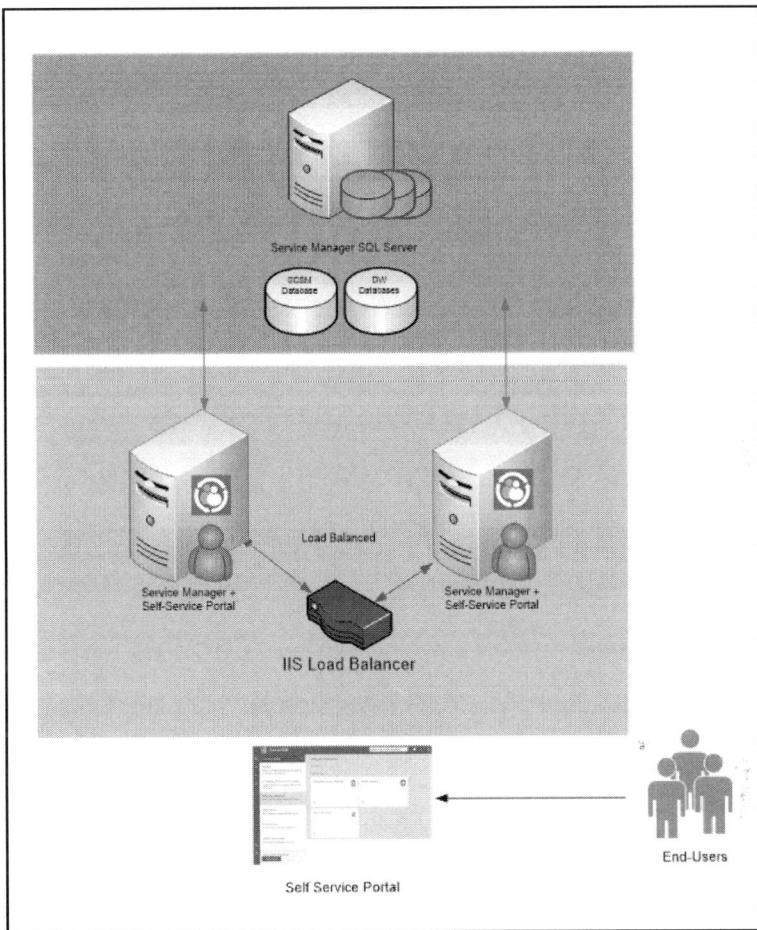

- The load balanced topology is a popular choice because it gives you the ability to have high availability and load balancing in your portal deployment. The load balancing in this topology can be managed by any load balancer such as by IIS, an F5, or Kemp. Much like the single server deployment, the portal server will contain a management server install of Service Manager plus the new HTML5 portal. Utilizing this topology gives you load balancing and high availability, but also requires more servers.

How it works...

The HTML5 Self-Service Portal (SSP) is a standard IIS website created using ASP.NET MVC Razor, Bootstrap with support from CSS, and JavaScript.

The new portal, while caching data on the web server for performance, does not persist data locally, making it easy to deploy as a load balanced web farm.

There are no additional services that get installed with configuration of the utilized management server that are stored in `web.config`, making it easy to separate, co-locate, or change the SDK server the portal is pointed to at any time.

Windows authentication is used by default and therefore provides a single sign-on experience for end users.

Deploying the HTML5 Self-Service Portal

Installing Service Manager's HTML5 Self-Service Portal is a straightforward process. Before deployment you should know the deployment topology you want to go with, you will also need to ensure that you have met all the prerequisites.

Getting ready

Make sure that Service Manager is up and running and that you install the portal using an account that has the administrator role in Service Manager. Ensure that you meet the following hardware and software requirements.

Hardware requirements for the new Self-Service Portal are as follows:

System Center 2012 R2 servers	Processor (min)	Processor (rec)	RAM (min)	RAM (rec)	Hard drive space (min)	Hard drive space (rec)
Self-Service Portal + Secondary Service Manager (Recommended)	8-Core 2.66 GHz CPU	8-Core 2.66 GHz CPU	16 GB	32 GB	80 GB	80 GB
Self-Service Portal (Standalone)	4-Core 2.66 GHz CPU	8-Core 2.66 GHz CPU	8 GB	16 GB	80 GB	80 GB

Software requirements are as follows:

- Windows Server 2012 R2

How to do it...

Install the HTML5 Self-Service Portal prerequisites. The prerequisites consist of the following:

- IIS Web Server
- .NET 3.5
- HTTP activation
- ASP.NET 4.5

The following role services under Web Server Role (IIS) also need to be installed:

- Basic authentication
- Windows authentication
- Application development:
- .NET Extensibility 4.5, ASP
- ASP.NET 4.5

A shortcut to adding all the prerequisites is to add them via an elevated PowerShell session by running the following PowerShell code:

```
Install-WindowsFeature -Name Web-Server, Web-ASP, Web-Asp-Net, Web-Asp-
Net45, Web-Net-Ext45, Web-Windows-Auth, Web-Basic-Auth, Web-Mgmt-Tools,
Web-Mgmt-Console, NET-HTTP-Activation, NET-Framework-45-Features
```

Next, the actual portal needs to be installed. To do this, follow these steps:

1. Launch the Service Manager Setup Wizard by clicking on the **SetupWizard.exe** in the setup folder from your download.
2. Choose **Service Manager Self Service Portal** under the **Install (Optional)** section of the splash screen.
3. Enter your name or another name, enter your organization name, check the license terms box to accept the EULA, and then click **Next**.
4. Change the desired installation location or leave the default and click **Next**.
5. Review the System check results to make sure everything is OK. If there are any issues resolve them and rerun the check. Once everything is OK, click **Next**.

6. On the **Configure the Self Service Portal Server** screen, provide the following information and then click **Next**:

- A name for the IIS Website
- The Service Manager management server name (FQDN or BIOS)
- The desired portal port (typically 80 or 443 if using SSL)
- If using SSL check the enable SSL box and select the SSL certificate to use

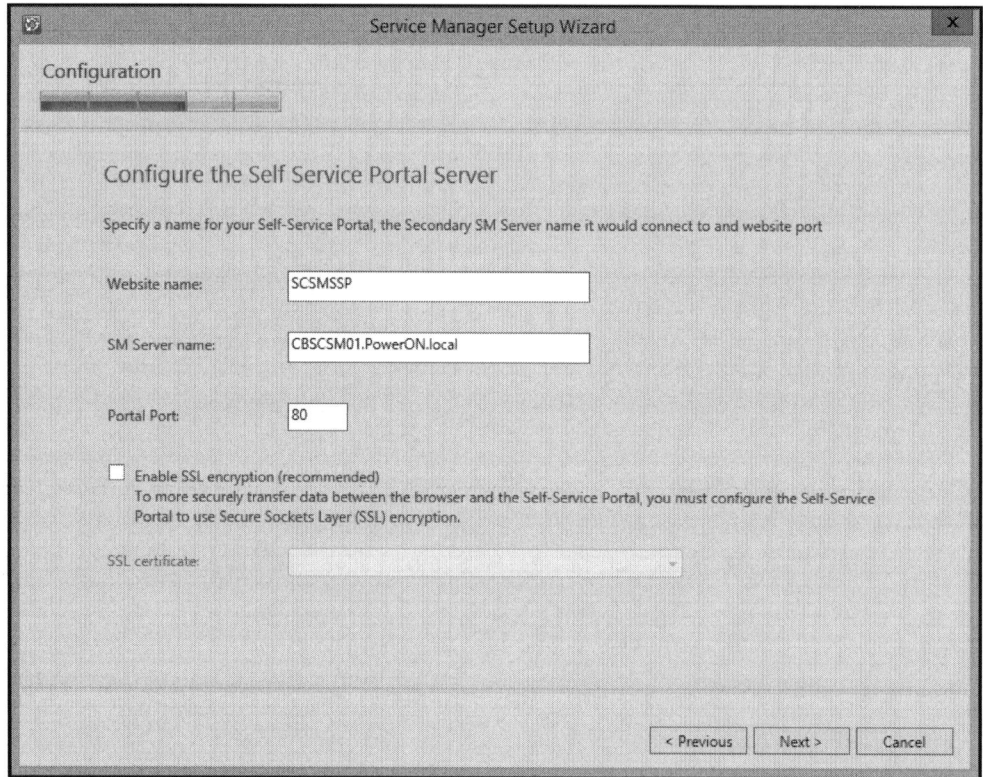

7. On the **Configure the account for the Self Service Portal** screen, select an account that the portal will use to run. It is recommended to use a domain account.

8. Test the credentials and then click **Next**.

9. On the Diagnostic and usage data notification information screen, you will see a notification that Diagnostic and usage data is sent to Microsoft by default. Click **Next** to continue.

If you want to turn this off for the Self Service Portal, it has to be done in the `web.config` file by changing the line `EnableTelemetry` from `true` to false.

10. You may be presented with a screen asking to select either to automatically install Microsoft updates for the Service Manager portal or not. Choose an option and click **Next**.

Updates for Service Manager are not released via the MU, WSUS channels at present so this option has little impact on Service Manager.

11. Review the **Installation summary** screen and then click **Install** when you are ready to proceed.

The setup should continue and you will see a setup completed successfully or failed screen. If the setup fails, click on the **Open the Setup Log** link and review the log for details on why the setup failed.

How it works...

The installation will create a new IIS website, bound to the port and installed in the directory chosen during the setup wizard.

An Application Pool is also created and run under the user context chosen during the setup wizard.

This website is then accessible for end users to browse to and will show any Service Offerings and Request Offerings that have been scoped to the end users.

An "out of the box" installation will have default brandings and information related to Microsoft and one of the first tasks should be to customize this for your organization.

See Customizing the Self-Service Portal recipe in this chapter for more information on these tasks.

There's more...

If attempting to upgrade the 2012 R2 HTML5 portal released with UR8 to the 2016 release, you must first ensure that a hotfix has first been installed.

You can find SSP Upgrade Fix, which will prep the portal for upgrade here:

`https://www.microsoft.com/en-us/download/details.aspx?id=54060`.

As an alternative to deploying the Self-Service Portal via the GUI wizard, you can do this via command line. To deploy the portal via command line, use the following syntax:

```
SetupWizard.exe /Install:SelfServicePortal /silent /accepteula
/CustomerExperienceImprovementProgram:No /EnableErrorReporting:No
/PortalWebSiteName:<Portal Name> /SMServerName:<SDK Server Name>
/PortalWebSitePort:<PortNumber> /PortalAccount:<domain>\<user>\<pwd>
```

Configuring permissions

The HTML5 portal is a Role Based Access capable portal. This means that the services offered to the end users can be varied and controlled based upon the groups the users are members of.

As a part of configuring the HTML5 portal you will need to set up permissions to control what users can see. Configuration of the portal permissions are done inside Service Manager within the service catalog, catalog items groups, and user role areas.

Getting ready

Make sure that Service Manager is up and running, the HTML5 portal is installed, and that you are using an account that has the administrator role in Service Manager.

How to do it...

To set up permission for the portal in a nutshell we need to create a catalog group, add all the Service Offerings and Requests we want to be shown in that group, create a user role and give it access to the catalog group, and lastly add users to the new user role.

After all of that is completed, users will see the intended service offerings and request offerings within the HTML5 portal. In order to set this up, follow these steps:

Setting up the catalog group

1. Start the Service Manager console and go to the **Library** workspace.
2. Right-click **Groups** and select **Create a Catalog Group**.
3. If the **Before You Begin** page of the wizard is shown, click **Next**.
4. Enter a name for the new Group and choose to store the group in either an existing management pack or create a new custom management pack within which to store the group.

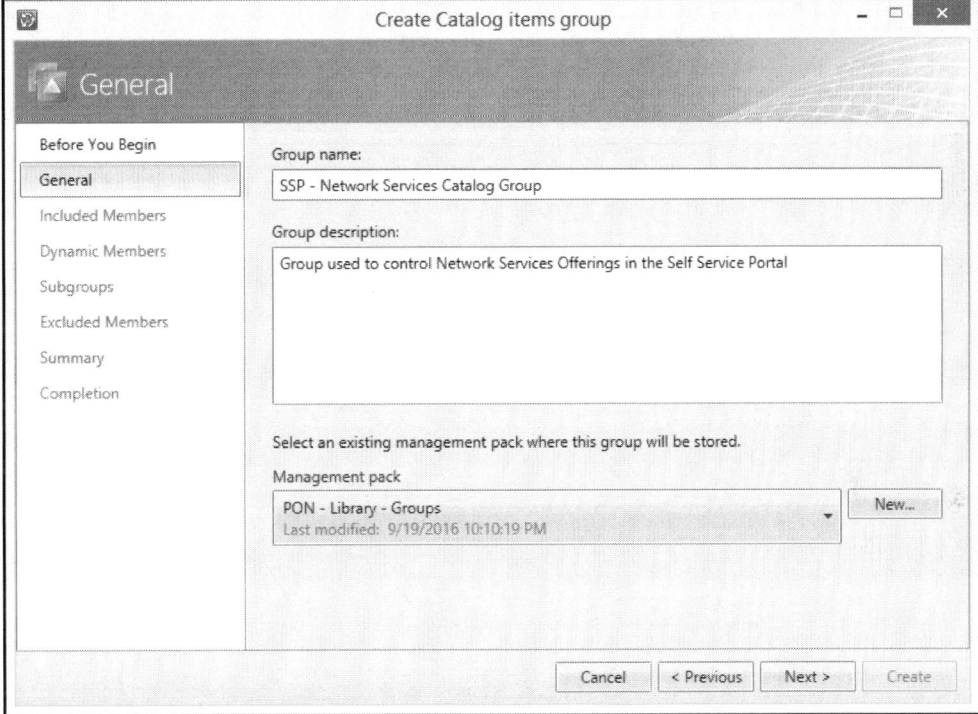

5. Click **Next**.
6. On the **Included Members** page click on **Add...**.

7. Select the Service Offerings and Requests that you want users of this new group to view, for this example we are choosing items relating to network services.

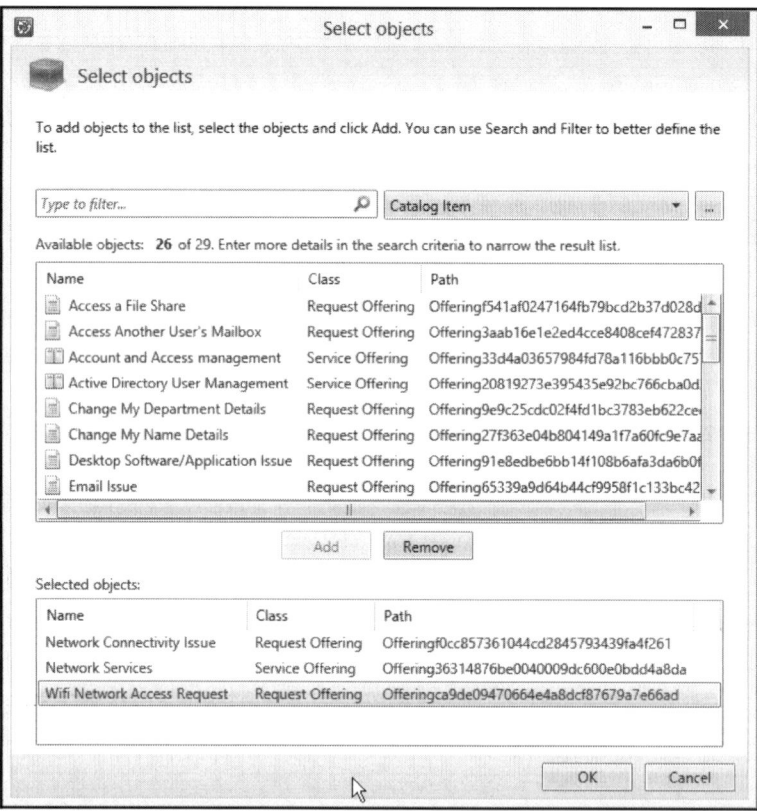

8. On the **Dynamic Members**, **Subgroups**, and **Excluded Members** pages of the wizard, click **Next** until you reach the **Summary** screen, and then click **Create**.
9. Once the catalog group has been created, click **Close**.

Setting up the User Role

1. Navigate to the Administration workspace | **Security** | **User Roles** node within the Service Manager console.
2. On the right-hand side, click on **Create User Role,** and then select **End User**.
3. If prompted with the **Before You Begin** screen of the wizard, click **Next**.
4. Give the user role a name, such as **Self Service Portal Users**.

5. On the **Management** Packs screen, select the Management pack(s) that contain the Service Offerings, Request Offerings, and the catalog groups you want to scope to the users.

 If in doubt, use the **Select All** option at the bottom of the Wizard page. Be aware though that this will not scope the next pages in the wizard down any further, meaning you will have more items to wade through to find the ones you want.

6. Click **Next** on the **Queues** screen of the wizard, accepting the default of **All work items can be accessed**.
7. Click **Next** on the **Configuration item Groups** screen of the wizard, accepting the default of **All configuration items can be accessed**.
8. On the **Catalog item Groups** screen, select **Provide access to only the selected groups**, and only choose the catalog group that was created in earlier steps.

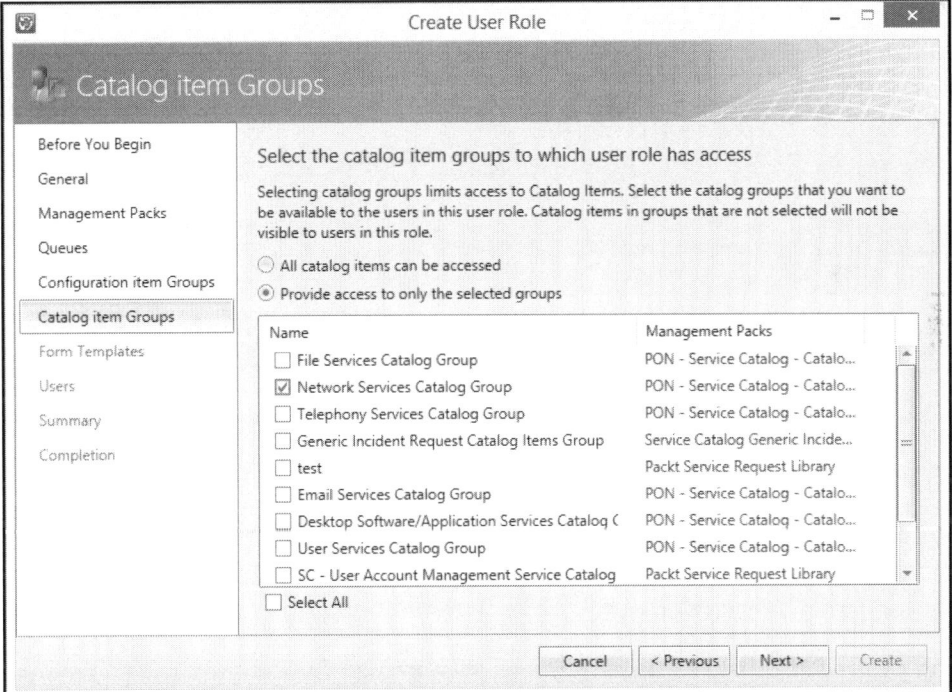

9. Click **Next**.
10. Click **Next** on the **Form Templates** screen of the wizard, accepting the default of **All forms can be accessed**.

11. **11.** On the **Users** screen, add the user/s and or groups from Active Directory that you want to have access to the Service Offerings and Request Offerings that were added to the catalog group and this Security Role, and then click **Next**.
12. Review the information on the **Summary** screen and then click **Create**.
13. Once the Security Role has been created, click **Close**.

How it works...

After you have gone through the previous steps you can log into the Service Manager HMTL5 portal as one of the users you just added to the new user role to see the intended Service Offerings and Request Offerings.

There's more...

NOTE: When creating the Catalog items group, if only Service Offerings and no Request Offerings are added, nothing will show up on the HTML5 portal. It is required to add Request Offerings for them to display along with Service Offerings.

Configuring cache settings

The new Service Manager HTML5 Self-Service Portal comes complete with caching technology. This caching technology ensures faster speeds for the end users that are using the portal. The caching technology consists of two types.

The first type is a user-specific cache. This is called **UserCacheTimeout**. Think about this in terms of status of requests a user has put in, comments on requests, and more.

The second type is a generic data cache used to cache global data that is shared among all users, think of images, icons, the service catalog, and more. This is called **DataCacheTimeout**. `DataCacheTimOut` by default is set to `1800` seconds (30 minutes).

Overall, having caching technology is good. There are times when an admin will make a change in the service catalog and needs this to show right away on the portal. Well the cache needs to be cleared or settings dialed back so they show sooner. This recipe will show you how to access the cache settings to clear cache or adjust settings.

Getting ready

Make sure that Service Manager is up and running, the HTML5 portal is installed, and that you are using an account that has the administrator role in Service Manager. You will also need access to IIS on the server/s hosting the HTML5 portal.

How to do it...

Clearing the HTML5 portal cache

Simply run **IISReset** from an elevated Command Prompt. Note that this will temporarily take the HTML5 portal down. The website will be unavailable during this time. The IISReset is normally a fast process. It is not recommended to perform this during business hours or high traffic times.

Modifying the cache settings

1. On the web server that is hosting the HTML5 portal, open IIS Manager.
2. Navigate to the HTML5 portal site within IIS.
3. Double-click the Application Settings for the site. The **Application Settings** configuration pane should open.
4. Go ahead and modify. You can modify **DataCacheTimeOut** or the **UserCacheTimeOut** settings as needed to increase or decrease the cache time refresh interval.

Customizing the Self-Service Portal

After the Service Manager HTML5 portal is deployed, there is typically a need to customize the look and feel of the portal. One of the many benefits of this new portal versus the old Silverlight portal is that it is easier to customize.

Customizing the portal consists of officially supported customizations and customizations that can be done, but are not officially supported. In this recipe, we will cover just the basic supported customization.

The main difference between the officially supported customizations and other types of customizations is that the official ones are guaranteed by Microsoft and will stay intact through updates and upgrades. Any customizations not on the official supported list may not survive an update or upgrade, therefore it is critical to back them up.

Here is a link to Microsoft's blog on the officially supported customizations:

```
https://blogs.technet.microsoft.com/servicemanager/2016/03/15/basic-ui-customiz
ation-in-new-self-service-portal-html5
```

Now let's explore some recipes on customizing the HTML5 portal.

Getting ready

Make sure that Service Manager is up and running, the HTML5 portal is installed, and that you are using an account that has the administrator role in Service Manager as well as a local administrator on the web server.

How to do it...

There are many customizations you can make to the new HTML5 portal. We will list the most common customizations.

General customizations

For general customizations such as title, logo, number, and e-mail, you will need to edit the `web.config` file:

1. Find the section: `<!- Customizable fields starts here ->`

Title

1. To change the title of the portal (seen at the top along the default blue bar as **Self-Service Portal**), find the following: `<add key="CompanyName" value=" Self-Service Portal"/>`
2. Change the value text to something that your end users will identify with, for example, "IT Service Desk Portal".

Logo

1. To change the logo of the portal (seen at the top left of the default blue bar as the Microsoft Logo by default), find the following: `<add key="CompanyLogoLocation" value="../Content/images/Logo_Transparent.png"/>`

2. Change the value text to point at the location of a PNG image file containing the logo you wish to display in the portal.

The company logo image works best as a 32×32 image.

All images are stored in: `c:\inetpub\wwwroot\SelfServicePortal\Content\images` if using the default installation path.

Service Desk phone number

1. To change the phone number displayed to users in the portal to ring for assistance (seen at the bottom of the side panel fly out), find the following: `<add key="ITPhone" value="612-532-4143"/>`

2. Change the value text to the phone number you wish to display in the portal.

Service Desk e-mail

1. To change the e-mail address displayed to users in the portal to use for assistance (seen at the bottom of the side panel fly out), find the following: `<add key="ITEmail" value="support@domain.com"/>`

2. Change the value text to the e-mail address you wish to display in the portal.

How it works...

These easy, general customizations are the main ones supported by Microsoft and are all contained within the single `web.config` file.

They are the first ones to start with and they enable a quick and easy customization of the portal to make it feel more like it belongs within your organization.

There's more…

The next recipes within this chapter will explorer further customizations that can be done, including some that are not on the officially supported list in terms of continuity of customizations across updates and upgrades.

Customizing the Self-Service Portal further

Customizing the portal consists of officially supported customizations, and customizations that can be done, but are not officially supported. In this recipe, we will cover both.

The main difference between the officially supported customizations and other types of customizations is that the official ones are guaranteed by Microsoft and will stay intact through updates and upgrades. Any customizations not on the official supported list may not survive an update or upgrade; therefore it is critical to back them up.

Here is a link to Microsoft's blog on the officially supported customizations:

```
https://blogs.technet.microsoft.com/servicemanager/2016/03/15/basic-ui-customiz
ation-in-new-self-service-portal-html5
```

Now let's explore some recipes on customizing the HTML5 portal.

Getting ready

Make sure that Service Manager is up and running, the HTML5 portal is installed, and that you are using an account that has the administrator role in Service Manager as well as a local administrator on the web server.

How to do it…

There are many customizations you can make to the new HTML5 portal. This recipe will show some different customizations that can be done within different areas and using different methods.

Lower-left side of fly out menu

To change the lower-left side of the menu shown in the following screenshot, above and beyond simply editing the values in `web.config`, try the following:

1. Navigate in Windows Explorer to `c:\inetpub\wwwroot\SelfServicePortal\Views\Shared` (assuming the portal is installed in the default location).
2. Open the `Sidebar.cshtml` file in Notepad or a code editor.
3. Find the following section:

```
<div class="side_nav_bottom">
<div class="side_nav_report">
<div>@Resources.SelfServicePortalResources.PoweredBy :
</div>
<img src="~/Content/images/msft_logo.png" alt="Microsoft"
style="max-width: 12em;" />
```

4. Modify the `<img src="~/Content/images/msft_logo.png" alt="Microsoft" style="max-width: 12em;" />` line to reference a logo image file of your choice, for example, `<img src="~/Content/images/logo1.png" alt="Private Cloud" style="max-width: 12em;" />`.

The Powered By: logo image works best as a 36×26 image.

All images are stored in: `c:\inetpub\wwwroot\SelfServicePortal\Content\images` if using the default installation path.

1. Find the next two lines within this same code section:

```
<div>@Resources.SelfServicePortalResources
.CantFindSolution</div>
<div>@Resources.SelfServicePortalResources
.ContactUs</div>
```

2. Comment them out by adding <!-before the line and –> after:

```
<!--<div>@Resources.SelfServicePortalResources
.CantFindSolution</di v>-->
<!--
<div>@Resources.SelfServicePortalResources
.ContactUs</div>- ->
```

3. Add your own descriptive text to be displayed instead, for example:

```
<div>Service Desk Contact Info:</div>
```

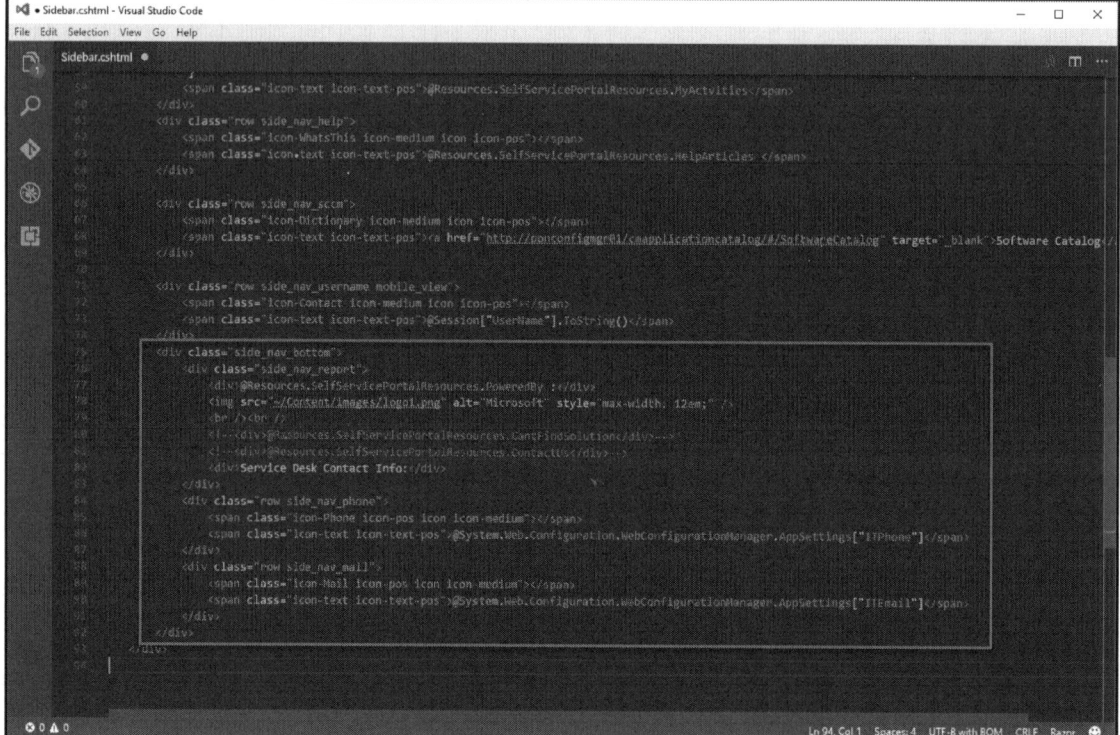

4. Save the file and reload the website to view the changes.

Icons

To modify icons do the following:

1. Go to `C:\inetpub\wwwroot\SelfServicePortal\Content\CSS` and edit the `main.css` file.

2. In this file, search for the `[class^="icon-"].icon-medium{` section.

3. Here you will see all the font icons. You can add the font icons you want to be available for use in the portals CSS. You can find icons that will work with the portal here: `http://modernicons.io/segoe-mdl2/cheatsheet`.

4. In the following screenshot, you will see an example of icon fonts that have been added, they are highlighted in yellow:

Side bar links

To add side bar links, do the following:

1. Go into `C:\inetpub\wwwroot\SelfServicePortal\Views\Shared` and modify the `Sidebar.cshtml` file.

2. In this file, under `<div class="side_nav_bar col side_menu">`, add something like the following:

```
<!- Custom side bar link Begin ->
<div class="row side_nav_IT Mission" accesskey="I" tabindex="4"
data-toggle="tooltip" >
<a href="http://portal.domain.com" target="_blank">
<font color="white">
<span class="icon-PreviewLink icon icon-pos icon-medium"></span>
</font>
</a>
</div>
<!- Custom side bar link End ->
```

Colors look and feel

Microsoft has a method for modifying the look and feel. Here we will show you another way to modify the look and feel.

The Microsoft method is to modify the `main.css` file, and it can be found here:
https://blogs.technet.microsoft.com/techlazy/2016/03/13/service-manager-new-html5-portal-basic-customizations-35-colors-and-tiles/

1. Create a new file named `custom.css` in `C:\inetpub\wwwroot\SelfServicePortal\Content\CSS` (assuming the default portal installation location).

2. Add the following code in the `custom.css` file:

```
.top_bar {
background :black
}
.top_bar .anouncement_count {
width: 1.5em;
background-color: #d2d2d2;
height: 1.5em;
border-radius: 50%;
position: absolute;
top: 5px;
```

```
right: 6px;
text-align: center;
}
.btn:hover {
background-color: green;
cursor: pointer;
}
/*media all*/
.btn {
background-color: black;
border: none;
color: white;
padding: 0.625em 2em;
margin-right: 1.5em;
font-size: 1.25em;
}
/*media all*/
[class^='icon-'].icon-fill {
color: #f00;
}
.vertical_list .list_header, .my_reg_container .list_header{
background: black;
}
/*@media screen and (min-width:1024px)*/
/*.main_body .side_nav_bar .row, .main_body .side_nav_bar_expand
.row {
height: 4em;
position: relative;
background-color: red !important;
}*/
/*@media screen and (min-width:1024px)*/
.main_body .side_nav_bar .row:hover, .main_body
.side_nav_bar_expand .row:hover {
cursor: pointer;
background-color: #777!important;
}
div[style*="background-color: rgb(37, 95, 133)"]
{
background-color : blue !important;
}
```

3. Save the CSS file.

4. From an elevated Command Prompt run IISReset to restart the self-service portal.

Custom error message

Something else that might come in handy is to have the portal produce a custom error when an error occurs. For example, you could display the service desk info with the actual error message. To show a custom error you need to modify the `Error.cshtml` file in `\inetpub\wwwroot\SelfServicePortal\Views\Shared`:

```
<hgroup>
<h1>Error.</h1>
<h2>An error occurred while processing your request. For further help
contact the service desk at support@domain.com.</h2>
</hgroup>
```

7
Working with Incident and Problem Management

In this chapter, we will cover the following topics:

- Configuring incident and problem lists
- Creating an incident template
- Creating a subscription to notify the affected user upon the creation of an incident
- Adding a task to the incident form
- Creating a view to display the problem records created in the last 30 days
- Configuring the Global Operators Group
- Downloading, installing, and configuring the Exchange Connector
- Making the description field in the incident form auto-grow
- Extending the Incident class with a new property
- Using Advanced Search to find very specific incidents

Introduction

In this chapter, we will look at recipes for two of the core processes within ITILÂ©: incident and problem management.

Any company following the ITILÂ© framework probably started their journey with the incident process, as it is one of the easiest processes to adapt and understand. Since the incident process is central to both ITILÂ© and **Service Manager** (**SCSM**), this is one of the areas where you might find yourself spending some extra time fine-tuning SCSM.

Configuring incident and problem lists

Lists are widely used in SCSM and appear in almost any form. These lists are used to offer the analysts predefined choices rather than having them enter text manually. This is really handy for fields where you want to limit the input options, to save time for the analyst and to make sure that the input is standardized.

Getting ready

Make sure that SCSM is up and running and that you have sufficient privileges to edit a list. In order to complete this and the rest of the recipes in this chapter, you need to be a member of the Author or Administrator user role within SCSM.

How to do it...

The following lists are available in incident and problem management:

- Incident Tier Queue
- Incident Status
- Incident Source
- Incident Classification
- Incident Resolution
- Problem Status
- Problem Resolution
- Problem Classification
- Problem Source
- Urgency
- Impact

Any of these lists can be configured through the Service Manager console. Here's an example of how to add a hardware option with two sub-categories to the **Problem Classification** list:

1. Open the **Service Manager Console** and go to the **Library** workspace.
2. Select **Lists** in the navigation pane.

3. To locate the **Problem Classification** list, enter `Problem classification` in the filter field, as shown in the following screenshot:

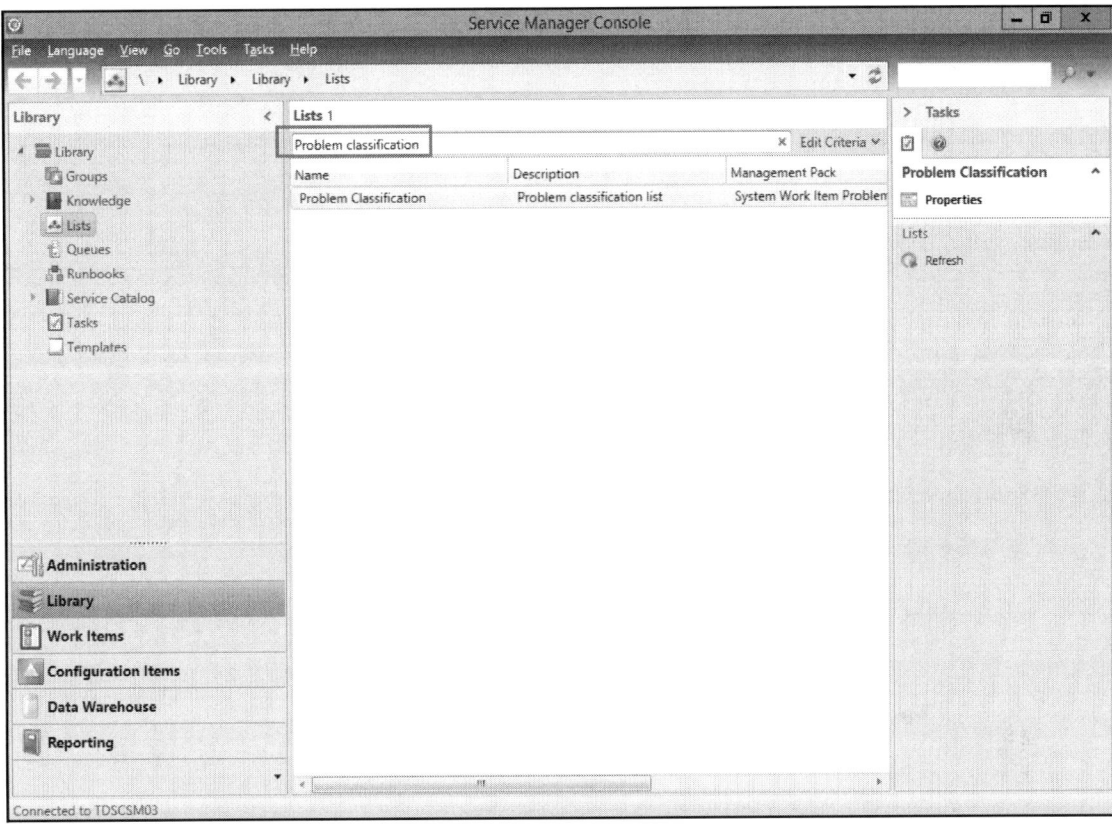

4. Double-click the **Problem classification** list to open it.
5. Click on **Add Item** to add a new value to the list.
6. At the bottom of the list, a new value named **List Value** should appear. Select this item and change the name to `Hardware`.
7. With **Hardware** still selected, click on the **Add Child** button.
8. A child item with the name **List Value** should appear under **Hardware**. Select this item and change the name to **Client**.
9. Select **Hardware** and click on **Add Child** again. Change the name of the new list item to **Server**.

10. Now select **Hardware** again and click on the **Move Up** button until the **Hardware** option is placed right under **Facilities**:

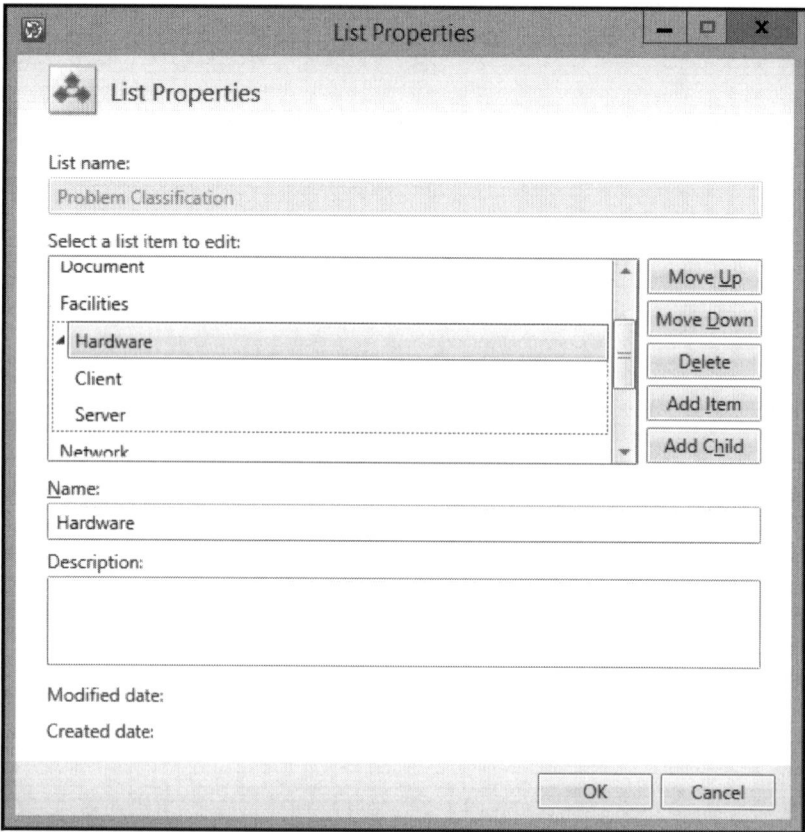

11. Click on **OK** when you are done.

How it works...

All these lists come predefined out of the box, but most of them will need to be modified by you to fit your organization and processes. Every time you edit a list, this change is reflected in a management pack. This makes it easy to work with lists in a pre-production environment and then copy them all to production by exporting, copying, and importing the management pack.

In the preceding example, all changes are stored in the management pack named **Service Manager Problem Management Configuration Library**.

There's more...

This way of working with lists applies to all lists in SCSM, and not only lists related to the incident and problem processes. If you add your own list to the system, by creating it in the Authoring Tool or by writing your own XML code, you will be able to see and edit it in the same fashion.

Renaming list items

If there's a predefined list item that you do not want, you should avoid renaming it something different that you would like to have in your list. Instead, remove the list item and add a new one. The reason for this is that if you rename an option, you are only changing the so-called display strings for that particular list item in the language that you are running the console.

 For instance, if you are running a Swedish console and rename the list item named **Configuration Data Problems** in the **Incident Classification** list to `Terminal Server Problems`, any users running a console in another language than Swedish will still see **Configuration Data Problems** in their respective language!

Impact and Urgency

When working with lists for the incident and problem processes, there are two lists that are special, **Impact** and **Urgency**. These two lists are used to calculate a priority and are shared between the two processes, which means that you will be unable to have different values in these lists for the two processes.

If you modify any of these lists, this will be reflected in the **Priority Calculation** under both Problem and **Incident Settings**:

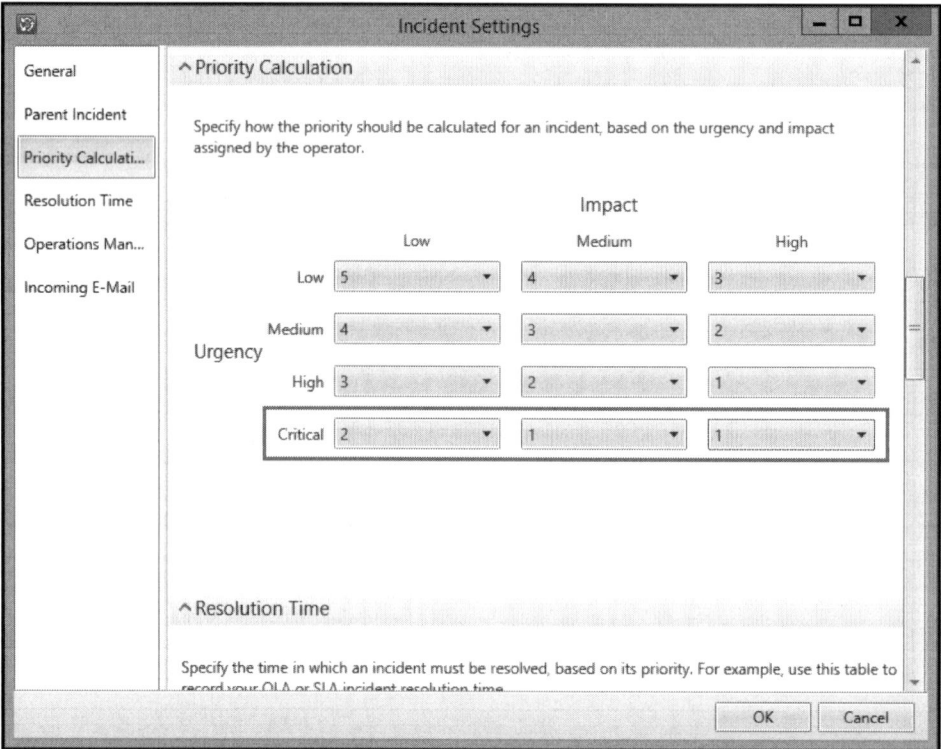

See also

- For more information regarding management packs, please see the *Creating Management Packs to save your SCSM personalization* recipe in `Chapter 2`, *Personalizing SCSM 2016 Administration*
- For more information regarding Impact, Urgency, and Priority, please see the *Configuring Priority and Urgency for your SLA targets* recipe in `Chapter 2`, *Personalizing SCSM 2016 Administration*
- For more information regarding lists, please see the *Creating Support Groups for Service Requests* recipe in `Chapter 5`, *Deploying Service Request Fulfilment*
- For more information regarding the Authoring Tool, please see *Using the SCSM Authoring Tool* in `Chapter 11`, *Extending SCSM with Advanced Personalization*

Creating an incident template

There are certain types of work item that occur frequently, and this is where the use of templates is valuable. Templates are used to speed up the creation of new work items and give us a way to standardize the information in them.

A template consists of one or more predefined properties of a certain class. For instance, an incident template used for registering local printer incidents might have the title, description, classification category, impact, and urgency predefined.

Getting ready

Make sure that SCSM is up and running and that you have sufficient privileges to create new templates.

How to do it...

As an example, we will create a template for registering local printer issues. In order to do so, follow these steps:

1. Start the **Service Manager Console** and go to the **Library** workspace.
2. Select **Templates** in the navigation pane.

3. A list of all available templates should now be displayed. Click on **Create Template** in the task pane on the right-hand side:

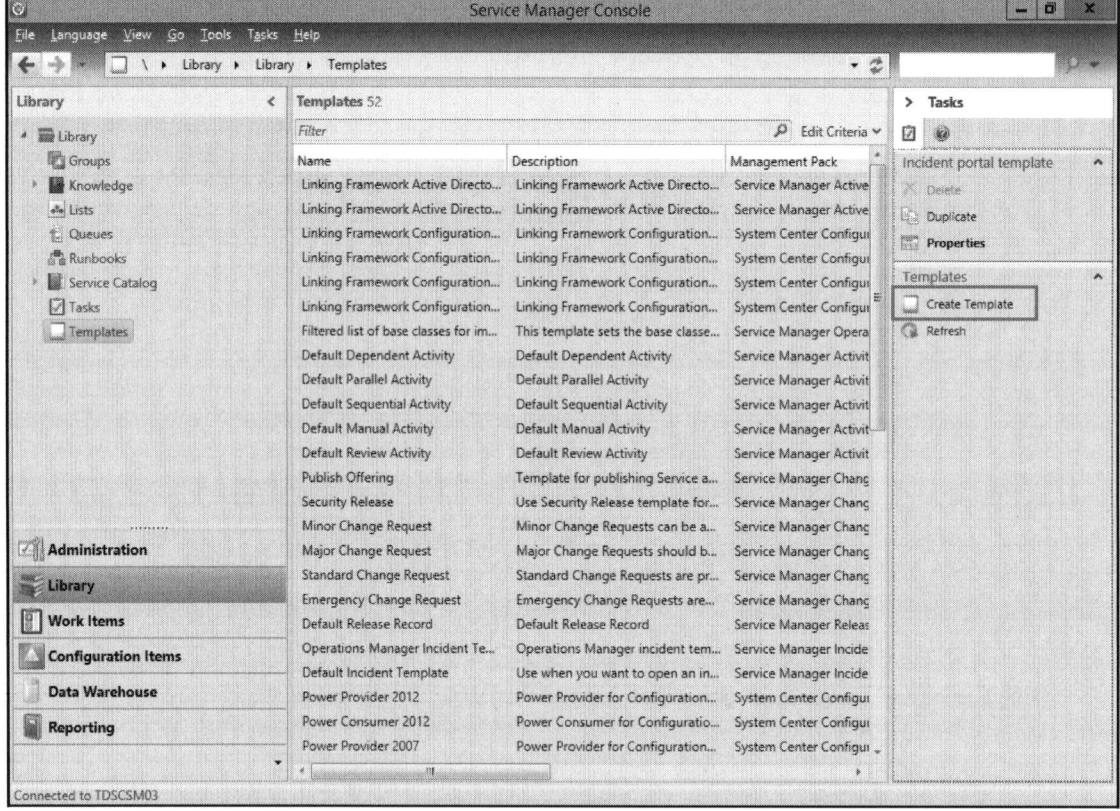

4. This will launch a new dialog form where you have to enter the **Name** and **Description** of the template. You also have to choose a targeted class and a management pack to store this template in.
5. Enter **Local Printer Incident** as the **Name** of the template.
6. Enter **Use this template to register any issues related to Local Printers** as the **Description** of the template.
7. Click on the **Browse...** button, select the **Incident** class, and click on **OK**.

8. Select a management pack to store the template in, just ensure that the selected management pack is intended to for this purpose. If there isn't a management pack for this, create a new one by clicking the **New...** button. When the desired management pack is selected, click on **OK**:

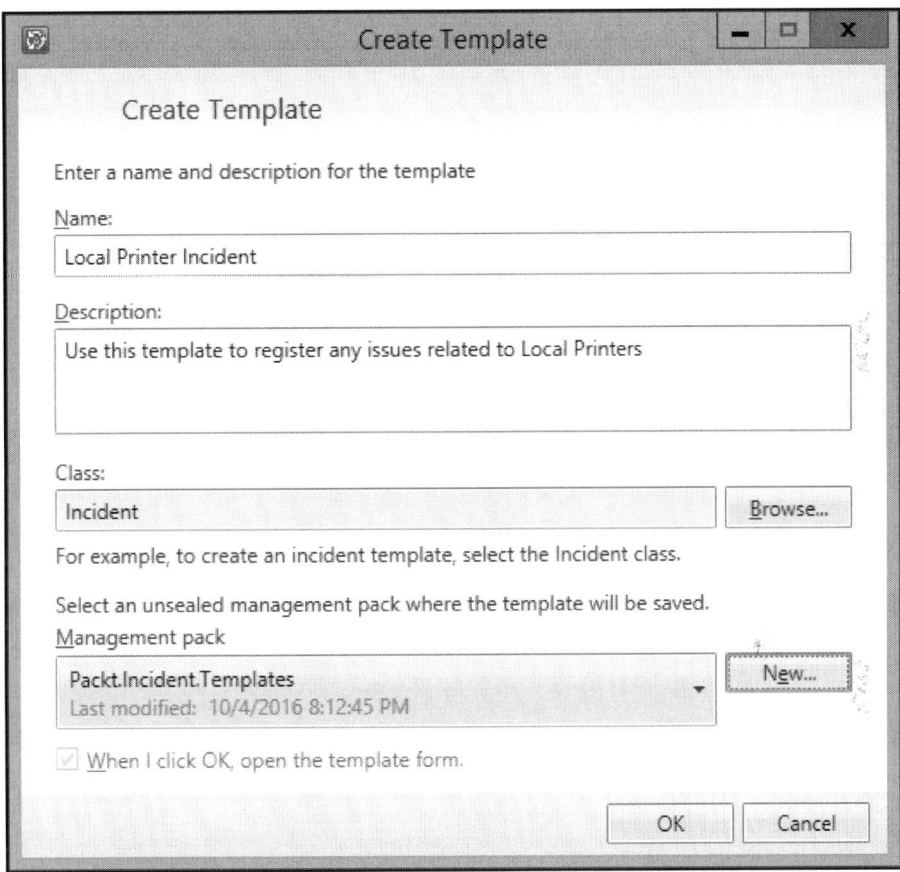

9. The Incident form should now be displayed. Enter the following information:
   - **Title**: `Local Printer issue`
   - **Classification Category**: `Printing Problems`
   - **Impact**: `Low`
   - **Urgency**: `Low`

10. Then click on **OK** to finish the creation of the template.

How it works...

After you have created a template, you can use this template to create a new incident with the **Create Incident from Template** task. If you do so, all the fields that you entered information in when creating the template will be pre-populated with that piece of information in this new incident.

It is also possible to apply a template to an already existing incident with the **Apply Template** task. Just bear in mind that all the fields that you have specified within your template will be written into the incident regardless of the information currently in those fields.

There's more...

Templates can be used in other ways as well. For instance, the Exchange Connector is using templates when creating new incidents or service requests upon receiving e-mails. In the same fashion, it also uses templates when updating existing work items.

You may also apply templates to work items from a workflow. This can be useful to route specific incidents to a person or group for instance.

 The problem management process within Service Manager does not support templates while all other work item classes does. It's possible to create templates for problems, but there is no way to actual apply these from the console.

See also

- For more information regarding the Exchange Connector, see the *Downloading, installing, and configuring the Exchange Connector* recipe in this chapter
- For more information regarding Management Packs, please see the *Creating Management Packs to save your SCSM personalization* recipe in Chapter 2, *Personalizing SCSM 2016 Administration*
- For more information regarding templates, please see the *Creating Service Request templates* recipe in Chapter 5, *Deploying Service Request Fulfillment*
- For more information regarding applying templates with workflows, see the *Routing incidents automatically using workflows* recipe in Chapter 12, *Automating Service Manager 2016*

Creating a subscription to notify the affected user upon the creation of an incident

Many IT departments often hear that they need to improve their information flow to the end users during the life cycle of a work item. To improve this, we can create subscriptions or workflows to automatically send e-mail notifications when working with work items, such as an incident. Subscriptions and workflows can be triggered when a work item fulfills a criterion. For instance, this could be when the status if an incident changes from **Active** to **Resolved**, or when the **Escalated** checkbox is checked.

Getting ready

In order to send outgoing mails from SCSM, you need to configure a notification channel. If you haven't done so, follow these steps:

1. Open the **Service Manager Console** and go to the **Administration** workspace.
2. Expand **Notifications** and select **Channels**.
3. Double-click on the **E-mail Notification Channel** to open the properties.
4. Enable e-mail notifications by checking the **Enable e-mail notifications** checkbox.
5. Enter the **Return e-mail address** (if you are using the Exchange Connector, the reply address should match the incoming address for the connector).
6. Now click on the **Add...** button.
7. Enter the **SMTP server** address and set **Authentication Mode** to **Windows Integrated**.
8. Click on **OK** to close the **Add SMTP server** dialog.
9. Click on **OK** to close the **Configure E-Mail Notification Channel** dialog.

How to do it...

In this example, we will take a look at how to create a subscription to notify the affected user that a new incident has been created. To do so, follow these steps:

1. Open the Service Manager console and go to the **Administration** workspace.
2. Expand **Notifications** and select **Subscriptions**.
3. Click on **Create Subscription** in the task pane on the right-hand side.
4. Skip the **Before You Begin** step by clicking on **Next**.

5. Enter **Incident – New Incident Notification** as the name of the subscription.

6. In the **Description** field, enter **This notification is used to notify the affected user upon creating a new incident**.

7. Make sure that the **When to notify** drop-down box has **When an object of the selected class is created** selected.

8. Click on **Browse...** next to **Targeted Class**, select the **Incident** class, and click **OK**.

9. Specify in which management pack you want to save this workflow and then click on **Next**:

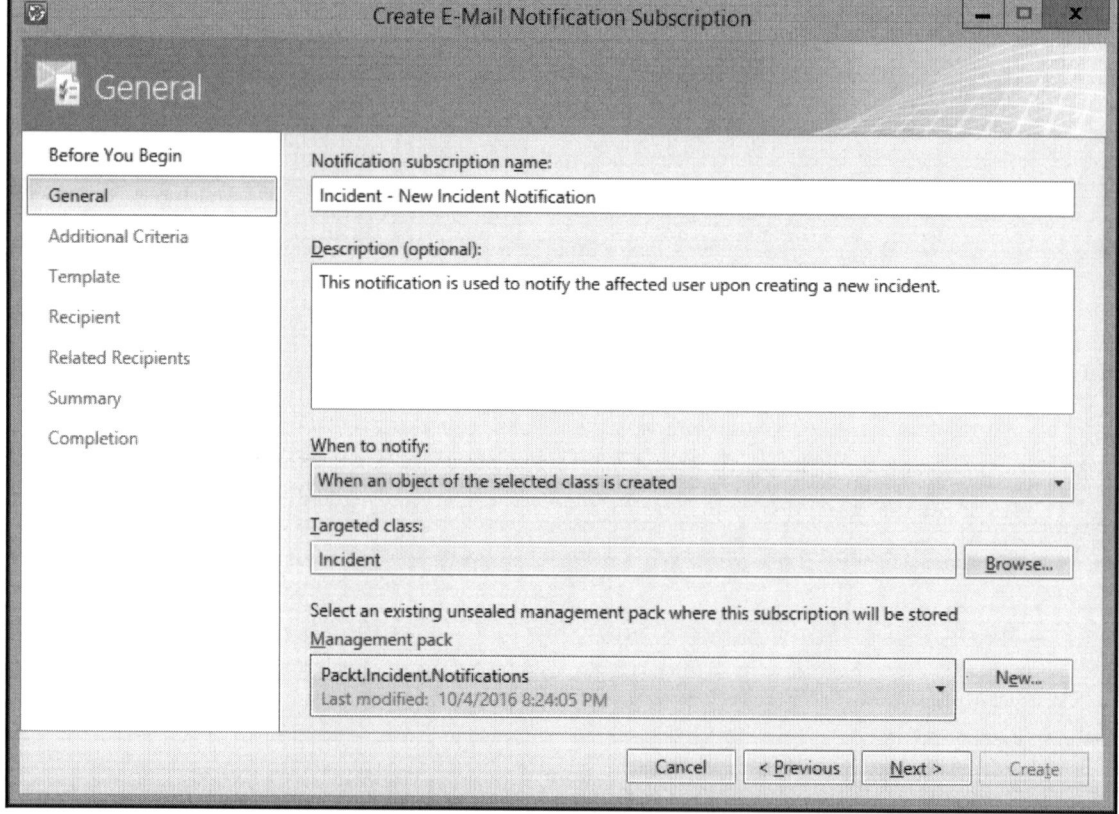

10. In the **Additional Criteria** step, don't enter anything and click on **Next**.

11. In **Template** step, click on **Select...** and select the **End User Notification Template**. Click **OK** followed by **Next** to move to the next step.

12. In the **Recipient** step, don't enter anything and click on **Next**.

13. In the **Related Recipients** step, click on **Add...** and while **Incident** is selected on the left side in the dialog box, select **Affected User** on the right side. Click **Add** to add this recipient.

14. Click on **Next** to get to the **Summary** step and then click **Create** followed by **Close**.

How it works...

Whenever a new incident is created and fulfills the criteria specified in our subscription, SCSM will send an e-mail to the affected user using the End User E-mail notification template. Since we didn't specify a criterion, this workflow will be triggered on the creation of all incidents.

There's more...

When creating the subscription as described, we used an out-of-the-box notification template to send our e-mail. Even though this works, you should consider creating your own e-mail notification templates for subscriptions and workflows. By doing so, you can specify the exact wording and format of the e-mail, and you can choose to insert properties of the actual incident that triggered the outgoing e-mail into the template.

If you are using the Exchange Connector to handle incoming e-mails, you are required to add the ID of the work item within square brackets (for instance, [IR319]) in the subject of the e-mail. By doing this, replies to notifications from the system will be added in the action log of the work item instead of creating a new work item.

If you have configured the notification channel in SCSM and created the subscription as described in the recipe, and still don't receive an e-mail, there might be an issue with your e-mail server or antivirus application. Many e-mail servers won't allow other servers to send e-mails (relay) and would require an authorizing configuration by an administrator. Additionally, some antivirus applications block outgoing e-mails from servers. You may have to configure exceptions in the relevant antivirus application to allow the SCSM workflow server to send e-mails.

Subscriptions and workflows

Subscriptions and workflows are mentioned in this recipe but we only looked at creating a subscription. However, both of these can be used to send outgoing e-mail notifications.

So, when should you use one or the other? To start with, workflows can only be created for activities, change requests, incidents, release records, and service requests, while subscriptions can be created for any class in the system (including configuration items). Next, workflows can use different notification templates for different recipients; in subscriptions, all recipients will get the same notification template. Workflows also have the ability to apply a work item template to the work item triggering the workflow, which can be very useful in certain scenarios.

Subscriptions, on the other hand, can send periodical notifications, and notifications to a certain user even if that user does not have a relation to the actual item triggering the subscription. This can be useful for sending notifications to the management team when an SLA is breached for instance.

So, the answer to the question is, it depends on the situation. If you don't know which one to use, try to stick with subscriptions as it gives you an easier overview of all the created notifications and also supports all classes in the system.

See also

- For more information regarding notification channels and notification templates, please see the *Creating formatted e-mail notification templates* and *Configuring global e-mail notification infrastructure settings* recipes in `Chapter 2`, *Personalizing SCSM 2016 Administration*
- For more information regarding workflows and notifications, please see the *Creating Service Request notifications* recipe in `Chapter 5`, *Deploying Service Request Fulfillment*

Adding a task to the incident form

Tasks are different type of action that you can perform on an object from the Service Manager console. Some tasks are essential for SCSM to work, such as the Create and Edit tasks, while other tasks are used to facilitate the troubleshooting process. A good example of this is the Ping Related Computer or Remote Desktop tasks that are available when working with incidents.

Getting ready

Make sure that SCSM is up and running and that you have sufficient privileges to create a new task.

How to do it...

In this example, we will create a custom task for executing an nslookup on a computer related to an incident:

1. Start the Service Manager console and go to the **Library** workspace.
2. Select **Tasks** in the navigation pane.
3. If you have created any tasks previously, these tasks should now be displayed, otherwise you should get the **No items found** message. To create a new task, click on the **Create Task** console task.
4. The **Create Task** wizard should now launch. In the **Before You Begin** step, click on **Next**.
5. Enter a name for your task; in this example, we will give the task the name Nslookup.
6. As a description, enter Perform an Nslookup on a computer related to the Incident.
7. Click on the browse button marked with **...** next to **Target Class**.
8. Select the **Incident** class and click on **OK**.
9. Specify whether you want to save this task in an existing management pack or if you want to create a new one to save it in. Then click on **Next**.
10. You will now be asked to specify where this task should be visible in the console. If you don't choose anything specific here, it will only show up when an object of the selected class is selected.
11. Don't select anything and click on **Next**.
12. Now, we have to specify where the executable is located, and which parameters we want to launch the program with. In the **Full path to command** field, enter %windir%\System32\nslookup.exe.
13. Now click on the **Insert Property** button, select **About Configuration Item** on the left side of the dialog box and then enter principal name in the search field for available properties. Select **Principal Name** under the **Windows Computer** heading and click on **Add**.

14. Make sure that the checkboxes for **Log in action log when this task is run** and **Show output when this task is run** are checked. Then click on **Next**:

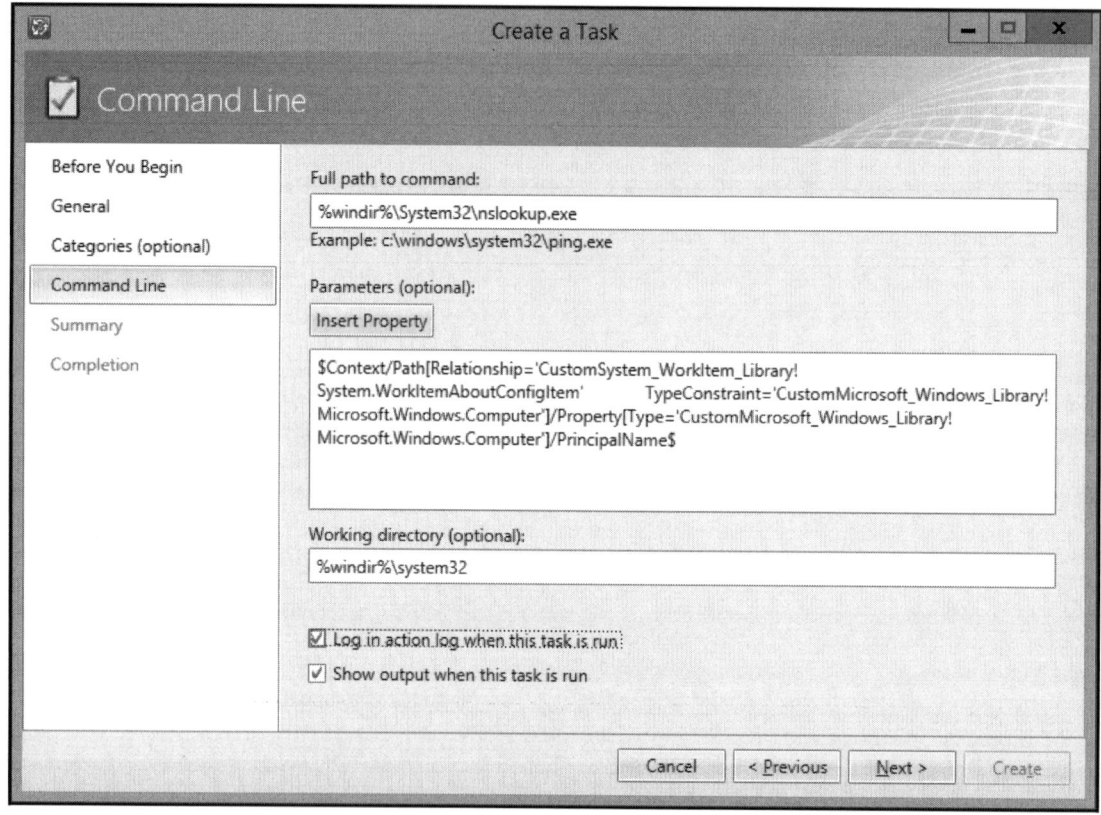

15. Review the summary, and then click on **Create** followed by **Close**.

How it works...

This task will be available in all consoles as long as the user running the console has the permissions to see it. When using the task, it will execute the `nslookup` command **from the computer running the console with the user's credentials**. This is important and something to keep in mind when creating tasks.

Before creating a new task, make sure that the executable is located in the same path on the computers where the Service Manager console is used, or is available through a network share. Otherwise the task won't work as it can't find the files.

There's more...

The tasks created from SCSM are simply an easier way of executing a command. There are, however, more advanced tasks that you create using Visual Studio. Those kinds of task require developer skill and knowledge of the Service Manager SDK, and are not covered in this book.

If your tasks are using input properties and the fields used for this don't contain any information, you will be asked to enter this manually. Additionally, if your field contains more than one object, you will be asked to select which object to run this task against.

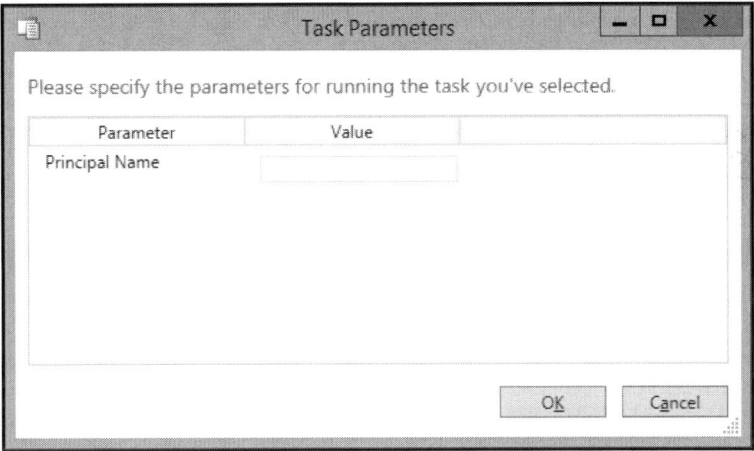

See also

- For more information on how to create custom tasks in Visual Studio, please see these two blog posts on the official Service Manager blog:
  `https://blogs.technet.microsoft.com/servicemanager/2010/02/11/tasks-part-1-tasks-overview` and

- `http://blogs.technet.com/b/ servicemanager/archive/2010/12/22/tasks-part-2-custom-console-tasks-for-create-edit-delete.aspx`

Creating a view to display the problem records created in the last 30 days

Views are used everywhere in the Service Manager console to display objects of a certain class and for a given criteria. If you take a look at the views for the problem management process, there are a few predefined views, as follows:

- Active Known Errors
- Active Problems
- Closed Problems
- My Problems
- Needing Review
- Resolved Problems

These are all good and useful views, but there's a good chance that you might want to create a couple of additional views. For instance, you might want a view that shows all the problem records that have been created in the last 30 days, regardless of their status.

Getting ready

Make sure that SCSM is up and running and that you have sufficient privileges to create a new view.

How to do it...

Here's how you create a view to display all the problem records that have been created in the last 30 days:

1. Open the **Service Manager Console** and go to **Work Items**.
2. Select **Problem Management**.
3. Click on the **Create View** task in the task pane.
4. Enter **All Problems last 30 days** as the name of the view.
5. Enter **This view displays all Problem Records created in the last 30 days** as the description.
6. Select a management pack to store this view in.
7. Go to the **Criteria** section, click on the **Browse** button, select the **Problem** class, and click on **OK**.

8. In the search field for **Available properties**, enter C**reated date**.

9. Check the **Created date** property and click on **Add**.

10. Created date should now appear in the **Criteria** section. Click on the drop-down box next to **Created date** and select **is greater than or equal to**.

11. Now check the **relative** checkbox and enter [now-30d] in the text field, as shown in the following screenshot:

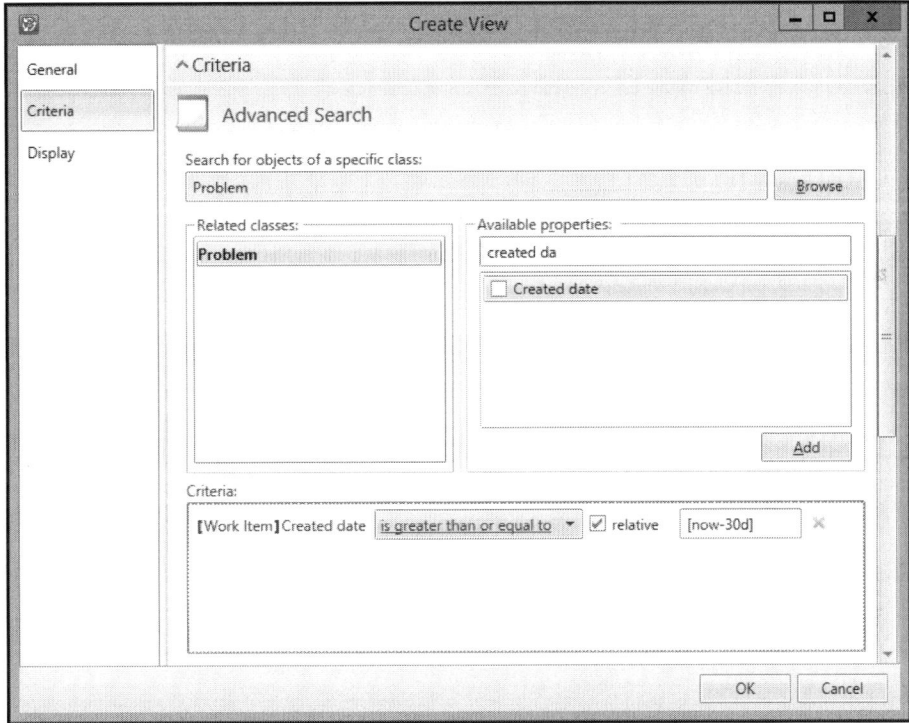

12. Next go to the **Display** section and make sure that the only columns that are selected are as follows:
    - **Created date**
    - **Id**
    - **Known Error**
    - **Status**
    - **Title**

There are two properties in the display section named ID. One of these is the actual ID of the problem request, and the other one is the internal ID (also known as GUID). Unfortunately, there is no good way to tell these apart, so if you select the wrong one, just edit the view and select the other ID instead.

13. Click on **OK** to create the view.

How it works...

The view will display all objects for the given class and criteria. In our example, we created a view targeting the Problem class. We used a special criteria property, **now**, for creating the view, which is known as a token. Because we used [now-30d], SCSM will deduct 30 days from the current date and use that as the criteria when querying the database.

There's more...

Views can be created for any class in the system using a similar series of steps. You could even create a view to display all incidents where the affected user belongs to the marketing department. In order to create such a view, you would have to base your view on a combination class instead of the regular incident class since we are traversing relationships.

When creating your view and choosing which class to target, click on the drop-down menu at the top-right corner and choose Combination classes. You will then get a list of all available combination classes. If you would like to create the view for all incidents where the affected user belongs to the marketing department, you could base your view on the incident (typical) combination class, for instance.

There's a catch in using Combination classes for your views; the bigger your combination class is, the more complex the SQL query behind the scenes are and the more objects will have to be retrieved from the database, which in turn decreases the performance for loading the view. Because of this, you should avoid using Combination classes if it's not necessary, and if you need to use them, always use the narrowest one. Using too large Combination classes in views, queues, groups, and so on is one of the most common mistakes when configuring SCSM and can greatly decrease performance.

Combination classes are actually another name for type projections, and the term type projection is far more common when searching for more information regarding this on the Web.

Available tokens in SCSM

There are three tokens available in SCSM:

- `[me]`
- `[mygroups]`
- `[now]`

All three tokens can be used when creating views. If you take a look at the views displaying **My Incidents** or **My Problems**, you can see how these tokens are used. Tokens cannot be used for anything other than view criteria.

See also

- For more information regarding views, please see the *Personalizing and organizing configuration item views* recipe in `Chapter 4`, *Building the Configuration Management Database (CMDB)*
- For more information regarding Combination Classes/Type Projections and views, please see these blog posts on the official SCSM blog:
  - `http://blogs.technet.com/b/servicemanager/archive/2010/02/02/creating-views-that-use-related-property-criteria-type-projections-software-views-example.aspx`
  - `http://blogs.technet.com/b/servicemanager/archive/2010/12/02/faq-why-is-my-custom-incident-view-so-slow.aspx`

Configuring the Global Operators Group

There are certain fields in the different forms of SCSM where you are supposed to add a user or group. These fields are called User Pickers, and if you take a look at the incident form there are three User Pickers on the **General** tab:

- **Affected user**
- **Assigned to**
- **Primary owner**

Some of these User Pickers target the end users, such as the **Affected user** field, while others target users or groups from the IT department, such as the **Assigned to** and **Primary owner** fields.

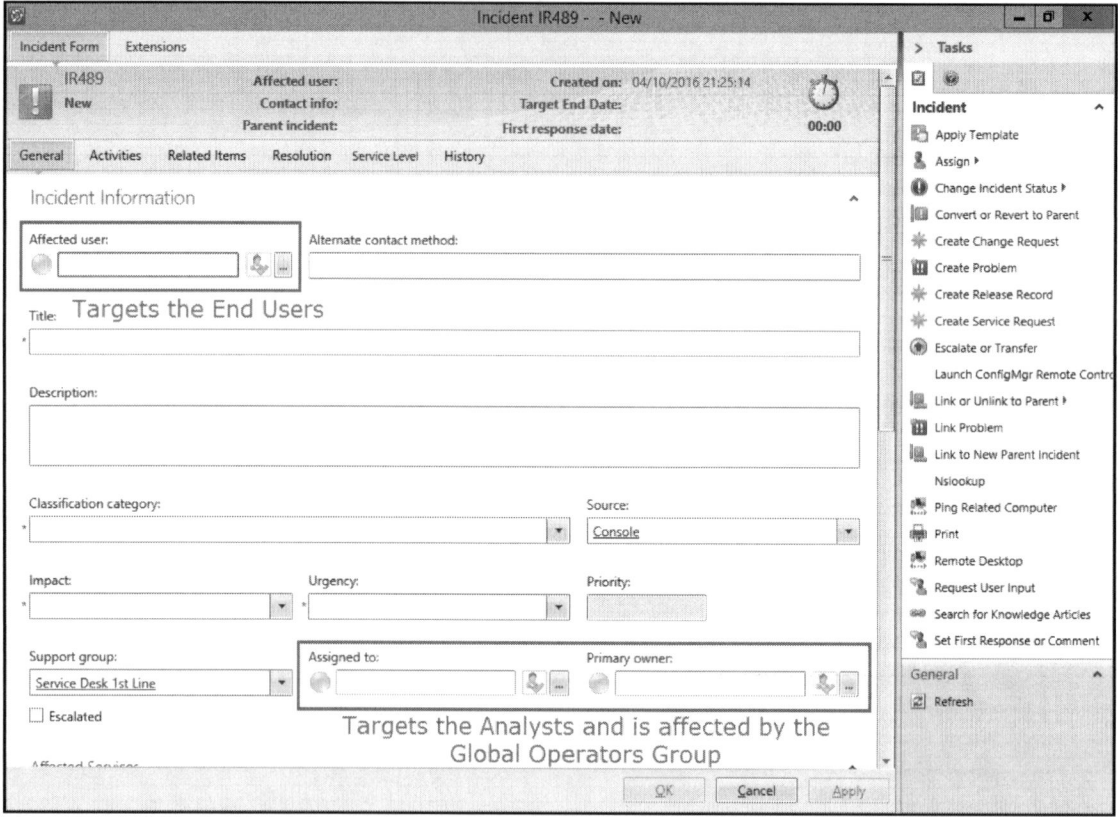

When searching for a user to add to the User Picker, SCSM will by default search the whole CMDB for users and groups. This is exactly what we want for the User Pickers targeting the end users, but for the User Pickers targeting the IT department, we are not interested in retrieving any users outside of the IT department.

It's very unlikely that we will assign an incident to a person outside of the IT department for instance. To narrow the scope of the User Pickers targeting the IT department, you will have to configure something called the Global Operators Group.

Getting ready

Make sure SCSM is running and that you have sufficient privileges to configure the Global Operators Group.

Ensure that you have users in your CMDB, preferably by configuring and running the Active Directory connector. Also, identify a property that is common for everyone that you would like to add to the Global Operators Group. In this recipe, we'll use the department property of the AD users.

How to do it...

The Global Operators Group is pre-created in SCSM, but in order for it to work properly you will have to configure it. To configure the Global Operators Group to include dynamic members, follow these steps:

1. Start the Service Manager console, go to the **Library** workspace, and select **Groups** in the navigation pane.
2. Double-click on **Global Operators Group** to view its properties.
3. Go to the **Dynamic Members** section and locate **Department** in the list of available properties.
4. Check **Department** and click **Add**.
5. Change the value of the list next to **Department** in the **Criteria** section to **equals** and then enter IT in the text field right next to it.
6. Click on **OK** to save your changes and close the Global Operators Group properties.

How it works...

After the internal group calculation has occurred in SCSM (which can take a minute or two), the Global Operators Group will include all users that fulfill the criteria specified in the Dynamic Members. This means that if you now browse a User Picker targeting the IT department (such as the **Assigned to** field in an incident), *you will now only see users where the department is set to IT for the actual user object in the CMDB.*

You can, of course, specify another criterion than the one used in the recipe to create a more specific dynamic membership.

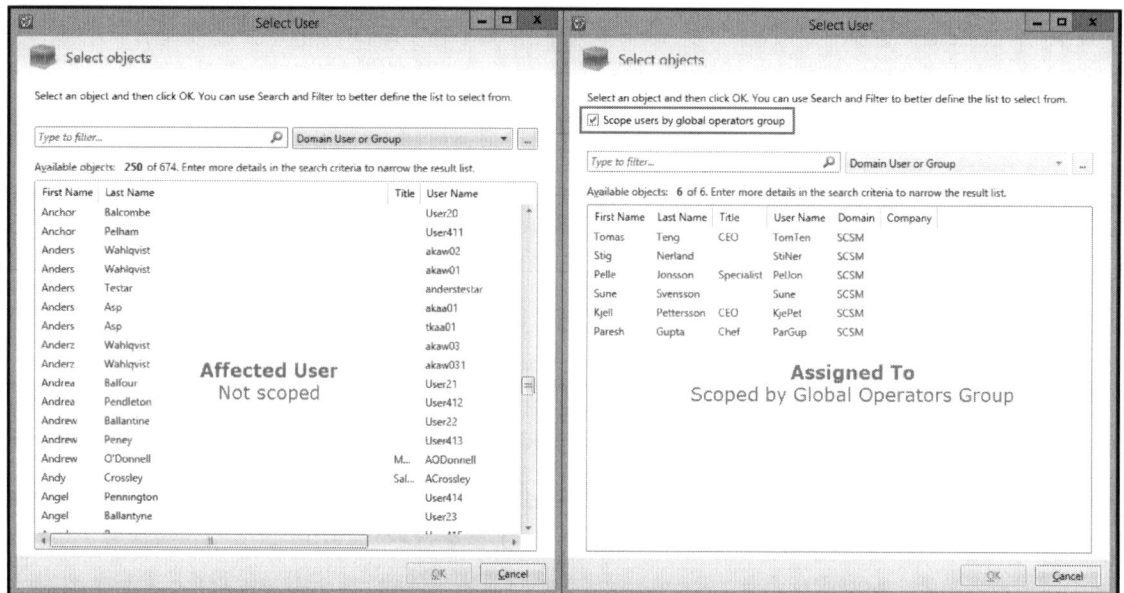

You can temporarily disable the Global Operators Group scope in a User Picker by deselecting the **Scope users by global operators group** checkbox when browsing for users or groups.

There's more...

When configuring the Global Operators Group, you have two options for membership:

- Static Members (Included Members)
- Dynamic Members

Static members are added to the **Included Members** section. Here, you get the option to specify exactly which users and groups to include in the Global Operators Group. The downside of this is that you will have to maintain this manually.

Dynamic members are added to the **Dynamic Members** section. Here, you have the option to create a criterion for the Domain User or Group class. Any user or group that fulfills this criterion will automatically be added to the Global Operators Group. If a user or group doesn't fulfill the criteria anymore, it will be removed as a member of the Global Operators group.

You also have the option to exclude members from the Global Operators Group. This is only useful when you use Dynamic Membership.

See also

- For more information regarding Groups in general, please see the *Creating a configuration item group* in `Chapter 4`, *Building the Configuration Management Database (CMDB)*
- Read more about the Global Operators Group in this blog post on the official SCSM
  blog: `https://blogs.technet.microsoft.com/servicemanager/2012/12/14/faq-why-does-it-take-so-long-to-find-users-in-the-assigned-to-and-primary-owner-fields/`

Downloading, installing, and configuring the Exchange Connector

SCSM has a built-in function to handle incoming e-mails. Unfortunately, this built-in function can be challenging to configure and is also very limited. Here's a few limitations:

- It can only handle incidents
- It doesn't handle updates to existing work items
- It requires an SMTP server to drop e-mails as a file in a folder within Windows

Because of these limitations and the need to have a working incoming e-mail channel, the Exchange Connector was developed by members from the SCSM product group, but was initially released as an unsupported solution. Nowadays, the solution is supported but is still handled as a separate download and is not included in the product itself.

Using the Exchange Connector, you will be able to monitor one or more mailboxes for new e-mails. When a new e-mail is discovered, the Exchange Connector will either update an existing work item, if it can find the work item ID encased in square brackets in the subject, or create a new incident or service request.

Getting ready

Make sure SCSM is running and that you have sufficient privileges to create a new connector.

Download the Microsoft Exchange Web Service Managed API 1.2 from Microsoft at `https://www.microsoft.com/en-us/download/details.aspx?id=28952`.

> Please note that you need Microsoft Exchange Web Service Managed API 1.2 – a newer version of this will not work.

Download the Exchange Connector from Microsoft at `https://www.microsoft.com/en-us/download/details.aspx?id=45291`.

> The download site for the connector doesn't list SCSM 2016 as a supported software at the time of writing. However, the connector is working fine beside from a small bug when configuring new connectors, and is supported to run on SCSM 2016 until a new version is released.

You will also have the option to use your own predefined incident and service request templates for creating and updating work items when configuring the connector. In a non-test environment, you have to create these templates before creating the connector, but in the recipe we will use some of the out-of-the-box templates.

How to do it...

This is how to install and configure the Exchange Connector for Service Manager. The process of installing the connector is split into three parts.

Part 1 – Installing the Exchange Web Service Managed API

1. Log on to the Primary Service Manager Management Server and make sure you have downloaded the Exchange Web Service Managed API installer.

The Primary Management Server is the first server you install and handles all the internal automation, such as connectors, workflows and subscriptions.

2. Double-click on the `EwsManagedApi.msi` file to start the installation.
3. In the first page of the installation wizard, click on **Next**.
4. Read the EULA, select **I accept the terms in the License Agreement**, and click on **Next**.
5. Make a note of the installation folder and select **Everyone** to install the EWS Managed API for everyone. Then click on **Next** followed by **Next** again.
6. Once the installation is finished, click on **Close**.
7. Now browse to the installation folder of the Exchange Web Service Managed API and copy the `Microsoft.Exchange.WebServices.dll` file.
8. Browse to the installation folder of SCSM and paste this DLL file. (The default installation folder for SCSM 2016 is `C:\Program Files\ Microsoft System Center\Service Manager`).

Part 2 – Installing the Exchange Connector

1. Log on to the Primary Service Manager Management Server. Make sure that you have downloaded the Exchange Connector.
2. Double-click on the `System_Center_Service_Manager_Connector_3.1_for_Exchange.exe` file to extract it.
3. On the welcome page, click **Next**.
4. Read and accept the EULA by checking **I accept the agreement** and clicking **Next**.
5. Choose a destination folder and click **Next** followed by **Extract**.
6. When the extraction is completed, click **Finish**.
7. Go to the extracted folder and open the `en-us` subfolder.

8. Copy the `Microsoft.SystemCenter.ExchangeConnector.dll` and `Microsoft.SystemCenter.ExchangeConnector.resources.dll` files.

9. Browse to the installation folder of SCSM and paste the DLL files.

10. Open the Service Manager console and go to the **Administration** workspace. Then select **Management Packs** in the navigation pane.

11. Click on the **Import** task in the task pane.

12. Browse to the `ServiceManager.ExchangeConnector.mpb` file that's located in the `en-us` directory from where you extracted the Exchange Connector. Remember to change the file extension in the bottom-right corner to **MPB files(*.mpb)** in order to be able to browse the file.

13. Select the `ServiceManager.ExchangeConnector.mpb` file and click on **Open**.

14. The **Import Management Packs** dialog should now be displayed. Click on the **Import** button to import the management packs.

15. Once the import has finished, click on the **OK** button.

Part 3 – Configuring the Exchange Connector

1. In the Service Manager console, go to the **Administration** workspace and select **Connectors** in the navigation pane.

2. Click on **Next** in the **Welcome** step.

3. Click on the **Create Connector** task in the task pane and select **Exchange Connector**.

4. Give the Exchange Connector a **Name**, a **Description**, and the **Active Directory Forest(s)** to search for users in:

   - Check **Attach each email as a .eml file...** if you want to save a copy of the e-mail within the actual work item that the connector creates. This can be used but if you have a large number of incoming e-mails or e-mails with big attachments, this could fill up your database so be careful with this option.

   - Check **Only process emails from users in the CMDB** if you don't want to allow other users to update or create new work items. If this is unchecked and a user that doesn't exist in the CMDB sends an e-mail to the system, the connector will create this user object in the CMDB.

   - Check **Move email to Deleted Items after processing** to ensure that the mailbox doesn't fill up over time.

   - Check **Append the full body of the email message...** if you want to save the whole e-mail as a post in the Action Log.

- Make sure that **Enable this connector** is checked to actually enable the connector.
- Click **Next** once you're done configuring this step.

5. On this page of the wizard you can use different methods to connect to the Exchange server. In this recipe, we will use Autodiscover to connect to a mailbox in Office 365.

6. Check the checkbox to **Use Autodiscover** and leave the **Validate only Office 365 autodiscover options** checked.

7. Click the **New...** button to create a new **Run As account**. Give the **Run As** account a display name and enter the username and password of the account of which you would like to import e-mails from. Enter a username like `username@domain`, just as in the following screenshot:

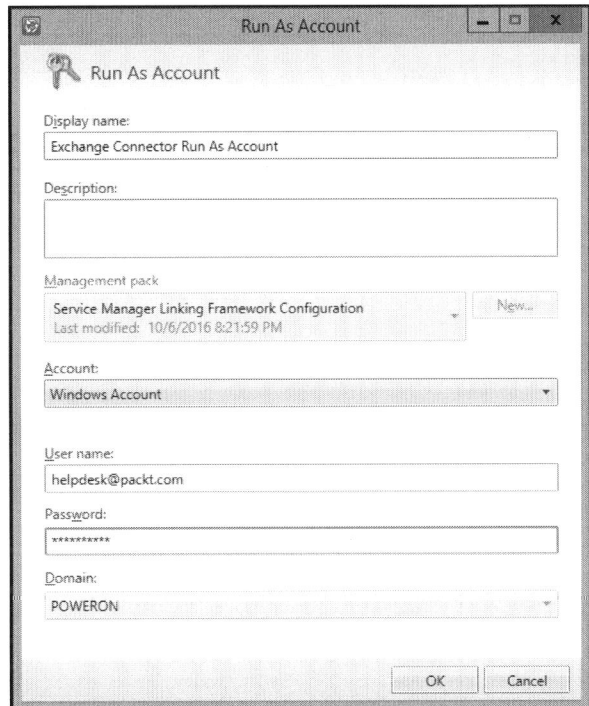

8. When done, click **OK** to create the new **Run As Account** and then click **Next** to proceed to the next step of the wizard.

9. You will now be prompted for the Run As account password again. Enter the password and click **OK**.

 **Important!** Do not click the **Test Connection** button as this will cause the wizard to crash with an error saying **Could not load type...**This is due to incompatibility issues with the Exchange Connector 3.1 and SCSM 2016. Similar errors will show up if you entered invalid information in the wizard and try to proceed to the next step. This issue will be resolved in an upcoming release of the connector, according to Microsoft.

10. You will now be asked to enter a number of parsing keywords. The suggested keywords work very well, and you can always go back and change this later if you realize that you should have used something different. Click **Next** to proceed.

11. In the **Routing and Schedule** step you have to choose some templates to apply when creating and updating incidents and service requests.

12. You should create specific templates to use for the Exchange Connector, but in our example here, select the **Default Incident Template** for new work items and incident updates, and select the **Default Service Request** template for Service Request updates.

13. It's not recommended to change the polling interval of the connector, so complete the configuration of the Exchange Connector by clicking on **Next** followed by **Create** and **Close**.

How it works...

The Exchange Connector will connect to the mailbox of the user specified using the Exchange Autodiscovery service on the specified interval, and will then look for new e-mails. Upon receiving a new e-mail, the Exchange Connector will take a look at the subject. If the subject includes a work item ID in square brackets (such as [SR921]), it will try to update the action log of that work item with the text in the body of the e-mail.

If the subject doesn't contain a work item ID enclosed in square brackets, the Exchange Connector will create a new work item based upon the template specified when configuring the connector.

It's also possible to resolve, close, vote on review activities, and so on using the connector. This is based upon the parsing keywords specified in step 9 of the *Part 3 – Configure the Exchange Connector* section. For instance, if you would like to resolve the incident with ID IR562, you could simply send an e-mail to the configured mailbox, with the incident ID enclosed in square brackets in the subject ([IR562]) and specifying the parsing keyword for resolving an incident in the body of the e-mail ([Resolved]).

There's more…

When using the Exchange Connector, you will have to make sure that every notification template in use has the work item ID enclosed in square brackets in the e-mail subject. Otherwise, replies to automatic notifications might result in new incidents/service requests instead of updating an existing one.

To be able to edit and create Exchange Connectors from any machine beside the Primary Management Server, you need to copy the Exchange Connector DLL files to the Service Manager console directory on that machine, as we did in Part 2 of this recipe.

See also

- For more information regarding the Exchange Connector, please take a look at the following blog posts on the official SCSM blog:
    - `https://blogs.technet.microsoft.com/servicemanager/2013/04/26/scsm-exchange-connector-3-0-rtm-released-supported/`
    - `http://blogs.technet.com/b/servicemanager/archive/2011/02/11/how-to-notify-the-assigned-to-user-when-an-incident-is-updated-via-the-exchange-connector.aspx`
    - `http://blogs.technet.com/b/servicemanager/archive/2011/02/08/tricky-way-to-handle-review-activity-approvals-with-the-exchange-connector.aspx`

Making the description field in the incident form auto-grow

By default, the description field of an Incident or a Problem only displays three rows of text. If you enter more than three rows of information into that field, you will have to scroll in order to read it all. This makes it hard to read and to get a quick overview of the actual issue. The solution to this is to change the behavior of the **Description** field to automatically grow with its content.

This is probably the most common form of customization for any organization using SCSM, and is a great way to start learning the Authoring Tool.

Getting ready

Make sure you have downloaded and installed the Authoring Tool. Note that the version of the Authoring Tool has to match the version of your Service Manager installed.

Download the Service Manager Authoring Tool available at
`https://www.microsoft.com/en-us/download/details.aspx?id=54059`

How to do it...

In this example, we will take a look at how to change the behavior of the **Description** field in the **Incident** form to auto grow with its content:

1. Start the **Authoring Tool**.
2. Go to the **Form Browser** and click on the **Reload Content** button:

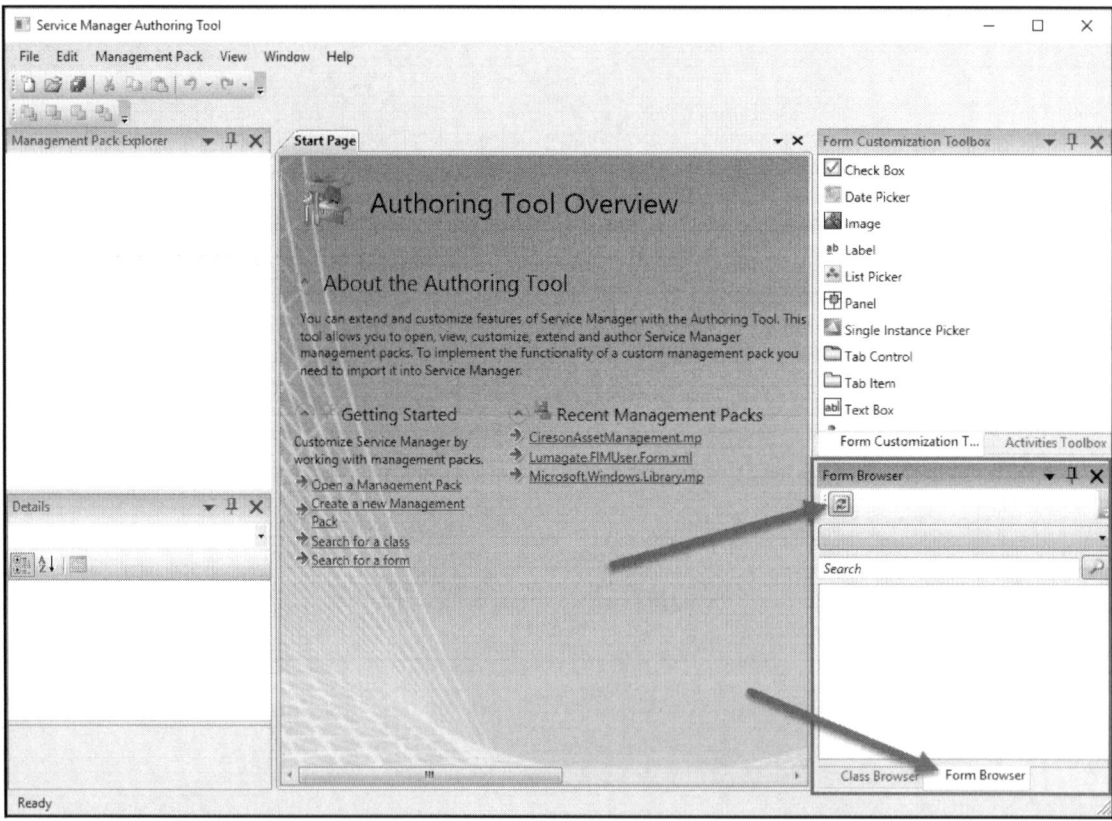

3. Enter `Incident` in the search field and locate **System.WorkItem.Incident. ConsoleForm**.

4. Now right-click on **System.WorkItem.Incident.ConsoleForm** and select **View**.

5. The Incident form should now be displayed in read-only mode. Click on the **Customize** button, which is located on the orange header just above the actual incident form.

6. You will now be prompted for a management pack to store your form customizations in.

 If you have made any customizations to the Incident form previously, you **must** save the changes you are about to make in the same management pack. Otherwise, you should create a new management pack to store this and all future incident form customizations.

7. Once you have browsed to your existing management pack or created a new one, make sure that it is select and click **OK**.

8. The incident form should now be displayed in an editable mode.

9. Select the **Description** field by clicking on it.

10. With the **Description** field selected, go to the **Details pane** and locate the **Height** property. The value of **Height** should be set to 55, and that's why there's only room for three rows of text.

11. Change the value of the **Height** property to **Auto**.

12. That's all we have to change for the **Description** field to auto grow. Save the management pack by going to the **File** menu and selecting **Save All**.

13. Next, we should actually seal the management pack, but as we will look into what that is and the requirement for doing so in later chapters of this book, we will skip that in this example. Instead, we will go on and import this unsealed management pack into Service Manager.

14. Open the **Service Manager console** and go to the **Administration** workspace. Then select **Management Packs** in the navigation pane.

15. Click on the **Import** task in the task pane.

16. Browse to the management pack you just created or edited, select it and click on **Open**.

17. The **Import Management Packs** dialog should now be displayed. Click on the **Import** button to import the management pack.

18. Once the import has finished, click on the **OK** button.

19. Restart the console and try your customization.

As a best practice, always restart the console after you've customized a form or done a class extension; otherwise, your changes might not be reflected or work properly.

How it works...

Once you have imported this management pack into SCSM, the **Description** field of new and existing incidents should automatically grow with its content. This behavior is much more convenient and makes it much easier to read.

Note that the exact same procedure can be used to change the behavior of the **Description** field in the **Problem** form:

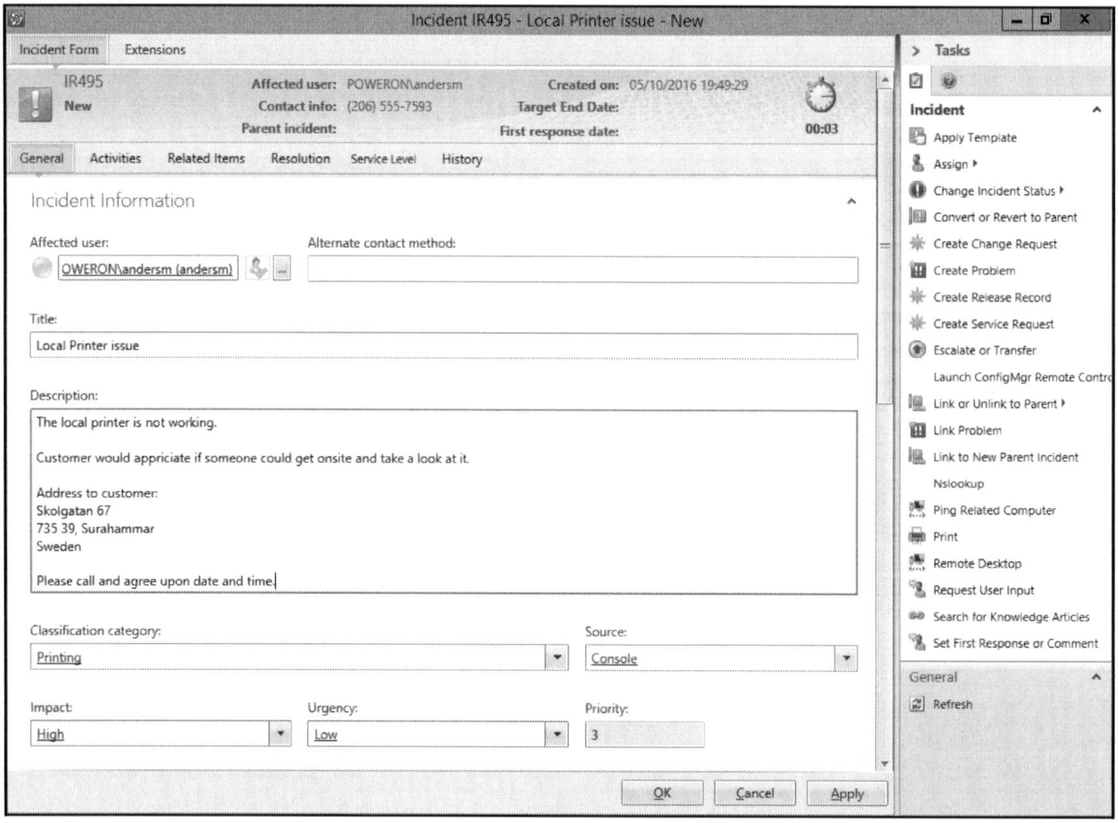

There's more...

The Authoring Tool is great for doing these kinds of customization. It's easy and pretty straightforward. There is one thing to keep in mind when customizing forms in the Authoring Tool, though, and that is you need to actually keep track of every single change you make to the form.

What does that mean? Well, if you first set the height of the description field to Auto, then change it to 100, and then finally set it back again to Auto, the Authoring Tool will actually write three sections of code into the management pack for all these changes. This makes it hard to read the XML code if you ever are going to modify it by hand. It could also affect the performance of loading the form.

To get around this, make sure that you don't play around too much when editing a form. It might be better to play around first then start all over and redo it when you are certain of which properties you want to configure. Another option is to clean the XML code in an XML editor, such as Notepad, when you are done with the customization in the Authoring Tool.

The authors recommend that you always seal your management pack if you have customized any forms.

See also

For more information regarding the Authoring Tool and how to use it to customize and extend Service Manager, see the *Customizing default forms* and *Sealing management packs* recipes in Chapter 11, *Extending SCSM with Advanced Personalization*

Extending the Incident class with a new property

In this recipe, we will take a look at extending the incident class with a new property. This can be done when you want to keep track of something that isn't available by default. You might want to keep track of the incident discovery date, for instance. That's not a property of the incident class by default, so if you would like to do so, you will have to extend the class, as described in this recipe.

Getting ready

Make sure you have downloaded and installed the Authoring Tool. Note that the version of the Authoring Tool has to match the version of your Service Manager installed.

Download the Service Manager Authoring Tool available at
`https://www.microsoft.com/en-us/download/details.aspx?id=54059`

How to do it...

1. Start the Service Manager Authoring Tool.
2. Locate **Class Browser** and click on the **Reload Content** button to load the list of all classes in SCSM.
3. Enter **Incident** in the **Search field** and hit **Enter**.
4. Locate the **Incident** class, right-click on it and select **View**.
5. The incident class should now be displayed in a read-only mode. In order to extend the incident class, right-click on the **Incident** class in the **Management Pack Explorer** and select **Extend class**:

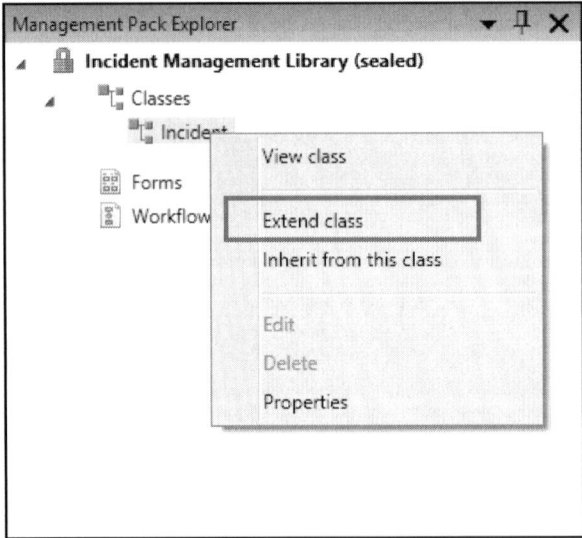

6. You will now be asked in which management pack you want to store your class extension. Click on **New...** to create a new management pack to store it within.

7. Give it a proper name, such as `Packt.Incident.ClassExtension`, and click on **Save**.

8. Make sure your new management pack is selected in the **Target Management Pack** dialog and click **OK**.

9. To add a new property to the incident class, click on the **Create property...** button located right above the list of all properties.

10. Change the **Internal name** to **IncidentDiscoveryDate** (without spaces) and click on **Create**.

11. With the new property selected, go to the details window and change the name to **Incident Discovery Date** (with spaces). This is actually the Display String of our new property and what we will see in the console later.

12. Then change the **Data Type** from **String** to **Date Time**.

13. Save your management pack by going to **File** and select **Save All**.

14. Next, we should actually seal the management pack, but as we will look into what that is and the requirement for doing so in later chapters of this book, we will skip that in this example. Instead, we will go on and import this unsealed management pack into Service Manager.

15. Open the Service Manager console and go to the **Administration** workspace.

16. Go to **Management Packs** and click on the **Import** task.

17. Browse to the management pack we just created and click on **Open**.

18. In the **Import Management Packs** dialog, click on **Import**.

19. For now, ignore the warning about the management pack not being sealed and click on **OK**.

How it works...

After you have imported the management pack created in the Authoring Tool, the incident class has been extended with a new property. This new property is available under the **Extensions** tab in the incident form:

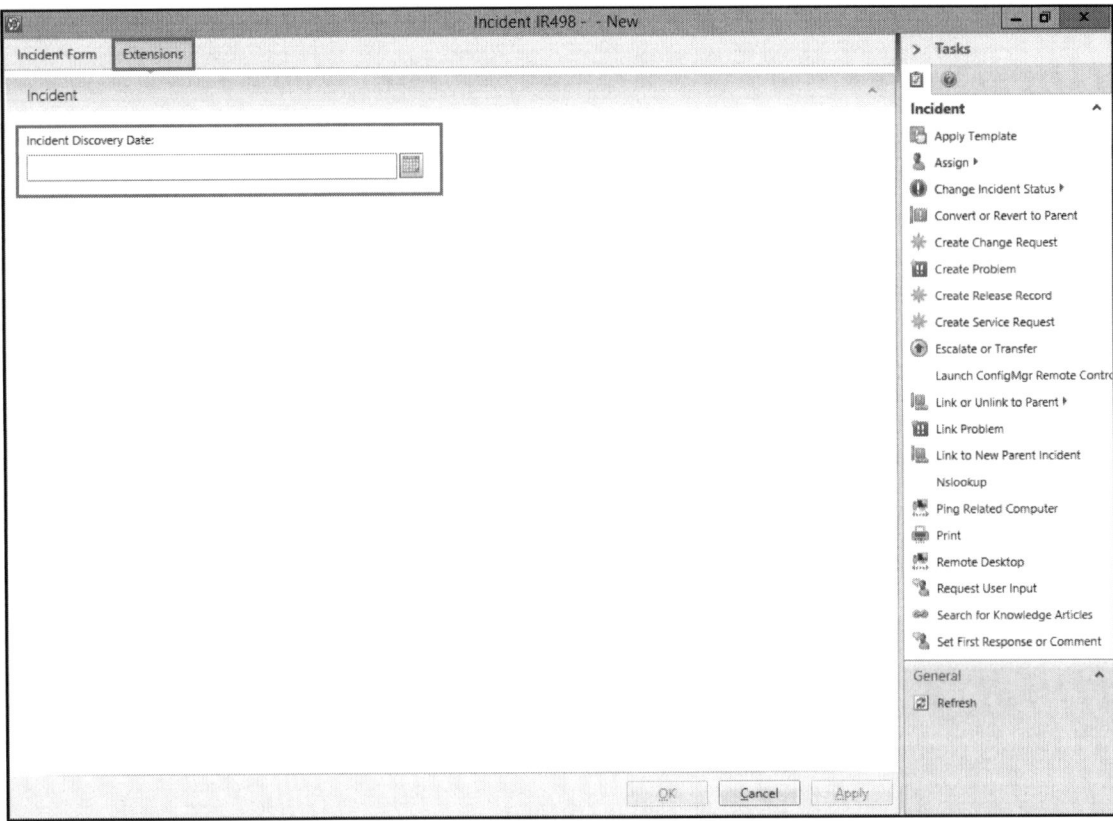

This is a simple way of extending an existing class in Service Manager with new properties that you might need. Even though you haven't modified the form, SCSM has made it possible to enter data in this field by presenting it on the **Extensions** tab. The next step would be to add a field for the new property on the actual form to avoid people forgetting to enter the information.

All management packs that include class extensions should be sealed before they are imported into SCSM. There are a few reasons for this, but the main ones are as follows:

- You want to protect your management pack from being modified
- Only sealed management packs are copied to the data warehouse
- You are not able to reference unsealed management packs from other management packs

There's more…

To get a grasp of the properties of each class, you could use the Authoring Tool to locate each class and then display it. You might be surprised that the property you want to extend your class with already exists, it's just not displayed on the form. But an even better way to get an understanding of the SCSM class hierarchy and model would be to take a look at the System Center Common Model for Service Manager Visio drawing. Unfortunately, this Visio drawing hasn't been updated since SCSM 2010, but is still a very good foundation to get an understanding of the classes. This Visio is included in the Service Manager Job Aids package for SCSM 2012 and is downloadable from Microsoft at `http://www.microsoft.com/en-us/download/details.aspx?id=27850`.

Relationships

Besides properties, classes can also have relationships to other classes. In this way, we can connect two or more objects with each other to create a richer experience for the analysts working in the system and to make powerful reports. A good example of a relationship is the Affected User relationship in the different work item classes. This relationship is used to connect the actual user object in the CMDB with the work item in which they are the affected user.

New relationships can be created in the Authoring Tool in the same way as we added a new property in this recipe, but unlike new properties, new relationships will not show up on the **Extensions** tab.

See also

- For more information about sealing a management pack, please see the *Sealing management packs* recipe in `Chapter 11`, *Extending SCSM with Advanced Personalization*

- For more information regarding the Authoring Tool and how to use it to customize and extend SCSM, see the *Using the SCSM Authoring Tool* recipe in `Chapter 11`, *Extending SCSM with Advanced Personalization*

Using Advanced Search to find very specific incidents

When working in the Service Manager console, you can use the different views to browse existing incidents. But if you're searching for very specific incidents and don't have a view with that given criteria, it can be very hard to locate those tickets. Besides, you're only looking for that right now and do not want to create a view to find them. This is when the search function in SCSM comes very handy.

The search bar is located in the top-right corner of the console and if you enter some text here and press *Enter*, the system will actually search the display name of all work items. As the display name is a combination of the ID and title of the work item, this means that if you're looking for something with a specific title or ID, it's very easy to find – just enter the information in the search bar and press *Enter*.

But let's say that you're looking for incidents where the affected user is working on a particular department and where the description field contains a certain keyword – that's when you have to use the advanced search function.

Getting ready

No specific preparations or rights is needed for this recipe.

How to do it...

In this recipe, we will search for incidents where the affected user is working in the marketing department and where the **Description** field contains the word `Intranet`.

1. Start the Service Manager console and press the little arrow next to the search bar in the top-right corner of the console.
2. Click **Advanced Search** to initiate a new search.
3. To specify a class to search for, click the **Browse** button.

4. When the **Select a Class** dialog is launched, click the drop-down menu in the top-right corner that reads **Frequently used basic classes** and change it to **Combination classes**.

5. We need to do this since we are going to traverse the affected user relationship to find incidents with affected users that are working in the marketing department.

6. In the filter field, enter **Incident**. Then locate and select the combination class named **Incident (typical)** and click **OK**.

7. Locate and select the **Description** property. Click **Add** to add it as a search criteria and enter `intranet` as the search string.

8. Now click the little arrow next to **Incident** to list all relationships in this particular combination class. Select **Affected User** and locate and add the **Department** property as another search criterion.

9. Change **contains** to **equals**, and then enter **Marketing** as the search string. This ensures that we get an exact match of the string:

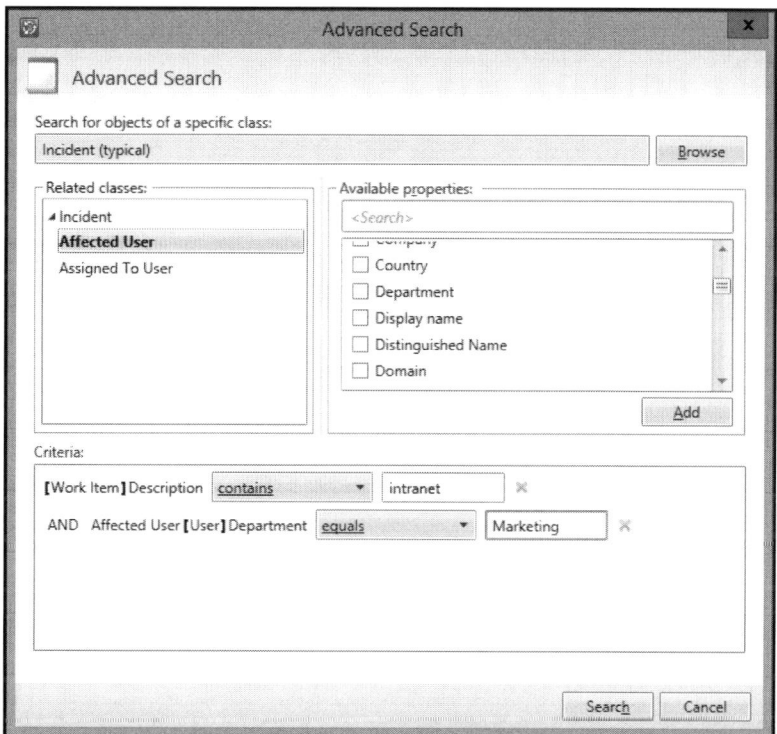

10. Click **Search** to find all incidents matching these criteria.

How it works...

Using the advanced search function you can do very advanced searches to locate any type of objects. The function is very useful to find those very specific work items or to do some quick analytics. One thing to keep in mind though, is that the search function does only search for active data in SCSM. Hence, objects that has been groomed and only exist in the SCSM Data Warehouse cannot be found using the search functions!

Avoid doing very generic searches as that could affected the performance of the system for all users. Using a very large combination class (or type projection) such as the Incident (advanced) and searching for any incident that have a description that contains the letter A is a very bad idea.

There's more...

Using the different combination classes, you can basically search for anything. A common request is to be able to search the action log for certain keywords – this can be achieved using by using this function. If you would like to search for all incidents which have an action log comment from the analyst that contains the word test can be achieved, such as in the following screenshot:

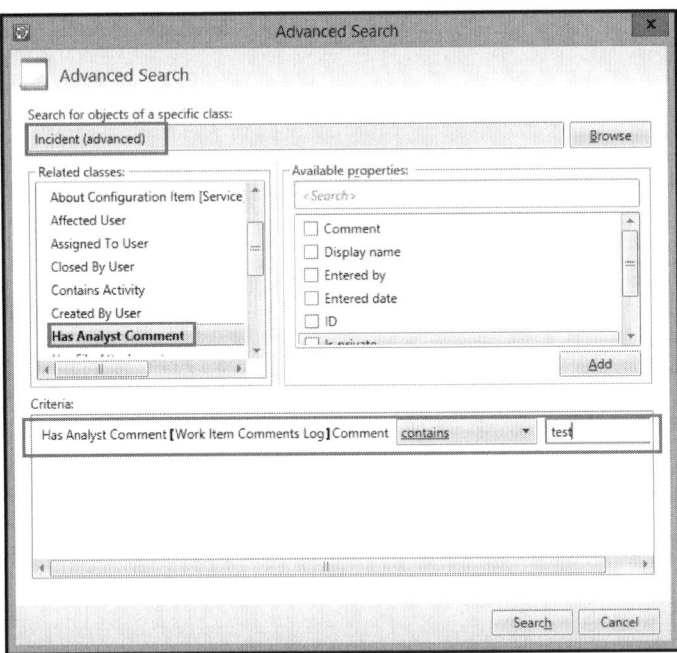

See also

- For more information on how to retrieve data from the Data Warehouse, including data that has been groomed, please see Chapter 10, *Working with the Data Warehouse and Reporting*
- For more information regarding grooming, please take a look at the following blog posts on the official SCSM blog:
  `https://blogs.technet.microsoft.com/servicemanager/2009/09/18/data-ret`
  `ention-policies-aka-grooming-in-the-service-manager-database/`
- `https://blogs.technet.microsoft.com/servicemanager/2015/11/16/an-in-de`
  `pth-look-at-grooming-in-system-center-service-manager-part-1/`

8
Designing and Configuring Change Management and Release Management

In this chapter, we will cover:

- Creating and configuring Change Request Templates
- Creating and managing Change Management Review Activities
- Creating Manual Activities for Change Management
- Creating and managing Dependent Activities in Change Management
- Creating and personalizing Change Management Parallel Activities
- Creating and personalizing Change Management Sequential Activities
- Creating and personalizing Change Management Activity notifications
- Creating and managing Build and Environment Release Records
- Creating and managing Release Record Templates
- Working with Change Requests and Release Records
- Filling in all related Activity Descriptions with Descriptions from parent Change Requests

Introduction

In this chapter we provide recipes to configure Service Manager to your environment. Specifically, we cover the Change and Release Management of Service Manager.

System Center 2016 Service Manager supports the "Change and Release Management" processes based on ITILÂ© or MOF.

In Change Management any change related to the IT infrastructure can be planned controlled and executed. Typical changes in IT are:

- Deploying service packs, hotfixes, patches, and updates
- Provisioning of new hardware components
- Updates to hardware infrastructure and implementing new software on servers and clients

In SCSM 2016 different types of activities can be used relating to Change Requests or Change Request Templates. Activities can be sequential and/or parallel in order to reflect the individual parts of the process.

To deploy changes to the IT infrastructure the Release Management process in ITILÂ© provides the opportunity to create different releases based on builds and environments, as well as activities.

In this chapter we provide recipes to configure the basics of Change Management, Release Management, and related Activities. We also see how Change Requests, Release Records, and Activities are related and work together.

The basic settings of Change Management and Release Management are described in Chapter 2, *Personalizing SCSM 2016 Administration* of this book.

Creating and configuring Change Request Templates

Change Request Templates can be used to pre-fill information in the Change Request form. These can be for instance a predefined Title, Description, Impact, Risk, and Priority.

This recipe will describe the steps to create a new Change Request Template.

Getting ready

In the SCSM 2016 console, navigate to **Library** | **Templates**.

How to do it...

To create a Change Request Template, follow these steps:

1. Click on **Create Template** in the **Tasks** pane.
2. Enter a name. In this recipe, we use `Change Request Service Pack Installation Template`.
3. Enter a description. For instance, `This template can be used for Change Requests regarding deployment of Service Packs`.
4. Choose the **Change Request** class by clicking on **Browse** next to the **Class** field, and then click on **OK**.
5. Choose an existing management pack or create a new one to store the Change Request Template (the *Creating Management Packs to save your SCSM personalization* recipe in `Chapter 2`, *Personalizing SCSM 2016 Administration* describes how to store your customizations in management packs as well as the best practice for naming conventions of the XML files).
6. Click on **OK**.

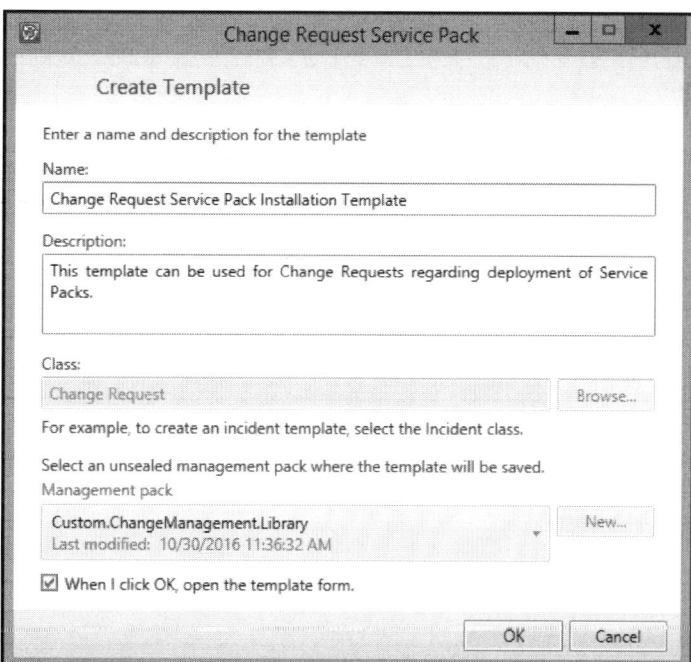

7. Fill in the information in the related fields of the form. In this recipe, we pre-fill the fields **Title**, **Description**, **Reason**, **Area** (select **Software** from the drop-down box), and **Priority** (select **Medium** from the drop-down box), in the **General** tab of the Change Request Template.

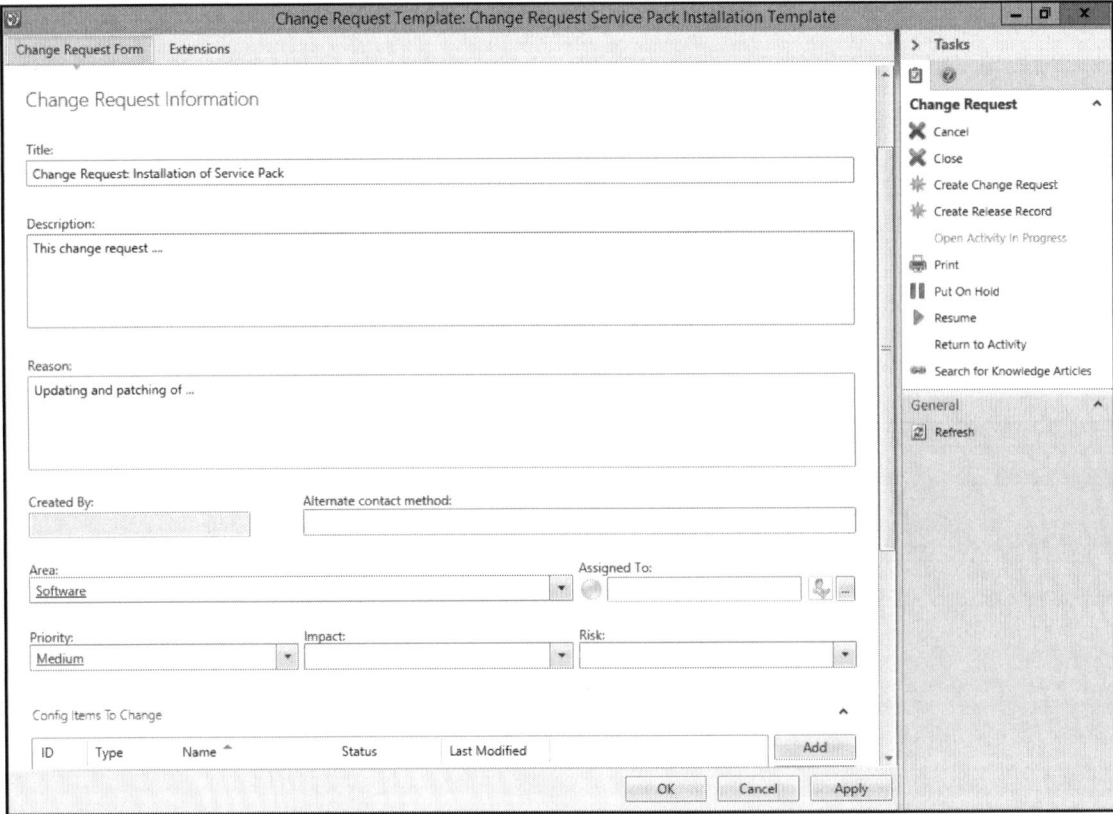

8. Pre-fill all fields you need in the **Planning** tab of the Change Request Template. In this recipe, we use **Implementation Plan**, **Risk Assessment Plan**, **Test Plan**, and **Back out Plan**.

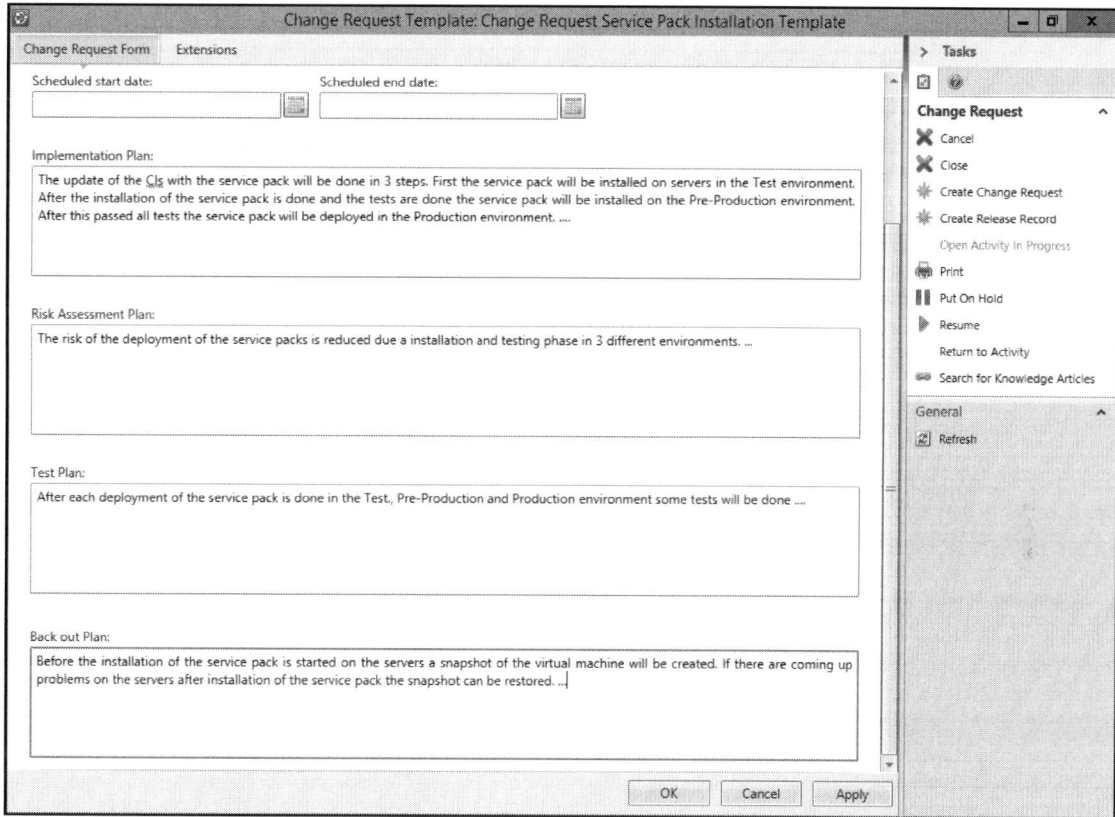

9. Click on **OK** to save and close the Change Request Template.

How it works...

Basically a pre-filled template in SCSM 2016 can be used to create new Work Items (for instance Incident Records, Change Requests, and Service Requests). Using templates keeps the content and information of forms consistent. Using pre-filled templates will also reduce the time each individual spends initiating the relevant Work Item.

There's more…

Change Management reporting is important due to the visibility and tracking provided, which is key to continually improving the process.

Reporting scheduled and actual date information

Providing the Scheduled Start and End Time of change requests is very helpful for reporting on the progress of the Change Management process. These key performance indicators offer a good overview on how many change requests are completed within the planned time.

To get more information about reporting please look at the recipes in `Chapter 10`, *Working with the Data Warehouse and Reporting* of this cookbook.

See also

Microsoft TechNet Library: *Managing Changes and Activities in System Center – Service Manager*: `https://technet.microsoft.com/en-us/system-center-docs/sm/manage/ops-managing-changes-and-activities-in-system-center-2016-service-manager`.

Creating and managing Change Management Review Activities

Review Activities in SCSM 2016 are used for approval of all the approval related steps and activities in a Change Request. This recipe will show how the different fields of a Review Activity can be configured.

Getting ready

To create Review Activities in a Change Request Template open the SCSM 2016 console and navigate to **Library** | **Templates**. Open the **Change Request Service Pack Installation Template** we created in the previous recipe.

How to do it...

To add a Review Activity in a Change Request or Change Request Template, follow these steps:

1. Click on the **Activities** tab in the Change Request form.
2. Click on **+ Activities**.
3. Choose the **Default Review Activity** in the list of templates and click on **OK**.

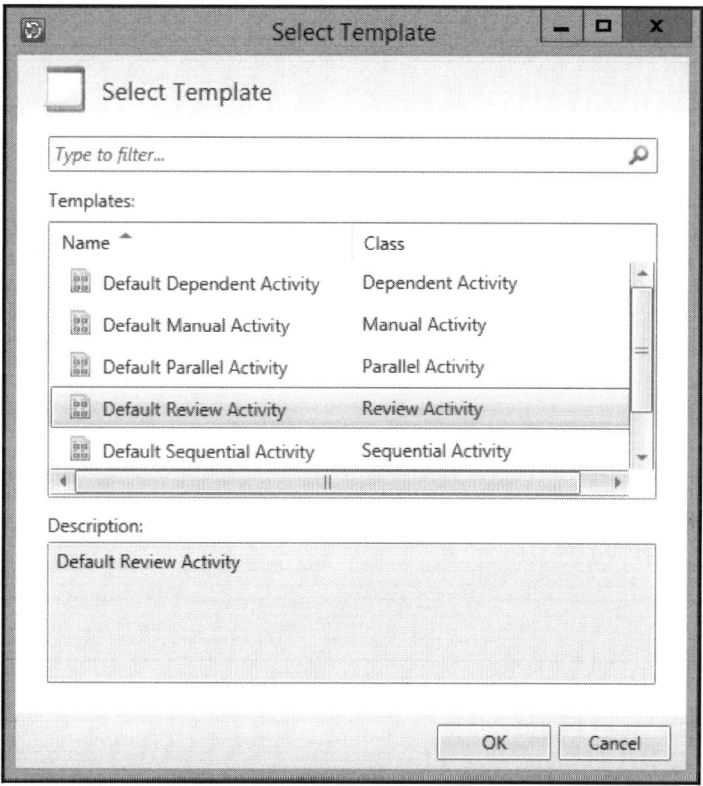

4. In the **Review Activity Template** we fill in the **Title** and **Description** fields.

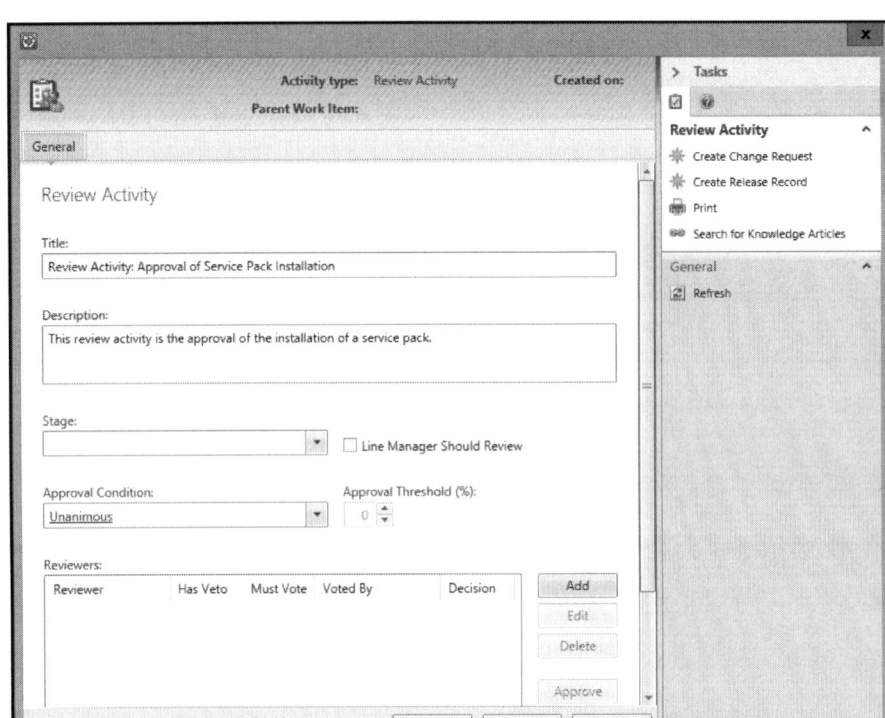

5. If the Line Manager of the requester should review, select the **Line Manager Should Review** option. If enabled, the manager of the user is discovered by the Manager attribute of the user in the CMDB (synced by the AD Connector from Active Directory).

6. Add **Reviewers** manually by clicking on **Add** in the **Reviewers:** section. Select the **Has veto** or **Must Vote** option if required by your process.

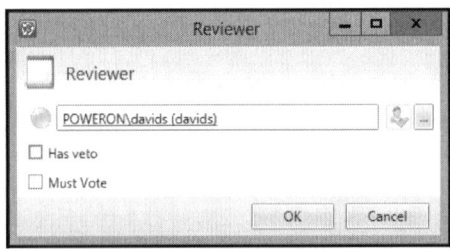

7. Click on **OK**.

8. Add more reviewers manually.

9. If you add more than one reviewer you can define the approval condition:

- **Unanimous**: All reviewers have to vote
- **Automatic**: The approval is done without anyone having to vote
- **Percentage**: For example, only 50% (**Approval Threshold (%)**) of the reviewers need to vote

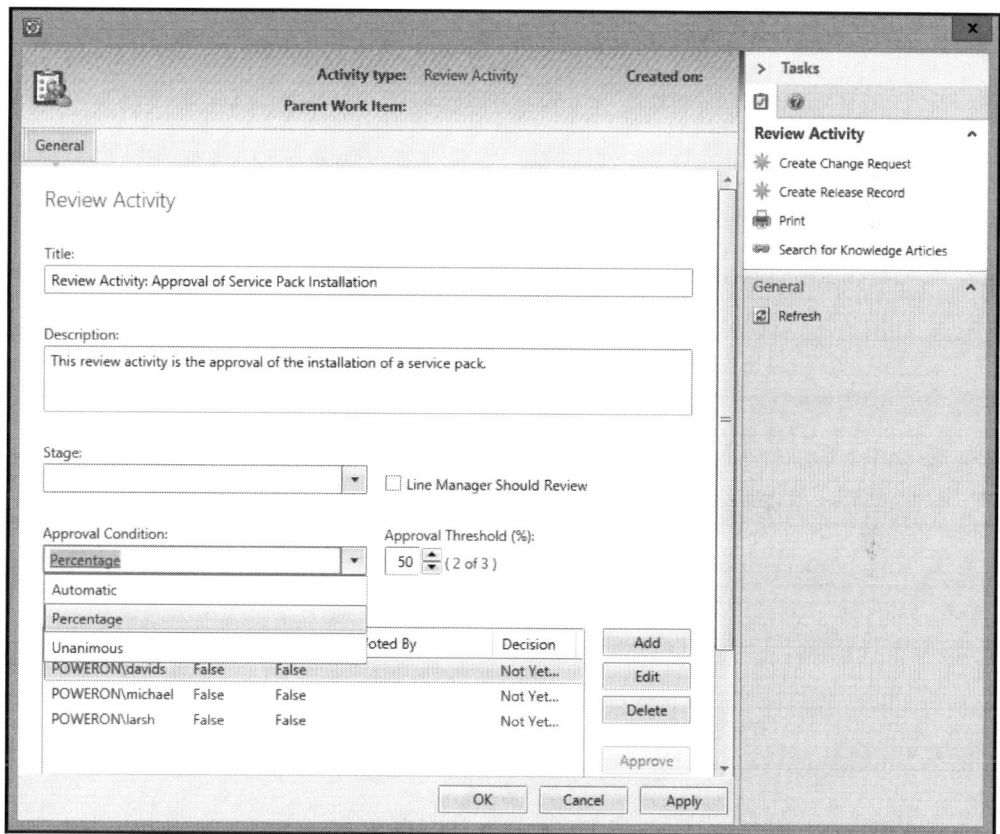

10. Click on **OK** to close the Review Activity form.

11. In the next recipe, we will add more activities, so don't close the Change Request Template.

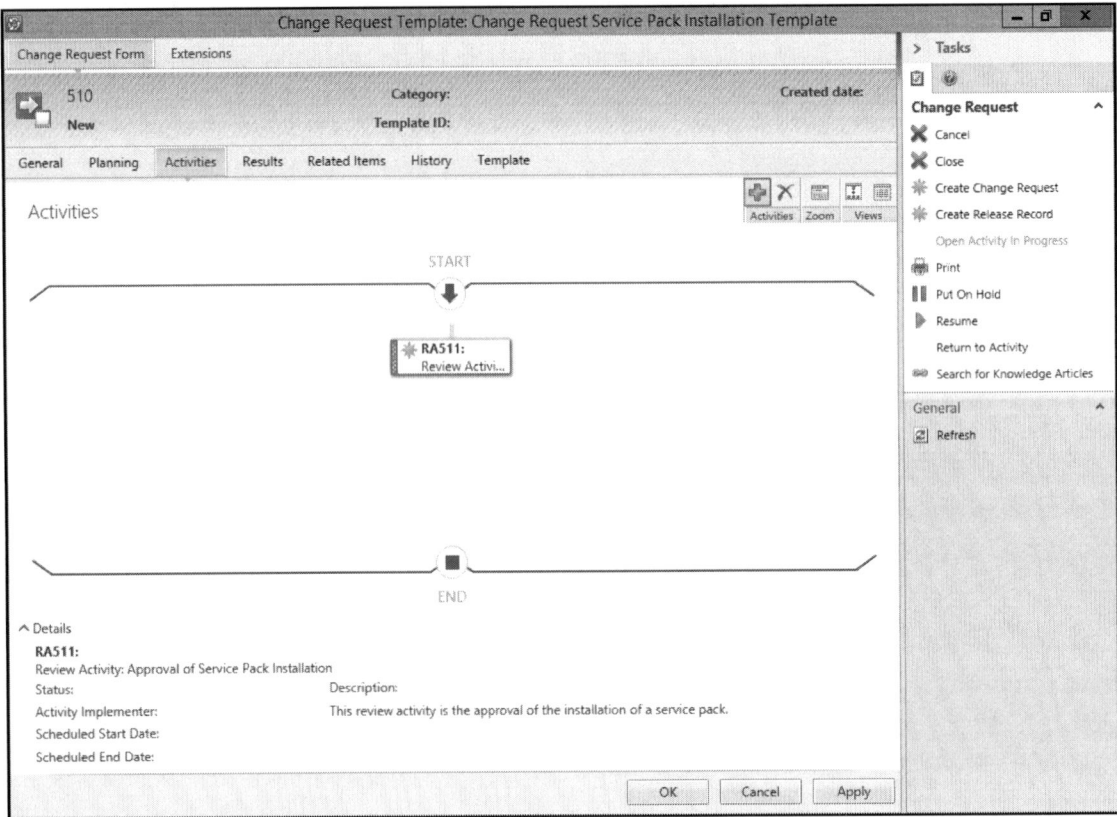

How it works...

If the Change Request Template is applied to a new Change Request, all pre-filled fields and all activities are automatically populated in the newly-created Change Request.

A SCSM 2016 workflow will set the first activity to the status of **In Progress**, all other activities will be set to the status of **Pending** by default. The Change Request will also get the status of **In Progress**.

The Review Activity provides the option to determine the manager of the requester automatically. The manager information is synced automatically from Active Directory by the AD Connector of SCSM 2016. The line manager information is only available if this has already been set in Active Directory.

Also, it is possible to require that a reviewer "must vote" and "has a veto".

You can configure a Review Activity so that all, or only subsets of reviewers have to review and provide approval.

There's more…

Notifying reviewers and adding additional activities are common tasks and requirements in the Change Management process.

Notification of reviewers

To see how to notify a reviewer if a Review Activity gets updated to the status of **In Progress**, please look at the *Creating and personalizing Change Management Activity notifications* recipe in this chapter.

Adding more activities to a Service Request created on a template

You can add additional activities to a Change Request that was created using a template during the process of working with the Change Request.

 You can add more activities as long as the last activity in the Change Request isn't completed.

See also

Microsoft TechNet Library: *Managing Changes and Activities in System Center – Service Manager*:

```
https://technet.microsoft.com/en-us/system-center-docs/sm/manage/ops-managing-c
hanges-and-activities-in-system-center-2016-service-manager
```

Creating Manual Activities for Change Management

Manual Activities in SCSM 2016 can be used to reflect the different manual steps during the Change Management process.

This recipe will show how to configure the different properties of Manual Activities in SCSM 2016.

Getting ready

If you closed the Change Request Form in the last recipe after creating a Review Activity, open the Change Request Template we created in the recipe before by navigating to **SCSM 2016 console** | **Library** | **Templates** | **Change Request Service Pack Installation Template**. Click on the **Activities** tab in the Change Request form.

If the form of the Change Request Template is still open just continue with the *How to do it...* section.

How to do it...

To add a Manual Activity in a Change Request or Change Request Template, follow these steps:

1. Click on **+ Activities** and select **Default Manual Activity** from the list. Click on **OK**.

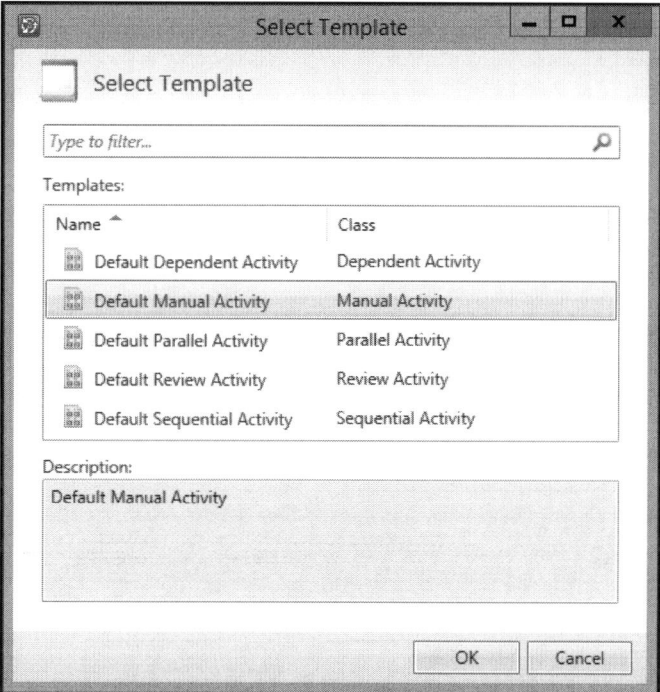

2. Fill the **Title** and **Description** fields.
3. Pick a **Priority** and **Area**. We will choose **Medium** from the **Priority** drop-down box and **Software** from the **Area** drop-down box, because the Change Request Template is related to the Installation of a Service Pack.

4. Click on **OK** to close the Manual Activity Template form.

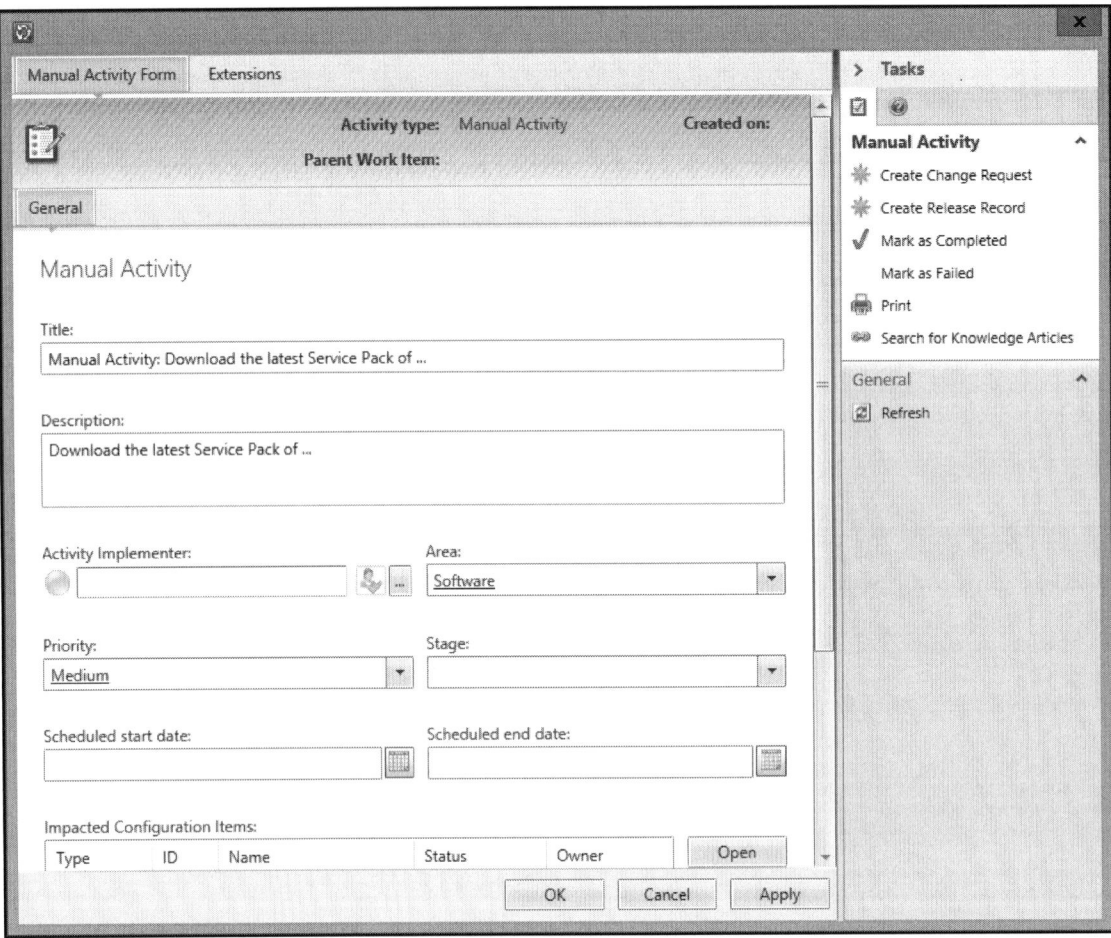

5. Click on **OK** to close the Manual Activity form.

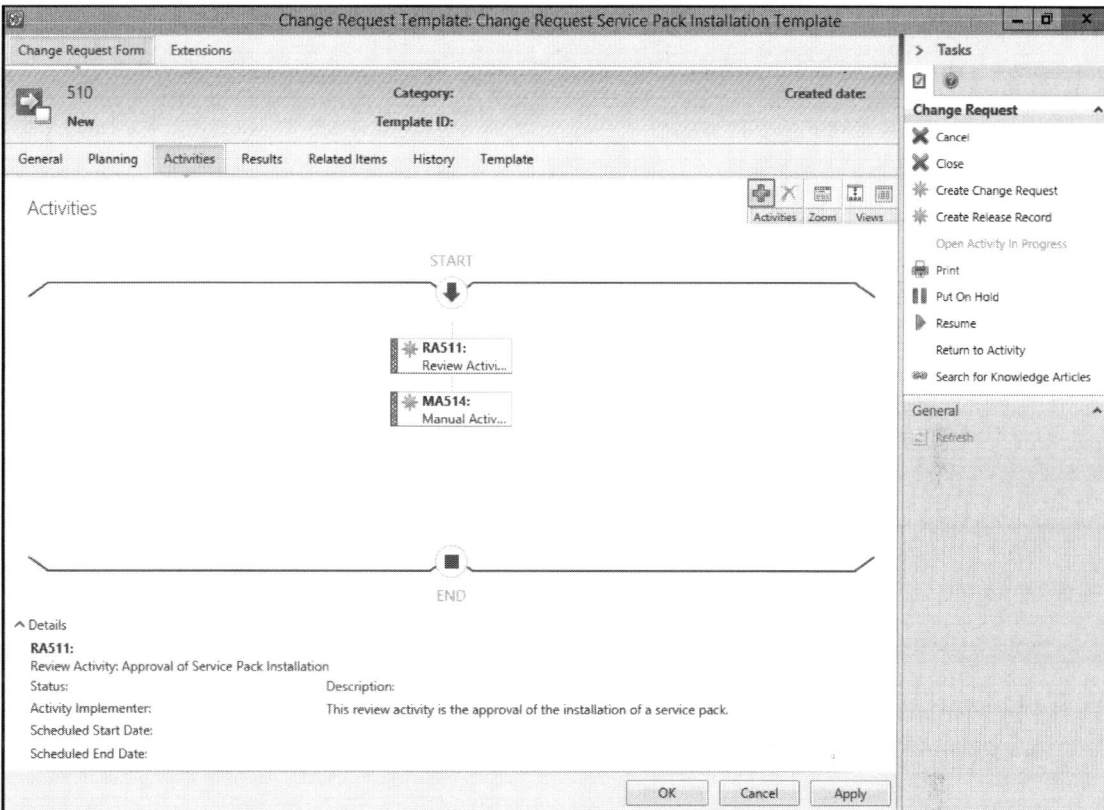

6. Click on **OK** to close the Change Request Template.

How it works...

A SCSM 2016 workflow will set the first activity to the status of **In Progress**, all other activities will be set to the status of **Pending**. The Change Request will also get the status of **In Progress**.

The Manual Activity allows you to capture the manual steps required in your defined Change Management process.

Typically, an Implementer is assigned to the Manual Activity. The Implementer is the person responsible for carrying out the manual action specified in the manual activity. Using the information in the Activity you are able to send a notification to the relevant individuals when the activity status is set to **In Progress**.

Also, you can configure the **Scheduled Start** and **Scheduled End Date**. This can be key to reporting as it provides visibility on how many activities are performed and completed in the scheduled time.

There's more…

Note that the Activity Implementer helps to optimize the process. Also reporting offers a good opportunity to improve the Change Management process.

Notificating the Activities Implementer

To see how to notify an implementer if a Manual Activity is updated to status **In Progress** please look at the *Creating and personalizing Change Management Activity notifications* recipe in this chapter.

Reporting Scheduled and Actual Date information

Providing the Scheduled Start and End Time of Manual Activity is very helpful for reporting.

To get more information about reporting in SCSM 2016, please take a look at the recipes in Chapter 10, *Working with the Data Warehouse and Reporting* of this cookbook.

See also

Microsoft TechNet Library: Managing Changes and Activities in System Center – Service Manager: https://technet.microsoft.com/en-us/system-center-docs/sm/manage/ops -managing-changes-and-activities-in-system-center-2016-service-manager.

Creating and managing Dependent Activities in Change Management

Dependent Activities in SCSM 2016 can be used to link activities between different Change Requests and Release Records, if relationships between the management processes are required. This recipe will show how to create Dependent Activities in a Change Request template.

Getting ready

To create a Dependent Activity in a Change Request Template, open the SCSM 2012 console and navigate to **Library** | **Templates**. Open the *Change Request Service Pack Installation Template* we created in an earlier recipe.

How to do it...

To create a Dependent Activity, follow these steps:

1. Click on the **Activities** tab in the Change Request form.
2. Click on + **Activities**.
3. Choose **Default Dependent Activity** in the list of templates and click on **OK**.

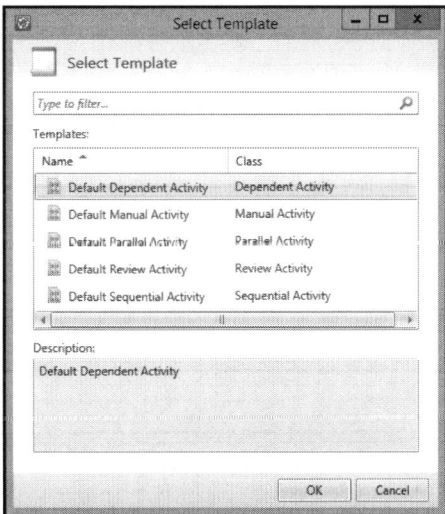

4. In the Dependent Activity Template form add the **Title** and **Description** information. If the **Owner** or **Assigned To User** is static for all Change Requests based on this Template you can add the Users in the corresponding fields. The **Owner** is responsible for the Dependent Activities related to the process; the **Assigned To User** is the user who works on the task of the activity. For instance, the **Owner** is responsible for installing the service pack. The **Assigned To User** will install the service pack.

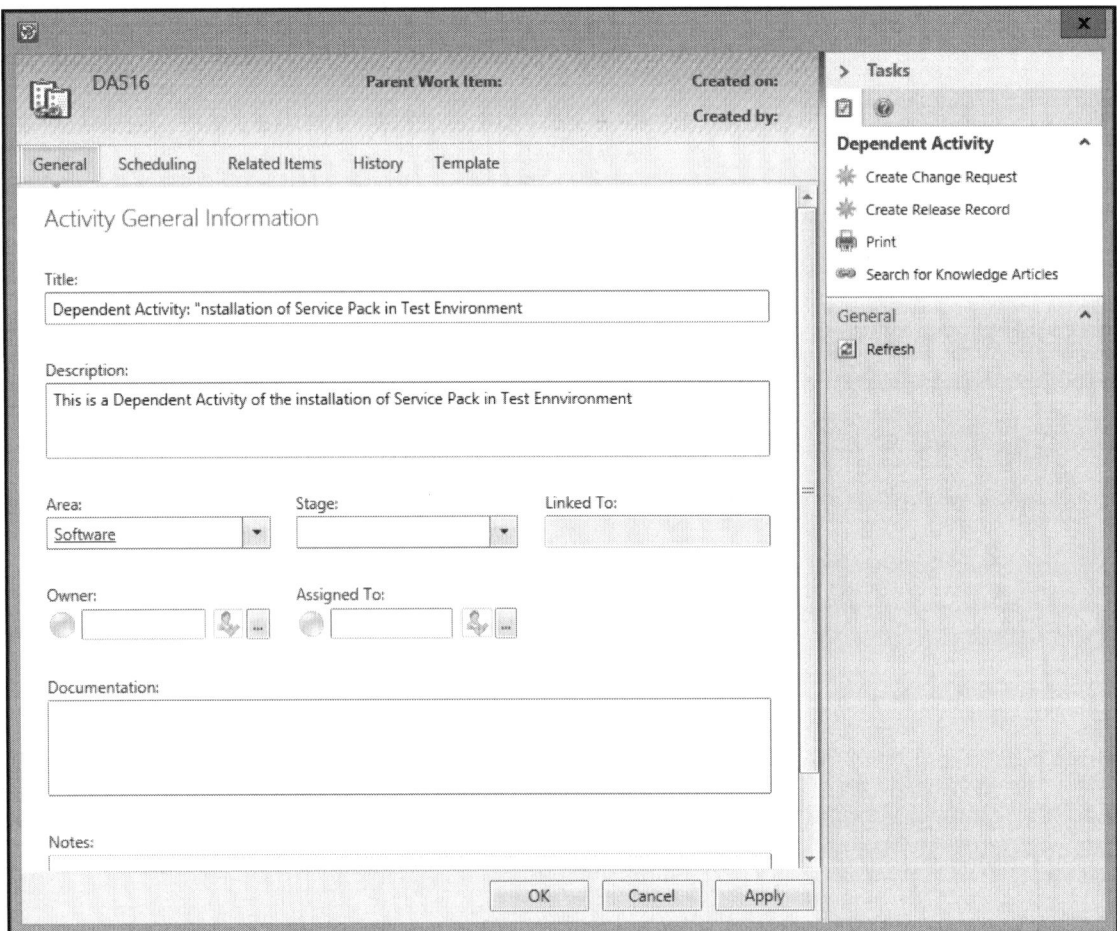

5. Click on **OK** to close the Dependent Activity Template.
6. Click on **OK** to close the Change Request Template.

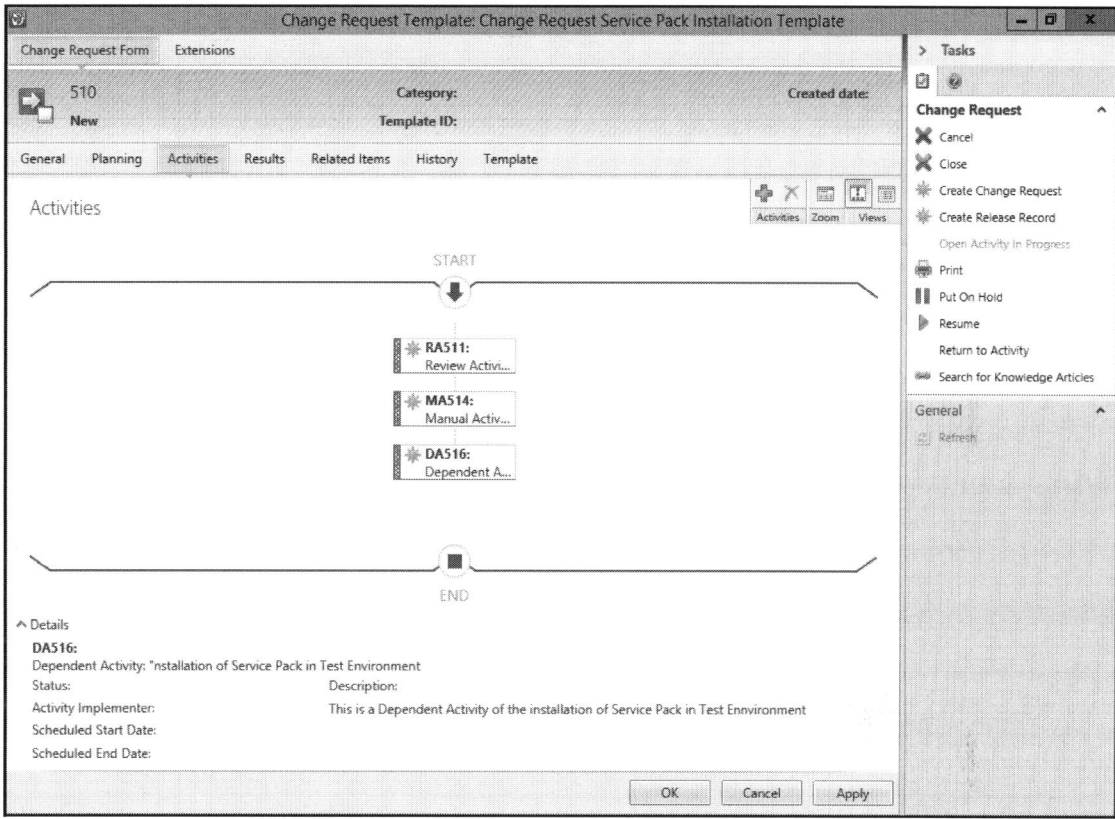

How it works...

Dependent Activities are used to relate activities in Change Request to an activity in a Release Record. This offers the option to link different process steps of Change Management to the corresponding steps in Release Management.

For instance: The Change Request for installing a Service Pack (only one Change Request) might have three Dependent Activities to three different Release Management Records (Installing the Service Packs to three different environments; Test-, Pre-Production-, Production-Environment).

There's more...

Change Management and Release Management are related. Dependent Activities are how this relationship is reflected in SCSM 2016.

Linking activities in Change Requests to activities in Release Records

The linking of Dependent Activities in Change Requests to activities in Release Records can't be done in a Change Request Template. You have to create a new Change Request based on a Change Request Template and a new Release Record before you are able to link a Dependent Activity of a Change Request to an activity in the Release Record. For more information on how to do this please look at the *Working with Change Requests and Release Records* recipe in this chapter.

See also

Microsoft TechNet Library: Managing Changes and Activities in System Center – Service Manager: `https://technet.microsoft.com/en-us/system-center-docs/sm/manage/ops -managing-changes-and-activities-in-system-center-2016-service-manager.`

Creating and personalizing Change Management Parallel Activities

Activities in SCSM 2016 are executed sequentially by default. To run different activities in parallel we need a Parallel Activity container.

This recipe will show how to create and work with Parallel Activities in SCSM 2016.

Getting ready

To create Parallel Activities in a Change Request Template open the SCSM 2012 console and navigate to **Library** | **Templates**. Open the *Change Request Service Pack Installation Template* that we created in an earlier recipe.

How to do it...

The following steps describe how to create and personalize Parallel Activities:

1. Click on the **Activities** tab in the Change Request form.
2. Click on **+ Activities**.
3. Choose the **Default Parallel Activity** from the list of templates and click on **OK**.

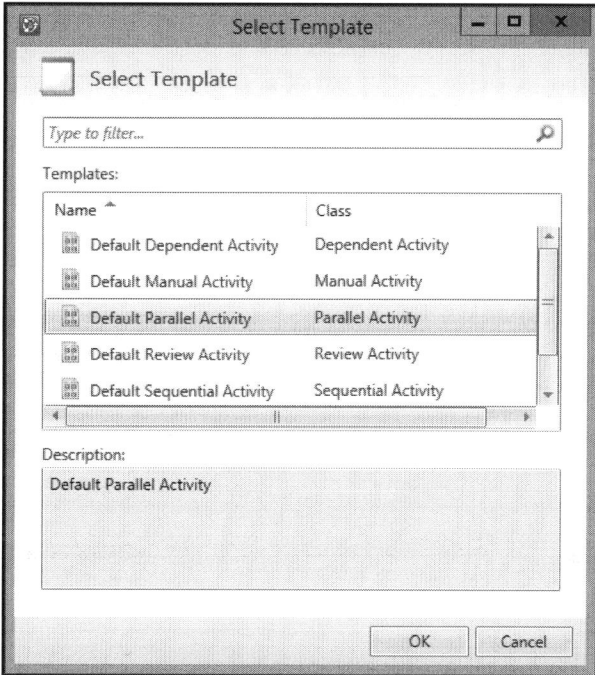

4. In the **General** tab we will fill the **Title** and **Description** field. We will select **Software** from the **Area** drop-down box.

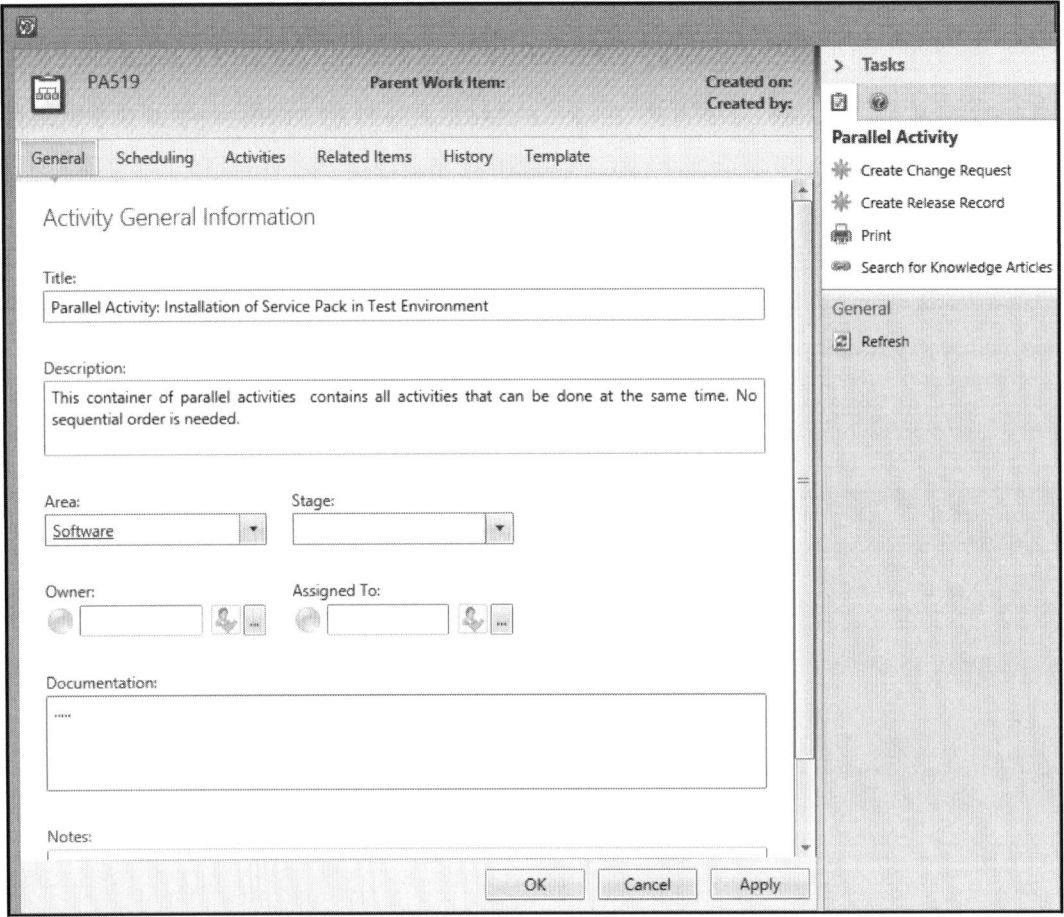

5. Click on the **Activities** tab.
6. Add Manual Activities to the Container Activity Template. In this recipe we add the following three Manual Activities:
   - Install Service Pack on x86 Clients in Test Environment
   - Install Service Pack on x64 Clients in Test Environment
   - Install Service Pack on Server 1 in Test Environment

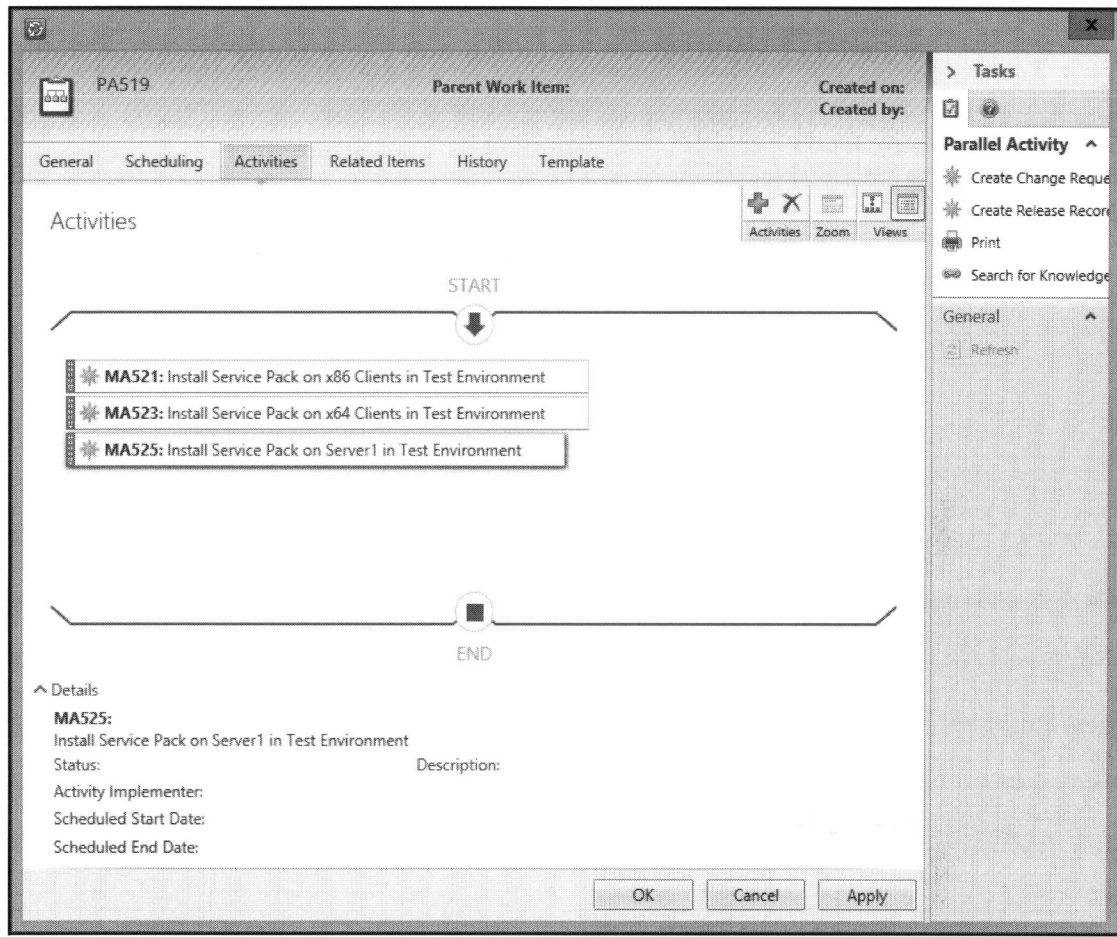

7. Click on **OK** to close the Container Activity template.
8. Click on **OK** to close the Change Request template.

How it works...

A Parallel Activity in SCSM 2016 works like a container. Each activity added to this container will get the same status update, **In Progress** when the Parallel Activity is changed from **Pending** to **In Progress**. This provides the ability to execute some Change Management process activities in parallel. For instance, if we want to perform the same activities on different systems (install Service Pack x86 version on some systems and install Service Pack x64 version on some other systems, or install the Service Pack on clients and servers in parallel). When all activities within the container are completed, the Parallel Activity will also be marked as **Completed**.

There's more...

Here is some more information about the different types of activities in SCSM 2016.

How to work with Review, Manual, and Dependent Activities

Please look at the following recipes to see how to work with different types of activities in SCSM 2016:

- *Creating and managing Change Management Review Activities*
- *Creating Manual Activities for Change Management*
- *Creating and managing Dependent Activities in Change Management*

How to work with Sequential Activities inside Parallel Activities

If you need to add Serialized/Sequential Activities inside a Parallel Activity container look at the next recipe of this chapter.

See also

Microsoft TechNet Library: *Managing Changes and Activities in System Center – Service Manager*:

```
https://technet.microsoft.com/en-us/system-center-docs/sm/manage/ops-managing-c
hanges-and-activities-in-system-center-2016-service-manager
```

Creating and personalizing Change Management Sequential Activities

If you have configured Parallel Activities as described in the previous recipe, all activities will be set to the status of **In Progress** at the same time. If you need to serialize activities inside a Parallel Activity container you must use Sequential Activities.

This recipe will show you how to work with Sequential Activities inside a Parallel Activity container.

Getting ready

To create Sequential Activities in a Change Request Template open the SCSM 2016 console and navigate to **Library | Templates**. Open the *Change Request Service Pack Installation Template* that we created in an earlier recipe.

How to do it...

Follow these steps to create a Sequential Activity:

1. Click on the **Activities** tab in the Change Request form.
2. Open the **Parallel Activity** we created in the previous recipe. (Right-click on the title of the Parallel Activity and select **Open**.
3. Click on the **Activities** tab in the Container Activity Template form.
4. Click on the **+ Activities**.

5. Choose the **Default Sequential Activity** from the list of templates and click **OK**.

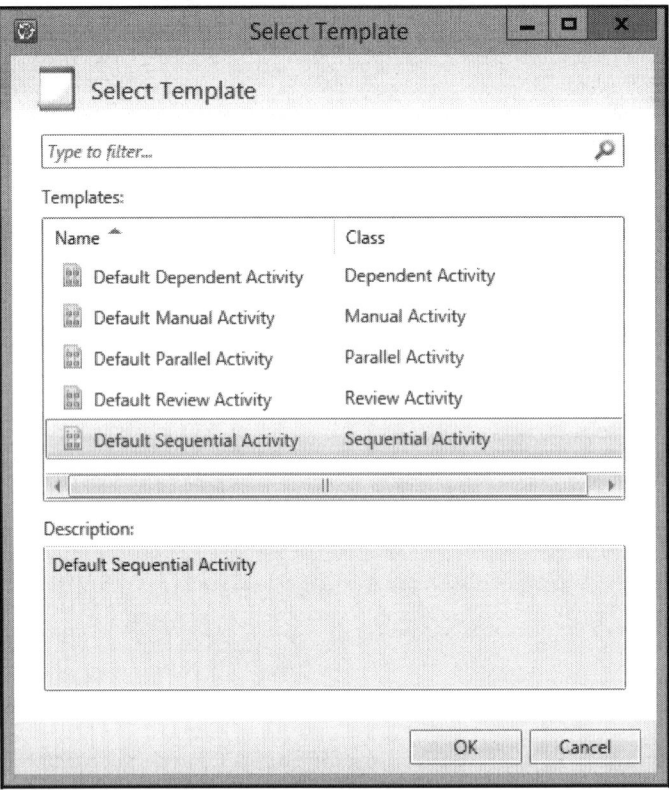

6. Fill the **Title**, **Description**, and **Area** fields.

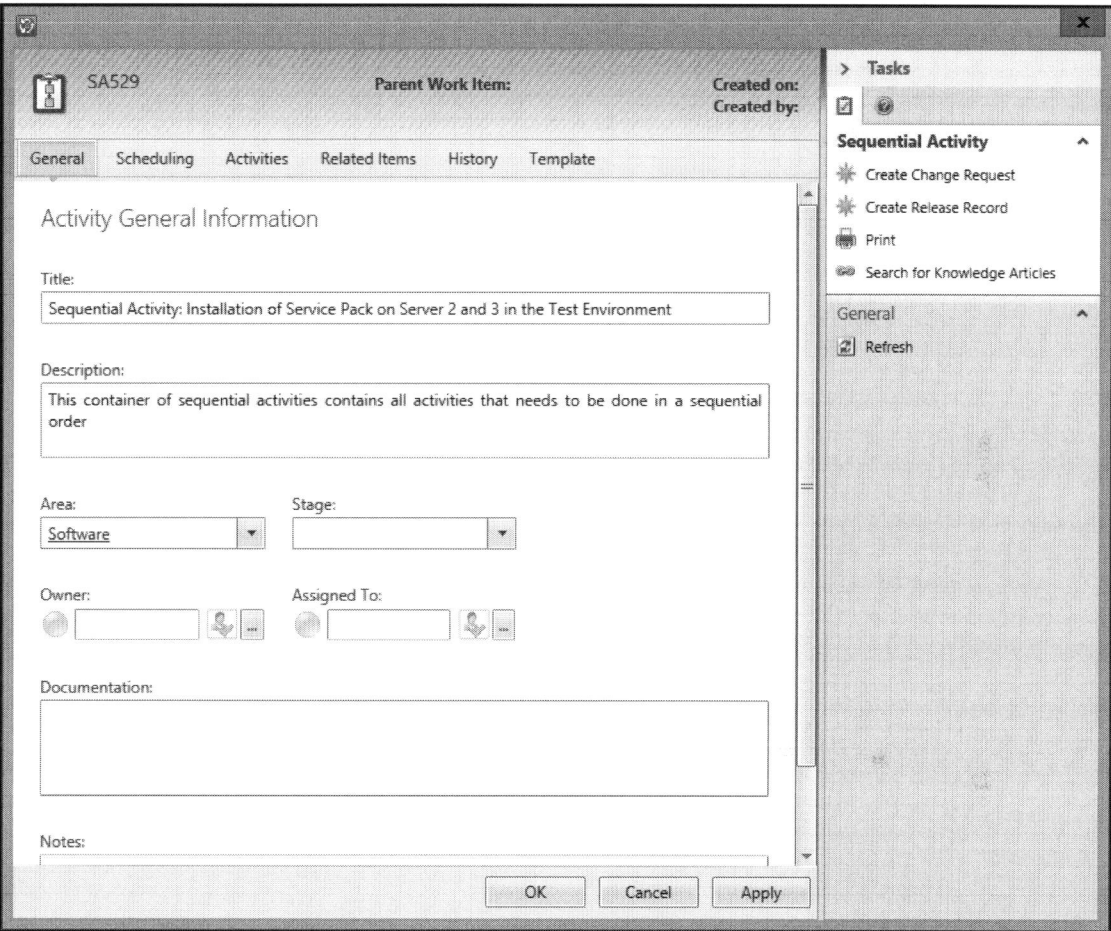

7. Click on **Activities**.

8. Add Manual Activities to the Container Activity Template. In this recipe we add two Manual Activities:

- **Install Service Pack on Server 2 in Test Environment**
- **Install Service Pack on Server 3 in Test Environment**

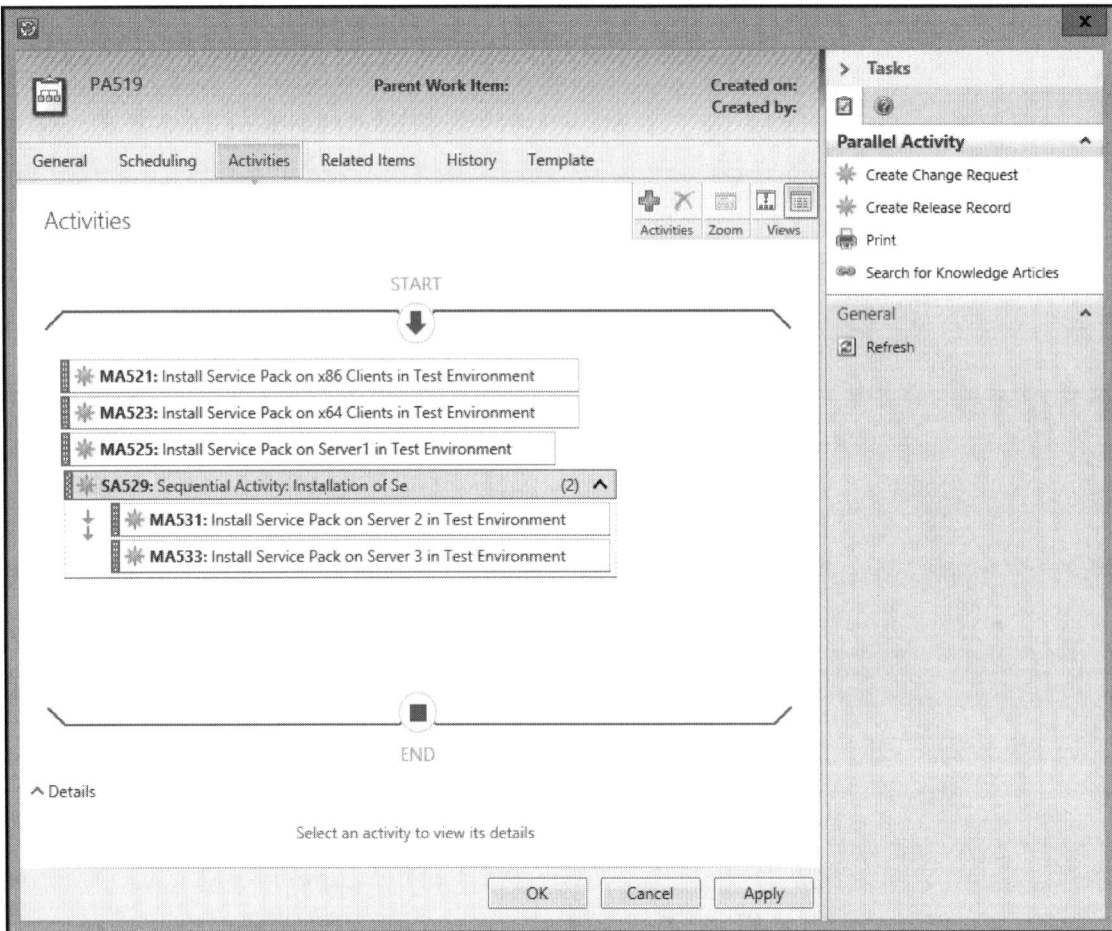

9. Click on **OK** to close the Container Activity Template.
10. Click on **OK** to close the Change Request Template.

How it works...

Sequential Activities in SCSM 2016 work like the Parallel Activities described in the previous recipe by providing a single container for one or more activities.

All activities inside a Sequential Activity container are processed in a serialized order. If the Sequential Activity changes to **In Progress**, the first activity inside it will get the same status. All other activities will be in the status of **Pending**. When the first activity moves to a **Completed** status, the next activity will change to **In Progress**, and so on. When the last activity in a Sequential Activity container is marked as **Completed** the Sequential Activity container will also be marked as **Completed**.

Sequential Activities can be used inside a Parallel Activity container if some activities need to be serialized. For instance, in this recipe we used the example of installing the Service Pack in parallel on different systems, but we need to install the Service Pack on two servers in a sequential order.

There's more...

Here is some more information on how to work with the different types of Activities in SCSM 2016.

How to work with Review, Manual, and Dependent Activities

Please look at the following recipes in this chapter to see how to work with different types of activities in SCSM 2016:

- Creating and managing Change Management Review Activities
- Creating Manual Activities for Change Management
- Creating and managing Dependent Activities in Change Management

How to work with Parallel Activities in SCSM 2016

Please take at the previous recipes to see how Parallel Activities work in SCSM 2016.

See also

Microsoft TechNet Library: Managing Changes and Activities in System Center – Service Manager: `https://technet.microsoft.com/en-us/system-center-docs/sm/manage/ops -managing-changes-and-activities-in-system-center-2016-service-manager`.

Creating and personalizing Change Management Activity notifications

In SCSM 2016 it is possible to send notifications to "Reviewers" of Review Activities and "Implementers" of Manual Activities. This is helpful because different activities in a Change Request will change their status during the Change Management process. For instance, a Manual Activity status changes from **Pending** to **In Progress** after a previous Review Activity is approved.

This recipe will show how this notification workflow can be configured.

Getting ready

There are two ways to create a notification in SCSM 2016.

The first one is to navigate to **Administration** | **Notification** | **Subscription** | **Create Subscription**. The wizard will lead you through the creation of the notification.

The second method is to configure a workflow by navigating to **Administration** | **Workflows** | **Configuration** and selecting the relevant process type.

We will use the second method and it is described in detail in this recipe. The major difference between these two methods is the option to apply a template to the activity with additional information when you use the workflow option.

To create an Activity Notification workflow, open the SCSM 2016 console and navigate to **Administration** | **Workflows** | **Configuration**.

How to do it...

To create a new notification, follow these steps:

1. Double-click on **Activity Event Workflow Configuration**.
2. In the **Select a Class** form select **Review Activity** and click on **OK**.

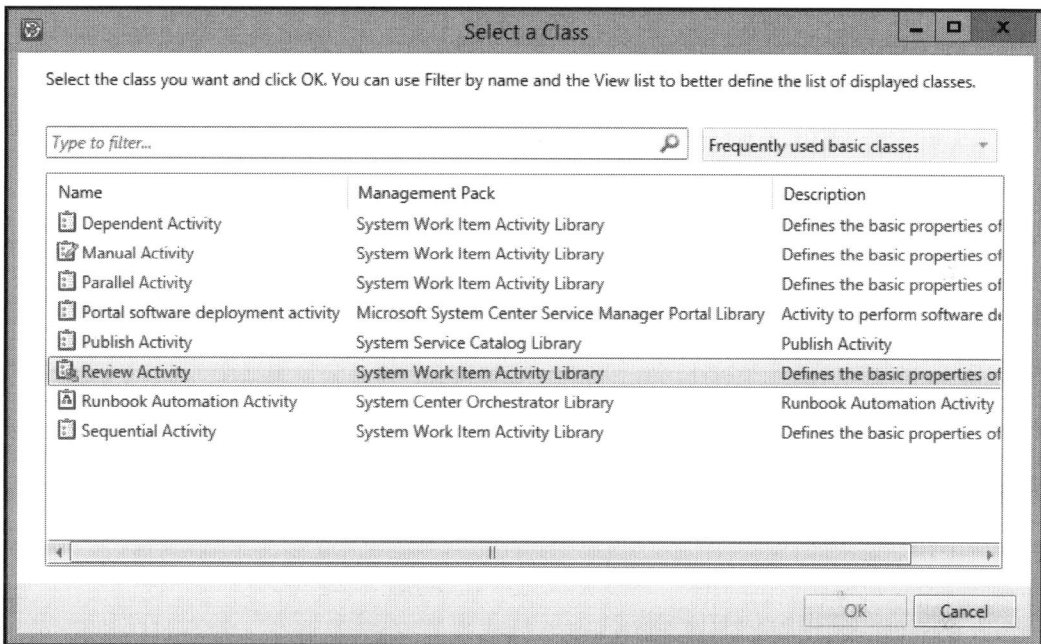

3. In the **Configure Workflows** window, click on **Add**.
4. Read the instructions and information on the **Before You Begin** page.
5. Click on **Next**.
6. Fill in the **Title** (Change Request Reviewer Notification Workflow) and a **Description** (This workflow will send a notification to the reviewer if a Review Activity status changed from "Pending" to "In Progress") fields in the **Workflow Information** page.
7. Select **When an object is updated** from the **Check for events:** list.

8. Select a management pack to save the workflow in (for example, **Custom. ChangeManagement.Library**).

9. Click on **Next**.

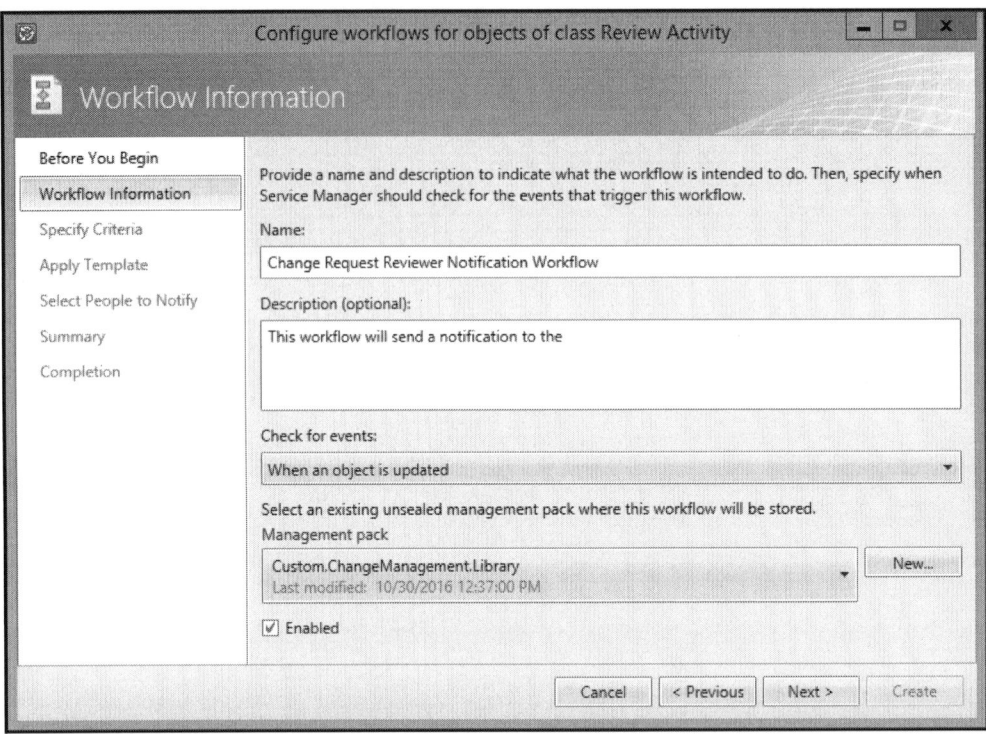

10. In the **Specify Criteria** page, click on **Changed from**.

11. In the **Available Properties** list search for **Status**, select the checkbox, and click on **Add**.

12. In the **Criteria** section, beside **[Activity] Status** click on the list with conditions and select **equals**.

13. In the **Criteria** section, beside **[Activity] Status** click on the list with status and select **Pending**.

14. In the **Specify Criteria** page, click on **Changed to**.

15. In the **Available Properties** list search for **Status**, select the checkbox, and click on **Add**.

16. In the **Criteria** section, beside **[Activity] Status** click on the list with conditions and select **equals**.

17. In the **Criteria** section, beside **[Activity] Status** click on the list with status and select **In Progress**.

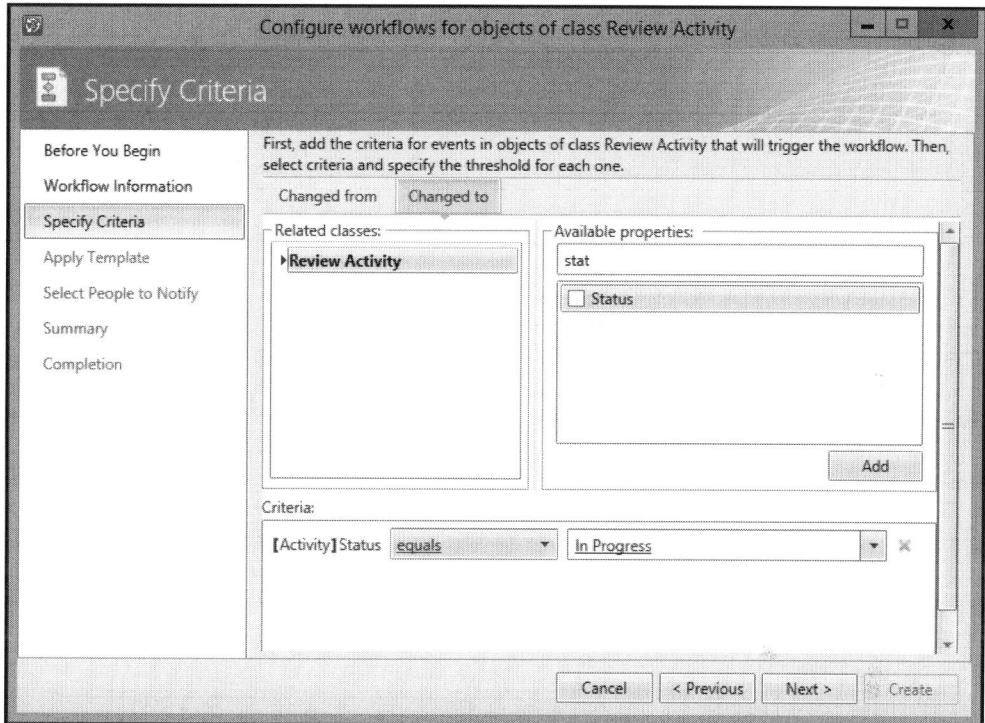

18. Click on **Next**.
19. In the **Apply Template** page, do not apply any template.
20. Click on **Next**.
21. In the **Select People to Notify** page, check the **Enable notification** checkbox.

22. Select **Reviewers** from the **User** drop-down box.

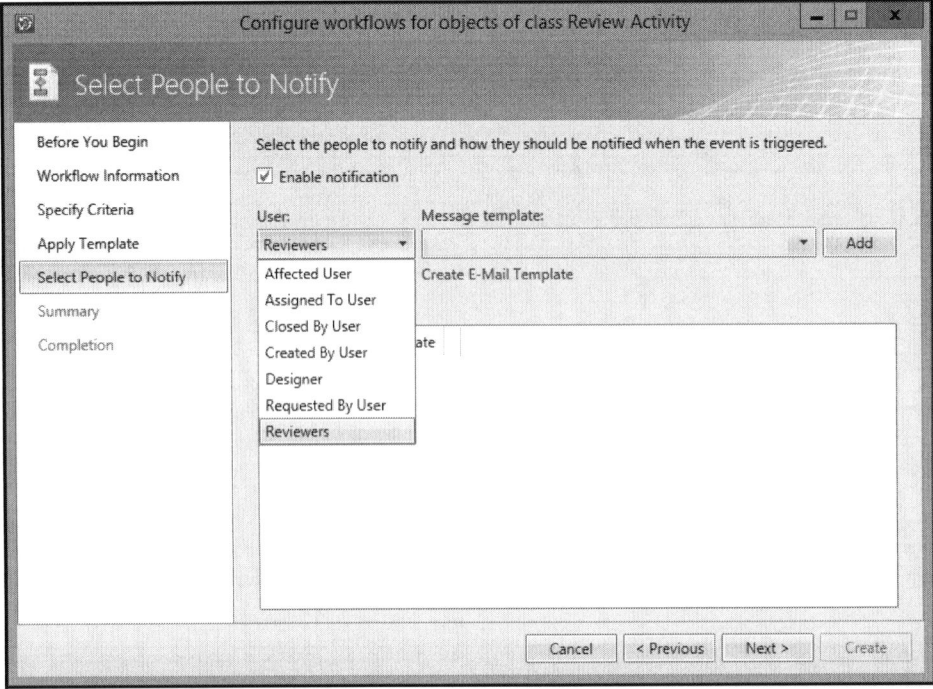

23. Select an existing message template from the list or create a new notification template by clicking on **Create E-Mail Template**.
24. Click on **Add**.
25. Click on **Next**.

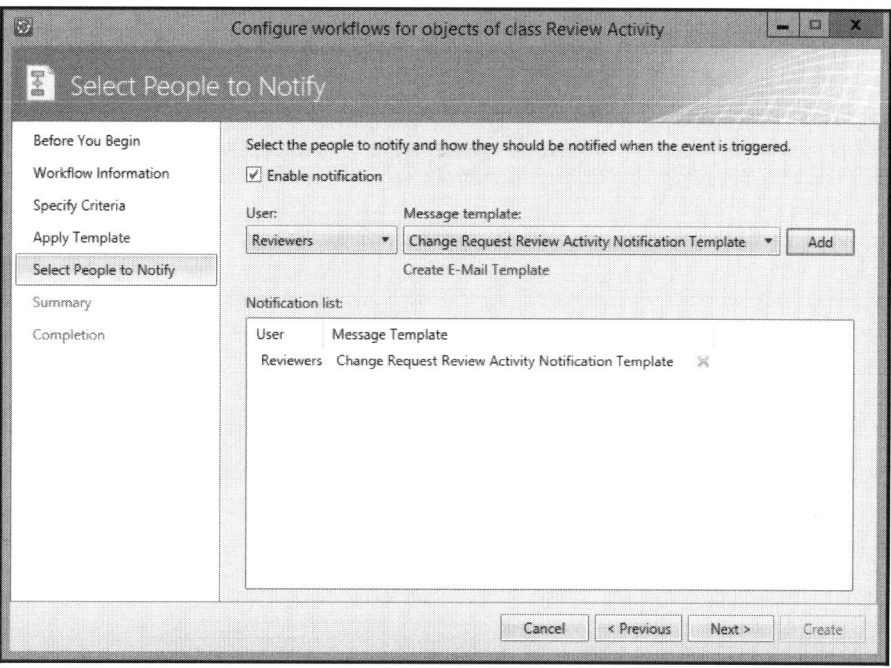

26. Verify the summary and click on **Create**.
27. In the **Configure Workflow** window click on **OK**.

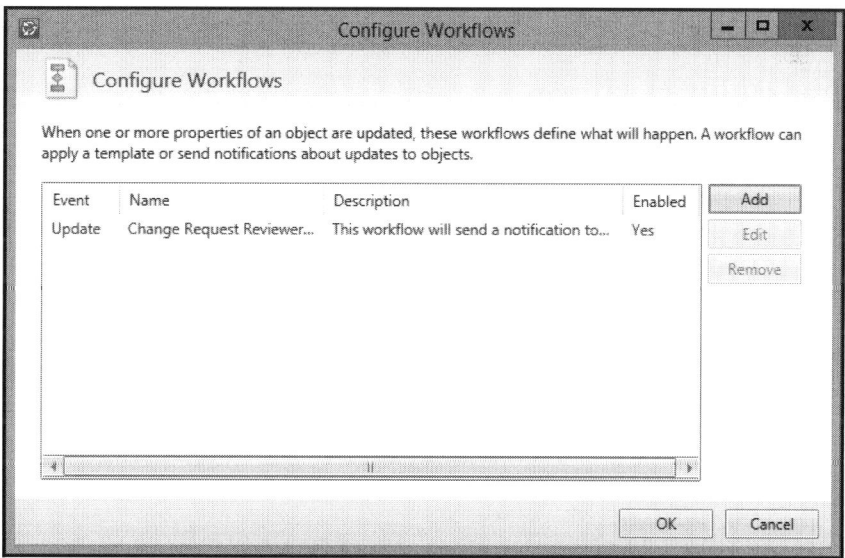

How it works...

The notification workflow will be initiated when the specified condition is met. In our workflow example, the notification will be sent to the reviewer when the status of the review activity changes from **Pending** to **In Progress**.

There's more...

Notification on activities is a good way to automate the Change Management process. An e-mail is sent to the reviewer or activity implementer of the activity when it becomes "active".

Notifying the Implementer of a Manual Activity

The notification of an implementer of a Manual Activity works similar to notifying the reviewer of a Review Activity There is one difference during the creation: you need to select **Assigned To User** because Implementer is not listed as an option. The **Assigned To User** in the list of possible recipients correlates to the **Implementer** of a Manual Activity.

Working with Notification templates

For more information on how to create and work with notifications, please look at the *Creating formatted e-mail notification* templates recipe in `Chapter 2`, *Personalizing SCSM 2012 Administration*.

See also

Microsoft TechNet Library: Managing Changes and Activities in System Center – Service Manager:
`https://technet.microsoft.com/en-us/system-center-docs/sm/manage/ops-managing-c hanges-and-activities-in-system-center-2016-service-manager`.

Creating and managing Build and Environment Release Records

In SCSM 2016 Release Management you can define different Builds and Environments of your IT infrastructure.

For instance, Builds can be different versions of software (different versions for x86 and x64 operating systems).

An Environment can be a test, pre-production, and/or production environment in your IT infrastructure.

This recipe will show you how to create Builds and Environments in the Release Management process of SCSM 2016.

Getting ready

To create and manage Environments of Release Records, open the SCSM 2016 console and navigate to **Configuration Items** | **Environments** | **All Environments**.

To create and manage Builds of Release Records open the SCSM 2016 console and navigate to **Configuration Items** | **Builds** | **All Builds**.

How to do it...

To create a new Environment, follow these steps:

1. Click on **Create Environment** in the **Tasks** pane.
2. Fill in the information in the **Display Name**, **Title**, and **Description** fields.
3. Choose **Deployed** from the **Asset Status** drop-down box.
4. Choose **Pre-Production** from the **Category** drop-down box.

5. Click on **OK** to close the form.

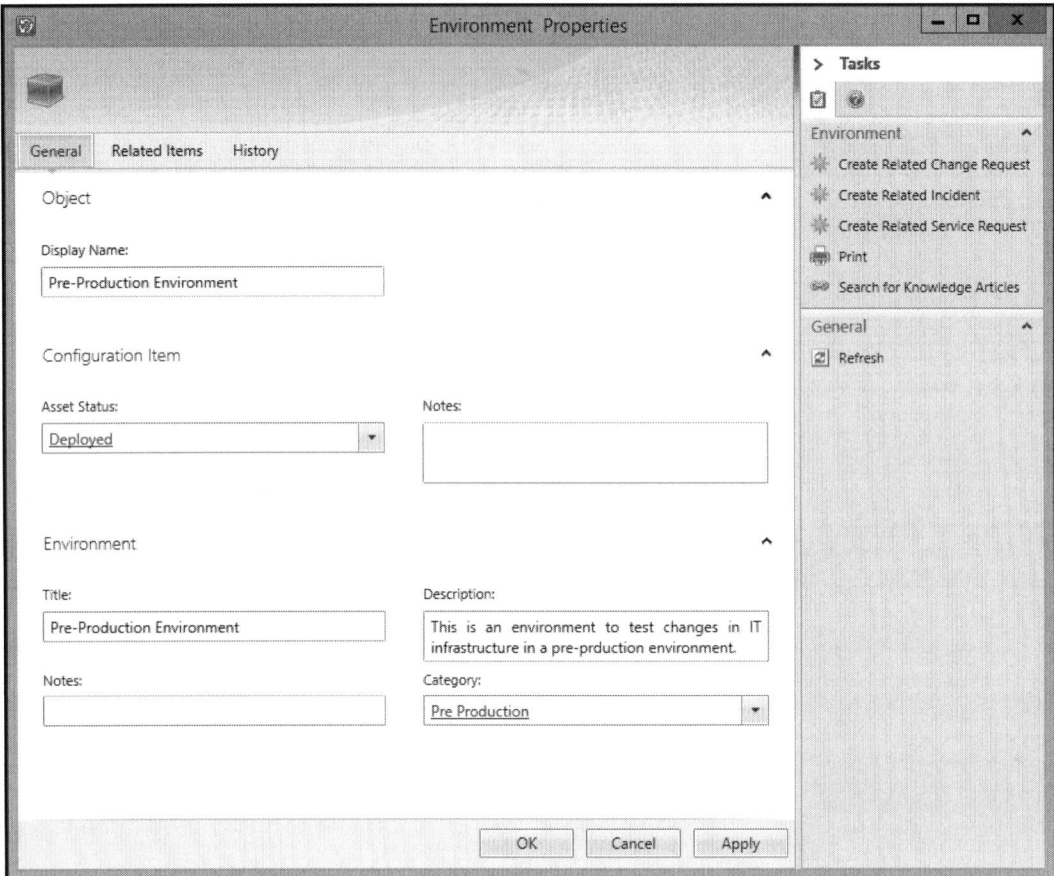

6. Create multiple environments to reflect your IT infrastructure.

To create a new Build, follow these steps:

1. Click on **Create Build** in the **Tasks** pane.
2. Fill in the **Display Name**, **Title**, **Version**, **Description**, and **Source Path** fields.
3. Choose an asset status from the **Asset Status** drop-down box, for example, **Undefined**.

4. Choose a category from the **Category** drop-down box. In our recipe we have selected **Software**.

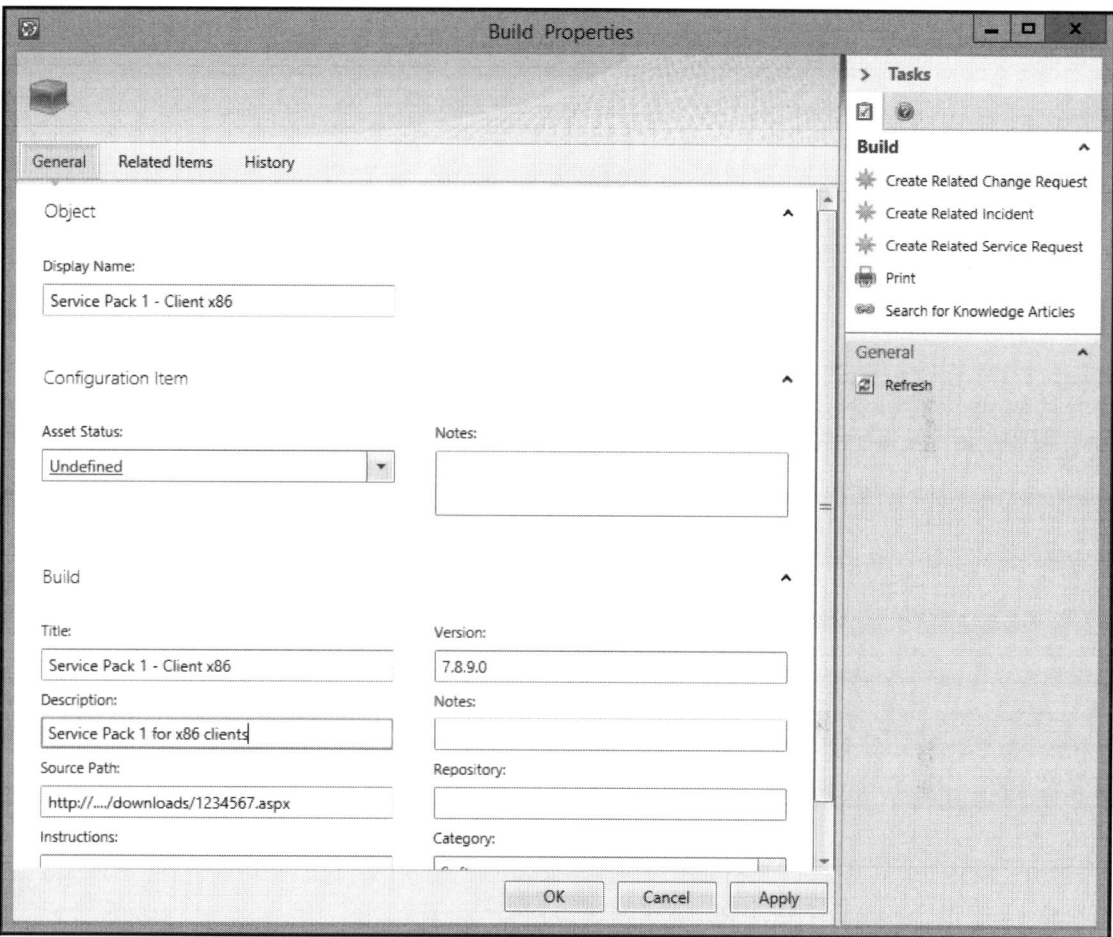

5. Click on **OK** to close the **Build** window.
6. Create new Builds for all the different versions you need:
   - Service Pack 1 – Client x86
   - Service Pack 1 – Client x64
   - Service Pack 1 – Server x64

How it works...

Builds and Environments can be used in Release Records to relate the release of a Build of software or hardware modification to a specified environment. This will also define the scope of the release.

There's more...

A Build is logical and is therefore not limited to a software version only.

Builds are not only software-related

A Build can describe different hardware Builds as well. For instance, different CPU architectures such as "Intel-processor based" or "ARM processor based". Another example might be different types of servers (physically or virtual).

See also

Microsoft TechNet Library: Managing Release Records in Service Manager: `https://techn et.microsoft.com/en-us/system-center-docs/sm/manage/ops-managing-release-rec ords-in-system-center-2016-service-manager`.

Creating and managing Release Record Templates

Release Record Templates can be used to pre-fill information in the Release Record form. For instance, these can be a predefined Title, Description, Impact, Risk, and Priority.

This recipe will describe the steps required to create a new Release Record Template.

Getting ready

In the SCSM 2016 console, navigate to **Library** | **Templates**.

How to do it...

To create a Release Record Template, follow these steps:

1. Click on **Create template** in the **Tasks** pane.
2. Enter a name in the **Name** field. In this recipe, we will use `Release Record Service Pack Installation Template`.
3. Enter a description in the **Description** field. For instance, `This template can be used for Release Records regarding deployment of Service Packs`.
4. Choose the **Release Record** class by clicking on **Browse** next to the **Class** field, and then click on **OK**.
5. Choose an existing management pack or create a new one to store the Release Record Template(the *Creating Management Packs to save your SCSM personalization* recipe in `Chapter 2`, *Personalizing SCSM 2012 Administration* describes how to store your customizations in management packs as well as best practice naming conventions of the XML files).
6. Click on **OK**.

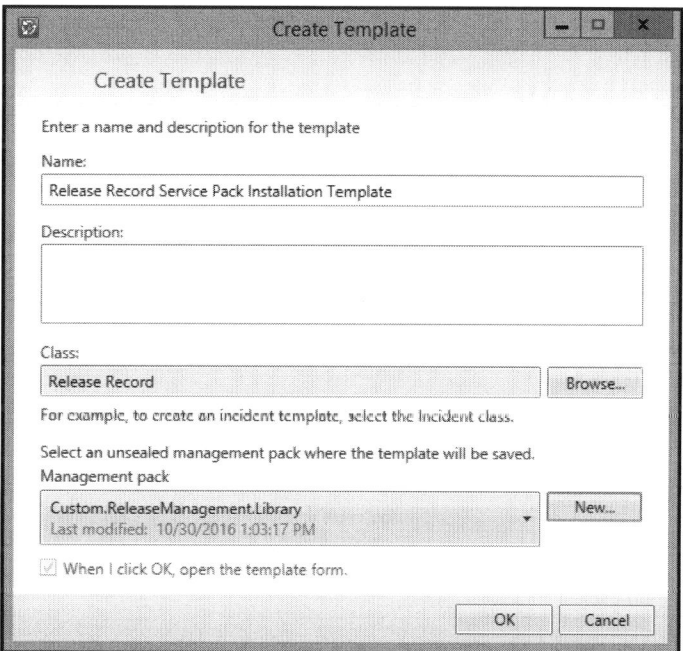

7. Fill in the information in all fields of the form. In this recipe, we will pre-fill the fields **Title**, **Description**, **Type** (select **Planned** from the drop-down box), **Category** (select **Fix** from the drop-down box), **Impact** (select **Standard** from the drop-down box), **Risk** (select **Medium** from the drop-down box), and **Priority** (select **Medium** from the drop-down box) fields in the **General** tab of the Release Record Template.

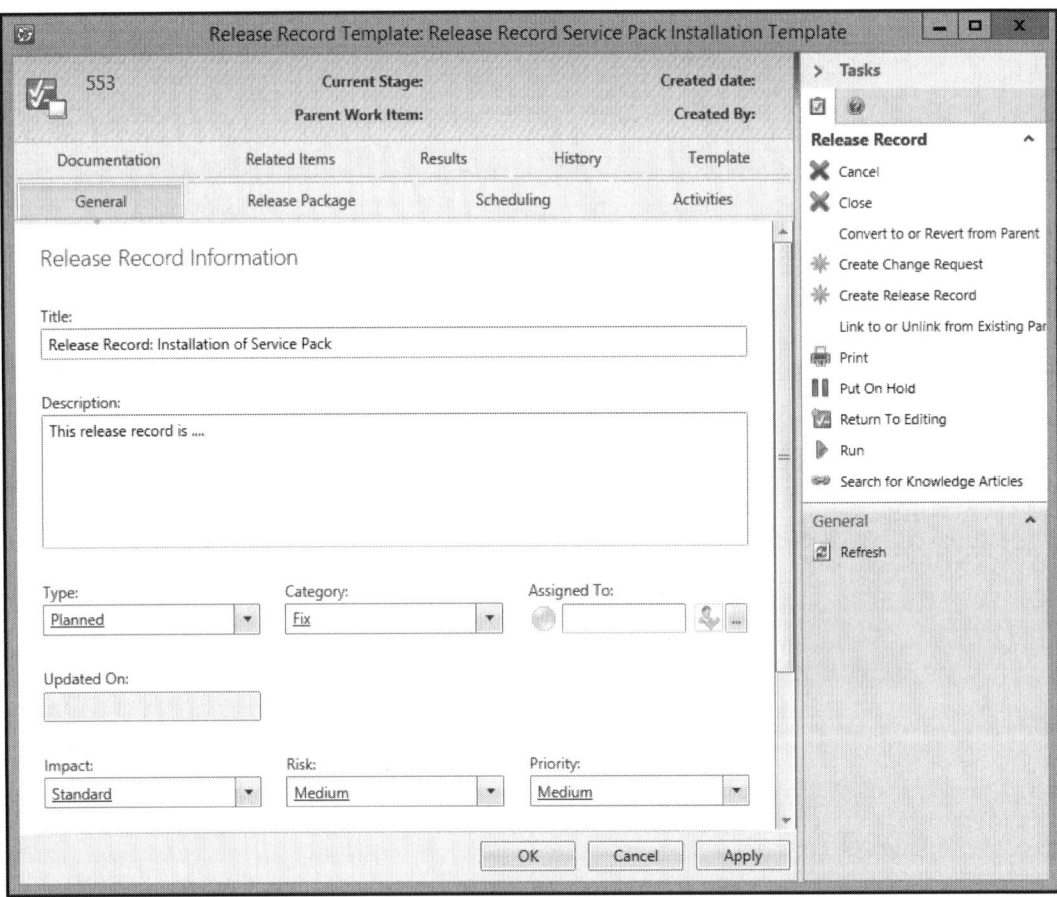

8. In the **Documentation** tab, add some information regarding this Release Record Template. For instance, some information on how the release is done.

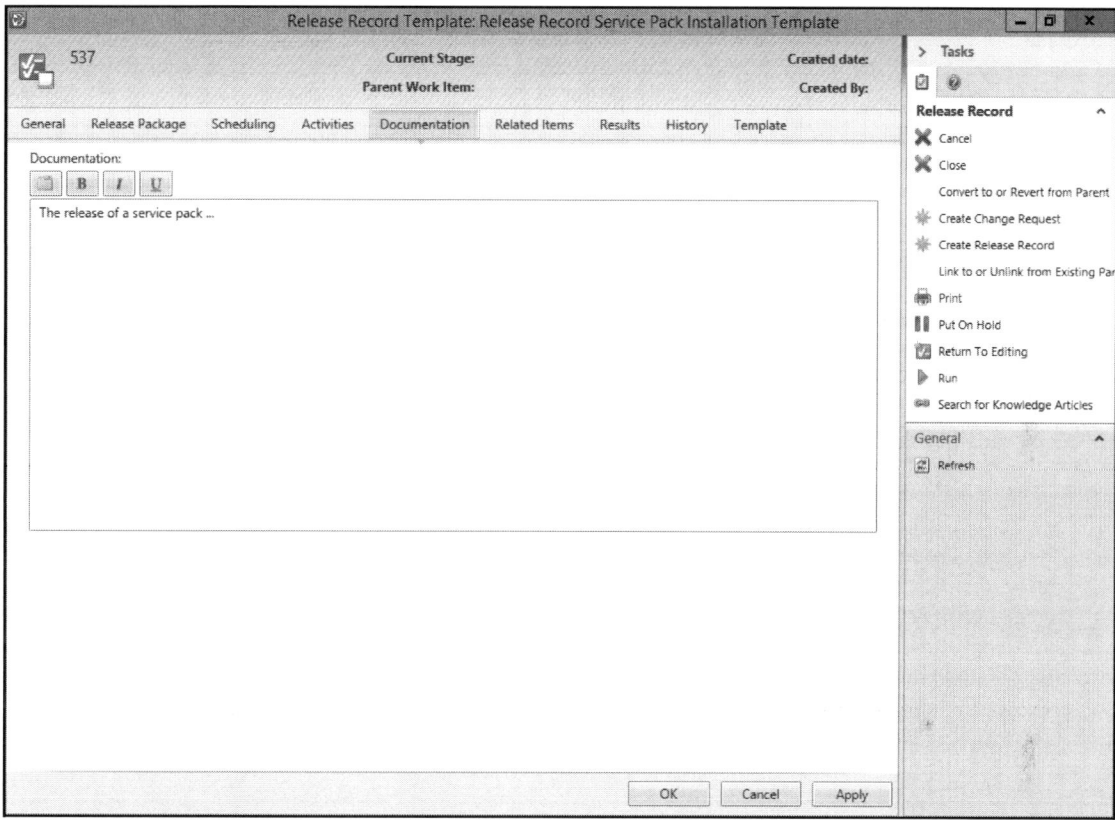

9. Click on **OK** to close the template.

How it works...

Basically, a pre-filled template in SCSM 2016 can be used to create new work items (for instances of Release Records, Incident Records, Change Requests, and Service Requests). Using templates keeps the content and information of forms consistent. Using pre-filled templates will also reduce the time each individual spends initiating the relevant Work Item.

There's more...

In this recipe, we did not talk about how to work with the different types of activities in a Release Record template. That topic is covered in the following recipes of this chapter:

- *Creating and managing Change Management Review Activities*
- *Creating Manual Activities for Change Management*
- *Creating and managing Dependent Activities in Change Management*

Here is an example scenario using the activities described in the previous recipes for a release record.

We will start with a Dependent Activity to link a Change Request configured as follows:

- Change Request name: `Install Service Pack`

Add a Parallel Activity Container named "`Install Service Pack`" with the following two Manual Activities:

- Install Service Pack on x86 clients
- Install Service Pack on x64 clients

We will then create a Sequential Activity container for this Change Request called:

- Install Service Pack on Servers

Containing the following Manual Activities:

- Install Service Pack on Server1
- Install Service Pack on Server2
- Install Service Pack on Server3

Adding more specific information to a Release Record Template

Optionally, you can add some more specific information to a Release Record Template as required and relevant to your processes:

Release Package tab:

- **Configuration Items to Modify**: Specific CIs that are related to this Release Record
- **Affected Services**: Business Services that are affected by these Release Records

Scheduling tab:

- It doesn't make sense to provide this information in a template. This tab should be filled out during the creation of a Release Record based on this template.

See also

Microsoft TechNet Library: Managing Release Records in Service Manager: `https://techn et.microsoft.com/en-us/system-center-docs/sm/manage/ops-managing-release-rec ords-in-system-center-2016-service-manager`.

Working with Change Requests and Release Records

After setting up the Change and Release Management in SCSM 2016 this recipe will show you how to create a new Change Request and Release Record. Also, it will show you how to add links between these two management processes.

Getting ready

To create a new Change Request in SCSM 2016 open the console and navigate to **Work Items | Change Management**.

To create a new Release Record in SCSM 2016 open the console and navigate to **Work Items | Release Management**.

How to do it...

Follow these steps to create a new Change Request:

1. Click on **New Change Request** in the **Tasks** pane.
2. Choose **Change Request Service Pack Installation Template**, which we created in an earlier recipe in this chapter.
3. Click on **OK**.

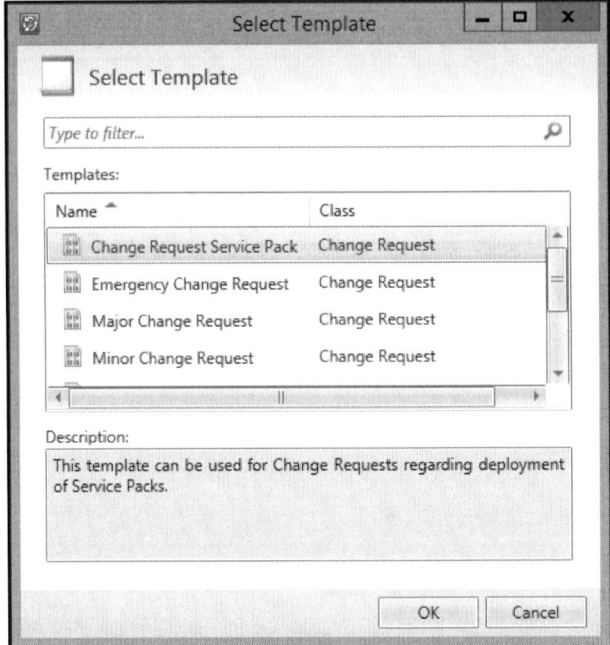

4. As we provided a lot of the information already in the Change Request Template only a few things need to be added:
   - Add the related computers to **Config Items To Change**. For instance, we will add **Client1**, **Client2**, **Server1**, **Server2**, and **Server3** in this recipe. Click on **Add** and pick the computers from the list, then click on **OK**.
   - Select **Standard** from the **Impact** drop-down box and **Medium** from the **Risk** drop-down box.

5. Click on **OK** to close the form and create the Change Request.

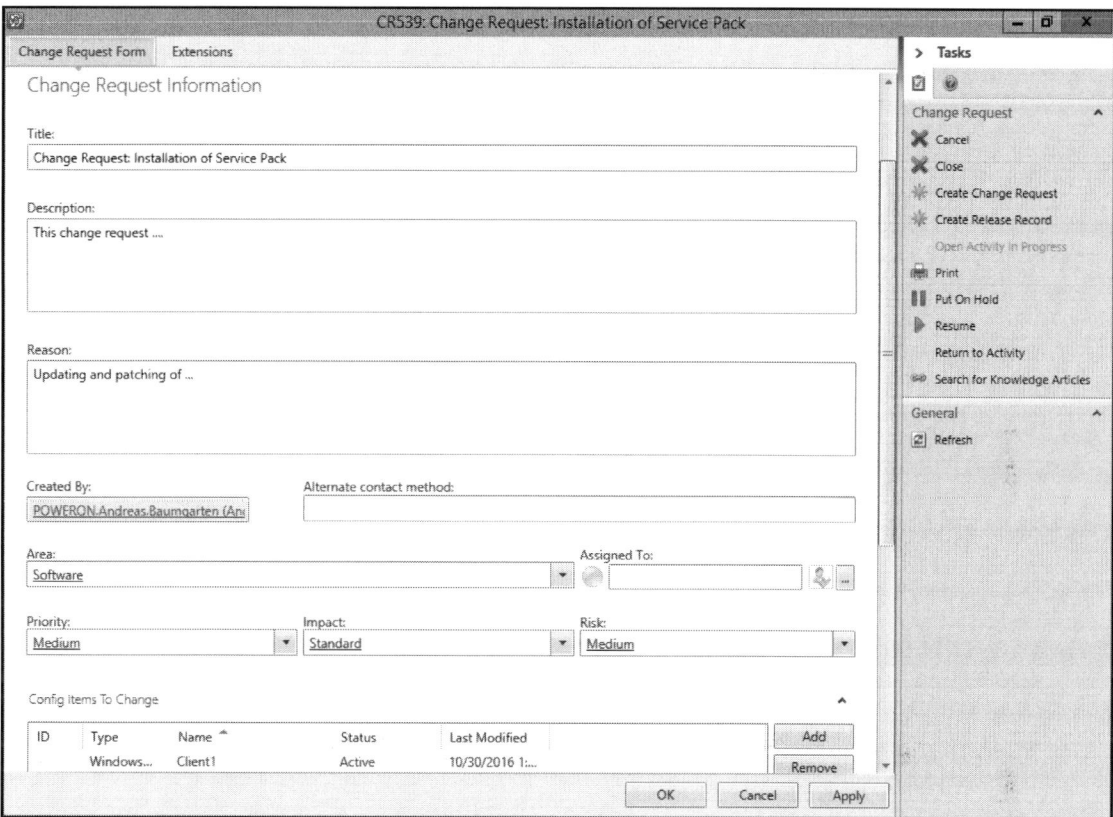

Follow these steps to create a new Release Record:

1. Click on **New Release record** in the **Tasks** pane.
2. In the **Select Template**, choose the Release Record Template we created earlier in this chapter called **Release Record Service Pack Installation Template**.
3. Click on **OK**.

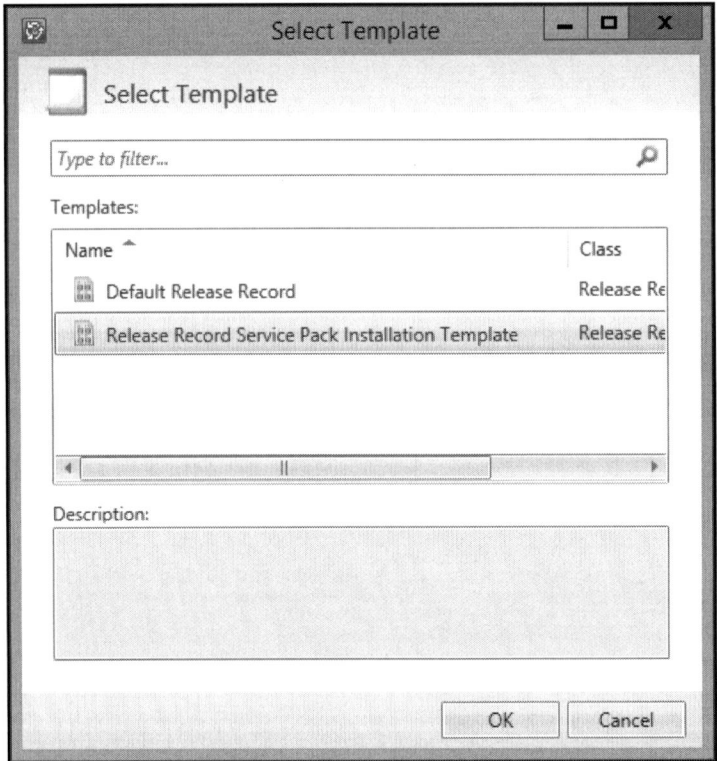

4. All the required information in the **General** tab is provided by the template.

5. Click on the **Release Package** tab and add the related computers to **Configuration Items to Modify**. For instance, we will add **Client1**, **Client2**, **Server1**, **Server2**, and **Server3** in this recipe. Click on **Add** and pick the computers from the list, then click on **OK**.

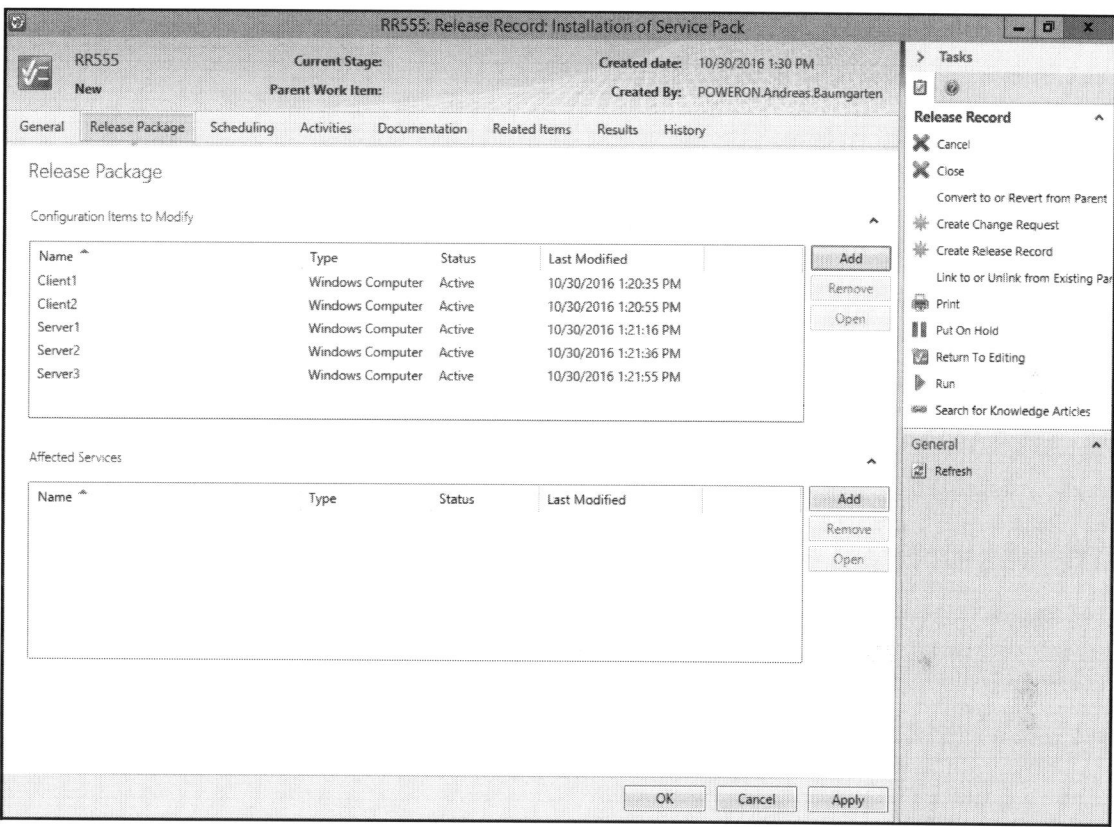

6. In the **Scheduling** tab, provide the scheduled (planned) time information, planned work, and planned costs.

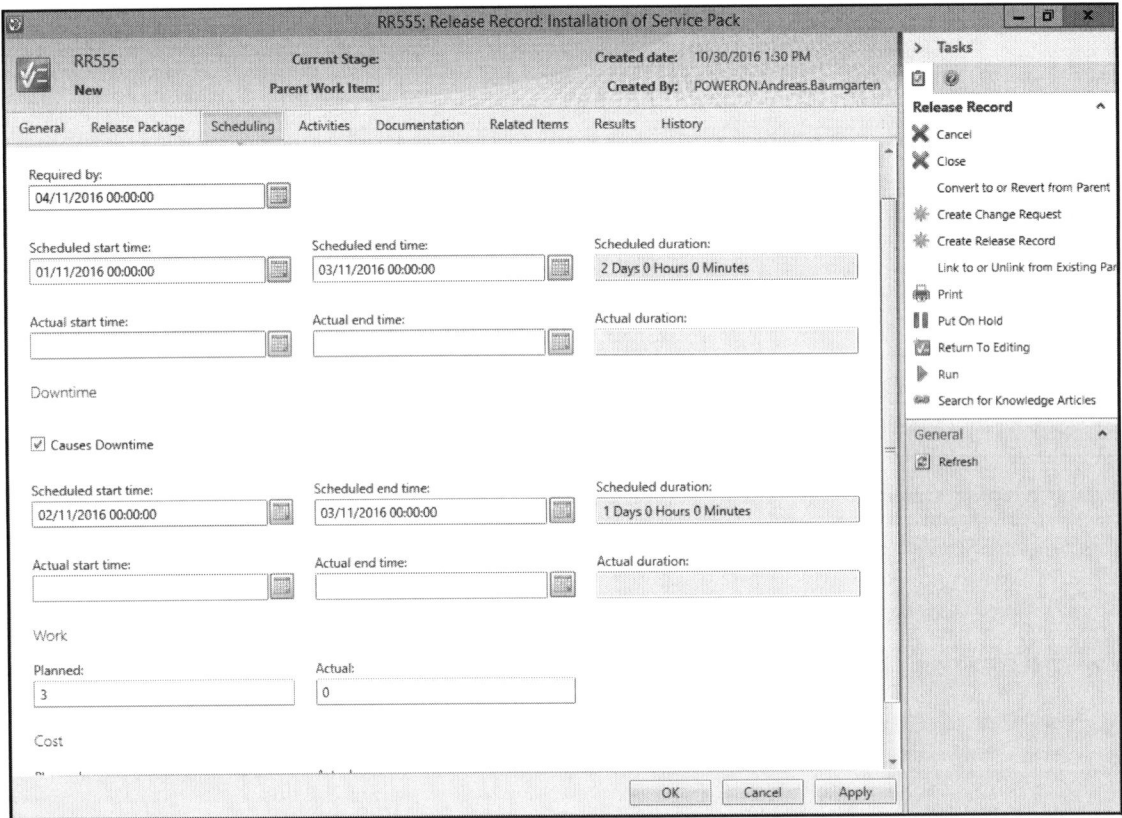

7. In the **Activities** tab you can use the activities we added in the previous recipe or you can build your own activities for this specific release. We will start with a Dependent Activity to link a Change Request configured as follows:

•   Change Request name: `Install Service Pack`

    Add a Parallel Activity Container named "Install Service Pack" with the following two Manual Activities:

•   Install Service Pack on x86 clients

- Install Service Pack on x64 clients

  We will then create a Sequential Activity container for this Change Request called:

- Install Service Pack on Servers

  Containing the following Manual Activities:

- Install Service Pack on Server1
- Install Service Pack on Server2
- Install Service Pack on Server3

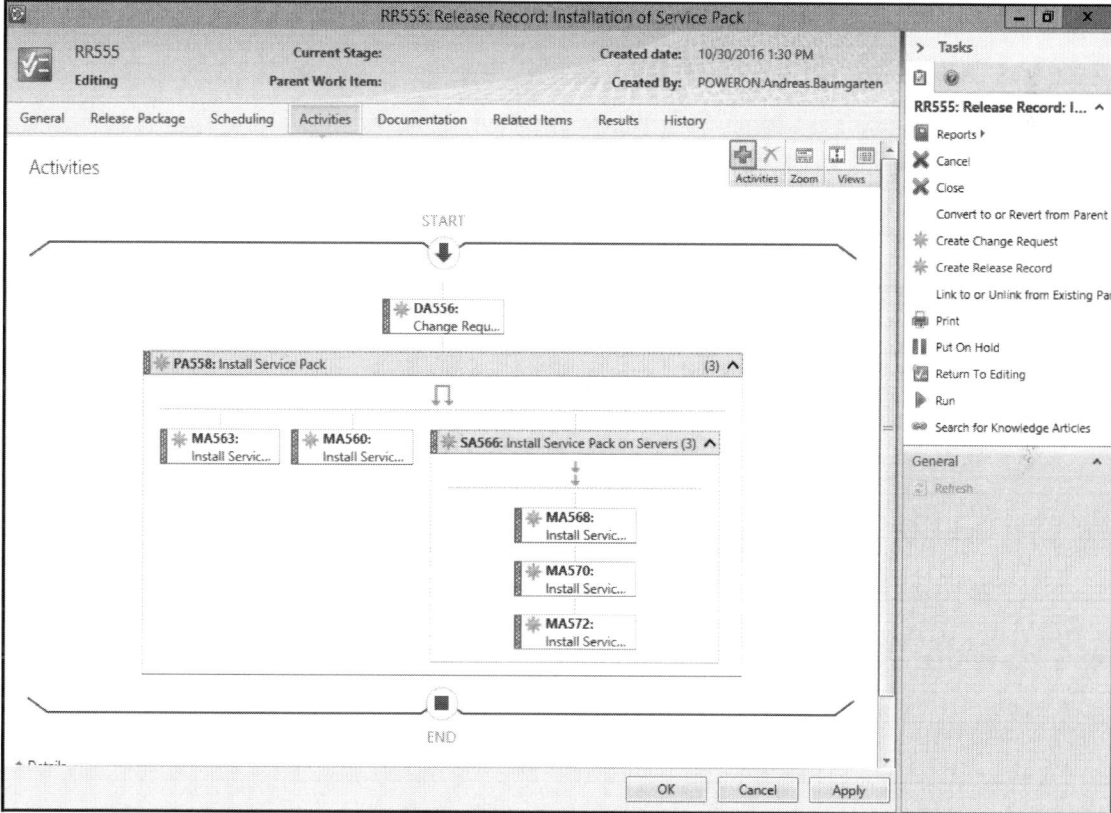

8. You can add additional specific information to each activity you added, such as **Impacted Configuration Items** and **Implementer**.

9. Right-click on the **Dependent Activity** and choose **Link to Change Request Activity**.
10. Choose the Dependent Activity from the Change Request we created earlier in this recipe and click on **OK**.

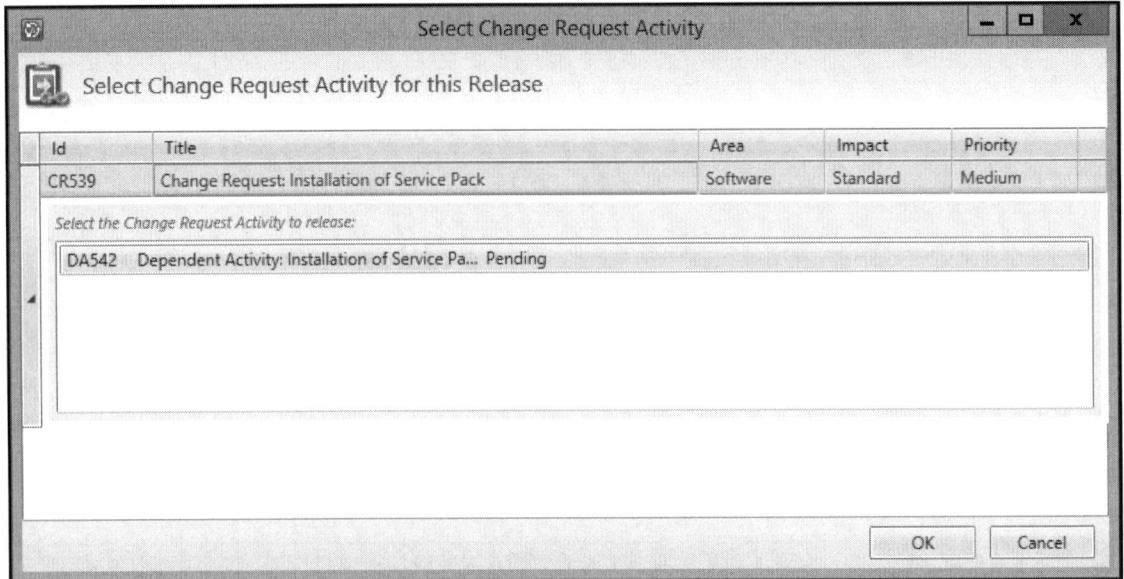

11. Click on **OK** in the Release Record form to close the form.
12. After providing all the information in the Release Record select the Release Record we created, and click on **Run** in the **Tasks** pane and add a comment to start the release process. After the Release Record is started you can switch to the editing mode by clicking on **Return to editing** in the **Tasks** pane.

How it works...

If you create a new Change Request based on a Change Request template, all pre-filled fields will be applied to the new Change Request object. You can modify or delete the template at any time. Also, the pre-defined activities within the template are added to the new Change Request. These activities can also be modified or deleted. Another option could be to skip activities once the actual Change Request has been created instead of deleting the activities from the template. To skip an activity, select the activity, right-click and choose **Skip Activity** from the context menu, enter a comment, and click on **OK**.

If you create a new Release Record based on a Release Record template the predefined fields of the template will be applied to the new Release Record. Similar to a Change Request you can modify or delete the pre-filled fields of the activities of the Release Record template. As in the Change Request, the activities can be modified, deleted, or skipped. To start a Release Record process, you need to click on **Run** in the **Tasks** pane and add a comment.

There's more…

To combine different configuration items you can add this to Builds. For complex and large releases it can be helpful to use Parent/Child Release records.

Using Environments and Builds

Instead of adding each individual CI, which will be affected by the release record you can add the environments and/or the builds in the Release Package tab.

Using Parent/Child Release Records

If a release is very complex you can use Parent/Child release records instead of creating a lot of different activities. This offers the option to split a complex release process into smaller pieces.

For instance, take a look at the following figure:

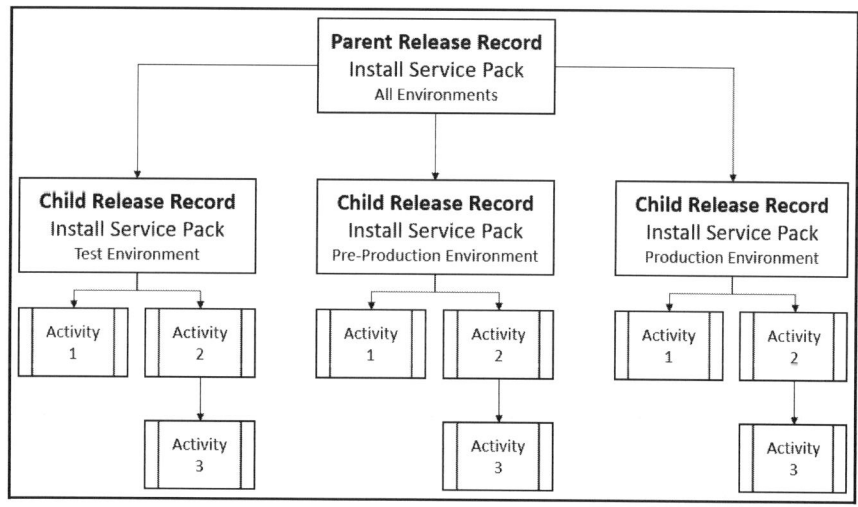

Reporting Scheduled and Actual Date information

Providing the Scheduled Start and End Time of change requests, release records, and all the different activities and also, providing the Actual Start and End Time is very helpful for reporting on how the Change Management and Release Management processes are performing. These key performance indicators offer a good overview on how many change requests, release records, and activities are completed in the planned time.

To get more information about reporting please take a look at the recipes of Chapter 10, *Working with the Data Warehouse and Reporting* of this cookbook.

See also

Microsoft TechNet Library: *Managing Release Records in Service Manager*: https://technet.microsoft.com/en-us/system-center-docs/sm/manage/ops-managing-release-records-in-system-center-2016-service-manager.

Filling in all related Activity Descriptions with Descriptions from parent Change Requests

It could be very helpful to have the description of the parent Change Request in every related Activity (especially the Review and Manual Activities).

One use where this can be helpful is the notification of Reviewers and Implementers by mail with the details in the Change Record description.

To solve this requirement a PowerShell script can be used to write the content of the Description filed of a parent Change Record in every Description field of a related Activity.

Getting ready

A Change Request must be submitted in SCSM 2016 before we start. The required steps to create a Change Request are described in the recipe *Working with Change Requests and Release Records* in this chapter. We need the ID of the created Change Request, in our example it is "CR575". If you like to run the PowerShell script remotely (not on the SCSM 2016 management server), we need the name of the SCSM 2016 management server as well. In our example, the name of the server is "TDSCSM03".

You must download and install the SCSM PowerShell Cmdlets found at `http://smlets.codeplex.com/` (see the *Downloading and installing SMLets* recipe in `Chapter 12`, *Automating Service Manager 2016*).

How to do it…

On the SCSM 2016 management server, start the Windows PowerShell ISE:

1. Type the following code into a new script window in **Windows PowerShell ISE**:

```
# Import SMlets module
Import-Module SMlets

#------ Variables ------

# ID of the Service Request
$id = "CR575"

# Name of the SCSM Management Server
$smDefaultComputer = "TDSCSM03"


#------------------------

# Definition of function to find all related activities

function Add-ActivityDescriptionRecursive($activity,
$description)
{
# Set internal activity id
$activityId = $activity.Displayname
# Get activity object
$activity = Get-SCSMObject -Class $activityClass -Filter
"Displayname -like $activityId*"
# Call function "Add-ActivityDescription" to write description of
activity
```

```
    Add-ActivityDescription -activity $activity -description
$description
  # Get related child activities
  $workItemContainsActivityRelationship = Get-SCSMRelationshipClass
  -Name System.WorkItemContainsActivity$
  # Get related activity objects
  $recursiveActivities = Get-SCSMRelatedObject -SMObject $activity
  -Relationship $workItemContainsActivityRelationship
  # For each related actvity found
  foreach($obj in $recursiveActivities)
  {
    # Call function "Add-ActivityDescription" to write description
  of activity
     Add-ActivityDescriptionRecursive -activity $obj -description
  $description
  }
  }
  # Definition of function
  function Add-ActivityDescription($activity, $description)
  {
  # Exists a description in the Activity?
  if ($activity.Description)
  {
    # Build PropertyHash if Activity Description is not empty
    $newDescription = $activity.Description +
  [Environment]::NewLine +  "--------------" +
  [Environment]::NewLine + $description
    $propertyHash = @{Description = $newDescription}
  }
  else
  {   # Set PropertyHash if Activity Description is empty
    $propertyHash = @{Description = $description}
  }
  # Update Description of activity
  $activity | Set-SCSMObject -PropertyHashtable $propertyHash
  }

  # Get Activity and Service Request classes
  $parentClass = Get-SCSMClass -Name System.WorkItem.ChangeRequest$
  $activityClass = Get-SCSMClass -Name System.WorkItem.Activity$

  # Get relationship between Service Request and all related
  Activities
  $workItemContainsActivityRelationship = Get-SCSMRelationshipClass
   -Name System.WorkItemContainsActivity$

  # Get configured Service Request and its description
  $parentRequest = Get-SCSMObject -Class $parentClass -Filter "Id =
```

```
$id"
$description = $parentRequest.Description

# Get all related Activities of Service Request
$activities = Get-SCSMRelatedObject -SMObject $parentRequest -
Relationship $workItemContainsActivityRelationship

# For each related Activity
foreach ($activity in $activities)
    {
        # Call function "Add-ActivityDescription" to write
description of activity
    Add-ActivityDescriptionRecursive -activity $activity -
description $description
    }
```

2. Save the file as a PowerShell file with a `.ps1` extension to a filesystem location (for example, `C:\ Set-DescriptionActivities.ps1`).

3. Modify line 9 and line 12 in the script with your CR ID and the SCSM 2016 management server name (marked in yellow).

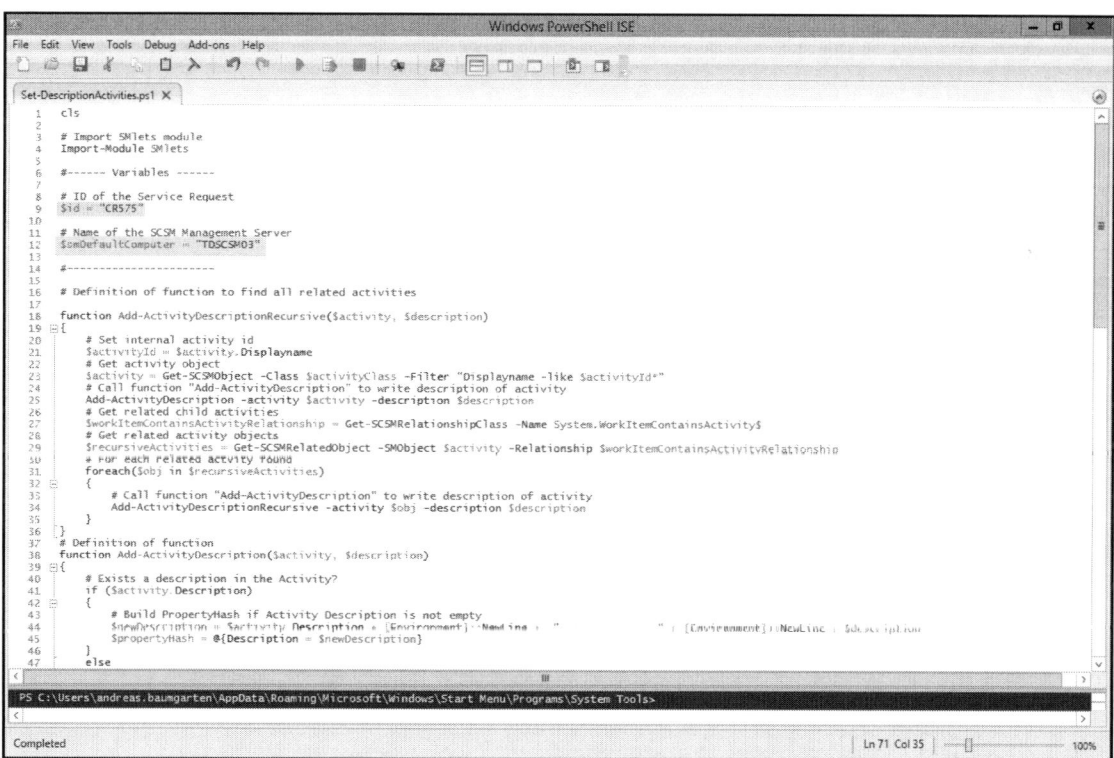

4. Press *F5* or click on **Run Script in Windows PowerShell ISE.**

5. Verify in the Output window of Windows PowerShell ISE that there is no error message.

6. Verify the result in the **SCSM 2016 console** ꟾ **Work Items** ꟾ **Change Management** by opening the Change Request (CR575 in our example) and related Activities on **Activities** tab. The result should look like this in all activities related to the Change Request:

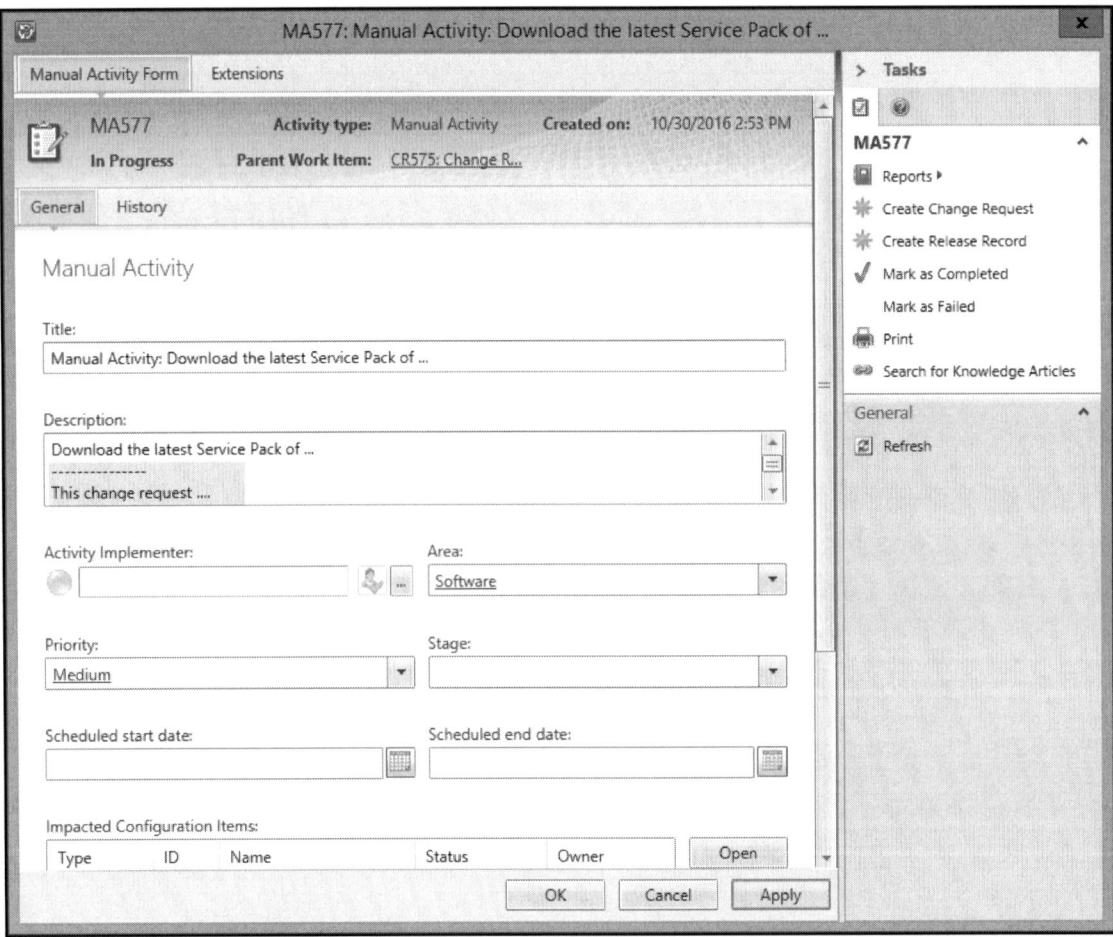

How it works...

The script contains two functions:

Function 1: **Add-ActivityDescriptionRecursive** (line 18-36)

- This function discovered all related activities of a Change Request recursive (if you have nested activities such as Parallel Activities containing other related activities)
- A second function is called (**Add-ActivityDescription**) for each discovered related activity

Function 2: **Add-ActivityDescription** (line 37-54)

- This functions checks if a description in the related activity already exists. If yes, a new line and the Description of the parent Change Request is added. If there is no content in the **Description** field of the activity only the Description of the Change Request is added.

Line 56-75 gets the parent Change Request details and description, the required classes, and the relationship details *System.WorkItemContainsActivity*.

There's more...

Setting the Description for all activities related to a Service Request

You can use the same script with minor changes to set the description of all activities related to a Service Request as well:

- Modify line 9 with a Service Request ID, for instance, **SR453**
- Modify line 57 with the class of Service Request: `$parentClass = Get-SCSMClass -Name System.WorkItem.ServiceRequest$`

- Run the script

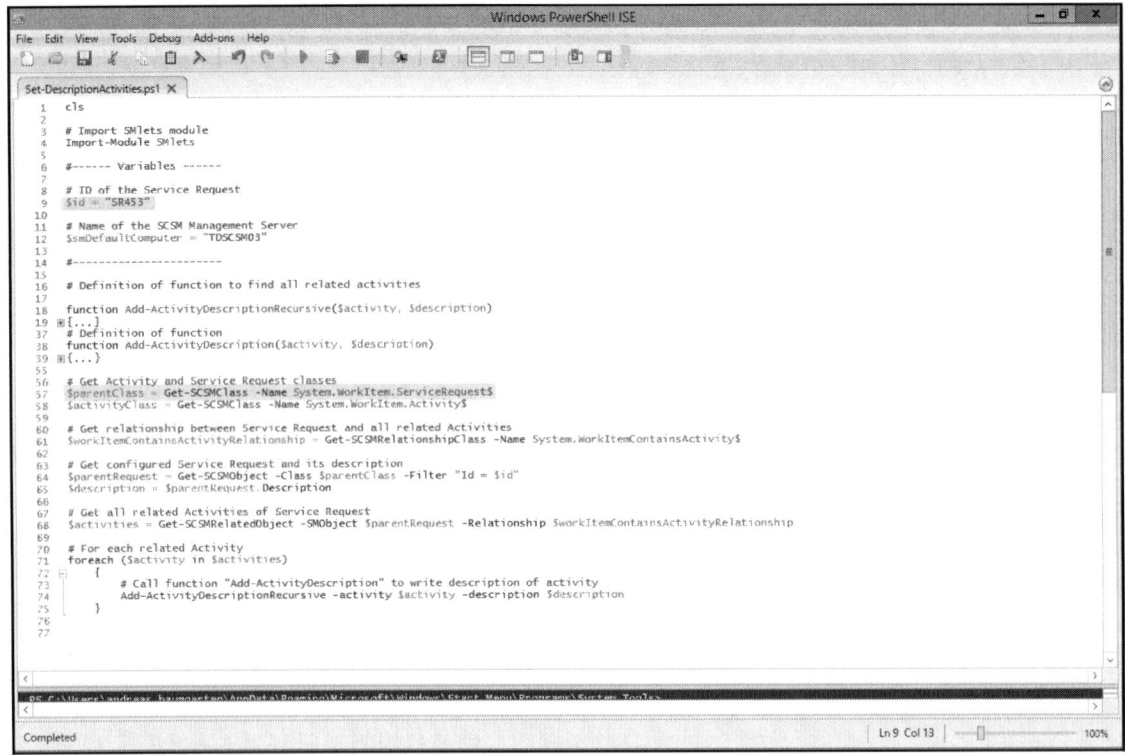

Implementing Security Roles

9

In this chapter, we will cover the following topics:

- Viewing basic settings for Security roles
- Adding users to the End Users role
- Creating and managing Service Request roles
- Creating and managing Incident Management roles
- Creating and managing Problem Management roles
- Creating and managing Change and Release Management roles
- Creating hybrid roles
- Configuring the Self-Service Catalog security role
- Listing SCSM security role details with PowerShell
- Getting SCSM security roles of a specific user with PowerShell

Introduction

This chapter discusses the security model used in System Center 2016 Service Manager (SCSM) and provides the configuration steps required to personalize the security model to your needs.

Security is applied across all objects you can manage in SCSM. The security model in use is commonly known as **Role Based Administration (RBA).** The RBA model provides a consistent method of delegating security control over what a user can interact with and what actions they can perform. System Center 2016 Service Manager has 13 default security roles.

The 13 default roles are as follows:

- Activity Implementers
- Administrators
- Advanced Operators
- Authors
- Change Initiators
- Change Managers
- End Users
- Incident Resolvers
- Problem Analysts
- Read-Only Operators
- Release Managers
- Service Request Analysts
- Workflows

The default security roles cannot be removed and have only one editable option; you can assign users or groups to a default role. The actions and implied actions of SCSM security roles can be found in the official product administrative guide and online at `https://techn et.microsoft.com/en-us/system-center-docs/sm/manage/admin-managing-user-role s-in-system-center-2016-service-manager`.

The security settings you apply to your SCSM environment require you to plan and test your scenarios. The recipes in this chapter will provide us with the technical steps required to implement your personal security model.

Viewing basic settings for Security roles

This recipe provides the steps required to view the out-of-the-box SCSM security roles available to you.

Getting ready

You need to have successfully installed the SCSM product, be a user in the SCSM Administrators role and have the SCSM console open.

You must be a member of the SCSM Administrators role to perform the tasks in this recipe. The default members of the SCSM Administrators role are, the user account used to install SCSM and the members of the Administrators group specified during the installation.

How to do it...

In this recipe, we will review the default End Users role in the SCSM console:

1. Navigate to **Service Manager Console** | **Administration** | **Security** | **User Roles**.

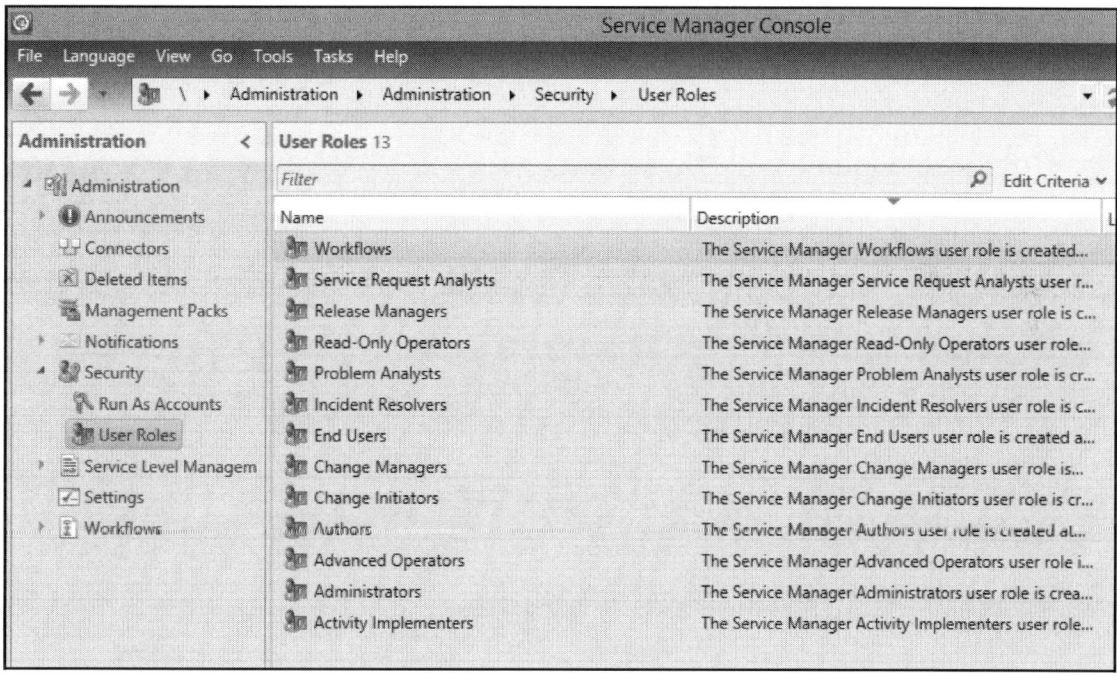

2. Select the **End Users** role in the middle pane and click on **Properties** under the **Tasks** options:

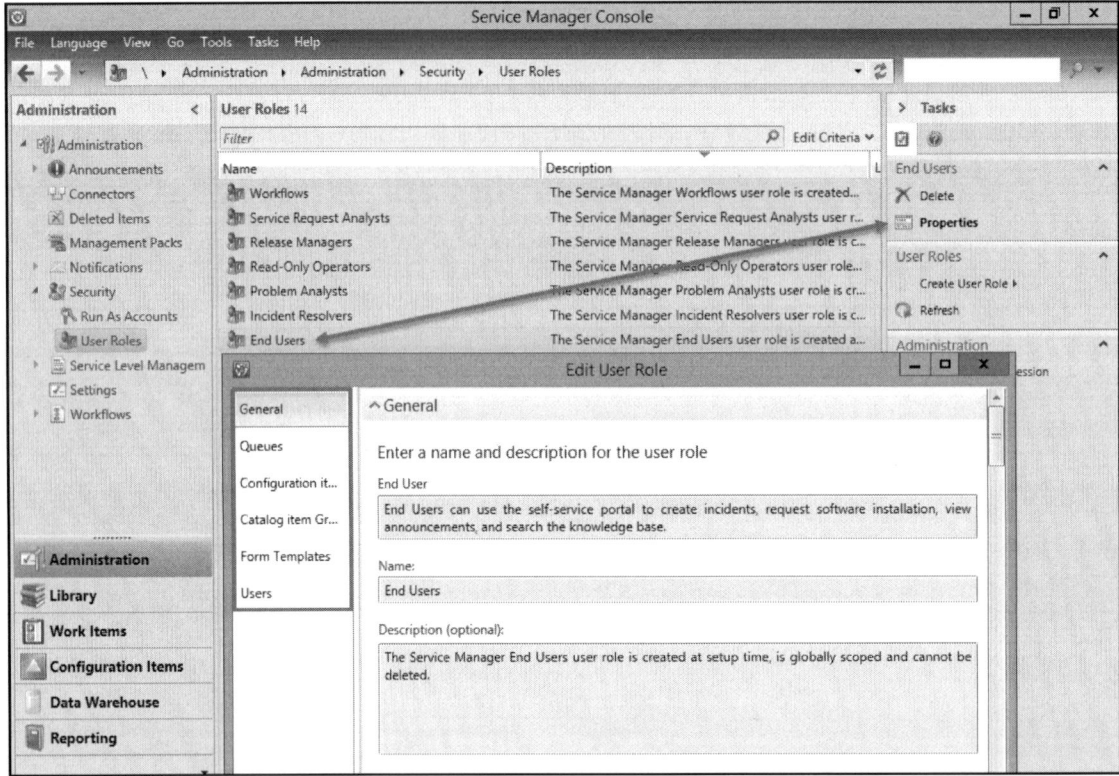

3. Review the default settings for each section of the security role to understand the scope of the security role.

How it works...

The general section of each role provides an overview of the role and the scope of access to the securable items in SCSM.

The default security roles have all sections set to read-only (cannot be edited) except the users section. You can add or remove users to a security role to grant them rights to preconfigured permissions.

There's more…

The default roles are templates for custom roles you create, except for two special roles:

- **Administrators**: This role cannot be used as a template and by default, has the user account used to install SCSM, the service manager service account and the SCSM Administrators group specified during the installation as members
- **Workflows**: This role cannot be used as a template and by default has the account specified for the workflow as the only member

Data Warehouse User Roles

There are two additional roles in a SCSM implementation where a Data Warehouse Management Server is installed and registered with an instance of SCSM. The registered Data Warehouse roles are as follows:

- **Report Users**: Users in this role are granted access to the reporting node and their SQL Reporting Service Rights determine what interaction the user can have with the published reports.
- **Administrators:** Users in this role are granted administrative access to the Data Warehouse node. Users added to this administrator's role do not automatically become members of the Administrators role defined under SCSM Administrator Security roles.

To view the Report Users or the Data Warehouse Administrators role, select **Data Warehouse | Security | User Roles**.

See also

The *Configuring report permissions* recipe in `Chapter 10`, *Working with the Data Warehouse and Reporting*, provides additional information on the Report User role.

Adding users to the End Users role

This recipe provides the steps required to add a user or group to a default SCSM security role.

We will use the End Users role to demonstrate these steps.

Getting ready

You need to have successfully installed the SCSM product, be a user in the SCSM Administrators role and have the SCSM console open.

The default members of the SCSM Administrators role are the user account used to install SCSM and the members of the Administrators group specified.

How to it...

The following are the steps you need to perform to add a user to a default SCSM role:

1. Follow steps 1 and 2 of the Viewing basic settings for the Security roles recipe to select the properties of the End Users role.

2. By default, this role has the special group Authenticated Users assigned to it. Select the **Users** section in the **End Users Role** window and click on **Add**. Type the name of the user or group and click on **Check Names...** to validate the user or group. Click on **OK**:

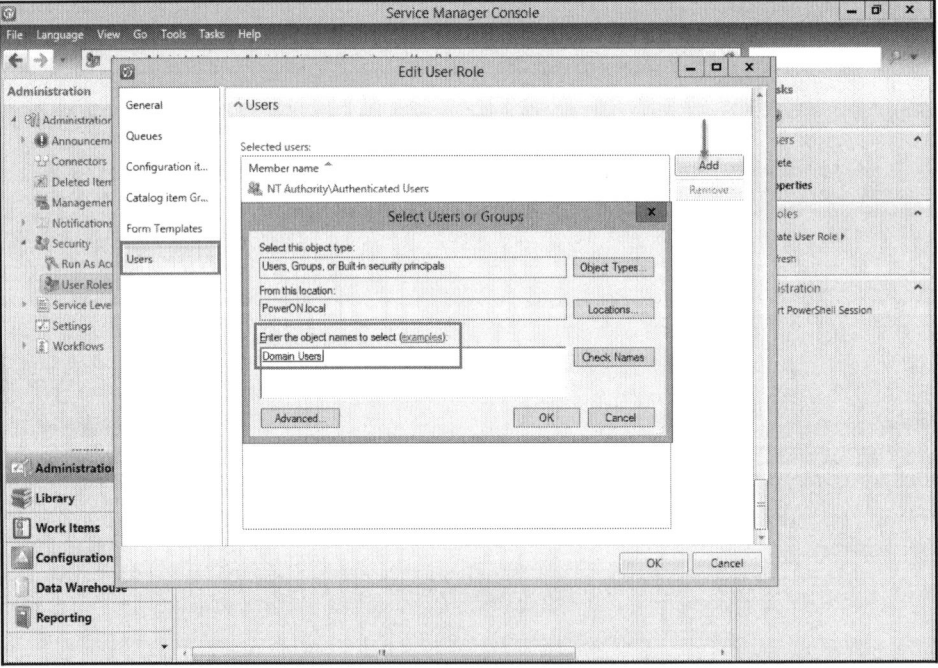

3. Repeat the previous steps for all users or groups you want to add to the role. Note that you can add multiple accounts in one step by separating your selection with a semicolon.

How it works...

The user(s) or members of the groups you add to a default SCSM security role will be granted the rights associated with the role.

A user can be a member of more than one role. The rights of a user in multiple roles are cumulative (for example, a user assigned the End User and Activity Implementer roles will have the combined rights of both roles).

There's more...

Here are some additional real-world tips to consider.

Beware of the Authenticated Users

The End Users and Report Users roles have the NT/Authenticated Users automatically assigned. Plan to remove this default setting and replace it with your specific users or groups. The default setting adds additional implied permissions (for example, a read-only operator will be able to create incidents because NT/Authenticated Users is part of the End Users role, which has the rights to create a work item).

Creating and managing Service Request roles

This recipe provides the steps required to complete the creation of a Service Request role.

Getting ready

You must meet the following prerequisites before you complete this task:

- **Planning:** Agree the support group analysts and categories for Service Requests (for example, use a table to capture the planning information). Plan for views and queues for security scope filtering. We will use a Service Request support team called Service Desk in this recipe. The table below shows the required planning information:

Process	Process role	SCSM Security role (template)	AD group	Categories (classification)
Service Request Fulfillment	Service Desk	Service Request Analysts	SCSM – SR SCSM – Service Desk	User account Password resets, printer, consumables

- **Installation and authorization:** You need to have successfully installed the SCSM product, be a user in the SCSM Administrators role and have the SCSM console open.
- **Console tasks:** Create custom Service Request queues and views to reflect the organization process for managing service request fulfillment.

In this recipe, we assume you have configured the following:

- A queue called **Custom SR – Service Desk** (scoped to the Service Request Class | Criteria support group = SR – Service Desk). See `Chapter 3`, *Configuring Service Level Agreements (SLAs)*, for detailed steps on how to create SCSM queues.
- A view called **Custom SR – All Service Desk Requests** (Criteria support group = SR – Service Desk).

How to do it...

Follow these steps to create and manage a Service Request security role:

1. Navigate to **Service Manager Console** | **Administration** | **Security** | **User Roles**.
2. Select **User Roles** | **Create User Role** | **Service Request Analyst** from the **Tasks** menu:

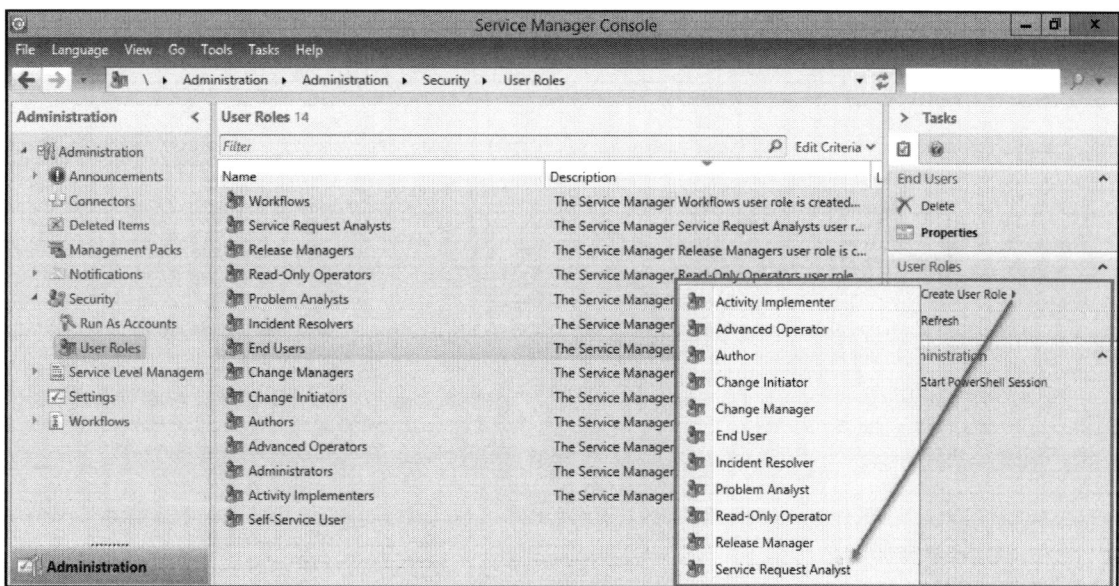

3. Click on **Next** in the **Before You Begin** wizard page.
4. On the **General wizard** page, type the following mandatory and optional information:
   - **Name:** SR - Service Desk Team
   - **Description (optional):** Service Request Role scoped for the Service Desk support group

5. On the **Management** Packs wizard page, select only the management packs related to Service Requests. (Include custom management packs used to store Service Request configurations.)

 You can select the management packs only while creating a new User role. If you edit an existing User role this section in the wizard is not available anymore.

6. On the **Queues wizard** page, select **Provide access to only the selected queues**. Select the custom queue for the role (for example, **Custom SR – Service Desk**). Click on **Next**:

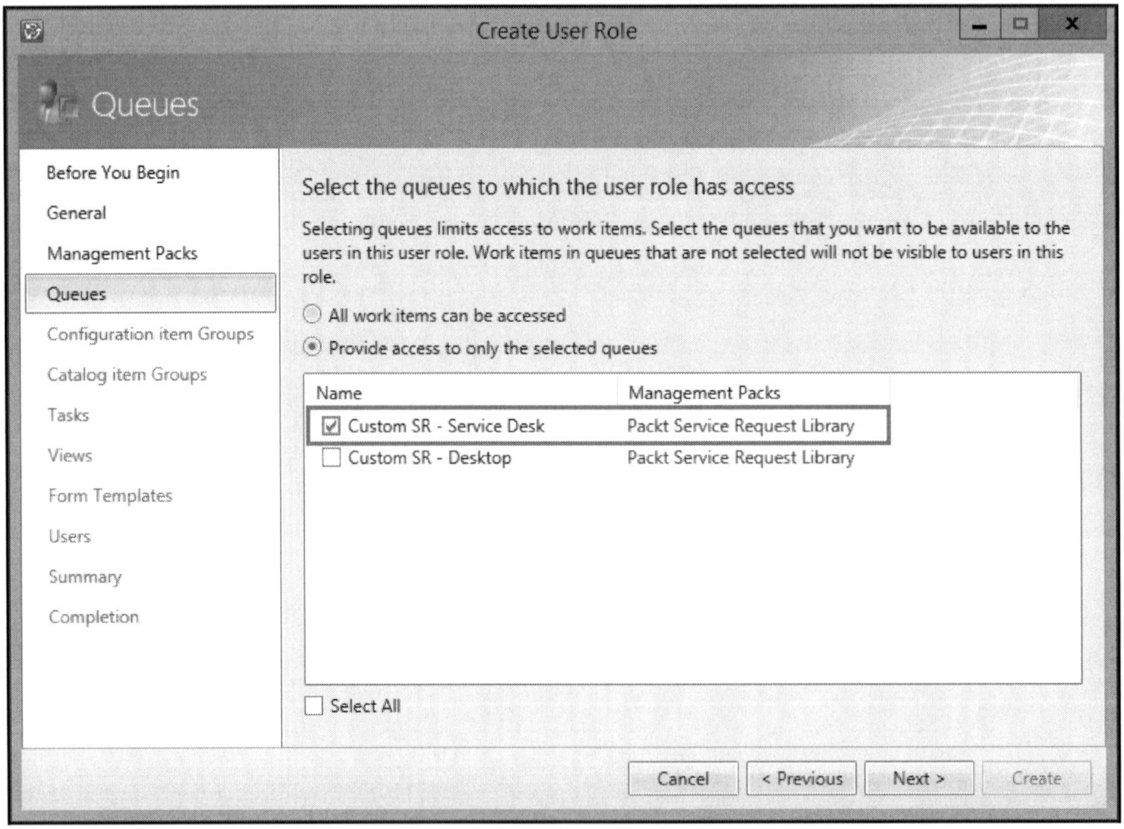

Create User Role

Queues

- Before You Begin
- General
- Management Packs
- Queues
- Configuration item Groups
- Catalog item Groups
- Tasks
- Views
- Form Templates
- Users
- Summary
- Completion

Select the queues to which the user role has access

Selecting queues limits access to work items. Select the queues that you want to be available to the users in this user role. Work items in queues that are not selected will not be visible to users in this role.

○ All work items can be accessed
◉ Provide access to only the selected queues

Name	Management Packs
☑ Custom SR - Service Desk	Packt Service Request Library
☐ Custom SR - Desktop	Packt Service Request Library

☐ Select All

Cancel < Previous Next > Create

7. Click on Next on the **Configuration item Group** and **Catalog item Group** wizard pages.

8. On the **Tasks** wizard page, select **Provide access to only the selected tasks**. Select the specific tasks relevant to the role (for example, we will not select **Configure Workflow Rules** for this analyst role). Click on **Next**:

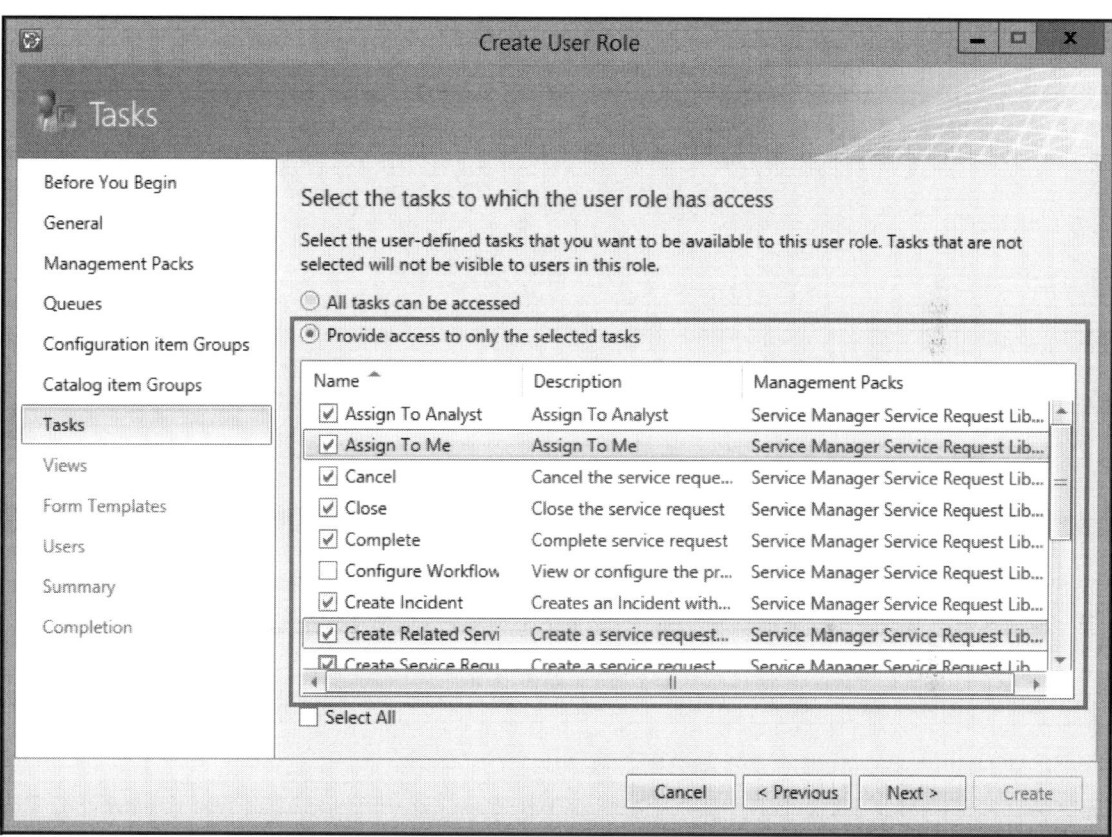

9. On the **Views** wizard page, select **Provide access to only the selected views**. Select the specific views relevant to the role and click on **Next**:

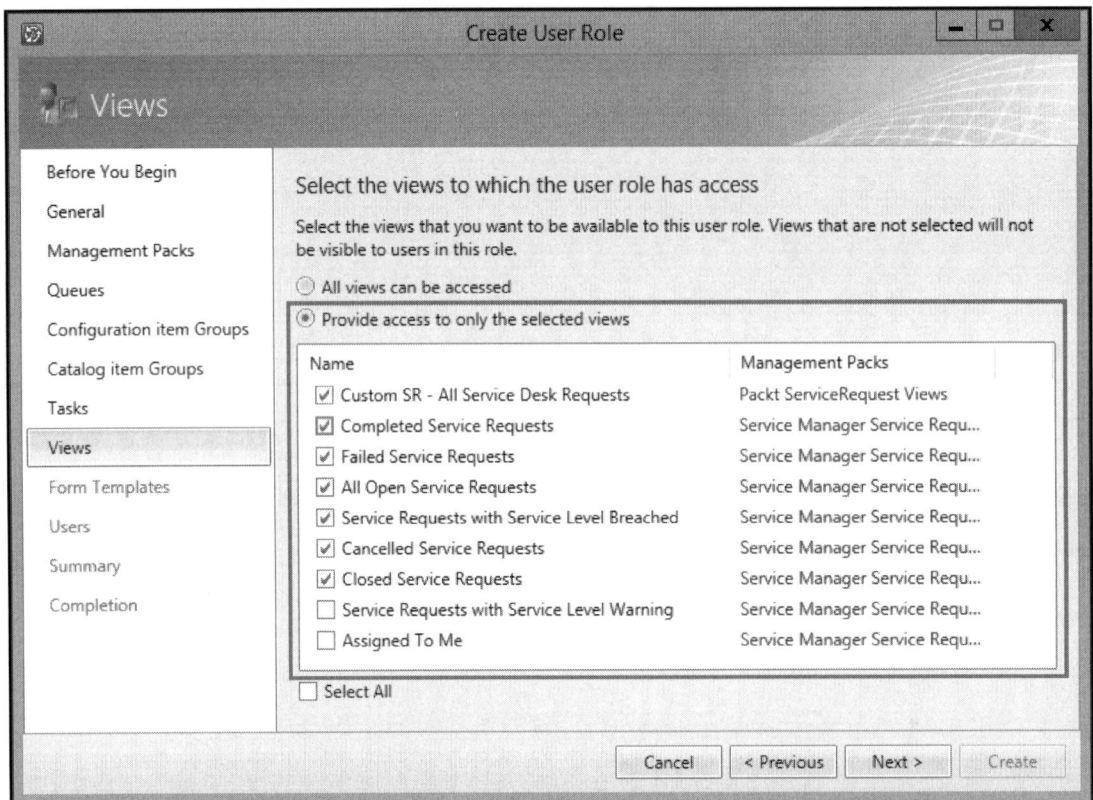

10. On the **Forms** Templates wizard page, select **Provide access to only the selected forms**. Select the specific forms relevant to the role and click on **Next**:

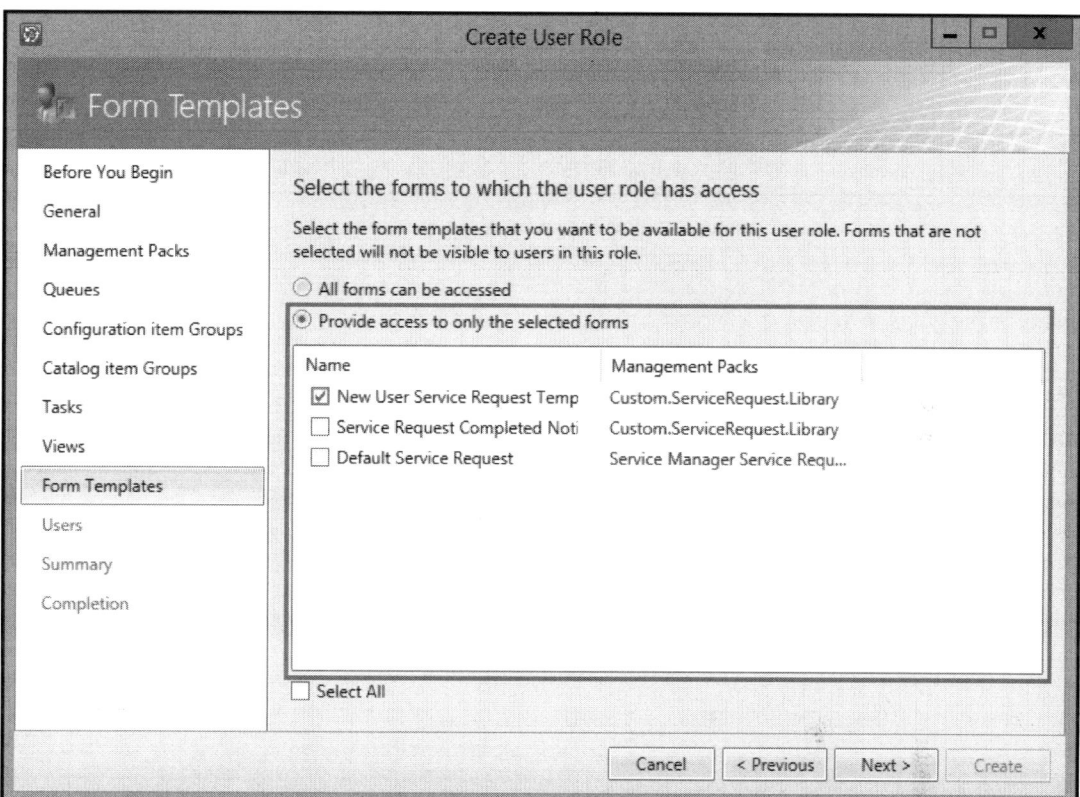

11. On the **Users** wizard page, follow the **Adding Users to the End User Role** task steps to select the Active Directory group for the role (as discussed in the Getting ready section of this recipe). Click on **Next**.

12. Review the **Summary** page; click on **Previous** to correct any configurations in previous wizard pages. Then, click on **Create** to complete the role creation.

13. Click on **Close** on the **Completion** wizard page.

How it works...

Role-based security configuration and management is similar to computer file access security. Compare SCSM security delegation to granting access to files stored in a particular network location. You need to plan for the following:

Computer files Access Network Share	SCSM console or portal
Folders structures grouped by file type, department, or content	SCSM Access Categories: Administration, library, Work Items, and Configuration Items
Create shares to represent a logical view and abstract the physical structure	SCSM Queues and Views
Grant action permissions on the content of the folders	SCSM Create, Delete, Edit, and category specific actions
Grant permissions for actions on the host machine of the shares	SCSM Infrastructure Administrative Settings
Local Security Groups (for example, Power Users)	SCSM built-in roles that you copy to create custom roles
Grant access permission by user or groups	Active Directory users or groups
Windows Explorer and other file access tools including file processing applications	SCSM console and portal

The following figure presents a graphical illustration of how role-based security works in SCSM:

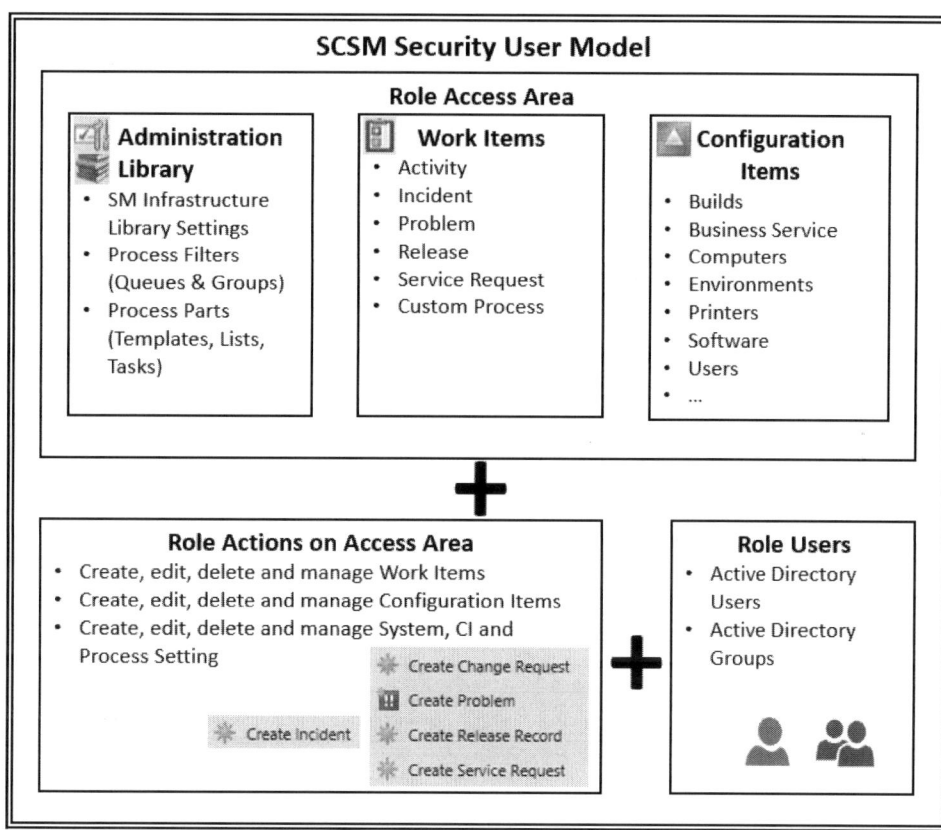

The principles of file access delegation apply to SCSM; in both cases, you must plan for roles to support the processes. In this recipe, we focused on Service Request fulfillment as a process and created a role with access to perform actions on the process objects in the scope of management. The following table is a breakdown of the wizard selection categories:

SCSM wizard page	Description and notes
Management packs	This provides the means to filter what you select in subsequent wizard pages when you are creating a role. This is a major benefit of organizing your configuration in specific management packs.
Queues	Queues are similar to the principle of a fairground ticket. By default, all work items can be accessed based on the SCSM security role template (get in line for all rides). You use a queue to grant access to a subset of work items (get in line for these specific rides).
Configuration Item Groups	These are similar to queues but applicable to configuration items. For example, you can create a group for all workstation class computers and grant access to only those groups for the role.
Catalog Item Groups	These groups are specific to the service catalog and grants the role access to specific categories accessed by using the Self-Service Portal.
Tasks	The actions you can perform relevant to the process category and infrastructure settings. For example, you may be able to create and modify service requests but not be able to cancel a service request.
Views	The views selected here control what is displayed in the SCSM console for the specific role. By default, this would be the built-in system views. You must configure custom views before you create the role if you want to assign the views at the role creation stage. Views created after the security role wizard completion can be granted by editing the role.
Forms templates	These are the process templates a role user can select when creating objects in a specific process. For example, you can create a new service request using a pre-configured template. You are only presented with templates assigned to the role. The default option grants access to all process specific templates.
Users	This is where you associate the SCSM specific role with the console or portal users.

Plan and create roles for the process instead of creating roles for specific people within a team.

There's more...

There is a hidden but very important security configuration for SCSM security roles and full implication for members of the security roles. The hidden configuration is better known as implied and inherited security.

Implied permissions

Review the product documentation for the inherited and implied permissions when you select the role template.

See also

Appendix B, *Useful Websites and Community Resources*, provides links to useful resources on complex security models for SCSM and official online product documentation

Creating and managing Incident Management roles

This recipe provides the steps required to complete the creation of an Incident Management role.

Getting ready

You must meet the following prerequisites before you complete this task:

- **Planning:** Agree the support group analysts and categories for Incident Management (for example, use a table to capture the planning information). Plan for views and queues for security scope filtering. We will use an Incident Management team called Desktop Support in this recipe.

Process	Process role	SCSM Security role (template)	AD group	Categories (classification)
Incident Management	Desktop Support	Incident Resolvers	SCSM – IM Desktop Support	Hardware\clients, software\client application

- **Installation and Authorization:** You need to ensure you have successfully installed the SCSM product, be a user in the SCSM Administrators role and have the SCSM console open.
- **Console Tasks:** Create custom Incident Management queues and views to reflect the organization process for Incident Management.

In this recipe, we assume you have configured the following:

- A queue called Incident – Service Desk 1st Line (scoped to the Incident Class | Criteria support group = IM – Desktop Support). See `Chapter 3`, *Configuring Service Level Agreements (SLAs)*, for detailed steps on how to create SCSM queues.
- Two Views called Custom – IM All Desktop Support Incidents (Criteria support group = IM – Desktop Support and all the states of an IM except closed) and Custom IM All Unassigned Desktop Support Incidents (Criteria support group = IM – Desktop Support, all the status of an Incident except closed and Assigned User is null).

How to do it...

Follow these steps to create and manage incident class related security roles:

1. Navigate to **Service Manager Console** | **Administration** | **Security** | **User Roles**.
2. Click on **Next** in the **Before You Begin** wizard page.
3. Select **User Roles** | **Create User Role** | **Incident Resolvers** from the **Tasks** menu.

4. On the **General** wizard page, type the following mandatory and optional information:

- **Name:** IM - Desktop Support Team
- **Description (optional):** Incident Management Role scoped for the Desktop support group

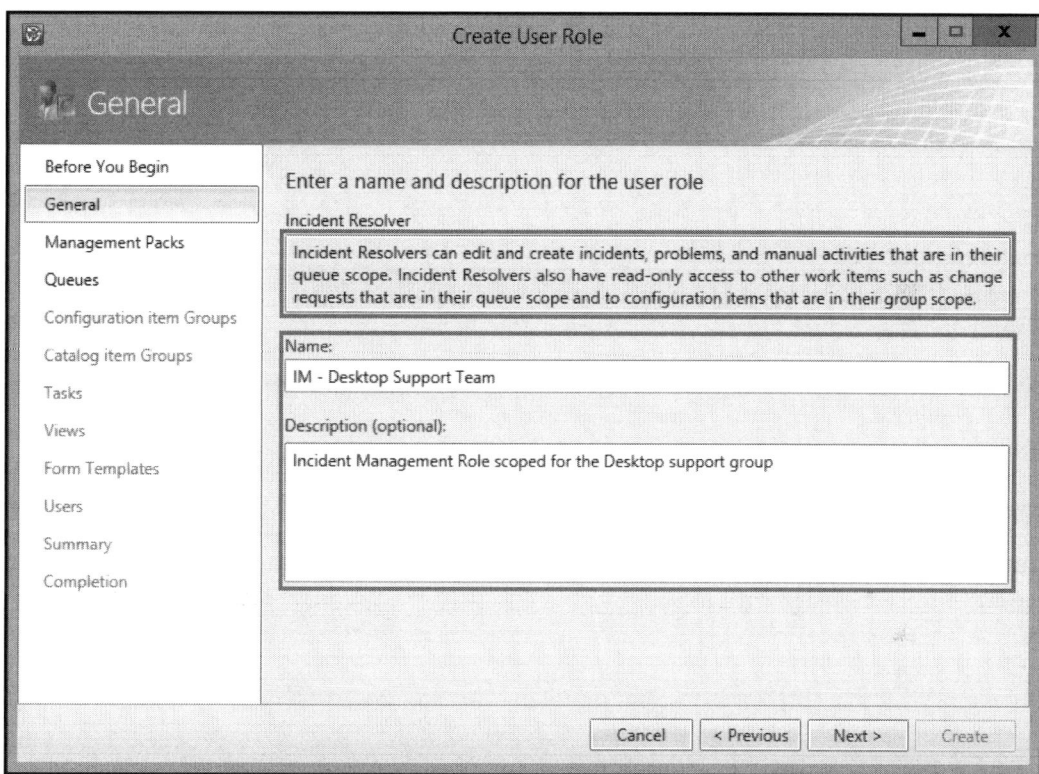

5. On the **Management Packs** wizard page, select only the management packs related to Incident Management (including custom management packs used to store Incident Management configurations).

6. On the **Queues** wizard page, select **Provide access to only the selected queues**. Select the custom queue for the role (for example, **Incident – Service Desk 1st Line**). Click on **Next**:

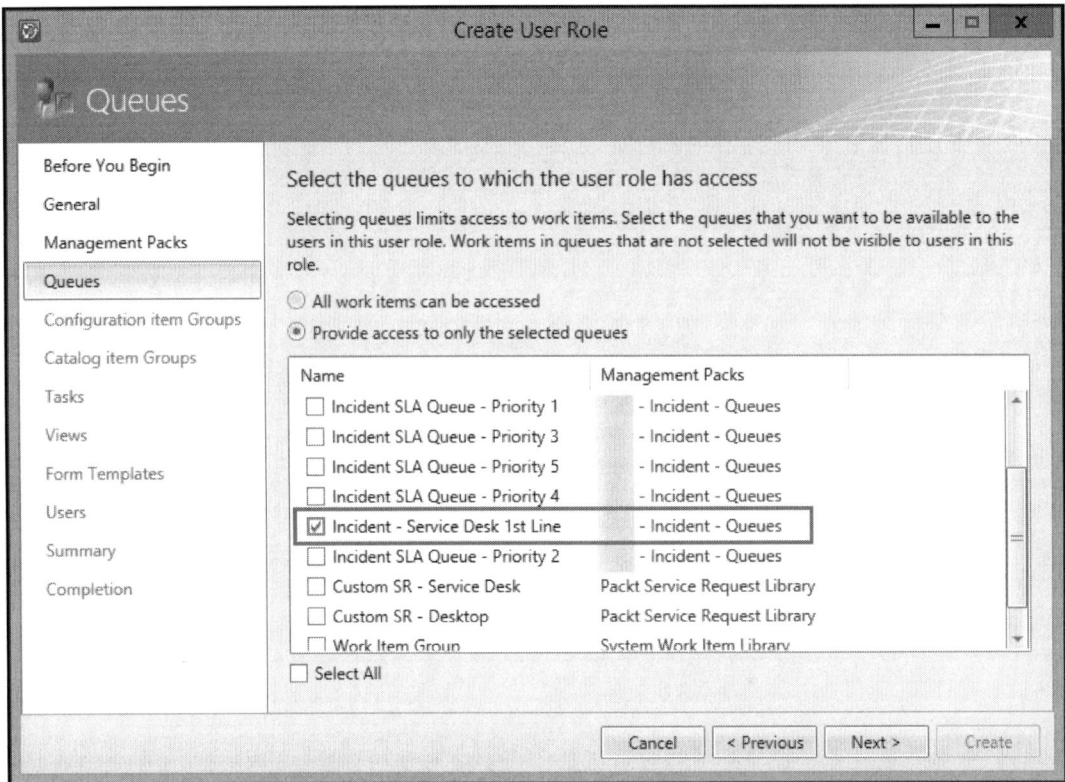

7. Click on **Next** on the **Configuration Items Group and Catalog items Group** wizard pages.

8. On the **Tasks** wizard page, select **Provide access to only the selected tasks**. Select the specific tasks relevant to the role (for example, we will not select **Configure Workflow Rules** for this Incident Management role). Click on **Next**:

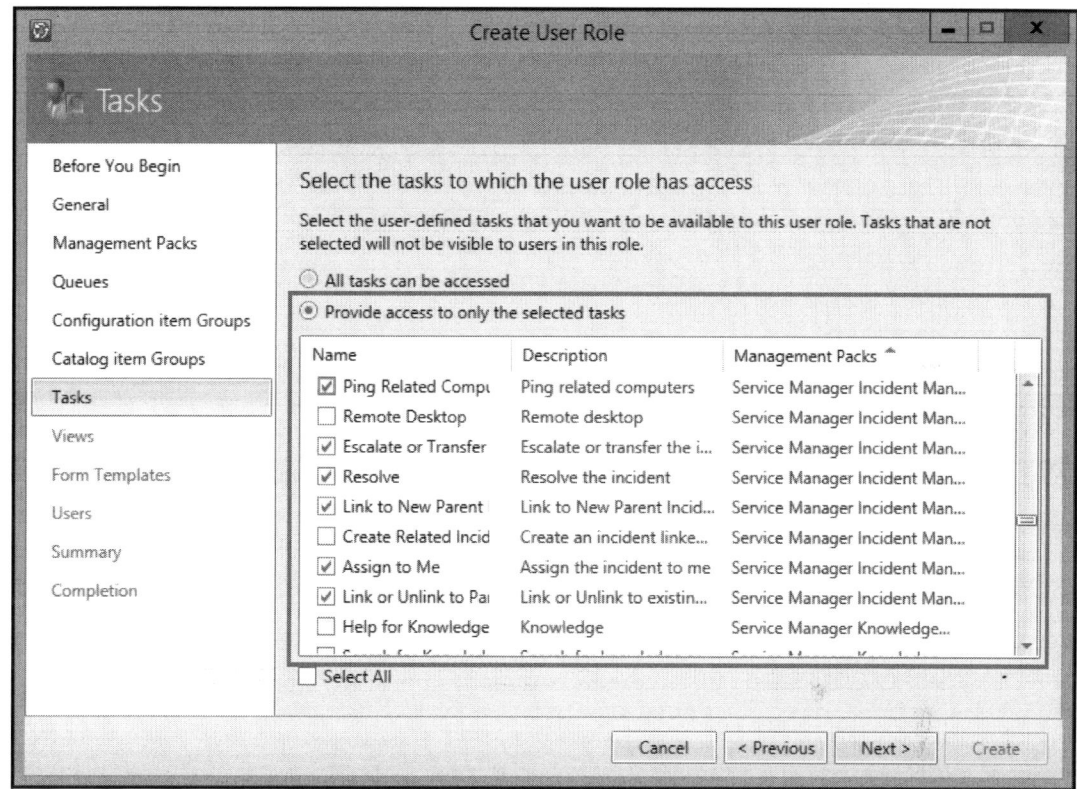

9. On the **Views** wizard page, select **Provide access to only the selected views**. Select the specific views relevant to the role and click on **Next**.

10. On the **Form Templates** wizard page, select **Provide access to only the selected forms**. Select the specific forms relevant to the role and click on **Next**:

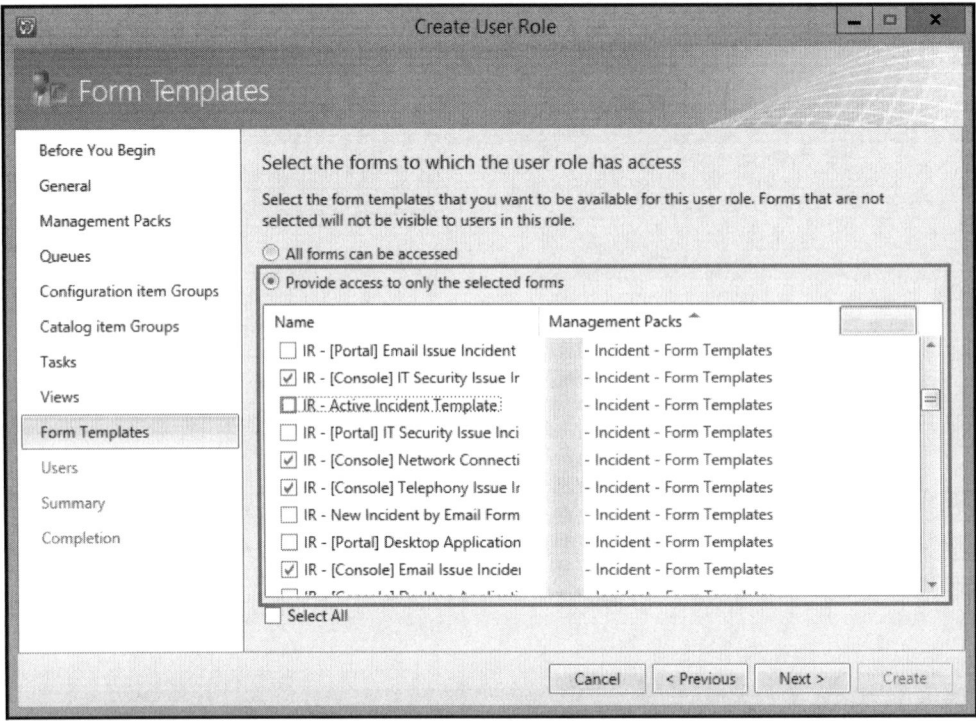

11. On the **Users** wizard page, follow the *Adding users to the End User role* recipe steps to select the Active Directory group for the role, as discussed in the planning information for the role creation. Click on **Next**.

12. Review the **Summary** page; click on **Previous** to correct any configuration in the previous wizard pages. Click on **Create** to complete the role creation.

13. Click on **Close** on the **Completion** wizard page.

How it works...

The *How it works...* section in the *Creating and managing Service Request roles* recipe in this chapter is applicable to this recipe. You must plan specifically for the Incident Management process.

There's more...

In some cases, SCSM has inconsistencies with the naming of list items and how they appear in forms. Here is a real-world common setting example that can be confusing to the SCSM console user.

Support Group alias (Incident Tier Queue)

The **Support group** field referenced in the Queue and Views for Incident Management has a specific name in the **Library**, **Incident Tier Queue**:

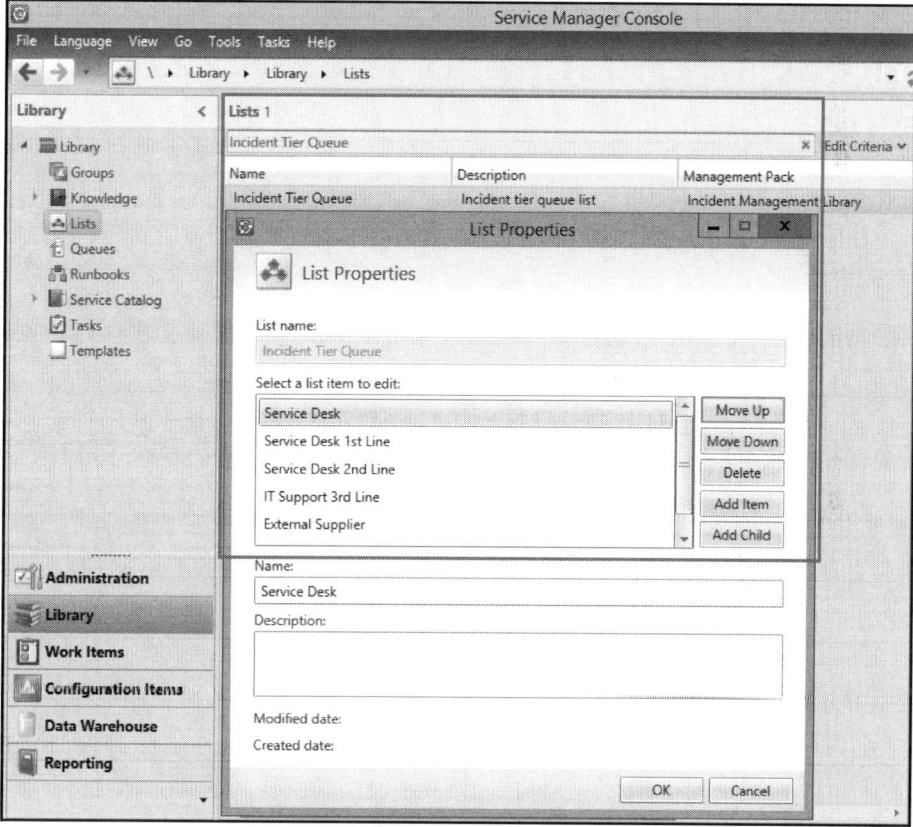

This Support Group is not shared with the Service Request process, though they appear as the same list name in the respective forms of the processes.

See also

Appendix B, *Useful Websites and Community Resources*, provides links to useful resources on complex security models for SCSM and official online product documentation.

Creating and managing Problem Management roles

This recipe provides the steps required to complete the creation of a Problem Management role.

Getting ready

You must meet the following prerequisites before you complete this task:

- **Planning:** Agree the logical support group analysts and categories for Problem Management (for example, use a table to capture the planning information). Plan for views and queues for security scope filtering. We will use a Problem Management team called Escalation Analysts in this recipe:

Process	Process role	SCSM Security role (template)	AD group	Categories (classification)
Problem Management	Escalation Analysts	Problem Analysts	SCSM – PR Escalation Analysts	Escalation/client related problems, escalation/server related problems, escalation/infrastructure related problems

- **Installation and Authorization:** You need to have successfully installed the SCSM product, be a user in the SCSM Administrators role and have the SCSM console open.
- **Console Tasks:** Create custom Problem Management queues and views to reflect the organization process for Problem Management.

In this recipe, we assume you have configured the following:

- A queue called Custom PR – Escalation Analysts (scoped to the Problem Class | Criteria Classification = Escalation\Client Related Problems OR Escalation\Server Related Problems, PR Escalation\Infrastructure Related Problems). See Chapter 3, *Configuring Service Level Agreements (SLAs)*, for detailed steps on how to create SCSM queues.
- Three Views called Custom – PR Client Related Escalations, Custom – PR Server Related Escalations and Custom – PR Infrastructure Related Escalations (Criteria is the problem classification category related to the respective escalation).

How to do it...

Here are the steps to create and manage a Problem Management class security role:

1. Navigate to **Service Manager Console** | **Administration** | **Security** | **User Roles**.
2. Select **User Roles** | **Create User Role** | **Problem Analysts** from the **Tasks** menu.
3. Click on **Next** on the **Before You Begin** wizard page.
4. On the **General** wizard page, type the following mandatory and optional information:
    - **Name:** PR - Escalation Analysts
    - **Description (optional):** Problem Management Role scoped for the Escalation Analysts group
5. On the **Management Packs** wizard page, select only the management packs related to Problem Management (including custom management packs used to store Problem Management configurations).

6. On the **Queues** wizard page, select **Provide access to only the selected queues**. Select the custom queue for the role (for example, **Custom – PR – Escalation Analysts**) and click on **Next**:

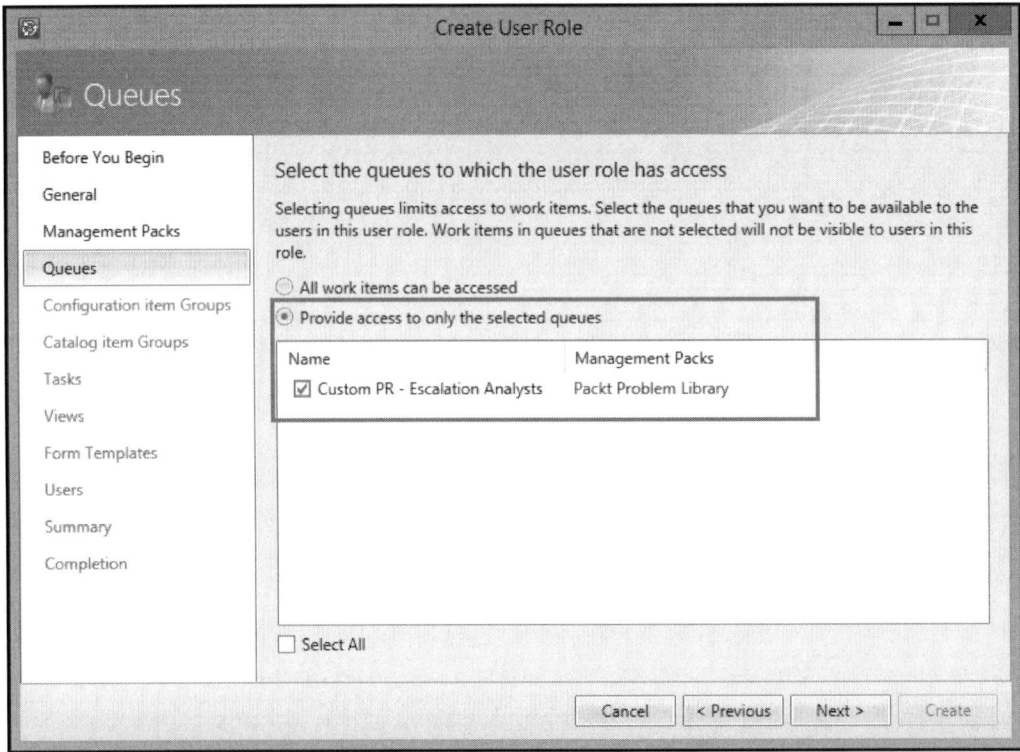

7. Click on **Next** on the **Configuration item Group and Catalog item Group** wizard pages.
8. On the **Tasks** wizard page, select **Provide access to only the selected tasks**. Select the specific tasks relevant to the role (for example, we will not select **Configure Workflow Rules** for this Problem Management role).

9. Click on **Next**:

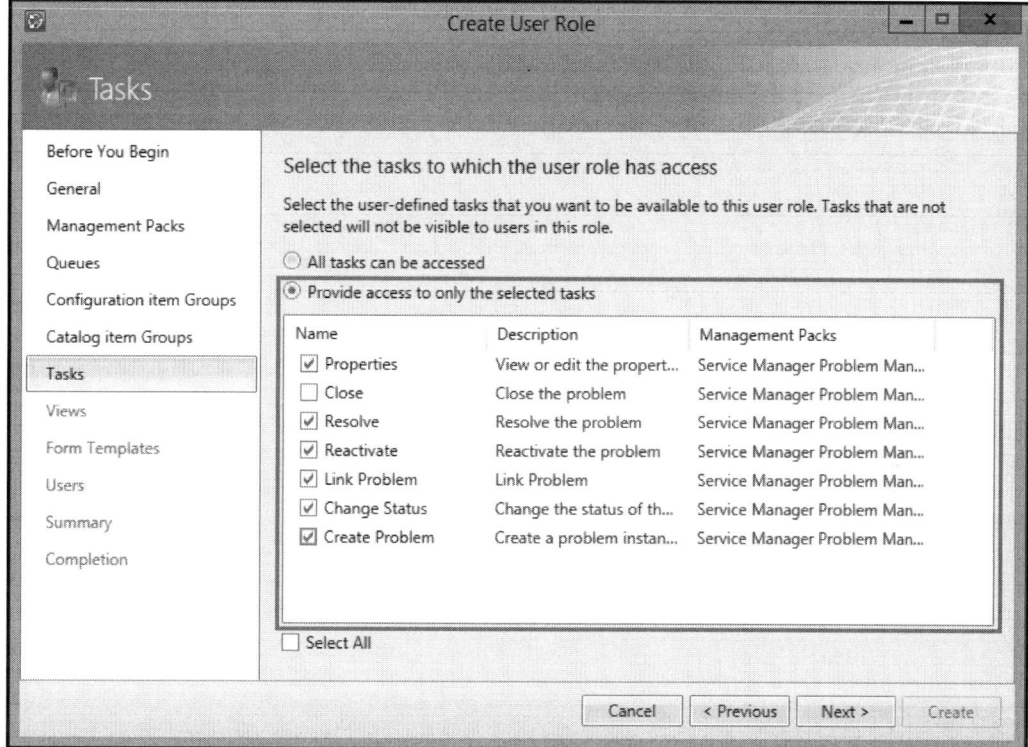

10. On the **Views** wizard page, select **Provide access to only the selected views**. Select the specific views relevant to the role and click on **Next**.

11. On the **Form Templates** wizard page, select Provide access to only the selected forms. Select the specific forms relevant to the role and click on **Next**:

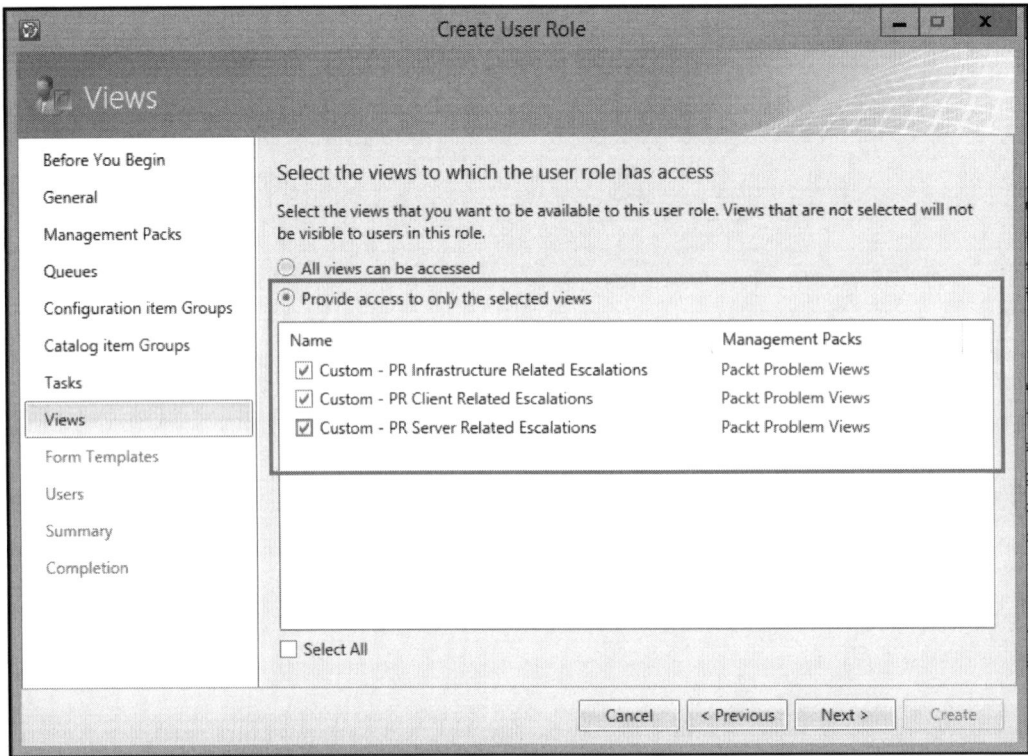

12. On the **Users** wizard page, follow the *Adding users to the End User role* recipe steps to select the Active Directory group for the role, as discussed in the planning information for the role creation. Click on **Next**.

13. Review the **Summary** page; click on **Previous** to correct any configurations on the previous wizard pages. Click on **Create** to complete the role creation.

14. Click on **Close** on the **Completion** wizard page.

How it works...

The *How it works...* section in the *Creating and managing Service Request roles* recipe earlier in this chapter is applicable to this recipe. You must plan specifically for the Problem Management process. The Problem Management process does not have a support group configuration option in SCSM.

This recipe demonstrates the difference in approach to role creation based on a process. The approach for Problem Management requires you to use a different category for organizing and managing the role. The recipe is organized using the classification category. A similar approach is used for the views, which allows us to structure the Problem Management role creation and management:

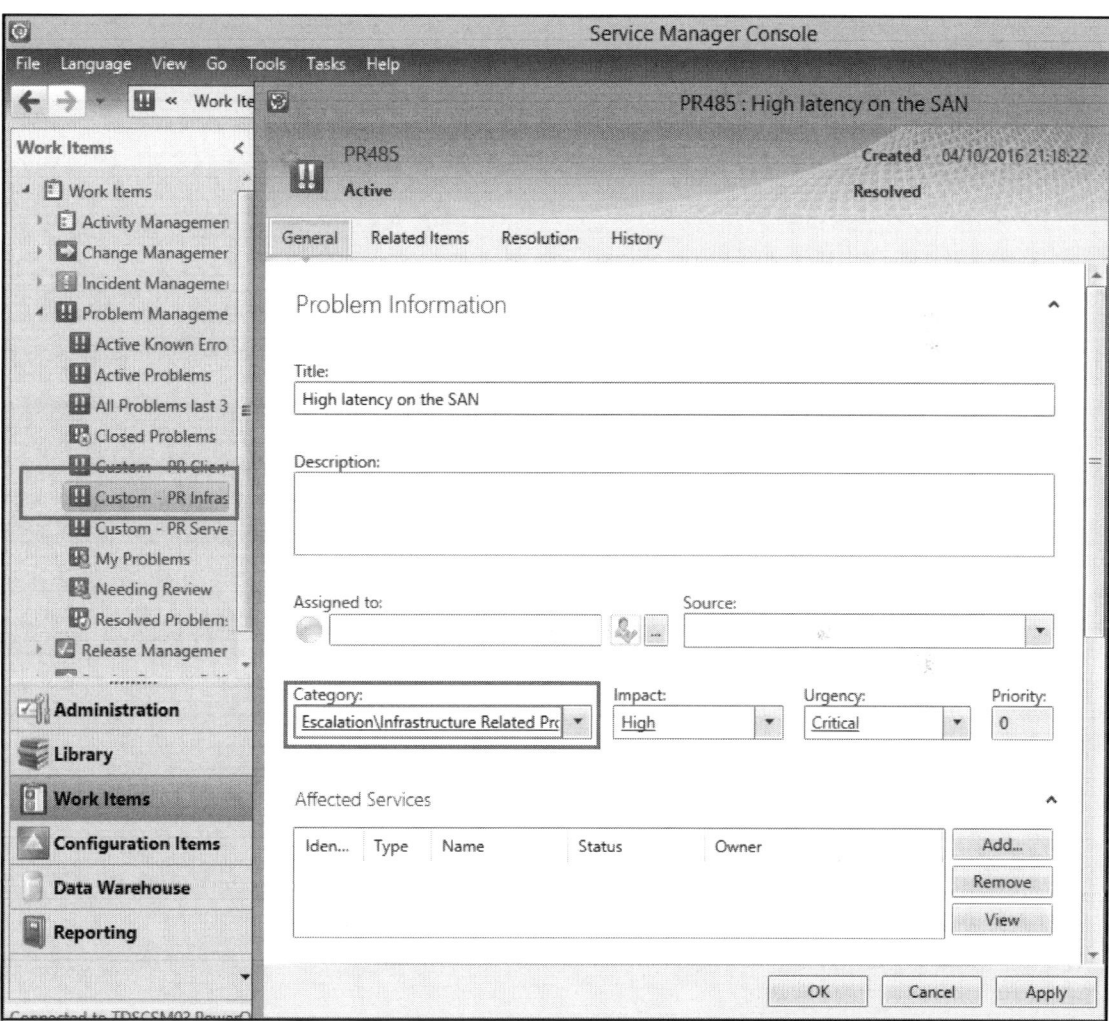

See also

`Appendix B`, *Useful Websites and Community Resources*, provides links to useful resources on complex security models for SCSM and official online product documentation.

Creating and managing Change and Release Management roles

This recipe provides details on creating and managing the roles required for Change and Release Management using SCSM.

Getting ready

You must plan to meet the following prerequisites before you complete this task:

- **Planning:** Agree the Change and Release Management categories and roles (for example, use a table to capture the planning information). Plan for groups and queues for security scope filtering:

Process	Process role	SCSM Security role (template)	AD group	Categories (area)
Change Management	Change Initiators	Change Initiator	SCSM – CR Change Analysts	Standard – infrastructure
Change Management	Change Owners	Change Managers	SCSM – CR Change Managers	All Change Management categories
Release Management	Release Owners	Release Managers	SCSM – RR Release Managers Analysts	All Release Management categories

- **Installation and Authorization:** You need to have successfully installed the SCSM product, be a user in the SCSM Administrators role and have the SCSM console open.

How to do it...

Follow these steps to create Change and Release management class security roles:

1. Create SCSM Groups for Configuration Items in the scope of Change Management. Use the steps in the *Creating a configuration item group* recipe in `Chapter 4`, *Building the Configuration Management Database (CMDB)*.
2. Create SCSM views by using Change and Release category.
3. Follow the steps detailed in the *Creating and managing Service Request roles* recipe to create the Change and Release management roles based on Change Initiators, Change Managers and Release Managers. Use the groups and views you create for the Change and Release management process to limit the scope of authority.

How it works...

The *How it works...* section in the *Creating and managing Service Request roles* recipe is applicable to this recipe. You must plan specifically for the Change and Release management process.

There are two typical scenarios for Change and Release Management process roles in organizations:

- Virtual roles of the Incident Management team
- Dedicated Change and Release Management team

In the first scenario, plan to use the AD groups created for the Incident Management roles as the assigned users of the Change and Release Management role. The authors recommend the best practice of creating dedicated groups by processing and adding the same users as members.

In the second scenario, plan the Change and Release Management roles using the **RACI (Responsible, Accountable, Consulted and Informed)** model as a guide. Use the agreed role plan to implement the SCSM role model.

There's more...

Built-in security roles that you can use as templates are great for testing, as they have implied and inherited permissions over all objects by default.

Using the built-in roles

The built-in roles provide a means to delegate SCSM security roles to the specific process areas. Plan to use custom roles to avoid granting unnecessary access to SCSM. The built-in roles are assigned global scope access to all work and configuration items. You must limit the scope of access using groups and views to avoid unplanned access to SCSM process areas.

Creating hybrid roles

This recipe discusses the steps required to create hybrid roles in SCSM. Hybrid role members require delegation across multiple SCSM processes.

Getting ready

You need to have successfully installed the SCSM product, be a user in the SCSM Administrators role and have the SCSM console open.

Review and document the role areas required for the hybrid roles.

How to do it...

Follow these steps to create hybrid roles (roles that are combined of two or more classes):

1. Document the hybrid process role (for example, users of the hybrid role need to have access to the following: Service Request, Incident Management and Problem Management):

Process	Process role	SCSM Security role (template)	AD group
Service Request Fulfillment	Service Desk	Service Request Analysts	SCSM – SR Service Desk
Incident Management	Desktop Support	Incident Resolvers	SCSM – IM Desktop Support
Problem Management	Problem Analysts	Problem Analysts	SCSM – PR Escalation Analysts

2. In the SCSM console, validate the users or groups assigned to each role in scope. In the console, navigate to the **Administrators** | **Security** | **User Roles** and select a role. Select **Properties** on the **Tasks** pane and click on **Users**. Add the hybrid role users to the group assigned to the role:

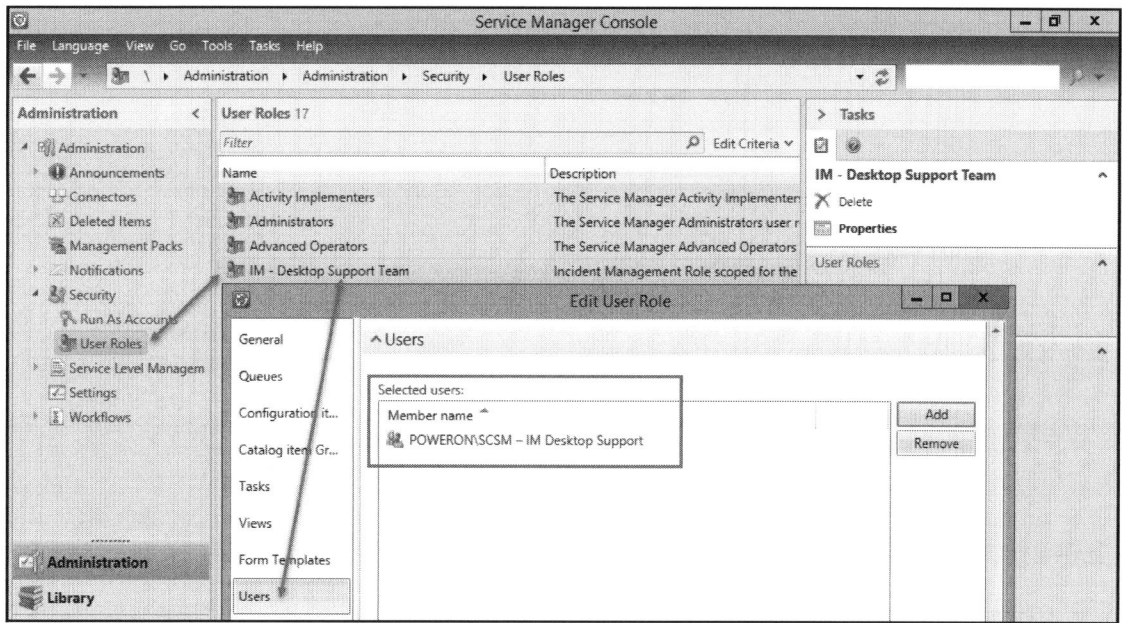

3. Repeat step 2 for all roles in the scope of the hybrid role.

How it works...

SCSM implements its role-based model by the class of process and objects. The notion of a hybrid role for a standard installation requires you to add users to the specific roles dedicated to each process.

The security and rights delegated to a single user across multiple roles is cumulative.

There's more…

SCSM as a product is highly customizable and as a result, you may have an environment that has different classes or extensions to the existing classes discussed in this chapter.

Advance extensions

You can extend the SCSM product to create a hybrid class to support a hybrid delegation model. The extension of SCSM is discussed in `Chapter 12`, *Automating Service Manager 2016*. If you have extended SCSM, follow the steps for role security creation in general. Plan to tailor the queues and views to the extended configuration or work items.

Configuring the Self-Service Catalog security role

System Center 2016 Service Manager has a role-based security model for its Self-Service Portal. This recipe discusses the security delegation configuration required to implement this model for an organization.

Getting ready

You need to have successfully installed the SCSM product, are a user in SCSM Administrators role and have the SCSM console open.

You need to have created at least one Service Offering or Request Offering as discussed by following the task steps in the *Creating Service Catalog Service Offerings* or *Creating Service Catalog Request offerings* recipes in `Chapter 5`, *Deploying Service Request Fulfillment*.

How to do it…

Here are the steps to create a self-service catalog security role:

1. In the SCSM console, navigate to **Library** | **Groups**:

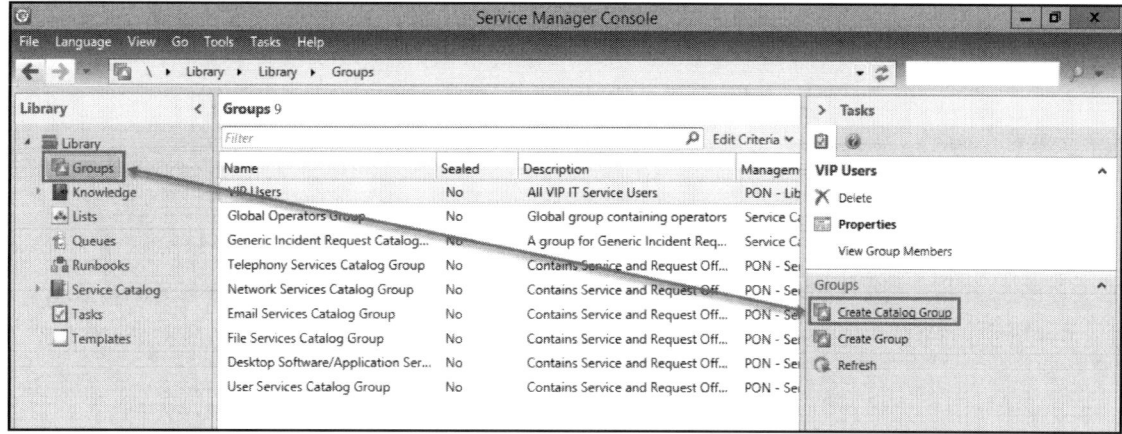

2. Under **Tasks** select **Create Catalog Group**.

3. Read the **Before You Begin** information and click on **Next**.

4. On the **General** page, fill in the mandatory group name and optionally provide a description for the group. Select a management pack and click on **Next**:

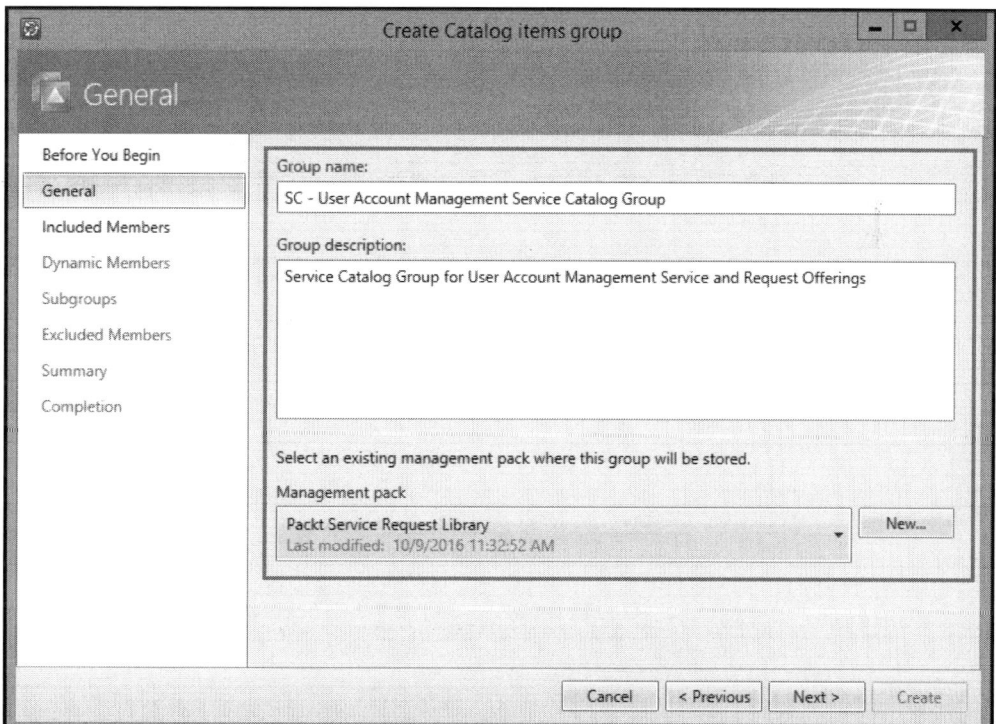

5. On the **Included Member** page, click on **Add**. Select the Service and Request offering you want to include in the catalog group and click on **Add**. Click on **OK** and then click on **Next**:

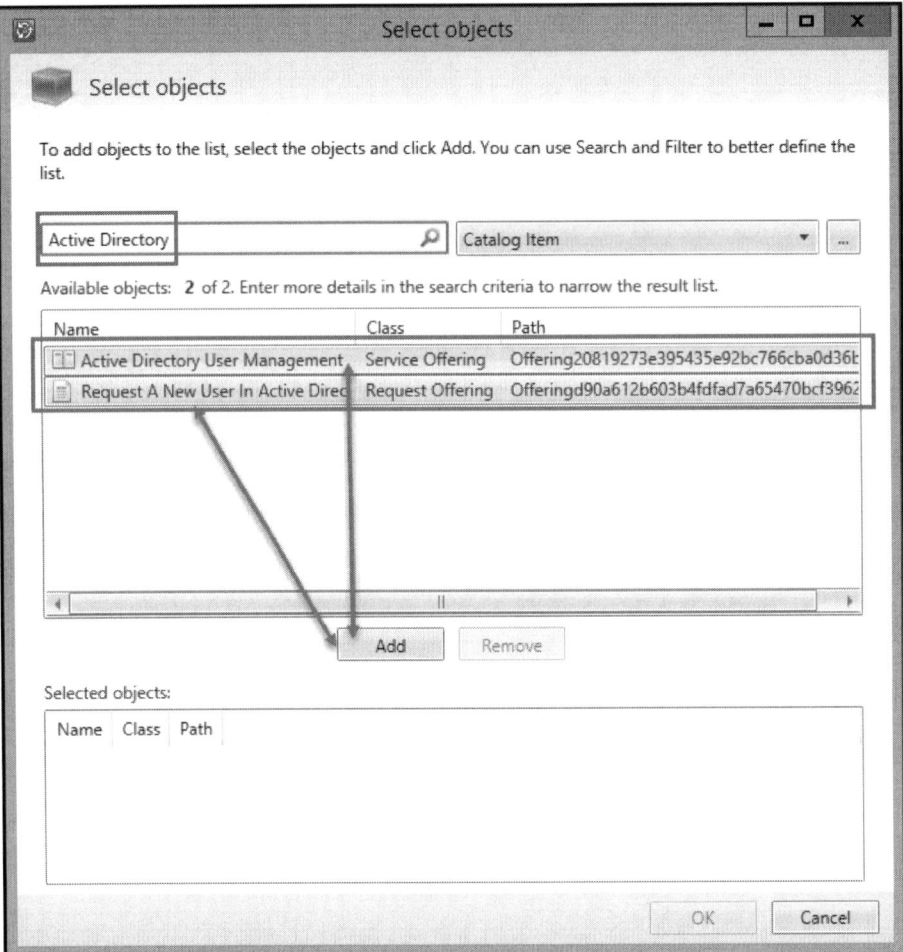

6. Click on **Next** on the **Dynamic Members, Subgroups** and **Excluded Members** pages.
7. Review the **Summary** page and click on **Create** to complete the group creation.
8. Navigate to **Administration** | **Security** | **User Roles**. Select Create **User Role** | **End User**. Provide a name for the role (for example, SC - Account Management Portal Role) and optionally type a description for the role. Click on **Next**:

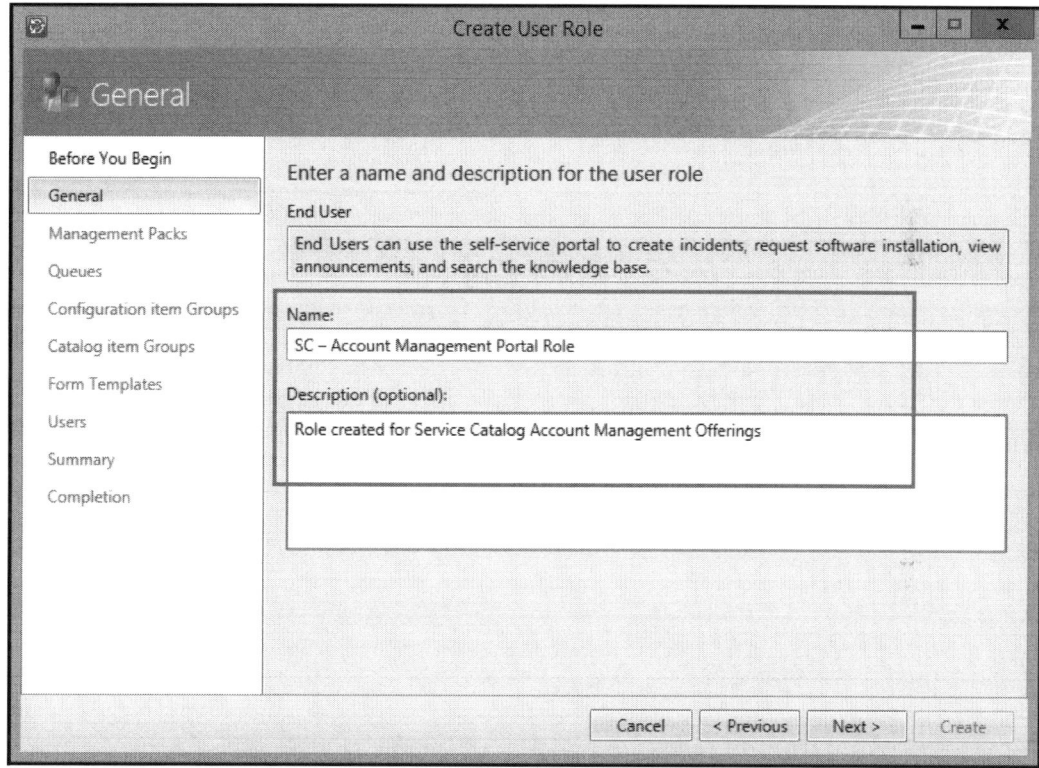

9. On the **Management Pack** page, select the management pack the catalog group is saved in and click on **Next**.
10. Leave the default selections for **Queues** and **Configuration Item Groups** and click on **Next**.

11. On the **Catalog Item Groups** page, select the catalog group we created and click on **Next**:

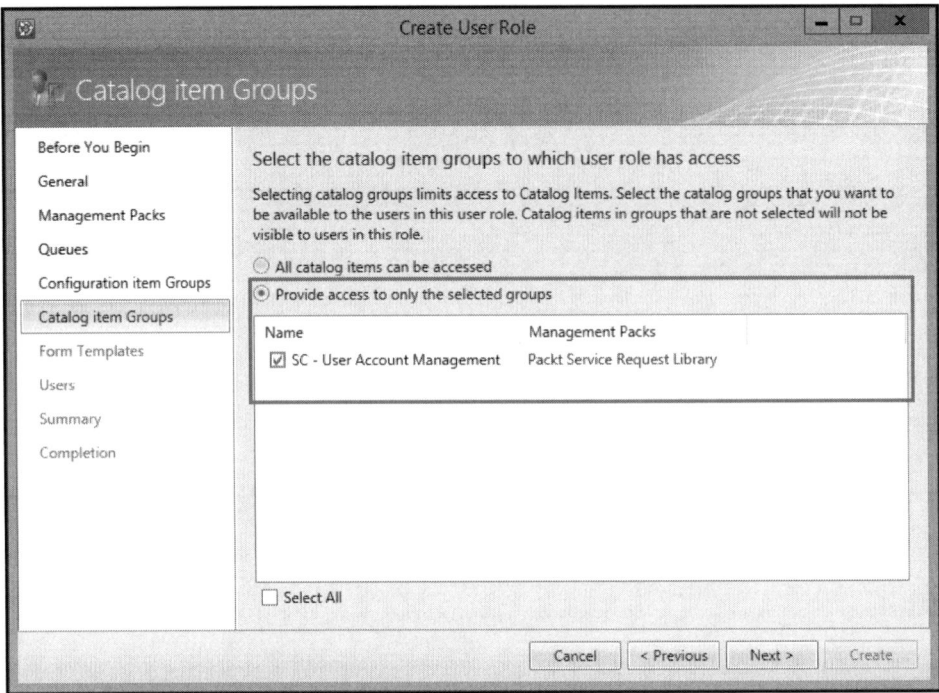

12. Leave the default option in the **Forms Templates** page and click on **Next**.
13. On the **Users** page, click on **Add** to select the users or groups you want to assign the role to and then click on **Next**.
14. Review the **Summary** page and click on **Next** to complete the role creation.

How it works...

Service catalog groups are used to implement role-based security on the self-service portal. You must assign Service and Request offerings to a Catalog group and assign the Catalog group to a user role. Only administrators can access a published self-service offering if a catalog group with the offerings are not assigned to a user role.

The continual management of the self-service is performed by assigning Active Directory users and groups to the user roles.

A real-world scenario is to assign the User Account Management offerings to only the human resources department. We achieve this objective by creating an SCSM role as discussed in this recipe and allocate an Active Directory group for the human resources department.

There's more...

Here are some additional real-world tips and tricks on creating and managing security roles.

Dynamic membership

You can use keywords in the creation process to automatically assign service offerings and request offerings to a catalog group. You must specify criteria similar to the process used to create views (discussed in `Chapter 2`, *Personalizing SCSM 2016 Administration*) to achieve this objective.

Excluded members

Dynamic groups are great, but we may want to protect specific offerings (for example, offerings tied to automated approved processes). During the catalog group creation process, select the offerings you want to exclude in the Excluded Members page.

Editing the catalog group

You can maintain and edit the catalog groups by viewing the properties and editing the relevant wizard pages.

See also

- The *Creating Service Catalog Service Offerings, Creating ServiceCatalog Request Offerings* and *Publishing Service Offerings and Request Offerings* recipes in `Chapter 5`, *Deploying Service Request Fulfillment* provide steps for creating and publishing Service and Request Offerings associated with the Catalog groups

Listing SCSM security role details with PowerShell

SCSM Security Role delegation can be managed using PowerShell commands. In this recipe, we discuss and provide steps to list the typical settings for all configured SCSM Security User roles using the SCSM PowerShell commands.

Getting ready

You need to ensure you have successfully installed the SCSM product, be a user in the SCSM Administrators role and have the SCSM console open.

You must download and install the SCSM PowerShell Cmdlets found at `http://smlets.co deplex.com/` (see the *Downloading and installing SMLets* recipe in `Chapter 12`, *Automating Service Manager 2016*).

How to do it...

Here are the steps you must follow to list the configuration of security roles using PowerShell commands:

1. Type the following code into a notepad or a plain text editor:

```
Import-Module SMLets
    # Name of the SCSM Management Server
$smDefaultComputer = "TDSCSM03"

$Roles = Get-SCSMUserRole
ForEach ($Role in $Roles)
{
    $RoleOutputName = $Role.DisplayName + " (" +
    $Role.ProfileDisplayName +")"
Write-Output "=================================================="
Write-Output $RoleOutputName
Write-Output $Role.Description
Write-Output "=================================================="
Write-Output "USERS"
ForEach ($User in $Role.Users)
    {
        Write-Output " " $User
    }
    Write-Output " "
```

```
Write-Output "VIEWS"
ForEach ($View in $Role.Views)
{
    Write-Output " " $View.DisplayName
}
Write-Output " "
Write-Output "OBJECT SCOPES"
ForEach ($Object in $Role.Objects)
{
    Write-Output " " $Object.DisplayName
}
Write-Output " "
Write-Output "TEMPLATES"
ForEach ($Template in $Role.Templates)
{
    Write-Output " " $Template.DisplayName
}
Write-Output " "
Write-Output "CLASSES"
ForEach ($Class in $Role.Classes)
{
    Write-Output " " $Class.DisplayName
}
Write-Output " "
Write-Output "CONSOLE TASKS"
ForEach ($CredentialTask in $Role.CredentialTasks)
{
    $T = Get-SCSMConsoleTask $CredentialTask.First
    Write-Output " " $T.DisplayName
}
}
}
```

2. Save the file as a PowerShell file with a .PS1 extension to a filesystem location (for example, **C:\AllSCSMUserRoles.ps1**).
3. Start a PowerShell command prompt as an administrator.
4. Run the following command:

Set-ExecutionPolicy RemoteSigned

5. Press the *Y* and *Enter* keys.
6. In the PowerShell command window, navigate to the location of the script. Type `C:\ AllSCSMUserRoles.ps1`.

7. Press the Enter key.

8. A list of all the default SCSM roles and any custom roles you have created is presented:

```
1    Import-Module SMLets
2    # Name of the SCSM Management Server
3    $smDefaultComputer = "TDSCSM03"
4
5    $Roles = Get-SCSMUserRole
6    ForEach ($Role in $Roles)
7    {
8        $RoleOutputName = $Role.DisplayName + " (" + $Role.ProfileDisplayName +")"
9        Write-Output "==========================================================="
10       Write-Output $RoleOutputName
11       Write-Output $Role.Description
12       Write-Output "==========================================================="
13       Write-Output "USERS"
14       ForEach ($User in $Role.Users)
15       {
```

```
SC - Account Management Portal Role (End User)
Role created for Service Catalog Account Management Offerings
=============================================================
USERS

VIEWS

OBJECT SCOPES

Global Settings

Star Rating

Configuration Item

Data Warehouse SDK Resource Store (internal)

Work Item

SC - User Account Management Service Catalog Group

TEMPLATES

CLASSES

CONSOLE TASKS
=============================================================
```

How it works...

The script is an example of using the SMLets commands to get information from SCSM. Using PowerShell, you can perform many of the console actions, including managing SCSM Security roles. You can find additional examples and usage options at http://technet.microsoft.com/en-us/library/hh316214.

There's more…

Running a script and seeing the output is great, but you may want to save the results of the script.

Piping the script output to a text file

You can save the output of the PowerShell script to a text file by following these steps:

1. In the PowerShell command window, navigate to the location of the script. Type `C:\ AllSCSMUserRoles.ps1 >> C:\<yourfilename.txt>`.
2. Press the *Enter* key.

See also

See the *Using SMLets to delete a Work Item* and *Autoclose resolved Incidents with SMLets and a custom workflow* recipes in `Chapter 12`, *Automating Service Manager 2016*, for additional SCSM management examples using PowerShell commands.

Getting SCSM security roles of a specific user with PowerShell

SCSM security role delegation can be managed (listed and modified) using PowerShell commands. In this recipe, we discuss and provide steps to list all SCSM security roles a specific user is a member of using the SCSM PowerShell commands.

Getting ready

You need to ensure you have successfully installed the SCSM product, are a user in the SCSM Administrators role and have the SCSM console open.

You must download and install the SCSM PowerShell Cmdlets found at `http://smlets.co deplex.com/` (see the *Downloading and installing SMLets* recipe in `Chapter 12`, *Automating Service Manager 2016*).

How to do it...

Here are the steps you must follow to list the configuration of security roles using PowerShell commands:

1. Type the following code into a notepad or a plain text editor:

```
Param([string]$userName)

# Name of the SCSM Management Server
$smDefaultComputer = "TDSCSM03"

Import-Module SMLets
Import-Module ActiveDirectory

If (!$userName)
    {
    Write-Host -ForegroundColor Red "Please start the script with
    a valid username! ... For instance: Get-UsersSCSMRoles.ps1
    andreas.baumgarten"
    Break
    }

$memberInAdGroups = Get-ADUser -Identity $userName -Properties
MemberOf
$memberInAdGroups = $memberInAdGroups.MemberOf

$scsmRoles = Get-SCSMuserRole
foreach ($scsmRole in $scsmRoles)
{
    if ($scsmRole.users)
        {
        $scsmRoleName = $scsmRole.Displayname
        if ($scsmRole.users -like "*$userName*")
            {
            Write-Host -ForegroundColor Blue "=== SCSM Role:
        $scsmRoleName ==="
            Write-Host -ForegroundColor Green "User $userName is
            direct member of this SCSM user role"
            }
        if ($scsmRole.Users -like "*Domain Users*")
            {
            Write-Host -ForegroundColor Blue "=== SCSM Role:
            $scsmRoleName ==="
            Write-Host -ForegroundColor Green "User $userName is
            member of this SCSM user role by AD groupmembership:
            Domain Users"
```

```
        }
    if ($scsmRole.Users -like "*Authenticated Users*")
        {
        Write-Host -ForegroundColor Blue "=== SCSM Role:
        $scsmRoleName ==="
        Write-Host -ForegroundColor Green "User $userName is
        member of this SCSM user role by AD groupmembership:
        Authenticated Users"
        }
    foreach ($adGroup in $memberInAdGroups)
        {
        $adGroupName = Get-ADGroup -Identity $adGroup
        $adGroupName = $adGroupName.SamAccountName
        if ($SCSMrole.Users -like "*$adGroupName*")
            {
            Write-Host -ForegroundColor Blue "=== SCSM Role:
            $scsmRoleName ==="
            Write-Host -ForegroundColor Green "User $userName
            is member of this SCSM user role by AD
            groupmembership: $ADgroupName"
            }
        }
    }
}
```

2. Save the file as a PowerShell file with a `.PS1` extension to a filesystem location
    (for example, **C:\Get-UsersSCSMRoles.ps1**).

3. Start a PowerShell command prompt as an administrator.

4. Run the following command:

Set-ExecutionPolicy RemoteSigned

5. Press the *Y* and *Enter* keys.

6. In the PowerShell command window, navigate to the location of the script. Type
    `C:\ Get-UsersSCSMRoles.ps1 <username>`. Replace *<username>* with any
    valid AD username.

7. Press the Enter key.

8. A list of all the SCSM user roles the user is a member is presented:

```
Get-UsersSCSMRoles.ps1  X
1    Param([string]$userName)
2
3    # Name of the SCSM Management Server
4    $smDefaultComputer = "TDSCSM03"
5
6    Import-Module SMLets
7    Import-Module ActiveDirectory
8
9    If (!$userName)
10      {
11         Write-Host -ForegroundColor Red "Please start the script with a valid username! ... For ins
12         Break
13      }
14
15   $memberInAdGroups = Get-ADUser -Identity $userName -Properties MemberOf
16   $memberInAdGroups = $memberInAdGroups.MemberOf
17
18   $scsmRoles = Get-SCSMuserRole
19   foreach ($scsmRole in $scsmRoles)
20      {
```

```
PS C:\Andreas> .\Get-UsersSCSMRoles.ps1 andreas.baumgarten

User andreas.baumgarten is direct member of this SCSM user role

User andreas.baumgarten is member of this SCSM user role by AD groupmembership: CBAdmins

User andreas.baumgarten is direct member of this SCSM user role

User andreas.baumgarten is member of this SCSM user role by AD groupmembership: Domain Users

User andreas.baumgarten is member of this SCSM user role by AD groupmembership: Authenticated Users


PS C:\Andreas>
```

How it works...

The script gets the group membership of the user specified by the username from Active Directory and the list of all SCSM user roles. The script then checks what SCSM roles the user is a member of based on their AD group membership. This assumes the delegation of SCSM roles is done with AD groups (this is the recommended practice).

There's more...

Running a script and seeing the output is great, but you may want to save the results of the script.

Piping the script output to a text file

You can save the output of the PowerShell script to a text file by following these steps:

1. In the PowerShell command window, navigate to the location of the script. Type `C:\ Get-UsersSCSMRoles.ps1 <username> >> C:\<yourfilename.txt>`.

2. Press the *Enter* key.

See also

See the *Using SMLets to delete a Work Item* and *Autoclose resolved Incidents with SMLets and a custom workflow* recipes in `Chapter 12`, Automating Service Manager 2016, for additional SCSM management examples of using PowerShell commands.

10
Working with the Data Warehouse and Reporting

In this chapter, we will walk you through the various options of using the Service Manager Data Warehouse to gain insight into the data stored in the Service Manager database. We will specifically cover using reporting and advanced analytics with the following tasks:

- Viewing SCSM reports
- Creating favorite and linked reports
- Understanding the Service Manager Data Warehouse data mart
- Creating reports with Report Builder
- Configuring report permissions
- Delivering reports automatically using report subscriptions
- Analyzing data with Microsoft Excel
- Using the Analysis Library to publish Excel reports

Introduction

Service Manager periodically transfers data that is stored in the operational database to the Service Manager Data Warehouse databases through a process called **Extract Transform and Load** (**ETL**). The processes required for keeping the data in the Data Warehouse in sync with the operational database are controlled by the Service Manager Data Warehouse Management Server role.

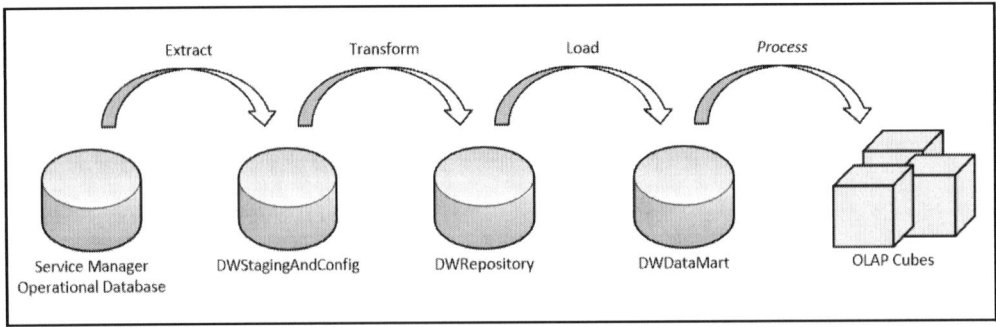

The ETL process is started on a scheduled interval. The first step is the extract workflow, which reads new data from the operational database and writes it to the **DWStagingAndConfig** database. The raw data is then picked up by the transform workflow, which does any reformatting required for bringing the data into the final format optimized for reporting prior to storing it in the **DWRepository** database. The load workflow then transfers the data to the **DWDataMart** database where it can be used for reporting.

The reasons for transferring data to the databases of the Service Manager Data Warehouse are the following:

- Offload data from the Service Manager operational database to improve performance.
- Provide a long-term storage of historical data stored in Service Manager.
- Optimize and provide data for reporting.

The DWDataMart database is the database used for all reporting needs. In addition, Service Manager comes with a set of predefined OLAP cubes to facilitate advanced analysis of data. An OLAP cube is a multi-dimensional data structure that is optimized for aggregating and analyzing large amounts of data while also allowing access to the most granular information. The SCSM Data Warehouse leverages Microsoft SQL Server Analysis Services to provide OLAP cubes to end users.

With both the `DWDataMart` database and the OLAP cubes, Service Manager provides powerful means for creating simple reports as well as gaining advanced insight into the data by analyzing it from multiple perspectives.

Within this chapter we will provide recipes to work with common reporting tools that allow you to access and analyze data stored in the `DWDataMart` database and the OLAP cubes.

Viewing SCSM reports

In this recipe, we will show you how to navigate through the reporting section of the Service Manager console and how to work with the built-in reports that are shipped out of the box with Service Manager.

Getting ready

Before you can work with reports, it is required that you have already installed a Service Manager Data Warehouse Management Server and that it has been registered with the Service Manager server installation. You also need to ensure that the initial synchronization of the management packs is complete and the ETL jobs have run. Information on how to complete these two tasks can be found in the TechNet library at the following URL:

`https://technet.microsoft.com/en-us/system-center-docs/sm/deploy/deploy-registering-with-the-service-manager-data-warehouse-to-enable-reporting`. This process normally takes several hours to complete from the time the Data Warehouse Management Server was registered.

How to do it...

We will now walk you through the steps required for viewing SCSM reports through the Service Manager console:

1. Navigate to the **Reporting** section of the Service Manager console.
2. Under the **Reports** node, you will see a couple of folders that contain predefined reports for different types of work items and configuration items. Click the **Incident Management** folder.
3. You will see the built-in reports for incident management listed in the view. In this example, we want to retrieve a list of all incidents concerning hardware problems. Click the **List of Incidents** report and then click **Run Report** from the tasks bar.

4. In the parameter section of the report window, under **Classification Category**, unselect the **(All)** option and check the **Hardware** option.

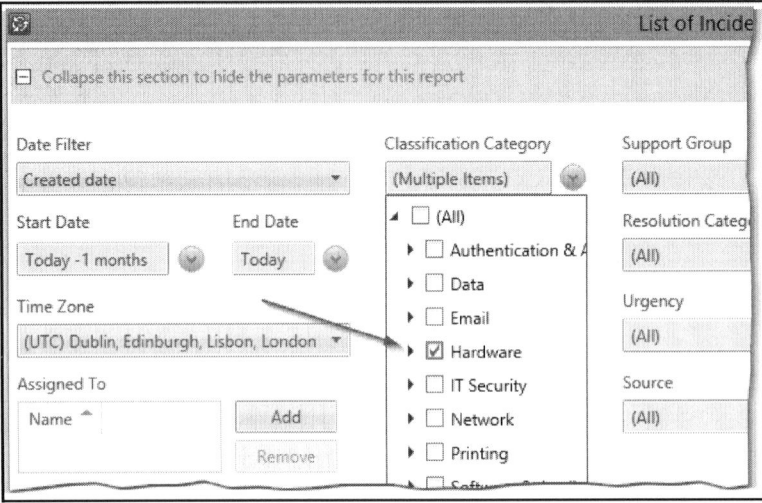

5. Click on the **Run Report** option from the task bar to generate and view the report in the console.

6. Click on the floppy disk icon and choose the desired format to export the report.

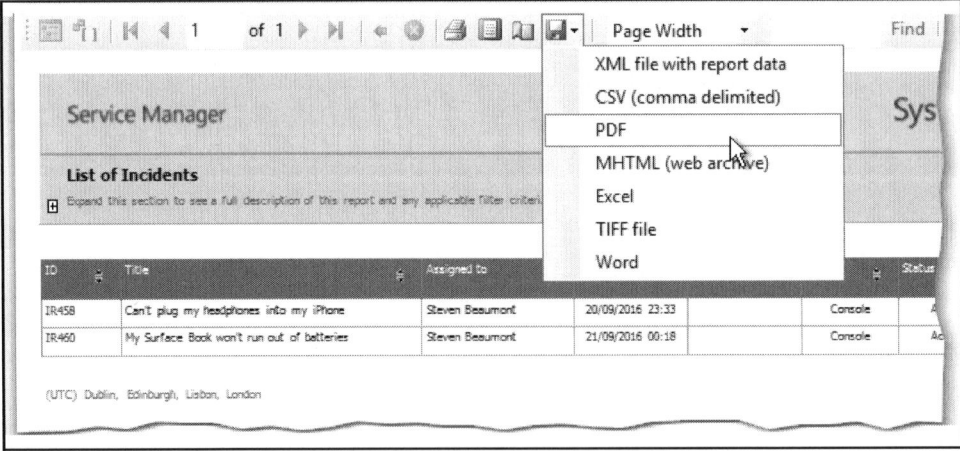

How it works...

Service Manager uses SQL Server Reporting Services to provide its reporting capabilities. The folders and reports that are listed under the **Reporting** section of the Service Manager console represent the way how the reports are organized in SQL Server Reporting Services.

When a report is opened in the console, Service Manager loads the report definition and displays its parameters to allow for filtering data in the report. The options and controls available for filtering data can be defined by using management packs.

There's more...

In this section, we will show you how you can access reports from a web browser, which is particularly interesting for users that do not have access to the SCSM console

Accessing reports from a browser

The **Reporting** section in the Service Manager console is a very comfortable way of accessing reports quickly from within the console. However, a common scenario is to allow the users that do not work with the Service Manager console to access reports. For instance, you might want to run incident statistics by your users' departments and hand out a report to each department head.

Creating such a report using the Service Manager console, exporting it to a suitable format, and sending it to each department head is quite cumbersome. Instead, you can grant your department heads access to the reports through the web browser.

Open your web browser and navigate to the following URL:

```
http://[SCSMDWSQL]/Reports
```

Replace [SCSMDWSQL] with the fully qualified domain name of the SQL server, which is used for reporting. If SQL Server Reporting Service is running as a named instance, the syntax of the URL will be the following:

```
http://[SCSMDWSQL]/Reports_[InstanceName]
```

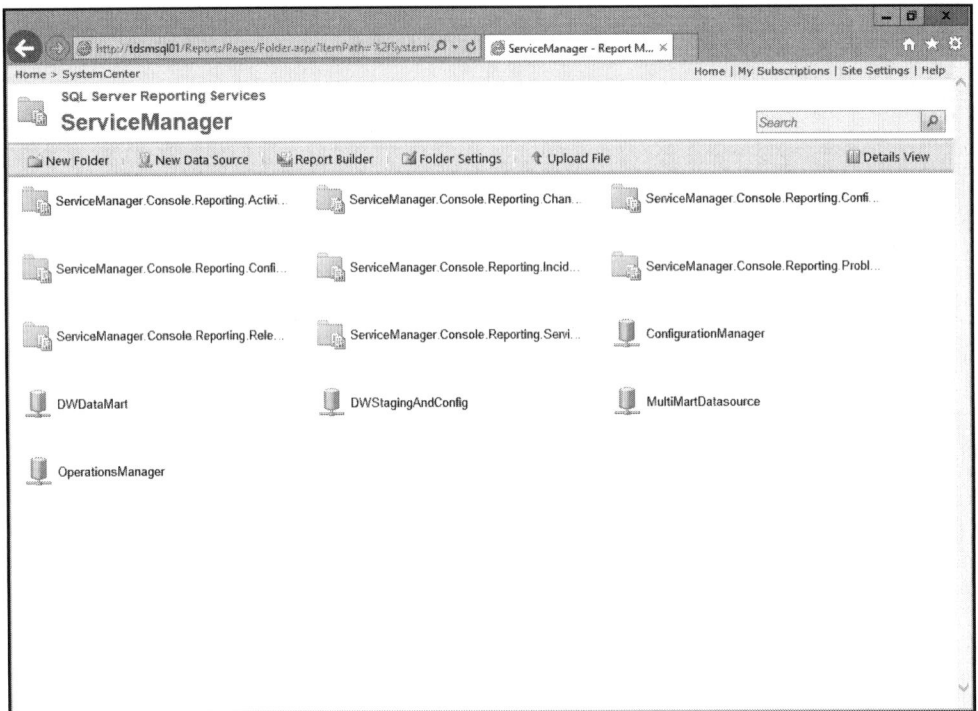

You will notice that the folder and filenames, as well as the controls used for defining your report parameters are much less comprehensive than when the reports are consumed through the Service Manager console. If you use the web browser to navigate the reports, SQL Server Reporting Services represents the actual file and folder names and also renders the default controls for the report parameters. This behavior can be overridden when accessing reports through the Service Manager console by using corresponding directives in management packs.

If you want to provide reports to users through the web browser, we recommend that you create custom reports for your end users that do not make use of advanced management pack features, but are comprehensively consumable through the web browser instead. You can create your own folder and report file structure in SQL Server Reporting Services and limit access to only the folders you want your users to see.

See also

Refer to the following recipes for more information on how to manage report permissions and folder structures:

- The *Configuring report permissions* recipe later in this chapter

Creating favorite and linked reports

System Center 2016 Service Manager allows you to save the selections you make in the parameters section of the report window for future use. You can either save your settings for just yourself or create a linked report that will also be available to other users.

Getting ready

It is recommended that you follow the instructions from the previous recipe, *Viewing SCSM reports*, to get familiar with how to open reports using the Service Manager console.

How to do it...

The selections that you make in the parameter section of the report window can be stored as a **favorite report**, allowing you to access the report with the same selections at a later point in time. Favorite reports are personal and cannot be accessed by other users:

1. Open the report of your choice in the Service Manager console.
2. Make the desired selections in the parameters section of the report window. For example, follow the instructions in the *Viewing SCSM reports* recipe to create a list of incidents about hardware-related problems.
3. In the task pane on the right-hand side, click on **Save as Favorite**, enter a name for the report, and then click on **OK**.

4. The favorite report will now appear under the **Favorite Reports** folder in the **Reporting** section of the Service Manager console.

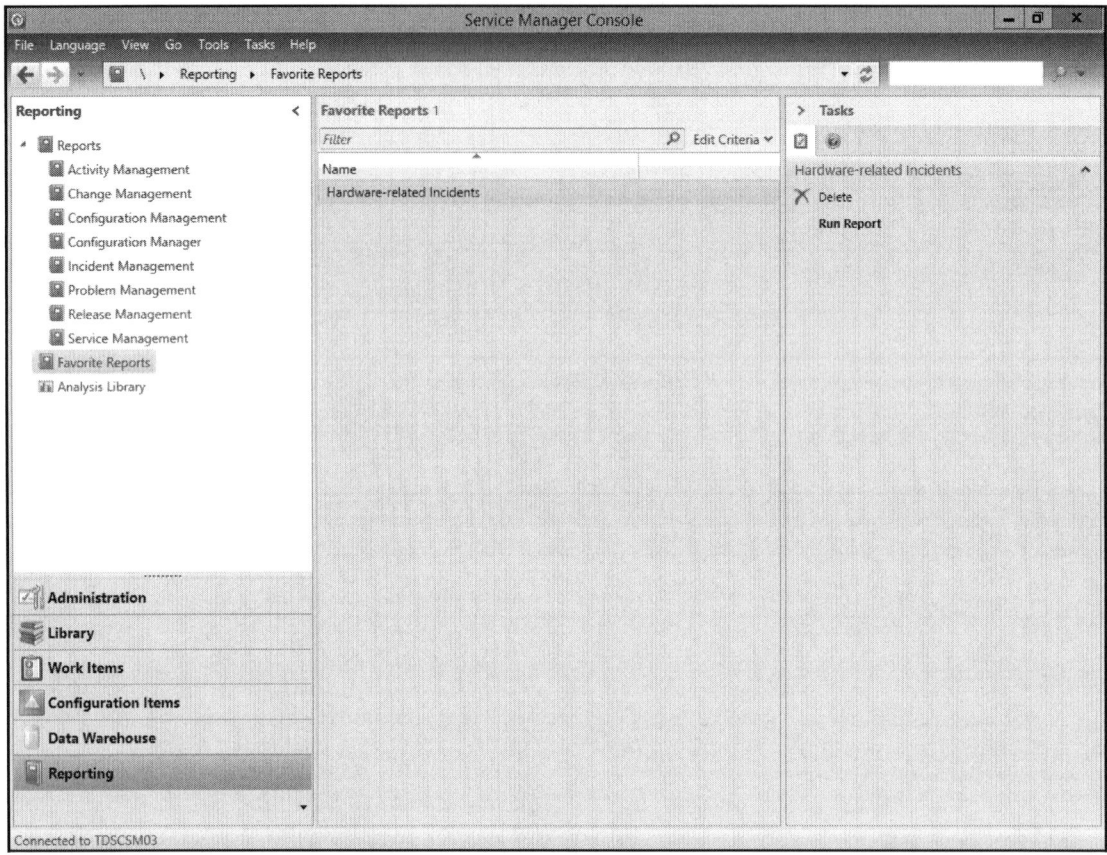

A **linked report** is a favorite report that can be accessed by other users. You can create linked reports only from reports that were imported through management packs. Follow these instructions to create a linked report:

1. Open the report of your choice in the Service Manager console.
2. Make the desired selections in the parameters section of the report window. For example, follow the instructions in the *Viewing SCSM reports* recipe to create a list of incidents about hardware-related problems.
3. In the task pane on the right-hand side, click on **Save as Linked Report**.
4. Enter a name for the report, and choose the management pack where you would like to save the linked report definition to.

5. Under **Select Folder**, choose the folder where you would like your report to show up under. Click on **OK**.

6. All the users with access to Service Manager reports and to the destination folder can now access the linked report by navigating to the respective location in the **Reporting** section of the Service Manager console.

> You require **Publisher** or **Content Manager** permissions in SQL Server Reporting Services to be able to create **Linked Reports**.

How it works...

Favorite reports are stored directly in the Service Manager database, whereas Linked Reports are actually a feature of SQL Server Reporting Services, which allows users to create a view on the underlying report with predefined selections for its parameters.

See also

Refer to the following recipes for more information on how to view reports and manage report permissions:

- The *Viewing SCSM reports* recipe in this chapter
- The *Configuring report permissions* recipe later in this chapter

Understanding the Service Manager Data Warehouse data mart

The purpose of this recipe is to describe the database schema of the Service Manager Data Warehouse data mart. Knowing the anatomy and the design of the data mart is key to successfully creating custom reports for System Center Service Manager.

Getting ready

The central repository that stores all data available for Service Manager reporting is the DWDataMart database. This database is located on the SQL Server, hosting the Service Manager Data Warehouse databases, and is also referred to as the Service Manager data mart.

Although SQL Server Report Builder and other tools used for authoring reports offer visual wizards for creating the queries that will be used for retrieving data from the Service Manager Data Warehouse data mart, it is hardly possible to work with reporting effectively without at least knowing the basics of the SQL used for querying relational databases.

The Service Manager Data Warehouse data mart is documented and is part of the SM Job Aids, which can be downloaded from the Microsoft website:

http://www.microsoft.com/en-us/download/details.aspx?id=27850.

How to do it...

All data relevant for reporting are exposed in views inside the DWDataMart database. You should not access the tables directly in your report queries. The DWDataMart is a Data Warehouse that uses three types of entities:

- Dimensions
- Facts
- Outriggers

Dimensions

A dimension in the database is roughly analogous to a class in Service Manager. Each class in Service Manager has a list of properties, while each dimension contains a list of attributes. Each dimension attribute will map to one property in a class.

Dimensions are exposed in views that normally end with the string . . .`Dimvw`, such as `ComputerDimvw`.

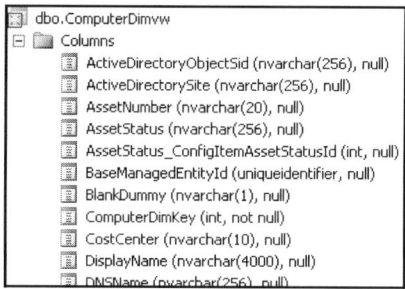

To get a list of all computers, you can execute the following query:

```
SELECT * FROM ComputerDimvw
```

Please note that data is never deleted from the Data Warehouse. Instead, deleted rows are marked accordingly. Each dimension has an attribute named `IsDeleted`. To get a list of all undeleted computers, you can execute the following query:

```
SELECT * FROM ComputerDimvw WHERE IsDeleted = 0
```

Furthermore, each dimension includes an attribute representing the primary key for each row in the dimension. This attribute is named `[DimensionName]DimKey`. The primary key attribute for the `Computer` dimension is named `ComputerDimKey`:

```
SELECT ComputerDimKey, * FROM ComputerDimvw WHERE IsDeleted = 0
```

Facts

A fact in the Data Warehouse is analogous to a relationship in Service Manager. Each relationships allows for a source instance and a target instance (both are typically represented by dimensions) to be joined together.

An example of a fact is the relationship between a computer and the operating system running on the computer. This relationship is exposed in a view named `ComputerHostsOperatingSystemFactvw`.

To create a query that returns data from both the computer and its operating system, you need to join the two dimensions together using the view representing the relationship fact.

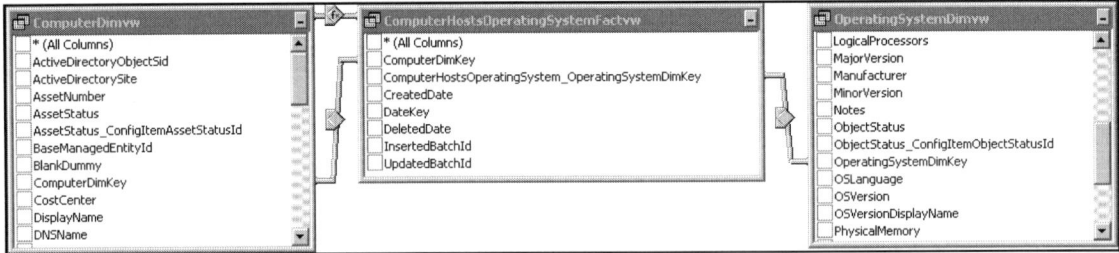

The join between the source dimension and the fact needs to be established using the dimension key attribute. To establish the join between the fact and the target dimension, use the corresponding target dimension key attribute. Please note that you can exclude deleted relationships by filtering the `DeletedDate` attribute by `IS NULL`:

```
SELECT     co.PrincipalName,     os.PhysicalMemory FROM     ComputerDimvw co
LEFT OUTER JOIN ComputerHostsOperatingSystemFactvw coHos ON
co.ComputerDimKey = coHos.ComputerDimKey          AND coHos.DeletedDate IS
NULL     LEFT OUTER JOIN OperatingSystemDimvw os ON
coHos.ComputerHostsOperatingSystem_OperatingSystemDimKey =
s.OperatingSystemDimKey WHERE     co.IsDeleted = 0
```

Outriggers

An outrigger is a list that can logically group together a set of values. Outriggers in the Data Warehouse can target one or more class properties and consolidate them into a single set of discrete values. These class properties are typically enumerations (also known as **Lists** in Service Manager).

An example of an outrigger is the **Status** property of the **Incident** class. This property is represented as a list in Service Manager.

If you execute the following query, you will notice that the values in the Status attribute contain internal names only:

```
SELECT Id, Status FROM IncidentDimvw
```

In order to retrieve the actual string values for the statuses, you need to join the corresponding view representing the outrigger, `IncidentStatusvw` in this case. The join needs to be established between the `[DimensionAttributeName]_[OutriggerName]Id` attribute of the dimension and the `[OutriggerName]Id` attribute of the outrigger.

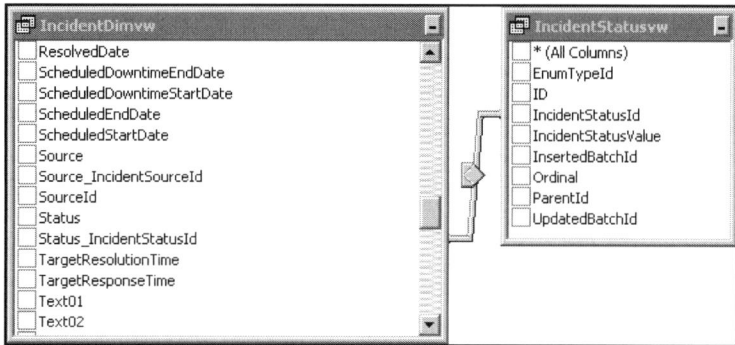

The string value for the outrigger is represented by the `[OutriggerName]Value` attribute, `IncidentStatusValue` in this case:

```
SELECT     i.Id,    i.Status,     s.IncidentStatusValue FROM     IncidentDimvw
i    LEFT OUTER JOIN IncidentStatusvw s ON
i.Status_IncidentStatusId = s.IncidentStatusId WHERE    i.IsDeleted = 0
```

How it works...

System Center Service Manager makes the data from the operational CMDB database available in a separate data mart named `DWDataMart`. The schema of the data mart is optimized for reporting.

Each entity type in the CMDB has its own representation in the data mart. Classes are represented as dimensions, relationships are represented as facts, and enumerations (also known as Lists) are represented as outriggers. Service Manager creates views in the SQL database that you can use to write queries for your reports.

The translation of entities in the CMDB to their respective representation in the data mart is defined in management packs. These management packs are synchronized from the operational database to the data mart as part of the `MPSyncJob` Data Warehouse job.

Creating custom database objects for reporting

Although the `DWDataMart` database ships with System Center Service Manager, its intended purpose is to act as the source for reporting, hence it is allowed to create database objects such as views, stored procedures, and user-defined functions to accommodate your reporting needs.

Whenever possible, use stored procedures for your reports. Stored procedures have advantages over views when it comes to optimizing the query and the ability to do complex queries that wouldn't be possible in views.

Try to come up with a naming standard for all custom objects that you create in the `DWDataMart` database. This allows you to easily distinguish them from out-of-the-box objects.

A sample naming standard would be:

```
[ObjectTypeAbbreviation]_[Company]_r_[Name]
```

Examples would be:

- `usp_MyCompany_r_IncidentSLA` for a stored procedure
- `udf_MyComany_r_GetStatusDisplayName` for a user-defined function
- `v_MyCompany_r_ListOfComputers` for a view

It is recommended not to use white spaces in the name of database objects.

Database permissions required for reporting

During the installation of the Service Manager Data Warehouse management server, you had to specify a reporting service account. The setup process automatically added this account as a SQL Server Login and added it as a member of the `reportuser` database role in the `DWDataMart` database.

In order for your custom-created reports to render successfully, you will need to grant explicit permissions to the `reportuser` database role for the objects you created in the `DWDataMart` database, such as Views, Stored Procedures, or User-Defined Functions.

Creating reports with Report Builder

This recipe will walk you through the steps of using Report Builder 3.0 to create new reports for Service Manager. We will also show you how to create a custom folder structure in SQL Server Reporting Services to store your reports in.

Getting ready

Although Report Builder offers a visual wizard for creating the queries that will be used for retrieving data from the Service Manager Data Warehouse database, it is hardly possible to work with reporting effectively without at least knowing the basics of the SQL used for querying relational databases.

Furthermore, you will need to get familiar with the database model of the DWDataMart database. Please refer to the *Understanding the Service Manager Data Warehouse data mart* recipe earlier in this chapter.

Also, you must install Microsoft .NET Framework 3.5 on all computers you intend to run Report Builder from.

How to do it...

First, we will create a custom folder structure in SQL Server Reporting Services to store our reports:

1. Open your web browser and navigate to the following URL:
   `http://[SCSMDWSQL]/Reports`.

2. Replace [SCSMDWSQL] with the fully qualified domain name of the SQL server that is used for reporting. If SQL Server Reporting Service is running as a named instance, the syntax of the URL will be the following:
   `http://[SCSMDWSQL]/Reports_[InstanceName]`.

3. Click on the **SystemCenter** folder, and then click on the **ServiceManager** folder.

4. Click on **New Folder**, enter a name for the folder, such as `Custom Reports`, and optionally enter a description. Click on **OK**.

5. Click on the newly created folder and then click on **New Folder** to create a new subfolder. Enter a name for the folder, such as `Incident Management`, and optionally enter a description. Click on **OK**.

6. Click on the newly created subfolder. Note that the permissions applied to the newly created folder will be inherited from the parent `ServiceManager` folder. You can break inheritance and apply custom permissions to your folders. Instructions on how to manage report permissions can be found in a later chapter.

With the folder structure created, we are now going to create the report:

1. Click on the **Report Builder** button from the toolbar. Report Builder will be streamed to your computer.

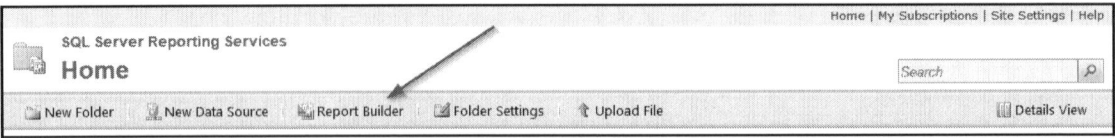

2. If you see the error message **To use Report Builder, you must install .Net Framework 3.5 on this computer** and you made sure .NET Framework has already been installed, you will need to run Internet Explorer in IE8 mode (you can switch mode by using the Developer Tools (F12)), or install Report Builder on your computer (see the following *There's more...* section).

3. If you see a security warning, click on **Run** to start the application.

4. Once Report Builder has started, on the **Getting Started** window, choose **New Report | Table or Matrix Wizard**.

5. In the **Choose a dataset** dialog, select **Create a dataset**, and then click on **Next**.

6. In the **Choose a connection to a data source** dialog, select the **DWDataMart** data source. If it is not displayed in the list, click on **Browse**, navigate to the **SystemCenter\ServiceManager** folder, and choose **DWDataMart**. Click on **Open**. Finally click on **Next** to proceed.

7. The **Enter Data Source Credentials** dialog will be displayed because Report Builder needs credentials to access the database. If the user account that you are using to run Report Builder has access to the `DWDataMart` database, you can choose the **Use the current Windows user** option and click on **OK**. Otherwise, you will need to provide the password of the Service Manager Reporting Account.

8. The **Design a query** dialog will open.

9. In the Relationships section, create the following relationships:

Left Table	Join Type	Right Table	Join Fields
IncidentDimvw	Inner	WorkItemDimvw	EntityDimKey = EntityDimKey
WorkItemDimvw	Left Outer	WorkItemAffectedUserFactvw	WorkItemDimKey = WorkItemDimKey
WorkItemAffectedUserFactvw	Left Outer	UserDimvw	WorkItemAffectedUser_UserDimKey = UserDimKey
IncidentDimvw	Left Outer	IncidentClassificationvw	Classification_IncidentClassificationId = IncidentClassificationId
IncidentClassificationvw	Left Outer	DisplayStringDimvw	EnumTypeId = BaseManagedEntityId

To do so, repeat the following steps 10 to 15 for each relationship in the preceding table.

10. On the left-hand side of the **Design a query** wizard, expand **dbo\Views**, which is under the **Database** view:

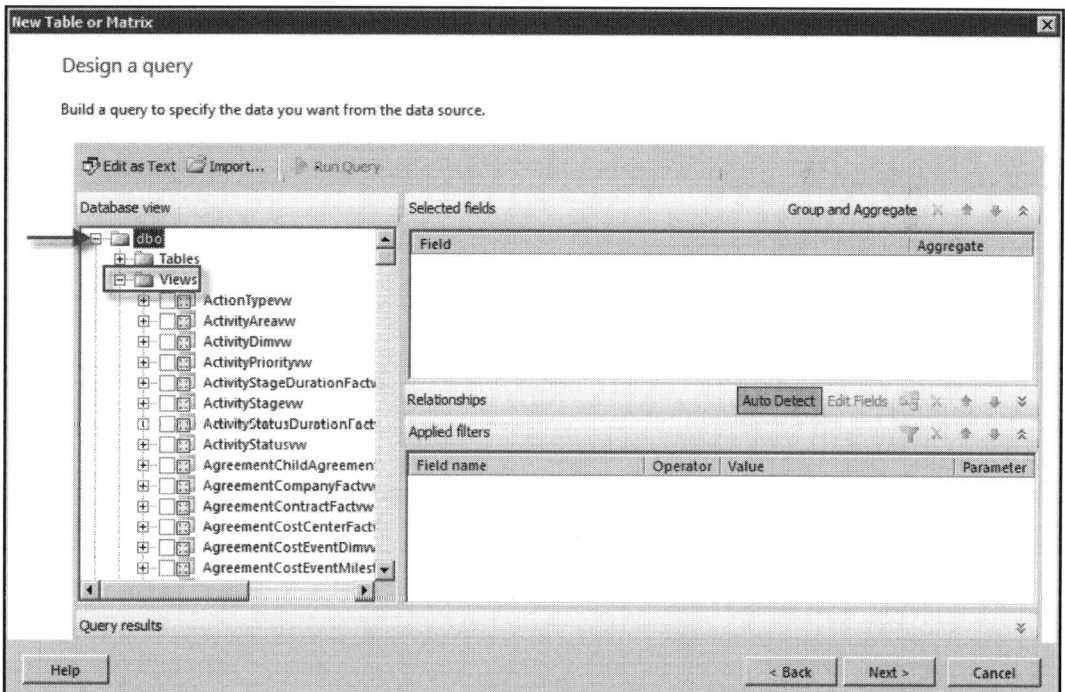

11. In the middle pane navigate to the **Relationships** section (you may have to expand the **Relationship** pane). Click on **AutoDetect** to activate the relationship button.

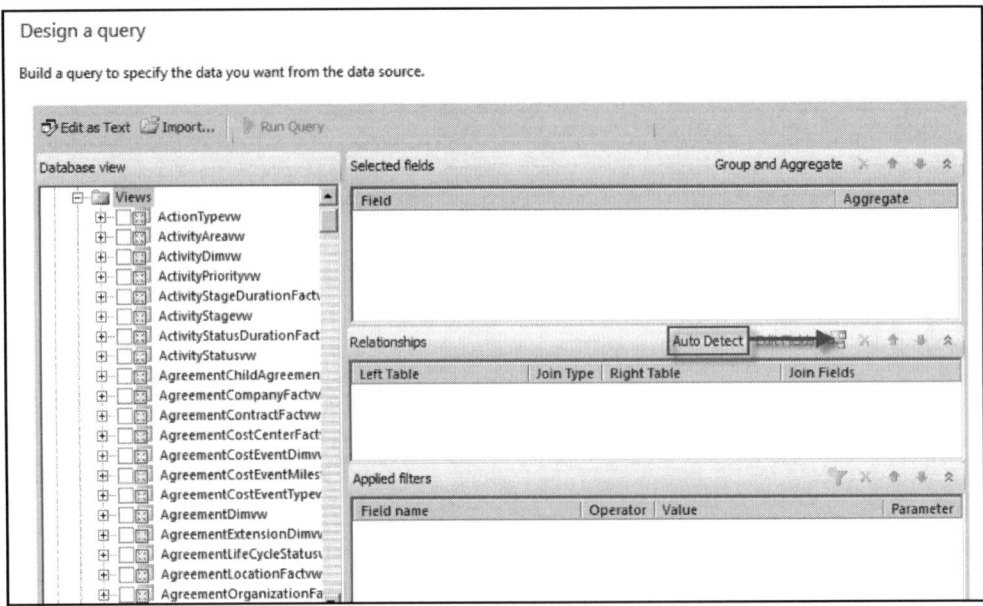

12. Click on the icon for adding a relationship, as indicated in the previous screenshot. An empty relationship entry is added to the **Relationships** section.

13. Click on the left part of the relationship. A new window is presented showing the dataset schema. Navigate to and expand **dbo\views**. Select the table on the left-hand side view, for instance **IncidentDimvw**.

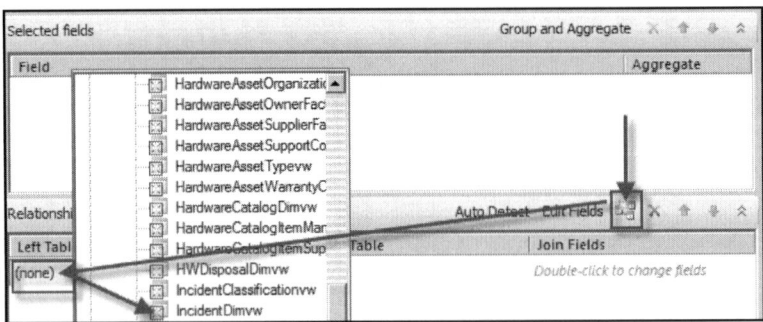

14. Click on the right part of the relationship. A new window is presented showing the dataset schema. Navigate to and expand **dbo\views**. Select the right table view, for instance **WorkItemDimvw**.

15. To select the `join` field, double-click the space below the join field and click on the **Add Field** icon. Select the left and right join fields.

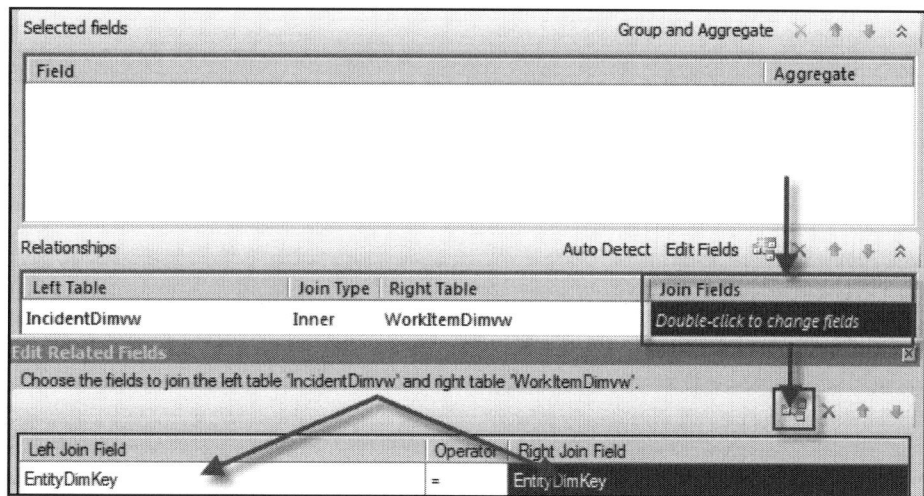

16. The following screenshot shows the required configuration of the **Relationships** section:

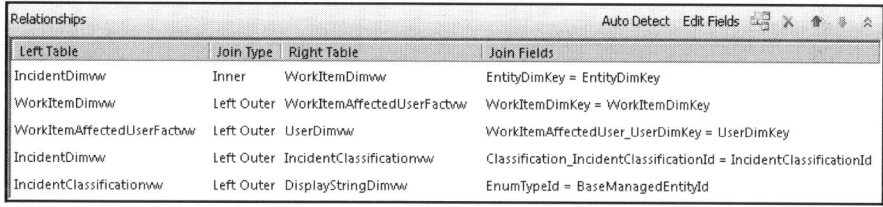

17. From the **Database view** section, select the following fields from the **dbo\Views** folder to add them to the **Selected fields** section, and configure the fields as follows:

Field	Aggregate
IncidentDimvw.Id	Count Distinct
DisplayStringDimvw.DisplayName	Grouped by
UserDimvw.DisplayName	Grouped by

18. In the **Applied filters** section, add the following filters:

Field name	Operator	Value
WorkItemAffectedUserFactvw.DeletedDate	is	(null)
DisplayStringDimvw.LanguageCode	is	ENU

19. Please see the following screenshot that shows all the required settings for designing the query:

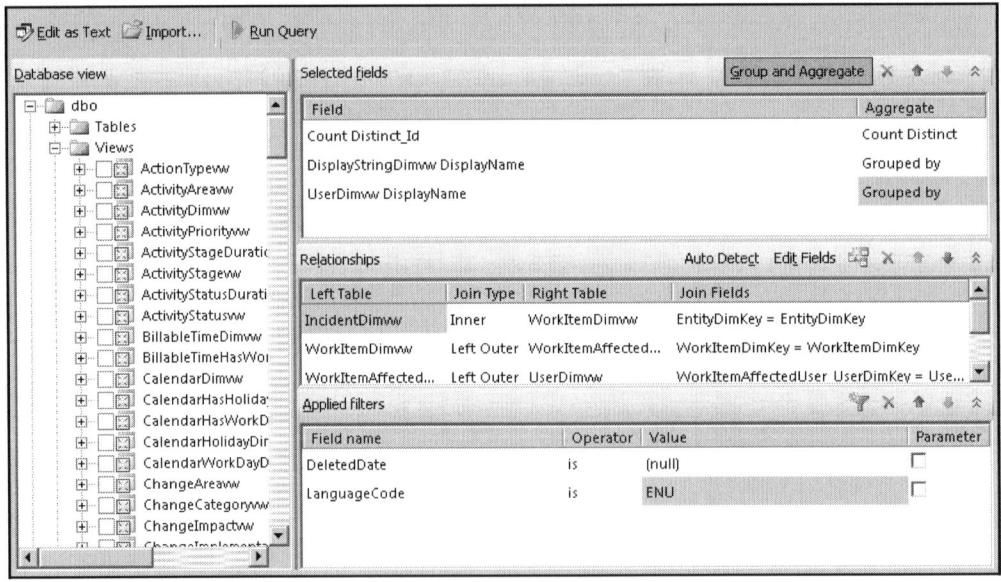

20. Click on **Next** to proceed to the **Arrange fields** dialog.

21. Drag the **DisplayStringDimvw_DisplayName** field to the **Column** groups area.

22. Drag the **UserDimvw_DisplayName** field to the **Row** groups area.
23. Drag the **Count_Distinct_Id** field to the **Values** area. Click on the arrow next to the fieldname and choose **Sum**. Click on **Next**.
24. In the **Choose the layout** dialog, make sure **Show subtotals and grand totals** is selected, and then click on **Next**.
25. In the **Choose a style** dialog, choose a style of your choice, and then click **Finish**. The wizard is now finished and you will see the report in the design view of Report Builder.
26. Replace the text, **Click to add title**, with a title such as Incidents by Affected User.
27. Replace the top-left column heading with Affected User.
28. Now it's time to test our report. Click **Run** from the Report Builder toolbar.

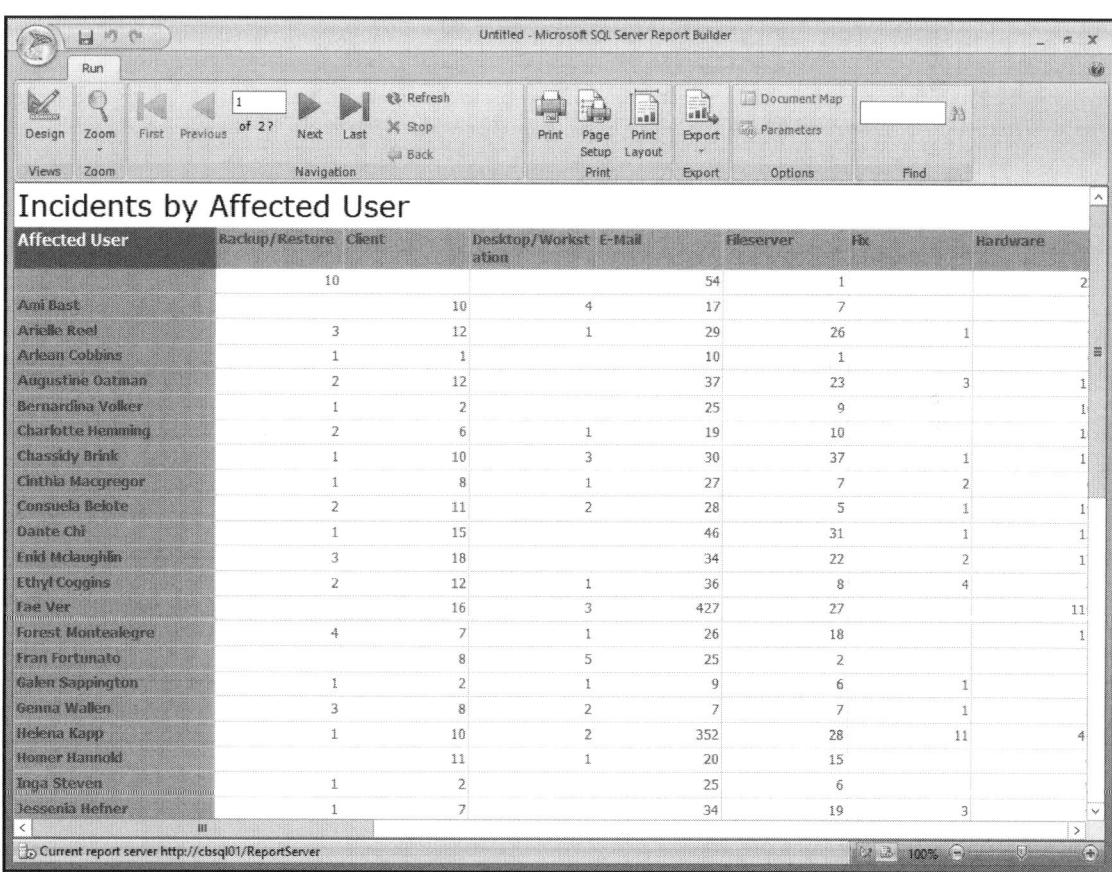

29. Press *Ctrl+S* or click on the floppy disk icon to save your report. In **the Save As Report** dialog, navigate to the newly created folder in the SQL Server Reporting Services folder structure, enter a name such as `Incident by Affected User`, and then click on **Save**.

30. Open the Service Manager console. If it was already started, you might need to restart the console for the newly created folders and reports to show up.

31. Navigate to the **Reporting** section of the Service Manager console.

32. Under the **Reports** node, you will see the newly created folders, and the report will show under the folder you saved it to.

As you can see, the report that you created can now be opened either through the Service Manager console or by accessing SQL Server Reporting Services directly through your browser.

If you would like to edit the report, navigate to the folder where it is stored using your browser, hover over the report file, click the arrow next to the report, and then click on **Edit** in Report Builder.

How it works...

Service Manager leverages SQL Server Reporting Services for providing rich reporting functionalities to the end users. As an administrator, you can create your own reports that access the `DWDataMart` database provided by the Service Manager Data Warehouse server.

SQL Server Report Builder is a powerful tool that you can use to design your reports and save them to SQL Server Reporting Services. Using folders and security settings, you can establish a custom reporting structure with permissions that correspond to your organization's needs. All reports can be accessed either through the web browser, or you can use the Service Manager console to browse and consume your reports.

There's more...

If you are authoring reports often, you might prefer to install Report Builder to your local computer. In this section, we will show you how to do this. We will also walk you through the process of editing SQL queries for your reports and copying existing reports.

Installing Report Builder 3.0 on your computer

Report Builder ships with SQL Server. As you have seen in the *How to do it...* section of this recipe, Report Builder can be streamed to your computer by clicking on the **Report Builder** button on the SQL Server Reporting Service web page. This allows you to manage your reports from virtually anywhere without the need to comply with any software requirements on the computer that you are working with.

However, if you mostly use the same computer to work with reports, you might want to install Report Builder, eliminating the need to stream the software to the computer every time you launch it.

You can download SQL Server 2102 Report Builder from the following URL:

`https://www.microsoft.com/en-us/download/details.aspx?id=29072`. During the installation procedure, the setup will ask you for the default target server URL. Enter the following URL if you are running SQL Server Reporting Services as a default instance:

`http://[SCSMDWSQL]/reportserver`.

Replace [SCSMDWSQL] with the fully qualified domain name of the SQL server that is used for reporting. If SQL Server Reporting Service is running as a named instance, the syntax of the URL will be the following:

`http://[SCSMDWSQL]/reportserver_[InstanceName]`.

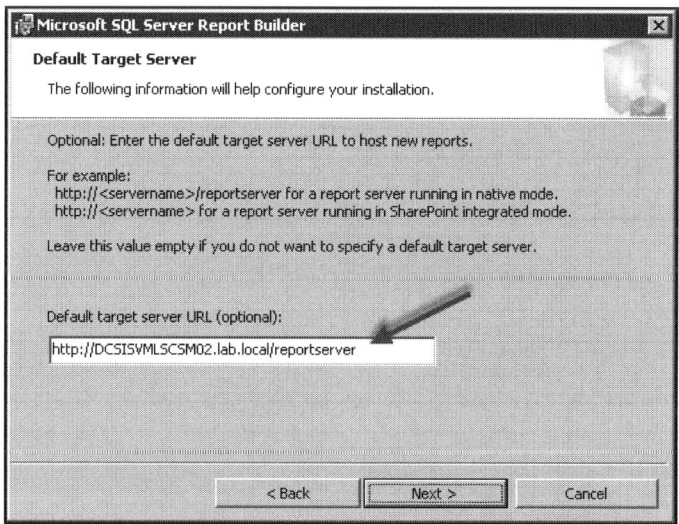

Writing SQL queries for your reports

When you are familiar with SQL, you might be faster to write the queries directly in SQL Server Management Studio. Use this query instead of walking through the wizard as described in this recipe. Click on the **Edit as Text** option in the **Design a query** dialog and paste the query directly in the editor. The following is the query that was used for the example in this recipe:

```
SELECT
    COUNT(DISTINCT IncidentDimvw.Id) AS [Count Distinct_Id]
    ,DisplayStringDimvw.DisplayName AS [DisplayStringDimvw
    DisplayName]
    ,UserDimvw.DisplayName AS [UserDimvw DisplayName]
FROM
    IncidentDimvw
    INNER JOIN WorkItemDimvw
        ON IncidentDimvw.EntityDimKey = WorkItemDimvw.EntityDimKey
    LEFT OUTER JOIN WorkItemAffectedUserFactvw
        ON WorkItemDimvw.WorkItemDimKey =
        WorkItemAffectedUserFactvw.WorkItemDimKey
    LEFT OUTER JOIN UserDimvw
        ON WorkItemAffectedUserFactvw.WorkItemAffectedUser_UserDimKey =
        UserDimvw.UserDimKey
    LEFT OUTER JOIN IncidentClassificationvw
        ON IncidentDimvw.Classification_IncidentClassificationId =
        IncidentClassificationvw.IncidentClassificationId
    LEFT OUTER JOIN DisplayStringDimvw
        ON IncidentClassificationvw.EnumTypeId =
        DisplayStringDimvw.BaseManagedEntityId
WHERE
    WorkItemAffectedUserFactvw.DeletedDate IS NULL
    AND DisplayStringDimvw.LanguageCode = N'ENU'
GROUP BY
    DisplayStringDimvw.DisplayName
    ,UserDimvw.DisplayName
```

Copying existing reports

Designing reports can be a very time consuming process. Once you have established and designed a report, you might want to copy the report instead of starting from scratch. This allows you to maintain the layout of the reporting controls and other settings that you made in your report definition:

1. Open the report in Report Builder.

2. Click on the Report Builder logo on the top left, and then click on **Save As** to save the report under a new name at the desired location.

3. In the **Report Data** section, under **Datasets**, delete any existing datasets.

4. Add a new dataset by right-clicking the **Datasets** folder and clicking on **Add Dataset**.

5. Give it a name and choose the option, **Use a dataset embedded in my report**.

6. Select the **DWDataMart** data source. Then either copy and paste the SQL query into the **Query** textbox or launch the wizard by clicking on **Query Designer**.

7. Once you have created your dataset, make sure that all the reporting controls point to the newly created dataset. For a table report, right-click the top left corner and choose **Tablix Properties**. Then change the **Dataset name** to the new dataset.

8. Add new columns to the table and make sure you delete any columns that still reference fields from the old dataset.

See also

Refer to the following recipe for more information on how to manage report permissions:

- The *Configuring report permissions* recipe later in this chapter

Configuring report permissions

A common issue when working with reporting is that some users cannot see the report folders and files in the **Reporting** section of the Service Manager console. It is important to know that access to the reports is controlled by the permissions configured in SQL Server Reporting Services.

When you first install the Service Manager Data Warehouse Management Server, the setup will automatically add the Service Manager Service Account as well as the Management Group Administrators group or user as Content Managers to SQL Server Reporting Services. Any other users that work with Service Manager need to be granted access to the reports manually.

Getting ready

Before you can configure report permissions, it is important to have a concept of how you would like your reports to be organized and structured in folders, and whom you will need to grant the access to.

How to do it...

In this example, we will grant a user or group read access to all reports of Service Manager:

1. Open your web browser and navigate to the following URL:
   `http://[SCSMDWSQL]/Reports`.
2. Replace [SCSMDWSQL] with the fully qualified domain name of the SQL server, which is used for reporting. If SQL Server Reporting Service is running as a named instance, the syntax of the URL will be the following:
   `http://[SCSMDWSQL]/Reports_[InstanceName]`.
3. Navigate to **Folder Settings** | **Security** | **New Role Assignment**.
4. In the **Group or user name** box, type the domain and name of the group or the user you would like to grant access to in the format `[Domain]\[User/Group]`. Check the **Browser** option and then click on **OK**.

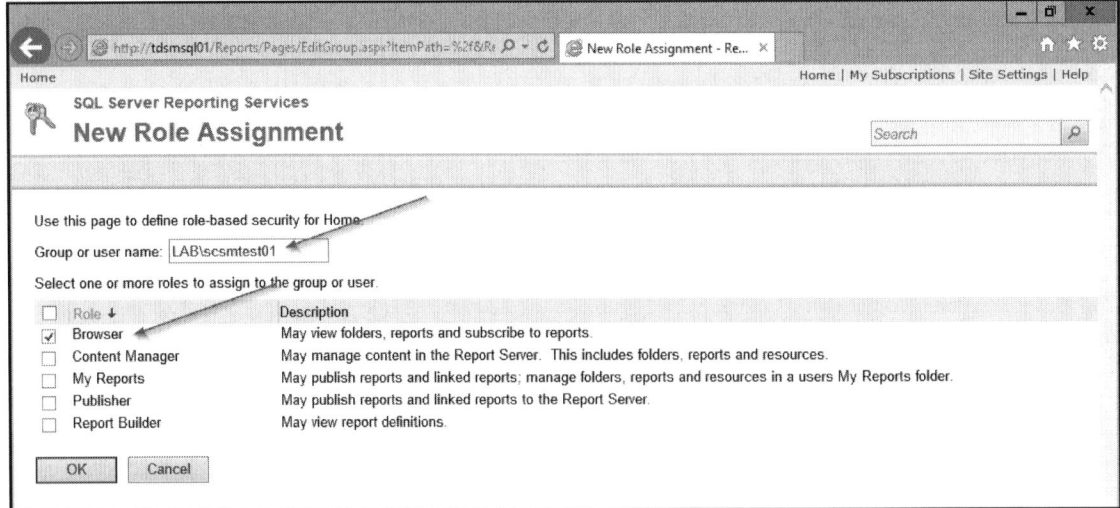

5. In the menu to the top-right, click on **Home** to get back to the root folder view. Click on the **SystemCenter** folder. Then click on the **ServiceManager** folder.

6. Repeat the procedures described in steps 2 and 3 to grant the same permissions to the **ServiceManager** folder.

The user or the members of the group that you configured will now be able to access the Service Manager reports through both the Service Manager console as well as the web browser. Please note that the users will have to restart the Service Manager console to be able to see the folders and reports.

How it works...

The way how permissions are configured in SQL Server Reporting Services is very similar to what you might know about configuring permissions in an NTFS filesystem. You can work with permissions on folders that are inherited to subfolder and files, and also, break inheritance where needed. This allows you to control which folders and reports are made available to your end users.

There's more...

When working with permissions in SQL Server Reporting Services, you should know about the basic concepts of security roles and the inheritance of permissions. We will cover these two topics in this section.

Security roles

Configuring permissions for reports requires deciding which actions the users are allowed to perform on the corresponding permission level. These actions can be configured by the use of security roles.

The following three security roles are important to know about when working with SQL Server Reporting Services security settings:

- The **Browser** security role allows the members to view folders, reports, and subscribe to reports.
- The **Publisher** security role allows the members to publish reports and linked reports.

- The **Content Manager** security role allows the members to manage content in the report server. This includes folder, reports, and other resources such as data sources, datasets, and so on.

Security settings inheritance

If you thoroughly plan and configure report permissions for Service Manager, and provided that the instance of SQL Server Reporting Services is not used for other purposes than Service Manager, you can revert the security settings on the `ServiceManager` folder back to parent security. You will, then, only configure permissions on the root folder, and you will have the ability to apply less restrictive permissions on any subfolder you want by breaking inheritance from the parent.

To revert the security settings of a folder back to its parent, proceed as follows:

1. On the SQL Server Reporting Services website, open the folder for which you would like to change the security settings.
2. Click on **Folder Settings | Security**.
3. Click on **Revert to Parent Security**.
4. A warning message will appear. Confirm by clicking on **OK**.

To break inheritance of the security settings of a folder's parent folder, proceed as follows:

1. On the SQL Server Reporting Services website, open the folder for which you would like to change the security settings.
2. Click on **Folder Settings | Security**.
3. Click on **Edit Item Security**.
4. A warning message will appear. Confirm with **OK**.

Delivering reports automatically using report subscriptions

SQL Server Reporting Services allow your users to subscribe to reports. Using report subscriptions, you can deliver reports to your end users' mailbox in the desired format on a scheduled interval.

Getting ready

Before you can make use of report subscriptions, e-mail delivery options need to be configured for SQL Server Reporting Services:

1. Log on to the server that hosts SQL Server Reporting Services with an account that has administrative privileges on both the local computer and SQL Server.
2. Start **Reporting Services Configuration Manager**.
3. Check the **Server Name** and **Report Server Instance** to make sure that you are connecting to the correct instance of SQL Server Reporting Services. Click on **Connect**.
4. Under **E-mail Settings**, enter the e-mail address that you want to use as the sender address for report delivery.
5. Enter the SMTP Server hostname or IP address, and then click on **Apply**. Click on **Exit** to close the Reporting Services Configuration Manager window.

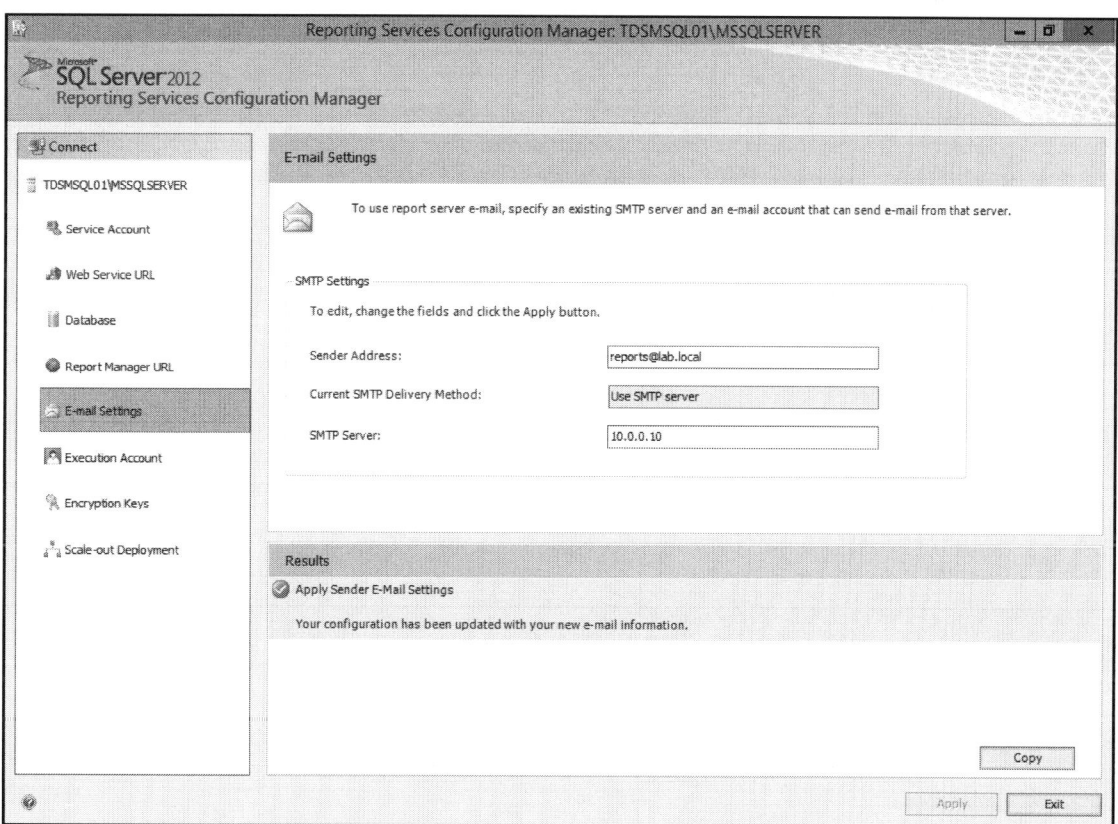

For e-mail delivery to work, the SMTP server you entered in the Reporting Services Configuration Manager must be configured to allow relaying from the IP address of the computer that SQL Server Reporting Services is running on.

SQL Server Reporting Services uses SQL Server Agent to schedule and run the report subscriptions. For this to work, SQL Server Agent needs to be configured to start automatically when the operating system starts:

1. Log on to the server that hosts SQL Server Reporting Services with an account that has administrative privileges on both the local computer and SQL Server.
2. Start **SQL Services Configuration Manager**.
3. Under **SQL Server Services**, double-click on **SQL Server Agent**.
4. Under the **Service** tab, choose **Automatic** as the **Start Mode**. Click on **OK**.

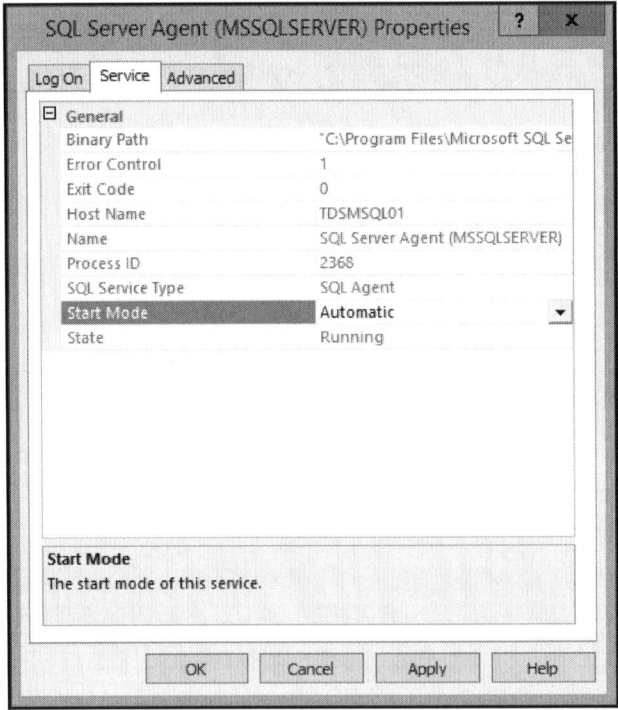

5. Right-click on **SQL Server Agent** and click on **Start**.

How to do it...

Next, we will walk you through the steps required for creating and managing report subscriptions in SQL Server Reporting Services:

1. Open your web browser and navigate to the following URL:

   `http://[SCSMDWSQL]/Reports.`

2. Replace [SCSMDWSQL] with the fully qualified domain name of the SQL server, which is used for reporting. If SQL Server Reporting Service is running as a named instance, the syntax of the URL will be the following:

   `http://[SCSMDWSQL]/Reports_[InstanceName].`

3. Navigate to the report that you would like to create a subscription for. In this example, we are creating a subscription for the report we created in the *Creating reports with Report Builder* recipe. Navigate to the **SystemCenter** | **ServiceManager** | **Custom Reports** | **Incident Management** folder.

4. Hover over the report file and click on the arrow next to the report; then click on **Subscribe**.

5. Enter the e-mail address you would like the report to be delivered to. Optionally, enter e-mail addresses in the **Cc** and **Bcc** fields. You can also enter a custom **Reply-To** address, if replies from users should be sent to a different e-mail address from the sender address.

6. If you want the report to be attached to the e-mail, check the **Include Report** option and choose the desired render format. We are going to choose **PDF** in this example.

7. Optionally, check the **Include Link** option, if you would like a URL to be added to the e-mail that allows the recipient to navigate directly to the report using a web browser.

8. Click **Select Schedule** and define the delivery frequency for this subscription. Click on **OK**.

9. Click **OK** to save and activate the subscription.

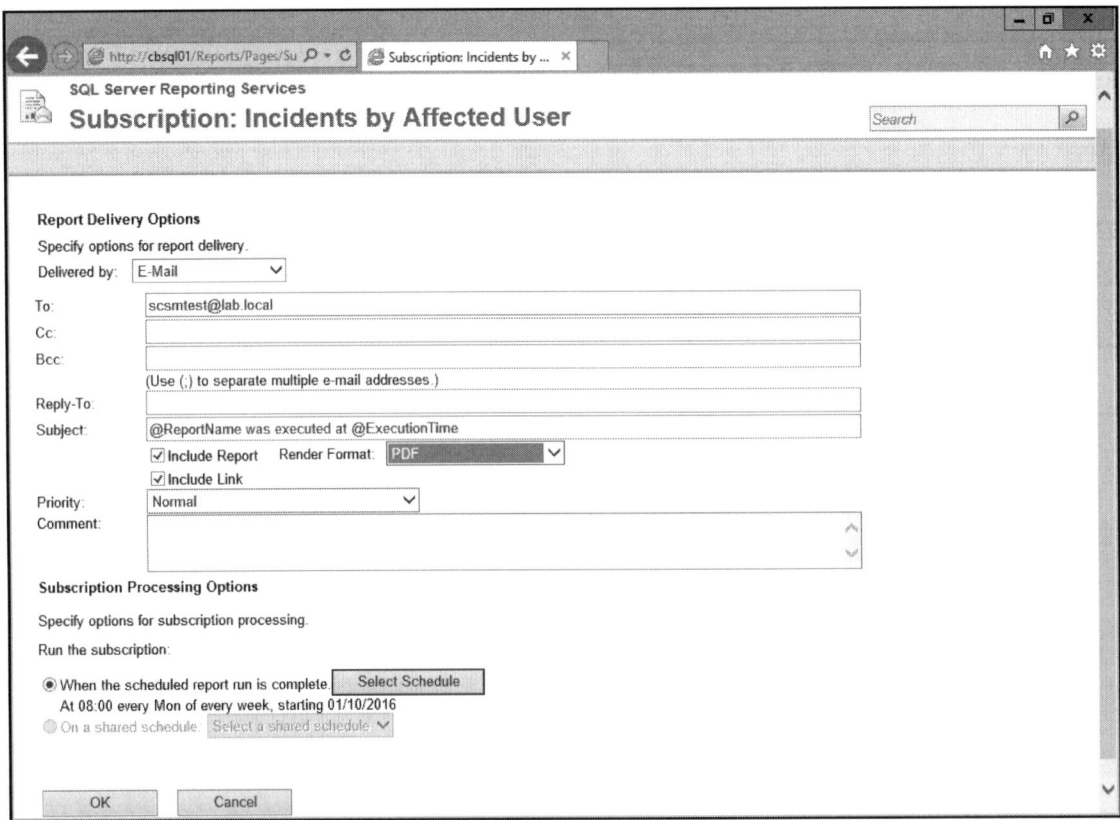

To manage your subscriptions, click on the **My Subscriptions** link from the top-right menu bar of the SQL Server Reporting Services web page. From here you can edit and delete the existing report subscriptions.

How it works...

SQL Server Reporting Services uses SQL Server Agent for scheduling and running report subscriptions. Each subscription creates a job for SQL Server Agent with a random GUID as the job name. When subscription jobs are executed, SQL Server reads the configuration of the subscription from the ReportServer database, calls SQL Server Reporting Services to run the report, and then sends the result to the recipients using the SMTP server configured for SQL Server Reporting Services.

There's more...

A common request when working with report subscriptions is to offer the ability to send reports to user-defined recipients. This section walks you through the steps required to fulfill this request.

Allowing non-Content Managers to define e-mail addresses

When users that are not a member of the Content Manager security role create subscriptions, the recipient name in the **To:** field is self-addressed using the domain user account of the person creating the subscription.

If you are using an SMTP server or forwarder that uses e-mail accounts that are different from the domain user account, the report delivery will fail when the SMTP server tries to deliver the report to that user.

To work around this issue, you can modify configuration settings that allow users to enter a name in the To: field:

1. Open `RSReportServer.config` with a text editor. The file can be found on the server hosting SQL Server Reporting Services in the SQL Server installation directory under the `MSRS10_50.[InstanceName]\Reporting Services\ReportServer` sub-folder.
2. Set `SendEmailToUserAlias` to `False`.
3. Set `DefaultHostName` to the DNS name or IP address of the SMTP server or forwarder.
4. Save the file.

Analyzing data with Microsoft Excel

Online Analytical Processing (OLAP) cubes are a feature in System Center 2016 Service Manager that leverages the Service Manager Data Warehouse infrastructure to provide self-service Business Intelligence capabilities to the end user.

An OLAP Cube is a data structure that overcomes limitations of relational databases by providing rapid analysis of data. Cubes can display and sum up large amounts of data while also providing users access to the most granular of data. These cubes are stored in SQL Server Analysis Services databases. Self-service BI tools such as Excel and SQL Server Reporting Services can target these cubes and allow the user to analyze the data from multiple perspectives.

In this recipe, we are going to show you how you can use Microsoft Excel to allow your users to quickly and easily create simple reports by directly accessing OLAP cubes from Service Manager.

Getting ready

Before you can work with OLAP cubes, it is a requirement that you have already installed a Service Manager Data Warehouse Management Server and that it has been registered with the Service Manager server installation. You also need to ensure that the initial synchronization of the management packs is complete and the ETL jobs have run. In addition, you need to make sure that the cubes that are defined in the Management packs have been created and fully processed. This normally takes several hours to complete from the time the Data Warehouse Management Server was registered.

How to do it...

In this example, we are going to create a report in Microsoft Excel that displays the number of incidents by affected user and incident classification. The output will be the same as from the report we created using Report Builder in the *Creating reports with Report Builder* recipe:

1. Open the Service Manager console and navigate to **Cubes** in the **Data Warehouse** section.
2. Click on the **Service Manager WorkItems Cube**. Ensure that the Status indicates **Processed**. Then click on **Analyze Cube In Excel** from the task pane on the right-hand side. Microsoft Excel will start and automatically establish a connection to the respective cube in SQL Server Analysis Services.
3. The list of measures and dimensions in the **PivotTable Field List** can be overwhelming. Hence we can reduce the size of it by selecting the measure group **IncidentDim** from the **Show Fields related to** dropdown.

4. Now select the following fields from the list:

- **IncidentDim\IncidentDimCount**
- **AffectedUserDim\Display Name**
- **IncidentDim_IncidentClassification\More fields\IncidentClassificationValue**

5. Move the **IncidentClassificationValue** field from the **Row Labels** area to the **Column Labels** area.

With only these few mouse clicks, we have created a report with the same content like the one created with Report Builder in the *Creating reports with Report Builder* recipe.

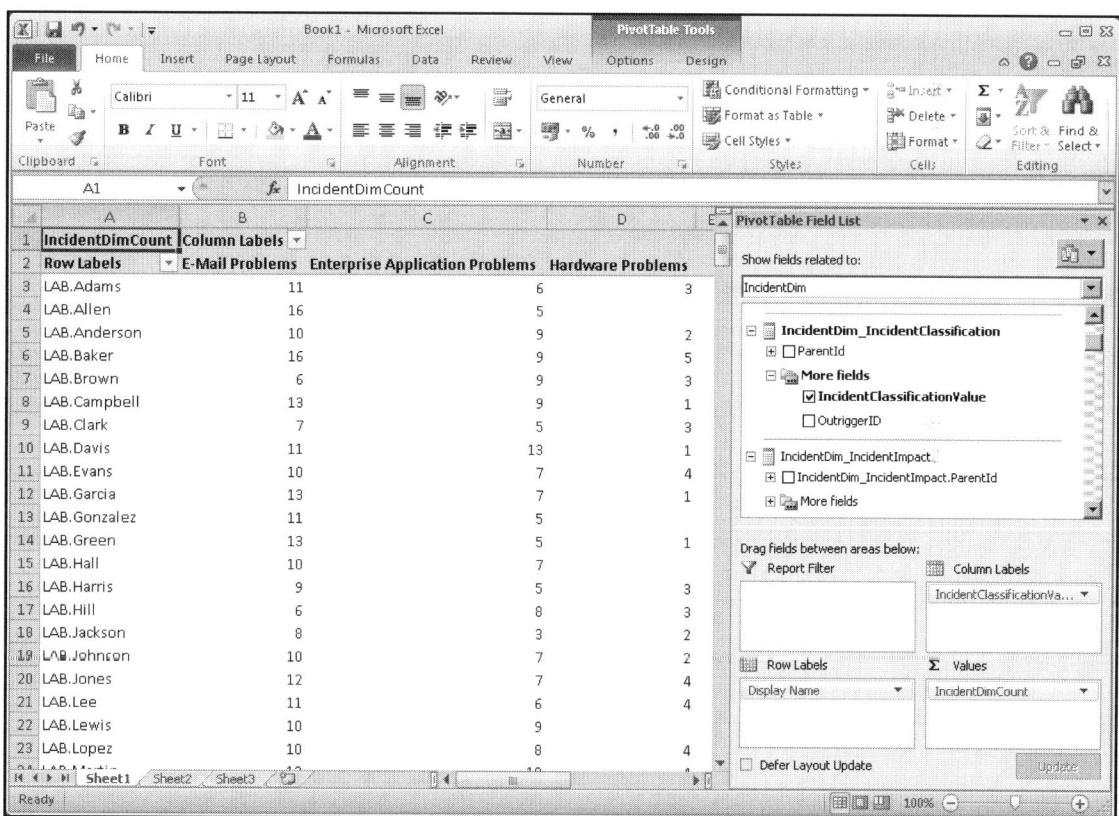

You can now use regular Microsoft Excel features to further customize your report. In order to refresh the data in your report, simply right-click anywhere in the PivotTable and click on **Refresh**.

How it works...

Microsoft Excel uses an active connection in the background to connect to the OLAP cube in SQL Services Analysis Services. By making your selections using the PivotTable feature, Excel dynamically creates **MultiDimensional eXpression (MDX)** queries in the background that are sent to SQL Server Analysis Services. The results returned are then displayed in the PivotTable.

There's more...

Excel comes with many more features for reporting than we could cover in this book. Next, we are going to show you one example of using Slicers to filter your data.

Using Slicers to filter data

Slicers are easy-to-use filtering components that allow you to filter the data in the PivotTable with a set of buttons. For instance, you can create a slicer for filtering the PivotTable we created earlier by the status of the incident:

1. With the PivotTable report in Microsoft Excel still open, click anywhere in the PivotTable area, switch to the **PivotTable Tools** | **Options** ribbon, and then click on **Insert Slicer**.
2. Select the **IncidentDim_IncidentStatus\More fields\IncidentDim_IncidentStatus.IncidentStatusValue** field and click on **OK**. The Slicer appears in Excel.
3. Now you can click on the buttons to filter data. For instance, click on the **Resolved** button to show only resolved incidents in the PivotTable

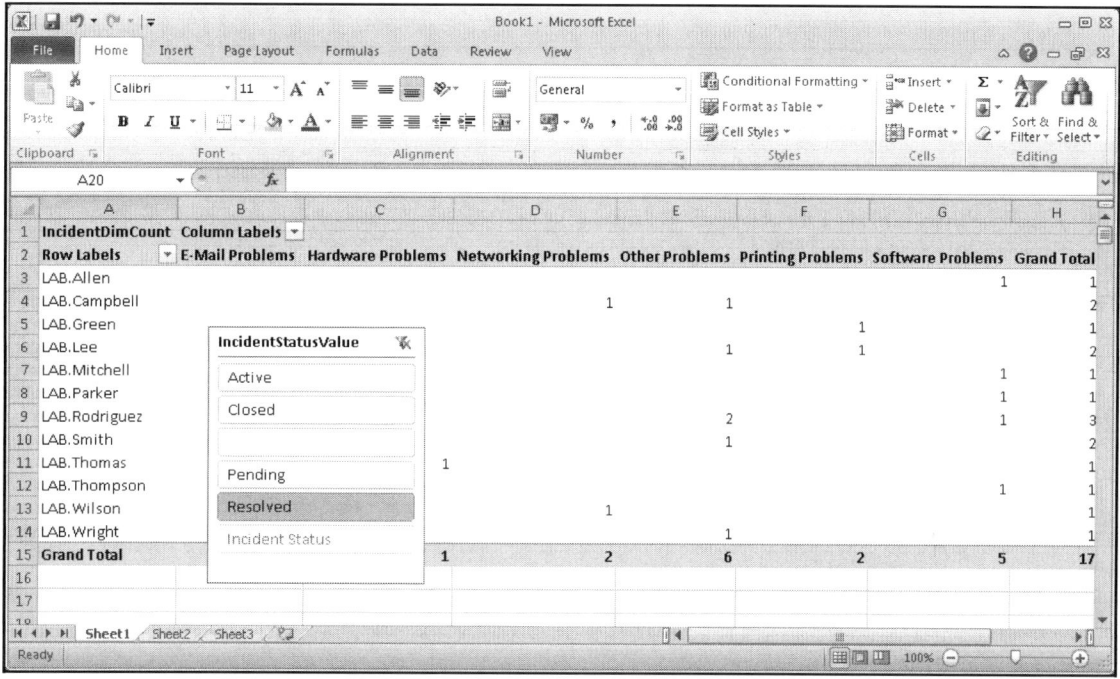

See also

Refer to the following recipe to see how reports created in Microsoft Excel can be made available to other users from within the Service Manager console:

- The *Using the Analysis Library to publish Excel reports* recipe later in this chapter

Using the Analysis Library to publish Excel reports

System Center 2016 Service Manager features **Analysis Libraries** that allow you to make reports created in Microsoft Excel available to other users from within the Reporting workspace in the Service Manager console.

Getting ready

Before you can save reports to the Analysis Library, you must create at least one storage area and map it to an Analysis Library. You might want to create many Analysis Library folders for different departments or ITSM processes.

In this example, we are using a file share on the Service Manager Management Server to serve as an Analysis Library:

1. Log on to the Service Manager Management Server with an account that has administrative privileges on the local computer.
2. Open Windows Explorer and create a new folder, such as `C:\AnalysisLibraries`.
3. Create a new subfolder named `IncidentManagement` under the newly created folder.
4. Right-click on the **IncidentManagement** folder, click on **Properties**, and then click on the **Security** tab.
5. Ensure that all the users you would like to be able to read reports have **Read and Execute** permissions. Change the security settings if required.
6. Ensure that all the users you would like to be able to save new reports or modify existing reports have **Read and Execute** and **Write and Modify** permissions. Change the security settings if required.
7. Change to the **Sharing** tab and click on **Advanced Sharing**.
8. Check **Share this folder**, click on **Permissions**, select **Everyone**, and make sure that both **Change** and **Read** are selected in the **Allow** column.
9. Click on **OK** to close the **Permissions** dialog. Click on **OK** to close the **Advanced Sharing** dialog, and then click on **Close**.
10. Open the Service Manager console with an account that has administrative rights in the Service Manager Data Warehouse. Navigate to the **Analysis Libraries** folder in the **Data Warehouse** workspace.
11. Click on **Add Library Folder** from the task pane on the right-hand side.
12. Enter a name, such as `Incident Management Reports`, and a description for the Analysis Library.
13. In the UNC Path field, enter `\\[ServerName]\IncidentManagement`, replacing `[ServerName]` with the name of your Service Manager Management Server.

14. Click on **OK** to create the Analysis Library.

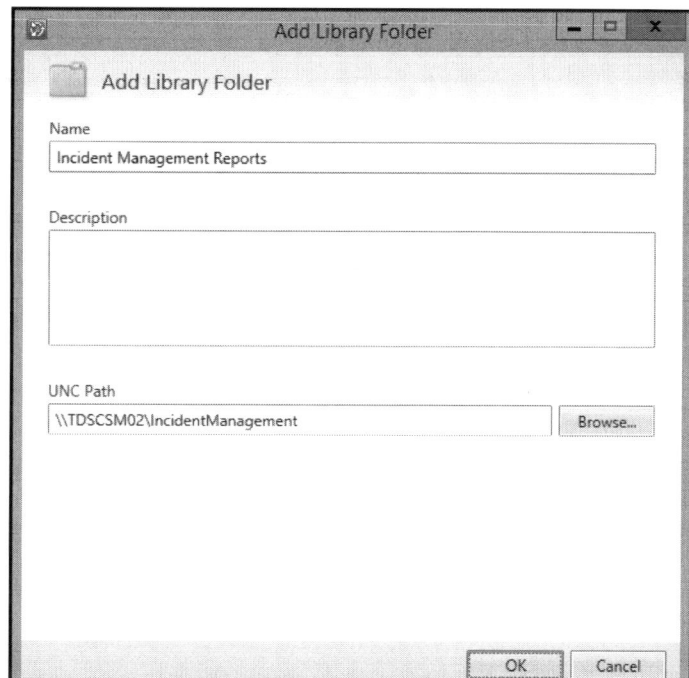

How to do it...

Now we are going to show you how you can save reports that were created in Microsoft Excel to an Analysis Library:

1. Follow the procedures in the *Analyzing data with Microsoft Excel* recipe to create an Excel report.
2. In Microsoft Excel, click on **File** | **Save As**.
3. In the **File name** textbox, enter `\\[ServerName]\IncidentManagement`, replacing `[ServerName]` with the name of your Service Manager Management Server. Press Enter to navigate to the network share.
4. In the **File name** textbox, enter a filename for the Excel report, and then click on **Save**.
5. Close Microsoft Excel.

This report has now been saved to the Analysis Library and other users can access it directly from the Service Manager console:

1. Open the Service Manager console and navigate to the **Reporting** workspace.
2. Under **Analysis Library** you will see the Analysis Library that we created.
3. When you select the Analysis Library, the Excel report is displayed in the list view of the Service Manager console.
4. Select the report, and then click on **Open Excel File** from the task pane on the right-hand side.

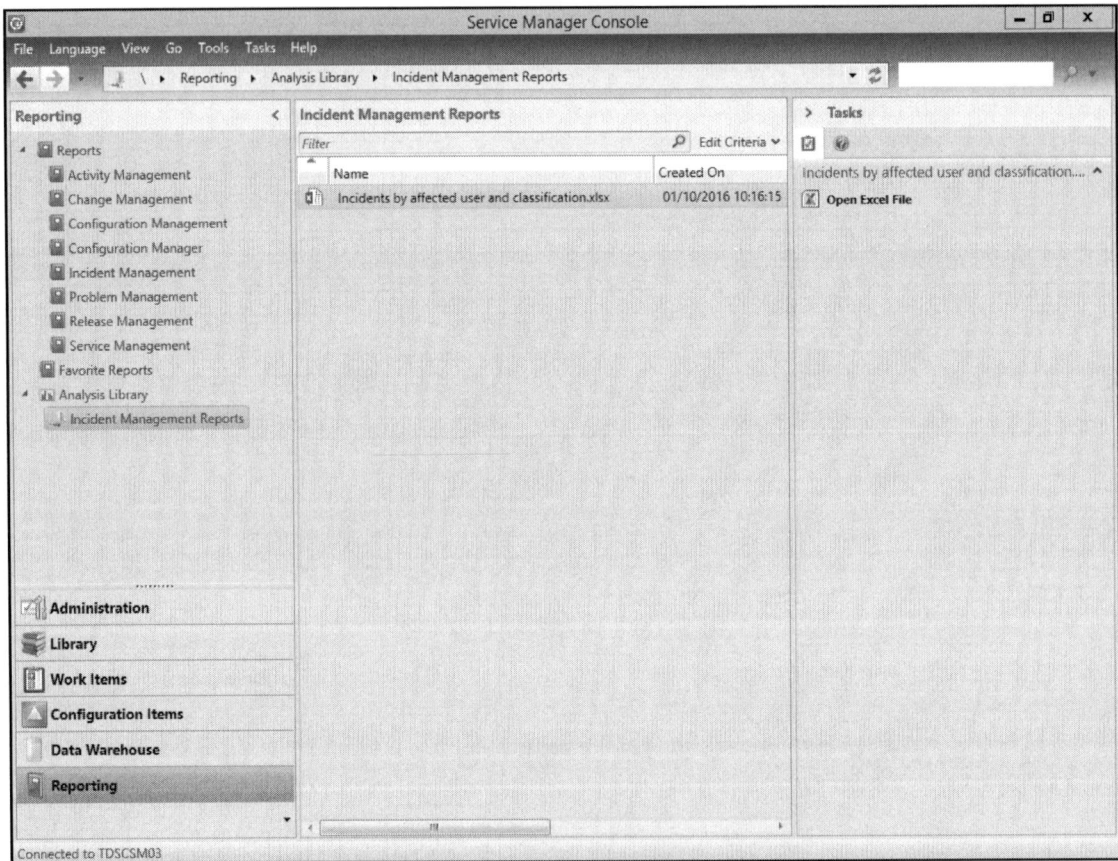

How it works...

An **Analysis Library** is effectively a file share on the network that is used to save Excel files to. You can create many network shares for different users, departments, ITSM processes, and so on, to best reflect your reporting requirements. Also, the network shares can be created on any computer, such as a file server, provided the security is configured properly so that your users can access the files on the network.

See also

Refer to the following recipe to see how reports can be created by using Microsoft Excel:

- The *Analyzing data with Microsoft Excel* recipe previously mentioned in this chapter

11
Extending SCSM with Advanced Personalization

In this chapter, we will walk you through the use of the System Center 2016 Service Manager Authoring Tool and advanced management pack authoring techniques for extending, customizing, and personalizing your installation of Service Manager. In particular, we will be covering the following tasks:

- Using the SCSM Authoring Tool
- Sealing management packs
- Extending Service Manager classes
- Creating new classes
- Customizing default forms
- Creating your own forms
- Using an XML editor to modify management packs
- Editing the XML of a view to alter the criteria to include AND instead of OR

Introduction

Service Manager uses management pack files that contain definitions for the various features in the product. The features available in Service Manager as well as the behavior of the product can be customized by modifying or adding management packs. Chapter 2, *Personalizing SCSM 2016 Administration,* walked you through the basic concepts of management packs and here we will look even deeper into the subject.

Basically, there are three methods that you can use to customize Service Manager. While all the three methods result in changes to a management pack file, they differ in scope and in the complexity of the customization that they provide:

- Using the Service Manager console
- Using the Service Manager Authoring Tool
- Directly editing the Management Pack XML

The most basic and common settings as well as customizations can be performed by using the Service Manager console. Most of this can be configured in the Administration and Library workspace, but other things can be configured in other workspaces as well, such as creating or editing views. Throughout this book you have seen plenty of ways to customize Service Manager.

While using the Service Manager console is sufficient for most customization requirements, there are certain limitations that require you to use the Service Manager Authoring Tool. The Service Manager Authoring Tool allows for the following kinds of advanced customizations:

- Extending Service Manager classes
- Creating new classes
- Customizing Service Manager forms
- Creating new forms
- Creating advanced workflows

The recipes in this chapter and the next will walk you through all of these advanced personalization scenarios.

For extensive or complex customizations and for customizations that require coding, you have to edit the XML file of the management pack directly. Working directly with management pack files requires in-depth knowledge in several areas, such as the System Center Common Schema and the structure of management packs. Also, manual editing is prone to errors.

Using the SCSM Authoring Tool

In this recipe, we will introduce you to the System Center 2016 Service Manager Authoring Tool, which we will use for subsequent recipes in this chapter.

Getting ready

The System Center 2016 Service Manager Authoring Tool is a separate product that is part of the System Center 2016 Service Manager Component Add-ons and Extensions. The Authoring Tool can be obtained as a free download from the following URL:

`https://www.microsoft.com/en-us/download/details.aspx?id=54059`.

You can install the Authoring Tool on Windows 8.1 and Windows 10, or on Windows Server 2012 R2 and Windows Server 2016. The Authoring Tool has some prerequisites that need to be installed prior to installing the Authoring Tool itself:

- .NET 3.5 framework
- .NET 4.5 framework
- Microsoft Visual Studio Shell 2008: `https://www.microsoft.com/en-us/download/confirmation.aspx?id=19670`
- Microsoft Visual C++ 2012 Redistributable (x86): `https://www.microsoft.com/en-us/download/details.aspx?id=30679`

Follow these steps to install the Authoring Tool:

1. Download the System Center 2016 Service Manager Authoring Tool, Visual C++ 2012 Redistributable, and Microsoft Visual Studio Shell 2008 from the preceding links.
2. Install **Visual C++ 2012 redistributable (x86)** and **Microsoft Visual Studio Shell 2008**.

Note that Microsoft Visual Studio Shell 2008 is actually an **extractor** and that you will have to run the setup itself from the folder in which the files were extracted (`C:\VS 2008 Shell Redist\Isolated Mode`).

Note that Microsoft Visual C++ 2012 Redistributable needs to be **x86**.

3. Run **SC2016_SCSM_Auth.exe** and click **Next** on the Welcome page.
4. Check **I accept the agreement** and click **Next**.
5. Specify the folder to where you would like to extract the files and click **Next** followed by **Extract**. Click **Finish** when the extract is completed.

6. Navigate to the directory you extracted the files to, right-click **Setup.exe,** and click **Run As Administrator**. Verify that you would like to run the installation as administrator by clicking **Yes** on the question that appears.

7. Click **Install the Service Manager Authoring Tool** to initiate the installation.

8. Enter your **Name**, **Organization**, and check "**I have read…**" to accept the EULA. Click **Next**.

9. Select an installation location and click **Next**.

10. Verify that you meet all the prerequisites and click **Next**.

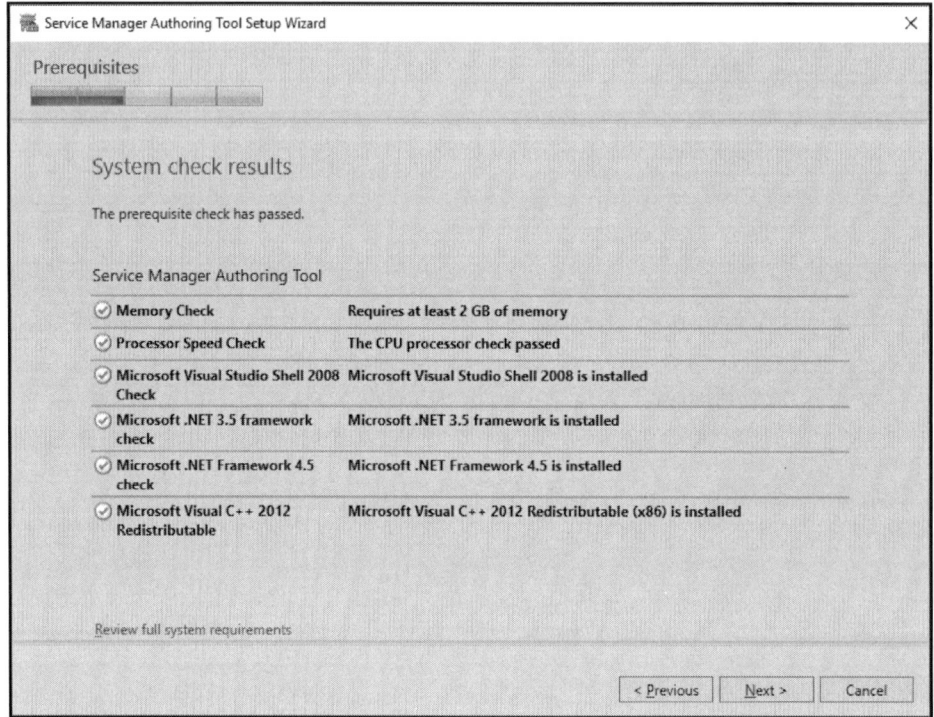

11. Click **Install** to install the product and when the installation is completed, click **Close**.

How to do it...

To understand and work with the Authoring Tool, we will now walk you through the different areas of the user interface.

The user interface is made up of various areas that you will use while authoring your management packs. Please note that you can rearrange and group the areas within the user interface by using the drag-and-drop feature. This allows you to tailor the user interface to your personal preferences. If any of the marked areas are missing, you can display them through the **View** menu.

The following screenshot shows a typical layout of the Authoring Tool user interface:

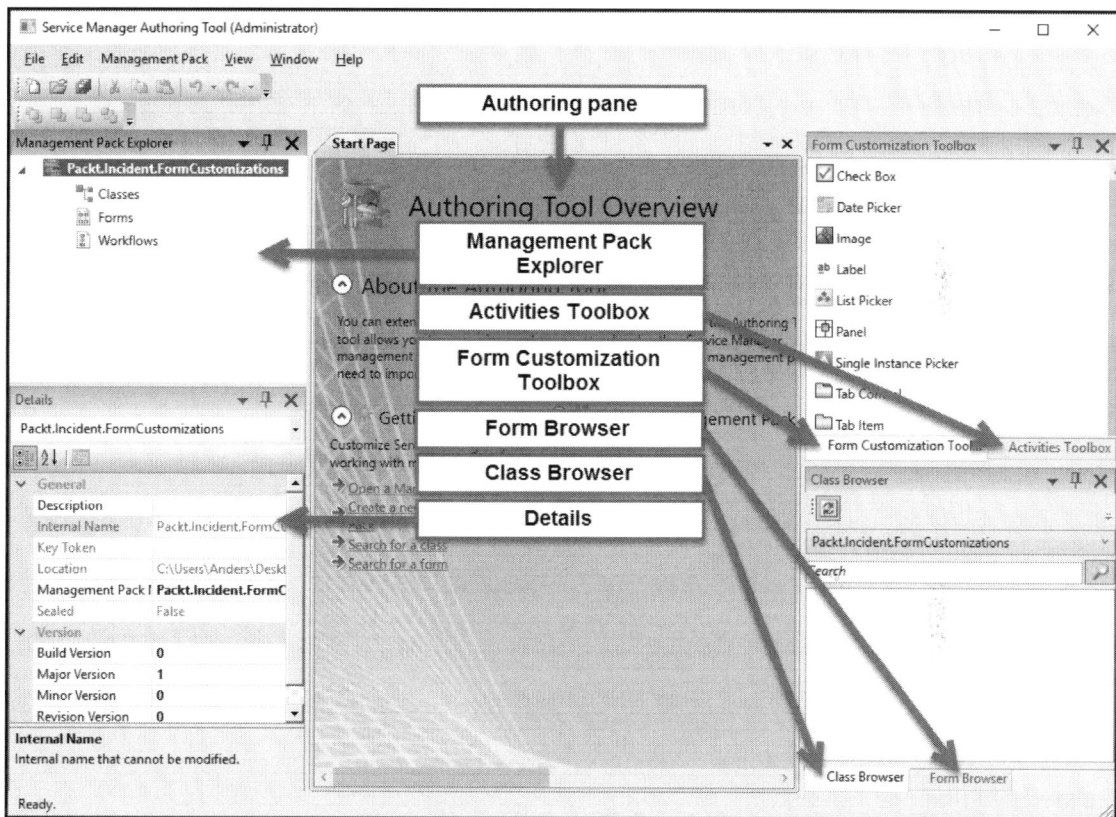

The Authoring Tool is made up of the following panes:

- **Authoring Pane**
- **Management Pack Explorer**
- **Activities Toolbox**
- **Form Customization Toolbox**
- **Form Browser**
- **Class Browser**

- Details

The following is a detailed explanation of all the panes:

- The **Authoring Pane** is the work area where you perform your customizations. The user interface will be different based on the type of object that you are working with: classes, forms, or workflows. You can open several objects and switch between them using the tabs at the top of the **Authoring Pane**.
- The **Management Pack Explorer** displays all the management packs that are part of the solution you are working on. You can view the classes, forms, and workflows that are included in each management pack. When you click on an object, such as a class, in **Management Pack Explorer**, you can view and edit its properties in the **Details** pane.
- The **Activities Toolbox** contains all out-of-the-box activities that you can use in custom workflows that you build using the Authoring Tool. The **Activities Toolbox** can be extended by custom **Activities** that you create using the Windows Workflow Foundation, which is part of the .NET Framework.
- The **Form Customization Toolbox** contains all controls that are available for being added to form extensions or newly created forms. Controls can be added to the form in the **Authoring** Pane by using the drag-and-drop feature.
- The **Form Browser** displays the forms available in all the management packs that are in the `Library` folder or from custom management packs that you have opened. You can narrow down the list of classes by filtering by management pack (using the pull-down menu), or by entering a search term in the Search field. The **Form Browser** is your starting point for form customizations.
- The **Class Browser** displays the classes available in all the management packs that are in the Library folder or from the custom management packs that you have opened. You can narrow down the list of classes by filtering by management pack (using the pull-down menu) or by entering a search term in the **Search** field. When you expand a class by clicking on the plus sign next to it, you will be able to see all properties of the class.
- The **Details** pane allows you to view the properties of the selected object. Also, you can use the **Details** pane to modify properties of the currently selected object. The **Details** pane is updated every time you select an object in **Management Pack Explorer**, the **Authoring** Pane, **Class Browser**, or **Form Browser** pane.

If the Form or Class Browser is empty, hit the **Refresh** button to load the objects.

How it works...

The System Center 2016 Service Manager Authoring Tool is built on the Visual Studio integrated development environment framework. Service Manager leverages core functionalities of the .NET Framework, such as the Windows Presentation Foundation (WPF) Framework and the Windows Workflow Foundation (WF) Framework to allow for extensive customizations to the product.

Any customizations that you perform using the Authoring Tool are stored in a management pack XML file. You can then import the XML file into Service Manager to apply the customization to your Service Manager environment.

See also

Refer to the following section for more information on how to work with management packs:

- The *Creating management packs to save your SCSM personalization* recipe in `Chapter 2`, *Personalizing SCSM 2016 Administration*

Creating workflows with the System Center 2016 Service Manager Authoring Tool is covered in two recipes of `Chapter 12`, *Automating Service Manager 2016*:

- *Creating a custom workflow in the Authoring Tool – exporting your unsealed management packs*
- *Autoclose resolved incidents with SMLets and a custom workflow*

Sealing management packs

When planning your customizations in Service Manager, one of the most important decisions to make is whether you are going to seal your Management packs or not.

As explained in `Chapter 2`, *Personalizing SCSM 2016 Administration*, a sealed management pack is a read-only management pack, which cannot be written to once it has been imported into Service Manager. Furthermore, sealing a management pack enables it to be referenced from within other management packs.

Some examples of when you need to reference another management pack are described here:

- Creating an extension of a class: In this scenario, you create a reference to the management pack that holds the base class.
- Customizing a form: This involves creating a reference to the management pack that defines the base form.
- Creating a view: Normally, you would want to create your view through the console, which means you are going to save it in an unsealed management pack. This means that the class you are referencing in your view must be part of a sealed management pack.

Sealing management packs also ensures upgradeability. When you import a later version of a sealed management pack into Service Manager, Service Manager checks whether an upgrade is possible or not, and will reject non-upgradeable management packs. For instance, if you have your own custom class with a set of properties and decide that you do not want a couple of these properties anymore, and try to import a new version of the management pack where these properties have been removed – Service Manager would reject the import. In order to import this new version of the management pack you would actually have to delete the older version from the system first, which also would remove any instances of that class in the database.

As a general rule, always seal management packs that contain the following:

- Classes
- Class extensions
- Forms
- Form extensions

Getting ready

To seal a management pack, you need a Strong Name Key (SNK) file. You can use the **sn.exe** tool to create a new SNK file. This tool is part of the Service Manager Authoring Tool, but it can also be found in the Windows Software Development Kit (SDK), which can be downloaded from the following URL:

```
http://www.microsoft.com/en-us/download/details.aspx?id=8279
```

To create your own strong name key file, first check on your computer for the existence of the sn.exe tool. On computers running the Authoring Tool, sn.exe should be located in `C:\Program Files (x86)\Microsoft SDKs\Windows\v6.0A\bin\`

If it isn't present there, you can try searching for it using this method:

1. Click on **Start**, type `cmd`, and then press *Enter*.
2. Type `cd\` and press *Enter*.
3. Type `dir sn.exe /s` and press *Enter*. This process will take a while and should output all locations where the sn.exe tool has been found. You can cancel the process with *Ctrl-C* once you find the tool. Write down the location of the sn.exe tool.

Creating the SNK file

Follow these steps to create your own SNK file:

1. Click on **Start**, type **cmd**, and then right-click on cmd.exe. Click on **Run as administrator**. Click on **Yes**.
2. Type `cd <full Path to sn.exe directory>` and press *Enter*.
3. Type `sn.exe -k <myfilename>.snk` and press *Enter*, where <myfilename> is the name you want to give the file.
4. Browse to the location and copy the SNK file to the directory where you store your Service Manager customizations.

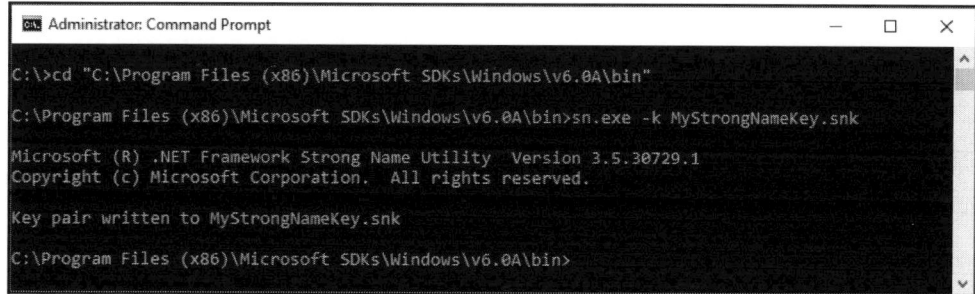

Make sure that you keep a backup of this file and that you use this SNK for all your customizations.

How to do it...

Now that you know the concept of sealed management packs and have created your SNK file, we are going to show you how you can seal management packs using the Authoring Tool:

1. Open the **Authoring Tool**, go to **File**, and then select **Open**. Browse to, and open the management pack that you want to seal (if you don't have such a management pack right now, you can create a new one just to try it out).

2. Right-click on the management pack in **Management Pack Explorer** and click on **Seal Management Pack**.

3. Change the **Output Directory** to the location where you would like to store your sealed management pack. Then, specify your **SNK file** and type the **Company** name.

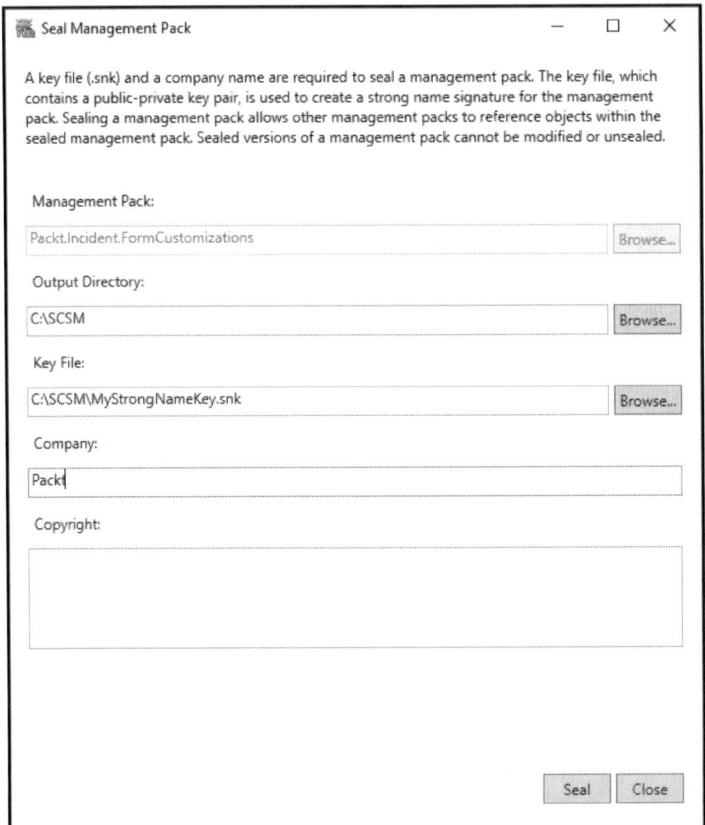

4. Click on **Seal**, wait until the message **Seal succeeded** is displayed, and then click on **Close**.

5. The management packs have now been sealed and can be imported to Service Manager.

6. Remember that you now have two management packs – one editable file with the .XML file extension and one sealed management pack with the .MP file extension. Both files should be kept as you need to have the unsealed management pack if you would like to update it in the future.

Please note that the Authoring Tool automatically increases the version of the management pack every time you seal it.

There's more...

If you have to seal management packs often or would like to do it without using the Authoring Tool, we recommend you use FastSeal.exe.

FastSeal.exe

Instead of using the System Center 2016 Service Manager Authoring Tool for sealing your management packs, you can also use the FastSeal.exe command-line utility. This tool is very convenient if you need to seal management packs in bulk or if you want to automate the seal process.

You can download the FastSeal.exe utility from the following URL:

http://blogs.technet.com/b/servicemanager/archive/2009/12/25/sealing-management-packs.aspx.

To seal a management pack with FastSeal, you simply run this command:

```
FastSeal.exe ManagementPackToSeal.xml /Company YourCompany /KeyFile
YourKeyfile.snk
```

See also

Refer to the following recipe for more information on how to work with management packs:

- The *Creating management packs to save your SCSM personalization* recipe in `Chapter 2`, *Personalizing SCSM 2016 Administration*

Extending Service Manager classes

Service Manager 2016 includes a very flexible class model that allows you to extend existing classes and create new classes. There are two main types of classes in Service Manager-Configuration Items and Work Items.

Configuration Items are items stored in your CMDB, such as Windows Computers, Users, Printers, and so on. These items are normally viewed in the Configuration Items section of the Service Manager console. Please refer to `Chapter 4`, *Building the Configuration Management Database (CMDB)*, for more information about the CMDB in Service Manager.

Work Items are classes that are used to support your ITSM processes, such as Incident, Service Request, Change Request, and so on. Work Items are typically viewed in the Work Items section of the Service Manager console. More information about ITSM processes covered by SCSM can be found in Chapter 1, Chapter 5, Chapter 7, and Chapter 8.

In this recipe, we will walk you through the process of adding additional properties to an existing Service Manager class similar to what we did in `Chapter 7`, *Working with Incident and Problem Management* in the *Extending the Incident class with a new property* recipe.

Getting ready

It is recommended that you follow the instructions in the first recipe, *Using the SCSM Authoring Tool*, to get familiar with the user interface of the System Center 2016 Service Manager Authoring Tool. Also, you will need to be familiar with the process of sealing management packs, as explained in the previous recipe, *Sealing management packs*.

Working with Service Manager classes requires knowledge of the class concepts, models, and hierarchies within the system. Each object in Service Manager is an instance of a particular base class. All instances of a base class have a common set of properties. Properties are used to represent the details of the actual object, that is, the instance of the class.

Each property has a predefined data type that defines the type of values that it can hold. There are data types for text values, numeric values and dates, among others.

Every class in Service Manager must specify a base class that identifies an existing class that the new class will specialize. The new class will inherit all properties defined in the base class, and also all properties that are defined in all parent classes of the base class.

To give you a better understanding of the concept of class inheritance, we will look at the following sample class diagram of the `System.Domain.User` class:

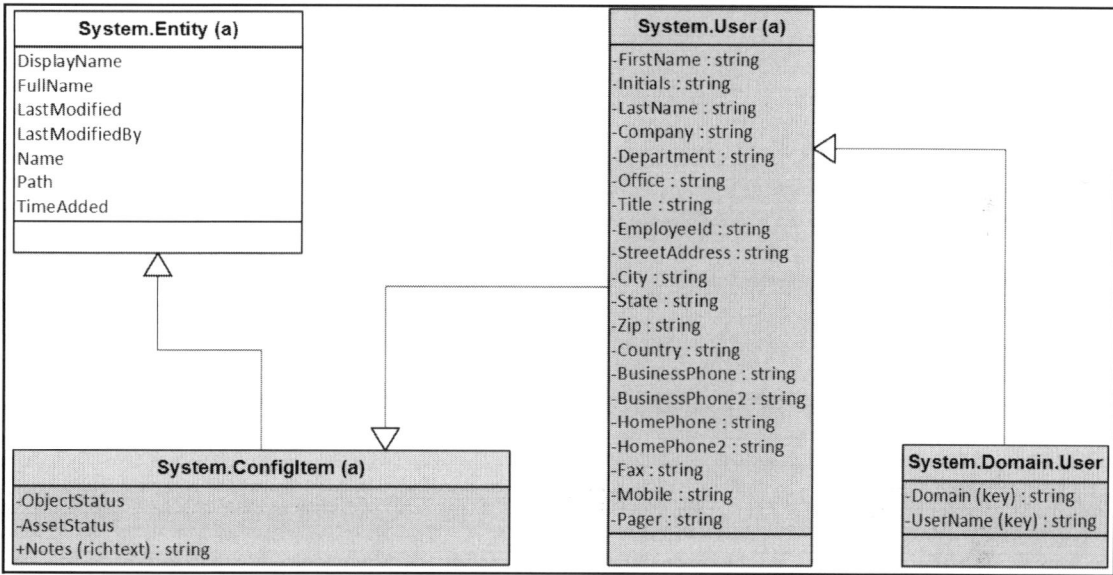

The `System.Domain.User` (which has the display name "Domain User or Group") only contains two properties named `Domain` and `UserName`. However, when you look at the class instances in the **Users** view of the **Configuration Items** section in the **Service Manager** console, you will notice that there are many more properties displayed. Through the concept of inheritance, the `System.Domain.User` class inherits all the properties of its base class – `System.User`. `System.User` also inherits from `System.ConfigItem`, which in turn inherits from `System.Entity`. As a result, the `System.Domain.User` class includes all properties of the parent classes in the entire hierarchy. The `System.Entity` class is the top-most class in Service Manager, which all the other classes inherit from. The (a) denotes that the class is an abstract class. Abstract classes can't have any instances and exist only to act as a base class for other classes.

How to do it...

Now that you have a basic understanding of **Service Manager** class concepts, we are going to extend one of the existing classes using the **Authoring Tool**.

Our head of server infrastructure has requested the ability to store special reboot instructions as well as the person who is technically responsible for the particular servers. **Service Manager** uses the **Windows Computer** class to store computer objects, such as client computers and servers, so we are going to extend this class to be able to store this information.

The special reboot instructions need to be defined as a text property, allowing the users to enter free text in the field. The field that will hold the technical responsible person, however, is a not a property of the class, but rather a relationship to another object. A relationship allows you to store relationships to one or more instances of a predefined target class (Domain User or Group in our example):

1. Start the **Service Manager Authoring Tool**.
2. Locate **Class Browser** and click on the **Reload Content** button to load the list of all classes in Service Manager.
3. Enter **Windows Computer** in the **Searchfield** and hit *Enter.*
4. Locate the **Windows Computer** class, right-click on it, and select **View**.
5. The management pack that includes the Windows Computer class will now be loaded by the Authoring Tool and displayed in the **Management Pack Explorer**.
6. In **Management Pack Explorer**, right-click on the **Windows Computer** class and select **Extend class**.
7. In the **Target Management pack** pop-up window, click on **New...** to create a new management pack. Give it the name **Packt.WindowsComputer.ClassExtension.xml** and click **Save**.
8. Make sure that the newly created management pack is selected, and then click on **OK**.
9. You will now see that a new class has been added to your management pack, and the class will also be displayed in the **Authoring Pane**.
10. In the **Authoring Pane**, change the class name to **Custom Windows Computer Extension** and the description to **Extension of class Windows Computer to hold additional information**.

11. To create the property to hold the special reboot instructions, click on **Create property…** in the **Authoring Pane**, enter **RebootInstructions** as the internal name, and click on **Create**.

12. Click on the newly created property from the list of available properties in the **Authoring Pane**. In the **Details pane**, change the **Name** property to **Reboot Instructions** (with a space) and set the **Maximum Length** property to **2000**.

13. To create the technical responsible person relationship, click on **Create relationship…** in the **Authoring Pane**. Enter **Technical Responsible** as the internal name and click on **Create**.

14. Click on the newly created relationship from the list of available properties in the **Authoring Pane**. In the **Details pane**, change the **Name** property to **Technical Responsible** (with a space). Under the **Value Constraints (target)** section, change the **Target Class** from **Object** to **Domain User or Group**.

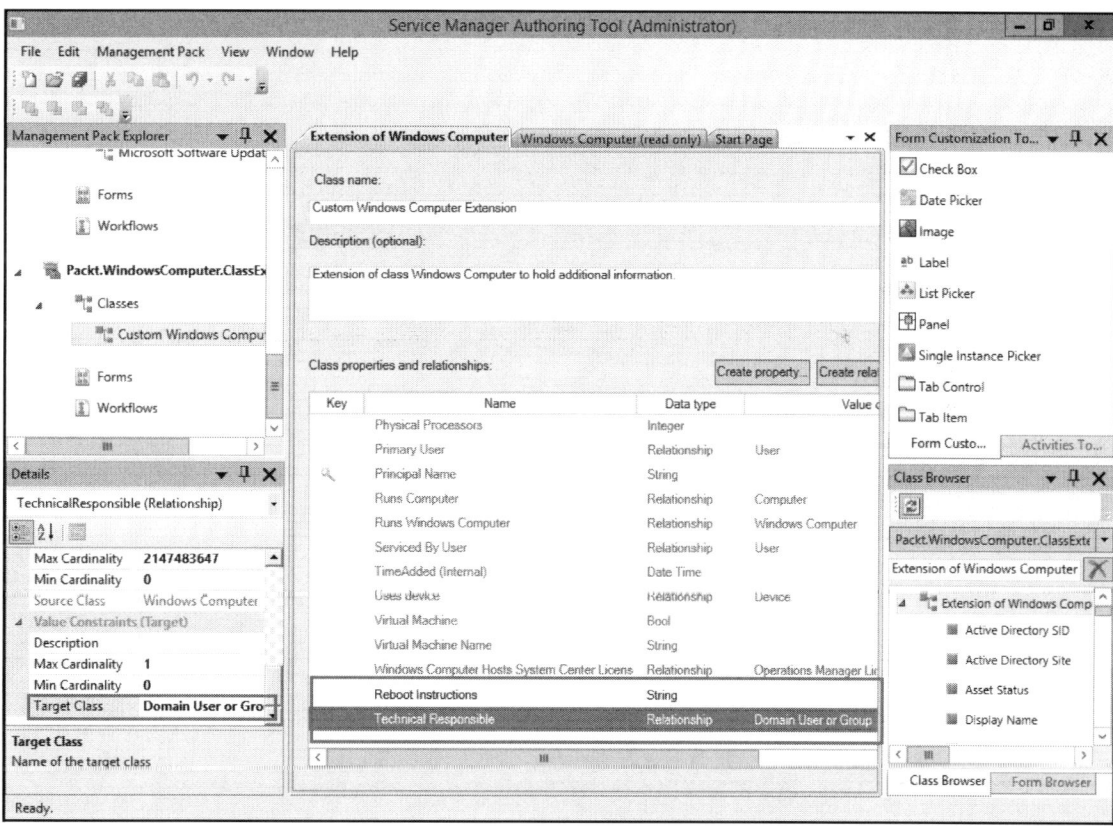

15. Save the management pack using the **Save All** option from the **File** menu.

16. Now seal the management pack by right-clicking it in the **Management pack Explorer** and select **Seal.** More details around this can be found in the previous recipe, *Sealing management packs*.

17. Open the Service Manager console and navigate to the **Management Packs** view in the **Administration** workspace.

18. In the task pane, click on **Import**, browse to the location where you stored your management pack, and click on the **Packt.WindowsComputer.ClassExtension.mp** file. Click on **Open**, and then click on **Import**.

> If you receive a warning saying that unsealed management packs should not contain type definitions, you either didn't seal your management pack, or you accidently imported the .XML file instead of the .MP file.

19. Go to the **Configuration Items** workspace, open the **All Windows Computers** view under **Computers**, and double-click on any of the listed computers.

20. When you switch to the **Extensions tab**, you will see the newly created **Reboot Instructions** field as a textbox allowing you to enter special reboot instructions for your instances of **Windows Computer**. However, the technical responsible relationship is not available as Service Manager does not dynamically add relationship properties to forms. We will be covering how to add this field later in this chapter, when we customize forms using the Authoring Tool.

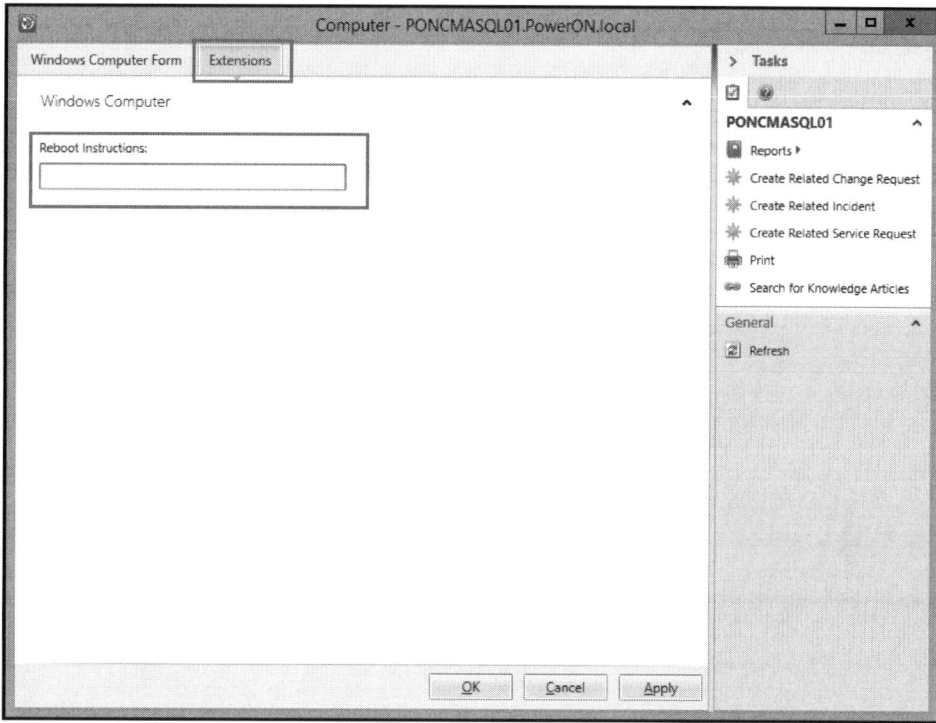

How it works...

Extending a class doesn't require any deep technical knowledge on how to edit XML or such, but it's important to understand how classes and class hierarchy works in Service Manager. When importing the management pack with a class extension, Service Manager will actually extend the Service Manager database with new columns to hold this information.

When Service Manager detects properties that were added to existing classes using class extensions, it will display the **Extensions** tab on the corresponding form. Each property will be added to the **Extensions** tab using a default control that is based on the property's data type.

Please note that Service Manager does not support dynamically displaying relationship properties in the **Extensions** tab. You will have to customize the form using the Authoring Tool to accomplish this task. Furthermore, you can define the layout and the arrangement of the controls used for your extended properties by extending the base forms contained in Service Manager. We will cover this scenario later in this chapter.

There's more...

An important choice to make when defining class properties is the correct data type. In the following section, you can find information about the data types available in Service Manager, as well as instructions on how you can use enumerations as data types.

The data type of each property can be defined in the **Details** pane of the **Authoring Tool**. The available data types are as follows:

- Integer: Signed integer (-2,147,483,648 to 2,147,483,647)
- Decimal: Precise fractional or integral type ($\pm 1.0 \times 10e{-}28$ to $\pm 7.9 \times 10e28$)
- Double: Double-precision floating point type (-1.79769313486232e308 to 1.79769313486232e308)
- String: Text type
- Date Time: Date/Time type
- GUID: Global Unique Identifier
- Bool: true/false
- Rich Text: Text in RTF form
- Binary: Binary data such as files
- List: Enumeration type

Lists aka enumeration types

The List data type can be used to create a property that will allow the user to select a value from one of the lists available in Service Manager, such as the Incident Classification property of the Incident class. Lists are special data types named Enumeration Types. You can target any existing list from any management pack in Service Manager, or create your own list using the Authoring Tool.

To define a property as a list, do the following:

1. In the Authoring Tool, add a new property that you would like to be defined as a List type, and then, in the **Details pane**, change the **Data Type** property to **List**.
2. In the **Select a list** dialog, either select an existing list, or create your own list using the **Create List...** option.
3. Save and seal your management pack and import into Service Manager
4. If you chose to create your own list, you can now define the available values under **Lists** in the **Library** section of the Service Manager console.

See also

Refer to the following recipe in this chapter for more information on how to customize the form to display controls for your newly created properties:

- *Customizing default forms*

Creating new classes

Sooner or later you are likely to come into the situation where you want to store data in your CMDB for which you are unable to find a matching class. Some examples might be monitors, mobile phones, racks, buildings, locations, cost centers, and so on. The Service Manager 2016 class model not only allows for classes to be extended, but also offers the capability to add new classes to the class model.

In this recipe, we will walk you through the steps required to create your own custom class using the Authoring Tool.

Getting ready

It is recommended that you follow the earlier recipes in this chapter to get an understanding on how the Authoring Tool works, how you seal management packs, and how the Service Manager class hierarchy works.

How to do it...

We will now use the Authoring Tool to create a new generic class named Peripheral Device to store data about monitors, scanners, and locally attached printers.

When you create a new class in Service Manager, you have to define one or more primary key properties. The primary key property uniquely identifies each instance of the class. In other words, the value of the unique key property, or the combination of values if you define more than one unique key property respectively, must be unique and cannot occur in any other instance of the class. As an example, the unique key property for the **Windows Computer** class is the **PrincipalName** property, which holds the Fully Qualified Domain Name (FQDN) of the computer. The **Domain User or Group** class defines both the **UserName** and **Domain** properties as the primary key.

In our example, we will name the primary key property **PeripheralDeviceID**. In addition to the ID, we will define properties for Device name, Description, Serial number, and Asset tag of the device. Also, in order to distinguish between the different device types, we will create an enumeration type property called Device type, which is bound to a custom list:

1. Open the **Authoring Tool**, go to **File**, and select **New**. Create a new management pack named **Packt.PeripheralDevice.Class.xml**.

2. Right-click on the **Classes** node in **Management pack Explorer** and click on **Create Configuration Item Class…**. Enter **Packt.PeripheralDevice** as the **Internal name**, and then click on **OK**.

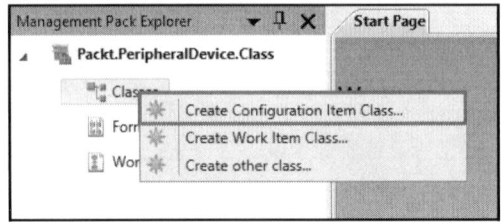

3. You will now see that a new class has been added to your management pack and the class will also be displayed in the **Authoring Pane**.

4. In the **Authoring Pane**, change the class name to **Peripheral Device**, and clear the description field.

5. Scroll to the bottom of the properties list in the **Authoring Pane**. You will see an automatically created property named **Property_4** defined as the key property of your class (indicated with the little key icon). Click on the red cross next to it, in order to delete the property. Click **Yes** on the question that appears.

6. A warning message will then appear that tells you that there is no key property available for your class. We are now going to create our custom key property, so you can ignore this message and click **OK**.

 The reason for us to delete and recreate the key is that we want to specify our own name for the attribute. Property_4 isn't a good name for a key property.

7. Click on **Create property...** in the Authoring Pane, enter **PeripheralDeviceID** as the **Internal name**, and click on **Create**. Ignore the warning message and click on **OK**.

8. Click on the newly created property from the list of available properties in the **Authoring Pane**, and then, in the **Details** pane, change the following:
   - **Key** = True
   - **Required** =True
   - **Auto Increment** = True
   - **Default Value** = PD{0}

 The {0} in **Default Value** will tell Service Manager that it should automatically assign auto incremented values to this property, and a prefix of PD will be used.

9. Click on **Create property...**, enter **DeviceType** as the **Internal name**, and then click on **Create**.

10. In the **Details** pane, change the **Data Type** property to **List**.

11. In the **Select a list** dialog window, click on **Create List...**, enter **PeripheralDeviceTypeList** as the **Internal name**, and **Peripheral Device Type** as the **Display name**. Click on **Create** and then click on **OK**.

12. Click on **Create property...**, enter **DeviceName** as the **Internal name**, and then click on **Create**. Change the **Name** property to **Device Name**.

13. Click on **Create property...**, enter **Description** as the **Internal name**, and then click on **Create**. Change the **Maximum Length** property to **4000**.

14. Click on **Create property...**, enter **SerialNumber** as the **Internal name**, and then click on **Create**. Change the **Name** property to **Serial Number**.

15. Click on **Create property…**, enter **AssetTag** as the **Internal name**, and then click on **Create**. Change the **Name** property to **Asset Tag**.

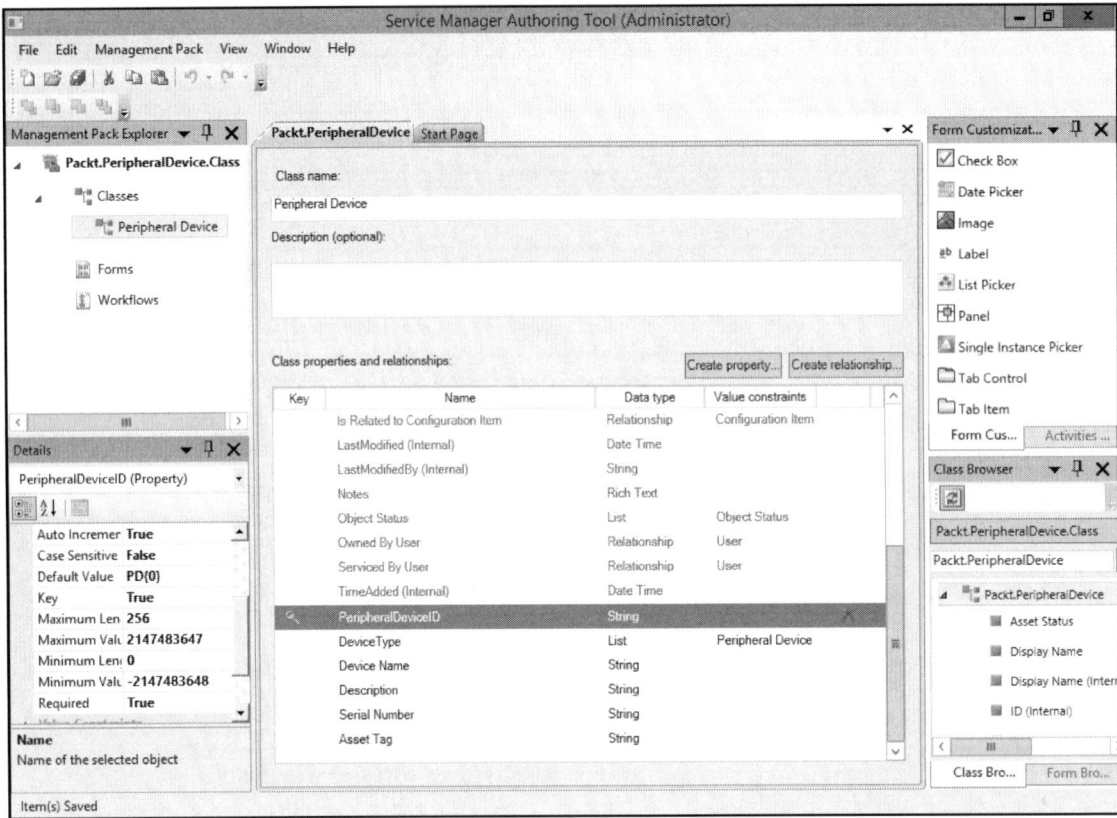

16. Save the management pack using the **Save All** option from the **File** menu.

17. Seal the management pack. For more information on how to seal a management pack, please refer to the previous recipe, *Sealing management packs*.

18. Open the **Service Manager** console and navigate to the **Management Packs** view in the **Administration** workspace.

19. In the task pane, click on **Import**, and browse to the location where you stored your sealed management pack. On the lower-right, change **MP files(*.xml)** to **MP files(*. mp)**, click on the **Packt.PeripheralDevice.Class.mp** file, click on **Open**, and then click on **Import**. When the import process is finished, click on **OK**.

20. Navigate to the **Library** workspace and click on **Lists**.

21. Locate and double-click on the **Peripheral Device Type** list and add the following values: **Monitor**, **Scanner**, and **Local Printer**. Note that you will have to specify a management pack where you want to store these list values in. This is because we sealed the management pack that holds the definition of the list.

> Your newly created class is now ready to be used for storing data in Service Manager. However, you might wonder how you will be able to manage your peripheral devices, as there are no corresponding views available in the Service Manager console. Instead, you have to create at least one view yourself.

22. Navigate to the **Configuration Items** workspace, right-click on the **Configuration Items folder**, and then click on **Create Folder**.

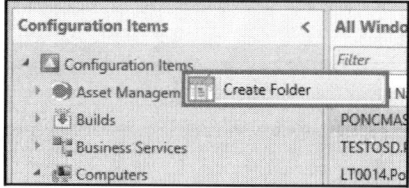

23. Enter **Peripheral Devices** as the **Folder name**. Select any of your custom management packs that you use for storing configuration management views, or create a new management pack for this purpose. Click on **OK**

24. Right-click on the newly created folder, **Peripheral Devices**, and then click on **Create View**.

25. In the **Create View** dialog, under **General**, enter **All Peripheral Devices** as the **Name**.

26. Under **Criteria**, click on **Browse**. In the drop-down menu in the top right corner, select **All basic classes**. Find and mark the **Peripheral Device** class, and then click on **OK**.

27. Under **Display**, make sure that the following properties are selected:
    - PeripherialDeviceID
    - Device Type
    - Device Name
    - Serial Number
    - Asset Number
    - Last Modified

28. Click on **OK** to save the view.

29. Click on the newly created view, and then, in the task pane, click on **Create Peripheral Device**.

30. **Service Manager** will load the generic form for the **Peripheral Device** class that allows you to enter data about your peripheral devices. Notice how the **PeripherialDeviceID** field is automatically populated according to our definition when we created the property in the **Authoring Tool**.

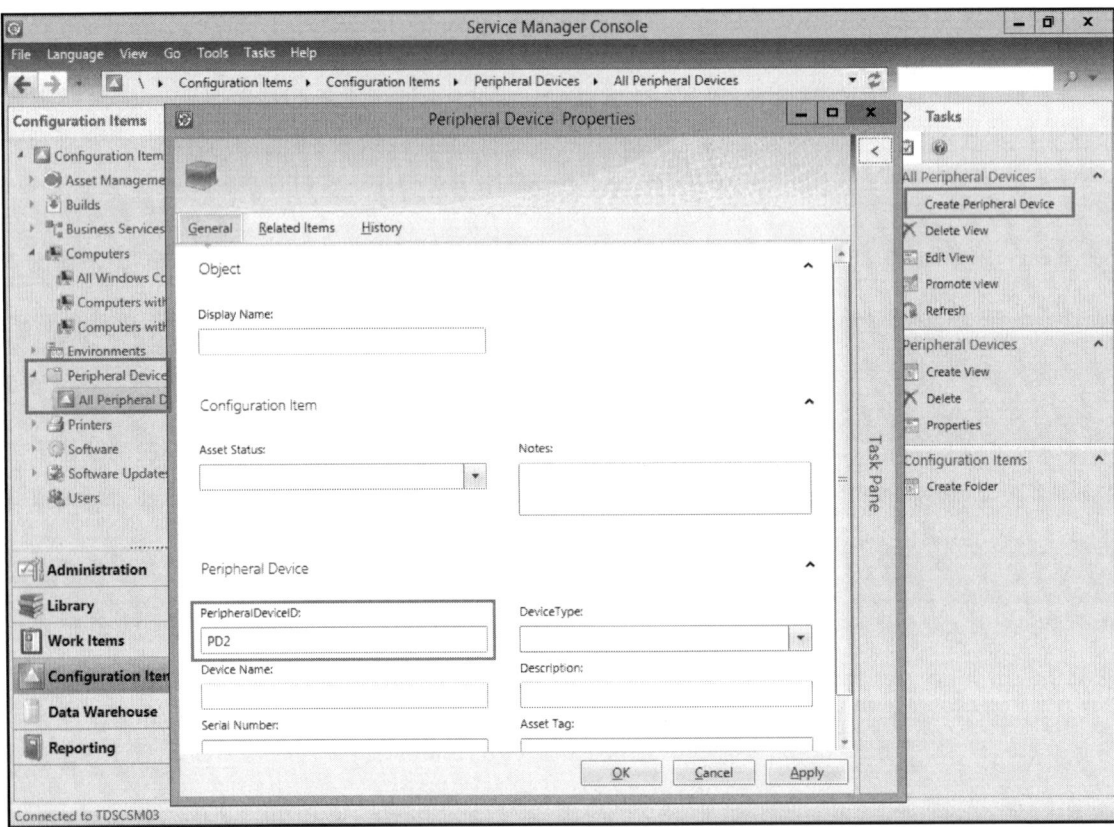

How it works...

Extending Service Manager with new classes is rather easy and straightforward as you can see. The work done in the Authoring Tool results in a management pack that contains all the information needed for the system to support these new objects. I encourage you to examine the management pack with a simple text editor to get a better understanding on how the actual XML code looks like – it might be easier than you think! Just make sure that you look at the .XML file and not the sealed .MP file.

The generic form

Whenever Service Manager has to open a form for a class for which no class-specific form exists, it will open a generic form that lists all available properties for the corresponding class. Service Manager uses default controls that are based on the data type of each individual property. As with class extensions, the generic form will not display any controls for relationships. You might also have noticed that the generic form includes properties that are inherited from parent classes.

If you will be using the Service Manager console often for working with instances of your user-defined classes, it is recommended that you also create a user-defined form for your custom class that accommodates your individual requirements and thus improves the usability over the generic form. We will cover the creation of new forms later in this chapter.

There's more...

Instead of creating new classes with all new properties, Service Manager also allows you to inherit the properties of an existing class. The next section explains the process of inheriting from an existing class, and talks about the System Center Common Model.

Inheriting from a different class

When you create a new Configuration Item or Work Item class using the right-click on option on the Classes node in the Management Pack Explorer of the Authoring Tool, your custom class will always have System.ConfigItem or System.WorkItem as its base class. However, you might want your custom class to inherit from a class further below in the class hierarchy.

As an example, you might want to create a special type of Incident class that is used for incidents raised by your monitoring system. These incidents should include all fields of the built-in Incident class, but also have some additional properties to hold the details of the monitoring alert. Instead of extending the Incident class with these properties (which would then be available to all kinds of incidents), you can create a new class that inherits from the Incident class.

To do so, simply use the third option called **Create other class...** and select the base class from which you would like to inherit from.

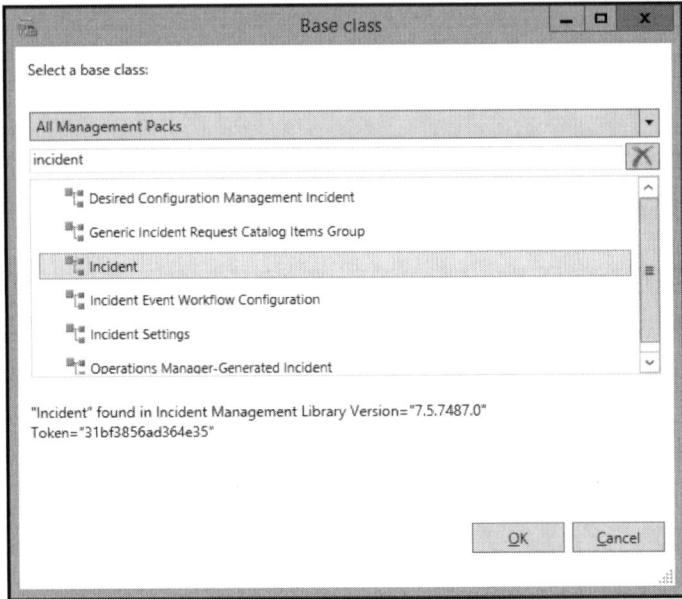

System Center Common Model

When creating new classes in Service Manager, you might find it difficult to identify an appropriate base class that your custom class could inherit from. The most commonly used classes in Service Manager are documented in the Visio UML class diagram named the **System Center Common Model**, as implemented in System Center Service Manager. This document is part of the **SCSM Job Aids**, which can be downloaded from the following URL:

http://go.microsoft.com/fwlink/p/?LinkID=232378

Unfortunately, there is no updated Job Aids package for Service Manager 2016 at the time of writing. Also, the System Center Common Model included in the available Job Aids package is created for Service Manager 2010. It is still very relevant though, as the later versions of Service Manager simply has extended the hierarchy with more classes.

See also

Refer to the following recipe in this chapter for more information on how to create a custom form for your newly created class:

- *Creating your own forms*

Customizing default forms

In the previous recipes, we have learned how to extend and create new classes in Service Manager 2016. Obviously, when you do this you would want to be able update or create forms to include all of this new information.

Although Service Manager 2016 includes a generic form for classes missing their own forms, and the Extensions tab for custom class extensions, you might want to have control over how the forms look like in order to improve the usability of the console. This is where the System Center 2016 Service Manager Authoring Tools can help you, as it allows you to customize existing forms and also create new forms for your custom classes.

In this recipe, we will walk you through the process of adding controls to the existing Windows Computer form. We will use the class extension we created in the Extending Service Manager classes recipe earlier in this chapter.

Getting ready

In addition to having knowledge on how to use the Authoring tool and how you seal management pack, you need to have completed the *Extending Service Manager classes* recipe earlier in this chapter.

Working with forms requires knowledge about the forms infrastructure of Service Manager. Whenever you open an object in the Service Manager console (using the Edit or Properties task, or by double-clicking on a class instance) or whenever you create a new object (using the Create task), Service Manager evaluates which form to load. During this evaluation, the class type of the object is evaluated. If a form is assigned to this class type, the form is loaded. If not, Service Manager retrieves the parent class (base class) of the object, and checks if a form is bound to this class. This process is repeated until a form is found.

As you have noticed in the previous recipe when we created the class for peripheral devices, Service Manager will also load a form of "no form exists" up the class hierarchy. The reason for this is that Service Manager has a so called Generic Form. One generic form is bound to the `System.Entity` class, which ultimately all the classes inherit from. Furthermore, generic forms exists for type projections with seed class `System.ConfigItem` and `System.WorkItem`.

How to do it...

Now that you have a basic understanding of Service Manager form concepts, we are going to extend one of the existing forms using the Authoring Tool. We will add the special reboot instructions and technical responsible properties from the Custom Configuration Items Computer Extension management pack that we created in the *Extending Service Manager classes* recipe:

1. Open the **Authoring Tool** and go to **File** and click **New**. Give the new management pack the name **Packt.WindowsComputer.FormCustomization.xml** and click **Save**.

2. Now go to **File** and click **Open**. Browse to the **sealed** management pack holding our class extension for the **Windows Computer** class. If you followed the previous recipes this should be named **Packt.WindowsComputer.ClassExtension.mp**.

3. With both of these management packs opened in the **Authoring Tool**, go to the **Form Browser** and click the **Reload button**.

4. Locate and right-click on the **ComputerForm** form and click on **View**.

5. The Management pack that includes the **ComputerForm** form will now be loaded by the **Authoring Tool** and displayed in the **Management Pack Explorer**. Also, the form will be shown in read-only mode in the **Authoring Tool**.

6. In the **Authoring Pane**, click on **Customize** in the yellow/orange header.

7. In the **Target Management pack** pop-up window, make sure that the newly created management pack is selected, and click on **OK**.

8. You will now see that the form has been added to your management pack, and that the form is being displayed in the Authoring Pane to be edited.

9. Click on the **ComputerForm (Customized)** form in the **Management Pack Explorer** and then go to the **Details** pane. Now change the **Name** property to **Custom Windows Computer Form** and clear the **Description** property.

10. Aligning controls on forms can be a bit tricky. Start with dragging a **Label** control from the **Form Customization Toolbox** to the form in the **Authoring Pane**. Still holding the mouse button, move the cursor slightly to the right of **Principal Name** until both the label and textbox are surrounded with a selection box. Drop the label control by releasing the mouse button. The label should appear right underneath the **Principal Name** textbox.

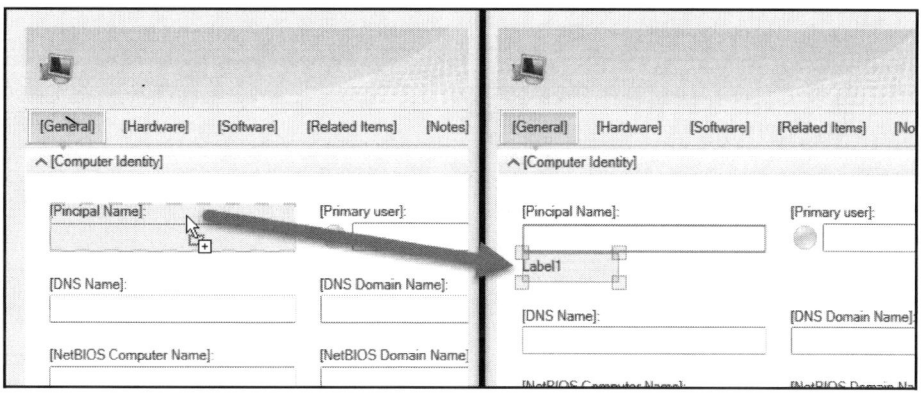

11. Select the newly added Label control by clicking on it. In the **Details** pane, change the following properties:
    - Width: Auto
    - Horizontal Alignment: Stretch
    - (Margin) Top: 10
    - Content: Special Reboot Instructions

12. Now, drag a **Text Box** control from the **Form Customization Toolbox** to the form in the **Authoring Pane**. Still holding the mouse button, move the cursor slightly to the right of Principal Name and release the mouse button – exactly as we did with the label. The textbox should appear right underneath the **Special Reboot Instructions** label.

13. Select the newly added **Text Box** control, and then, in the **Details** pane, change the following properties:

      - Height: Auto
      - Width: Auto
      - Minimum Height: 23
      - Horizontal Alignment: Stretch

14. With the control still selected, locate and click on the **Binding Path** property in the **Details** pane. Click on the browse button marked with **...** that now appears. Select the **Reboot Instructions** property from the Binding Path pop-up window, and click on **OK**.

15. Drag another **Label** control from the **Form Customization Toolbox** to the form in the **Authoring Pane**. Still holding the mouse button, move the cursor **precisely to the pixel** between the **Primary User** label and the Primary User control. Ensure that both the label and the user picker control are surrounded with the dashed selection box, as seen in the previous screenshot. Drop the label control by releasing the mouse button. The label should appear right underneath the **Primary User** user picker control.

16. Select the newly added **Label** control, and then, in the **Details** pane, change the following properties:

      - Width: Auto
      - Horizontal Alignment: Stretch
      - (Margin) Top: 10
      - Content: Technical Responsible:

17. Now drag a **User Picker** control from the **Form Customization Toolbox** to the form in the **Authoring pane**. Still holding the mouse button, move the cursor to the empty space between our new label called **Technical Responsible,** and the **Primary User** user picker. Ensure that all the controls are surrounded with the dashed selection box. Drop the **User Picker** control by releasing the mouse button. The **User Picker** should appear right underneath the **Technical Responsible** label.

18. Select the newly added **User Picker** control, and then, in the **Details** pane, change the following properties:

      - Height: Auto
      - Width: Auto

- Minimum Height: 25
- Horizontal Alignment: Stretch

19. In the Details pane click the **Binding Path** property, and then click on the **...** button. Select the **Technical Responsible** relationship from the Binding Path pop-up window, and click on **OK**.

20. Verify that the alignment of the controls match with the following screenshot:

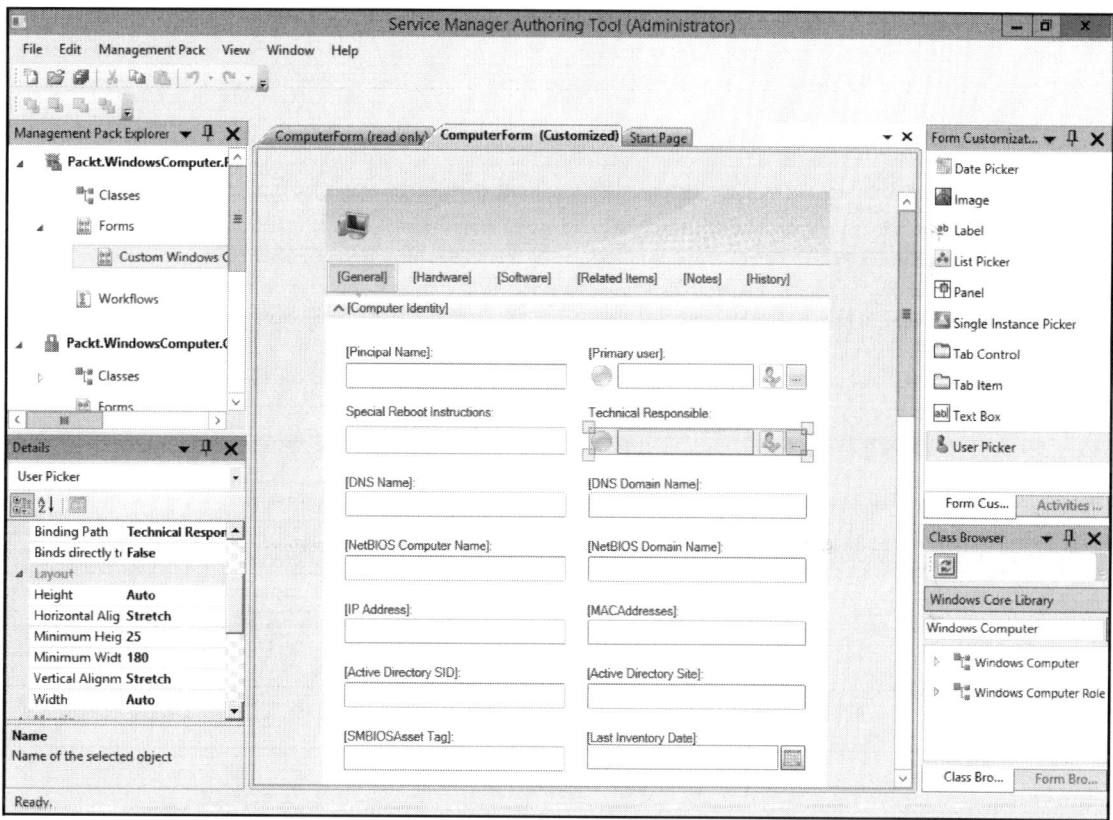

21. Save the management pack using the **SaveAll** option from the **File** menu.

22. Seal the management pack. For more information on how to seal a management pack, please refer to the Sealing Management packs recipe earlier in this chapter.

23. Open the **Service Manager** console and navigate to the **Management Packs** view in the **Administration** workspace.

24. In the task pane, click on **Import**, and browse to the location where you stored your sealed management pack. On the lower-right, change **MP files(*.xml)** to **MP files(*.mp)**, click on the **Packt.WindowsComputer.FormCustomization.mp** file, click on **Open**, and then click on **Import**. When the import process is finished, click on **OK**.

25. Go to the **Configuration Items** workspace, open the **All Windows Computers** view, and double-click on any of the listed computers.

You will now see the newly added fields displayed on the computer form. If the fields do not show up, try closing and restarting the Service Manager console, as the form could be stored in your local Service Manager cache.

How it works...

Service Manager forms are based on Windows Presentation Foundation (WPF), which is part of the Microsoft .NET Framework. Each form is technically a WPF user control that is compiled into a DLL file. By extending a form, you are referencing the base form in your management pack. All the customizations are contained in the management pack XML code as tags that can be interpreted by WPF. When Service Manager loads the extended form, during the rendering process, it applies the customization tags to the base form before it is displayed to the end user.

There's more...

When you extend classes in Service Manager, you might notice a tab titled Extensions on the form of the extended class. The nature of this tab is explained in the following section.

The Extensions tab

When Service Manager loads a form, both the class of the object that is being displayed as well as the class to which the form that is being displayed is targeted are evaluated. If these classes differ, and if the form that is being displayed is not a generic form, an Extensions tab is added to the form. This tab displays all properties of any extension classes in the class hierarchy of the object. We learned about the Extensions tab when we originally created the Windows Computer class extensions in the Extending Service Manager classes recipe.

As we have now added the properties we want to the General tab of the computer form, we might want to remove the Extensions tab. This can be done by manually editing the management pack XML code. We will cover this scenario in the *Using an XML editor to modify Management packs* recipe later in this chapter.

See also

Refer to the following recipe for more information on how to create class extensions:

- Extending Service Manager classes

Creating your own forms

In the Creating new classes recipe, we have added a class to Service Manager to store instances of peripheral devices in our CMDB. While the generic form that was used to manage the devices might be sufficient, you are still likely to come into the situation where you want to have control over what controls to display, and the layout of the form.

The Service Manager 2016 form infrastructure not only allows for the existing forms to be customized, but also offers the capability to add new forms.

In this recipe, we will walk you through the steps required to create your custom form using the Authoring Tool.

Getting ready

In addition to having knowledge on how to use the Authoring tool and how you seal management pack, you need to have completed the *Creating new classes* recipe earlier in this chapter.

You will need a basic understanding of the form infrastructure in Service Manager. It is therefore recommended that you read through the Getting ready section of the previous recipe, *Customizing default forms*.

How to do it...

We will now use the **Authoring Tool** to create a new form for the **Peripheral Device** class that we defined in the *Creating new classes* recipe earlier in this chapter:

1. Open the **Authoring Tool**, go to **File**, and click **New**. Give the new management pack the name **Packt.PeripheralDevice.Form.xml**.

2. Go to **File** and click **Open**. Locate and open the **sealed** management pack that holds the **Peripheral Device** class (**Packt.PeripheralDevice.Class.mp**).

3. With both management packs opened, right-click **Forms** under **Packt.PeripheralDevice.Form** in the **Management Pack Explorer**, and click on **Create**.

4. In the **Base class** pop-up window, select the **Peripheral Device** class, and click on **OK**.

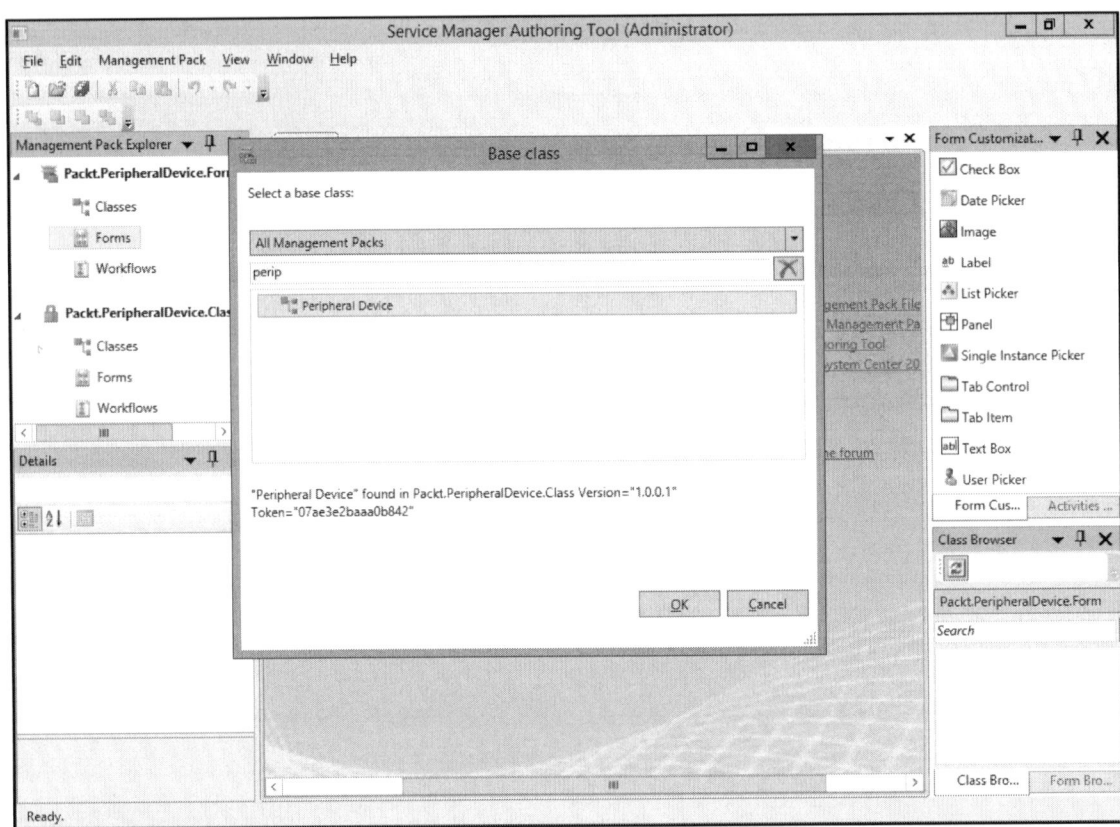

5. In the **Create** form pop-up windows, enter **PeripheralDeviceForm** as the **Internalname**, and then click on **OK**.

6. You will now see that the form has been added to your management pack, and the form will also be displayed in the **Authoring Pane** and can now be edited.

7. Click on the **PeripheralDeviceForm** form in the **Management Pack Explorer**. In the **Details** pane, change the **Name** property to **Peripheral Device Form**, and clear the **Description** property.

8. Drag and drop a **Label** control from the **Form Customization Toolbox** to the form in the **Authoring Pane**.

9. Select the newly added **Label** control, and then, in the **Details** pane, configure the following properties:

   - Height: 20
   - Horizontal Alignment: Left
   - Minimum Height: 0
   - Minimum Width: 0
   - Vertical Alignment: Top
   - Width: Auto
   - (Margin) Bottom: 0
   - (Margin) Left: 20
   - (Margin) Right: 0
   - (Margin) Top: 20
   - Content: ID:

10. Now, drag a **Text Box** control from the **Form Customization Toolbox** to the form in the **Authoring Pane** and drop it somewhere on the form. We will configure the margins to get the correct placement in the next step.

11. Select the newly added **Text Box** control, and then, in the **Details pane**, configure the following properties:

    - Binding Path: PeripherialDeviceID
    - Height: 23
    - Horizontal Alignment: Left
    - Minimum Height: 0
    - Minimum Width: 0
    - Vertical Alignment: Top
    - Width: 120
    - (Margin) Bottom: 0

- (Margin) Left: 20
- (Margin) Right: 0
- (Margin) Top: 45
- Is Enabled: False

12. We are disabling this particular control because the ID value is defined to be automatically assigned.

13. Now add labels and controls for the following properties:

- Device Name
- Description
- Device Type
- Serial Number
- Asset Tag

14. Aside from the Is Enabled property (which shouldn't be touched for these controls) use the similar preceding configuration. You will have to play around with the margins to find a layout that fits your need. Don't try to use the mouse to move the controls around as it will write excessive rows of XML in the management pack, but it is also very hard to get exact placement using the mouse.

15. When adding the **DescriptionTextBox** it might be a good idea to make it a bit higher than the other controls as it may contain some more text. It might also be a good idea to set the **Text Wrapping** to **Wrap with overflow** and **Accepts the ENTER key** to **True** for this control.

16. If you want, you can also add a **User Picker** control for the **Owned By User** relationship that is inherited from the `System.ConfigItem` class to indicate the owner of the device.

17. When you're finished with the design, save your management pack by using **Save all** under the **File** menu. The following screenshot shows how the form design might look:

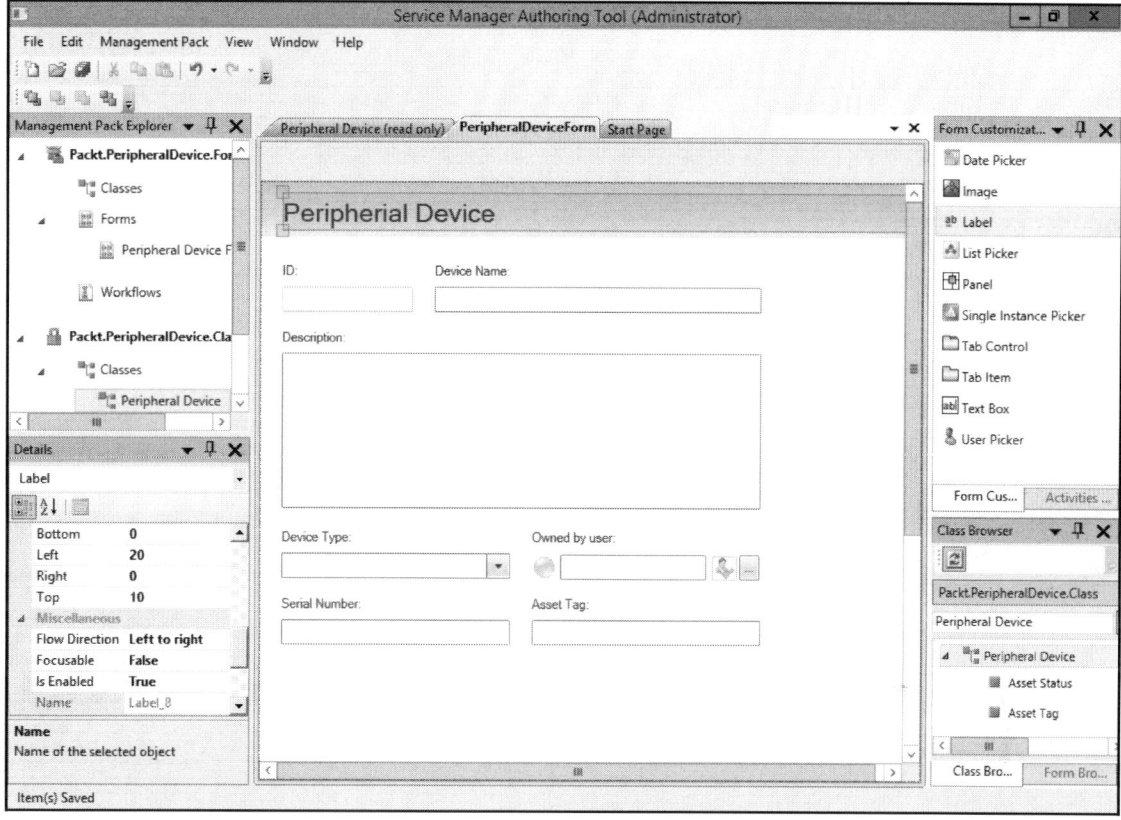

18. **Seal** the management pack. For more information on how to seal a management pack, please refer to the *Sealing Management packs* recipe earlier in this chapter.

19. Open the **Service Manager** console and navigate to the **Management packs** view in the **Administration** workspace.

20. In the task pane, click on **Import**, and browse to the location where you stored your sealed management pack. On the lower-right, change **MP files(*.xml)** to **MP files(*.mp)**, click on the **Packt.PeripheralDevice.Form.mp** file, click on **Open**, and then click on **Import**. When the import process is finished, click on **OK**.

21. Go to the **Configuration** Items workspace, open the **All Peripheral Devices** view created in the *Creating new classes* recipe and double-click on any of the listed peripheral devices, or create a new one using the **Create Peripheral Device** task in the task pane.

From now on, Service Manager will use the newly added form when you work with instances of the **Peripheral Device** class.

How it works...

With the creation of a custom form for the Peripheral Device class, Service Manager now no longer displays the generic form. By creating your custom form, you have total control over which properties are displayed on the form, over the layout of the controls, and also on the design of the form.

For more advanced forms you can use Visual Studio to create these. Using Visual Studio you can also create your own custom WPF user controls that can be used in your custom forms. Unfortunately, using Visual Studio for advanced customization of Service Manager is out-of-scope for this book.

See also

Refer to the following recipe in this chapter for more information on how to create a custom class for Service Manager:

- *Creating new classes*

Using an XML editor to modify management packs

By following the instructions in all recipes so far in this book you have gained an insight of the vast personalization and extensibility options available to Service Manager.

But using the Service Manager console and the Authoring Tool are only two possible ways of customizing Service Manager. There are much more options available to customize Service Manager, for instance, by directly editing the XML code of your management packs.

It is beyond the scope of this book to cover all possible customization scenarios you can address by modifying the management pack XML. However, there are a lot of examples available in the community that you can apply to your environment. Refer to Appendix B for a list of some of the most important community websites to visit.

The goal of this recipe is to become familiar with the general process of modifying the XML code of a management pack.

Getting ready

In order to work with the XML code of management packs, you need to use software for opening and editing XML files. Even though you can use Notepad to edit XML files, it is recommended that you use a more advanced tool that offers color schemas and XML validation.

The first recommended choice would be to use the Visual Studio integrated development environment from Microsoft. Visual Studio is available in various commercial editions, and there is also two free editions named Visual Studio Express and Visual Studio Community.

If you are not into developing software, Visual Studio is not the best choice, as the user interface might be too complex for simple XML editing. One of the many alternatives is the free tool Notepad++ that you can download and install from the following URL:

```
http://notepad-plus-plus.org/
```

How to do it...

In this example, we are going to create a new management pack that will hide the **Extensions** tab from the Windows Computer form. After we have extended the Windows Computer by following the instructions in the *Extending Service Manager classes* recipe, we have noticed that the **Extensions** tab, which displays the extended properties, has been added to the form. As we have later customized the form in the *Customizing default forms* recipe to include the extended properties in the **General** tab, we would now like to hide the **Extensions** tab from the Windows Computer form.

Note that it is required that the sealed management packs that you created in the *Extending Service Manager classes* and *Customizing default forms* recipes are available and imported into Service Manager:

1. Open the **Authoring Tool**, go to **File,** and click **Open**. Locate and open the **sealed** management pack that includes the **Windows Computer form** extension from the Customizing default forms recipe, **Packt.WindowsComputer.FormCustomization.mp**.

2. Click on the management pack in **Management Pack Explorer**, and then, in the **Details** pane, write down the values of the following properties:

    - Internal Name
    - Key Token
    - Version (in the form: Major.Minor.Build.Revision)

3. In **Management Pack Explorer**, expand the **Forms** node, click on the **Custom Windows Computer Form**, and then, in the **Details** pane, write down the value of the **Internal Name** property.

4. Click on **Close Solution** from the **File** menu.

5. Go to **File** and click **New** to create a new management pack. Give this new management pack the name **Packt.WindowsComputer.HideExtensionsTab.xml**.

 We're using the Authoring Tool to create this new management pack to do our XML editing in. Doing this we don't have to write all the base XML code that construct the actual management pack.

6. Save the management pack using the **Save All** option from the **File** menu, and then close the **Authoring Tool**.

7. Use the XML editor of your choice to open the management pack XML file (we will be using Notepad++ in this recipe).

8. First, we will need to add a reference to the management pack that hosts the actual Windows Computer form extension. The management pack references are always in the beginning of the XML and is listed between the <References> tag. Add the following code to the References section just before the </References> tag (the easiest way is to copy an existing reference and edit the values):

```
<Reference Alias="ComputerFormExtension">
<ID>Custom.ConfigurationItems.ComputerFormExtension</ID>
<Version>1.0.0.1</Version>
```

```
<PublicKeyToken>249f95ca48020739</PublicKeyToken>
</Reference>
```

9. Replace the values for `ID`, `Version`, and `PublicKeyToken` with the corresponding values you wrote down in Step 2.

10. Next, we will need to add another reference to the UI Administration management pack. Add the following code to the References section just before the `</ References>` tag:

```
<Reference Alias="Admin">
<ID>Microsoft.EnterpriseManagement.ServiceManager.UI.
Administration</ID>
<Version>7.5.7487.0</Version>
<PublicKeyToken>31bf3856ad364e35</PublicKeyToken>
</Reference>
```

11. Now locate the `<Categories>` section, and add the following just before the `</Categories>` tag:

```
<Category ID="HideComputerFormExtensionTab"
Target="ComputerFormExtension!CustomForm_dc869531
_a7b9_46fb_9ac3_9ff6
2066e829"
Value="Admin!Microsoft.EnterpriseManagement.
ServiceManager.UI.Administration.Enumeration.HideExtensionTab" />
```

12. Replace the `CustomForm_dc869531_a7b9_46fb_9ac3_9ff62066e829` string in the Target with the internal name of the form you wrote down in Step 3.

13. Save the XML file and import it into Service Manager. When you now open the Windows Computer form, the **Extensions** tab will no longer be displayed. Please note that you might need to restart the Service Manager console for the changes to take effect.

The final code should look similar to the following screenshot. The only thing that could be somewhat different are the values that you wrote down in Step 2 and 3. (Please note that Word Wrap has been enabled just for the sake of fitting all code into the screenshot!)

There's more...

The following section gives you information about where you can find the XML Schema Definition (XSD) for Service Manager Management packs.

Management pack schema

Microsoft has released the XML Schema Definition (XSD) of the management pack XML structure used in Service Manager. The schema allows for better understanding of the content of the management pack XML code and enables schema validation when you work with management pack XML files.

The XSD file is part of the SCSM Job Aids that can be downloaded from the following URL:

```
http://go.microsoft.com/fwlink/p/?LinkID=232378
```

See also

See the next recipe, *Editing the XML of a view to alter the criteria to include AND instead of OR*, on how to do some more XML editing.

Editing the XML of a view to alter the criteria to include AND instead of OR

Another time when some XML editing comes in handy is when you're trying to create some more customized views. Sure, you're able to create views from the console, but the Create View dialogue doesn't allow you to do things such as renaming column headers, set the order of columns, or something as simple as creating a view criteria that includes the same property twice, constructed with an AND instead of OR.

In this recipe, we will do just that – modify the view criteria through some XML editing so it is constructed with an AND instead of an OR.

Getting ready

In order to follow this recipe you will need to create a view from the console for us to edit in XML:

1. Start the **Service Manager** console and go to the **Work Item** workspace.
2. Right-click **Incident Management** and select **Create View**.
3. As the **Name** of the view, enter **All Active Incidents** and select a management pack to store the view in.

4. Click on **Criteria** on the left side of the dialogue window to get to the **Criteria** section. Click **Browse** and select the **Incident** class.

5. Now, locate and add **Status** twice to the **Criteria**. Set the first row to **Status Does Not Equal Resolved** and set the second row to **Status Does Not Equal Closed**. Notice how Service Manager has added an OR between these two rows.

6. As the criteria is constructed right now, it will always show **all incidents** regardless of status – just because of the OR.

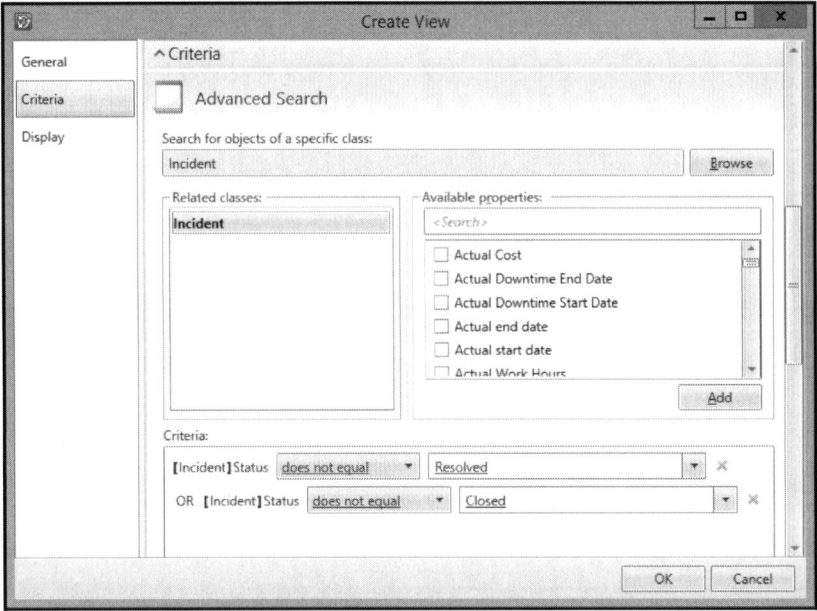

7. Proceed to the **Display** section and select the following properties:

- Classification Category
- Created Date
- ID
- Last Modified
- Status
- Support Group
- Title

8. Click **OK** to create the view.

How to do it…

So we have our view that we need to edit in order to work, this is how you would fix the criteria:

1. Open **Service Manager** and go to **Management Packs** in the **Administration** workspace.
2. Locate the management pack in which the view you want to edit is stored, and **Export** it.
3. Open the management pack with your favorite XML editor – in my case Notepad++.
4. Now we need to locate our specific view within this management pack, in order to do so, search for **All Active Incidents**. This should take you to the `DisplayStrings` section of the management pack, which should look similar to this:

```
<DisplayString
ElementID="View.baa0288a02d149b4a2f8e5124dc4e247">
<Name>All Active Incidents</Name>
</DisplayString>
```

5. Unless you have several views named **All Active Incidents**, this piece of code gives us the **ElementID** to our view. Copy the **ElementID** (in my case `View.baa0288a02d149b4a2f8e5124dc4e247`) and do a search for this until you find a row starting with **<View ID=** When you've located that row, you've found the actual view definition of the **All Active Incidents** view.
6. Scroll a couple of rows down until you find the `<Criteria>` tag. This is where the view criteria is defined.
7. Within the criteria, you should see a couple of `<Expression>` tags, but there should also be a tag called `<Or>` and another one called `</Or>`. The code between these two tags are the code that defines that the **Status Should Not Equal Resolved** or **Status Should Not Equal Closed**.

8. In order to change the criteria from OR to AND, simply replace the **Or** in the tag to **And**. Then save your management pack.

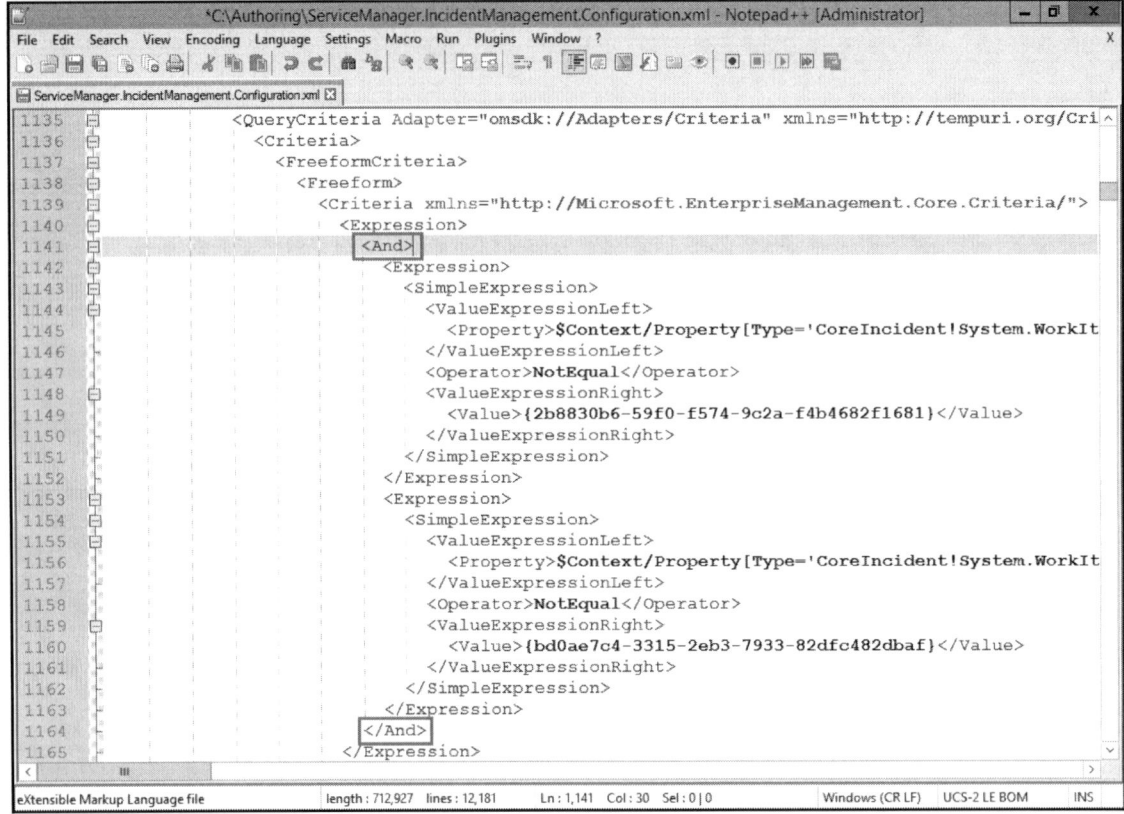

9. Open the **Service Manager** console and go to **Management Packs** in the **Administration** workspace.
10. Import the management pack that we just edited and the view criteria should be updated.

In order for our changes to apply, you might need to restart your Service Manager console since the view might be cached.

How it works...

After you've made the change in the management pack by editing the XML and re-imported it into Service Manager, the view criteria should now contain an AND instead of an OR.

To see how our changes are reflected in the console, locate the **All Active Incidents** view, right-click it, and then select **Edit View**. Now if you go to the Criteria section of this view, there should now be an AND instead of the OR, but what is also worth noting, is that the criteria section is now disabled. This is because we've edited the criteria directly in the management pack and that the Edit View wizard doesn't support the modification.

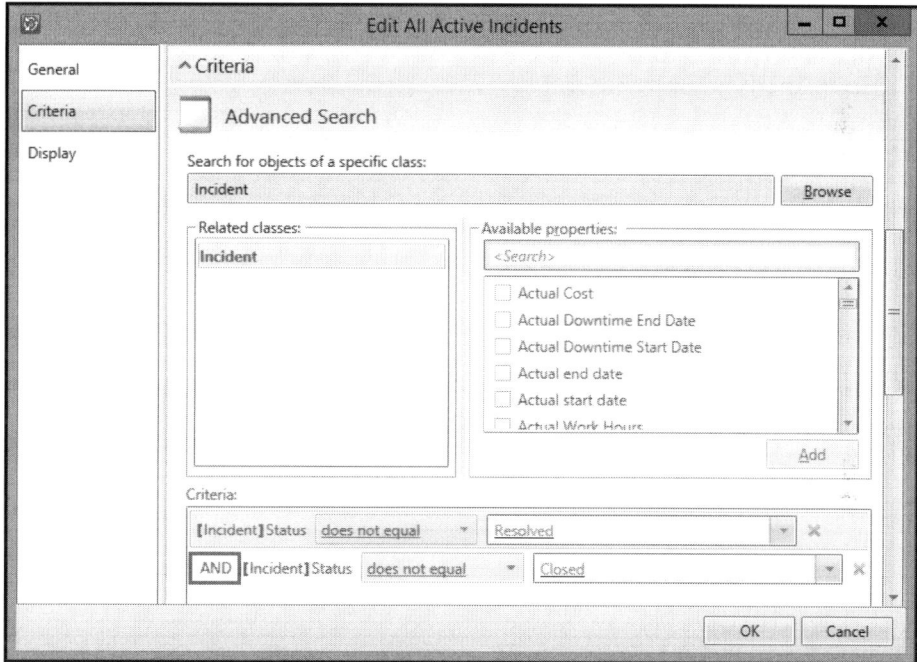

There's more...

There are plenty of other modifications that you can do to views by doing some XML editing – as mentioned earlier changing column names and order is two of them. You might also change things such as column width, how sorting should be handle in different columns, the view icons, and so on.

See also

See the following recipe on how to do some other XML editing:

- *Using an XML editor to modify management packs*

12
Automating Service Manager 2016

In this chapter, we will cover the following:

- Routing incidents automatically using workflows
- Downloading and installing SMLets
- Using SMLets to delete a work item
- Exporting your unsealed management packs using SMLets
- Creating a custom workflow in the Authoring Tool – exporting your unsealed management packs
- Autoclosing resolved incidents with SMLets and a custom workflow
- Automating your request offerings with Orchestrator
- Creating new work items with SMLets

Introduction

In this chapter of the cookbook, we will take a look at different scenarios for automating Service Manager. Besides working with the standard workflows within Service Manager, we will create custom workflows through the Authoring Tool and use SMLets to automate tasks. Also, we will take a look at how we can use System Center Orchestrator to automate our work items.

Routing incidents automatically using workflows

We will start by taking a look at a simple workflow to route incidents to a certain user or a group. This functionality can be created using the built-in workflows within Service Manager.

Getting ready

Be sure that you have read and understood the creation of templates as described in the *Creating an incident template* recipe in `Chapter 7`, *Working with Incident and Problem Management*.

Make sure that Service Manager is up-and-running and that you have sufficient privileges to create workflows and templates (administrator permissions are needed).

How to do it…

In this example, we will create a workflow to route any incidents with the classification category, **E-mail Problems**, to the dispatcher of the Exchange group:

1. Start the Service Manager console and go to the **Library** workspace.
2. Select **Templates** and create a new template based upon the **Incident** class. The only thing that you should define in this template is the **Assigned To** user – in our case, the dispatcher of the Exchange group.

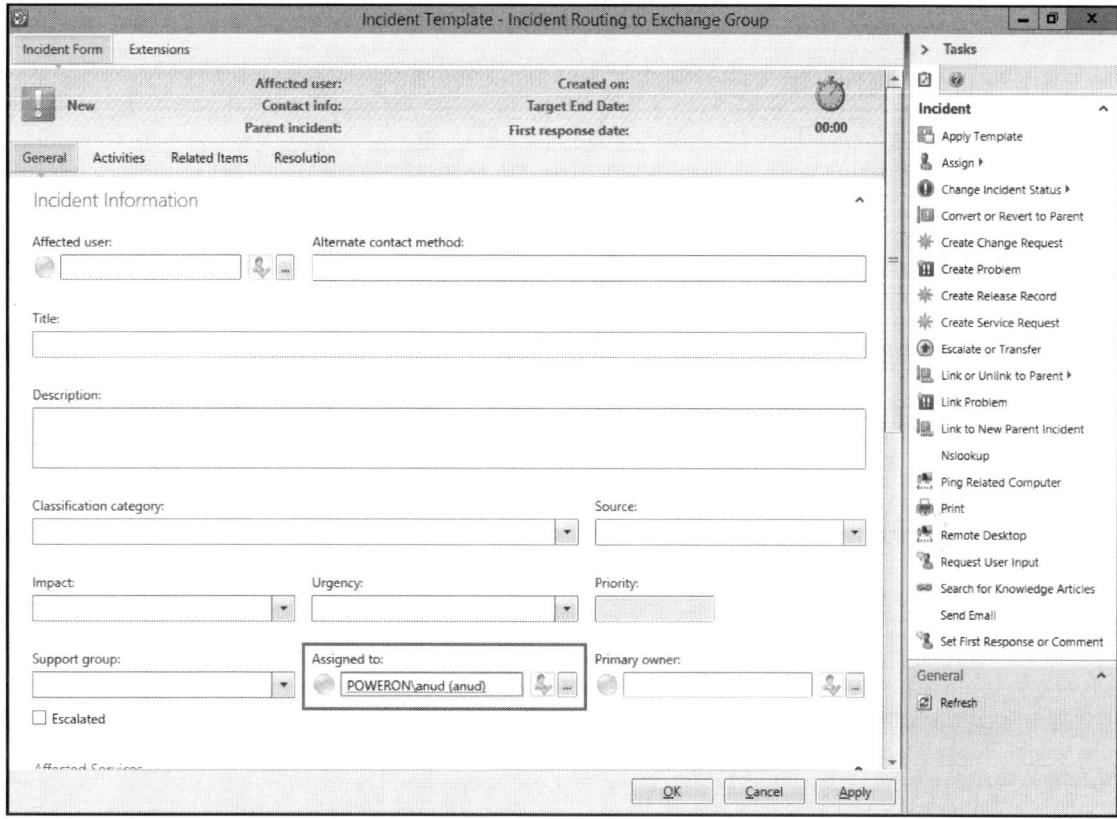

3. When you've created your template, go to the **Administration** workspace.

4. Expand **Workflows** and select **Configuration**.

5. Double-click on **Incident Event Workflow Configuration** to open the properties of it.

6. To create a new incident workflow, click on the **Add** button.

7. Click on **Next** in the **Before You Begin** step of the wizard.

8. As the **Name** of the workflow, enter Incident - Route E-mail incidents to Exchange group. In the **Description** field, enter This workflow will route all new incidents with the Classification Category set to E-mail Problems to the dispatcher of the Exchange group.

9. Make sure that **When an object is created** is chosen in the **Check for events** drop-down and then create a new or select an existing management pack to store your workflow in. Then click on **Next**.

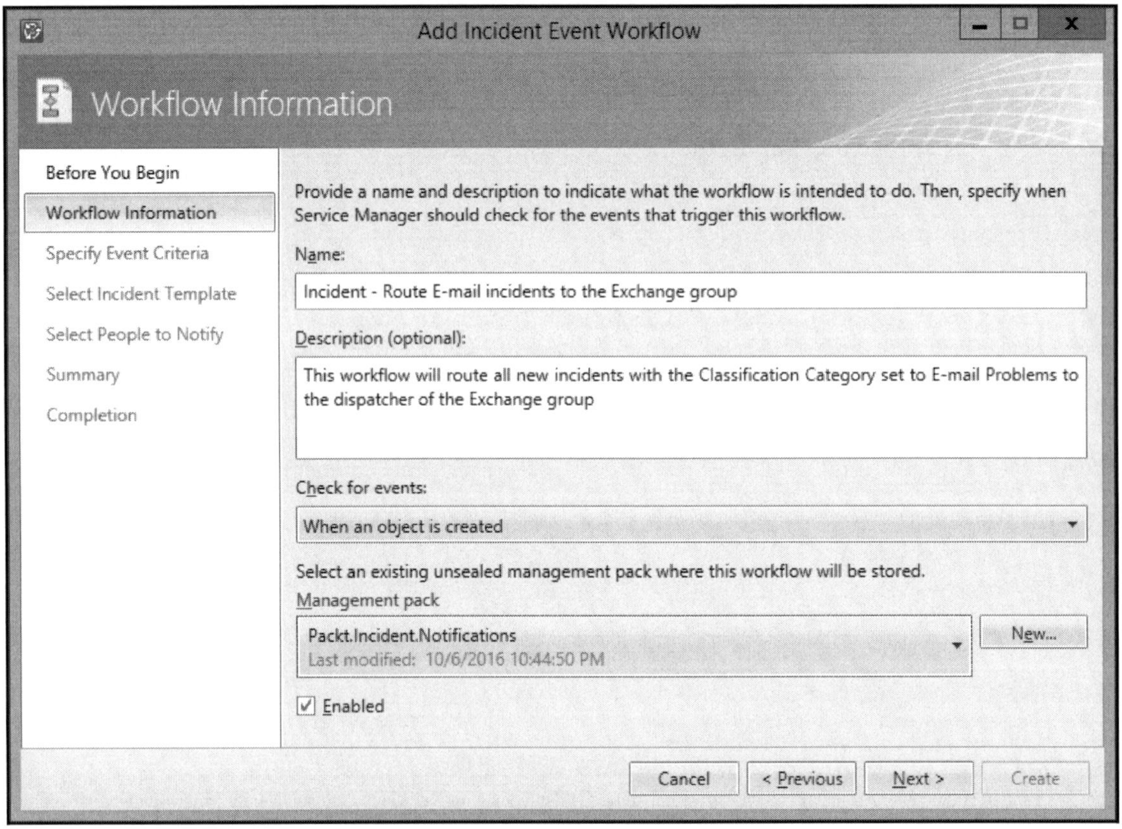

	Add Incident Event Workflow	— □ X

Workflow Information

Before You Begin

Workflow Information

Specify Event Criteria

Select Incident Template

Select People to Notify

Summary

Completion

Provide a name and description to indicate what the workflow is intended to do. Then, specify when Service Manager should check for the events that trigger this workflow.

N̲ame:

> Incident - Route E-mail incidents to the Exchange group

D̲escription (optional):

> This workflow will route all new incidents with the Classification Category set to E-mail Problems to the dispatcher of the Exchange group

C̲heck for events:

> When an object is created ▾

Select an existing unsealed management pack where this workflow will be stored.
Management pack

> Packt.Incident.Notifications
> Last modified: 10/6/2016 10:44:50 PM ▾ | N̲ew...

☑ Enabled

Cancel | < P̲revious | N̲ext > | Create

10. In the **Specify Event Criteria** page, locate the **Classification Category** in the **Available Properties**, select it, and click on **Add**. This will add the **Classification Category** to the **Criteria** section and all you have to do now is select **E-Mail problems** from the list. Click on **Next**.

With this criteria specified, the workflow will now trigger on every new incident where the **Classification Category** is set to **E-Mail Problems**.

11. On the **Select Incident Template** page, choose to apply the template that you created in Step 2, by checking the **Apply the following template** option and selecting your template from the list. Click on **Next**.
12. Do not enable notifications. Click on **Next** followed by **Create** and **Close**.
13. Click on **OK** in the **Incident Event Workflow Configuration** to close the workflow properties.

How it works...

When an incident is created and the **Classification Category** is set to **E-Mail Problems**, the workflow will trigger and apply the template in which the Assigned To user is set to the dispatcher of the Exchange group. This will happen regardless of the incident being created from the portal, by e-mail, or by an analyst in the console.

To test this workflow, create a new incident and make sure that the **Classification Category** is set to **E-Mail Problems**. Once you've created the Incident, give the workflow a minute to run. After that, open the incident to confirm that the Assigned To user is set to the dispatcher of the Exchange group.

See also

- For more information regarding templates, please see the *Creating an incident template* recipe in Chapter 7, *Working with Incident and Problem Management*
- For more information regarding workflows, please see the *Creating a subscription to notify the affected user upon the creation of an incident* recipe in Chapter 7, *Working with Incident and Problem Management*, to notify the affected user upon the creation of an incident

Downloading and installing SMLets

SMLets are a set of PowerShell cmdlets (pronounced as command-lets) to do administrative tasks and automate things in Service Manager. By using the different cmdlets in SMLets you can do things that you are unable to do from the console and create some very powerful scripts. This makes the SMLets a vital part of any Service Manager administrator's toolbox.

There are in fact an official Service Manager PowerShell module included in the product, and even if it's becoming better and better, the SMLets still offers more powerful capabilities.

 Please note that SMLets is a community-driven open source project and is not officially supported by Microsoft. Members of the Service Manager product group was the original creators for SMLets and have done almost all the development.

Getting ready

Make sure that you have local administrator rights on the Service Manager management server in order to install the SMLets.

How to do it...

To download and install SMLets, follow these steps:

1. Open your favorite browser and go to `http://smlets.codeplex.com`.
2. Click on the large purple **Download** button on the right-hand side of the site and select a folder to save the file to.
3. Once the download is completed, locate the `SMLets.msi` file, right-click on it, and select **Properties**. Now click on the **Unblock** button in the lower-right-hand side of the **Properties** dialog. Click on **OK**. This step might not apply to your environment depending on your current security settings.
4. Log on to your **Service Manager management server** and copy the **SMLets.msi** file there.
5. Double-click on the **SMLets.msi** file to start the installation.
6. On the first page of the installation wizard, click on **Next**.
7. **Check the checkbox** to agree on the license agreement and click on **Next**, followed by **Next** and **Install**.
8. Once the installation is done, click on the **Finish** button.

How it works...

The SMLets should now be installed on your Service Manager management server and you are now ready to use the cmdlets.

 In order to use the SMLets you might have to change your PowerShell Execution policy settings. To do so, start a PowerShell prompt with administrator rights and run this command:
`Set-ExecutionPolicy remotesigned`

To confirm the installation, follow these steps:

1. Open a PowerShell prompt and import the SMLets module by running this command:

   ```
   Import-Module SMLets
   ```

2. Once the SMLets module are imported, run this command to verify that it's working:

   ```
   Get-SMLetsVersion
   ```

If everything is working correctly, you should see some information regarding the SMLets version, as shown in the following screenshot:

```
Administrator: Windows PowerShell                                    _  □  X

PS C:\Users\anders.asp> Import-Module smlets
PS C:\Users\anders.asp> Get-SMLetsVersion


TargetProduct        : Microsoft System Center 2012 R2 Service Manager
WorkingCopyRootPath  : D:/My Documents/Visual Studio 2012/Projects/SMLets/SMLets
URL                  : https://smlets.svn.codeplex.com/svn/Main/Source/SMLets/SMLets
RepositoryRoot       : https://smlets.svn.codeplex.com/svn
RepositoryUUID       : e17a0e51-4ae3-4d35-97c3-1a29b211df97
Revision             : unknown
LastChangedAuthor    : gritsenko
LastChangedRev       : unknown
LastChangedDate      : 07/01/2015 03:23:23
IsPrivate            : True
Changes              : {}
SMCompiledVersion    : 7.5.3079.0
SMInstalledVersion   : 7.5.7487.0
SM2012               : True


PS C:\Users\anders.asp> _
```

There's more…

SMLets will be used in several of the upcoming recipes in this chapter, so we won't be giving any examples on how to use SMLets in this particular recipe.

See also

`http://smlets.codeplex.com`

Please see the recipes *Using SMLets to delete a work item* and *Autoclosing resolved Incidents with SMLets and a custom workflow* in this chapter for examples of how to use SMLets.

Using SMLets to delete a work item

In this recipe, we will take a look at how you can use SMLets to delete a work item. This is something that you cannot perform from the console for several reasons. One of them being that this goes against all the rules of ITIL.

So why would someone need to delete a work item? Well, you might have created a couple of test work items to verify the production environment or to test a workflow, or something similar.

Getting ready

Make sure that you have downloaded and installed SMLets as described in the previous recipe, *Downloading and installing SMLets*.

You also need administrator rights within Service Manager to be able to delete a work item.

How to do it…

In this particular example, we will take a look at how to delete an incident. To do so, follow these steps:

1. Log on to the Service Manager management server where you installed the SMLets and start Windows PowerShell ISE.

2. In the ribbon menu of PowerShell ISE, click **Show Script Pane Maximized**, and then type the following:

```
Import-Module SMLets
```

3. Now execute the script by pressing *F5* on your keyboard.

The reason for executing this part of the script is to be able to use the PowerShell autocomplete function for SMLets. The autocomplete function allows you to press the Tab key on your keyboard to complete the command syntax. Try it out in the next step! Type `Get-SCSMC1` and press the Tab key; PowerShell should now autocomplete the command syntax.

4. Press *Ctrl* + *I* to get back to the script pane and type the following on a new line:

```
$IncidentClass = Get-SCSMClass System.WorkItem.Incident$
```

The `Get-SCSMClass` cmdlets are used to retrieve a class from Service Manager and as we are going to remove an incident, we need to retrieve the `Incident` class.

5. On the next line, type the following:

```
$Incident = Get-SCSMObject -Class $IncidentClass -Filter "Id -eq
IR495"
```

We are now retrieving a particular incident using the `Get-SCSMObject` cmdlets. The `Get-SCSMObject` cmdlets can retrieve any object in the Service Manager database. The `-Class` parameter tells `Get-SCSMObject` that we are looking for an object of the Incident class, and the `-Filter` parameter is used to specify which object of the incident class we want to retrieve. In this example, we are looking for an Incident where the ID equals `IR495`.

You can use the `-Filter` parameter for filtering the objects you are retrieving by any `property` of the class. However, you cannot use the `-Filter` parameter to filter on several properties at the same time or to filter on relationships.

6. Replace IR495 with the ID of the incident you want to delete. Then enter the following on a new line and press F5 to execute the script:

```
$Incident
```

7. The script will now run and display the incident. Before proceeding to the next step, confirm that this is the particular incident that you want to delete. There is no undo button if you accidentally delete the wrong work item!

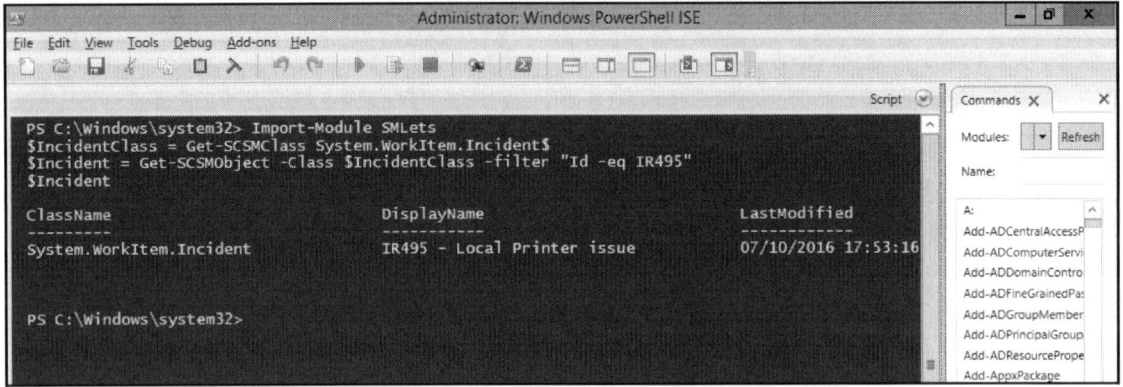

8. Press *Ctrl + I* to get back to the script pane again and add the following on line 4, right after $Incident (there's a space right before the pipe sign):

```
| Remove-SCSMObject -Force
```

9. This completes the script and it should now look like the following:

```
Import-Module SMLets
$IncidentClass = Get-SCSMClass System.WorkItem.Incident$
$Incident = Get-SCSMObject -Class $IncidentClass -Filter "Id -eq
IR495"
$Incident | Remove-SCSMObject -Force
```

10. Press *F5* to execute the script and delete the incident.

How it works...

This script effectively removes the particular work item from the database. By defining another filter parameter you can remove several incidents at once and if you skip the filter parameter, you may remove all your incidents from the database. This is both good and bad so think twice before running your scripts in a production environment!

 Deleting all work items in an environment doesn't mean that the ID counter will get reset. It will still continue to count from the last known value.

There's more...

If you would like to delete other type of work items, all you have to do is pass another class to the `Get-SCSMObject` command. The name of each class can be tricky to figure out if you are new to Service Manager, and especially to the SMLets, so here is a quick list of the most common ones:

- **Incident class** = `System.WorkItem.Incident$`
- **Problem class** = `System.WorkItem.Problem$`
- **Change Request class** = `System.WorkItem.ChangeRequest$`
- **Service Request class** = `System.WorkItem.ServiceRequest$`
- **Release Record class** = `System.WorkItem.ReleaseRecord$`

If you want to list all the available classes in Service Manager, you could run `Get-SCSMClass` without any parameters.

 The dollar sign (`$`) at the end of each class name isn't actually a part of the class name itself. It's used as a stop character, telling SMLets to not retrieve anything that starts with the class name. If you don't add the dollar sign, SMLets will actually retrieve subclasses of the class when running the `Get-SCSMClass` cmdlets. Try this by running `Get-SCSMClass System.WorkItem.Incident` and `Get-SCSMClass System.WorkItem.Incident$` and compare the results!

See also

`http://smlets.codeplex.com`

Please see the recipe *Autoclosing resolved Incidents with SMLets and a custom workflow* in this chapter for examples of how to use SMLets.

Exporting your unsealed management packs using SMLets

As part of your backup routines for Service Manager you should always take a backup of your unsealed management packs. But in order to take backup of these, you will have to export them from Service Manager first and doing so manually from the Service Manager console every day isn't really an option. A better way of doing this is using the SMLets.

Getting ready

Make sure that you have downloaded and installed SMLets as described in the earlier recipe, *Downloading and installing SMLets*.

How to do it…

The following is a pretty simple script that uses the SMLets to export your management packs:

1. Log on to the Service Manager management server where you have the SMLets installed. Make sure that the account used for logging in has Administrator privileges in Service Manager.

2. Open a PowerShell prompt and run this command to import SMLets:

   ```
   Import-Module SMLets
   ```

3. Once the module has been imported, run the following command (make sure that the target directory exists prior to running the command):

   ```
   Get-SCSMManagementPack | where{$_.Sealed -eq $False} | Export-
   SCSMManagementPack -TargetDirectory "C:\MP Backup"
   ```

4. That's all you need to type in order to export all unsealed management packs.

 If you try to run this command with both SMLets and the out of the box Service Manager PowerShell modules loaded, you will get an error saying **A parameter cannot be found that matches parameter name 'Path'**. This is because both contain a similar cmdlet expecting different parameters. The solution to this is simply not to load both in the same PowerShell session.

How it works...

So, all you have to do is run a single line of code to export all unsealed management packs. Let's take a close look at that line of code:

```
Get-SCSMManagementPack | where{$_.Sealed -eq $False} | Export-
SCSMManagementPack -TargetDirectory "C:\MP Backup"
```

The code consists of three different commands. The first one is `Get-SCSMManagementPack`, which is used to list all the management packs within Service Manager. But as we only want the unsealed management packs, we are piping the results to a where statement such as the following: `where{$_.sealed -eq $False}`. This part of the command will make sure that only the management packs where the Sealed property is set to `False` is retrieved. Now we can pipe the results to our third command, `Export-SCSMManagementPack -TargetDirectory "C:\MP Backup"` that simply exports the unsealed management packs to the directory we specified.

There's more...

You can also use the SMLets to import management packs. This is especially useful when testing management packs that you are working with in other tools, such as the Authoring tool.

To import a management pack with SMLets, simply do this:

```
Import-SCSMManagementPack C:\MPs\Packt.Custom.Workflows.xml
```

See also

`http://smlets.codeplex.com`

Please see the recipes *Downloading and installing SMLets* and *Autoclosing resolved Incidents with SMLets and a custom workflow* in this chapter for examples of how to use SMLets.

Creating a custom workflow in the Authoring Tool – exporting your unsealed management packs

We have seen how we can use workflows to send notifications or apply templates in the other chapters and earlier in this, but now we are going to take it one step further and create our own custom workflow. So when do you need to create a custom workflow? Well, you might want to do something else than applying a template or sending a notification, or you might want to target another class than the ones you are able to target from the console.

Getting ready

Make sure that you have completed the previous recipe, *Exporting your unsealed management packs using SMLets*, and that the Authoring Tool is installed and working properly.

How to do it…

In this example, we are going to create a workflow that takes a backup of all our unsealed management packs every day. To do this we will use the PowerShell script we created in the previous recipe as a base:

1. Start the **Service Manager Authoring Tool**.
2. Go to **File** and click on **New** to create a new management pack to store our custom workflow in.
3. Give the management pack a proper name and click on **Save**.

4. In the **Management Pack Explorer**, right-click on **Workflows** and select **Create**.

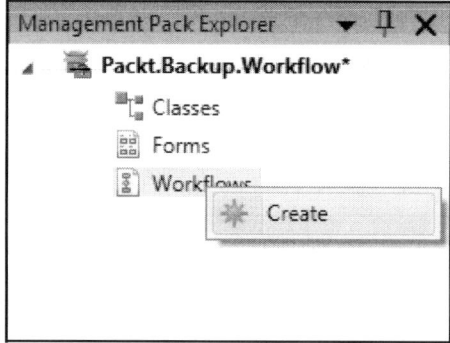

5. For the name of the workflow, enter BackupOfUnsealedManagementPacks (spaces are not allowed in the internal workflow name) and then click on **Next**.
6. In the **Trigger Condition** page, select **Run at a scheduled time or at scheduled intervals** and click on **Next**.
7. Specify whenever you want the workflow to run and click on **Next**, followed by **Create** and **Close**.

 Keep in mind that we want the unsealed management packs to be a part of our regular backup job, so make sure this workflow runs every day before the regular backup starts.

8. Now when we have defined the trigger to our workflow, we need to define what actually happens when it triggers. You should now have an empty workflow workspace in the Authoring Tool. Grab the **Windows PowerShell Script** activity from the **Activities** toolbox and drag it onto the workspace and release it on top of the text saying **Drop Activities to create a Sequential Workflow**.
9. Make sure that the **WindowsPowerShellScript1** activity is marked in the workspace and go to the details windows and change the **(Name)** to **RunBackupScript**. Then go to the **Script Body** field and click on the **...** button to launch the **Configure a Script Activity** dialog.

10. Click on the blue **View or Edit** Script bar and enter the following code:

```
Import-Module SMLets
$RootPath = "C:\Service Manager MP Backup"
$Date = Get-Date
$Path = $RootPath + $Date.ToString("yyyy-MM-dd")
if ( ! (test-path $Path))
{
$CreateOutput = New-Item -ItemType Directory $Path
}
Get-SCSMManagementPack | where{$_.sealed -eq $False} | Export-
SCSMManagementPack -TargetDirectory $Path
$DeleteFolder = $Date.AddDays(-14)
$DeletePath = $RootPath + $DeleteFolder.ToString("yyyy-MM-dd")
if (test-path $DeletePath)
{
$RemoveOutput = Remove-Item $DeletePath -Recurse
}
Remove-Module SMLets
```

11. The script is a refined version of the one we created in the previous recipe, we will go through all the code in the *How it works...* section later. It might be a good idea to run this in a PowerShell prompt before pasting it into the workflow script activity, in order to ensure that it works properly. When done, click on the **OK** button to close the **Configure a Script Activity** dialog.

12. That's all we need to do in the Authoring Tool. So let's save everything by going to **File** and selecting **Save All**.

13. We now need to copy the `BackupOfUnsealedManagementPacks.dll` file that the Authoring Tool has created for us to the installation directory of Service Manager on the management server (`C:\Program Files\Microsoft System Center\Service Manager`). The DLL file is located in the same folder as your management pack that you created in Step 2.

14. When the DLL file is copied, we need to import the management pack into Service Manager. So start the Service Manager console and go to **Administration** and select **Management Packs**.

15. Click on the **Import** task, locate your **Management Pack**, and click on **Import** followed by **OK**, when the import is done.

16. Now expand Workflows and select **Status**. Verify that our custom workflow is present by locating it in the list of workflows.

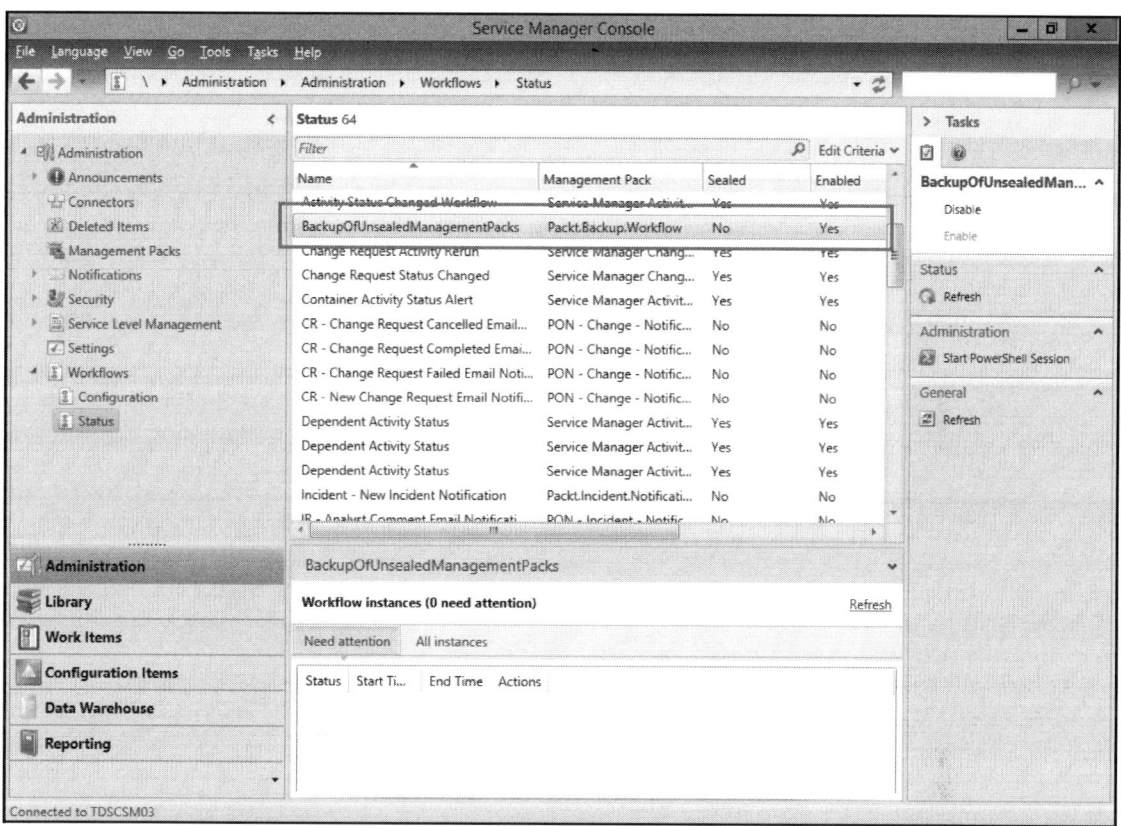

How it works...

So we created a custom workflow that triggers on a schedule and that runs a PowerShell script. The script itself exports all the unsealed management packs from Service Manager to a folder in a predefined path where the folder name matches the current date. If there's a folder in the same path with the name of the current date minus 14 days, it will also delete that folder to avoid filling up the disk.

The creation of the actual workflow is easy and pretty straight forward. Select a management pack to store the workflow in, define a trigger (schedule or database criteria), and create your actions (in our case, run a PowerShell script).

Let's go through the script:

```
Import-Module SMLets
$RootPath = "C:\Service Manager MP Backup"
$Date = Get-Date
$Path = $RootPath + $Date.ToString("yyyy-MM-dd")
```

The first line of code loads the SMLets module (as discussed in the previous recipe) and the next three lines calculate the target path, based on the current date. If you want to change the root folder for your management pack backup, you can simply change the $RootPath variable.

```
if (! (test-path $Path))
{
$CreateOutput = New-Item -ItemType Directory $Path
}
```

We then check if the folder exists and if it doesn't, we simply create it.

```
Get-SCSMManagementPack | where{$_.sealed -eq $False} | Export-
SCSMManagementPack -TargetDirectory $Path
```

This line of code is from the previous recipe and does the actual export of the unsealed management packs.

```
$DeleteFolder = $Date.AddDays(-14)
$DeletePath = $RootPath + $DeleteFolder.ToString("yyyy-MM-dd")
if (test-path $DeletePath)
{
$RemoveOutput = Remove-Item $DeletePath -Recurse
}
Remove-Module SMLets
```

Finally, we take the current date and subtract 14 days. We then calculate the path for the folder that were created 14 days ago and check if that folder exists. If it does, we simply delete it and all its content. The last line of code does simply unload the SMLets modules from the PowerShell session.

There's more...

The truth is that you might as well create a scheduled task within windows to achieve this, but when you are running the script as a workflow within Service Manager, you can use the console to check wherever it's executed or not. It also makes it easy to move this function between different environments – all you have to do is copy the DLL and import the management pack.

See also

- *Creating Management Packs to save your SCSM personalization* in `Chapter 2`, *Personalizing SCSM 2016 Administration* for more information on Management Packs.
- To learn how to use the Authoring Tool, see *Using the SCSM Authoring Tool* in `Chapter 11`, *Extending SCSM with Advanced Personalization*.
- See *Exporting your unsealed management packs using SMLets* in this chapter on how to create the required script for this recipe.

Autoclosing resolved incidents with SMLets and a custom workflow

To automatically close incidents that have been resolved for a number of days is a pretty common request among customers who've been working with Service Manager in production for a while. Even though this can be handled manually, it's much more convenient to automate this process. The thought behind all of this is that when the Analysts change that status of the incident to resolved, the Affected User has a number of days to contact IT before the incident is closed. If the Affected User contacts IT before the incident is closed, the incident gets re-activated, otherwise a new incident has to be opened.

Getting ready

Make sure that SMLets and the Authoring Tool is installed and working properly and that you have read and understood these previous recipes in this chapter:

- *Downloading and installing SMLets*
- *Using SMLets to delete a work item*
- *Creating a custom workflow in the Authoring Tool – exporting your unsealed management packs*

How to do it...

In this recipe, we will be using the SMLets to handle the actual automatic closure of resolved incidents. We will then put the PowerShell script in a custom workflow and schedule it to run once a day-just as we did in the previous recipe.

 Keep in mind that we are creating a script/workflow to modify a large number of incidents and if you mistype something you might end up closing every incident in your system! I strongly suggest that you test this in a lab environment before implementing it into a production environment.

1. Start the Service Manager **Authoring Tool**.
2. Open an existing or create a new **Management Pack** to store this workflow in.
3. Create a new workflow by right-clicking on **Workflows** in the **Management Pack Explorer** and selecting **Create**.
4. Give the workflow a proper name, such as **AutocloseResolvedIncidents**, and then click on **Next**.
5. Make sure that the **Run at a scheduled time or at scheduled intervals** is selected and click on **Next**.
6. Now specify when you want the workflow to run and click on **Next**.

 It might be a good idea to trigger this workflow outside your business hours since doing it during the day might be confusing to your Analysts. What if they actually are trying to re-activate the incident when the script is executed?

7. In the **Summary** step, make sure that everything looks okay, and then click on **Create**, followed by **Close**.
8. Now drag the **Windows PowerShell Script** activity onto the workspace.
9. With the **Windows PowerShell Script** activity selected, go to the **Details** pane and change the name to **AutocloseResolvedIncidentsPS**. Then go to the **Script Body** field and click on the **...** button.
10. Click the blue **View or Edit Script** bar and enter the following code:

```
Import-Module SMLets
$NumberOfDaysResolved = 7
$Now = (Get-Date).ToUniversalTime()
$ResolvedDate = $Now.AddDays(-$NumberOfDaysResolved)
$IncidentClass = Get-SCSMClass System.WorkItem.Incident$
$ResolvedStatusId = (Get-SCSMEnumeration
IncidentStatusEnum.Resolved$).Id
```

```
$CriteriaType =
"Microsoft.EnterpriseManagement.Common.
EnterpriseManagementObjectCriteria"
$CriteriaString = "Status = '$ResolvedStatusId' and ResolvedDate
<= '$ResolvedDate'"
$Criteria = New-Object $CriteriaType
$CriteriaString,$IncidentClass

$ResolvedIncidents = Get-SCSMObject -Criteria $Criteria

if ($ResolvedIncidents -ne $null) {
$Propertyhash = @{"Status" = "Closed";
"ClosedDate" = $Now;}
$ResolvedIncidents | Set-SCSMObject -PropertyHashtable
$Propertyhash
}

Remove-Module SMLets
```

Before proceeding to the next step, you should **try this script in a lab environment** to make sure it works as planned. If something is mistyped, you might end up modifying every Incident in your system! We will go through each line of code in the *How it works...* section later on.

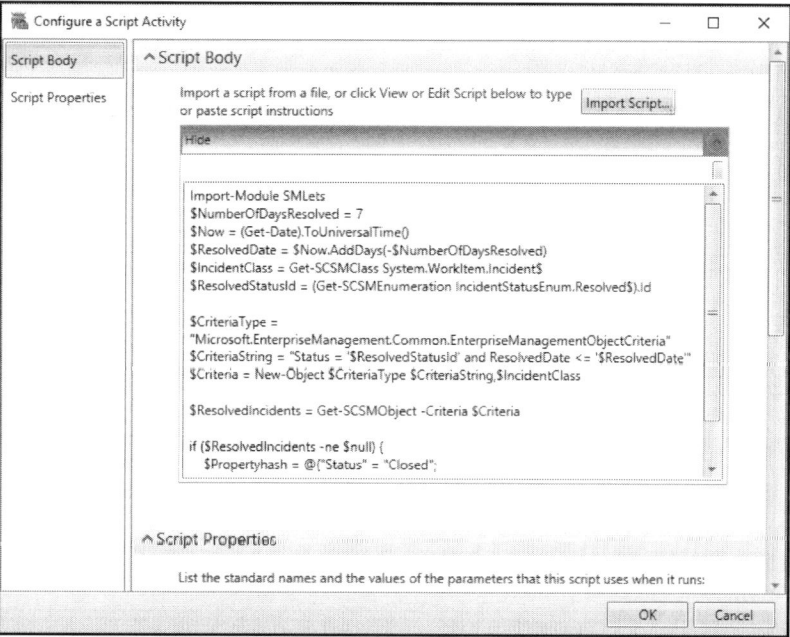

11. Click on the **OK** button to close the **Configure a Script Activity** dialog.

12. Now **Save** the management pack and copy the `AutocloseResolvedIncidents.dll` to the installation folder of Service Manager on the management server. When that is done, import the management pack.

13. Verify that the workflow is listed under **Workflows** | **Status**.

How it works...

The preceding steps are almost the exact same steps as in the previous recipe, what's interesting and new here is the actual script. So let's go through all the code:

```
Import-Module SMLets
$NumberOfDaysResolved = 7
$Now = (Get-Date).ToUniversalTime()
$ResolvedDate = $Now.AddDays(-$NumberOfDaysResolved)
```

As with most scripts, we start with importing the SMLets PowerShell module to be able to use all the commands. Then we set a variable to the number of days an incidents should have been resolved in order to be autoclosed. If you want the incidents to stay Resolved for another number of days, this is where you change that. Next we retrieve the current datetime in UTC format and then calculate the actual timestamp to use when looking for matching incidents to close.

```
$IncidentClass = Get-SCSMClass System.WorkItem.Incident$
$ResolvedStatusId = (Get-SCSMEnumeration
IncidentStatusEnum.Resolved$).Id
```

Here we use the `Get-SCSMClass` cmdlets to retrieve the incident class and the other line of code is to retrieve the GUID of the Incident resolved status enumeration. To get the actual enumeration object you can use the `Get-SCSMEnumeration` cmdlets, but in this case we are only interested in the GUID and that's why we are just getting the ID.

```
$CriteriaType =
"Microsoft.EnterpriseManagement.Common.EnterpriseManagementObjectCrit eria"
$CriteriaString = "Status = '$ResolvedStatusId' and ResolvedDate <=
'$ResolvedDate'"
$Criteria = New-Object $CriteriaType $CriteriaString,$IncidentClass
$ResolvedIncidents = Get-SCSMObject -Criteria $Criteria
```

This part of the code is pretty tricky. It is where we retrieve the Incidents with the `Get-SCSMObject` cmdlet. But instead of using the `-Filter` parameter, we are using another one called `-Criteria`. The reason for this is because `-Filter` can only handle **one** argument. So we could **either** retrieve the incidents with status Resolved **or** get the ones with a resolved date that is less than the one we calculated earlier. If you want to use several arguments when retrieving objects you will have to use the `-Criteria` parameter. The criteria type should always be `Microsoft.EnterpriseManagement.Common.EnterpriseManagementObjectCriteria`, but you will have to change the criteria string to fit your needs. See a link to an official blogpost on where to read more about this under *See also...*

If you run the code to this point, the `$ResolvedIncidents` variable should contain all the incidents that would autoclose if you ran the complete script. Use this to verify that your code is retrieving the incidents you expect it retrieve.

```
if ($ResolvedIncidents -ne $null) {
    $Propertyhash = @{"Status" = "Closed";
                      "ClosedDate" = $Now;}
       $ResolvedIncidents | Set-SCSMObject -PropertyHashtable
$Propertyhash
   }
    Remove-Module SMLets
```

The final part of the script will check if the `$ResolvedIncidents` variable contains any objects. If it does it will change the status of these to **Closed** and set the **Closed Date**. Finally, we unload the SMLets module from the PowerShell session.

See also

- Official blogpost – `Properly Querying SCSM Using SMLets Get-SCSMObject` cmdlet: https://blogs.technet.microsoft.com/servicemanager/2011/04/04/properly-querying-scsm-using-smlets-get-scsmobject-cmdlet/.

Automating your request offerings with Orchestrator

In Chapter 5, *Deploying Service Request Fulfillment*, we discussed how to create a Service Catalog and present your service offerings and request offerings on the self-service portal. This is great and allows the end users to report incidents and register service requests from the portal whenever they like. To make this even better we can automate the actual request by utilizing System Center Orchestrator.

> This recipe involves working in System Center Orchestrator and has some requirements within that product, which we don't have room to discuss in this book.
>
> For more information regarding System Center Orchestrator, see the official documentation on TechNet: https://technet.microsoft.com/en-us/system-center-docs/orch/orchestrator.

The whole process of creating automated request offerings can be summarized in these steps:

1. Create a Runbook in System Center Orchestrator.
2. Sync the Runbook to Service Manager through the Orchestrator connector.
3. Create a Runbook Automation Activity template-based on the Runbook created in step 1.
4. Create a Service Request template-that includes the Runbook Automation Activity created in Step 3.
5. Create a Request Offering based upon the Service Request template created in Step 4.
6. Add the Request Offering to a Service Offering and Publish these.
7. Test and verify.
8. Place into production.

This might seem like a lot of work to do, but the fact is that this is the easy job and once you get the hang of it you will be able to do it pretty quickly. The largest, most time consuming, and most important job is to get your idea documented and well thought through before starting these steps. Poor preparation leads to a bad result.

It's also important to test your automated request offerings in a test environment before publishing them to your end users in a production environment to make sure they are working as planned.

Getting ready

Make sure you have System Center Orchestrator up-and-running, that you have sufficient privileges to create new Runbooks and that you have the Integration Packs for Active Directory and System Center 2016 – Service Manager deployed.

In Service Manager you need to have the Self-service Portal installed and working properly as well as the System Center Orchestrator connector. You will also need Administrator permissions to perform the following recipe.

See the *Importing Orchestrator Runbooks* recipe in Chapter 4, *Building the Configuration Management Database (CMDB)*, on how to configure the Orchestrator connector and Chapter 6, *Deploying and Configuring the HTML 5 Self-Service Portal* for instructions on how to deploy the self-service portal.

How to do it...

In this recipe, we will create a fully automated request offering to create new users in Active Directory. As stated earlier, we will be working with Orchestrator, but won't have the opportunity to discuss Orchestrator in too much detail here.

Part 1 – Creating the Runbook in Orchestrator

1. Launch the **Orchestrator Runbook Designer**.
2. Expand **Runbooks** on the left-hand side and create a new Runbook in a suitable place.
3. **Check Out** the Runbook and change the name to **New AD User**.
4. Expand the **Runbook Control** integration pack on the right-hand side. Now drag the **Initialize Data** activity onto the workspace.
5. Double-click on the **Initialize Data** activity on the workspace to open the properties of it. Add two new parameters by clicking on the **Add** button. Rename one of the properties to **Firstname** and the other one to **Lastname**. Click on **Finish**

6. Drag the **Create User** activity from the **Active Directory** integration pack onto the workspace and place it on the right side of **Initialize Data**. Connect **Initialize Data** to this activity by dragging the small arrow next to **Initialize Data** to **Create User**.

7. Double-click on **Create User** to open its properties and click on the **Browse** button marked with **...** to select your **Active Directory connection** and click on **OK**.

The connection must be configured in Orchestrator for the Integration Pack, otherwise this menu will be empty.
For more information on how to do this, please see this link to TechNet: `ht tps://technet.microsoft.com/en-us/system-center-docs/orch/mana ge/active-directory-integration-pack`.

8. Click on the **Optional Properties** button and add **Display Name, First name, Last name, Password**, and **SAM Account Name**, and then click **Ok**.

9. Configure the properties like the following and click **Finish**:

- **Common Name** = `<Firstname from Initialize Data><Lastname from Initialize Data>`
- **Display Name** = `<Firstname from Initialize Data> <Lastname from Initialize Data>`
- **First name** = `<Firstname from Initialize Data>`
- **Last name** = `<Lastname from Initialize Data>`
- **Password** = `P@ssw0rd`
- **SAM Account Name** = `usr_<Firstname from Initialize Data>`

`<Firstname from Initialized Data>` means that you should get the information from the database by right-clicking the field and selecting **Subscribe | Published Data**.

10. Add the **Enable User** activity from the **Active Directory** integration pack to the workspace. Connect **Create User** to this activity and double-click on it to open its properties.

11. Click on the Browse button marked with **...** select your **Active Directory connection** and click on **OK**.

12. In the field for **Distinguished Name**, add the **Distinguished Name** from the **Create User** activity by subscribing to the database. Click on **Finish**.

13. Our simple Runbook is now complete and should look something like the following:

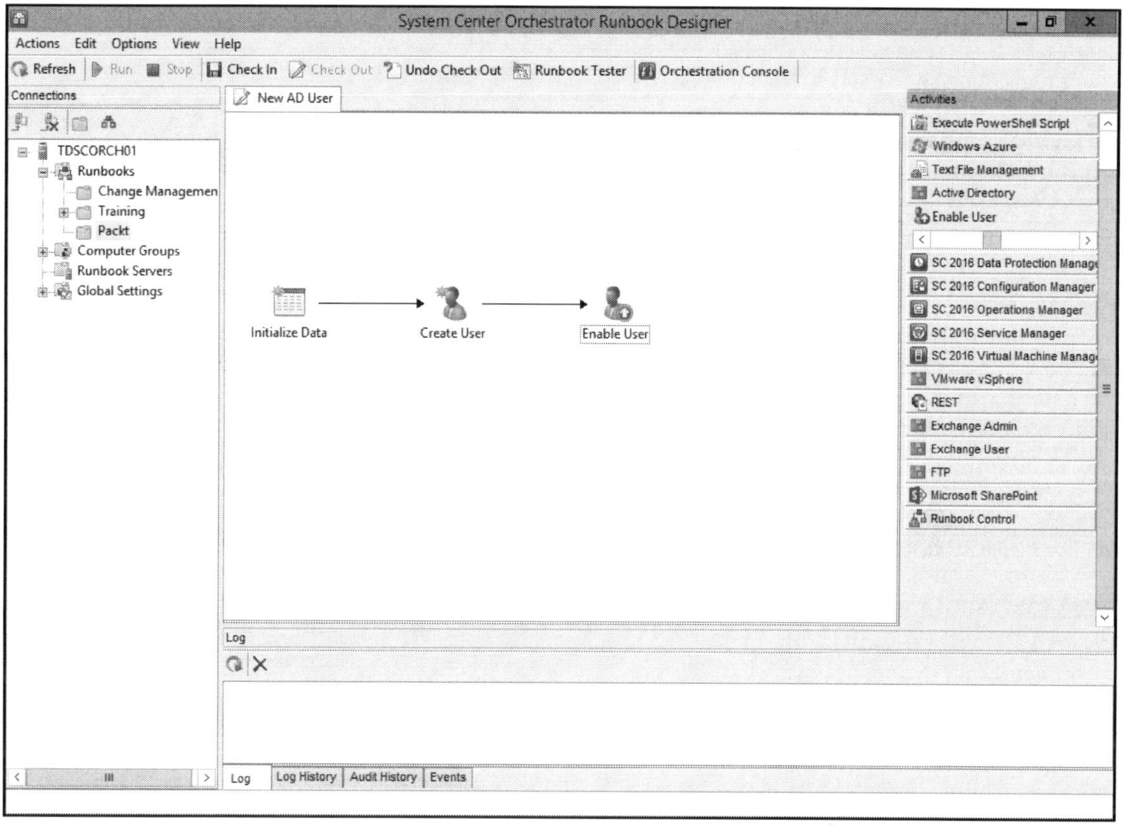

This is a really simple Runbook and should only be used for testing purposes. In a production environment you should considering adding logging, error handling, password generation, and so on.

14. Verify that the Runbook is working properly in the **Runbook Tester**. Once this is verified remember to **Check In** your Runbook!

Part 2 – Syncing the Orchestrator connector

1. Start the **Service** Manager console and go to the **Administration** workspace.
2. Go to **Connectors**, select your **Orchestrator connector**, and click on the **Synchronize Now** task.
3. Give the connector a couple of minutes to run, then go to the **Library** workspace, and select **Runbooks**.

4. Confirm that the **New AD User Runbook** we just created is listed.

Part 3 – Creating a Runbook Automation Activity template

1. Select the **New AD User** Runbook and click on the **Create Runbook Automation Activity Template** task.
2. Give the template a name, such as **RBA – New AD User**, select an existing management pack or create a new one to store this template in. Click on **OK**.
3. As the title of our Runbook Automation Activity enter New AD User then make sure to check the checkbox that says **Is Ready For Automation** in the top right corner.
4. Go to the **Runbook** tab and take note of how the **Parameter mapping** is done. By default, our properties should be mapped to **Text1** and **Text2**, as seen in the following screenshot:

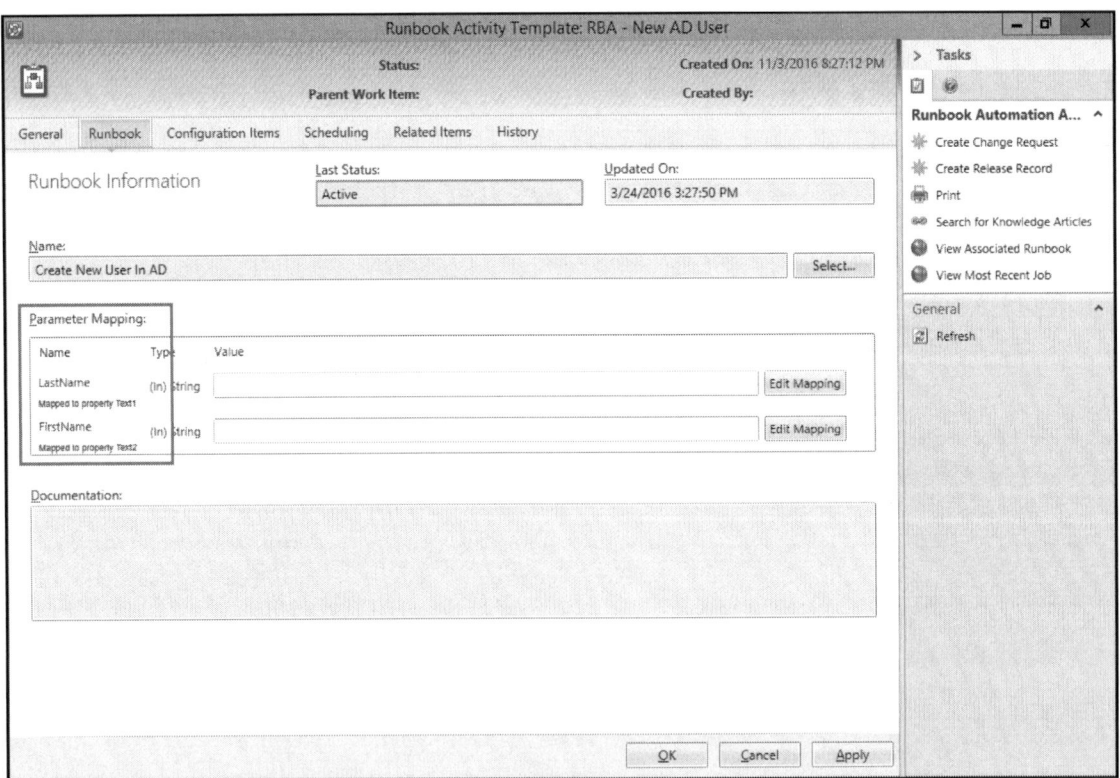

5. Click on **OK** to save the **Runbook Automation Activity Template**.

 You might of course specify more information in your template to make it more informative and seamless to your processes before saving it.

Part 4 – Creating a Service Request template

1. Next we need to create a **Service Request template** to use in our **Request Offering**. Go to **Templates** under the **Library** workspace.

2. Click on the **Create Template** task to create a new template.

3. Give it the name **SSP – New AD User** and use the **Browse...** button to select the **Service Request** class. Choose a management pack to store the template in and click **OK**.

4. Enter the following information on the **General** tab:
   - **Title** = Request of new Active Directory user account.
   - **Description** = The Affected User has requested a new Active Directory user account. See User Input for details.
   - **Urgency** = Low.
   - **Priority** = Low.
   - **Source** = Portal.
   - **Area** = Directory \ Account Management.

5. Go to the **Activities** tab and add our Runbook Automation Activity named **RBA – New AD User**. Click on **OK** when the **Runbook Automation Activity** opens.

6. Click on **OK** to save our **Service Request template**.

Part 5 – Creating a Request Offering

1. Now we will have to create a **Request Offering** to use when the end user request a new AD user account.

2. In the **Library** workspace, expand **Service Catalog** and select **Request Offerings**.

3. Click on the **Create Request Offering** task.

4. Click on **Next** in the **Before You Begin** step.

5. Enter **Request a new user** account as the title of the **Request Offering**. As the **Description**, enter `Use this Request Offering to request a new Active Directory user account.`

6. Click on the **Select Template** button, select the template that we just created called **SSP – New AD User**, and click on **OK**.

7. Select a **Management Pack** to store this **Request Offering** in and click on **Next**.

The management pack picker will be grayed out / disabled since our template is stored in an unsealed management pack, and since we can't create references to unsealed management packs, we are forced to store it within the same file.

8. In the **User Prompts** step add two text prompts. One prompt called **Please enter the first name of the new user** and the other one called **Please enter the last name of the new user**. Click on **Next**.

9. On the **Configure Prompts** page you can apply certain configurations to the prompts, but in our case we will skip this. Click on **Next** to move to the next step.

10. We will now get to an important step for the automated request offering scenario-**Map Prompts**. In order for Service Manager to pass the parameters to Orchestrator once calling the Runbook, we need to map our parameters to the same properties that we configured the **Runbook Automation Activity** to pass to the Runbook in *Part 3 – Creating a Runbook Automation Activity template*, Step 4.

11. To do this, mark the **New AD User – (Runbook Automation Activity)** in the object picker and map the **Firstname** prompt to **Text2** and the **Lastname** prompt to **Text1**. Click on **Next**.

Again, if this mapping is done incorrectly, the Runbook in Orchestrator won't get the necessary parameters to run the Runbook and the Runbook will fail. This will also cause the Runbook Automation Activity and the Service Request to fail.

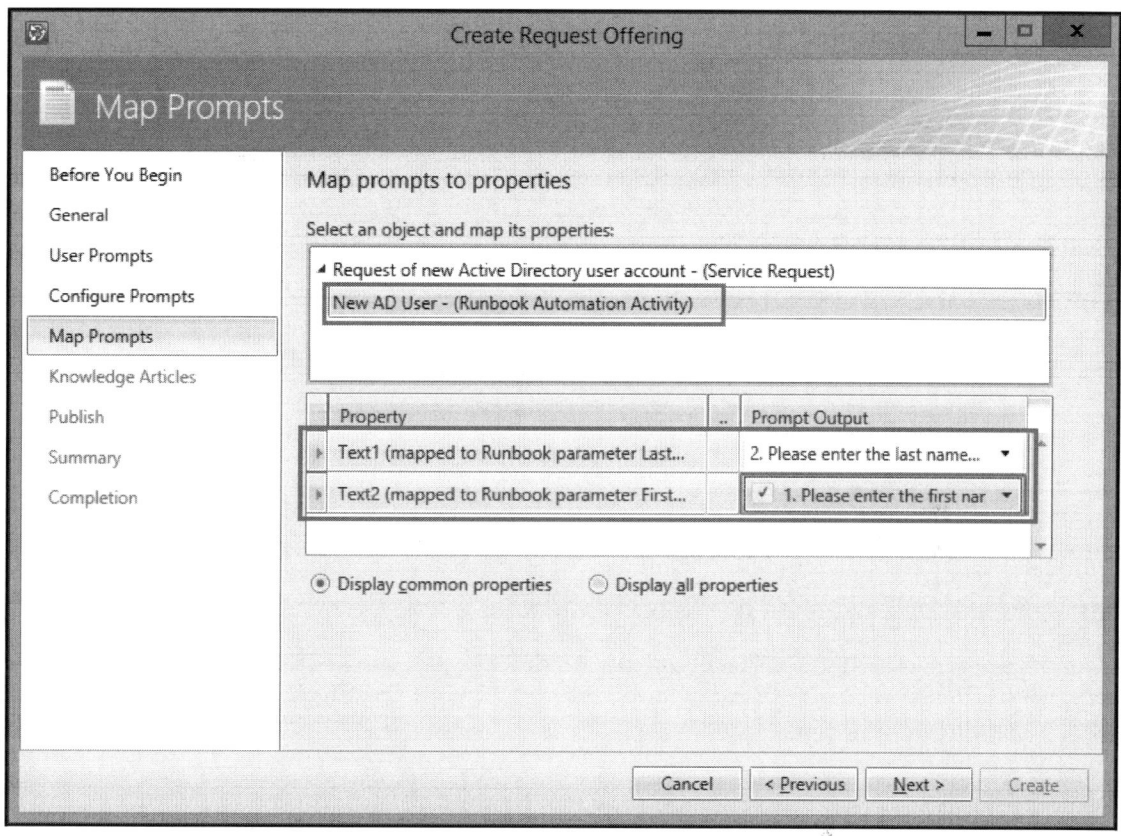

12. On the **Knowledge Article** step, click on **Next**.
13. Set the **Offering Status** to **Published**. Click on **Next** followed by **Create** and **Close**.

Part 6 – Creating a Service Offering

1. Select **Service Offerings** underneath **Service Catalog** in the **Library** workspace.
2. Click on **Create Service Offering**. Click on **Next** on the **Before You Begin** page.
3. Give the service offering the name **Account and Access management**. As the **Overview** and **Description**, enter `Includes Request Offerings such as Request New User, Request Group Membership etc.` Select a management pack to store the service offering in and click on **Next**.
4. Skip the **Detailed Information, Related Services**, and **Knowledge Articles** pages, by clicking on **Next** on each page.

5. In the request offering page, click on the **Add** button, locate and select our **Request Offering** called **Request a new user account**. Click on **Add** followed by **OK**.

6. Click on **Next** to get to the **Publish** page. Change the **Offering Status** to **Published**. Click on **Next**, followed by **Create** and **Close**.

Part 7 – Testing and verifying

1. Open the **Self-service** Portal and make sure that you can see our **Service Offering** called **Account and Access management**.

2. Click on **Account and Access management** and then click on **Request a new user account**, which is the request offering we also just created.

3. This will take you directly to the form where you should see our two prompts. Enter a first name and a last name and click on **Submit**.

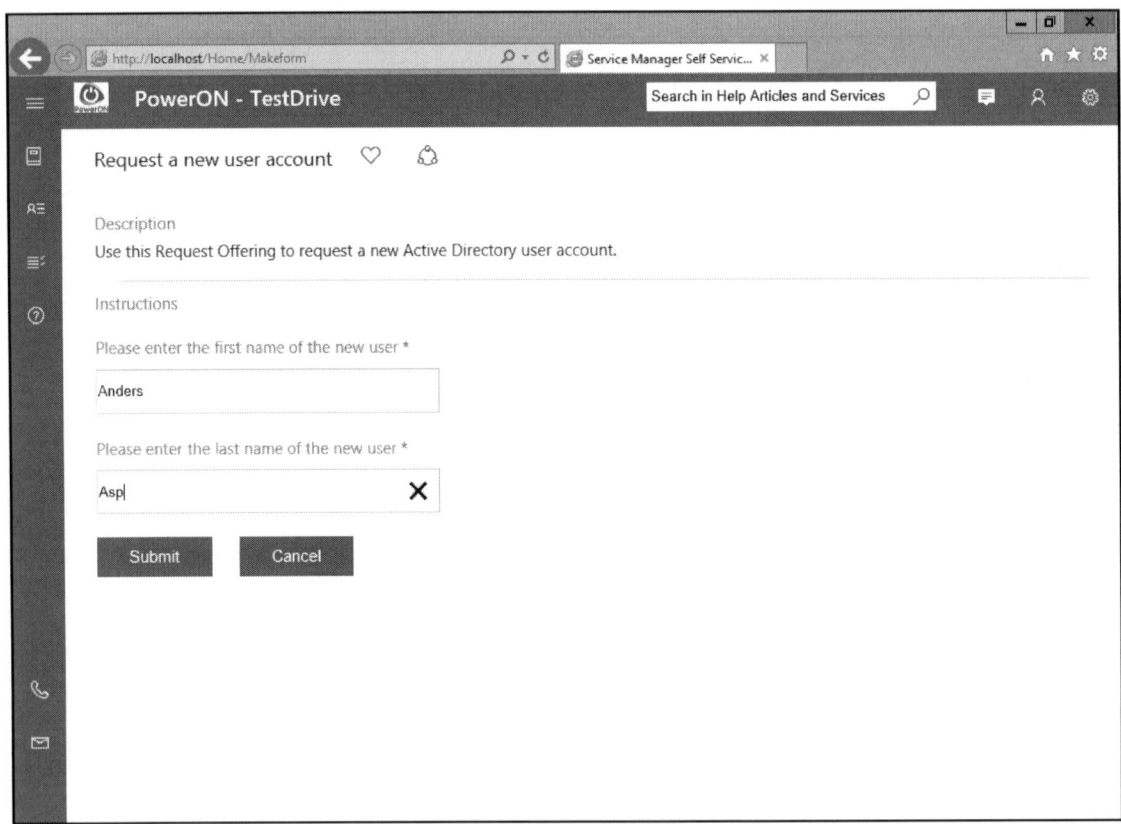

4. The service request will now be created and the **Service Request ID** will be shown in the blue header that is displayed for a short while. Take note of this ID.

5. Go to the **Work Items** workspace in the **Service Manager** console. Expand **Service Request Fulfillment** and select the **All Open Service Requests** view.

6. Locate and open the service request with the ID we noted in Step 4 above.

7. Verify that the information in the **User Input** section is correct and that the **New AD User** activity is **In Progress**.

 If you can't find the service request in the All Open Service Request view, it might already be completed or have failed. Look in the Completed Service Requests or Failed Service Request view to see if it's listed there instead.

8. Once you've verified that everything seems okay in Service Manager, open an **Active Directory Users and Computers** to see if the User account has been created.

9. When the account is created and the Runbook is finished, the Runbook Activity and the service request itself should change status to **Complete**.

How it works...

When you've created your Runbook in Orchestrator it can be synced to the Service Manager CMDB through the System Center Orchestrator connector in Service Manager. This Runbook object in Service Manager contains the information needed to trigger the Runbook through the Orchestrator web service, such as the Runbook GUID and required input parameters. From this Runbook object you can create a Runbook Automation Activity template to use in your different Work Items. Whenever this activity is used and the status of it is set to In Progress, Service Manager will call the Orchestrator web service and trigger the related Runbook together with the parameters mapped in the Runbook Automation Activity (as seen in *Part 3 – Creating a Runbook Automation Activity template*, Step 4).

There's more…

This was a very basic example of an automated request offering and as stated earlier you will need to plan and build all of this in more detail. There are many things to consider before you can create fully automated request offerings. Here are a few questions that might be good asking yourself when designing the automated request offerings:

- What do we want to achieve?
- How do we want it to be executed?
- Who is going to use this request offering?
- What kind of input do we need from the end user requesting this request offering?

When you have the answer to these questions the risk of having to redo the design of your automated request offering due to forgetting some details is much more unlikely.

Make sure that your Runbook is checked in

A Runbook that isn't Checked In cannot be triggered from Service Manager. This means that the Runbook Automation Activity within Service Manager will fail if it tries to trigger the Runbook.

Be careful when editing your Runbook!

It's pretty common that you need to go back to improve your Runbook or add new features to it, but be careful! If you edit or add new parameters in the Initialize Data activity, the Runbook object within Service Manager will be marked as Invalid. This means that it won't be able to trigger the Runbook ever again. The only fix for this is to delete the Runbook object and re-import it. This also mean that you have to redo everything that is based upon this Runbook object, such as Runbook Automation Activity templates, service request templates that includes the Runbook Automation Activity, and request offering based upon that template!

Service management automation and Azure automation

Unfortunately, Service Manager does not have a connector to either of the newer automation engines from Microsoft. However, there are ways you can use these tools anyways by calling them from PowerShell workflows, or you can use a third-party software that has custom created connectors for this.

See also

- For more information regarding request offerings, service offerings, service request, and the Self-Service Portal, please see `Chapter 5`, *Deploying Service Request Fulfillment*.
- For more details on how to create automated request offerings, take a look at the following blog posts on the official blog for Service Manager:
  - `http://blogs.technet.com/b/servicemanager/archive/2011/11/09/ demo-automating-service-request-fulfillment-from-the-scsm-service-catalog-with-orchestrator.aspx`
  - `https://blogs.technet.microsoft.com/hybridcloud/2011/11/04/introduction-to-service-manager-2012-service-catalog-part-1/`
  - `https://blogs.technet.microsoft.com/servicemanager/2011/11/08/request-offering-wizard-overview/`

Creating new work items with SMLets

When automating your ITIL processes, there will be situations where you will need to create new work items programmatically. For instance, you might have a scheduled change once a month or you would like to automatically create incidents when you discover an error in the event log of some LOB application.

In this recipe, we will take a look at how we can create a new service request with included activities directly from PowerShell.

The end result would look like this:

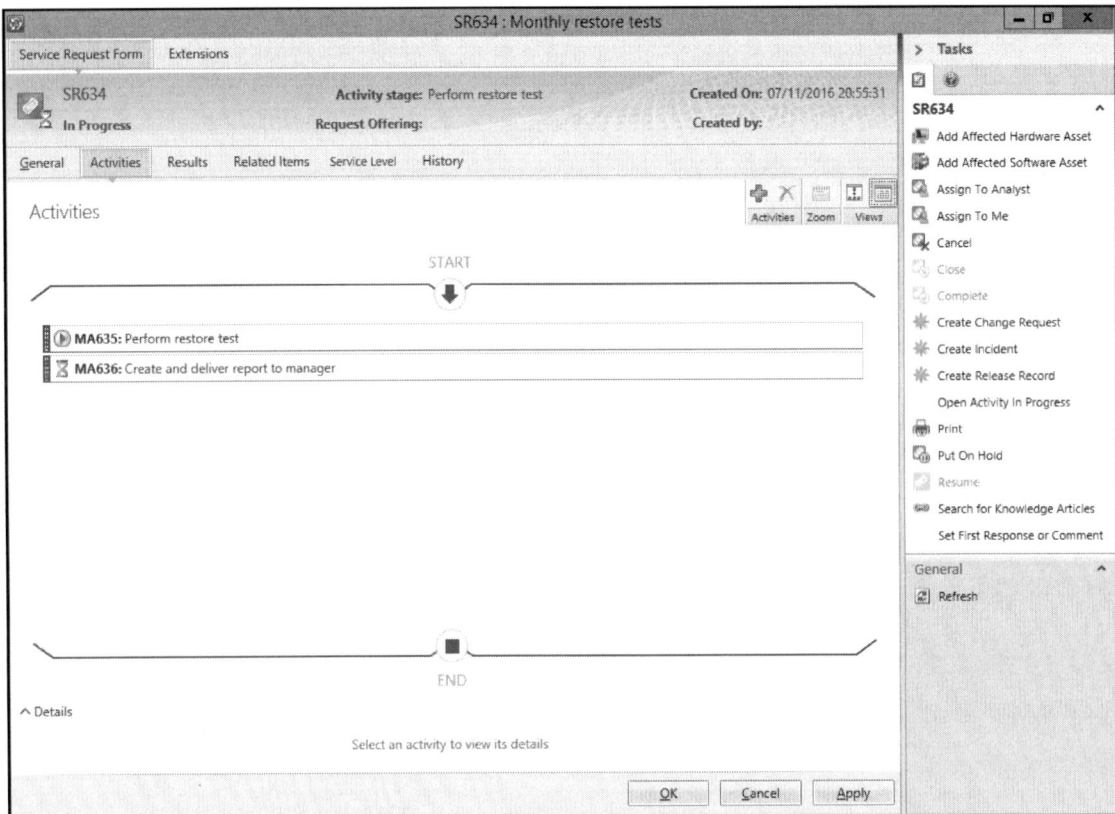

Getting ready

Make sure that you've followed the *Downloading and installing SMLets* recipe earlier in this chapter. It's also very good if you have tried the other recipes that have something to do with PowerShell and/or SMLets, as the syntax for what we are going to do here can be quite complex otherwise.

How to do it...

Using SMLets we will create a new service request that includes two manual activities. This service request is a part of the backup-teams routine to perform restore tests of the company's backups:

1. On a machine that has SMLets installed, start PowerShell ISE.

2. Write the following piece of code and press F5 on your keyboard. This will ensure that the module is loaded and that you can use tab-completion for commands in SMLets:

   ```
   Import-module SMLets
   ```

3. With the SMLets loaded, we will need to get some enumerations to use when creating our new service request:

   ```
   $UrgencyLowEnum = Get-SCSMEnumeration ServiceRequestUrgencyEnum.Low$
   $PriorityLowEnum = Get-SCSMEnumeration
   ServiceRequestPriorityEnum.Low$
   $SourceOtherEnum = Get-SCSMEnumeration
   ServiceRequestSourceEnum.Other$
   $StatusNewEnum = Get-SCSMEnumeration ServiceRequestStatusEnum.New$
   ```

4. With the enumerations retrieved, we can now continue to create our Property Hash Table for the **Service Request** itself:

   ```
   $SRPropertyHash = @{
   "Id" = "SR{0}";
   "Title" = "Monthly restore tests";
   "Description" = "This is a recurring Service Request to ensure
   that we do
   restore test of our backups";
   "Urgency" = $UrgencyLowEnum;
   "Priority" = $PriorityLowEnum;
   "Source" = $SourceOtherEnum;
   "Status" = $StatusNewEnum;
   }
   ```

5. Then we have the Property Hash Tables for our two **Manual Activities**:

   ```
   $FirstMAPropertyHash = @{
   "Id" = "MA{0}";
   "SequenceID" = "0";
   "Title" = "Perform restore test";
   "Description" = "Perform a restore test of a random backup that
   hasn't
   ```

```
been tested for a while";
}

$SecondMAPropertyHash = @{
"Id" = "MA{0}";
"SequenceID" = "1";
"Title" = "Create and deliver report to manager";
"Description" = "Create a report of the results of the restore
tests and
deliver it to the system owner and your manager";
}
```

6. Now that we have all the base code, we need to create our Object Projection. This is the piece of code that ties the **Service Request** and the **Manual Activities** together with the help of a Type Projection. This is where it will get a bit tricky since we are working with several nested Property Hash Tables (note the double underscores in there!):

```
$Projection = @{
__CLASS = "System.WorkItem.ServiceRequest";
__OBJECT = $SRPropertyHash;
Activity = @{__CLASS = "System.WorkItem.Activity.ManualActivity";
        __OBJECT = $FirstMAPropertyHash;
      },
    @{__CLASS = "System.WorkItem.Activity.ManualActivity";
        __OBJECT = $SecondMAPropertyHash;
      }
}
```

7. Then there's the last piece of code – the code that will commit the Object Projection to **Service Manager**. In other words, the step that create the **Service Request** with two containing **Manual Activities**:

```
New-SCSMObjectProjection -Type
"System.WorkItem.ServiceRequestAndActivityViewProjection"
-Projection $Projection
```

8. When you've entered all this code, it should look something like this:

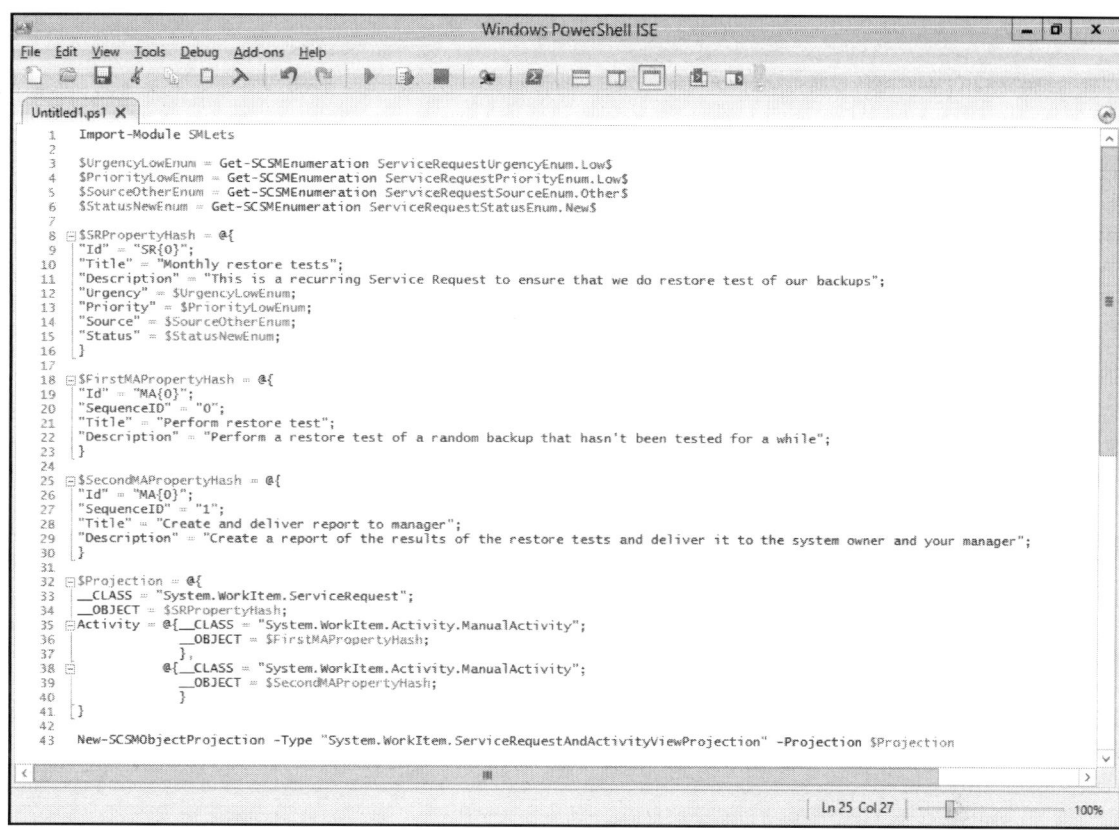

9. Execute the code by pressing F5 in **PowerShell ISE**. Make sure that the code is executed without any error and open a **Service Manager** console to ensure that the **Service Request** was created.

How it works...

Let's take a closer look at the code and analyze what each part does:

```
Import-Module SMLets

$UrgencyLowEnum = Get-SCSMEnumeration ServiceRequestUrgencyEnum.Low$
$PriorityLowEnum = Get-SCSMEnumeration ServiceRequestPriorityEnum.Low$
$SourceOtherEnum = Get-SCSMEnumeration ServiceRequestSourceEnum.Other$
$StatusNewEnum = Get-SCSMEnumeration ServiceRequestStatusEnum.New$
```

This first part is pretty straight forward and is something that we've worked with several times in this book already. We are simply loading the SMLets module and retrieving some enumerations to use in the script going forward.

```
$SRPropertyHash = @{
"Id" = "SR{0}";
"Title" = "Monthly restore tests";
"Description" = "This is a recurring Service Request to ensure that we do
restore test of our backups";
"Urgency" = $UrgencyLowEnum;
"Priority" = $PriorityLowEnum;
"Source" = $SourceOtherEnum;
"Status" = $StatusNewEnum;
}
```

Here we're creating a property hash table to store all the properties of the service request we are going to create. There are two key rows in this part, the first one is `"Id" = "SR{0}";` This little piece of code tells Service Manager to create a new ID for this service request and use the prefix `SR`. The `{0}` part simply tells the system to take the next ID number from the internal counter. The second part that is important in the preceding code, is where we define the status of the service request, `"Status" = $StatusNewEnum;`. You need to create the new service request with status `New` – otherwise the internal Workflow engine will not pick it up as an ordinary service request and set the status of containing activities as it should.

```
$FirstMAPropertyHash = @{
"Id" = "MA{0}";
"SequenceID" = "0";
"Title" = "Perform restore test";
"Description" = "Perform a restore test of a random backup
that hasn't been tested for a while";
}
$SecondMAPropertyHash = @{
"Id" = "MA{0}";
"SequenceID" = "1";
"Title" = "Create and deliver report to manager";
"Description" = "Create a report of the results of the
restore tests and deliver it to the system owner and your
manager";
}
```

Here's another two property hash tables, but these two are for the containing manual activities. Just like on the service request we have to define the ID with the prefix and the {0} ID counter. But another very important part of these two property hash tables is the SequenceID. The Sequence ID tells the system in which order the activities should be listed and also initiated when the service request is created. If you forget to set the Sequence ID, the internal workflow engine will not know in which order to execute the activities and you will be unable to complete any of them within the console.

```
$Projection = @{
__CLASS = "System.WorkItem.ServiceRequest";
__OBJECT = $SRPropertyHash;
Activity = @{__CLASS =
"System.WorkItem.Activity.ManualActivity";
            __OBJECT = $FirstMAPropertyHash;
            },
         @{__CLASS =
            "System.WorkItem.Activity.ManualActivity";
            __OBJECT = $SecondMAPropertyHash;
            }
}
New-SCSMObjectProjection -Type
"System.WorkItem.ServiceRequestAndActivityViewProjection" -
Projection $Projection
```

Then we have this complex part, where we are defining an Object Projection and submitting it to Service Manager. The reason for us working with New-SCSMObjectProjection instead of New-SCSMObject, is that the relationship between the service request and the containing activities is of the relationship type called Membership. This means that the activities live in the context of the service request and have to be created at the same time as the relationship, hence we are forced to use New-SCSMObjectProjection.

But how do you know how the Object Projection object should be constructed? Well as you can see in the last line of code we are working with a type projection called System.WorkItem.ServiceRequestAndActivityViewProjection. If you use SMLets to retrieve that type projection, you should get this:

```
PS C:\> Get-SCSMTypeProjection "System.WorkItem.ServiceRequestAndActivityViewProjection"

ProjectionType: System.WorkItem.ServiceRequestAndActivityViewProjection
ProjectionSeed: System.WorkItem.ServiceRequest
Components:
   Alias                    TargetType                              TargetEndPoint
                                                                    --------------
   Activity                 System.WorkItem.Activity                Activity
   Assigned...              System.User                             AssignedWorkItem

PS C:\>
```

With that information we can see that the Seed or Class should be of `System.WorkItem.ServiceRequest`. We can also see that there is a relationship to the `System.WorkItem.Activity` class with the alias `Activity`.

So the object projection we are creating has to have the base of an existing or new service request. Then in the __OBJECT part of this service request, we have a property hash table for all the service request properties, and then we are using the alias `Activity` with two other nested property hash tables for our two activities.

There's more...

If you already have an existing service request to which you would like to add one or more activities to, you would use the same approach. But instead of using __OBJECT and a property hash table in the first level of the object projection, you would use __SEED and the actual work item object to which you would like to add these activities. Modifying the last part of our script to fit this method would make it look something like this:

```
$SR = Get-SCSMObject -Class (Get-SCSMClass System.WorkItem.ServiceRequest$)
-Filter "Id -eq SR629"

$Projection = @{
__CLASS = "System.WorkItem.ServiceRequest";
__SEED = $SR;
Activity = @{__CLASS = "System.WorkItem.Activity.ManualActivity";
            __OBJECT = $FirstMAPropertyHash;
            },
          @{__CLASS = "System.WorkItem.Activity.ManualActivity";
            __OBJECT = $SecondMAPropertyHash;
            }
}
New-SCSMObjectProjection -Type
"System.WorkItem.ServiceRequestAndActivityViewProjection" -Projection
$Projection
```

See also

See this blogpost for more information:

https://blogs.technet.microsoft.com/servicemanager/2013/01/16/creating-membership-and-hosting-objectsrelationships-using-new-scsmobjectprojection-in-smlets/

13

What's New in SCSM 2016 and Upgrading from SCSM 2012 R2

In this chapter, we will discuss the versions and updates that Service Manager has gone through since the release of version 2012. We will discuss the important changes and new features, and we will also give guidance on upgrading to Service Manager 2016. We will specifically cover the following aspects:

- What's new in Service Manager 2016?
- Preparing for Service Manager 2016
- Upgrading to Service Manager 2016

Introduction

Since its initial release back in 2012, Microsoft released various updates for the product, each of which not only fixed shortcomings and bugs in the software, but also introduced new features.

A total of three major releases for System Center Service Manager 2012 exist. They are:

- Service Manager 2012
- Service Manager 2012 SP1
- Service Manager 2012 R2

For Service Manager 2016, there has only been one release at the time of writing. For each major release, there were several minor releases made publicly available, commonly referred to as Update Rollup (UR).

In order to understand which changes are to be expected when you upgrade your environment of SCSM 2012 to SCSM 2016, it is important to know which version you are using to date.

To check the version of Service Manager that you are using, log on to your SCSM Management Server, and then open **Control Panel**, **Programs**, **Programs and Features**, **Installed Updates**, and then find the list entry with the highest version number for program Service Manager.

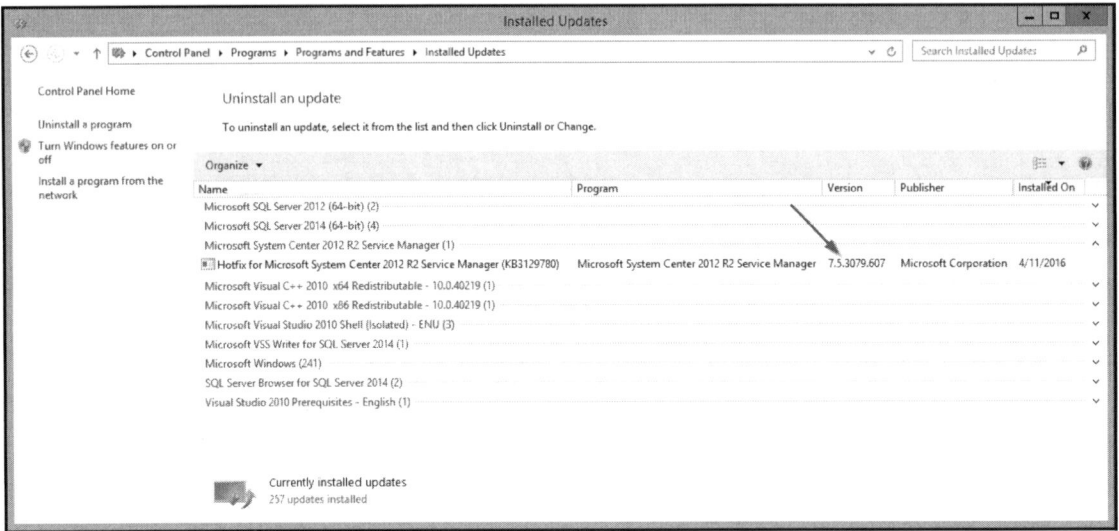

The preceding screenshot references a Service Manager 2012 R2 installation with Update Rollup 9.

Do not take a look at the **About Service Manager** dialog in the **Help** menu of the Service Manager console, as this dialog will only show the major version you have installed.

The following table lists all major and minor versions of SCSM since the initial release of Service Manager 2012. In the following chapters, when we talk about the important new features of SCSM, we will be referring to the major version and Update Rollup with which the feature was implemented.

Product	Update	Build	KB Article	Release Date
Service Manager 2012	Update Rollup 2	7.5.1561.106	KB2719827	07/24/2012
Service Manager 2012	Update Rollup 3	7.5.1561.116	KB2750615	12/04/2012
Service Manager 2012 SP1	–	7.5.2905.0		
Service Manager 2012 SP1	Update Rollup 2	7.5.2905.125	KB2802159	04/10/2013
Service Manager 2012 SP1	Update Rollup 4	7.5.2905.150 7.5.2905.158	KB2887775	11/14/2013
Service Manager 2012 SP1	Update Rollup 6	7.5.2905.179	KB2904726	04/22/2014
Service Manager 2012 SP1	Connector Update	7.5.2905.188	KB2970642	09/04/2014
Service Manager 2012 R2	–	7.5.3079.0		
Service Manager 2012 R2	Update Rollup 2	7.5.3079.61	KB2904710	05/26/2014
Service Manager 2012 R2	Update Rollup 3	7.5.3079.148	KB2962041	07/31/2014
Service Manager 2012 R2	Update Rollup 4	7.5.3079.236	KB2989601	10/29/2014
Service Manager 2012 R2	Update Rollup 5	7.5.3079.315	KB3009517	04/23/2015
Service Manager 2012 R2	Update Rollup 6	7.5.3079.367 7.5.3079.402	KB3039363	05/25/2015
Service Manager 2012 R2	Update Rollup 7	7.5.3079.442 7.5.3079.504	KB3063263	10/07/2015
Service Manager 2012 R2	Update Rollup 8	7.5.3079.507	KB3096383	10/11/2015

Service Manager 2012 R2	Update Rollup 9	7.5.3079.571 7.5.3079.601 7.5.3079.607	KB3129780	02/18/2016
Service Manager 2016	–	7.5.7487.0		09/26/2016

In November 2015, Microsoft released a new HTML5-based Self-Service Portal for end users, as a replacement of the former portal, which was based on Silverlight and SharePoint. Various updates have been released for this portal. They are listed in the following table:

Product	Update	Build	KB Article	Release Date
Self-Service Portal (HTML)	–	7.5.3079.507	KB3096383	10/11/2015
Self-Service Portal (HTML)	Hotfix #1	7.5.3079.523	KB3124091	12/14/2015
Self-Service Portal (HTML)	Hotfix #2	7.5.3079.548	KB3134286	01/26/2016
Self-Service Portal (HTML)	Hotfix #3	7.5.3079.572	KB3144617	05/11/2016

What's new in Service Manager 2016?

In this recipe, we will be discussing the important new features and fixes in Service Manager 2016. We will only cover changes that were introduced since the first release of Service Manager 2012 R2 (version number 7.5.3079.0).

If you want to read about the changes between Service Manager 2012 and Service Manager 2012 R2, please refer to the following online resource:

```
http://blogs.technet.com/b/thomase/archive/2013/10/29/service-manager-2012-r2-f
ixes-included.aspx
```

The chapter lists the important changes per Update Rollup. For a complete list of all changes, please refer to the following web resources:

Update Rollup 2: `https://support.microsoft.com/en-us/kb/2904710`

Update Rollup 3: `https://support.microsoft.com/en-us/kb/2962041`

Update Rollup 4: `https://support.microsoft.com/en-us/kb/2989601`

Update Rollup 5: `https://support.microsoft.com/en-us/kb/3009517`

Update Rollup 6: `https://support.microsoft.com/en-us/kb/3039363`

Update Rollup 7: `https://support.microsoft.com/en-us/kb/3063263`

Update Rollup 8: `https://support.microsoft.com/en-us/kb/3096383`

Update Rollup 9: `https://support.microsoft.com/en-us/kb/3129780`

Service Manager 2016:
`https://technet.microsoft.com/en-us/system-center-docs/sm/get-started/what-s-new-in-service-manager`

Important changes

The following important changes were introduced with the various Update Rollups for Service Manager 2012 R2:

- **Update Rollup 2**: When the Service Manager console runs in maximized mode, you encounter one or more of the following issues:
    - You experience slow performance in the console, and the console consumes excessive CPU resources.
    - Context menus in the console are not displayed as expected, and instead it is displayed at the upper-right hand corner of the main window.
    - Scroll bars for the work items preview pane do not display when you run in full-screen mode. Even if the scroll bars display, they are still inactive and you cannot move the slider.
    - Certain forms or wizards do not display appropriately. Specifically, only the left navigation pane displays and the right area is blank.
    - When you create or edit on a User Prompts page in a request offering, the page is not displayed appropriately.
    - When you scroll on an open work item or a configuration item form, the scrolling does not work. In this case, you can have the mouse held over the scroll bar for scrolling.

- **Update Rollup 4**: Data Warehouse Transform jobs have a hardcoded 60-minute time-out. Therefore, Data Warehouse jobs cannot be disabled for very long because the volume of data to be transformed can quickly pile up. This can cause an issue if the volume exceeds the amount that can be processed by the transform modules within the time-out period.

- **Update Rollup 5**: Enhanced in-event logging for DW jobs. Logging the batch start and completion events for all DW job categories in event log. The start and completion event will include the process category, process name, batch ID, batch start, or completion time.
- **Update Rollup 5**: Enhanced in-event logging for DW cube processing:
  - Time taken by Cube's batch ID to complete will be logged in seconds
  - Information about whether the Cube is processed under Analysis Services that are running in Microsoft SQL Server Standard Edition or in SQL Server Enterprise Edition
  - Event logs will be added during processing of each Dimension and Measure Group for each partition (if applicable) for both enterprise and standard editions of SQL Server
- **Update Rollup 5**: Added the new Windows PowerShell cmdlet Get-SCDWInfraLocations on the Service Manager management server to retrieve the following location information about its Data Warehouse infrastructure.
- **Update Rollup 6**: Service Manager 2012 R2 now supports Microsoft SQL Server 2014.
- **Update Rollup 6**: Several improvements for a significant reduction in sync time of the System Center Configuration Manager (CM) connector and the Active Directory connector.
- **Update Rollup 6**: The Active Directory connector sync schedule is now configurable through the console and Windows PowerShell.
- **Update Rollup 7**: Write collision avoidance. You can now save if another workflow or analyst has updated the same item simultaneously with disjoint changes. When a conflicting change occurs, an error will provide details about the conflicting fields to provide you a choice to incorporate disjoint updates and save the rest of the changes without refreshing the form. You can read more about the fix at the Service Manager blog.
- **Update Rollup 7**: Active Directory connector fixes. The Active Directory connector was updated to address a problem where the connector performed a complete sync after any domain controller failover. The issue put an unnecessary load on the workflow server, causing performance to degrade. Normally, the connector only syncs data that was changed since the last run.
- **Update Rollup 8**: New HTML5-based Self-Service Portal.

Along with the changes in the previous list, Service Manager 2016 comes with the following new features and changes:

- Performance improvements:
    - Improved work-item creation and update commit performance
    - Improved workflow processing
    - Higher work-item per second processing capacity
    - Group and queue calculations were improved significantly
    - Faster SCCM and Active Directory connector sync with optionally disabling ECL logging
- Support for Lync 2013 and Skype for Business
- New Date dimensions in Data Warehouse cubes
- Spell check is now enabled for work item forms in the SCSM console
- A new console task Open Activity in Progress, was added for service requests and change requests
- Changes to Setup supporting SQL AlwaysOn Availability Groups installation
- Support for .NET Framework 4.5.1
- Support for Microsoft SQL Server 2016
- Support for Windows Server 2016 with or without Desktop Experience

Features removed or deprecated

The following features and capabilities are not included anymore in the System Center 2016 Service Manager:

- Silverlight-based Self-Service Portal
- Microsoft IT GRC Process Management Pack SP1 for Service Manager
- Service Manager Cloud Service Process Pack (CSPP)

Preparing for Service Manager 2016

Although an in-place upgrade from Service Manager 2012 R2 to Service Manger 2016 is supported, there are some important aspects to be taken into account before you upgrade your environment to Service Manager 2016.

Supported upgrade paths

In order to do an in-place upgrade to Service Manager 2016, you must be running Service Manager 2012 R2 with Update Rollup 9 (version 7.5.3079.607 or later). If you are currently using an earlier version, you must first upgrade to Service Manager 2012 R2 and install the latest Update Rollup.

If you are running either or both Service Management Automation 2012 R2, and Orchestrator 2012 R2, in your environment, and you are using the Orchestrator connector to import runbooks into SCSM, you must first upgrade Service Management Automation and Orchestrator to version 2016.

Minimum hardware recommendations

Please make sure you meet the following minimum hardware recommendations before upgrading to Service Manager 2016:

Service Manager Management Server: 4-Core 2.66 GHz CPU, 8 GB RAM, 10 GB hard drive space

Service Manager Database: 8-Core 2.66 GHz CPU, 8 GB RAM (32 GB recommended), 80 GB hard drive space

Service Manager Data Warehouse Management Server: 4-Core 2.66 GHz CPU, 8 GB RAM (16 GB recommended), 10 GB hard drive space

Service Manager Data Warehouse Databases: 8-Core 2.66 GHz CPU, 8 GB RAM (32 GB recommended), 400 GB hard drive space

Service Manager Console: 2-Core 2 GHz CPU, 4 GB RAM, 10 GB hard drive space

Service Manager Self-Service Portal (standalone): 4-Core 2.66 GHz CPU (8-Core recommended), 8 GB RAM (16 GB recommended), 80 GB hard drive space

Service Manager Self-Service Portal + Secondary Management Server (recommended): 8-Core 2.66 GHz CPU, 16 GB RAM (32 GB recommended), 80 GB hard drive space

Operating systems compatibility

All server-side components of Service Manager 2016 can run on any of the following server operating systems:

- Windows Server 2012 R2 Standard, Datacenter
- Windows Server 2016
- Windows Server 2016 (Server with Desktop Experience)

Windows Server 2008 R2 and Windows Server 2012 are no longer supported.

The Service Manager console can run on any of the following operating systems:

- Windows 8.1
- Windows Server 2012 R2 Standard, Datacenter
- Windows 10 Enterprise
- Windows Server 2016 Standard, Datacenter

On January 3, 2017, Microsoft announced that the SCSM 2016 console is supported on Windows 7. More information can be found here: `https://blogs.technet.microsoft.com/servicemanager/2017/01/03/extending-the-support-of-platforms-for-sm-2016/`

SQL Server version compatibility

The Service Manager database and the Service Manager Data Warehouse databases can run on any of the following versions of SQL Server:

- SQL Server 2012 SP2 Enterprise, Standard (64-bit)
- SQL Server 2014 Enterprise, Standard (64-bit)

- SQL Server 2014 SP1 Enterprise, Standard (64-bit)
- SQL Server 2014 SP2 Enterprise, Standard (64-bit)
- SQL Server 2016 Enterprise, Standard (64-bit)

 SQL Server 2008 R2, and SQL Server 2012 with or without SP1 are no longer supported.

Browser support

The new HTML5-based Self-Service Portal is supported on the following browsers:

- Internet Explorer 10
- Internet Explorer 11
- Microsoft Edge
- Mozilla Firefox 42 and later
- Google Chrome 46 and later

Customizations and third party add-ons

While previous versions of Service Manager were using .NET Framework 3.5, Service Manager 2016 uses the .NET Framework 4.5.1. Consequentially, Service Manager SDK was also upgraded from .NET 3.5 to .NET 4.5.1.

 If you have customized Service Manager using compiled code and the SDK, your customizations are likely to stop working after the upgrade.

Any customizations using compiled code and the SDK must be recompiled using the new SDK binaries of Service Manager 2016. To fix your custom SCSM solutions, you have to:

- Recompile the solutions with the target .NET Framework 4.5.1.
- Some classes in some assemblies were moved to other assemblies. Modify your solutions to include references to the appropriate new SM assemblies.
- Remove version-specific references to SM assemblies. In Service Manager 2012 R2, some assemblies had a higher version (7.1.1000.0) than in Service Manager 2016. In Service Manager 2016, all assemblies have the same version (7.0.5000.0).

For more guidance on fixing your custom solutions, see the following blog post:

```
https://blogs.technet.microsoft.com/servicemanager/2016/08/03/scsm-2016-upgrade
-steps-for-custom-development/.
```

 If you are using third-party add-ons for SCSM, make sure to check with the manufacturer for updated version which will run on Service Manager 2016.

Once you have your reworked solutions and the new third-party add-ons at hand, you can perform an in-place upgrade to Service Manager 2016, and then import the new solutions into SCSM.

Self-Service Portal

The Service Manager Self-Service Portal was updated for Service Manager 2012 R2 and Service Manager 2016. The new HTML 5-based version replaces the Silverlight-based version. Use the following section that applies to the version that you want to replace.

Silverlight-based Self-Service Portal

If you are currently using the Silverlight-based Self-Service Portal, you must uninstall it before performing an upgrade to Service Manager 2016. The Silverlight-based portal is no longer supported.

If the Silverlight-based portal is **installed on a separate server that is not a Service Manager management server**:

- Uninstall the Silverlight-based portal

If the Silverlight-based portal is **installed on the same computer as a Service Manager secondary management server**:

- Uninstall Service Manager 2012 R2

If the Silverlight-based portal is **installed on the same computer as the Service Manager primary management server**:

- Add a new Service Manager 2012 R2 secondary management server to the management group
- Install the latest Update Rollup
- Promote the newly installed secondary management server to a primary management server role, which will move the current primary management server to a secondary role
- Uninstall Service Manager 2012 R2 from the server hosting the portal

HTML5-based Self-Service Portal

If you are currently using the HTML5-based Self-Service Portal, you must prepare the upgrade by following these instructions:

If the HTML5-based portal is **installed on a separate server that is not a Service Manager management server**:

- Upgrade the Self-Service Portal directly from Service Manager 2012 R2 to Service Manager 2016

If the HTML5-based portal is **installed on the same computer as a Service Manager management server**:

- Do not uninstall the Self-Service Portal or management server. Attempting uninstallation might create an unstable state.
- Download the **SM2016SSP_UpgradeFix_20160601.exe** patch, and install it on the server where the 2012 R2 Self Service Portal is installed. You can download the patch here: http://go.microsoft.com/fwlink/?LinkID=798214.
- Upgrade all management servers from Service Manager 2012 R2 to Service Manager 2016 (see the next recipe). The Self-Service Portal will also get upgraded along with the management server.

Remote SQL Server Reporting Services

If you are running SQL Server Reporting Services (SSRS) on a different computer than the Data Warehouse management server, you must use the following procedures to prepare the computer that hosts SSRS for the upgrade:

- Copy the `Microsoft.EnterpriseManagement.Reporting.Code.dll` file from the `Prerequisites` folder on the Service Manager installation media to the `\Program Files\Microsoft SQL Server\MSRS10_50.MSSQLSERVER\Reporting Services\ReportServer\Bin` folder on the SSRS server.

- On the SSRS server, open the `\Program Files\Microsoft SQL Server\MSRS10_50.MSSQLSERVER\Reporting Services\ReportServer\rsreportserver.config` file. Locate the `<Data>` code segment. There is only one `<Data>` code segment in this file.

- Add the following `Extension` tag to the `<Data>` code segment where all the other **Extension** tags are, and then save the file:

```
<Extension Name="SCDWMultiMartDataProcessor"
Type="Microsoft.EnterpriseManagement.Reporting.MultiMartConnection,
Microsoft.EnterpriseManagement.Reporting.Code" />
```

SQL Server 2014 Analysis Management Objects

You must install the SQL Server 2014 Analysis Management Objects on all management servers, the Data Warehouse Management Server, and on all computers hosting a Service Manager console. You can download the software from this link:

```
http://www.microsoft.com/en-us/download/details.aspx?id=42295.
```

Upgrading to Service Manager 2016

In this recipe, we will walk you through the steps of upgrading your environment from Service Manager 2012 R2 to Service Manager 2016.

Getting ready

Before performing an upgrade to Service Manager 2016, please make sure that you have carefully read the previous recipe, *Preparing for Service Manager 2016*, and that you have met all the requirements.

Before you start the upgrade, we recommend that you back up your Service Manager database, your Service Manager Data Warehouse databases, your reporting databases, and your encryption keys.

Due to the move to the .NET Framework 4.5.1 and changes to the SDK, the upgrade to Service Manager 2016 may break the custom solutions made in house or by third party (non-Microsoft), as discussed in the previous chapter. Make sure you have all new versions at hand before doing the upgrade.

 It is good practice to first test the upgrade in a lab environment.

How to do it...

The order in which you perform your upgrade tasks is important. You must start with the Data Warehouse management server, followed by the initial Service Manager management server, and then by any secondary management servers. Then you can optionally deploy the new Self-Service Portal or upgrade your existing portal.

Upgrading the Data Warehouse Management Server

You can skip this section and continue with the next chapter if you do not have a Data Warehouse in your deployment.

If you have installed a Data Warehouse in your Service Manager environment, you cannot perform and upgrade if you have not registered with the Service Manager data warehouse. Moreover, it is recommended that initial synchronization of the Data Warehouse is complete.

You will need to disable the Data Warehouse job schedules before you start the upgrade. To do so, log on to the Data Warehouse management server and start PowerShell, and then run the following script:

```
cd (Get-ItemProperty -path 'HKLM:\SOFTWARE\Microsoft\Microsoft Operations
Manager\3.0\Setup').InstallDirectory
Import-Module .\Microsoft.EnterpriseManagement.Warehouse.Cmdlets.psd1
Get-SCDWJob | ? {$_.Name -match 'Extract_'}  | foreach {Disable-
SCDWJobSchedule -JobName $_.Name}
Disable-SCDWJobSchedule -JobName Transform.Common
Disable-SCDWJobSchedule -JobName Load.Common
Disable-SCDWJobSchedule -JobName DWMaintenance
Disable-SCDWJobSchedule -JobName MPSyncJob
Start-SCDWJob -JobName MPSyncJob
```

In some cases, a problem with the upgrade process causes the MPSync job to fail after the upgrade is complete. To prevent this, please run the following script on the DWRepository database:

```
;WITH FactName
AS (
        select w.WarehouseEntityName from etl.WarehouseEntity w
        join etl.WarehouseEntityType t on w.WarehouseEntityTypeId =
t.WarehouseEntityTypeId
        where t.WarehouseEntityTypeName = 'Fact'
),FactList
AS (
    SELECT  PartitionName, p.WarehouseEntityName,
            RANK() OVER ( PARTITION BY p.WarehouseEntityName ORDER BY
PartitionName ASC ) AS RK
    FROM    etl.TablePartition p
        join FactName f on p.WarehouseEntityName = f.WarehouseEntityName
)
, FactPKList
AS (
    SELECT  f.WarehouseEntityName, a.TABLE_NAME, a.COLUMN_NAME,
b.CONSTRAINT_NAME, f.RK,
            CASE WHEN b.CONSTRAINT_NAME = 'PK_' + f.WarehouseEntityName
THEN 1 ELSE 0 END AS DefaultConstraints
    FROM    FactList f
    JOIN    INFORMATION_SCHEMA.KEY_COLUMN_USAGE a ON f.PartitionName =
a.TABLE_NAME
    JOIN    INFORMATION_SCHEMA.TABLE_CONSTRAINTS b ON a.CONSTRAINT_NAME =
b.CONSTRAINT_NAME AND b.CONSTRAINT_TYPE = 'Primary key'
)
, FactWithoutDefaultConstraints
AS (
```

```
    SELECT   a.*
    FROM     FactPKList a
    LEFT JOIN FactPKList b ON b.WarehouseEntityName = a.WarehouseEntityName
AND b.DefaultConstraints = 1
    WHERE    b.WarehouseEntityName IS NULL AND a.RK = 1
)
, FactPKListStr
AS (
    SELECT   DISTINCT f1.WarehouseEntityName, f1.TABLE_NAME,
f1.CONSTRAINT_NAME, F.COLUMN_NAME AS PKList
    FROM     FactWithoutDefaultConstraints f1
    CROSS APPLY (
                 SELECT   '[' + COLUMN_NAME + '],'
                 FROM     FactWithoutDefaultConstraints f2
                 WHERE    f2.TABLE_NAME = f1.TABLE_NAME
                 ORDER BY COLUMN_NAME
              FOR
                 XML PATH('')
              ) AS F (COLUMN_NAME)
)
SELECT   'ALTER TABLE [dbo].[' + f.TABLE_NAME + '] DROP CONSTRAINT [' +
f.CONSTRAINT_NAME + ']' + CHAR(13) + CHAR(10) +
         'ALTER TABLE [dbo].[' + f.TABLE_NAME + '] ADD CONSTRAINT [PK_' +
f.WarehouseEntityName + '] PRIMARY KEY NONCLUSTERED (' +
SUBSTRING(f.PKList, 1, LEN(f.PKList) -1) + ')' + CHAR(13) + CHAR(10)
FROM     FactPKListStr f
```

You can now start the upgrade process on the Data Warehouse Management Server by executing Setup.exe from the Service Manager installation media:

1. On the start screen, under **Upgrade**, click **Service Manager data warehouse management server**.

2. Confirm the two steps on the **Prepare for upgrade** screen and continue to the next screen.

3. On the **Product registration** screen, enter your name, the name of your organization, the product key, and accept the license agreement.

4. Make sure you meet all requirements on the **System check results** page. If you see the title **Installation cannot continue**, you will need to install some prerequisites before you can continue.

5. Setup will now read the configuration of your Service Manager environment and list the details on the **Configuration summary** page. Click **Install** to start the upgrade and wait for the process to finish.

6. On **The upgrade was completed successfully** page, if you have already backed up the encryption key, clear the **Open the Encryption Backup or Restore Wizard** checkbox, and then click **Close**.

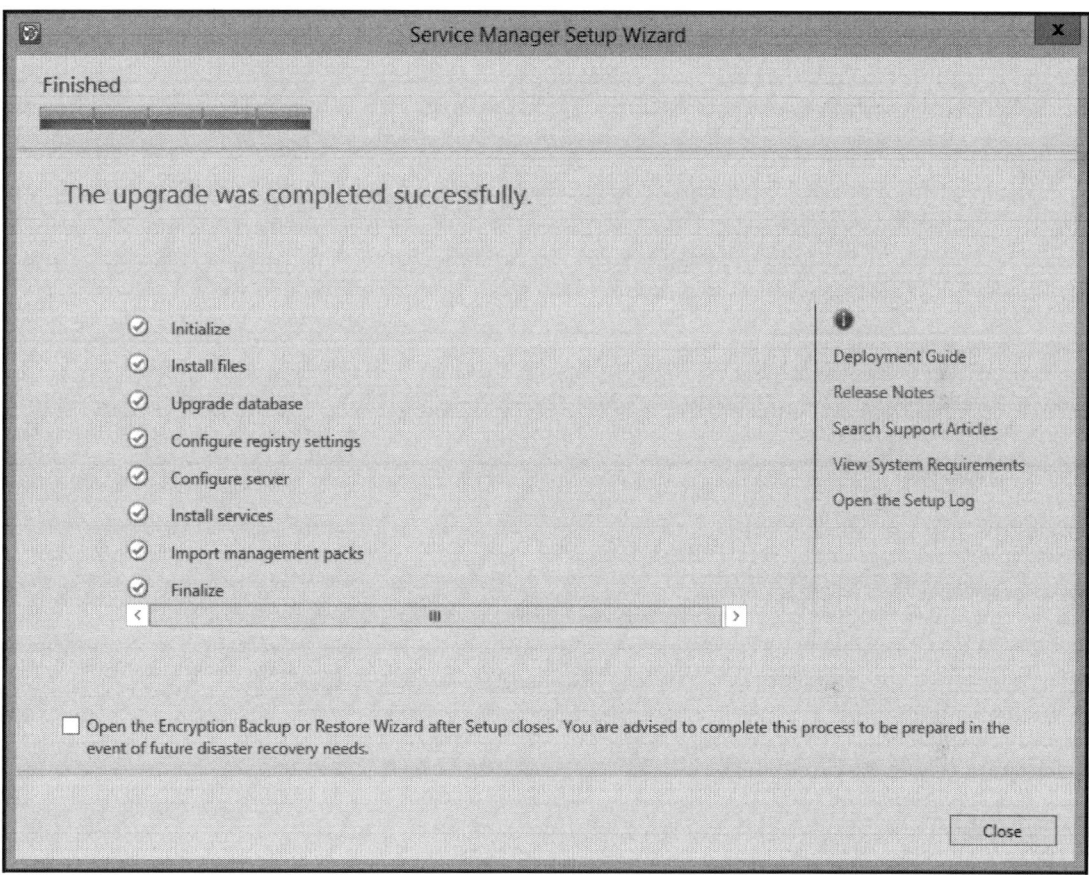

Upgrading the Service Manager Management Server(s)

You can now start the upgrade process on the management server(s). If you have multiple management servers in your environment, you must start with the workflow (primary) management server:

1. On the Service Manager installation media, double-click **Setup.exe** to start the Service Manager Setup Wizard.
2. On the start screen, under **Upgrade**, click **Service Manager management server**.
3. Confirm the two steps on the **Prepare for upgrade** screen and continue to the next screen.
4. On the **Product registration** screen, enter your name, the name of your organization, the product key, and accept the license agreement.
5. Make sure you meet all requirements on the **System check results** page. If you see the title **Installation cannot continue**, you will need to install some prerequisites before you can continue.
6. Setup will now read the configuration of your Service Manager environment and list the details on the **Configuration summary** page. Click **Install** to start the upgrade and wait for the process to finish.
7. On the **The upgrade was completed successfully** page, if you have already backed up the encryption key, clear the **Open the Encryption Backup or Restore Wizard** checkbox, and then click **Close**.
8. Repeat steps 1-7 for each additional management server in your environment.

Upgrading the Service Manager Consoles

Once all your servers are upgraded to Service Manager 2016, you can upgrade all your Service Manager consoles:

1. On the Service Manager installation media, double-click **Setup.exe** to start the Service Manager Setup Wizard.
2. On the start screen, under **Upgrade**, click **Service Manager console**.
3. Confirm the two steps on the **Prepare for upgrade** screen and continue to the next screen.

4. On the **Product** registration screen, enter your name, the name of your organization, and accept the license agreement.

5. Make sure you meet all requirements on the **System check results** page. If you see the title **Installation cannot continue**, you will need to install some prerequisites before you can continue.

6. Setup will now read the configuration of your Service Manager environment and list the details on the **Configuration summary** page. Click **Install** to start the upgrade and wait for the process to finish.

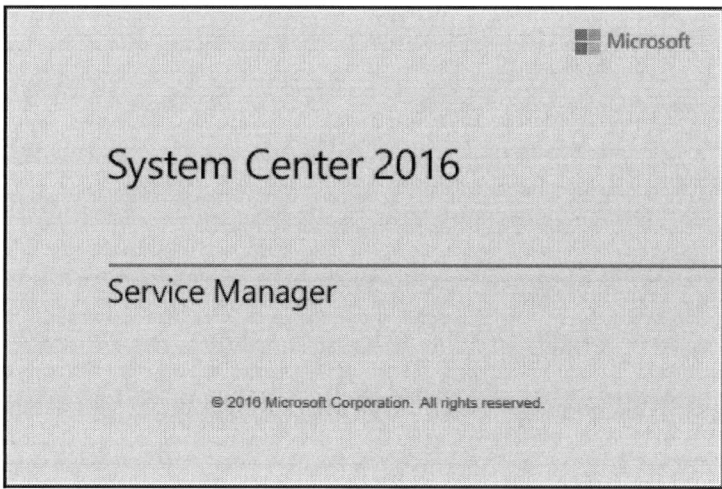

After Upgrading to Service Manager 2016

In case you have a Data Warehouse in your Service Manager environment, you will need to perform some post-upgrade tasks, which are explained in this chapter. You can ignore these steps if you do not have a Data Warehouse:

1. On the Data Warehouse management server, restart the **System Center Data Access Service** and the **System Center Management** service. You can do this by executing the following PowerShell command as an Administrator:

```
Restart-Service omsdk, omcfg
```

2. Enable and restart the Data Warehouse jobs by running the following PowerShell script on the Data Warehouse management server:

```
cd (Get-ItemProperty -path 'HKLM:\SOFTWARE\Microsoft\Microsoft Operations
Manager\3.0\Setup').InstallDirectory
Import-Module .\Microsoft.EnterpriseManagement.Warehouse.Cmdlets.psd1
Get-SCDWJob | ? {$_.Name -match 'Extract_'}  | foreach {Enable-
SCDWJobSchedule -JobName $_.Name}
Enable-SCDWJobSchedule -JobName Transform.Common
Enable-SCDWJobSchedule -JobName Load.Common
Enable-SCDWJobSchedule -JobName DWMaintenance
Enable-SCDWJobSchedule -JobName MPSyncJob
Start-SCDWJob -JobName MPSyncJob
```

3. On the computer that hosts SQL Server Reporting Services, restart the **SQL Server Reporting Services** service.

How it works...

Service Manager 2016 is designed in a way that supports an in-place upgrade from Service Manager 2012 R2 to Service Manager 2016, thus minimizing the efforts and risks involved with the upgrade procedure. However, there are still some important aspects that need to be carefully taken into consideration before performing the upgrade.

Community Extensions and Third-Party Commercial SCSM Solutions

Introduction

Similar to the majority of technology solutions in the market, Service Manager does not address every organization's specific requirements. Microsoft solution provider partners create solutions, which complement and extend the product to address some of the common requested extensions to SCSM. This appendix will provide you with a list of some vendor extensions to Service Manager.

Cireson solutions for Microsoft Service Manager

In this section, we will have a look at some solutions by Cireson for Microsoft Service Manager.

Cireson Self-Service Portal

The Cireson Self-Service Portal for end users is a complete replacement of the Microsoft Self-Service Portal for Service Manager. It empowers end users to perform everyday self-service tasks by providing an easy to use, personalized experience when reporting incidents, searching the knowledge base, and requesting services from the service catalog:

- Adaptive for any device to cater to the hyper-connected mobile world we live in
- 100% browser, mobile device, and OS agnostic
- Integrated HTML Knowledge Base for end users to solve their own problems
- Free download: `http://cireson.com/apps/self-service-portal-community`

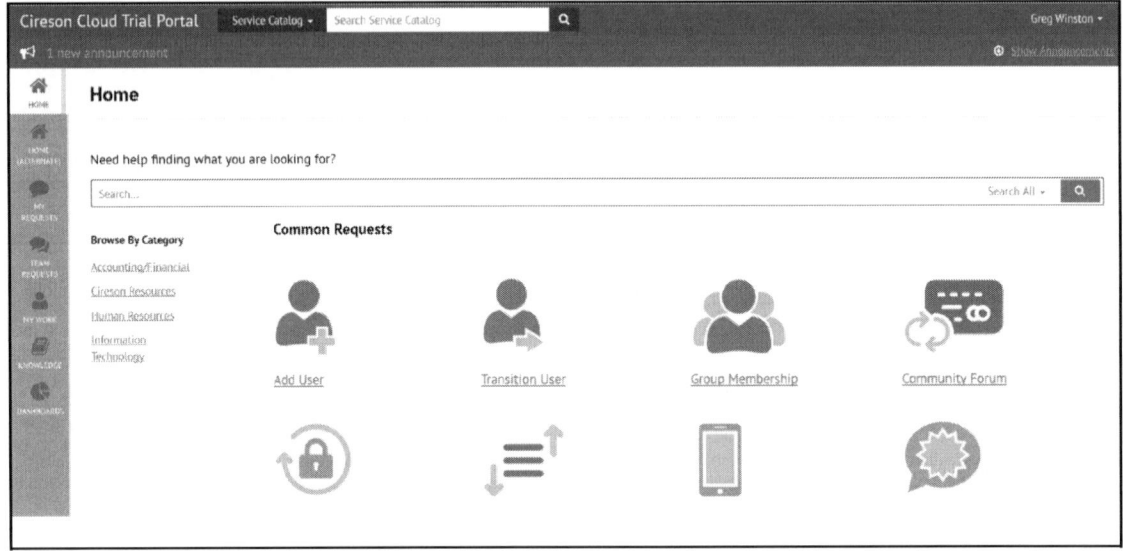

Provide end users with a single, consumer-friendly storefront experience

Cireson Analyst Portal

The Cireson Analyst Portal integrates seamlessly with Microsoft Service Manager to allow management of day-to-day activities on any browser, device, or OS. Built on cutting edge HTML5, the Analyst Portal is fast, adaptive, and highly functional, allowing for quick and easy access and management of items – with or without a desktop in sight:

- Cutting edge architecture with memory cache on web server for enhanced performance and scalability
- 100% browser, mobile device, and OS agnostic
- Integrated HTML Knowledge Base to create, edit, manage, search, and view articles in HTML format within the Portal

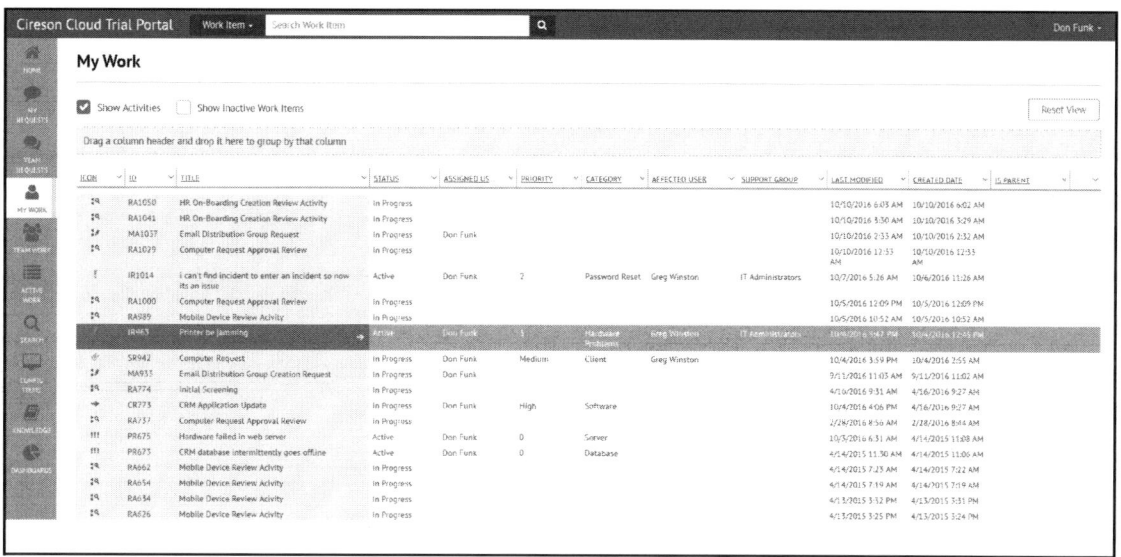

Easily manage all your active work in a single streamlined view

Cireson Dashboard Designer

Intelligent, dynamic, dashboards for business process domain areas provide insightful analytics to IT Managers including how a Service Management Team is performing, and helping to identify hot spots and data trends. Easily create your own dashboards with data from anywhere – Service Manager, System Center, or SQL data source.

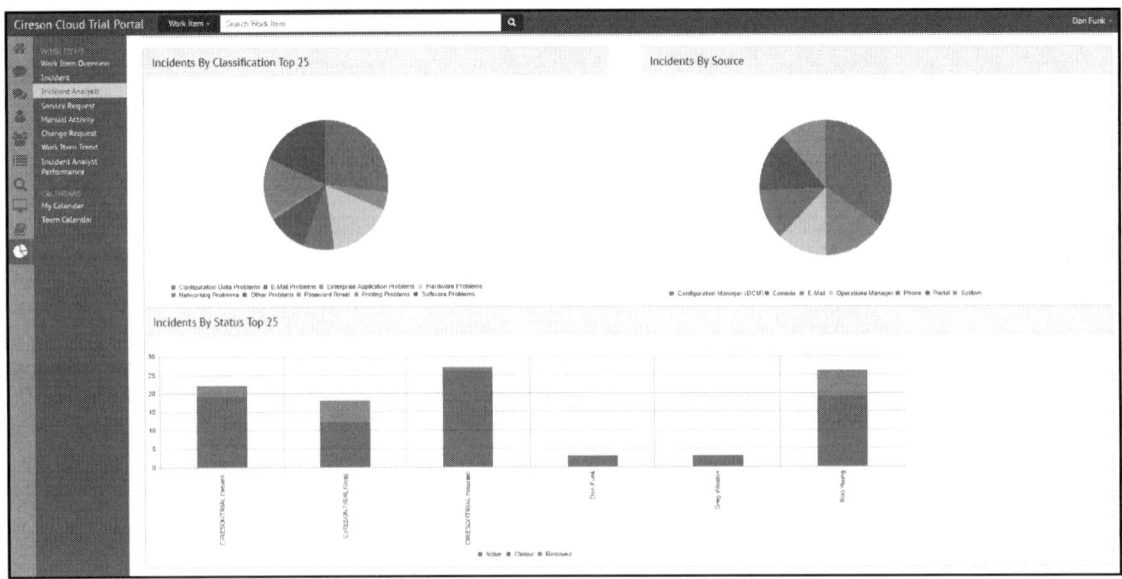

Create powerful, intuitive dashboards with 17 standard charts and gauges

Cireson Asset Management

Cireson directly integrates with Microsoft Service Manager, Configuration Manger, and other sources to manage every asset life cycle from purchase to retirement. Ensure compliance, reduce costs, and gain control for all of your business's hardware and software assets:

- Track all hardware and software assets
- Microsoft true-up readiness
- Windows 10 upgrade readiness
- Office 365 migration planning
- Technical, organizational, and financial alignment

Cireson Asset Management provides Asset Managers with an effective life cycle view, revealing precisely where a particular asset is at any given moment. Track all of your IT asset details from the asset status, location, department, cost center, owner, warranty, maintenance, and software licensing to gain control on your true IT operational costs.

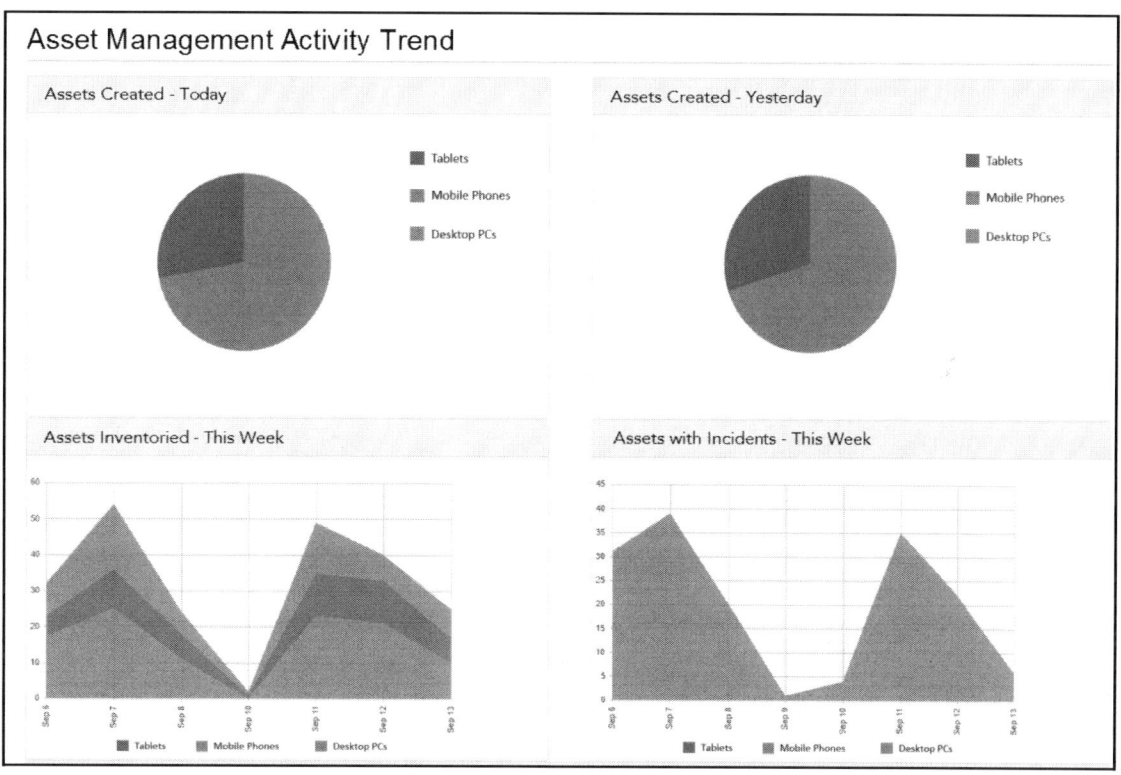

Comprehensive reporting based on asset data from the data warehouse and cube reporting engine within Service Manager

Cireson Asset Import

Perform scheduled data imports with built-in Microsoft System Center connectors, CSV file mapping, real-time Excel data updates, and other third-party sources via direct SQL Server access. No XML code knowledge required.

Cireson Asset Barcode

Easily handle asset receiving, inventory audits, and asset swaps from your smartphone or another Bluetooth device. Enhance mobile work and allow field technicians to update work on the fly.

Cireson Asset Excel

Modify data, bulk import assets, and modify administration items and warranties/contracts, all within Microsoft Excel. Modify software and hardware assets as needed using the search capability.

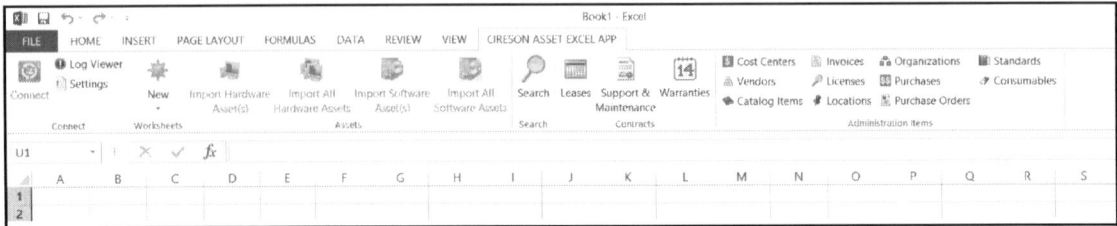

Utilize the power of Microsoft Excel to streamline data management

Cireson Life cycle Management

Greatly reduce manual migration efforts including cleanup and modification, while helping to ensure data integrity. Choose what data, configurations, and objects to migrate for a configurable and customized experience:

- Migrate from Service Manager 2012 to Service Manager 2016
- Refresh your current environment
- Service Manager consolidation between environments

Service Manager Community Apps from Cireson

Cireson offers free Service Manager apps for the community to help maximize your System Center investment.

Download for free at `http://cireson.com/free-community-apps`

- **Self-Service Portal**: A complete replacement of the Microsoft Self-Service Portal for Service Manager. 100% browser, device, and OS freedom. Includes an HTML knowledge base to help users easily resolve issues on their own.
- **Auto Close**: Configure how many days an incident, service request, and so on, should be closed within.
- **Advanced Send E-mail**: Send e-mails to an affected user within the Service Manager console.
- **Notify Analyst**: Quickly configure the essential communications around incident and service request management.
- **Action Log Notify**: Notify the assigned-to analyst when an end-user comment is added and notify the affected user when an analyst comment is added.
- **Service Desk** Ticker: Create an announcement within Service Manager and communicate those announcements directly to an employee's computer in real time.
- **Time Tracker**: Record the amount of time spent working on specific types of work items.

The Cireson Community

The Cireson Community is an active, collaborative forum for discussion, questions, resources and general industry information, and insights around Service Manager, Cireson solutions, and other System Center products. Connect and collaborate on all of your Service Manager needs with IT community members, Cireson employees and customers, partners, and other industry experts.

Join the conversation at `http://community.cireson.com`

itnetX

itnetX is a gold-certified Microsoft integration and software solutions partner which provides various extensions for SCSM, as well as development services for custom SCSM solution requirements.

ITSM Portal Suite

The ITSM Portal Suite for SCSM is a suite of products which consists of an Analyst Portal and a Self-Service Portal for System Center Service Manager.

The Self-Service Portal allows end users to browse the IT Service Catalog, create new requests, view and update open requests, and work on activities as part of ITSM workflows. Built on cutting-edge HTML5 and CSS3, with full support for smartphones and tablets, the ITSM Portal for SCSM is a fast and intuitive alternative for the out-of-box SCSM Self-Service Portal. It offers all features present in the out-of-box SCSM Self-Service Portal, and adds enhanced features leading to a better Self-Service user experience.

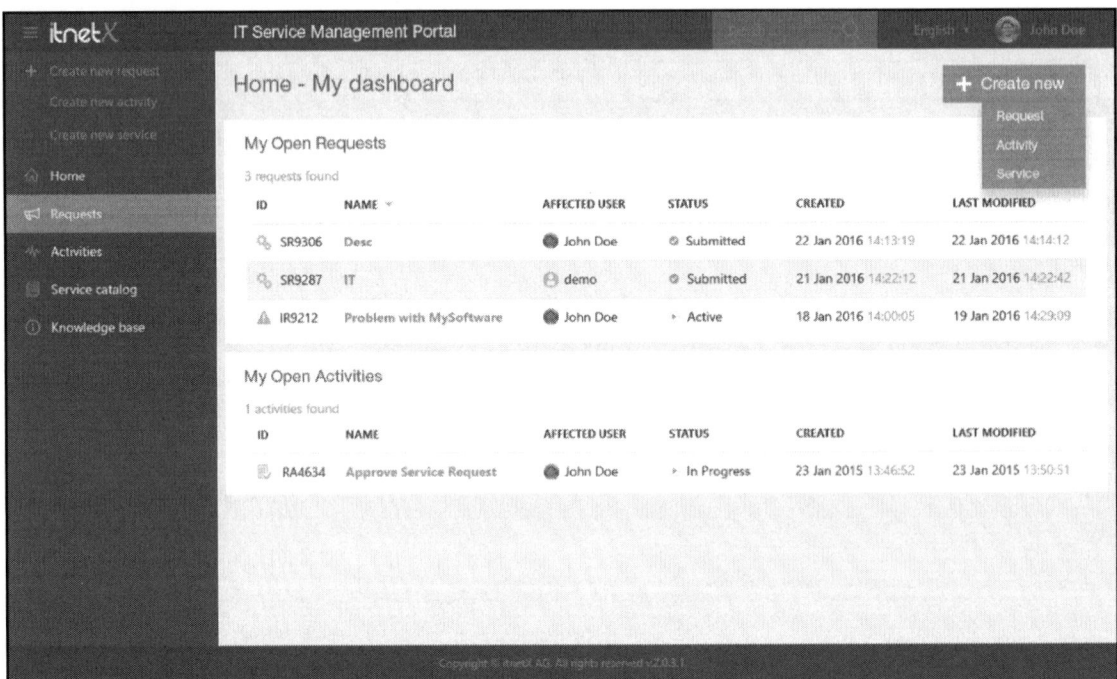

The Analyst Portal allows analysts to create and manage work items such as incident, service request, and change requests. It also allows analysts to view and edit items that live in the Service Manager CMDB. Both portals can be highly customized to accommodate your specific requirements. This not only includes the ability to customize the design and layout of the portals, but you can also bring in and manage your custom classes and objects from SCSM.

Using a web-based approach, the ITSM Portal Suite dramatically increases the flexibility and productivity of your team.

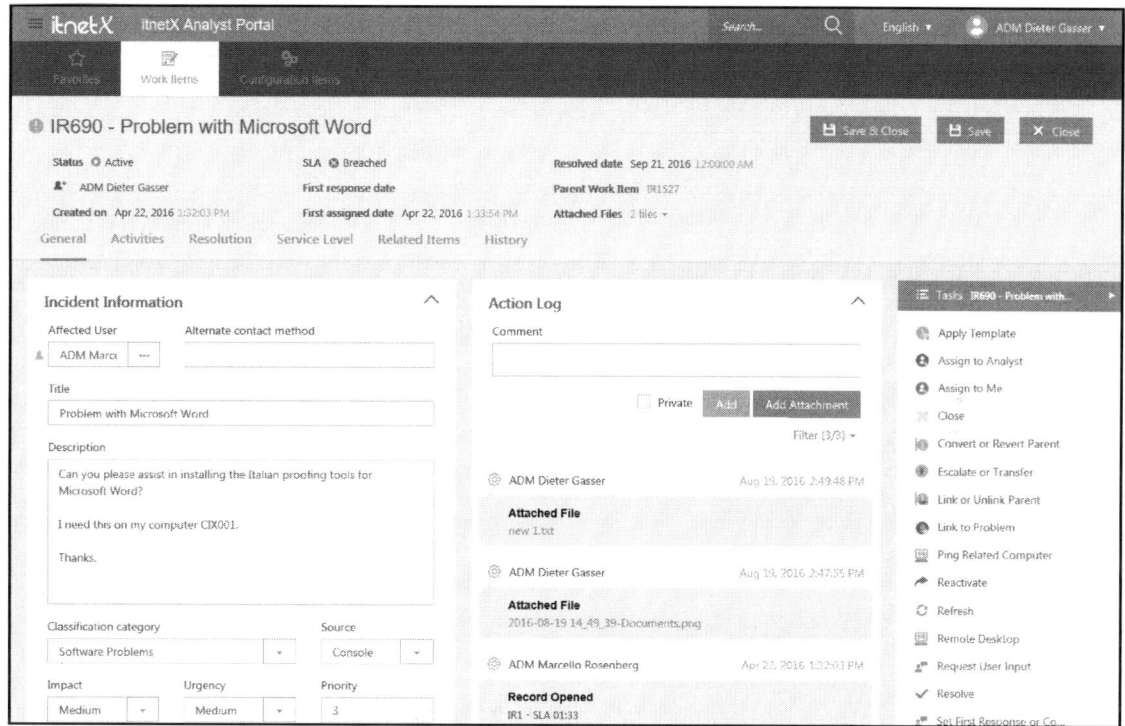

Built on cutting-edge HTML5 and CSS3, the itnetX ITSM Portal is a fast and intuitive alternative for the out-of-box SCSM Self-Service Portal. It allows end users to browse your IT Service Catalog, create new requests, view and update open requests, and work on activities as part of ITSM workflows. It offers all features present in the out-of-box SCSM Self-Service Portal, and adds enhanced features leading to a better Self-Service user experience.

Productivity Pack

The Productivity Pack for SCSM contains a variety of valuable extensions for your System Center Service Manager environment. These extensions were built to close important gaps in System Center Service Manager and add new valuable functionality to it. The main goal is to make your analysts and administrators more productive with a tailored System Center Service Manager experience. Productivity Pack extensions can be licensed as a bundle or individually – depending on your exact needs.

Advanced View Editor

Advanced View Editor for SCSM is an add-on for the Microsoft System Center Service Manager Console aimed at administrators. Advanced View Editor is designed to improve the existing built-in view editor to make managing folders and views in SCSM much easier. Use its power to create complex list views, tree views, and calendar views in seconds without using a XML editor ever again.

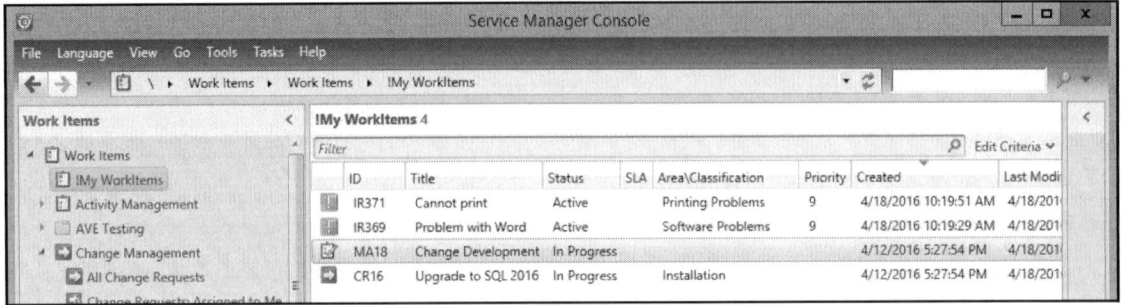

Billable Time

Billable Time for SCSM allows analysts to record the time they spend working with tickets directly to the appropriate work items. This enables organizations to gain more insights on the time spent on the different IT service management processes.

Checklist Activities

Checklist Activities for SCSM can be used to add multiple working steps as a simple checklist into a single activity. Once all steps are marked as completed, the activity will be completed and the process will be driven forward. You can use Checklist Activities just like you use manual activities and add them to your Service Request, Change Request, and Release Record templates.

CMDB Visualizer

CMDB Visualizer for SCSM lets you visualize any object that lives in the CMDB, including its relations to other objects. This enhances the visibility and transparency within the CMDB dramatically and helps you identify critical dependencies.

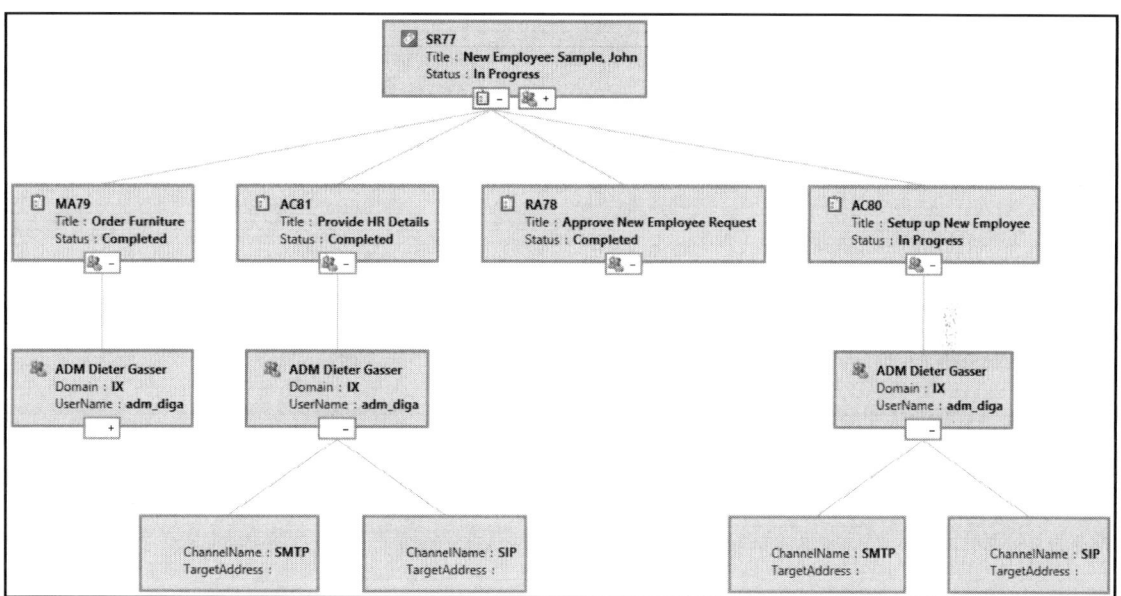

Desktop Alert

Desktop Alert for SCSM can be used to notify analysts whenever a ticket is assigned to them or when a service level objective status changes to warning or breached. The notification is shown as a balloon tip from the taskbar and helps reducing notification e-mails.

Power Print

Power Print for SCSM lets you configure printouts and PDF exports for configuration items in a very easy way. The extension allows you to bring object values to the printout and helps you to create handover documents by using the Service Manager notification template.

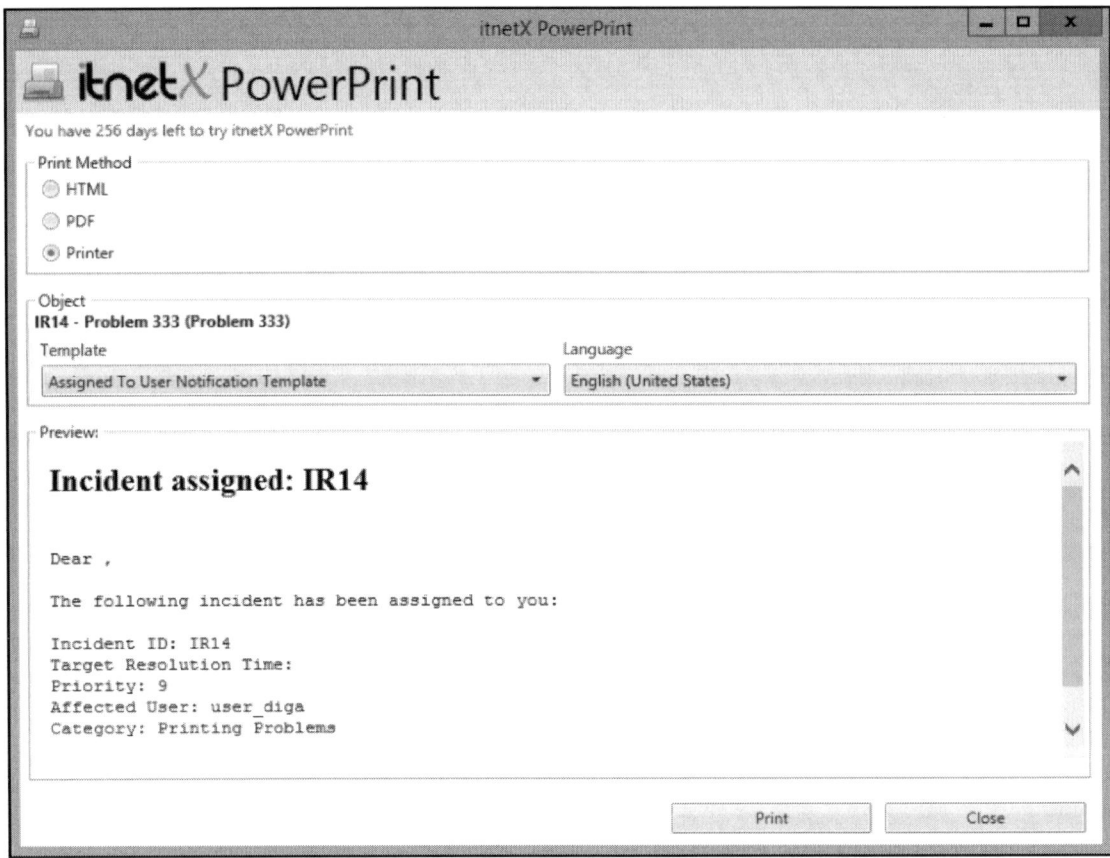

PowerShell Activity

PowerShell Activity for SCSM allow you to automate tasks in a very easy way. By introducing an activity which runs custom PowerShell scripts, you can flexibly use your automation as a step inside your business workflows. All automation scripts are stored in the CMDB and are triggered from PowerShell Activity within your processes.

You can use PowerShell Activity just like you use runbook activities and add them to your Service Request, Change Request, and Release Record templates.

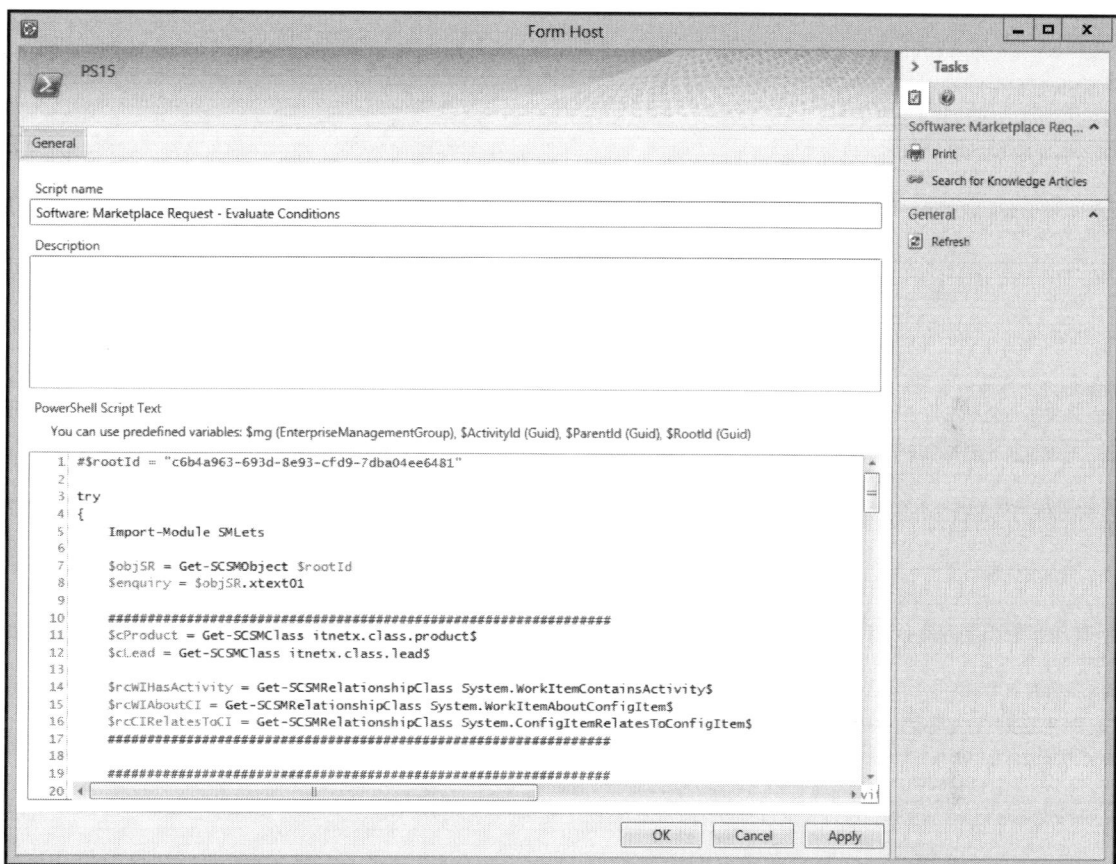

PowerShell Tasks

PowerShell Tasks for SCSM allow you to easily create tasks in the SCSM console that trigger PowerShell scripts that are stored within the CMDB. With this extension you don't need Visual Studio anymore for creating tasks that interact with the console context. This allows you to create tasks for things such as setting default values in a form, applying business rules to attributes, and bulk-modifying attributes, to name a few.

Preview Forms

Preview Forms for SCSM changes the preview pane for all work item types to make an analyst's life easier. The updated preview pane makes the most important properties of a work item accessible in the preview pane without even opening it.

Send Mail

Send Mail for SCSM is an extension which allows analysts to send e-mails such as questions or informational messages about requests they are working on. It allows you to send e-mails with screenshots and attachments quickly and easily from within the console.

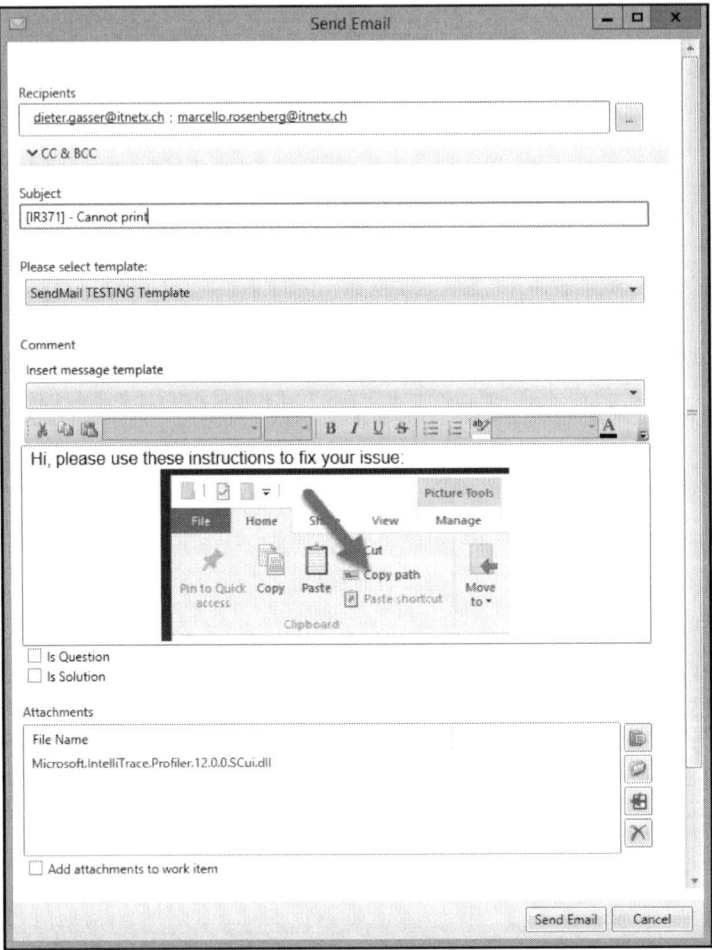

SMA Connector

SMA Connector for SCSM allows you to automate specific activities from a work item by using a SMA runbook. It works the same way as the out-of-the-box SCORCH connector does, but allows you to use the newer SMA automation platform.

Provance

Provance, a Microsoft integration and solutions partner, provides asset life cycle management extensions for SCSM.

Provance IT Asset Management

Provance IT Asset Management is a process management pack that runs within System Center Service Manager. Provance IT Asset Management works with both your IT and business systems to bring together isolated silos of asset-related operational and financial information into a unified actionable view.

Integration with Active Directory, Configuration Manager, Operations Manager, Orchestrator, Virtual Machine Manager, and Data Management Pack 2012, lets you easily import and associate detailed hardware and software configuration data with business data gathered from your ERP, finance, procurement, invoicing, and human resource systems. Provance IT Asset Management brings together and reconciles asset detail from multiple sources – auto discovery solutions, business systems, manual entry, CSV or flat files, spreadsheets, and databases – and provides you with a single, consolidated source of data for analysis and reporting. Process integration lets you expose this unified asset detail directly within Service Manager to support and improve incident, problem, change, configuration, release, and request management.

By leveraging and extending Service Manager platform technologies, Provance IT Asset Management provides additional capabilities that run within Service Manager:

- IT Asset Life Cycle Management for controlling IT costs and effectively managing hardware and software throughout their entire life cycle
- Software Asset Management for minimizing software costs and effectively managing licenses to avoid over and under-utilized licensed software titles

- Financial, contractual and organizational information to support more efficient and cost effective IT Service Management
- A comprehensive overview of contractual relationships with external companies which you need to efficiently manage the associated financial commitments
- Support for audits by giving you the flexibility of a point in time calculation for your software licensing position

An optional Software Intelligence SM subscription service simplifies software license optimization by standardizing your software assets. Ultimately, it provides an accurate inventory of your normalized software installations. Software Intelligence also augments the existing Best Fit Analysis TM technology to help asset managers understand their software license inventory and how it can be effectively managed to meet their business requirements.

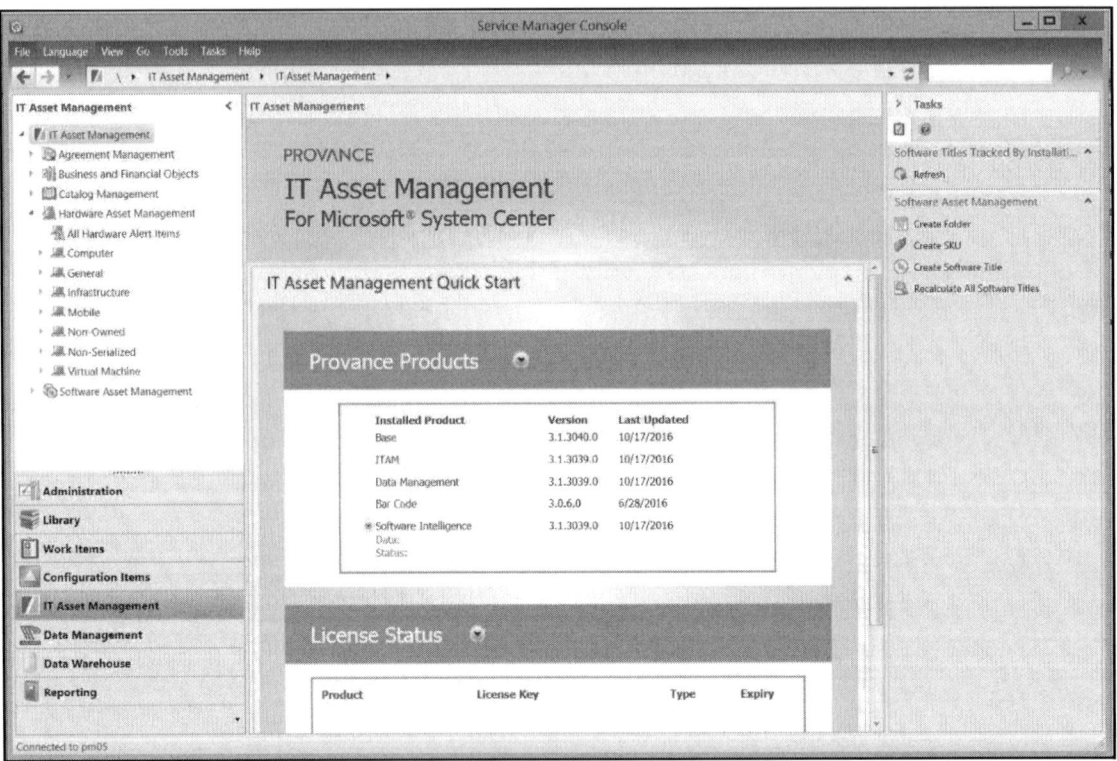

Provance Data Management Pack

The Provance Data Management Pack (DMP) uses a robust engine to simplify and automate the process of quickly getting data into and out of the Service Manager CMDB, while simultaneously improving data consistency and accuracy. The DMP has an easy-to-use graphical interface, making it simple to automate data import from files, databases, and your Active Directory domains, without coding or extensive knowledge of the CMDB structure. Depending on what it discovers during the import, the DMP may either update existing CIs with new data or create new objects. If the source data contains relationships, then they are maintained within the new objects. Related objects can also be created as part of the import.

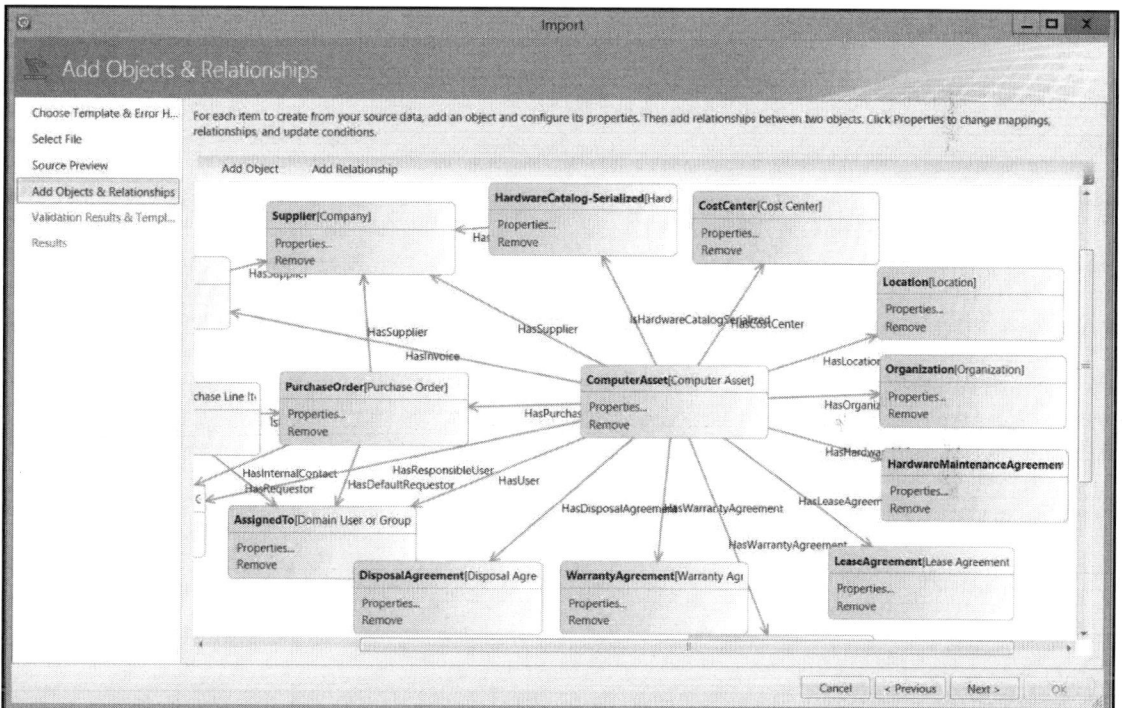

Provance Bar Code

Provance Bar Code is a mobile asset scanning software suite. With a minimum of data entry it gives you the freedom to receive new assets and to perform ad-hoc audits whenever you prefer. Use its simple three-task menu to receive new assets, track the movement of existing assets, and verify asset characteristics.

Provance Bar Code is integrated with System Center 2012 Service Manager, and hence Provance IT Asset Management, through a web service and a Service Manager connector.

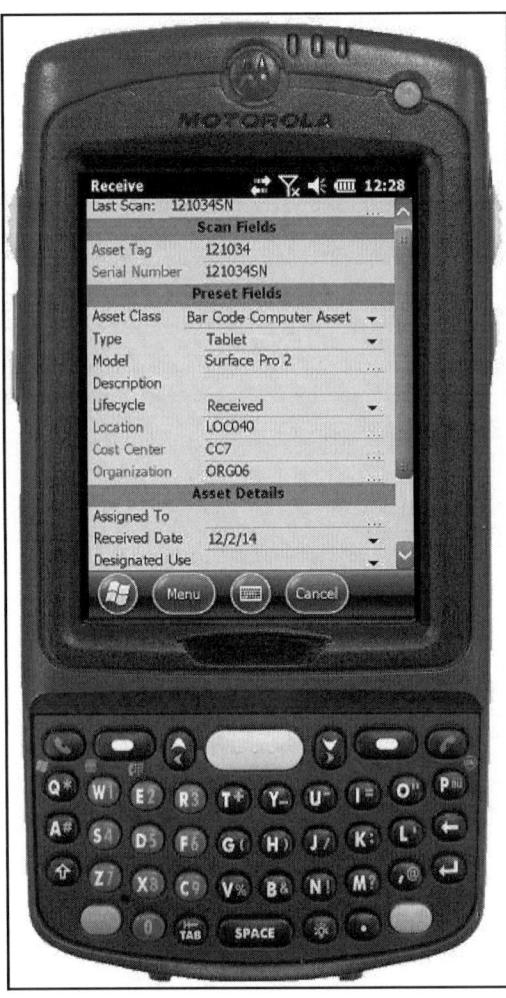

Derdack

Now, let's look at solutions from a company called Derdack.

Enterprise Alert®

Tired of managing all your alerts with SCOM subscriptions? Do you need reliable alert notifications after business hours? Too many alerts at night? No tracking, no escalations? No convenient on-call scheduling in System Center? No mobile app?

Derdack's Enterprise Alert® is a unique incident notification and response solution, extending Microsoft System Center, OMS/OI, and other IT monitoring and helpdesk solutions. It transforms basic alert notifications into a 24/7 anywhere engagement for on-call teams and introduces a new quality of on-call incident response.

Enterprise Alert comes with everything your IT line of business needs to respond to unexpected and major incidents quickly, reliably, and effectively. It delivers critical alerts to the right people via text, voice, IM, e-mail and push, tracks delivery, and escalates automatically. It introduces an entirely new level of incident accountability. With the Enterprise Alert mobile app, IT operations and remediation of critical incidents now truly rests in the palm of your hand. Your IT users will benefit from significantly shorter down times and your IT will see significant improvements on their KPIs. Customers confirm an up to 10x faster alerting and incident resolution in mission-critical IT and OT scenarios.

The following functionalities are added to Microsoft System Center and OMS:

- Automated, intelligent, and reliable alert notifications by voice, text, IM, push, and email (broadcast or sequence) with real-time tracking and escalations.
- Alert filtering, de-duplication, flood protection, severity checks, responsibility mapping, and alert auto-recovery support.
- Enrich alerts from SCOM with information from any source, for example, your customer CMDB, to create meaningful alert messages.
- Powerful mobile app for alert management, collaboration and remote troubleshooting, and remedial. Native app for iOS, Android, and Windows Phone.
- Intuitive drag and drop on-call, 24/ and follow-the-sun team scheduling including "who's on call" dashboard, even on a mobile device. Comprehensive scheduling including auto-rotation, back-ups, stand-ins, and so on.
- App-enabled execution of SCO runbooks and PowerShell scripts for "anywhere" incident troubleshooting and remediation. Results in a much faster response and resolution.
- Create and manage service tickets on-the-go. Notify analysts automatically from SCSM.
- The industry's only plug and play two-way integration for all System Center components: SCOM, SCSM, and SCO, enabling alert status updates from a mobile device or via text reply into SCOM. Active Directory-based user management.

Derdack's Enterprise Alert® is the innovation-leading enterprise notification system for on-prem and hybrid cloud deployments. Find more on `http://www.derdack.com`.

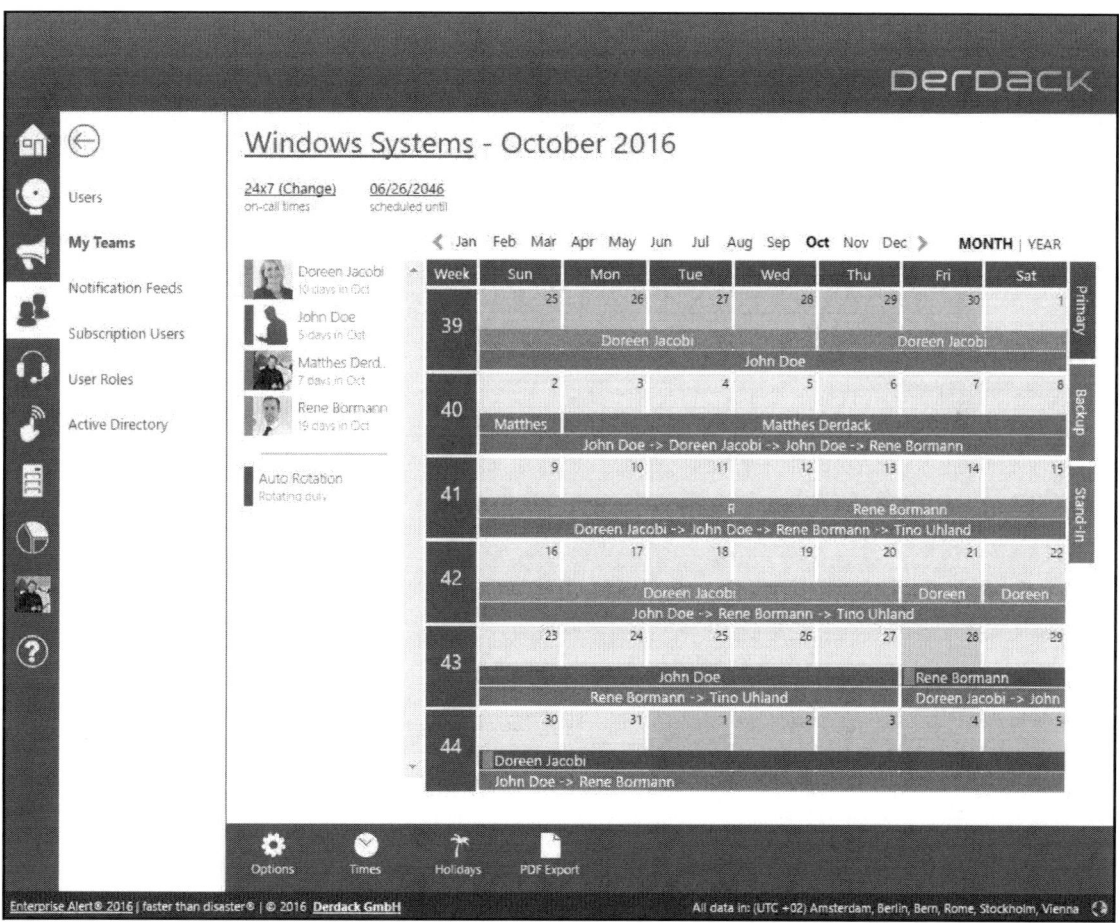

Gridpro

Gridpro, a Microsoft integration and solutions partner, provides Web Analyst Console, Productivity Tools, and Datacenter Request Management for Microsoft System Center Service Manager.

WebFront for Service Manager

WebFront is a responsive web console used for managing your daily work in Microsoft System Center Service Manager . It enables common tasks usually only accessible by using the standard console to be available in web on any device, with the option to enable CTI and Skype integration.

It removes the need to install the standard console software locally, delivers a familiar interface that lets users transition between standard and web console without additional training, and enables hyperlinks to work items or configuration items to be used in e-mail notifications.

PowerPack for Service Manager

PowerPack is a collection of powerful add-ons for Microsoft System Center Service Manager . Receive guidance on work item assignment by using preconfigured support groups or affected configuration items with PowerAssign. Avoid the painful process of registering the wrong type of work item by first documenting the request and then deciding what type of work item to create using PowerForm. Create and manage your own combination views of different work item types directly in the Service Manager console using PowerView.

Request Management for Windows Azure Pack

Windows Azure Pack delivers Microsoft Cloud technologies and capabilities to your data center and includes both a unified cloud platform framework and federated authentication. Add business processes, custom services, and customer support by integrating Microsoft System Center Service Manager with Windows Azure Pack using Request Management for Windows Azure Pack.

SCUtils

In this section, we'll look at some solutions and tools offered by SCUtils.

SCUtils Email Connector 2016

The **SCUtils Email Connector 2016** is a powerful connector for Microsoft System Center 2016 Service Manager. The connector supports all email messaging systems including Microsoft Exchange, Microsoft Office 365, IBM Lotus Domino, Gmail, Outlook.com, and so on, using IMAP/POP3 protocol.

SCUtils Email Connector 2016 has many unique features like processing signed and encrypted messages, reactivating incidents by email, allowing Active Directory group's members to vote on behalf of the group, and many others. SCUtils Email Connector 2016 can filter files smaller than a certain value like company logos, social network icons and the like that are often contained in user's email signatures to avoid generating unnecessary attachments.

For organizations that do not use Microsoft Exchange infrastructure, SCUtils Email Connector 2016 provides an effective way to integrate with an email messaging system. For those with Microsoft Exchange, the product extends the capabilities and creates new ways for an automation.

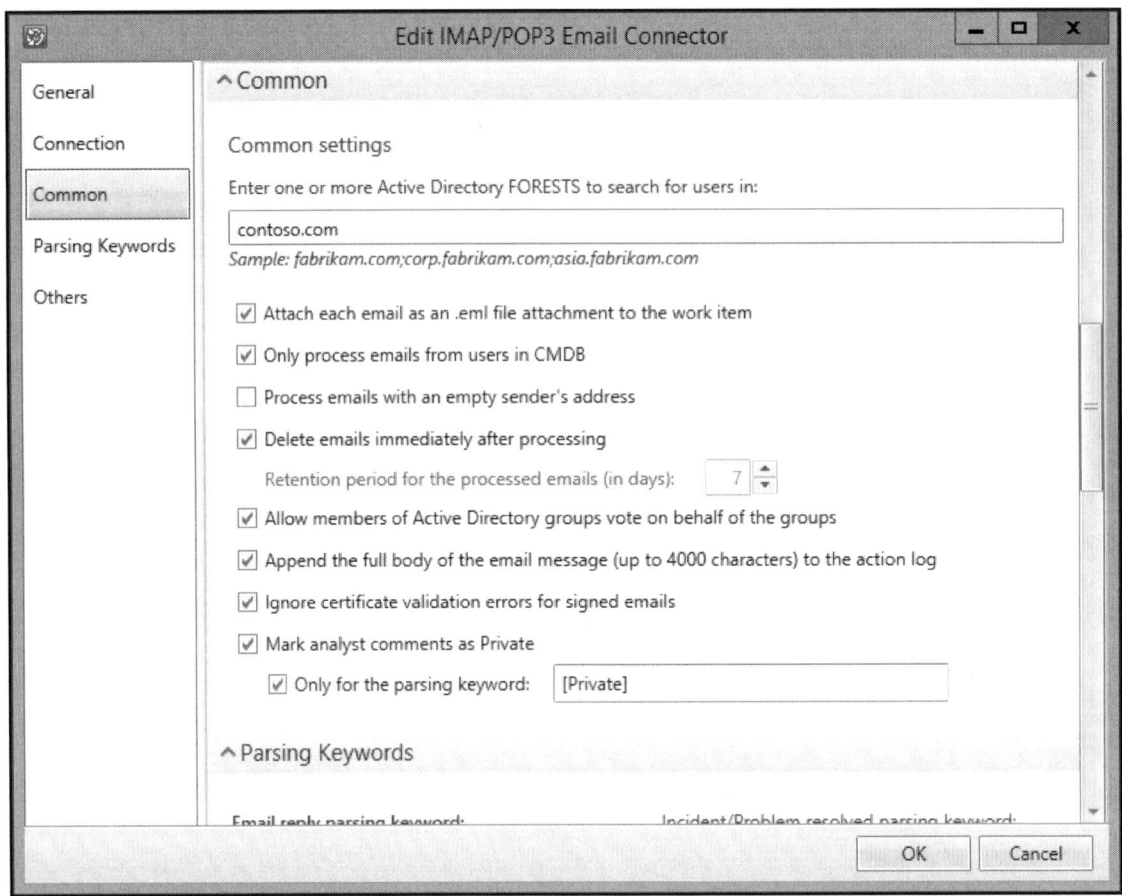

SCUtils ConvertTask 2016

End users often do not see any difference between Incidents and Service Requests. Sometimes users or even IT analysts create Incident instead of Service Request or Service Request instead of Incident. Occasionally, Service Manager connectors or other connected systems generate work items of the wrong type.

SCUtils ConvertTask 2016 transforms new or existing Incidents to Services Requests and vice versa. The flexible settings of product define a way in which values of the specific type will be converted. Besides values, the product also copies relations like affected users, affected configuration items, related knowledge articles, and so on.

Different scenarios for converted work items can be defined using other settings. It is also possible to copy a work item's description into activities that might be useful for information and notifications.

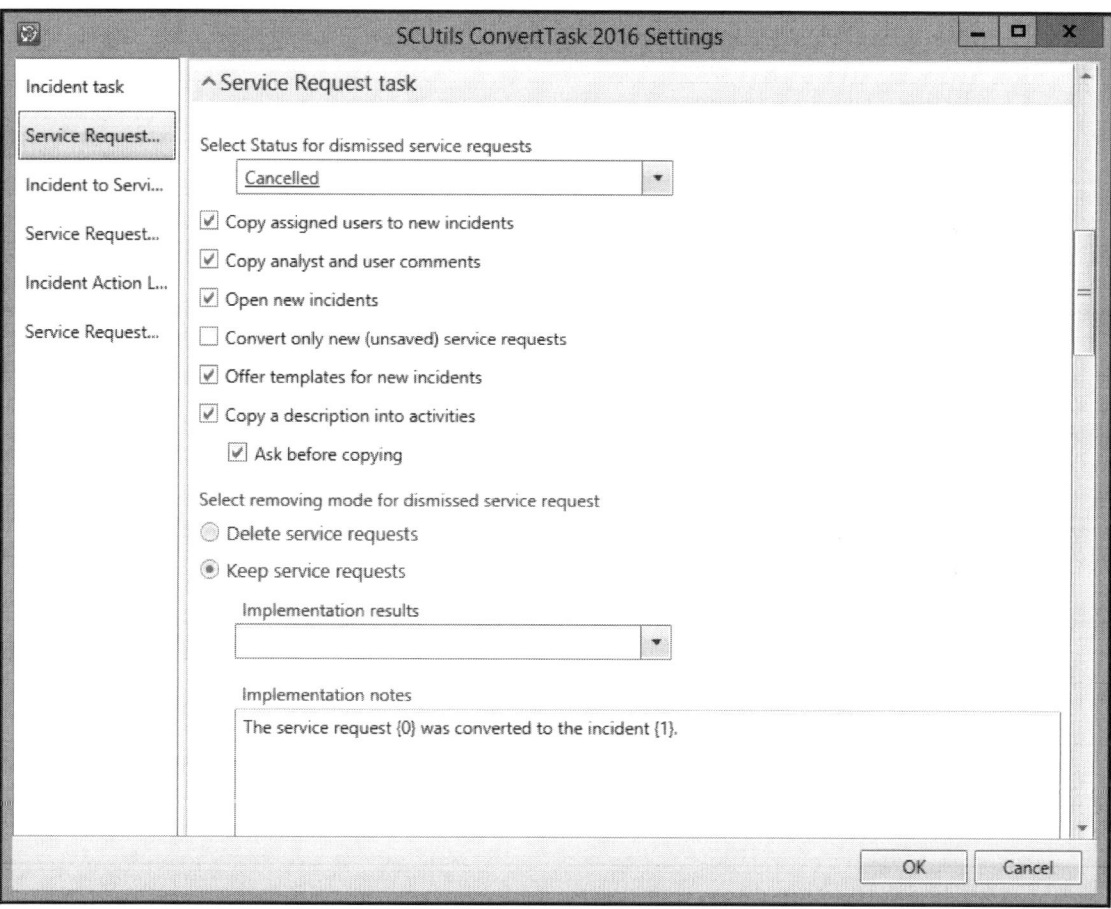

SCUtils WorkItem Scheduler 2016

Many types of IT tasks like maintenance jobs, update deployment, and releases have a repetitive nature. SCUtils WorkItem Scheduler 2016 automates the process of creating work items using different schedules.

SCUtils WorkItem Scheduler 2016 helps to implement various planned actions for all Service Manager work item's types using embedded capabilities of System Center 2016.

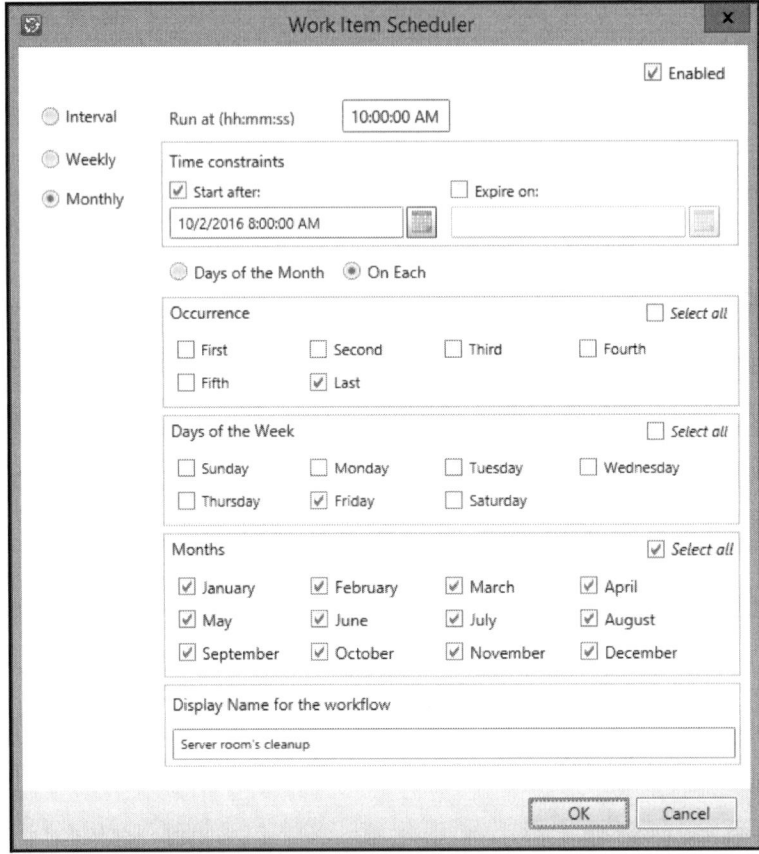

SCUtils SLAInstanceDuration 2016

Not all required data to assess the IT support team's performance are presented in Service Manager by default. SCUtils SLAInstanceDuration 2016 calculates the duration of each Service Level Objective's instance that helps to count many useful KPI-like mean elapsed time to achieve incident resolution considering only working hours.

Using the Service Level Objective's duration calculated taking into account only the working hours of the linked calendar, it is easy to get minimum, maximum, median, and average time for every period defined as Service Level Objective.

Some companies prefer to count only time when Incident or Service Request is in a "dynamic" status. SCUtils SLAInstanceDuration 2016 also computes the duration of SLOs for incidents/Service Requests when the work items are not in Pending/On Hold status.

Axians

Axians provides several useful solutions for SCSM 2016. Let's take a look.

Axians myOperations for System Center Service Manager

"Easier IT management with the myOperations family."

The **myOperations family** by Axians opens up an era of new freedom and control for IT managers and users. Developed by experienced consultants, it is the product of years of listening to customers' voices and needs. Its different modules give you the opportunity to develop Self-Services, standardize notifications, manage users, prepare migrations, and even analyze complex notes/domino infrastructures. Additionally, we offer you a nice and easy way to purchase software packages ready to roll out in our `software package shop`.

The myOperations Portal for System Center Service Manager

The **myOperations Portal** is an add-on for Microsoft System Center Service Manager, which delivers a flexible and complete replacement for the System Center Service Manager self-service portal and more, for example, service desk staff and administrators. The portal also allows users to interact fully with the corresponding information, such as resolving tickets, completing single activities, or starting new requests for user-based assets and devices. Send notifications to all users with a custom notification agent directly on the desktop.

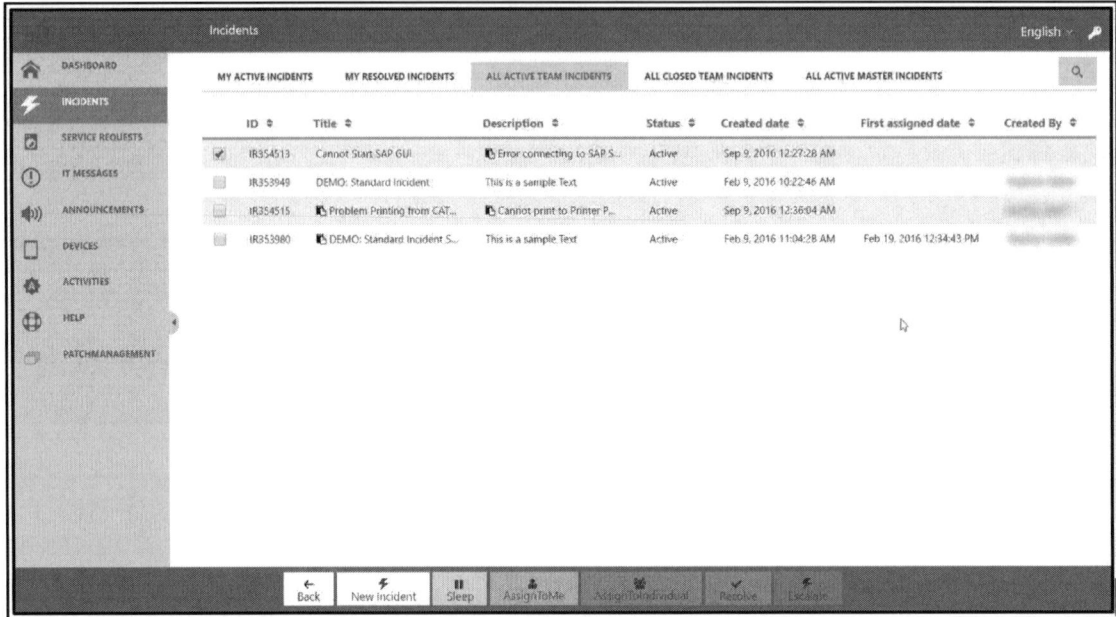

Incident management in the portal

The options to customize the portal for any use cases are endless, because custom defined actions to work items or configuration items are possible without the need of additional programming.

myOperations Portal dashboard and service request

The myOperations Enterprise Add-Ons

Enterprise Add-Ons deliver comprehensive functionalities for other IT processes and requirements. The upcoming version of the myOperations Portal integrates four main features: Server Patch Management, Change Management, Assets, and Service Designer. Enterprise Add-Ons are inspired by real-life customer situations. Future Enterprise Add Ons might be designed with you!

This is what the PatchManagement Configuration screen looks like:

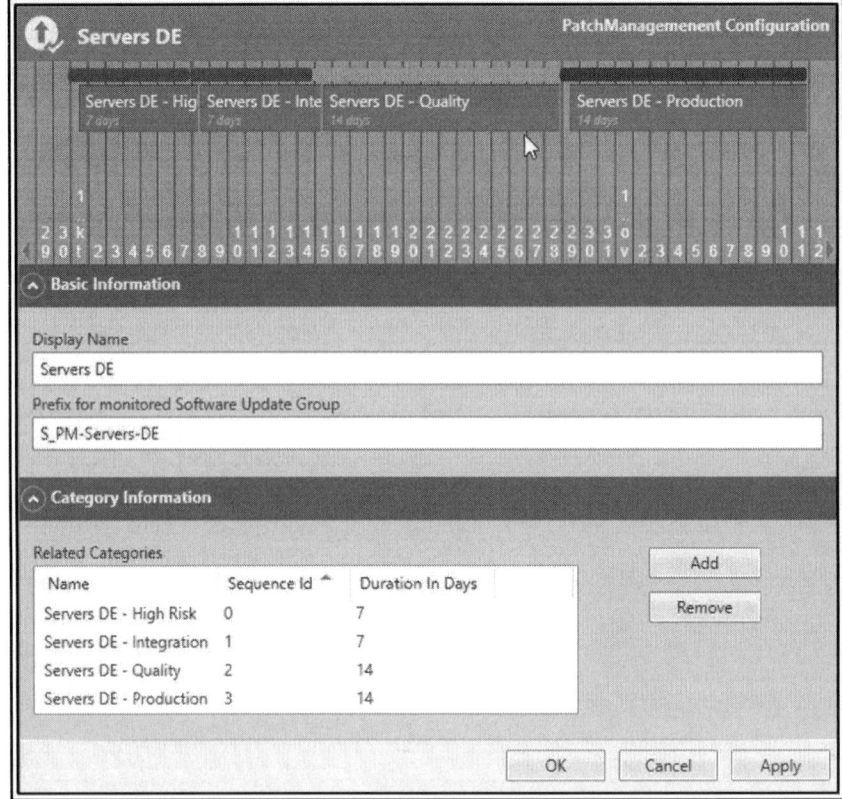

Enterprise Add-On Patch Management

Technology explained – customizing the myOperations Portal

With the myOperations Portal, endless possibilities to customize the Portal to your use cases and scenarios have been integrated. Based on the already existing myOperations user roles, you can customize the navigation, views, interactions, and more. The interactions work in a similar way as console tasks in SCSM, which can improve the user experience by replacing more complex tasks with simple and easy to use quick actions.

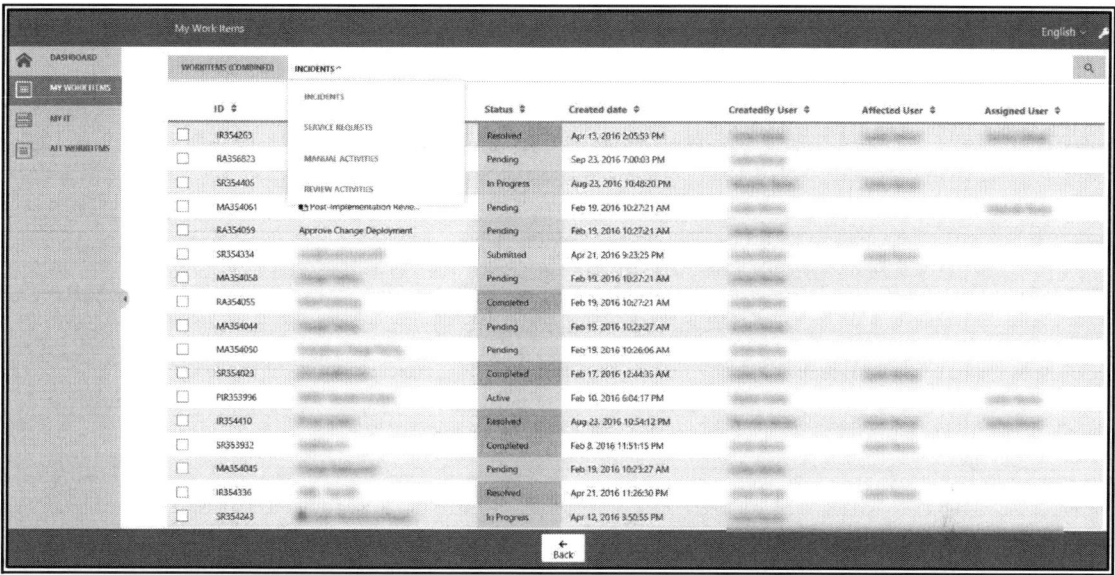

Overview work items

Technology explained – SCSM Extensions and the myOperations Portal

To leverage the full potential of System Center Service Manager, extending the data model by custom integrations is very common and also necessary in many situations. Use cases can be very different and so is the required data model. Before customizing can begin, you have to be fully aware of the data model provided with System Center Service Manager. Also, each scenario should be prepared and documented thoroughly. This will make it easier to understand some of the possible restrictions which could evolve in later stages due to unprepared changes or other common challenges.

myOperations Enterprise Add-On – Server Patch Management

The Server Patch Management Enterprise Add-on is a perfect example, for a result from our nearly 20 years of systems management consulting experience. Throughout the years we came across many large environments with problems regarding getting a server patch management in place. Patching servers is more cumbersome as one might think.

Even though you have the proper tools, a functional process, and the knowledge to successfully execute patching servers, one of the most problematic topics is to get the approvals for all the systems in the required time frame. Especially in larger environments with hundreds of servers, this is nearly unachievable.

The Server Patch Management Add-on to the myOperations Portal has been developed over the past years in several versions for different customer scenarios.

Finally, we created a generic version which still is highly customizable. The Server Patch Management Add-on comes with a highly-customizable frontend and a standard patch management workflow. The patch management workflow is just a suggestion of how server patch management can be done using System Center Configuration Manager.

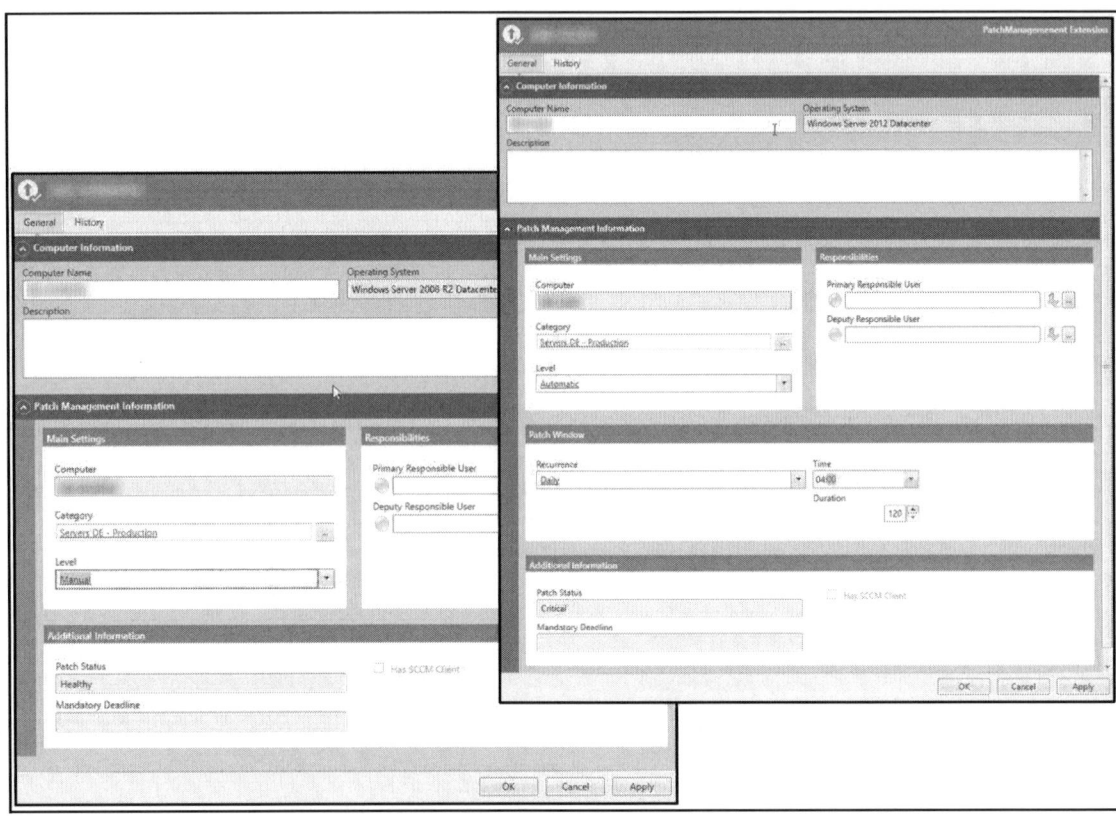

myOperations patch management forms in SCSM

The workflow can be customized to your needs. Do you have special requirements, like sending more notifications, require different approvals, or many other ideas you might have, this Enterprise Add-on in combination with SCSM gives you the flexibility to customize the workflow to fit your server patch process.

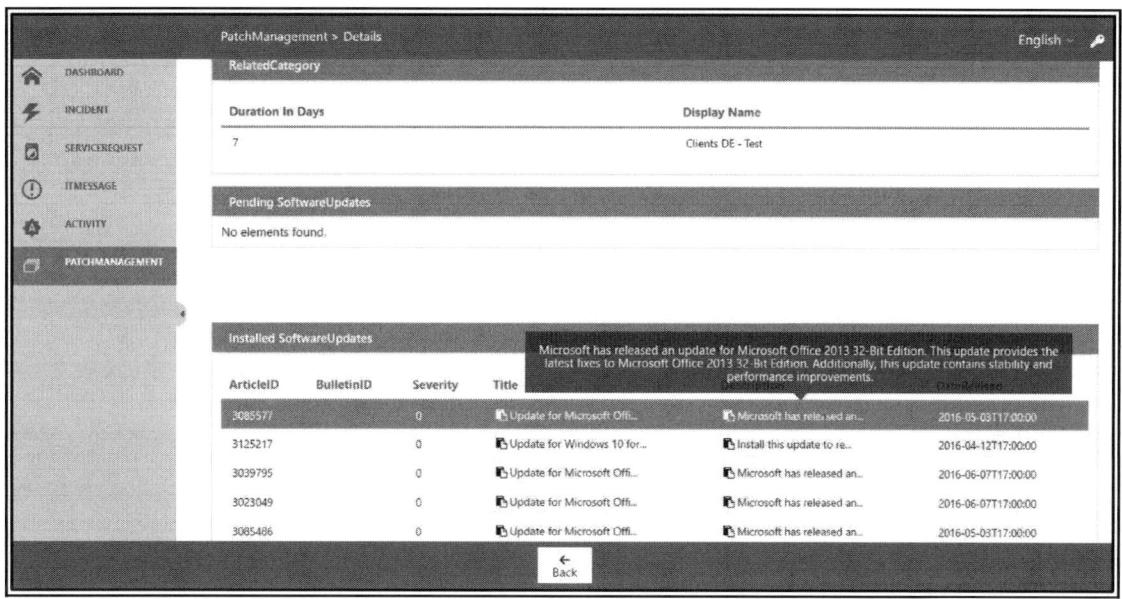

Patch managed computer view in myOperations

Design principles in the myOperations Portal solution

- The myOperations Portal can be integrated with all existing SCSM customizations and use cases without the need of additional programming. For example, if you have other third-party solutions which do extend the functionality of SCSM and therefore provide additional value, you can integrate the corresponding scenarios and processes into the myOperations Portal without modifying code. This applies also for SCSM customizations done by you directly.
- SCSM customizations coming with the myOperations Portal are designed in a way to not interfere with other possible customizations. This ensures that existing, but also possible future extensions and customizations can be used together with the myOperations Portal.

Learn more about the myOperations family and visit http://www.myoperations.de.

B

Useful Websites and Community Resources

Introduction

This appendix will list some helpful websites and communities for System Center Service Manager.

Useful community blogs

- **Anders Asp (MVP)**: http://www.scsm.se/
- **Steve Buchanan (MVP)**: http://www.buchatech.com/category/microsoft/system-center/scsm/
- **Steve Beaumont (MVP)**: http://systemscentre.blogspot.co.uk/
- **Dieter Gasser**: http://blog.dietergasser.com/
- **Andreas Baumgarten (MVP – German blog)**: http://startblog.hud.de/category/mssc/service-manager/
- **Samuel Erskine (MVP, MCT)**: http://www.itprocessed.com/
- **System Center: Service Manager Engineering Blog**: http://blogs.technet.com/b/servicemanager/
- **Marcel Zehner (MVP)**: http://blog.scsmfaq.ch/
- **Anton Gritsenko (MVP)**: http://blog.scsmsolutions.com
- **Maarten Goet (MVP)**: http://blogs.inovativ.nl/auteur?u=maarten
- **Kurt Van Hoecke (MVP)**: http://www.scug.be/scsm

- **Nathan Lasnoski**: `http://blog.concurrency.com/author/nlasnoski/`
- **Matthew Dowst**: `http://blogs.catapultsystems.com/author/mdowst/`

Frameworks and processes

- **Official ITIL© website**: `http://www.itil-officialsite.com/`
- **Microsoft Operations Framework**:
  `http://technet.microsoft.com/en-us/library/cc506049.aspx`
- **ISO official website**: `http://www.iso.org/iso/home.html`

Valuable community forums and user groups

- **TechNet Forums – System Center Service Manager (EN)**:
  `http://social.technet.microsoft.com/Forums/en-US/category/servicemanager`
- **TechNet Forums – System Center (DE)**:
  `http://social.technet.microsoft.com/Forums/de-DE/systemcenterde/threads`
- **System Center Central – Service Manager**:
  `http://www.systemcentercentral.com/forums-archive/forums/service-manager/`
- `http://www.systemcentercentral.com/blog/service-manager/`
- **MyITforums – System Center Service Manager**:
  `http://www.myitforum.com/forums/System-Center-Service-Manager-f154.aspx`
- **German System Center User Group**: `http://scsmug.de/`
- **Minnesota System Center User Group**: `http://www.mnscug.org`

Websites for SCSM solutions and extensions

- **CodePlex – SCSM PowerShell Cmdlets**: http://smlets.codeplex.com/
- **TechNet Library – System Center 2012 & 2012 R2 – Service Manager**: http://technet.microsoft.com/en-us/library/hh305220
- **TechNet Library – System Center 2016 – Service Manager**: https://technet.microsoft.com/en-us/system-center-docs/sm/service-manager
- **TechNet Gallery – Resources for IT Professionals – Service Manager**: http://gallery.technet.microsoft.com/site/search?query=service%20manager
- **TechNet Gallery – Resources for IT Professionals – SCSM**: http://gallery.technet.microsoft.com/site/search?query=SCSM
- **Provance Technologies** Inc: http://www.provance.com/
- **Derdack GmbH**: http://www.derdack.com/
- **Gridpro:** https://www.gridprosoftware.com/
- **Cireson:** http://cireson.com/cireson-platform
- **Expit:** http://expit.com
- **ITNetX AG**: http://itnetx.ch
- **Scutils:** http://www.scutils.com
- **Xapity PTY LTD**: http://www.xapity.com
- **Axians (Fritz & Macziol)**: http://www.myoperations.de/

Online wikis

- **Microsoft TechNet Wiki: Management Portal**:
  http://social.technet.microsoft.com/wiki/contents/articles/703.wiki-management-portal.aspx#System_Center_Service_Manager
- **Microsoft TechNet Wiki: System Center 2012 Service Manager Survival Guide (en-US)**:
  http://social.technet.microsoft.com/wiki/contents/articles/8113.system-center-2012-service-manager-survival-guide-en-us.aspx
- **Microsoft TechNet Wiki: Service Manager Survival Guide**:
  http://social.technet.microsoft.com/wiki/contents/articles/service-manager-survival-guide.aspx
- **System Center 2012 Service Manager Developer's Survival Guide**:
  http://social.technet.microsoft.com/wiki/contents/articles/13472.system-center-2012-service-manager-developer-s-survival-guide.aspx

Social network resources

- **System Center on Facebook**:
  https://www.facebook.com/search/top/?q=Microsoft%20System%20Center%20Support
- **System Center on Twitter**: https://twitter.com/system_center
- **Service Manager on Twitter**: https://twitter.com/ServiceManager

Index

Printed in Great Britain
by Amazon

36319470R00350